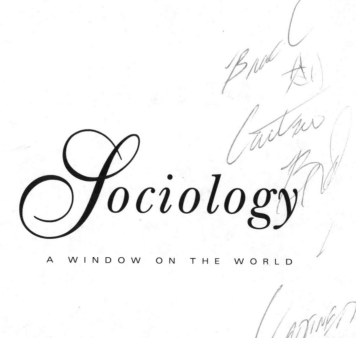

Sociology

A WINDOW ON THE WORLD

Third Edition

Sociology

A WINDOW ON THE WORLD

BARBARA D. WARME

ELINOR MALUS

KATHERINA L.P. LUNDY

· · · · · · · · · · · · · · · · · · · ·

Nelson Canada

ITP

International Thomson Publishing
The trademark ITP is used under licence

© Nelson Canada
A Division of Thomson Canada Limited, 1994

Published in 1994 by
Nelson Canada,
A Division of Thomson Canada Limited
1120 Birchmount Road
Scarborough, Ontario M1K 5G4

Canadian Cataloguing in Publication Data
Warme, Barbara
    Sociology : a window on the world

3rd ed.
Previous eds. by Katherina L.P. Lundy and Barbara D. Warme.
Includes bibliographical references and index.
ISBN 0-17-604196-6

1. Sociology. I. Malus, Elinor, 1948-   .
II. Lundy, Katherina L.P. Sociology : a window on the world. III. Title.

HM66.L8 1994   301   C94-930228-7

Acquisitions Editor	Charlotte Forbes
Editorial Manager	Nicole Gnutzman
Production Editor	Tracy Bordian
Developmental Editor	Heather Martin
Art Director	Liz Nyman
Design	Stuart Knox
Cover photo	COMSTOCK

Printed and bound in Canada
1 2 3 4 (BG) 98 97 96 95 94

In memory of Kitty Lundy
B.W.

To my students
E.M.

PREFACE

In this third edition, we have attempted to respond to the suggestions and criticisms offered by colleagues and students who have used the book in their courses. As well, we have profited from the comments of two sets of anonymous peer reviewers, drawn from across the country. The first set, addressing the previous edition, told us what they thought worked and what could be improved; the second set reviewed each chapter of the new manuscript. We were gratified by the careful consideration they gave both to the words and to the tune, and, wherever possible, we have incorporated their recommendations.

The first two editions of *Sociology: A Window on the World* were written when Barbara Warme and Katherina Lundy were colleagues at York University. Barbara was delighted that Elinor Malus of Champlain Regional College, St. Lambert, agreed to collaborate on this third round, and that Linda Deutschmann, University of Toronto, continued her participation by contributing Chapter 5, "Deviance and Social Control." Without the initiative of Kitty Lundy, the book would not have been written in the first place, and her legacy is most apparent in the historical dimension of each chapter.

The invitation to prepare another edition of the book provided a welcome opportunity to thoroughly rethink things and to do better. We approached this task with the same attitude we have encouraged students to adopt (in the Appendix, "Writing to Learn"). Namely, that one writes to learn and that the essence of revision is "re-seeing." As a result, the changes in the present edition are substantial. We have, of course, done the expected things. We have updated statistical material, drawn on recent publications, changed a number of the end-of-chapter exercises and suggested readings, and considered some of the issues that are gaining prominence in Canadian society. The inserts are now set off more clearly from the text; they are taken largely from magazine articles, newspaper reports, and letter-to-the-editor columns, and are intended to invite critical discussion in the classroom. However, there are no added "bells and whistles," nor is there change just for the sake of change. Rather, we have concentrated our energies on fundamentally reorganizing each chapter, as well as the sequence of chapters, to achieve what we think is a more logical development. Some of the chapters bear little resemblance to their counterparts in the previous edition, even though certain headings may have been retained. Chapter 9, " 'The Family' and Families," is new almost in its entirety.

The twelve chapters of the book are organized into five sections. Section 1, "Groundwork," paves the way by introducing students to the sociological frame of mind. We examine both the nature of the questions that intrigue sociologists and some of the strategies that they employ in seeking answers. We also discuss contributions made by several of the early major theorists who prepared the groundwork for the subsequent development of sociology as a discipline.

Section 2, "Culture and the Individual," emphasizes commonalities and the binding consequences of social interaction. Section 3, "Social Inequality and Power," focuses on differentiation, cleavage, and hierarchy. The chapters in this latter section deal with social stratification, minority/majority relations, and work. We have eliminated the chapter on organizations, choosing instead to examine bureaucracy as one of the contexts in which work is located.

Section 4 is devoted to social institutions. This time, we have only concentrated on three—the family, education, and religion—and have expanded our treatment of them, paying attention to their paradoxes and contradictions. Although social change is a theme of the entire book, it is also the subject of Section 5, in which we have included a discussion of social movements and countermovements.

As before, there is not a separate chapter on the subject of sex/gender, since it is germane to all areas of sociology. Instead, we give women's issues systematic treatment throughout the book. Feminist perspectives provide an important link from chapter to chapter, as do the functionalist, Marxist, and symbolic interactionist approaches. We have also made every effort to integrate the text through cross-references.

We wanted to present sociology as an absorbing, pleasurable, open-ended, and rather untidy (that is, human) activity, "disturbing" in the best sense, and possibly addictive, rather than as a closed world of established knowledge. We also hoped, above all, to persuade students that it *matters*.

Barbara Warme, Amsterdam, The Netherlands
Elinor Malus, Montreal, Canada

ACKNOWLEDGMENTS

In the course of preparing this third edition, we have incurred debts galore and are happy to acknowledge them.

We are grateful to the following people for good conversation and for various kinds of assistance: Ellen Baar, Ann Baulu, Janis Grobbclaar, Diana Hartmann, Michael Hartmann, Philippa Hunter, Dale Huston, Lorna Kelly, Vivienne Monty, Dorathy Moore, Jan Pretorious, Norene Popu, Alan Thomas, Sharon Thomas, Silvia Viljoen, and Sandra Ward. Ashleigh Hendry was as competent and amiable a research assistant as one could wish to have. From Meagan Thomas, we received valuable help with the reference list.

We are much indebted to our associates at Nelson Canada. Charlotte Forbes, Acquisitions Editor, helped us to overcome what were, at certain stages of the work, rather formidable geographic distances, and organized the extensive peer review process. The penetrating questions of Erika Krolman, our copy editor, sent us off to do our homework in more instances than we care to remember, but the book is better for them. We are particularly indebted to our fine production editor, Tracy Bordian, for her painstaking work on the manuscript. We are also grateful to Camille Isaacs and Heather Martin for their contributions.

While it is required by academic convention to "cite" one's sources, it is not required to "thank" them. The writing, or revising, of an introductory textbook, however, is a special case, because it obliges one to venture well beyond the narrow precints of one's own research interests. This rewarding exposure to the recent work of so many others has given us a renewed sense of how varied, rich, and imaginative are the projects in which our colleagues in the discipline are engaged. A nod of appreciation to all!

To Robert Jacobs and Bastiaan van Gent, a thousand thanks for as many acts of generosity, over and above the steady gifts of partnership that we have come almost to take for granted. It's your turn now.

Contents

SECTION

1

ONE

· · · · · · · · · · · · · · · · · · ·

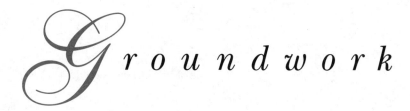

Groundwork

CHAPTER ONE

Groundwork

In your mind's eye, scan your classroom. Picture the seating arrangement, the students, the instructor, the layout of the room. Imagine a class. Step back. You are entering the classroom and it already contains a few people. Is one of them the instructor? How do you know? The class begins. Picture the next few minutes of the class and ask yourself the following questions. Who moves around the classroom? How are most people in the room sitting? Who writes on the board? Who asks most of the questions? Who does most of the talking? Who is looked at most often? Can you generate answers to these questions without getting so mired in numerous qualifications and exceptions that the exercise becomes impossible?

Exploring, examining, and explaining recurring patterns in human life is the concern of sociology.

Courtesy Ryerson Polytechnical Institute.

Of course, it's simple. Your responses reflect your awareness of what transpires almost daily involving millions of individuals across the country for hours at a time. Everywhere people work together to carry on the business of daily life, whatever that might entail. Exploring, examining, and explaining recurring patterns in human group life is the concern of sociology. Two characteristics typify sociological enquiry. First, the level of enquiry is general and abstract. It is not about the peculiarities of a certain concrete situation or about the singularity of a specific individual. Second, the answers focus on an individual's involvement in group life. The groups can be formally identified and constituted or consist of individuals unknown to each other who merely share a particular trait.

Your classroom imaginings fit both criteria. If there were not common patterns of behaviour in a classroom you would not have been able to engage in the exercise. Membership in the group, whether as student or instructor, has a determining influence on the participants' behaviour. Usually, it is apparent who the instructor in the classroom is. That person commonly stands at the front of the classroom facing the others, the students, who face the front and sit in their seats. The instructor usually asks more of the questions, speaks more, is more mobile, and has more room to move around, in addition to having a larger desk and control of the board. (If all this seems obvious to you, imagine the same room and students' behaviour without the instructor present!) Expand your enquiry by asking yourself how you came to be in the classroom. Did most of your family members pursue an education, or are you the exception, breaking ground for "people like you"? Do you think that your classmates followed a similar path? Are there characteristics that mark one group of students from another? These questions may be more difficult to answer as you may be unaware of the larger social processes that favoured or hindered your educational advancement. The structure of power in the society, the distribution of resources, your gender, race, ethnicity, and class each contribute to your biography. Illuminating the workings of these forces also falls into the sociological domain.

Thus the stuff of sociology can range from the mundane—your classroom—to the extraordinary or awesome—the dismantling of the Berlin Wall. In his book *Invitation to Sociology*, Peter Berger observes that the sociologist

> ...investigates communities, institutions and activities that one can read about every day in the newspapers. Yet there is another excitement of discovery beckoning in his investigations. It is not the excitement of coming upon the totally unfamiliar, but rather the excitement of finding the familiar becoming transformed in its meaning. The fascination of sociology lies in the fact that its perspective makes us see in a new light the very world in which we have lived all our lives (1963:21).

The article on women and poverty (see Box 1.1) provides a springboard for sociological enquiry. What explanations can there be for the statistic that from 50 to 70 percent of single, elderly Canadian women are likely to be poor? Such a high proportion indicates that this cannot be a personal problem arising from character flaws, but is a social issue that some have labelled the "feminization of poverty."

Return to the classroom you envisioned at the beginning of the chapter and continue the scenario. The instructor asks how many students in the class do well in math. Which students raise their hands? Which students raise their hands when the instructor asks who "can't do math?" Do the students answering

BOX 1.1

SINGLE ELDERLY WOMEN LIKELY TO BE POOR

Single elderly women are among the most likely victims of poverty, especially in Quebec—the province with the highest over-all poverty rate in 1990, says a [recent] federal study...

Seven in every 10 unattached women 65 and older in Quebec were poor in 1990, compared with five in every 10 in Canada.

"One possible explanation for Quebec's high rate is the lack of any provincial income supplement for low-income seniors," says the report of the National Council on Welfare.

Single elderly Quebec women make up one of the three highest-risk groups for poverty.

Four in every 10 unattached Quebec women under 65 are poor—again the highest rate in the country—as are six in 10 single-parent mothers, which is the national average.

The poverty rate for male seniors in Quebec fell from 34 per cent to 19 per cent in the last decade—again, higher than the 13 per cent rate across Canada.

In Montreal, poor for a single person means living on less than $14,155 a year—sometimes on a lot less.

For single poor women, the average national income was 43 per cent below the poverty line, meaning just $8,068 a year.

In all, there were 1.2 million Quebecers living below the poverty line in 1990, including 292,000 children. That's 18 per cent of the province's population, a bigger proportion than in any other province. Manitoba was next (17.8 per cent), then Saskatchewan (16.6) and Newfoundland (15.6).

The national average was 14.6 per cent, representing 3.8 million Canadians, including more than one million children.

In 1980, Newfoundland led the nation with a poverty rate of 23.6 per cent, followed by Quebec at 18.6 per cent.

For the first time, the council attempted to measure the "depth of poverty"—that is, how poor the poor are, how far below the poverty line they are.

In Quebec, the average poor unattached individual is trying to get by with an income of 65 per cent of the poverty line, while for families it's 70 per cent.

Source: Terrance Wills, "Single Elderly Women Likely to Be Poor," Gazette *(Montreal) (1 December 1992), p. A1. Reprinted with permission.*

either question share another category of group membership? Is there a distinguishing characteristic among the students in either group? Typically male students report that they succeed in math, and the females are the ones who say that they can't do it very well. Usually, if anyone is planning to study math it is the males in the classroom, in contrast to the females who do not see their futures going in that direction. Is there a trajectory from here to poverty? A sociologist could hypothesize the following route.

A young woman in high school may already feel apprehensive about math, given her upbringing and school experiences. (We will have more to say about socialization in Chapter 4.) She carries with her the knowledge from peers, mass media, and parents that there is another arena in which she must succeed that depends more on her outward appearance and personality than on her academic achievement. This is the stage of personal relationships, particularly those with young men. For her, the goal of academic success in male preserves like the physical sciences vies with that of popularity, and her choice is weighted in the direction of social success. Her preparation then suits her for work that is not the most lucrative. In all probability, the work she finds will be in the clerical or service area where she will earn about 68 cents for every dollar that a male worker receives. Typically, this young woman will marry, have children, and be responsible for the double duty of family care and work in the labour force, which further limits her ability to be financially successful in her own right. Her marriage may endure or not. If it does not, given her training, labour force experience, and resources, she may ultimately find herself among the 50 to 70 percent of poor women described in Box 1.1.

Philosopher and economist Karl Marx (1818–1883) noted that human beings make their own history, but not under conditions of their own choosing. Often, invisible social forces channel lives. Understanding the workings of those social forces gives people a new measure of freedom and power. According to C. Wright Mills in *The Sociological Imagination* (1959, 15), "The sociological imagination ... is a quality of mind that seems most dramatically to promise an understanding of the intimate realities of ourselves in connection with larger social realities."

An excellent historical illustration of this sociological perspective and group influence on behaviour is provided in the classic study *Suicide* (1897), by Emile Durkheim (1858–1917), one of the founders of sociology. Durkheim, who lived in France at a time when the social order was changing rapidly, reasoned that one manifestation of loss of social cohesion would be an increase in the rate of suicide. For him, the group, not its members, was the appropriate unit of sociological analysis. He contended that one can analyze group phenomena without focusing on the motivations and characteristics of individuals. Consonant with this emphasis, Durkheim studied how suicide rates varied with the state of society and with the extent to which individuals were integrated into a particular group (*Suicide*, 1897). It was a brilliant choice of study, for, until then, suicide had been treated as a phenomenon that could be explained only by the state of mind of the individual who engaged in this behaviour. Durkheim was concerned with suicide as a "social fact," a product of social forces external to the individual.

Durkheim was interested in the impact of social bonds on suicide rates in the complex and fragmented society that emerged in the century following the French Revolution.

The Bettman Archive.

He posited that suicide rates would be higher at times of rapid change, when **anomie**, a lack of clarity about established rules for conduct, was likely to prevail, and that they would be higher for people who lacked family ties—those who were either single or married but had no children.[1] The content of religious beliefs, Durkheim thought, would be another important factor. Thus, he predicted that Protestants, whose religion emphasized individual responsibility for ethical decisions, would be more prone to commit suicide than Roman Catholics, who had available the psychic relief of confession and, moreover, could look to their church as an authoritative guide to conduct. Statistical analysis of suicide rates supported Durkheim's assumptions.

The data, and the statistical tools for analyzing them, that Durkheim had available for his study on suicide would be considered unacceptably crude by present-day standards. Yet, he made a vital contribution with his method for analyzing social problems, such as suicide, in the light of the social organization or disorganization of a particular society or group.

Most modern social scientists agree that, ultimately, the person who commits suicide cannot be left out of the equation. Durkheim has, therefore, been criticized for neglecting the individuals who make up social groups in his eagerness to establish the primacy of social phenomena. He has also been criticized for neglecting to take into account the ways in which suicide statistics (the "social fact" with which he was concerned) are constructed by the decisions of coroners. Though there is justification for this criticism, Durkheim's preoccupation with wholes must be seen as a reaction to the mode of explanation used in his time, which, for the most part, sought reasons for behaviour in the motives and actions of individuals. In Box 1.2, suicide is attributed to the phenomenon of anomie that Durkheim describes.

BOX 1.2

SUICIDE RATE HIGH BECAUSE TEENS FEEL LESS SECURE

The deaths of two teenage girls in Longueuil in an apparent suicide pact are sad but not surprising, a Montreal suicide-prevention worker says.

The bodies of Katia Arpage, 15, and Geneviève Poirier, 14, were found near the train tracks in the CN Rail yard... Both lived in St. Hubert.

Police speculate the girls stood hand-in-hand facing the early morning train.

Melanie Faille, of Suicide Action Montreal, said she is angry that girls so young have problems so grave, they feel they have no options left.

Statistics Canada figures for 1989 show suicide is the second-biggest killer of Canadians aged 15 to 24.

Quebec teenagers have the fourth-highest suicide rate in the industrial world, Faille pointed out.

Faille said the rates are high because today's teens feel less secure than young people did a generation before, and face a much more competitive world.

The situation is even worse in Quebec than in other provinces, she said, because of the rapid social changes the province has undergone in the last 40 years.

Faille said the large families common in Quebec before the Quiet Revolution meant teens had more of a sense of community, and people were always around to help with problems.

Nowadays, parents have less time for their kids and are less strict, she said.

"Parents wanted to make sure kids didn't have the kind of background they did," Faille said. "But they gave too much. We forgot to say no."

Eighty-four Quebecers aged 10 to 19 killed themselves in 1989, Faille said. A 1991 study by the Université Laval community-services research centre showed one in five Quebec teens said they were profoundly unhappy. One in 10 said they had attempted suicide.

Parents worried about their children should press school boards to run suicide-prevention courses for teachers, students and families, Faille said.

She also suggested the provincial government give half the money now used each year to treat the 57,000 Quebecers who attempt to kill themselves to suicide-prevention groups.

Source: Stephanie Nolen, "Suicide Rate High Because Teens Feel Less Secure," Gazette (Montreal) (28 November 1992), p. A3. Reprinted with permission.

SETTING THE AGENDA

To look at the world from a sociological perspective is to discover the fascinating and sometimes surprising patterns of human behaviour. But before proceeding, a working definition of what we mean by sociology—a definition that will take on fuller meaning as you work your way through this book—is necessary. **Sociology** is the scientific study of relationships among and within groups. Over time, patterns of relationships crystallize into social structures. These structures constrain group and individual action, and are in turn shaped and reshaped by the push and pull of such action.

As noted in our working definition and our initial illustrations about classrooms and poverty, sociologists are concerned with the study of groups in society—for example, industrial workers, community college students, and women in the work force—and with the processes of interaction that take place among groups and between individuals. Under what circumstances does dissension arise among groups, and how is it resolved? A labour strike reflects an instance of such dissension between employer and workers. Each group seeks to maximize its share of the benefits; the workers may want higher pay and shorter working hours, while the employer may want guarantees that overtime will be worked as required. Religious conflict, such as that now occurring in the former Yugoslavia, and political conflict, such as the dispute over the Canadian constitution, become more or less acute at various periods. When the lines of group conflict harden, individuals are significantly affected. A Catholic father may assert that his daughter will marry a Muslim "over my dead body"; white parents in the United States may fight unrelentingly against having their children bussed to racially integrated schools.

Examining the relationships among large groups is called studying society at the **macrolevel**. For example, how does the working of the mass media affect the political process in a society? Sociologists can also study society at the **microlevel**, investigating the relationships within and between small groups, such as particular families or schools. For example, how are relations in the family affected when a parent becomes unemployed? What happens when a new element is brought into a formerly homogeneous group—say, a male secretary or a female senior executive? **Macrosociology** and **microsociology** are not different disciplines; rather, they use different lenses to examine what is happening in society. To look at interaction within the family or the peer group, one uses a telephoto lens. On the other hand, a wide-angle lens is a more suitable instrument for recording how labour-contract negotiations are affected by such major forces as changes in technology and economic recession. Each vantage point requires different research methodologies. These will be discussed in Chapter 2, "Sociologists at Work."

One current example of sociological research should wrap up the points covered thus far. In early l993, newspaper headlines flagged the preliminary results of a cross-Canada study on dating abuse carried out by two sociologists from Carleton University. These results showed that 81 percent of young women had suffered some sort of abuse—verbal, physical, and/or sexual—on dates in the past year. The young men who were surveyed reported, in an almost equal ratio, that they had been the perpetrators of these types of abuse. Whether these specific results are sound or not (criticisms of the study are discussed in Chapter 2), what it highlights is the fact that young Canadian women are at risk of attack, not by strangers in public places as popular mythology would have it, but from intimate male partners or acquaintances. Sources of this pattern of violence need to be sought in social forces, not individual pathology. The solutions, it seems, will be found not in individual counselling, but in revising the perceptions, behaviours, and interaction patterns of young men and women. Revisions of this magnitude, however, are likely to require even broader changes in the economic, political, and social structures that play a part in shaping the relations between men and women. Thus, in looking at the issue of dating abuse, we can move from the microsociological level (the date) to the macrosociological level (the structure of society).

SOCIAL SCIENCE PERSPECTIVES

As complex as humans are, they cannot focus on all the stimuli occurring in even a single situation. If you stop now to consider all the input you are receiving at this moment, you will realize that the task is close to impossible. What people attend to in a given situation depends on a variety of factors both internal and external. A partial inventory might include: their health, their emotional needs, their past experience, the weather, and the time of day. In a more systematic but similar manner, each practitioner of a social science will highlight some aspect of an event. To get an approximation of this process, think about an artist and farmer looking at the same field. For an example from the social sciences, picture a group of people having a meal together in a Chinese restaurant to celebrate the eighteenth birthday of one of the participants. The group is made up of young men and women who are about the same age. Their discussions revolve around school, sex, families, and movies. What might professionals in various social science disciplines make of this fictitious birthday party?

An anthropologist might comment on their eating utensils, the age segregation of the group, and the behavioural differences among the Chinese workers in the restaurant and the non-Chinese diners. A psychologist might try to assess the personality configurations of the celebrants and describe their interaction with reference to motivations. An economist could discuss consumer preferences and spending patterns for this age group or the repercussions of increased restaurant eating for the labour market. A sociologist might examine gender differences in speaking, behaviour, and nonverbal communication.

Using an example on a societal or macro level, we approached a sample of social scientists from various fields and asked them what questions they might raise concerning wife assault. Their responses appear in Box 1.3. You will notice that the approaches are not as sharply differentiated as one might expect, reflecting the overlapping of interests among the disciplines.

As you can see from Box 1.3, other social and behavioural scientists besides sociologists are interested in broadening their enquiries (making them more abstract), seeking out the general patterns suggested by individual incidents. In addition, all of these social scientists, unlike philosophers, for

BOX 1.3

WIFE ASSAULT

Statistics vary but most social scientists will agree that wife assault, which was once thought to be a rare event, is a common occurrence. Estimates are that, in Canada, one in ten women is abused. Wife assault can be defined as mental, psychological, emotional and/or physical abuse by a man living in a marital or marital-like relationship with a woman. What would social scientists, including sociologists, ask about this problem?

Sociologist: What social forces underlie wife abuse and contribute to its continuance? What impact do gender roles have on the problem? What socialization patterns encourage this behaviour? What social sanctions are necessary? Are there different rates of wife abuse in different social classes, educational, religious, or occupational groups?

Psychologist: Are there personality profiles of abusers or victims? What characterizes women who leave their husbands after the first violent incident? What motivates perpetrators to seek and respond to therapy? Are there signs of dysfunction in the couple? What types of therapy are successful?

Political Scientist: Does the government have a role in what some may consider a private issue?

What role could the government play in alleviating this problem? Should resources be allocated by the government for people in this predicament? Are public service announcements in order?

Economist: What are the costs of hours lost at work? Can these costs be lessened by setting up shelters for women and their children? Could shelters be a potential source of employment? Is there a need for workers in this field? Should costs for treatment be covered by the government, by employee benefits packages, or by the individuals themselves?

Anthropologist: Are there cultures or subcultures in which this does not occur? Are there features of social organization that promote wife assault? How have different cultures coped with this problem?

Historian: Has wife abuse been documented historically? How has the issue been approached by different groups such as religious leaders, politicians, and community members? What social changes have led to increased attention to this topic?

example, test their ideas empirically, relying on evidence of the senses. Each type of social scientist, however, would have a different focus, and would, therefore, pose different types of questions in an attempt to make sense of what has been observed. A sociologist's first question is usually, "To which groups does the person belong: which sex, age, ethnic, economic, and educational category?" The situation remains the same. The points of view of the various social scientists are like the windows of a room. Each window offers a different perspective, directing attention to different aspects of the scene outside and influencing how one perceives and defines what is going on.

THE BENEFITS OF SOCIOLOGY

Sociological enquiry invites comparison of seemingly dissimilar events in order to identify their underlying structures and common characteristics. Numerous cognitive abilities are necessary in this endeavour. Thus, studying sociology can help you to develop your critical skills, that is, your ability to comprehend, analyze, and synthesize material, and to apply theories and concepts to concrete situations.

A background in sociology is also useful for many types of occupations, such as medicine, teaching, law, social work, architecture, urban planning, business administration and careers in government service. The diversity and calibre of jobs that 1982 sociology graduates were performing in 1987 is illustrated in Exhibit 1.1.[2]

Sociology can, moreover, sensitize you to dimensions of daily interaction of which you have been unaware and/or that you could not explain. Since most people spend most of their time interacting in groups—at home, work, school, and in leisure pursuits—such insight is valuable. Perhaps you have watched a male student join a hitherto all-female group of students and have noticed that the group seemed to become formal and constrained. Before knowing something about sociology, you might have simply regretted the change or attributed it to the personality of the male student, who tended to be somewhat loud and opinionated. In the light of your new knowledge, however, you might speculate that the newcomer felt out of place and conspicuous, being the only male, and so, to ease his discomfort, he behaved in an overly assertive manner. If you learned that his high-school classmates had always found him quiet and unassuming, this explanation, focusing on his group position rather than on his personality, would gain support. The females in the group might also have become overly demure. With the entrance of the male student the composition of the group changed, and the gender of the participants became salient. This heightened awareness of gender can lead to discomfort and disrupt the former "taken-for-granted" patterns of interaction.

To the extent that sociology hones people's awareness of the complex processes involved in social intercourse, it allows them to deal with situations more effectively and may expand their options. Inasmuch as sociology provides insights into why people act as they do, it may even help human beings become more tolerant and compassionate. Further, a sociological understanding may also encourage them to make a commitment to help bring about change in some area of society.

EXHIBIT 1.1

Industry of Employment, Occupation, and Average Salary of 1982 Sociology Graduates in 1987

Industry of Employment	M	F	T	Occupation	M	F	T
Manufacturing and Constr.	13.4	0.3	4.1	Managerial/ Administrative	47.4	27.7	33.0
Transportation and Comm.	1.8	4.2	3.5	Teaching	19.6	27.2	25.1
Trade	5.1	3.7	4.1	Social Science	7.6	11.1	10.1
Finance, Insurance, Real Estate	4.0	7.7	6.6	Health	—	6.4	4.7
Business Services	3.6	3.3	3.4	Other Highly Qualified	7.4	3.1	4.2
Other Commercial	17.6	12.7	14.0	Total Highly Qualified	81.9	75.4	77.2
Total Commercial Sector	45.3	31.8	35.7	Clerical	8.5	13.7	12.3
Public Service	19.3	10.0	12.7	Sales	4.3	3.4	3.7
Education	18.0	35.2	30.2	Service	5.3	5.8	5.7
Health and Social Services	17.4	22.9	21.3	Other Non- Highly Qualified	—	1.6	1.2
Total Public Sector	54.7	68.2	64.3	Total Non- Highly Qualified	18.1	24.6	22.8
Total Graduates	642	1,569	2,211	Total Graduates	567	1,531	2,098

Annual Incomes

M	(N)	F	(N)	Total	(N)
$30,109	(490)	$28,069	(1,231)	$28,649	(1,721)

Source: Society Société, Newsletter of the Canadian Sociology and Anthropology Association, *Université Concordia, Montreal, Quebec, Vol. 16, No. 2 (May 1992). Reprinted with permission.*

CONCERNS OF THE EARLY SOCIOLOGISTS

The sociologists who shaped the discipline in the nineteenth and early twentieth centuries lived at a time of social upheaval. Ways of explaining the world that had long been taken for granted were being challenged or appeared to have no further relevance. No longer was it automatic that a son would follow in his father's occupational footsteps. That occupation might be vanishing, as occurred with bellringing, town crying, and blacksmithing. At the same time,

Early sociologists were faced with the task of explaining the transformations engendered by the Industrial Revolution.

Metropolitan Reference Library.

new occupations were emerging, creating opportunities but also curtailing the autonomy of workers such as craftsmen. The Industrial Revolution had brought in its wake the transformation of society from a rural to an urban one. With the movement of population, people could no longer assume that their lives would be played out on the same little stage. The resultant uncertainty and dislocation engendered anxiety. Many people felt they had lost their sense of direction, though others welcomed the new horizons.

In the past, nature itself had been deemed uncontrollable and unpredictable, as likely to send ideal weather for a bountiful harvest as to deliver an outbreak of plague, destroying whole communities. With the acceleration of scientific breakthroughs, there seemed to be grounds for hope that natural forces could be understood and harnessed. The founders of sociology sought, each in a different way, to apply to the study of society the modern spirit epitomized by science. If the mysteries of nature could be deciphered, it was not unreasonable to expect that patterns and regularities could be discovered in society. Once these had been identified, social phenomena would become more predictable and subject to control.

Our purpose in introducing the contributions of some of the early sociologists is not to provide more facts to be memorized. Rather, we want to identify the various streams that have fed into present-day sociological perspectives. A perspective is developed by individuals; in turn, each one's perception of the world is influenced by the social context in which he or she lives. At the time of Auguste Comte, Karl Marx, Emile Durkheim, and Max Weber, the explosion of scientific knowledge and its attendant technological development were transforming the world and ways of thinking about it.[3]

A "BASTARD" SCIENCE

The term "sociology" (made up of the Latin "socio" meaning "groups" and the Greek "logy" meaning "study of"; note that "logy" is derived from "logos," the Greek word for reason, implying that the study will be conducted along rational lines) was coined by Auguste Comte (1798–1857) who sought to make the study of society scientific by removing it from the realms of philosophy and theology. In *Introduction to Positive Philosophy* ([1830–42] 1970), Comte divided his study into what he called "social statics" and "social dynamics." In the former, he examined the nature and interplay of mechanisms that contribute to stability. He isolated three factors as vital to the maintenance of social order:

- *language*, which provides a common medium for behaviour;
- *religion*, which cements society by providing shared rituals and beliefs; and
- the *division of labour* (the breaking down of work into specialized tasks), which brings about mutual interdependence.

For Comte, the major importance of a particular institution, such as the family or religion, was in the contribution it makes to maintaining society as a harmonious whole.[4] Stability and order were high on Comte's list of priorities, in part, perhaps, because they were conspicuously absent in the society in which he lived. Just before his birth, the French Revolution had occurred. In its aftermath, France was rocked by a series of further revolutions that wrought extensive social changes in the nineteenth century.

Under the heading of "social dynamics," Comte addressed questions of social progress and human evolution. In his law of three stages, he argued that every society must pass through the theological and the metaphysical stage to arrive at the positive stage. The dominant mode of explanation in the first stage is religious dogma and, in the second, abstract speculation. The positive stage is marked by the scientific approach, which combines empirical observations and analysis, both carried out according to specified rules.

Comte believed that, through scientific study, the laws that govern society could be discovered and, from this knowledge, society could be shaped and thus bettered. However, since he did not attempt to test whether the law of three stages applies in the "real" world, he did not put to work the scientific method he advocated.

Comte was, however, the first analyst to lay out a program for investigating society scientifically and to specify the types of enquiry to be used for this enterprise:

- *Observation* within the limits set by his theoretical framework of social statics and social dynamics. Without such a framework, observations are merely a jumble, an aggregation of unrelated items.
- *Comparison* between animal and human societies and among different types of human societies. In this way, the processes of evolution are made apparent.
- *Historical analysis*, since to understand what exists now (for example, a particular family form, such as the nuclear family), one must look back to how it developed.

These three prerequisites may seem obvious today. In Comte's day, however, this was a novel way to approach the study of society. His method has endured and is now taken for granted in the investigation of social issues.

THE STRUGGLE FOR POWER AS HISTORICAL REALITY

Describing someone as "Comtian" would have no meaning for the layperson, but the term "Marxist" is used throughout the world, attesting to the pervasive influence on modern thought of Karl Marx. For many people, the label "Marxist" is tied to left-wing (or radical, change-promoting) political views. This association is not incorrect, but it does not convey the substance of Marx's works. For sociologists, the term implies seeing society as an arena of conflict in which the advantage lies with those who are already privileged.

Marx viewed the history of societies as the struggle for societal rewards (power and possessions) between a dominant group and exploited groups. Exploiter and exploited assume different guises at different points in history, but disparities in power are a persistent characteristic of human societies. In ancient Greece and Rome, according to Marx, the basic struggle was between free men and slaves. Free Romans were themselves divided into the upper-crust patricians and the mass of plebeians, terms still used to connote class differences. However, slaves were the most exploited group; as individuals, they were without power and had minimal civil rights. In medieval Europe, the dominant groups were the nobility, the upper clergy, and the landowners (these groups sometimes overlapped). Peasants and serfs were the subordinated groups. Serfs were tied to the land; they could not move about, get married, or make any significant decisions about their lives without the consent of the landowner. Even the nominally free peasants had little latitude in what they could or could not do. In Marx's own time, the unequal contest was between the bourgeoisie and the proletariat. The bourgeoisie owned the **means of production**, that is, whatever was needed—other than human labour—to produce the goods and services required by the society. This included natural resources such as land for crops, animals, and buildings; capital such as factories, workshops, machinery, and tools; and the money to buy more of these material things. The proletariat was made up of landless workers who had nothing to sell but their labour.[5] The workers were "exploited" because capitalists paid them less in wages than the value their labour produced. The **surplus value** was appropriated by the capitalists, thus giving them economic power that increased on a cumulative basis.

In each historical case, the power of the dominant group was rooted in its control of the means of production. Marx did not claim that the position of a slave in Roman times was equivalent to that of a nineteenth-century factory worker. Their similarity lay in the fact that both were on the lowest rung of the social ladder. Indeed, one of Marx's most important contributions to the social sciences was his insistence that individuals, groups, and institutions must be studied in their specific social contexts. In other words, to understand the position of a teacher in a particular society, for example, one must look at the value that society places on education, at the way the educational system is organized, at the training required to become a teacher, and at the kinds of individuals likely to have access to this occupation.

The nature of the various contesting groups changes over time; the essential struggle, instead of being between free men and slaves, becomes, for Marx, one between owners and workers. Changes in these groups attest to changes in society. How does change come about? Marx argued that every social order, every economic system, develops internal contradictions (features that are inconsistent, that is, work against each other). Over time, these contradictions become so strong that they can no longer be handled within the confines of the existing order; when this occurs, the existing order is overthrown, and a new order comes into being. This new order encompasses novel features as well as the remnants of the previous system. However, Marx did not believe that transformations could be predicted on the basis of general laws. As we have noted, he stipulated that each situation must be analyzed empirically, that is, in its specific historical context.

For example, with the accelerating development of technology and other changes in the mode of production, workers had to be able to move to the location of jobs. Thus, since it was impractical to have a labour force that was partially tied to the land, the feudal system became obsolete. However, the capitalist system that emerged was, in turn, to be fractured by oppositional forces (internal contradictions) that, Marx predicted, would cause the demise of the system. From its ruins would arise a socialist order in which inequality would be abolished.

Marx was a German by birth, but his revolutionary journalism and other activities led to his living in exile for much of his life. Most of his best-known work was done in England, which, in mid-century, was experiencing the most blatant excesses of the Industrial Revolution (excesses well documented in the novels of Charles Dickens). Understanding the political and social chaos he lived in is a prerequisite to understanding his work.

Marx will be encountered again when we examine the bases on which societal rewards are allocated.

SOCIAL REGULATION AND SOCIAL COHESION

Following defeat in the Franco-Prussian war, Napoleon III was overthrown in 1871, and the Third French Republic was established. France was a latecomer to the Industrial Revolution. The migration of rural labourers to the cities, which Marx had observed in Britain a generation earlier, was therefore occurring only in the late 1800s, which was also the period in which Durkheim wrote most of his influential works.

When most people had lived in small, homogeneous communities, individuals had performed similar work, engaged in similar lifestyles, and, because of these similar circumstances, held common values and beliefs. This **mechanical solidarity**, as Durkheim labelled it, cemented the social order. In the agricultural society of preindustrial Europe, each family unit was relatively self-sufficient. Durkheim believed that the mechanical solidarity rooted in similarity and self-sufficiency would eventually be replaced by **organic solidarity**, a state of interdependence created by a highly specialized division of labour. Just as the liver, the heart, the brain, and other organs must perform particular work for the body to function as a whole, so must each group carry out its tasks in order for society to operate. In today's world, mutual interdependence is brought home dramatically when an occupational group, such as transit workers or nurses, goes on strike, seriously disrupting everyday life.

In Durkheim's time, the social order was changing so swiftly that the old communal values were eroding before appropriate new values had come to be held in common. As previously mentioned, Durkheim described this situation as anomie (normlessness, a lack of values). As we will discuss in Chapter 4, which deals with socialization, one of Durkheim's important contributions was to explain how societal values are internalized (made part of the individual). Social control thus also works in "invisible" ways, and is not solely imposed by external agents. People who have been socialized to one set of values become disoriented if they find themselves in a world in which these values no longer appear applicable. This happened to many new urbanites in the late nineteenth century; their familiar guideposts had disappeared, and no reliable new ones were available. It was this climate, Durkheim contended, that contributed to increasing numbers of suicides.

THE ESTABLISHMENT OF SOCIOLOGY AS AN ACADEMIC DISCIPLINE

Comte coined the term "sociology" and attempted to provide the infant discipline with a scientific basis. Marx's controversial theories of how a social order persists and changes thrust the study of society into the forefront of intellectual and popular debate. It was left to Durkheim to establish sociology as a legitimate area of academic study.

In 1913, Durkheim was appointed professor of the newly created chair of the Science of Education and Sociology at the prestigious Sorbonne in Paris. In this capacity and through his previous long and fruitful association with the faculty of education at the Sorbonne, Durkheim was able to influence the training of teachers and hence the way new generations of students would be socialized. With a group of brilliant young scholars, Durkheim founded *L'Année Sociologique* in 1898. The journal was an instant success in the academic community, allowing Durkheim to communicate his approach to sociology to other social scientists throughout the world. His impact on many areas of sociology means that we will encounter Durkheim's formulations, like Marx's, in subsequent chapters in this book.

THE SUBJECTIVE DIMENSION OF HUMAN ACTION

Like France, Germany was a relative latecomer to the Industrial Revolution. Max Weber (1864–1920) observed the struggle between the landed aristocracy, which still wielded a disproportionate degree of political power, and the new urban middle class, which was anxious to obtain some of this power. The tension between tradition and innovation informed much of Weber's research, notably his interpretation of the emergence of capitalism.

Like Durkheim, Weber influenced many areas of sociology. Some of his best-known works deal with the characteristics of bureaucracy, an organizational form with which all North Americans are familiar, having encountered it in hospitals, schools, private corporations, and so on. Long before bureaucracies actually became the dominant mode of organization, Weber anticipated this development. Although he believed this form was technically the most efficient one, he was concerned with its potential for depersonalizing and dehumanizing people. In another important area studied by Weber and explicated in *The*

Protestant Ethic and the Spirit of Capitalism (1958), he attempted to demonstrate that the collective values and beliefs of individuals were crucial to the emergence of capitalism.

Both of these contributions will be examined in some detail in subsequent chapters. Here we will focus on some of the dimensions Weber added to the study of society. He believed that to understand a culture, one has to immerse oneself in it. Knowing the language is invaluable in allowing the researcher to become sensitive to what is going on and to hear not only words but the meaning behind them. (Weber practised what he preached; he had a command of several languages, among them English, Latin, Greek, and Hebrew.) His concept of *Verstehen*, which is the German word for "understanding," but used by him to mean "empathic understanding," is now a basis for all qualitative sociological research methods, such as in-depth interviews and community studies, in which researchers try to think themselves as much as possible into the frame of mind of those they are studying. This kind of stance has pragmatic advantages: consider how much of the goodwill generated by aid projects to third-world countries is dissipated when project personnel are not attuned to the ways in which the native population lives and thinks.

Weber, like Marx, was a historical sociologist. He believed that to understand the characteristics of a society or of an organizational form, such as a bureaucracy, one needs to trace its evolution. Weber was concerned with understanding the meaning that individuals attach to their actions in a particular socio-historic context. This led him to study the migration patterns of East-Prussian tenant farmers. Their large-scale movement away from the estates (where many had worked for generations) into the rapidly growing cities was causing problems for contemporary landowners, who were left without experienced workers. Since most of the migrants did not have skills that were easily marketable in an urban setting, they lived there in abject poverty. In the short run, therefore, they were worse off than they had been. Weber reasoned that their actions had to be viewed in light of their belief that they were providing their children with the chance of a better life in the long run. In other words, one could not understand the actions or motives of these labourers without knowing the positive value they placed on giving their children opportunities to improve themselves and the belief that this could be accomplished in the cities. (Similar arguments can be put forward to explain the severe hardships many immigrants to North America have been willing to endure.)

Durkheim firmly believed that social scientists have a duty to help strengthen the moral basis of society. In contrast, Weber argued that the task of the scientist was to unravel the interplay of factors that gives rise to a chain of events—for instance, the Industrial Revolution—and to delineate further possible consequences of such occurrences. For Weber, however, prescription (a recommendation of what ought to be done) was inappropriate for someone engaged in a scientific enterprise.

Weber was aware, however, that values enter into the social scientist's choice of what to investigate. Selecting an area for study designates it as important, at least to some segment of society. In North America, for example, the high value placed on the preservation of human life is reflected in the huge resources devoted to medical research and health care. It is in the conduct of the actual research that the scientist must leave personal values aside. For example, you may be assigned an essay on a topic—say, euthanasia—on which you have adamant feelings. Nonetheless, if you are asked to write an essay and not an editorial, you have a responsibility to investigate the issue objectively and to avoid value-laden language when reporting your findings.

Comte, Marx, Durkheim, and Weber were concerned with the links between the individual and society, and with the tension between the autonomy of the individual and the coercive power of social structures. Marx focused on the coercive role of economic relations and the binding role of ideology, a form of control in modern society, while Comte and Durkheim emphasized the binding function of shared values and beliefs. Weber, too, recognized the importance of shared values, as well as the administrative mechanisms, such as government bureaus and business firms, that establish connections between individuals and the larger society.

PRESENT-DAY APPROACHES TO SOCIOLOGICAL QUESTIONS

The questions addressed by these men and by their contemporaries have continued to exercise the minds of sociologists. Although the range of social phenomena is vast, one can discern patterns in the ways sociologists choose to define and investigate questions. We will now briefly examine some major modern perspectives, or schools of thought.

FUNCTIONALISM

Functionalism is rooted in the tradition of Durkheim and more remotely in that of Comte. It treats society as a system, which is itself made up of smaller systems, such as armies or families. A system can be defined as an arrangement of interrelated and interdependent parts. Each performs functions that contribute to the well-being of the entire system. For a system to operate effectively, each of the component parts must perform its task. Although most functionalists do not take the organic analogy literally, they often cite the human body to illustrate the notion of a system. Clearly, a person cannot survive if a vital organ is out of kilter; heart failure will produce a lethal crisis even if all the other vital organs are sound.

Systems, such as an army, possess certain characteristics:

- *Boundaries.* One is either a member of the army or not.

- *Interdependence of parts.* Communication of commands and information, deployment of troops, and distribution of material are interdependent activities.

- *Needs.* An army needs recruits, weaponry, and food supplies.

- *Equilibrium state.* If an army increases in number, as in wartime, supply depots must be enlarged accordingly. For a system to persist, changes in one part must be compensated for by changes in its other parts. The result is a shifting balance called a dynamic equilibrium.

Functionalism has been a prominent orientation among North American sociologists, especially in the 1950s and 1960s, with Talcott Parsons (1902–1979) and Robert Merton (1910–) as its two leading exponents. Parsons's writing is not easy to understand, but his work has been highly influential. For a good discussion of what functionalism is (and is not), see Merton's *Social Theory and Social Structure* (1968). Scholars who held this perspective believed that correct identification of the functions assigned to various parts of the social system would facilitate performance of these functions. During the years immediately after the Second World War ended, hopes that poverty, racial discrimination, and other social problems could and would be eliminated were high. A society in which all could share in the good life was believed to be just around the corner.

In practice, however, social systems are never in a perfect state of equilibrium. Functionalists tend to view a society as a relatively homogeneous whole, characterized by shared values and beliefs. It is obvious, however, that a large, complex society, such as Canada's, contains groups whose interests and values are opposed. Thus, equal-opportunity legislation is functional for such groups as women or native peoples, who have hitherto been denied access to certain prestigious positions. On the other hand, such legislation can be seen as dysfunctional for those (in this case, white males) who must now compete with more contestants for desirable jobs.

As we shall see throughout the book, many other criticisms have been raised against functionalism, among them that the kind of harmonious society it posits simply does not exist any longer, if it ever did. A related charge is that functionalism places insufficient emphasis on the importance of power differentials and on their consequences for society, for groups and for individuals. With its emphasis on consensus and stability, it tells us more about how social phenomena persist than about how they change. The functionalist perspective has, nevertheless, made important contributions to sociological analysis. First, it has sensitized investigators to those shared values and assumptions often taken so much for granted that they remain implicit rather than explicit in the culture. This "hidden consensus" can be recognized most readily through contact with members of another culture who do not share one's values and assumptions. Thus, the discovery that some societies prize plump women reveals that the ideal of *Vogue* slimness is not universal. Second, researchers with a functionalist perspective have undertaken a great deal of research into many areas of social life. William Goode (1970), for instance, did cross-cultural studies of the relationships between industrialization and the ways in which families are structured and operate.

Although functionalism is no longer the overriding perspective in North American sociology, it continues to exert a strong influence on the work of many present-day sociologists.

THE CONFLICT PERSPECTIVE

Functionalists concentrate on the mechanisms by which society coheres. The **conflict perspective** is rooted in the writings of Weber and Marx, although not all conflict theorists accept all of their arguments. Conflict theorists focus on areas of dissent and strife. They look at opposed interest groups and at their attempts to gain (or maintain) power in order to further their own advantage at the expense of other groups. Take, for example, the debate over the elimination of grade 13 in Ontario. Proponents of both positions couched their arguments in terms of what would be most beneficial to the education of students. Conflict theorists point out, however, that beneath this debate smouldered a conflict between secondary school teachers, eager to keep students in their schools as long as possible to safeguard existing teaching jobs, and community colleges and universities, intent on maximizing their share of the educational tax dollar.

For a society or a group to persist, it clearly needs some consensus, but social scientists disagree as to how this consensus is attained and maintained. Where a functionalist points to shared values, the conflict theorist focuses on the ability of dominant groups to enforce their viewpoint by dint of force and misrepresentation. Immigrant workers unfamiliar with Canadian laws may, for example, be told by anti-union employers that union membership is illegal or that union dues would take a large bite from the workers' earnings; they may also be threatened, subtly or blatantly, with the spectre of plant closure or with dismissal.

The Hutterites provide a good example of social phenomena that are perceived quite differently when studied by researchers with either a functionalist or a conflict perspective.[6] The functionalists see a group united by shared values and sentiments, with each practice of the group making a contribution to that harmony. On the other hand, conflict theorists note that the group's stability is achieved in large part by its custom of restricting access to power to a minority—mature men. Hence, those who might want to institute changes are deprived of the means of doing so. Thus, some Hutterite women have expressed to researchers the desire to bear fewer children, but lacking money to obtain birth control devices, they have been powerless to do so.

Among the prominent modern conflict theorists are Ralf Dahrendorf (1929–) and C. Wright Mills (1916–1962). In *Class and Class Conflict in Industrial Society* (1959), Dahrendorf asserts that change, conflict, and coercion are persistent features of every society. In *The Power Elite* (1956), Mills argued that, in the United States, power is wielded by a relatively small group that controls the industrial, military, and government apparatus, and that this group uses power to further its own ends rather than seeking to benefit society at large.

By definition, conflict theorists are interested in areas of conflict and in the ways in which groups jostle for power so as to maintain or gain an advantage. In some circumstances, such as under slavery or in concentration camps, the power of the dominant group is virtually absolute. In North American society, groups and individuals can enter the push and shove of the political arena more freely, though not always effectively. Human rights legislation, which includes fair employment laws and the establishment of an ombudsman's office in many Canadian jurisdictions, are examples of attempts to equalize power between large collectivities and individuals or subordinated groups. The research study, *Making Fast Food* (Reiter 1991), discussed in Chapter 2, provides a recent example of a work that employs a conflict perspective.

Power and its deployment are central to a conflict view, just as emphasis on common values informs the functionalist perspective. Theoretical orientation affects whether a bottle is seen as half full or half empty. Sociologists have noted in connection with the Hutterites that functionalists may point to an observed consensus, while the researcher attuned to conflict asks at what cost the consensus is brought about. As tools for making sense of social life, both approaches have utility, but one should always be aware of what questions are being neglected.

SYMBOLIC INTERACTIONISM

While functionalists and conflict theorists address themselves to large-scale relationships—for example, those between the values of a society and institutions such as the family or education—symbolic interactionists focus on how individual actors interpret given situations. This is a microsociological approach. The assumption is that these interpretations are the basis for subsequent action. In other words, **symbolic interactionism** is concerned with how individuals subjectively construct, and react to, social situations. (Note symbolic interactionism's intellectual debt to Max Weber, who also concerned himself with the meanings people attach to events in social life.) The same situation need not evoke the same response in two people or in the same person in different circumstances. For example, individuals may react with pleasure, amusement, fear, or anger to a remark about their appearance, depending on the interpretation given to the words.

Symbolic interactionists attribute major importance to **symbols**, which can be defined as signs that have shared meaning to members of a group. Behaviour is then structured in terms of what a particular symbol means. The police officer's uniform acts as a symbol, and people react to the uniform rather than to the person wearing it. For some, the symbol may signify danger, for others safety. Words are symbols that collectively form the most important human symbolic code: language.

In focusing on how people behave in social units, such as families or offices, and in how a unit is shaped by the actions and interactions of its members, symbolic interactionists use the perspectives of both sociology and psychology. They are, therefore, often described as adopting a social-psychological viewpoint.

The theory of symbolic interactionism was first developed by Americans George Herbert Mead (1863–1931) and Charles Horton Cooley (1864–1933). They were intent on showing that human beings differ in kind from other animals because they are able to objectify themselves—that is, each can imagine the effect of his or her behaviour on others and the possible reactions of those others. We will encounter the ideas of these scholars in Chapters 3 and 4, the topics of which are culture and socialization.

Many present-day sociologists adhere to this perspective, and a large body of research is informed by it.[7] Howard Becker and Erving Goffman, among others, are prominent in this area; like many of their colleagues, they study familiar situations and discover that they are more complex than they appear. For example, Becker and Geer looked at the processes by which medical students are transformed into full-fledged physicians. Their study *Boys in White* (1961) provides fascinating illustrations of the changes that occur in the ways these students perceive themselves and the ways they are perceived by others, such as instructors and patients. Goffman joined the staff of a state mental hospital while doing his research for *Asylums* (1962), in which he focused primarily on the situation of inmates who must adapt to a role dramatically different from those they played on the outside. Goffman observed the ways in which staff and patients interacted among themselves and with each other. A patient who engaged in behaviour that might have been defined outside the institution as showing initiative or being innovative was likely to be labelled difficult to manage.

The functionalist and conflict perspectives outline the basic contours of social life; the symbolic interactionist approach shades in the details. Indeed, a criticism of symbolic interactionism is that it is so preoccupied with the trees that it loses sight of the forest. For example, Zeitlin (1973) argued that Goffman focuses on the minutiae of daily life without taking sufficient account of the larger context in which they occur. In other words, to really understand why state mental hospitals operate as they do, observers must look at the society of which these hospitals are a part, and at how that society defines mental illness. For an informative volume on symbolic interactionism, including a chapter on its methodology, see Blumer (1987).

FEMINIST APPROACHES TO SOCIOLOGY

Feminist contributions to sociology began to emerge in the 1970s in conjunction with the revival of the women's liberation movement and share its goal of valorizing women. (For a discussion of the women's movement itself, see Chapter 13.) Much feminist sociology is drawn from this political movement and from the sociological perspectives of Marxism and symbolic interactionism.[8] The term "feminist sociology," however, is a catchall. Feminists do not all agree on which issues are important or about how to tackle those issues, so a succinct synopsis of the diverse viewpoints is difficult.[9] What we will try to do in this section is to highlight the most basic commonalities of the feminist perspective and describe briefly the three main currents of feminist thinking.

One tenet of feminist sociology is that women and the worlds they inhabit have been disregarded. Most sociological inquiry has focused on industrialization, large-scale political and economic changes, and the public and formal worlds of male actors. The private, domestic, and informal realms inhabited by women have not been seen as problematic and therefore worthy of study. Women's roles have been considered unimportant and/or predominantly biologically based and therefore irrelevant. Men have been taken as the norm and research findings have been generalized to include women. To remedy this lopsided picture, feminist sociologists endeavour to incorporate women's concerns, experiences, and viewpoints into sociology.

If the task of sociology is to examine the relationship between people's own experiences and social structures, then the aim of feminist sociology is to relate women's experiences, hitherto ignored, to larger social forces. This idea is expressed in the feminist slogan of the sixties, "The personal is political." In other words, societal-level relationships of power and authority affect even the most intimate behaviour of men and women. That women still wait for men to "make the first move" in sexual relationships and that women must be "nice" by not "sleeping around" are examples of "the personal." They are reflections of the "political" fact that very few women have political power, that women are underrepresented (i.e., found in lower numbers than would be expected given their proportion of the population) in higher paying occupations in the labour force, and that they earn less, on average, than men.

There are three main currents of feminist sociology: radical feminism, socialist feminism, and liberal feminism. Each of them has a unique analysis of sexism and, therefore, a different focal point. Radical feminists see male dominance, rooted in women's biological capacities, as the basis of all other systems of oppression, such as class and race. They have shown both a scholarly and a practical concern with the matter of violence against women. Socialist feminists identify class and capitalism as the basis of women's lesser status, and challenge the power relations of the social and economic order. Liberal feminists believe that women can achieve equality of opportunity by promoting legal changes that do not involve the radical restructuring of society (Adamson, Briskin, and McPhail, 1988).

By exposing **sexism**, prejudice, and discrimination on the basis of sex, feminist sociology, then, not only includes women, it seeks to work for and empower them. Knowledge of how sexism works and is reproduced in daily interaction can be used to bring about changes in the system that will promote social equality between men and women.

Dorothy Smith (1987), notable in the field of Canadian feminist sociology, has conducted research on the work mothers do to help their children as students. She demonstrates that the school appropriates (or makes use of) the activities of mothers in helping their children participate in the educational system. She thus renders this "invisible" unpaid work visible, showing that the boundaries between the "private" domain of families and the "public" domain of education are less pronounced than they are generally conceived to be.

Feminist scholars also discuss the social construction of knowledge and argue that what is accepted as knowledge is influenced by social relations (Eichler, 1985). In other words, the vista one sees depends on one's location in the scene. Knowledge, too, usually reflects the vision of people in power (white men). Feminists assert that women are social actors whose location in society, different from that of men, is at least as worthy of examination, and that this examination may call for different assumptions and methodologies. The generating of sociological knowledge from a feminist perspective is considered in more depth in Chapter 2.

Much of the research cited in this text is informed by a feminist perspective. Throughout the text we have also included many examples and issues that particularly concern women. By avoiding a separate chapter on gender, we hope to emphasize that women share the world with men and that it is inappropriate to relegate them to a separate place either in a textbook or in society.

TRYING PERSPECTIVES ON FOR SIZE

The classroom scenario, again, can give you a feel for the contrasts of contemporary sociological schools of thought. A functionalist sociologist could examine the part played by tests and exams in education or determine the function of extra-curricular activities. At a macrolevel, the functionalist might be concerned with how what goes on in schools relates to what goes on in the work world. A conflict theorist might focus on the power differential between teachers and students, or between different categories of students, to identify who captures the privileges and who is excluded from them. On a macrolevel, one could trace which groups vie for control of educational institutions and how that struggle reflects the distribution of power in the society. Symbolic interactionists, who are by definition microsociologists, might check students' perceptions of a class. For students, is it an opportunity to learn, an occasion to catch up with friends, or a possible meeting place for a boyfriend or girlfriend? How do the students' perceptions square with the teacher's, and what are the results of these differing expectations? Feminists, as we shall see in Chapter 10, "Education: Winning and Losing," might be concerned with the sexist nature of classroom interaction or of the curriculum, and might examine the ways in which opportunities are structured differently for males and females.

By adopting one perspective rather than another, a sociologist illuminates particular aspects of social existence, leaving others in darkness. Therefore, it is best to use several different viewpoints in order to make sense of the world. People need to know how institutions and the relationships among them are moulded by processes of cooperation and conflict, but also important is discovering the interpretations individuals attach to situations and the ways in which such interpretations influence behaviour.

. . . .

OVERVIEW

In this introductory chapter the aim was to give you a sense of the sociological perspective. We have mapped some of the ways in which sociology sheds new light on familiar territory. The territory is large and variegated. It includes society as an entity and the many groups that make up this entity. Sociology calls attention to the continuous interplay between individuals and the social context in which they live out their lives.

The roots of modern sociology lie in the Europe that was shattered by a series of political revolutions and profoundly altered by industrialization and massive migration in the late eighteenth and nineteenth centuries. Comte, Marx, Durkheim, and Weber, each in his own way, sought to explain the bases of social stability and the dynamics of change. The insights they brought to the analysis of society have provided an underpinning for subsequent sociological study. In some cases, modern enquiry has followed the paths laid out by these founders. In other instances, sociologists have taken new approaches. Recently feminist scholars have challenged "mainstream" sociology.

One of the most important uses of sociology is to lay bare the connection between the general and the particular. You can recognize, for example, the disadvantaged position of individual women as a manifestation of inequality in the society. A sociological perspective enables you to move back and forth between these levels. Since, to a large extent, the everyday and the common-place provide the grist for the sociological mill, this agility is especially useful for understanding social life.

ASSIGNMENTS

1. We began this chapter by examining a concrete, rather ordinary, event: your class. Raise a sociological question about another situation you encounter in your everyday life. How is the question sociological and which of the perspectives that we have discussed might be useful in exploring it?

2. Try to determine how a sociologist from each perspective would approach some feature of your university or college. Do not answer questions, but pose ones that you think would be generated by each perspective.

3. For a combination of sociology, history, and literature, read Fay Weldon's *Letters to Alice on First Reading Jane Austen* (1984). With Weldon as a guide, use your sociological curiosity to examine another work of fiction, a biography, or an autobiography.

SUGGESTED READINGS

Bennet M. Berger, ed., *Authors of Their Own Lives: Intellectual Autobiographies by Twenty American Sociologists* (Berkeley: University of California Press, 1990). The first person singular does not come easily to most sociologists, since one of the conventions of academic writing, what Berger calls "the rhetoric of academic impersonality," has dictated that social scientists keep themselves as invisible as possible. Berger invited some well-known sociologists to reflect on the relationship between their lives and their work. The authors talk about what brought them to sociology in the first place, and what kept them there.

Peter Berger, *Invitation to Sociology: A Humanistic Perspective* (New York: Doubleday, 1963). Berger outlines the ways in which a sociological perspective can provide a clearer understanding of human interaction. One can readily relate to the examples he uses to illustrate his arguments. The writing is lively and commendably jargon-free.

Bertolt Brecht, *The Life of Galileo* (London: Eyre Methuen, 1981; first published in German in 1939). Brecht's play is about the suppression of scientific truths that threaten existing belief systems. In the early 1600s, Galileo's observations that the earth revolved around the sun contradicted the Church's teaching that God created the earth as the centre of the universe. Thus, these observations had to be declared in error, and Galileo was forced to recant. Brecht, a German with passionate anti-Nazi convictions, wrote the play in the late 1930s, a time when truth was being twisted in the service of political ideology.

William C. Carroll, Linda Christiansen-Ruffman, Raymond F. Currie, and Deborah Harrison, eds., *Fragile Truths: 25 Years of Sociology and Anthropology in Canada* (Ottawa: Carleton University Press, 1992). In the introduction to this collection of essays, the authors note that "The truths that our disciplines offer are not fast-frozen and absolute; they are historical, interpretive, and contingent—as are the social and cultural realities of which our disciplines speak." We are reminded that the study of society is a very human enterprise, optimistic, tentative, and flawed. The contributors examine the historical context that helped to shape the emergence and development of sociology and anthropology in Canada, and also review the contributions that members of the two disciplines have made to an understanding of Canadian society and to social policy.

C. Wright Mills, *The Sociological Imagination* (New York: Oxford University Press, 1959). In this critique of the sociological enterprise, Mills argues that the sociological imagination is properly exercised in that territory where "private troubles" and "public issues" meet. That is to say, the sociologist has a responsibility to explore the connections between the experience of individuals and the social structures in which they are located. Mills believed that sociology could help people to realize their dreams of a better world.

William Outhwaite and Tom Bottomore, eds., *The Blackwell Dictionary of Twentieth-Century Social Thought* (Oxford: Blackwell Publishers, 1993). Obviously, dictionaries are not meant to be read from cover to cover. This volume, however, is useful to consult. The entries have been commissioned from a wide range of experts in an attempt to address three themes: 1) the concepts that have been influential in social thinking; 2) the principal schools and movements, and 3) the institutions and organizations that have been important objects of social analysis or that have themselves produced major ideas and doctrines. In conjunction with this chapter of your textbook, you might, for example, consult the items "Conflict," "Feminism," "Functionalism," "Marxism," and "Symbolic Interactionism."

NOTES

1. Durkheim's powerful intellect did not prevent him from sharing the myth that marriage was more beneficial for women than men. On finding that recently widowed men were far more likely to kill themselves than recently widowed women, he reluctantly concluded that men might derive greater benefits and stability from marriage than was commonly believed.

2. For further information on occupational and educational opportunities for recent sociology BA graduates, you can order *Opportunities*, a brochure by Neil Guppy and Alan Hedley, c/o Concordia University, 1455 boul., De Maisonneuve Ouest, Montreal, Quebec H3G 1M8.

3. Two discussions of the development of sociological theory you might consult are Collins and Makowsky's *The Discovery of Society* (1984) and Swingewood's *A Short History of Sociological Thought* (1984).

4. A social institution is a patterned way of accomplishing an important social goal or solving an important social problem. It emerges from the interaction of a particular group's beliefs, value system, and coping strategies. Institutions are examined in Section 4, Chapters 9 to 11.

5. This very brief overview of Marx's does not do justice to the complexity of his arguments. See Chapter 8, "Work and Its Contexts," for an elaboration of Marx's theories.

6. The Hutterites are a fundamentalist Protestant sect with a number of rural colonies in western Canada and some adjacent American states. Their traditional, communal lifestyle is deeply rooted in their religious beliefs, and many aspects of it have changed little in 450 years.

7. When sociologists are described as working from a similar perspective, this does not mean that there are no differences in their views.

8. Ethnomethodology, a type of symbolic interactionism developed by Harold Garfinkel in the late 1960s, has provided theoretical input for feminist sociology. Ethnomethodologists try to discover the "background understandings," that is, the knowledge and rules shared by people that allow them to interact comfortably. The idea that the everyday world of ordinary reality is something problematic to be explored is in line with examining how sexism is recreated in everyday life. For a discussion of ethnomethodology, see Garfinkel's *Studies in Ethnomethodology* (1967).

9. Nor are all feminists women. Even this statement, however, brings up an example of the diversity of feminist viewpoints. Some feminists do not believe that men can be feminists, since they do not share the life experiences of being women themselves. Other feminists do not think that being male automatically prevents one from being a feminist. For an elaboration, see Pamela Abbott and Claire Wallace's *An Introduction to Sociology: Feminist Perspectives* (1993).

CHAPTER TWO

Sociologists at Work

The sociologist, then, is someone concerned with understanding society in a disciplined way. The nature of this discipline is scientific. This means that what the sociologist finds and says about the social phenomena he studies occurs within a certain rather strictly defined frame of reference.

Peter Berger, *Invitation to Sociology*

What do sociologists do? Most sociologists teach in academic institutions and usually also do research. Some sociologists work for private or public corporations as researchers. The research may be to determine social trends, public policy, consumer preferences, or to address some current social issue of interest. All sociologists, even those who do not carry out their own studies, must be able to evaluate the work of others, so a grounding in the conducting of research is essential.

Given this focus on research in whatever sector a sociologist works, in this chapter we will examine how one, occupationally, puts sociology into practice or "does sociology." (We have tried in Chapter 1 to show that even if you don't become a sociologist, the study of sociology can be immensely beneficial for you personally and occupationally.)

As a concrete illustration of a sociologist at work, we begin with a study by Ester Reiter (1991) on work in the fast foods industry, *Making Fast Food: From the Frying Pan into the Fire*. Before we proceed, think for a moment about your experiences with fast food. How much do you know about it? How often do you buy it? Have you worked at a fast food franchise? What was your experience as a customer or an employee?

The fast food phenomenon has become so common, even world-wide, that it is probably almost impossible to imagine a time when you couldn't, for a relatively small amount of money, walk up to a counter, order and obtain a meal, eat it, and clear away your debris all in about twenty minutes. Reiter starts by describing the growing permeability of the boundary between the public and private worlds of paid work and consumption in creating fast food consumers. She documents the expansion of the restaurant industry from a time when restaurant meals were unavoidable necessities for people away from home to the incredible proliferation of the factory-like fast food chains in the past few decades. In large metropolitan areas, fast food outlets occur every 17.2 blocks.[1] In 1988, McDonald's grossed over $1.4 billion in Canada (Reiter, 1991, 47).

Fast food outlets have become so common it's almost impossible to imagine being unable to order and eat a cheap meal in less than 20 minutes.

Ontario Ministry of Transportation.

Reiter herself worked in a Burger King franchise (employing the technique of participant observation, which is explained more fully later on in this chapter). Having tried unsuccessfully to attend McDonald's Hamburger University, Reiter attended a ten-week training course for food supervisors at George Brown College (1991, 78) and secured a position at a Burger King outlet in a suburban shopping mall she calls Briarwood.

In her study she describes the workers, the jobs, the management, and the day-to-day interaction in the restaurant. Infusing feminist perspectives into her descriptions, Reiter reveals the food industry's reliance on the existing gendered division of labour that allows it to offer poor working conditions and salaries. The explosive success of the industry could not have occurred without women who mainly work at home and young people who attend school. Burger King offers them an opportunity to earn money with supposedly minimal intrusion on their other responsibilities.

Reiter characterizes the conditions the Burger King workers face as exploitative, despite the contrary public relations pitch. Parents, she writes, have come to the franchise managers to demand that allowances be made in their teenaged children's schedules to enable them to do their schoolwork in addition to their Burger King jobs. Often the manager does not bend. Workers' dilemmas are private troubles, to be worked out by themselves. Scheduling problems often result in workers' being fired. Workers complain infrequently, as the training process in the restaurant encourages them to get along with everyone and dismisses any notion of workers' rights and corresponding employers' responsibilities. Reiter sums it up:

There is little personal space at Burger King. The "working knowledge" or "tacit skills" Burger King workers bring to their jobs give them little room to manoeuvre in moderating management directives. Even physical needs such as drinking water or using the washroom are regulated. Scheduling procedures do not take workers' interests into consideration: the hours and days when workers are scheduled vary weekly according to Burger King's wishes.

The informal social life of the workplace is used by Burger King to create identification with the company and management pays a great deal of attention to the employee's social aspects. Thus a human relations "sales pitch" is presented as a substitute for decent wages and benefits at Burger King. The company does not offer sufficient incentives to effectively reduce turnover. Rather it seeks to embody the image of a happy loyal team or family, even with a constantly shifting group of workers. Loyalty is defined as obedience rather than longevity of tenure (1991, 165).

Burger King jobs are not seen as the pivot in the workers' lives. As a consequence, the women and young people who make up the Burger King staff aren't always committed enough to their work to comply with all the arbitrary demands made on them by management. Many express their dissatisfaction in one of the only avenues available to them: they quit.

In the final chapter of her book, Reiter links the development of the fast food industry with the social patterns it exemplifies and helps establish. Having completed her examination of Burger King, Reiter asks the reader: Is this the best that can be done? Is this a vision of the kind of society you want for yourself?

Reiter's study reveals how the fast food industry has shaped people's private and public lives, demonstrating what Mills points out in *The Sociological Imagination*:

It is not only information that [people] need—in this Age of Fact, information often dominates their attention and overwhelms their capacities to assimilate it. It is not only the skills of reason that they need—although their struggles to acquire these often exhaust their limited moral energy.

What they need, and what they feel they need, is a quality of mind that will help them to use information and to develop reason in order to achieve lucid summations of what is going on in the world and of what may be happening within themselves. It is this quality, I am going to contend, that journalists and scholars, artists and publics, scientists and editors are coming to expect of what may be called the sociological imagination (1959, 5).

THE SCIENTIFIC APPROACH: THE CONDUCT OF SOCIOLOGICAL RESEARCH

The issues that occupy sociologists are in essence similar to those that have puzzled students of society since antiquity. As the quotation from Peter Berger's *Invitation to Sociology* (1963), which opens this chapter, states, what sociology has sought to add to the study of society is a scientific approach. The root of the word science is *scio*, which means, "I know." Science is a general agreement on one way of looking at the world. It offers a systematic description and explanation of natural phenomena, in an attempt to map out what the world is "truly" like.

Observation and conceptualization (forming mental pictures) are indispensable to science, and there should be constant interplay between the two. Unless ideas are rooted in factual observations, the thinker is working in the realm of speculation. However, observations must be ordered and interpreted with the use of reason. Without it, they become a meaningless tangle.

Science is a cooperative enterprise. It builds on work already done. Sociologists take into account previous formulations, whether they wish to support, modify, or refute them. In physics, Newton disclaimed sole credit for his breakthrough in formulating the law of gravity, pointing to the foundations laid by Copernicus, Keppler, Galileo, and others.

Much of scientific research is done most effectively by teamwork, in which the interplay of minds and perspectives can be brought to bear on a problem. The Manhattan Project, which led to the development of the atomic bomb, is a good example from the physical sciences. In the social sciences, researchers Belenky, Clinchy, Goldberger, and Tarule (1986) built on the work of Gilligan (1982) in examining how women come to learn and think for themselves, a process they claim is different from the developmental sequence based on men's experiences.

Once research is published, it becomes public property and invites challenge or confirmation. These findings may reach the general public via the mass media. Without training in social science research, however, few journalists are able to evaluate the research. In addition, bias creeps into the reporting. Faludi (1991, 365) cites the example of women in the labour force. Many reporters cheered the advance of women in nontraditional, male-dominated employment areas with headlines heralding women's "takeover" of the labour force. While women have made inroads in male-dominated spheres of employment, most of them, by far, still work in clerical and service jobs.

Faludi (1991) details the misinformation in another report with an attention-grabbing headline in the late 1980s that proclaimed a "man shortage" for women over thirty. Reporters uncritically accepted findings from a study by Harvard and Yale researchers that stated that a college-educated, never-wed woman, at the age of 30, had a 20 percent chance of marrying; at 35 she had a 5 percent chance; and at 40 she had no more than a 1.3 percent chance. Faludi ferreted out the real numbers. Women's marital odds were much higher than the study suggested. At 30, her chances of marrying were, at 58 to 66 percent, three times more than had been reported; at 35, they were seven times higher (32 to 41 percent); and at 40, a whopping twenty-three times higher, at 17 to 23 percent (1991, 11). The study's researchers had used an unusual and unproven statistical technique in their predictions and a sample of women that was unrepresentative (i.e., who were not similar to the majority of women in the population).

The two main tools that scientists use are: (1) empirical scrutiny of what is occurring in the world, and (2) analysis, which makes it possible to discern patterns in these perceptions. Doing research involves using structured, systematic observation. For example, a study of primary education might include an analysis of what is taught (which may not be what the curriculum list claims) and the methods by which the subject matter is communicated to students. In the course of analysis, researchers seek to shape observable data into a meaningful pattern. In fact, analysis precedes as well as follows observation. When a scientist embarks on a research project, he or she has a conceptual framework, an idea of what is sought. It has been observed, for instance, that until junior high school, girls, on average, do better academically than boys. After puberty, the pattern is reversed. This phenomenon has generally been explained as a consequence of girls becoming more interested in social relationships and, therefore, more preoccupied with their appearance than with academic effort. Today a team of sociologists might speculate that the raising of women's consciousness has changed the pattern. In science, such a speculation is referred to as a **hypothesis**, "an assertion that can be tested" (True, 1989, 37) and either verified or rejected. Hypotheses are statements of relationships among **variables**, concepts that change quantitatively or qualitatively. In each study the variable assumed to be the cause is the **independent variable**; the presumed effect is the **dependent variable**.

In our example, the hypothesis could be tested by selecting a number of high schools across Canada and examining the grades of boys and girls at the schools (the dependent variable) over the last ten years and noting variations in the pattern. The researchers would have to be very careful about reaching conclusions because, after all, they are not looking at the same individuals. If they consistently found different patterns, they could be somewhat confident that a change had occurred, though they would have to examine other possible explanations than just the girls' raised consciousness (the independent variable). On the other hand, they might find changes in the west but not in Ontario and Quebec. They would then need to search for reasons for these regional differences and test their explanations systematically.

Disconfirmation of a hypothesis—that is, the finding that a hypothesized relationship does *not* exist—adds to knowledge just as support would. Disconfirmation is not "failure" in the conventional sense of the word; indeed, it provides impetus to rethink the problem, and thus can be extremely productive. Goldenberg's *Thinking Sociologically* (1987) is a useful and clear introduction to what is involved in conducting sociological research.

THE COMPLEXITY OF SOCIOLOGY AS SCIENCE

Science aims at precision and therefore tends to become increasingly exact and quantitative. Because terms must be used carefully and consistently, each scientific discipline develops a specialized vocabulary, a "jargon," to ensure that terms mean the same thing to everyone working in the field. In the emergency room of a hospital, an ambulance attendant might report, "Upon arrival, patient was semicomatose. BP 60 over 100. Pulse weak and thready. Complaining of pain in chest and right arm. En route, he arrested, and CPR was initiated." All the medical personnel present know exactly what conditions and procedures, in what order, are subsumed in this shorthand report.

Sociology, like all disciplines that are concerned with human behaviour, encounters inherent obstacles to becoming scientific, in the sense of reaching the degree of quantification and precision that physics or mathematics can achieve; this occurs because people are complex and never wholly predictable. For example, you have probably experienced instances in which people you thought you knew extremely well "weren't themselves" and acted "out of character," in a manner quite different from their usual behaviour. In fact, you yourself may respond to an emergency situation in ways you would not have anticipated. (In Chapters 3, "Culture and Social Organization," and 4, "Socialization," we will discuss some of the processes that make individuals similar and predictable.)

Not only are people unpredictable, they can also choose to behave in ways that either help or hinder the researcher and, unlike inanimate objects of study, can be affected in unforeseen ways by the research process itself. The latter discovery arose while research was being conducted at the Hawthorne General Electric plant in Chicago in the 1920s. The purpose of the study was to measure worker output under a variety of conditions, but surprisingly, no matter which material conditions were modified, or even made worse, the employees were more productive. The researchers concluded that the attention the workers received improved their performance. The term "Hawthorne effect" has come to mean that research subjects may alter their behaviour simply because they are the subjects of study.

As the Hawthorne effect suggests, sociologists and all other social scientists can certainly be scientific by carefully testing observations and deriving general patterns from their data, but the physiological, psychological, and social factors that impinge on human action are so numerous and so complex that there are always exceptions to such patterns. In this sense, sociology and other social sciences can be said to provide "fragile truths." They are not "fast-frozen and absolute; they are historical, interpretive; and contingent—as are the social and cultural realities of which our disciplines speak" (cited in Carroll, Christiansen-Ruffman, Currie, & Harrison, 1992, 1). While the notion of the fragility of "truth" may initially seem disturbing to you, we hope that you will come to find it both intriguing and liberating.

THE QUESTION OF VALUES

A claim that is frequently made for science is that it is "value-free." As we noted in our discussion of Max Weber's work, this is both true and not true. Values enter into the selection of what is studied and into the construction of the conceptual framework used to decide what aspects of a problem are relevant. Box 2.1 on mother–infant bonding provides a good example of the sway of social values on research.

Scientists are also assumed to be objective and are seen as not allowing their personal values and biases to enter their research. This stance of objectivity as a practice and a goal, in both the natural and social sciences, has come under fire in the last decades particularly from feminist scholars. Many decry the idea of researchers distancing themselves from the subject matter, the research subject, and the uses to which the resulting knowledge is put.[2] Feminists argue that objectivity, as it is practised, reinforces the dichotomy of subject and object, ruler and ruled. Individuals being studied must be brought

BOX 2.1

INFANT BONDING AND GUILTY MOTHERS

Children should be fed on a schedule. Children should be fed when they're hungry. Infants should be picked up when they cry. They should be left to cry and remain unspoiled. New mothers should stay home for a year. Mothers can feel confident about returning to work in six weeks. Day care inhibits development. Day care accelerates development.

There is a common thread among these apparently contradictory opinions. Each at one time or another has been offered with utter confidence to its audience of new parents, mothers especially, as scientific truth. Delivered by doctors, nurses, psychologists and other child-rearing professionals, such expert advice has guided and intimidated parents for generations.

In science, facts are supposed to fall where they may. But as the contradictions suggest, not all "facts" and the theories that emerge from them have long shelf lives.

In "Mother–Infant Bonding: A Scientific Fiction," just published by Yale University Press, Diane E. Eyer examines mother–infant bonding, one theory that turned out to have a short but influential life span, roughly the 1970's.

Bonding managed to have a major impact despite slender evidence for its existence: a study by the original researchers of only 28 mothers, analogies from studies of mother-offspring attachment and rejection in nonhuman mammals as well as interpretations drawn from the behaviour of infants in pathological situations. Though the early research has largely been dismissed the theory of bonding continues to have an impact.

"One of the things I wanted to see," Ms. Eyer said in a recent interview about her work, "was how research that was so patently untrue was so credible to so many people. I didn't expect to find villains, but it was clear that medicine was benefiting more than women were."

As Ms. Eyer points out, while it lived, bonding—the notion that mothers and infants who spend quality time together right after birth will form a crucial psychological attachment—helped transform obstetrics and the experience of childbirth.

Scientific support for bonding gave credence to claims by reformers that the widespread hospital practice of isolating healthy newborns from their mothers was damaging. The "science," in fact, allowed a resistant medical profession to yield gracefully to the reformers.

Mothers and infants are central to her book, but Ms. Eyer, a psychologist with interests in the philosophy and sociology of science, says the real issue is how science can come to serve social values. "How is science socially constructed? All data involves interpretation, even if you are talking about nuclear physics," she said in a recent interview. "When you get into child development, you are up against a lot of unquestioned assumptions about women and infants."

It is not a coincidence, Ms. Eyer argues, that expert advice tends to reflect the Zeitgeist. In the 20's and 30's, during a period of economic growth and preoccupation with efficiency and productivity, childcare experts urged women to teach children discipline early on by establishing rigid routines and schedules. Picking up a crying child in essence trained the child to keep crying. By the 40's, science "discovered" that infants needed constant attention and a hovering mother. Mothers who failed to respond to every cry risked raising a neurotic at best, a criminal at worst.

The original bonding theory provoked many times its weight in anxiety and guilt, particularly among women who missed the critical early phase, because they were slow to recover from delivery or their newborns were ill or adopted.

Intentional or not, lack of bonding could have severe consequences, researchers said. As recently as the late 80's, one pediatric expert declared that infants who do not bond properly can become terrorists.

Even though the importance of postpartum bonding has receded somewhat in the neonate gospel, Ms. Eyer notes that some experts have argued that bonding—the same notion for which there is little scientific evidence—continues to occur throughout the first year and perhaps beyond, an insight, if it is true, that would put millions of children of working women at risk.

Ms. Eyer says she has already seen "the rise of another familiar twist to the tradition of mothering advice": a developmental psychologist who discovered women "selfishly overwhelming their infants with excess attention in order to alleviate their 'guilt' about working."

Ms. Eyer steps out of her role as historian of psychology for a moment to ponder the potential effects of her research: "I have gotten calls from all over. Relieving women of guilt has been a great pleasure."

Source: Barbara Presley Noble, "Infant Bonding and Guilty Mothers," The New York Times (21 February 1993), p. F25. Copyright © 1993 by The New York Times Company. Reprinted by permission.

into the research process, indeed their experiences should provide the starting point of enquiry. Connell et al. write:

> [A different model of research] should empower the people who are normally just the objects of research, to develop their capacity to research their own situations and evolve their own solutions. It should embody a relationship where expertise is a resource available to all rather than a form of power for a few (1982, 216).

Objectivity, as a goal, should be approached, according to Eichler (1988), by indicating the values underlying the research, by examining all contrary evidence, and by facilitating maximum replicability by including complete and explicit information in the reporting of the study. Once the information has been gathered, the scientist must present it impartially, even if it contradicts his or her original assumptions. For example, Lundy (1977) embarked on a study of executive secretaries assuming that a majority of these women yearned for the pay, prestige, and power enjoyed by their bosses. In fact, she found that only a small minority aspired to executive positions.

THE FEMINIST CRITIQUE OF SCIENCE

As we stated in Chapter 1, feminist sociology defies easy description. The same can be said for feminist critiques of research methodology. Messing (cited in Nemiroff, 1987, 104) listed the areas in which sexism permeates the research process, pointing out that it starts with the selection of scientists. As scientists are very much affected by the social world they inhabit, the fact that most scientists are not representative of the population at large, being predominantly white men, results in a skewing of the scientific enterprise. (Box 2.1 suggests this possibility.) Eichler (1988) refers to this as **androcentrism**, viewing the world from a (white) male perspective that assumes men's centrality in that world. On a very basic level, Smith (1987) reminds readers that male researchers are unlikely to have to take care of such mundane physical needs as buying and preparing food, cleaning, laundering clothing, or tending to families, which divorces them from a certain aspect of reality.

Topics chosen for research are those deemed worthy of study. What is deemed worthy depends on one's vantage point. Until the recent emergence of feminist scholarship, issues that affect women specifically, were at worst ignored, and at best treated as peripheral. Many theories were developed using only males as subjects. Women were seen as deviant if their behaviour did not conform, on the assumption that male behaviour set the standard.

Other stages of the research process are also infiltrated by sexism: the wording of hypotheses, the methods of study, the data analysis, the interpretation of the data, and the publication and popularization of the data and results (Messing, cited in Nemiroff, 1983). In some settings, sexism has a direct impact on the female researcher, as Burns (cited in Carroll et al., 1992) indicates in relating her experiences while studying West Coast fishing expeditions. Contrary to her expectations, sexism impeded her work from the beginning.

> ... I was made to feel uncomfortable. While I attempted to deny my femininity and assert a researcher identity, the fisher(men)s laughed at such presumption and imposed my "natural" role as woman, domestic labourer, and sexualized object[3] (1992, 180).

FORMULATING A RESEARCH PROBLEM

The goal of sociological research is to discover how a group, such as a society, a corporation, or a family, is structured and operates. To put this more formally, research is aimed at increasing knowledge about the structure and functioning of social groups and about relationships among and within groups. Feminists would add that this knowledge should be formulated with the help of those groups and be made accessible to them for their own use. Fundamental to investigation is the perception of a problem, of a state of affairs that appears anomalous, "out of sync." In other words, the starting point in a search for answers may be a sense of dissonance.

For example, it has been found that in Toronto, children from lower-income homes are streamed into vocational classes or special education classes for slow learners far more frequently than those from affluent homes (Wright, 1970). In the same vein, Porter (1965; 1973) and others (Harp & Hofley, 1971) have noted that a disproportionate percentage of students in law, medical, and other professional schools come from families in high-income groups. As sociologists, we might want to know the reasons for this state of affairs, which runs counter to Canadian society's professed commitment to equality of opportunity.

To start with, we would look at research that has been done on the relationship between socioeconomic class and formal education. (Remember, science is cumulative.) Among other things, we would want to know what facets of this relationship have been explored by previous researchers and whether the Canadian cases are isolated instances or fall into a more general pattern. What we would find is that it is indeed a frequently occurring pattern that poor children predominate in vocational classes and that affluent students are overrepresented in professional schools.[4]

Various aspects of the relationship between socioeconomic class and educational attainment could now be explored. Depending on the direction we decided to take, we could use qualitative methods or quantitative methods, or some combination of the two. **Qualitative method**s involve the collection of data through interviews, observation, or analysis of written material. We might speculate that most teachers are middle-class white people and hence find it difficult to relate to lower-class and/or black children; they may thus be inclined to view such children as slow learners. To test this assumption, we might conduct in-depth interviews with the teachers and principals of public schools in Toronto that have special education and vocational classes, in an attempt to find out what criteria are used to assign children to them. We might then want to know whether or not the teachers' own assessments of student performance confirm the judgment of those who assigned them to the particular classroom. In-depth interviews are an example of a qualitative method.

In using **quantitative methods**, data are obtained in numerical form through enumeration or measurement (as in surveys, for example). If, for instance, we decided to see if the percentage of affluent students in professional schools has changed over time, we would look for the requisite information—say, for 1970, 1980, and 1990—in university and other statistical records. Using computers, we could manipulate the data to make several internal comparisons, as between law and medical students, males and females, whites and people of colour in both schools, and within each school. We would then try to explain our findings in terms of what we know about inequality in Canada generally and about the relationship between socioeconomic class and formal education specifically. Computer analysis of statistical information is an example of a quantitative method.

RESEARCH METHODS

Qualitative and quantitative methods are the basic tools of sociological research. The categories are not hard and fast. For example, data from both in-depth interviews and content analyses are quantified. Ultimately, the method sociologists choose depends on the topic of enquiry and on the resources of labour, money, and time available. The ideal is to have the breadth provided by quantitative analysis and the insights qualitative investigation affords.[5]

Qualitative Methods

Important facets of qualitative research are: description; formulation of hypotheses (that may subsequently be explored by quantitative methods); and making inferences about causal processes. Some of the most frequently used methods of qualitative research in sociology include case studies, in-depth interviews, participant observation, and content analyses.

Case study involves an intensive and comprehensive investigation of a single unit, such as a community, business firm, prison, or hospital. Rosabeth Moss Kanter's study (1977) of INDSCO, a large, multinational company, focused on the relative positions of men and women in the firm, and on the effects of power and powerlessness on managerial behaviour. While serving as a chaplain at the Guelph Reformatory, W.E. Mann (1967) examined in rich detail the inmate culture, which stood in stark opposition to the official prison culture. He found that for the prisoners, most of them young and many of them first offenders, the reformatory in fact functioned as a school for crime. Historian Michael Bliss, in his book, *Plague* (1991), looked at the 1885 smallpox epidemic that killed more than 3,000 people in Montreal. He described the role of institutions in the epidemic and the conflicts that arose in a community straddling the traditional and modern eras. Garfinkel (1967), in a study of a transsexual, sheds light on the processes of gender socialization by illustrating "passing" (that is, being taken for a member of another group) and provides detailed information on how gender is socially constructed.

Case studies provide detailed descriptive information and generate questions that cannot be answered by the study itself. They invite study of other cases that are seemingly similar to or clearly different from one another in order to help identify, for example, what characteristics are likely to be present in all institutions in which people are housed involuntarily and those characteristics that are idiosyncratic to reformatories.

In-depth interviews give a researcher the opportunity to talk at length with people whose behaviour they wish to study. This approach can be both intensive and extensive (that is, respondents may be interviewed more than once as well as in more than one setting, such as at home and at the office). In-depth interviews can illuminate areas about which little is known and those areas that cannot be effectively explored through standardized questionnaires. Oakley's pathbreaking interviews with British housewives in *The Sociology of Housework* (1974) are an example. Oakley's aim was to describe housework as work and ascertain how women felt about it. Perhaps not surprisingly, she found that a large majority of the women reported being dissatisfied with housework, a perception that cut across economic lines. Oakley suggested that the dissatisfaction resulted from the nature of the work itself—from its being monotonous, fragmented, and solitary. Oakley's work was innovative, coming when it did, in applying concepts and theories from occupational sociology, which is centred on wage labour, to work in the home. Oakley found, however, that the theories were inappropriate for examining unpaid housework. Her study illustrated the "lack of fit" of traditional theories to the particular situation of women and led to the further development of feminist sociology. Lillian Rubin (1977) talked at length to working-class women, mostly in their own homes. In *Worlds of Pain* she conveyed how these women live, how they do or do not cope with the frequent crises in their lives, and how they themselves feel about their existence. Carol Gilligan (1982), studying moral development, interviewed women making abortion decisions. Her data led her to hypothesize a developmental path for women that differed from the standard theories and to formulate a higher stage of moral development based on her subjects' responses. This she labelled the ethic of care. Her theory is predicated on the idea that no one should be hurt by a decision, as opposed to the (masculine) ethic of justice in which everyone is treated in the same fashion irrespective of circumstances and context. Her book is aptly titled *In a Different Voice.*

Participant observation permits the researcher to become a part of the group being explored; he or she literally participates in its activities while doing the observing. This is what Reiter (1991), as mentioned previously, did at Burger King, working as a crew person for five months (without pay) and for another seven months as a shift worker. Prolonged interaction with a group can provide a rounded picture of what it is "really" like. Total immersion allows the researcher to become familiar, insofar as it is possible, in what the subjects are experiencing. There is the danger, however, that the researcher will become so involved with the group members that objectivity will be impaired. William Foote Whyte's classic study *Street Corner Society* (1943) shows that it is possible for the researcher to be an acute observer without sacrificing objectivity. While a graduate student at Harvard in the late 1930s, Whyte joined in the activities of a group of young men in an Italian slum in the north end of Boston. He built a colourful kaleidoscope of the ambitions, preoccupations, and daily lives of the "corner boys" and the ways in which they differed from those of the "college boys," the inhabitants of the slum who aspired to higher education as a way out. Burns (1992), in her participant observation of the men who fish on the Canadian West Coast, reported in "Caught in the Riptide: Female Researcher in a Patricentric Setting" (in Carroll et al., 1992), focuses on some drawbacks of participant observation.

Content analysis involves the systematic examination of a chosen medium (frequently mass media output) to discern perceptions of and attitudes toward certain groups or policies. Such analysis can be used for historical materials, making it possible to draw comparisons between different periods. Thus, in *The Feminine Mystique* (1963), Betty Friedan documented images of women in magazine stories and articles over two decades. She found that during the Second World War, when women were needed in the labour force, they were depicted as competent, able to cope with pressure and with a variety of demands. After the war, when the drive was to get women back into the home to free jobs for returning veterans, stories showed women as dependent, unsure of themselves, and confused, except when they discovered their true roles as wives and mothers.

Content analysis has been used often to examine gender and race in quantifying numbers of males, females, whites, and people of colour shown; the types of tasks they are engaged in; character traits they exhibit; and their role in the narrative. For instance, in analyses of primary school readers, researchers recorded the number of references to male characters and to female characters. (One can guess, in each instance, which group was mentioned more often.) MacBeth Williams and her colleagues (1986) found that gender stereotyping in Canadian and American television shows has changed little since television's inception in the 1950s. Men are still overwhelmingly overrepresented; women are still shown as "the weaker sex"; and women are shown more often than men as sex objects. The only progress has been in picturing women in non-traditional occupations. Another content analysis compared the values of the punk movement with those of both 1960s hippies and the American middle class (Lamy & Levin, 1986).

Like all approaches, qualitative research has advantages and drawbacks. An important advantage is its fleshing out of data, giving an idea of what life is like for the people being studied. Researchers are able to probe and establish whether the questions being asked address the problems under investigation. In charting out relatively unexplored areas, qualitative research can also provide a basis for larger-scale quantitative studies.

On the negative side, qualitative research runs the danger of interviewer bias; what is observed and recorded represents the researcher's interpretation, both of what is worth recording, and of what it means. Moreover, because the numbers that can be studied by qualitative methods are necessarily small and the cases to be studied must be selected with care, researchers must be cautious in generalizing the findings so as to fit ostensibly similar cases.

Quantitative Methods

Quantitative research in sociology can vary widely in detail. Two general types are experimental design and survey analysis.

Experimental design generally entails a systematic comparison of two groups before and after a stimulus has been applied. The immediate goal is to assess the effect of such a stimulus. Suppose we want to test the influence of media propaganda on attitudes toward illegal immigrants. We could compose a questionnaire on relevant attitudes and ask a class of students to complete it. Then we would divide the class into two parts, taking care to match the halves as closely as possible for such characteristics as gender, age, race, and ethnicity. We would apply no further treatment to one half, the control group. The other half, the experimental group, would be shown a movie portraying illegal immigrants in a favourable light, describing their plight in their home countries and showing the ingenuity and courage that were necessary for them to get to Canada. We would then ask both groups of students to complete the same questionnaire they had previously filled out. Our results might show that the control group, as we expected, demonstrated no change. But in the experimental group, we would likely find that a substantial number of students had changed their views. We could then say that the propaganda had an impact. A problem with experiments, however, is that one must be very careful about making generalizations about the findings: experiments are generally conducted under artificial (laboratory) conditions; the number of subjects is relatively small and, therefore, usually not representative of the population.

An exception to the typical experiment is Macbeth Williams and her colleagues' natural experiment (1986). She was fortunate to study a Canadian community, to which she gave the pseudonym Notel, that was on the verge of getting television for the first time in July 1973. For comparison, she looked at two similar communities in the area that already had, respectively, one and more than one television channel available for viewing. These were dubbed (appropriately) Unitel and Multitel. What is uncommon about his piece of research is that, unlike other experiments, it could avoid many of the usual pitfalls. The setting is "the real world," that is, it was not influenced by the researchers; the subjects did not volunteer to be subjects, which might have made them atypical in some way; and two other "control" groups in the adjacent communities of Unitel and Multitel were available.

Research on the effects of television has been carried out since television ownership became common in the 1960s, but it has been difficult to come up with definitive statements. The many laboratory experiments on violence and television that have been conducted are considered to be unrealistic. Field studies in natural settings make it difficult to limit the influence of extraneous variables, to control the situation as one is able to in a laboratory.

The three communities of Notel, Unitel, and Multitel were studied just before and two years after Notel received TV reception. The topics of investigation were those prior research had shown to be affected by television viewing.

Television is said to have an effect if there are differences among the groups in the different locales on the variables studied, such as creativity. These differences are determined and measured by statistical techniques. (For information on the variables, operational definitions, that is, how each concept was measured, and the specific tests used, see the study.)

What Williams and her colleagues found was that, contrary to some of their initial hypotheses, there were no beneficial effects from television, for example, on vocabulary. Television, they found, had a negative impact on creativity, on the acquisition of reading skills, and on participation in community activities such as sports. The study also indicated that students developed more stereotypical ideas about gender with the advent of television and that all children, regardless of sex or age, became more physically and verbally violent. Advocating additional research, which is common, the investigators stressed that the idea that television has no impact must be abandoned once and for all.

Survey analysis involves the collection of responses from large numbers of subjects and the statistical manipulation of the information obtained. The Canadian census is an example of survey analysis that provides a large data bank on which sociologists draw for further research. Armstrong and Armstrong used Canadian census data in their book *The Double Ghetto* (1978) to illustrate the segregation of women's work in the paid labour force and then, using different theoretical frameworks, to explain its occurrence and endurance. While the statistics have changed since then, this problem of two labour markets—the blue and white collars versus the pink—has not been ameliorated. The "double ghetto" of pink collar work in the labour force and housework still exists.

The General Social Survey (GSS) established by Statistics Canada in 1985 provides data on health, education, justice, and culture. The aim of the GSS is to track changes in Canadians' standards of living and to explore trends in contemporary social issues. Some specific subject areas covered by the GSS are friendship networks, computer use by Canadians, and the amount of time people spend working, doing housework, and shopping (*Canadian Social Trends*, Winter 1990). One survey that garnered much attention from the media, which was not surprising given its findings, was a study on campus dating abuse, conducted by two University of Carleton sociologists and published in 1993. The study found, using a broad definition of abuse, that 81 percent of women felt they had been abused on a date. Media reports stressing this statistic made the results immediately controversial. Examination of the actual data shows that this type of violence occurs frequently and needs to be addressed. A discussion of the study is provided in Box 2.2.[6]

Surveys have been criticized. As with experiments, the **sample** (the respondents or research subjects) is often atypical, limiting the people to whom one can apply the results. Question wording may be biased, leading respondents to answer in a certain fashion. Surveys may be done to reinforce sponsors' opinions (as happens with private political polling) and may be improperly reported as factual, as Box 2.3 illustrates.

Familiarizing yourself with the rigours of the scientific process of research gives you the ability to ask the proper questions and to assess findings. Results from social science research, particularly those deemed sensational, as we have shown, get reported in the media most often, and often incorrectly. This subject itself—the popular media's representation of social science research and its consequences—has generated sociological investigation. Singer and Endreny (1986), using the techniques of content analysis and interviewing with reporters, social scientists, and editors, alert people to the fact that the goals of social science reporting and those of the news media are different. The aim of news is to tell a story. The aim of science is to produce and share new knowledge. These objectives are not always compatible. In news reporting the source, context, method, and limitations of the specific piece of research are rarely provided, making such reports at best inadequate, since readers and viewers cannot properly evaluate their conclusions.

BOX 2.2

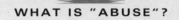

WHAT IS "ABUSE"?

The two Carleton University sociologists were unprepared for the reaction that greeted their report... Researchers Katharine Kelly and Walter DeKeseredy reported striking levels of abuse of women on Canadian college and university campuses, based on a written questionnaire filled out by 3,142 students. The key findings: 22 per cent of women surveyed said that they had been physically abused, and 29 per cent said that they had been sexually abused, by boyfriends or male acquaintances during the previous 12 months. And 81 per cent of female respondents said that they had suffered some form of abuse when the definition was broadened to include psychological abuses such as taunts and insults. The margin of error in the survey was plus or minus five per cent. In the ensuing days, the researchers said, they and their office staffs received about 40 telephone calls a day, mostly from men, many in support but some loudly and even crudely denouncing the professors and their survey. In editorial columns and on television and radio talk shows, writers and commentators debated the findings. The critics focused on the 81-per cent figure, saying that the broad definition of "abuse" was too all-encompassing. Still, there was no disagreement over the survey's major focus: there is a widespread problem across Canadian campuses. "The alarming thing to me is just how many women I know who have been assaulted by acquaintances," said William Dobie, 20, a third-year political science student at the University of British Columbia.

The survey, financed by a $236,000 grant from Health and Welfare Canada's Family Violence Prevention Division, was conducted by Kelly and DeKeseredy, who have been studying violence against women for five years, in 1992. Their questionnaire was divided into three categories—sexual, physical and psychological abuse. In a typical question, female respondents were asked: "Have you had sexual intercourse when you didn't want to because you were drunk or high?" In addition to the 81 per cent of 1,835 female survey respondents who claimed to have suffered some form of abuse during the previous year, 75 per cent of the 1,307 men admitted to having been abusive.

One expert in polling techniques, Michael Sullivan, senior vice-president of the Toronto-based polling and market research firm Decima Research, said that the broad definition of abuse produced some numbers that are "so high that they stretch the credibility of the results in the mind of the public." Sullivan said that the survey should also have asked men if they had been psychologically abused by women. "If you can show that psychological abuse is a two-way street," he said, "then it becomes a problem of civility." Still, Sullivan did not challenge the professors' results. "There's no problem with the methodology of the survey," he said, "and there's no reason to quibble with its findings."

The survey also reported a high incidence of "date rape"—when a woman is raped by her date, boyfriend or a male acquaintance.

"People don't see it as rape," said Carole Forsythe, 28, a third-year history student at the University of British Columbia. She told *Maclean's* that many men who commit date rape "feel that it is fine, that it was consensual. And no matter how much the woman protests, people say, "Well, you were friends, you should have made your protests clearer.'"

According to Kelly and DeKeseredy, who are both married and have children, the real number of women assaulted on dates could be higher than shown in the survey, because some are reluctant to report sexual or physical assault in cases that involve people they know. The incidence of date rape—nine per cent—reported in the Kelly–DeKeseredy survey was almost exactly the same as was found in a 1992 Decima poll for *Maclean's* that asked about date rape on campus.

Whether they had been abuse victims or not, many women on campus told *Maclean's* last week that they are aware of the possibility of male violence, and conduct themselves accordingly. Chloe Town, 20, a film and communications student at Montreal's McGill University, said that she became cautious after hearing of assaults on female friends and family members.

"I stay away from places that I don't feel are safe," Town said. "I think it's insulting that I can't walk the streets and the university grounds and feel as safe as men do."

The survey came under attack in newspaper columns and editorials for its definition of abuse. Robert Sheppard, a columnist for Toronto's *The Globe and Mail*, wrote that "to broaden the nature of abuse as the authors have done, and to cloak this with an air of academic respectability, is to trivialize the real problem" of sexual abuse in society. But while they knew their definition would likely raise concerns, Kelly and DeKeseredy stuck with it. "In many cases, women said that psychological abuse was worse than physical abuse," said Kelly. Added DeKeseredy: "It's not our job to define what women call abuse. If that's how they see it, we just report it."

For Kelly and DeKeseredy, the release of the survey may be only a beginning. As a next step, they say that they hope to study the causes of sexual, physical and psychological abuse, not just in universities, but in high schools and society in general. Meanwhile, DeKeseredy said that he hoped the initial findings would convince postsecondary institutions to set up mandatory courses on male–female relations, and to require students to sign a code-of-conduct agreement that, if breached, could result in expulsion. The two researchers also expressed the hope that their findings, by raising some troubling issues, may at least encourage a higher degree of male–female civility in campus life.

Source: James Deacon, Hal Quinn, John DeMont, and Ann McLoughlin, "What Is Abuse?" Maclean's (*22 February 1993*), p. 54. Reprinted with permission.

ETHICAL ISSUES IN SOCIAL SCIENCE RESEARCH

In the aftermath of the Second World War there was much concern about people's ability to be evil and the conundrum of obeying illegal, immoral, or inhuman orders. In a series of studies in the United States in the early 1960s, which have come to be known as the obedience experiments, Stanley Milgram (1974), a social psychologist, conducted a series of experiments designed to test how far someone would go in obeying orders. He found that research subjects would administer what they believed to be lethal shocks to another person if that person failed to memorize a list of words correctly. Close to half the participants "killed" their partners, some protesting but continuing to do as told nonetheless. The subjects were upset and humiliated when let in on the purpose of the study. The research is still cited as controversial.

In an interview with another psychologist, Carol Tavris, Milgram discussed this work:

Tavris: Some people criticized the obedience work by saying, "I knew that." After all, centuries of human history amply document the excesses of following orders. What advantage derives from an experiment that confirms history?

Milgram: The purpose of the obedience experiment was neither to confirm nor disconfirm history, but to study the psychological function of obedience; ... Moreover, we must ask whether people really do learn the lessons of history, isn't it always the "the other guy" who shamelessly submits to authority, even in violation of elementary morality? I think it is hard for many people to accept that they themselves have the potential to yield without limit to authority (Tavris, 1974).

A number of puzzling and important issues could be explored if it were permissible to run roughshod over people "in the interests of science." Fascinating questions such as the influence of environment and genetics on human behaviour might be explored. One could isolate a group of newborns and watch them as they grew up to determine if "human nature" is basically good or evil, cooperative or competitive. One might separate identical twins, raise them in entirely different settings, and see if they demonstrated similar behaviours, which then could be assumed to be biologically based. A less hypothetical debate surrounds the use of Nazi medical findings, obtained horrendously and inhumanely, to benefit people now (Suzuki, 1988). Should the conditions under which the findings were generated preclude their use?

A major concern in designing, implementing, and analyzing research is the ethical treatment of human subjects. The use of animals is, of course, also controversial. Professional organizations in many social science disciplines and many academic institutions have formal policies on this kind of research. Two basic principles in such policies are clear: informed consent and freedom from harm. As you might imagine, spelling out these principles concretely is not an easy process, and the prohibitions and prescriptions can be very detailed. The right to informed consent on the part of subjects may conflict with the aim of the researchers to gather uncontaminated data. If subjects are aware of the hypothesis, they may either try to help or hinder the investigators. Subjects must also be left unharmed by the research, not only physically but psychologically, socially, and emotionally. Many studies offer debriefing sessions for the participants (as in the Milgram experiments), but is debriefing always enough to counteract what may have occurred in the course of the research?

Tea Room Trade, by Laud Humphreys (1979), is a work that exemplifies the issue of consent. This study was one of the few to deal with "closet homosexuals," men who have not publicly asserted their homosexuality. Humphries acted as a lookout to protect the men who were using public washrooms for quick, impersonal sex. At the same time, he surreptitiously observed and recorded their behaviour and also noted the licence numbers of their cars, which allowed him to find out who they were. He then set up

BOX 2.3

THE POLLS DANCE TO ANYBODY'S TUNE

Consumers overwhelmingly preferred a Chrysler to a Toyota after test-driving both, contends a study sponsored by Chrysler. The vast majority of U.S. college students picked Levi's 501 jeans as the most "in" clothing, says a study sponsored by Levi's. And in separate studies funded by the cloth-diaper and disposable-diaper industries, guess what: Cloth diapers were shown to be better for the environment than paper—and vice versa.

In recent years, research studies like these have become one of America's most powerful and popular tools of persuasion. Once confined to a small circle of polling and research companies and a few universities, the business of studying public opinion and consumer habits has exploded in the past two decades. Today, studies have become vehicles for polishing corporate images, influencing juries, shaping debate on public policy, selling shoe polish and satisfying the media's—and the public's—voracious appetite for information.

Yet while studies promise a quest for truth, many today are little more than vehicles for pitching a product or opinion. An examination of hundreds of recent polls indicates that the business of research has become pervaded by bias and distortion. The result is a corruption of the information used every day by voters, consumers and leaders.

While described as "independent," a growing number of studies are actually sponsored by companies or groups with a real—usually financial—interest in the outcome. And often the study question is posed in such a way that the response is predictable:

When Levi Strauss & Co. asked students which clothes would be most popular this year, 90 per cent said Levi's 501 jeans. They were the only jeans on the list...

A Gallup poll sponsored by the disposable-diaper industry asked: It is estimated that disposable diapers account for less than 2 per cent of the trash in today's landfills. In contrast, beverage containers, third-class mail and yard waste are estimated to account for about 21 per cent of the trash in landfills. Given this, in your opinion, would it be fair to ban disposable diapers? Eighty-four per cent said no.

"There's been a slow sliding in ethics," says Eric Miller, who, as editor of the U.S. newsletter *Research Alert*, reviews some 2,000 studies a year. The scary part is, people make decisions based on this stuff. It may be an invisible crime, but it's not a victimless one.

The news media also play a role in disseminating sloppy or biased research to consumers. Journalists often publicize reports about a study without examining the study's methodology, or technical index, to see if it was conducted properly. Statistics are thrown around with abandon, even when sample sizes are so small they're meaningless...

There is still much good research being done, of course. In medicine and other physical sciences, research must be quantifiable and replicable to be taken seriously. Moreover, much consumer research is conducted strictly for internal consumption, not public distribution; it is therefore in a company's interest to get it right.

"We will eventually get to a dual standard of information," says Mr. Miller. "There will be a distinction made between research that's done with no hidden agenda, but to create useful information, and research that contains useful information that was generated for a very specific purpose."

In recent years, lean budgets have made everyone who does research, including formerly neutral colleges and universities, a little hungrier for work. "A funder will never come to an academic and say, 'I want you to produce finding X and here's a million dollars to do it,'" says Paul Light, associate dean at the Hubert Humphrey Institute at the University of Minnesota. The subtext, he continues, is that if researchers produce the right finding, more work—and funding—will come their way. "Once you're on that treadmill, it's hard to get off. Many universities, which often get a cut of the fee, don't monitor the outside work done under their imprimatur."

Shortages of money and time also contribute to diminishing sample sizes in polls. Researchers say it's best to have at least 1,000 respondents if you hope to project results onto a large population. Yet most of the dozen or more U.S. national polls taken about Clarence Thomas's confirmation interviewed only 500 to 700 people. When broken into subgroups, such as women or blacks, the margin of error goes off the charts—as high as 12 per cent. So when an ABC–*Washington Post* poll interviewed about 500 adults, roughly half women, and found that more women believed Clarence Thomas (38 per cent) than believed Anita Hill (28 per cent), the opposite could also have been true. (Other surveys, however, did bear out the poll's results.)

Besides interviewing too few people, there are other ways a survey can be flawed: Those surveyed may not be representative of the population, the analysis of the data may be faulty or the conclusions may be screened so only the best are reported. What's more, many studies tackle issues that are so complex they are virtually unresolvable.

And then there are those studies that, though conducted with correct scientific protocol, may have predictable conclusions because the researchers hired to do the studies are known to have come to similar conclusions in the past.

"You can't have an industry study done by that industry be 100 per cent objective," says Carl Lehrburger, who has studied the environmental impact of cloth versus disposable diapers for the cloth-diaper industry.

There are at least four widely publicized studies on diapers that explore the issue of whether disposables are disproportionately responsible for burdening U.S. landfills and fouling the environment. Two studies were sponsored by the cloth-diaper industry and conclude that cloth diapers are friendlier to the world; two others, sponsored by the paper-diaper industry, conclude the opposite.

In studies like these, assumptions and statistics are crunched by computers but entered by humans: Put in one slightly different assumption—that babies use 65 instead of 85 cloth diapers a week—and the picture changes...

But duelling studies can also paralyze decision-making.

"It's gotten to the point where someone will produce a study that statistically demonstrates X or Y, and then the other side will rush out and get an expert to do a study for them," says Ray Sentes, a professor at the

University of Regina, and a critic of many asbestos studies that minimize the effects the materials has on health. "For 10 years we flash studies at each other. If the practical outcome of a scientific study ends up being a delay of any activity, shouldn't a scientist say, 'You don't need this study'?"

One of the fastest-growing areas of research today is so-called advocacy studies. These are commissioned by companies or industries for public-relations purposes. Simplesse, maker of Simple Pleasures frozen dessert, did a study last summer showing, among other things, that 44 per cent of people who eat a lot of ice cream are likely to take a tub bath. "It was interesting to a lot of people," says Russ Klettke, a spokesman for Simplesse, part of Monsanto Co. "We timed the study for when the media want to write about ice cream, and we have gotten a number of clips back."

Kiwi Brands, a shoe-polish company, commissioned a study earlier this year on the correlation between ambition and shiny shoes. The study found that 97 per cent of self-described "ambitious" young men believe polished shoes are important...

...Surveys can be done with astonishing swiftness. With Computer Assisted Telephone Interviewing, called CATI, interviewers sitting in booths can see questions flash onto a computer screen. As each respondent's answer is recorded, the next question automatically flashes on the screen. Jack Honomichl, who publishes *Inside Research*, an industry newsletter, says: "You could, right now, develop a question, call a research company, do 1,000 interviews tonight and have the data on your desk tomorrow.

"But the research process, if done right, is much more difficult than people realize," adds Mr. Honomichl. "It takes time and money. When deadlines and budgets are short, a lot of those niceties go down the tubes."

The "niceties" include things such as careful wording of questions. But even meticulously crafted surveys can get skewed, particularly when they bump up against human shortcomings, like pride and guilt....

With the help of sophisticated statistical techniques, finding 1,000 Americans who can speak for 240 million others has become more reliable. Yet even here there are pitfalls. Poor people and minorities are notoriously underrepresented in telephone surveys; in surveys taken in shopping malls they are rarely interviewed. What's more, research companies say it's getting more difficult to find people willing to spend 15 minutes answering questions. How representative is a sample of people who will agree to that kind of invasion of privacy, they wonder.

So, in many cases, research simply relies on unrepresentative samples:—"There's good news for the 65 million Americans currently on a diet," trumpeted a news release for a diet-products company. Its study showed that people who lose weight can keep it off. The sample: 20 graduates of the company's program who endorse it in commercials.

The Chrysler study showing its cars were preferred to Toyota's included just 100 people in each of two tests. But more important, none of the people surveyed owned a foreign car, so they may well have been predisposed to U.S.-made vehicles. Chrysler says its intent was to survey people who might buy a foreign car...

The text of questions such as these, along with the methodology used in the studies, should be readily available to anyone who wants it. But in practice, technical indexes frequently are not offered, often on the ground that the material is proprietary. A survey done for a coupon-redemption company, Carolina Manufacturer's Service, found that a "broad cross-section of Americans find coupons to be true incentives for purchasing products." The technical index was available only for a price: $2,000...

In the end, it's the news media that disseminate the findings of studies—both good ones and bad. "Only if journalists aren't doing their jobs does the public have a problem," says Karen Anderson, public information manager for Battelle Human Affairs Research Centers. "It's the journalist's problem to look at the report or interview the researcher."

But if the journalist doesn't, the consumer of news is often left in a confusing stew of statistics. Many newspapers include explanations of methodology with their polls, but they can be difficult to understand. "The average consumer doesn't know what two standard deviations are," says Mark Clements, head of a New York research firm. Yet, they nonetheless seize on surveys and studies of all types.

Source: Cynthia Crossen, *"The Polls Dance to Anybody's Tune,"* The Globe and Mail *(7 December 1991), p. D5. Reprinted with permission.*

interviews with them and collected a great deal of information about their religion, their families, and their relationships with their wives. Humphreys protected the subjects' anonymity, but had the information not remained hidden, these men could have suffered enormously.

These discussions of Milgram and Humphreys's work illustrate another ethical principle: publishing and sharing scientific work. Researchers are exhorted to publicize their findings, so that others can build on them, and so that their results can be critically evaluated. For replication purposes, too, explicit details on the methodology used in the study are indispensable.

. . . .

OVERVIEW

A goal of the early sociologists was to apply to the study of society the tools science was developing in other areas. Central to a scientific way of doing things is a systematic alternation between observation and analysis. But scientists cannot escape from their own skin. They cannot ignore the values and beliefs that prevail in their own environment, and these must be accounted for in the research process. Current discussions on how this is to be done are fuelled predominantly by feminists, challenging the androcentrism of science.

Sociology uses qualitative and quantitative methods of investigation. Each has advantages and drawbacks, but the choice of method is usually determined by the subject being investigated. In turn, enquiry is influenced by the interests and theoretical orientations of the researcher. Knowledge of the process generating its conclusions is essential in appreciating its benefits.

ASSIGNMENTS

1. To get the flavour of doing research, administer the following brief questionnaire probing attitudes toward abortion. Choose six Catholics and six non-Catholics as your respondents; each group should be equally divided between men and women.

   What are the differences in responses between the two groups? How do responses differ within each group, for example, between the males and the females? Discuss with your instructor what these responses show about the influence of religion and gender on attitudes.

QUESTIONNAIRE

A. Under what circumstances do you consider abortion permissible? (You can choose more than one alternative.)
   a — Never
   b — In cases of dire danger to the mother's life
   c — When there is a likelihood of the baby being defective
   d — When there is danger to the mother's mental health
   e — In cases of economic necessity
   f — Upon demand

B. Who do you think should make the decision regarding an abortion?
   a — Hospital abortion committee
   b — Physician
   c — Physician and mother
   d — Both parents
   e — Mother alone

C. Where should abortions be performed?
   a — Hospital
   b — Abortion clinic (such as Dr. Henry Morgentaler's)

D. Should the current legislation (or proposed legislation) on abortion:
   a — Remain unchanged?
   b — Become more stringent?
   c — Become more lenient?

E. Please specify your gender and religion.
   Gender: Religion:
   — Male   — Catholic
   — Female   — Non-Catholic

2. Recently, much publicity has been given to the issue of televised violence. Do a content analysis of a particular type of television program, for example, children's shows, soap operas, crime shows, situation comedies. Construct an operational (working) definition of violence to measure the amount of violence shown. Then, modify your definition of violence. How does the new definition affect your assessment of the program?

3. Discuss the merits and drawbacks of using results of research obtained unethically. For example, the Nazis, during the Second World War, conducted "experiments" that were really torture. Should the results of those studies be used if they can be beneficial to people today?

SUGGESTED READINGS

Earl Babbie, *Observing Ourselves: Essays in Social Research* (Belmont, Calif.: Wadsworth Publishing Co., 1986). Babbie explores the underlying dynamics of the research process in this series of essays. What does it mean, for example, to ask someone for their opinion on an issue when conducting a survey? Babbie discusses such topics as the nature of enquiry and value-free science, showing how seemingly simple questions can generate indepth thinking about ourselves and the research endeavor.

Margrit Eichler, *Nonsexist Research Methods: A Practical Guide* (Winchester, Mass.: Allyn and Unwin, 1988). Eichler's book provides a systematic approach to identifying, eliminating, and preventing sexist bias in the research process. Using specific examples, Eichler clearly defines seven "sexist problems," including gender insensitivity, double standards, and andocentricity, and suggests concrete ways to avoid them.

Alison I. Griffith and Dorothy E. Smith, "Constructing Cultural Knowledge: Mothering as Discourse," in Jane Gaskell and Arlene McLaren, eds., *Women and Education*, 2nd ed. (Calgary: Detselig Enterprises, 1991:81–97). In this paper, the authors discuss their research on mothering as a personal and emotional experience, but also as *work*. They address some of the dilemmas involved in doing feminist research and propose strategies for dealing with them. For example, how is it possible to remain faithful to the experiences of the women they study, but also, as researchers, to interpret these experiences in the light of the larger social, economic, and political structures that help to shape the women's experiences? How is it best to cope with the unequal relation between researcher and respondent?

Phillip E. Hammond (ed.), *Sociologists at Work* (New York: Basic Books, 1964). Doing sociological research is likely to be a rather untidy process. In these essays, sociologists give a vivid account of their research projects and of the snags they encountered. The essays remind us that sociology is both an art and a science, and that imagination, flexibility, persistence, and tolerance for frustration are useful pieces of equipment.

Doris Lessing, *Prisons We Choose to Live Inside* (Concord, Ont.: House of Anansi Press, 1991). In this published version of her CBC

Massey Lectures, Lessing looks at the increasing violence and brutality in the world and wonders what future generations will make of what she sees as our inability to understand our social behaviour. She chides her audience for ignoring the insights of social science research and the attitudes they foster, which are "the most valuable thing we have in the fight against our own savagery" (25).

NOTES

1. According to the *Gazette* (Montreal), August 5, 1993.

2. Feminists are not the only sociologists to make the criticism. Some sociologists use the mass media to disseminate their findings. These researchers are action-oriented and believe that publishing their research results only for other academics is not enough. Their purpose is to lay bare the underlying material structures of people's lives and then to have research participants use this sociological knowledge to change the conditions under which they live. As an example, finding that landlords discriminate on the basis of race in renting housing units, these critical sociologists would meet with journalists and community organizers to encourage community political action to solve the problem. For a further discussion of critical sociology and other perspectives, see Lawrence W. Neuman's *Social Research Methods* (1991).

3. For further discussion of what feminist scholarship is attempting to do, see Kirby and McKenna (1989), Smith (1987), and Harding (1987). For an excellent example of a feminist at work, read Marilyn Waring's *If Women Counted* (1988), an examination of the process and consequences of the devaluation of women and their work.

4. If families with incomes of more than $30,000 form, say, 15 percent of the Canadian population, but 30 percent of the medical and law students come from such families, we say that such students are "overrepresented" in medical and law schools.

5. For an easy-to-follow discussion of research in the social sciences, see Agnew and Pyke (1987). See also Armstrong and Armstrong (1983).

6. For more critical appraisals of the study by sociologists, see Gartner (1993) and Fox (1993).

SECTION

2

TWO

· · · · · · · · · · · · · · · · · · · ·

Culture and the

Individual

CHAPTER
THREE
3

Culture and Social Organization

The idea, which we take for granted, that everyone usually sits round a table to eat is in fact very specific to our own culture. Many people sit on the floor to dine, round a tray or trays of food. Another widely followed custom is for each diner to have his or her own table, like the small tables we provide in the living room for drinks or tea. The formal Japanese diner has a beautiful little lacquered table all to himself; he might even have two or three of them. Greeks in the Classical period each had a small oblong three-legged table.

Margaret Visser, *The Rituals of Dinner*

The beauty myth tells a story: the quality called "beauty" objectively and universally exists. Women must want to embody it and men must want to possess women who embody it. An imperative for women and not for men, it is necessary and natural because it is biological, sexual and evolutionary: strong men battle for beautiful women, and beautiful women are more reproductively successful. Women's beauty must correlate to their fertility, and since this system is based on sexual selection, it is inevitable and changeless. None of this is true. [Emphasis added.]

Naomi Wolf, *The Beauty Myth*

SUNNI SYED, Urdu Muslim, employed in government of India, undertaking, MADRAS, fair, 32, 2,200 more or less, 163 cms., owns flat in Madras City, seeks suitable alliance from brides of same caste of Madras City. The girl should be very fair, beautiful, graduate, below 25 years, around 157 cms. height, from highly educated and officials' family of Madras. Write to Box No. 521, c/o WOMAN'S ERA, *New Delhi*

Personal ad, *Woman's Era* magazine, New Delhi, India

Consider the following exchange between an interviewer and a respondent.

Interviewer: "What do you mean when you say the Lord taught you a lesson about pride last Easter?"

Respondent: "I mean ... well ... I looked so fine! And I knew I looked fine. So I went to church and the Lord blessed me ... the Lord blessed me more than He ever had ... it was more than ever before in my life ... and I learned my lesson. About pride. He blessed me and I learned He would meet my pride ...

In order to understand this exchange you need to know that "blessing" for this religious group includes being seized by a spiritual fervor that results in physically demanding activity. This woman is saying that the Lord met her pride in her appearance by causing her to become disheveled. It was a lesson in humility.

June Audrey True, *Finding Out: Conducting and Evaluating Social Research*

The above items, although diverse in subject matter, have a feature in common hinted at in Margaret Visser's description of dining arrangements. Above all, humans are creators of, participants in, and products of culture.

WHAT MAKES HUMANS HUMAN? THE CONCEPT OF CULTURE

Human beings share approximately 98 percent of their genetic heritage with chimpanzees. The dissimilar 2 percent makes humans look distinct, but certainly physical appearance is not the major determinant of humanity. What singles out homo sapiens is the capacity for creating culture, which human biology both demands and permits. Humans are not governed by **instincts—** that is, uncontrollable, universal, innate, complicated behaviour patterns that emerge through maturation. As survival tales demonstrate, if different individuals were in identical life-threatening situations, one might freeze, another flee, another fight, and another scream. Instincts, if present, would demand that each person automatically react in exactly the same manner, exhibiting identical patterns of behaviour.[1]

What many people mean when they refer to "instinctive behaviour" are human reflexes and drives. **Reflexes** are simple, uncontrollable, innate responses to stimuli, like babies sucking and the kinds of behaviour commonly known as "knee-jerk" reactions. **Drives** are internal feelings of dissatisfaction or tension that press for resolution. Modes for satisfying drives such as hunger, thirst, fatigue, and sex, so that humans are able to survive and flourish, are not predetermined but learned. The mechanism that provides the means for satisfying drives and guaranteeing human survival is culture.

Humans have the exceptional ability to override drives and to create myriad ways of satisfying them. Chimps, if they are hungry, cannot decide, as you can, that they will wait to eat at a later time. Drives, even for our closest phylogenetic relatives, are demanding and take precedence. For North Americans and people in wealthier nations, the money, energy, and time spent dieting is a testament to this ability to curb even the most critical of biological needs. The range of eating patterns and foodstuffs across cultures illustrates the diversity of options groups have discovered (as the quotation at the beginning of the chapter shows).

Far from being a detriment, then, this lack of inbuilt solutions for survival has enabled people to surpass their physical limits and create vastly different worlds in incredibly varied physical environments such as the Arctic, the Sahara, under the sea, and in space. Your grandparents, a mere seventy years ago, might not have believed that people could fly, and now we know that teams can travel to the moon and return safely.

What, then, constitutes **culture**? In sociology, as in many other disciplines, there are particular definitions of words that may not be consonant with their meanings in common everyday usage. Culture is such a term. People often associate the word with highbrow activities, such as attending opera and ballet performances, visiting art exhibitions, and talking knowledgeably about philosophy. However, young people who go to rock concerts or become ardent fans of singers and movie stars also partake of culture, since the term incorporates almost every human behaviour. Given such an overarching concept, it is not surprising that even scholars have defined "culture" in different ways.

People often associate the word "culture" with highbrow events such as opera, but young people who go to rock concerts also partake of culture.

Bryce Duffy.

One of the most widely cited definitions of culture is that of E.B. Tylor (1832–1917):

> That complex whole which includes knowledge, beliefs, arts, morals, law, customs, and any other capabilities and habits acquired by man as a member of society (1958, 10).

Members of a particular group or society share a certain way of life and of doing things. One of the important factors providing that commonality is language. Language is a symbolic code, in that words make sense only if one knows what they represent. The quotation from True (1989) at the beginning of the chapter is an example. Studying such a code is one way of learning what is important to a group. For example, the Inuit have a variety of terms for different kinds of snow, just as Bedouin tribes have many words to describe varieties of sand. However, having command of a language sufficient to translate what is said does not ensure that one will understand, in the deeper sense, what is meant. A native English speaker is likely to receive different images if a woman is described as "aggressive" rather than "forceful," whereas someone whose native tongue is not English may not be sensitive to the distinction. A sincere "thank you," for example, does not have the same force or emotional content in an unfamiliar language, so the words may have to be repeated in the speaker's predominant tongue to "feel" sincere. Thus, a native English speaker, who is beginning to learn Arabic may follow "Shucran" with the words "Thank you" to transmit the requisite emotion, even though the English words may be incomprehensible to the recipient. Nonverbal communication, too, is symbolic and shared by members of a culture. A sideways shake of the head is a dismissive "no" in Canada, but in Greek culture it is an indication of assent.

Culture, then, provides a framework for perceiving and interpreting the world. It includes goals for which people learn to strive and it furnishes typical behaviour patterns to reach those goals. As is true of most Canadians, you likely believe the world is governed by scientific principles and not by the whims of numerous gods and goddesses. Similarly, you are likely to value success in economic terms. You have learned, as well, that the conventional way to reach that goal is to study, get a degree or degrees, and then land a lucrative job. It would probably not occur to you to petition Athena, the Greek goddess of wisdom, to help you excel scholastically, nor is it probable that you will quit school and rely on lottery winnings to assure your economic well-being.

ETHNOCENTRISM AND CULTURAL RELATIVISM

One consequence of the sharing of culture is the tendency toward ethnocentrism on the part of the members of that culture. **Ethnocentrism** is the belief that one's own group or culture is the best. It is demonstrated in the statements or questions of those who assume that all cultures do or should function in the same way as theirs and by derogating and/or mocking others' cultures. For example: "Why are the stores closed in the afternoon here? How can anyone do their shopping?" "Do you believe they all eat from the same plate, with their hands? It's disgusting." "Did you see how foolish those men looked in those long outfits that looked like dresses?" Recent large-scale examples of ethnocentrism abound. Wars in Somalia and the former Yugoslavia grab headlines. Neo-Nazism is attracting followers in Europe and North America. In inner cities rivalry among ethnic gangs tears neighbourhoods apart and accounts for the deaths of numerous young people.

Opposing ethnocentrism is the stance of **cultural relativism**, the attempt to understand other people's behaviour from the viewpoint of their own culture or group. (We will have more to say about this in Chapter 7, which discusses race and ethnicity.) "I see why the stores are closed. It's so hot here in the afternoons, almost all you can do is relax. It's a great time for a siesta." It is this ability to empathize and perceive a situation from another's perspective that allows an appreciation of both the commonality and diversity of human existence. A position of cultural relativism might lead one to describe both the makeup, ear piercing, and facelifts of one culture and the neck rings, facial scarring, and body painting of another as strategies of adornment.[2] An ethnocentric position would condemn some aspects of the other culture's adornment as "mutilation." One point is inescapable: groups have different ways of manifesting their humanity.

Adornment or protest?

Tee/Urban Primitive.

SOCIETY, INSTITUTIONS, AND SOCIAL ORGANIZATION

Aspects of culture are shared by members of a **society**, a group of people, usually living in the same geographical area, who have all the necessary institutions for meeting basic human needs. An **institution** is a social arrangement that defines expected behaviour in important areas of social life.

All societies develop family, economic, political, and religious institutions that are necessary for the sustenance of the group. Family institutions, for example, have rules designating appropriate marriage partners and care for dependent children. The form of each of these institutions, however, can differ cross-culturally. In Canada, the biological mother is considered most responsible for childcare; in others, wet nurses or collectivities of women perform childrearing tasks. In our culture, one is allowed only one marriage partner at a time. In some societies, several partners are allowed. A woman of Pahari culture, whose members live in the southern part of the Himalayas, marries the eldest of a group of brothers who are regarded as equivalent by people in the culture. Therefore, all the brothers become her husbands and her children consider all her husbands to be their fathers, and address them as such (Peoples & Bailey, 1988, 211).

What sometimes seems to us an immense chasm from culture to culture is simply an alternative institutional arrangement. Ethnocentrism arises when these different institutional forms are incorrectly seen as hierarchical.

Social institutions constitute the **social organization** of a society, giving social interaction regularity and predictability. Imagine all the things you take for granted just in going to school. Without shared ideas of time and punctuality, traffic regulations, teacher and student behaviour, having even one class would be almost impossible.

Changing rules about gender provide a sample of the quandaries that can result from a lack of social organization. In our society men have traditionally "made the first move" in heterosexual relationships by asking women out on dates. That rule now is being reconsidered by some, making it difficult to decide how to act. If a man is interested in a woman, should he call her? Will the woman wait for him to call or will she call him if she's interested? If she hasn't called, does that mean she's not interested? Will she be annoyed or appreciative if he takes the initiative? Will he think her aggressive or "easy" if she approaches him? This seemingly unimportant matter can cause confusion and upset for the participants. It illuminates the fact that without the predictability social organization provides, people would be exceedingly bewildered and uncomfortable. In the extreme, societies would be unable to function.

Social organization is controlled by the exercise of power. Weber (1958) defined **power** as the ability to impose one's will on others, to force groups or individuals to act in certain ways, even against their will. Power can come from physical strength, control of valued resources, or weapons. It may be wielded subtly, crudely, or in a manner falling between these extremes. For example, employers cannot wield power as crudely as they did in Marx's day; nevertheless, power relationships remain a pervasive facet of work life. (See the discussion in Chapter 1 on the conflict perspective.) Parents can control children's behaviour, if only because of their greater size. Thieves with guns are likely to be more successful than those without.

Authority is power that has become legitimated and institutionalized in a society or other social group. Because, from infancy on, individuals are taught to comply with authority, they may be unaware of the extent to which everyday life is shaped by external authority, most prominently by the authority of the state. This is expressed in laws, regulations, and ordinances that require one, for instance, to pay taxes, declare goods purchased abroad, and obey traffic signals.

In small groups, such as families, most children accept parents' authority most of the time. The team coach directs the activities of players; not every player may agree with the directions, but they usually comply with them because the coach's authority is seen as legitimate. Girls may go along with their boyfriends' requests because it makes them feel feminine to let the male take charge.

IDEOLOGIES

Existing structures of power and authority are reinforced and modified by ideologies. An **ideology** is a set of interrelated beliefs that serves to rationalize and justify a particular social order.

An important ideology in this culture is individualism, according to which success in almost any endeavour is seen not only as attainable, but also as being primarily dependent on individual effort (that is, if one tries hard enough and perseveres, one will succeed). This ideology discounts the impact of the social environment. It says that one must compensate for an unfavourable environment by trying harder—exemplars are those who make it against tremendous odds, providing evidence for the claim that individual effort is rewarded. Personal deficiencies, the ideology asserts, are the chief reason for failure. The rationale that personal characteristics are correlated with success is used to justify the superior position of people in power.

Another example of an ideology is that of male dominance, which serves as an underpinning in most cultures and permeates almost all aspects of social organization. **Male dominance** or **patriarchy** is defined as "a situation in which men have highly preferential access, although not always exclusive rights, to those activities to which the society accords the greatest value, and the exercise of which permits a measure of control over others" (Friedl, 1975, 7). Like all ideologies, this one purports to explain the social order, in this instance men's preferential access to social rewards, by making it seem natural, unquestionable, and immutable. The ideology of male dominance builds on the fundamental biological difference between men and women, that of childbearing. According to the ideology, women's place is biologically mandated to be in the home. There does not seem to be scientific proof of any mandatory connection between bearing and rearing a child (remember, there are no instincts, maternal or otherwise) and the varieties of family organization cross-culturally bear this out. Thus, the ideology obscures the social construction of male power. The idea that women's "natural" place is in the home extends to the notion that women are best suited for certain jobs—those that require nurturing and care-taking skills. Separate job spheres for men and women are created and maintained by stressing the biological suitability of women for (only) these types of jobs. Again biological difference is used in the service of male interests, as this "women's work" is less prestigious and less well remunerated than that allotted to males.

Many women and men are now challenging the prevailing ideology of male dominance, using the ideology of individualism to make their case. Women, as well as men, they contend, should be considered as individuals and have an equal opportunity to compete for society's rewards. (Individualism is not the only solution to the problem of dominance, as we shall see in Chapter 6, which discusses stratification.)

The idea that women's "natural" place is in the home extends to the notion that women are best suited for jobs that require nurturing and caretaking skills.

Courtesy International Business Machines Corporation.

VALUES

Ideologies gain moral justification from the values of the culture and, in turn, affect those values. **Values** are the overriding themes that designate goals worth striving for and lay out general standards for evaluating behaviour. The salient values in Canadian society, reflecting our ideology of individualism, involve individual freedoms—freedom of speech, freedom of choice with respect to religion, occupation, area of residence, and marriage partner. Success, as the result of individual effort, moving onward and upward in a particular field—whether this be in one's occupation, in athletics, or in an artistic endeavour—is one of the most pervasive values. Values are not usually explicit and may be difficult to discern, but nonetheless they provide the motives for action, shaping people's choices and helping them to justify their behaviour. For example, as in our culture, women in Mayan society (an advanced Indian culture found in a collapsed state by the Spaniards when they explored the New World) were valued for their beauty, but their operationalization of this ideal is very different from ours.

EXHIBIT 3.1

Valued Goals of Teenagers

Goals	Percent of Teenagers Viewing Goals as "Very Important"	
	1984	1992
Freedom	84	86
Friendship	91	84
Being loved	87	80
Having choices	—	79
Success in what you do	78	76
Being respected	—	75
A comfortable life	75	70
Concern for others	—	62
Family life	65	60
Being a Canadian	50	45
Recognition	42	28
Cultural-group heritage	—	24
Being popular	21	22
Religious-group involvement	—	11
Cleanliness	79	72
Honesty	85	70
Humour	—	69
Forgiveness	66	59
Intelligence	63	56
Politeness	64	53
Working hard	69	49
Creativity	—	45
Imagination	42	—
Generosity	—	40

Source: Reginald W. Bibby and Donald C. Posterski. Teen Trends: A Nation in Motion. *(Toronto: Stoddart, 1992), pp. 15, 19. Reprinted with permission of Stoddart Publishing, Don Mills, Ontario, Canada.*

"The classic beauty in Mayan culture, circa 700 A.D., had a pointed head, flattened between boards at infancy. She was cross-eyed due to a pitch ball hung between her eyes. Her teeth were filed to fine points, a beauty treatment carried out by old women with pumice stone. For the finishing touch, she would paint her face a shocking shade of red with the juice of the achiote seed" (Ferguson, 1993).

Exhibit 3.1 lists valued goals and means for Canadian teenagers in 1984 and 1992. As you can see, in the span of those years young people's values changed. Humour and generosity have become more important instrumental values, while all others have declined in priority. Goals such as friendship and being loved have decreased. Having choices, being respected, concern for others and religious-group involvement appear only on the 1992 list. To see if you share these priorities, rank the values yourself.

Conflicts over the priorities assigned to values arouse strong feelings. For example, the environmentalists' desire to save forests in order to ensure the survival of wildlife and help sustain clean air competes with the immediate and desperate need of people for jobs. People who fish on the East Coast wage campaigns to continue fishing even though the stock may be deteriorating. The values of immediate and deferred gratification are at odds with each other.

NORMS—FOLKWAYS, MORES, AND LAWS

Values, then, are general ideas of what is good or bad, desirable or undesirable. **Norms** are rules for behaviour in particular situations, the concrete ways in which the abstract conceptions of values are put into practice. Norms are contextual: they vary within a culture from situation to situation, and they vary from culture to culture. Wearing a bathing suit is unacceptable in a classroom but almost mandatory on a beach in the summer heat (unless, of course, if it is a nude beach). Wearing a bathing suit while men are present is forbidden to women in parts of Saudi Arabia.

Nonverbal conceptions of space are normative. Every culture has rules about personal space for distances among people. Canadians maintain a distance of about two and a half to four feet when talking with acquaintances. In other countries, such as India, the space is much smaller. Any disruption of the norm, whether intended or unconscious, disturbs the interaction and creates uneasiness for the participants. There is a sense that something is amiss even if they can't put their fingers on the problem. Those in intimate relationships signal their closeness by standing or sitting closer together. Distance of more than two and a half feet in this situation might signify that the relationship is cooling. Canadian culture, contrary to some others, limits touching between strangers. If your fingers, even gloved, accidently touch another's on a crowded bus, both hands jump as if scorched. Touching is the ultimate encroachment on another's space and is permitted only when people know each other well.

Norms can be divided into folkways, mores, and laws. Each differs in terms of the strength of the resulting **sanctions** (rewards or punishments) used to enforce them. They can also be distinguished by the individual or group that is responsible for doing the sanctioning. **Folkways** are norms, usually not encoded in law, that change quite frequently. Examples are personal space, etiquette, fashions, minimum standards of politeness, and other everyday practices. For instance, one is not supposed to push ahead of others in a line-up or cut into a conversation. Sanctions for violations of folkways are not considered to be harsh and are informal (that is, they can be meted out by anyone). They include teasing or verbal reprimands, such as "Well, you certainly are in a hurry," or "Some people just have no manners." It must be stressed, however, that although folkways may not seem serious, most of people's behaviour falls into this category of norms. Being laughed at or stared at, reprimanded, mocked, or pointed at are not severe sanctions, but they do have the power to make us feel ashamed, worthless, isolated, and wrong. Thus even folkways are potent enough to make transgression very uncomfortable, and the damage to our sense of self from repeated misbehaviour can be devastating. Should you be skeptical, try an exercise in norm violation. Keep asking questions about what people mean when they speak. "How are you?" "Fine." "What do you mean by fine?" "I'm

While the "new year" may be ushered in worldwide, vastly different cultural norms govern when and how celebrations occur.

Canapress.

149, 309/John Issac/UN Photo.

okay." "What's okay? I'm not sure what you're talking about." Or, you might like to try addressing your parents formally as "Mr." and "Mrs." Persisting in either task can require more perseverance than you might imagine.

Mores are norms considered so crucial to group maintenance that violations must be severely sanctioned. In an industrialized society like that of Canada, mores form the basis of most laws, so it becomes difficult to draw hard and fast lines distinguishing the two. Mores underlie laws such as those that safeguard people against murder and sexual or physical assault, and those that protect property against robbery, theft, and embezzlement. Adultery was never illegal in Canada but was regarded as an unspeakable act, particularly for a woman, providing the husband with grounds for divorce. Similarly, being pregnant without being married was not illegal but, until recently, the resulting child was labelled a bastard and not protected by law. Ostracism is one of the most potent punishments meted out for disregarding a mos (the seldom-used singular form of "mores").

Precisely, mores are informally sanctioned norms, like folkways, while **laws** are norms formally enforced by public officials. Legal sanctions range from warnings for violations to imprisonment and, in some cultures, capital punishment. They can be reinforced informally for those who have been convicted of crimes deemed especially repugnant. Child molesters, for example, often have to be isolated from other prisoners for their own safety. The other inmates may demonstrate their sense of outrage against violation of such a sacred norm by attacking or even murdering the offenders.

ROLE AND STATUS

Individuals play particular roles within a social organization. Here again there is a need to be precise about the meanings of terms that are also used in everyday speech but with quite different connotations. Take the term "role," for example. In everyday language, "playing a role" means enacting a public part. You might say of a newly appointed manager, "She seems a little unsure of how to play the role." To understand how role is used in sociology, you must understand another concept, that of status. Robert Merton delineates status as a "position in a social system involving designated rights and obligations" and role as "the behaviour oriented to the patterned expectations of others" (1968, 110). The Crow Indians of North America had a third gender status called Berdaches. Berdaches were men who rejected the usual male role of bison hunter, raider, and warrior. Instead they dressed, spoke, and styled their hair like women and pursued traditionally female activities such as cooking and sewing. Certain key rituals could be performed only by Berdaches, confirming their position in Crow life (Kottak, 1991, 344). Berdaches, although uncommon, were far from being viewed negatively; they were often sought out as healers, artists, matchmakers, and companions of warriors because of the vast spiritual powers attributed to them (Haviland, 1991).

As you can see, status and role are closely linked. **Status** refers to position in the social structure, while **role** is the active dimension, the behaviour stemming from occupancy of a certain position. Box 3.1 on classroom etiquette lists recommendations for the role of those whose status is that of student. It was generated by an ombudsperson at a community college to help students who were having trouble adjusting to the college environment. You might like to produce a parallel set of expectations geared to teachers.

What do these pictures illustrate about status and role?

Canapress.   Mir Lada/MARAT.

To be a father is a type of social status. Associated with it are prescriptions for the behaviour expected of a father in a given group. In western society, for example, there is an expectation that a father will give his children economic and moral support. Many people would now say that emotional support also belongs on this list, although a few decades ago this obligation was often viewed as falling mainly within the mother's purview.

With changing economic conditions, the majority of women are adding the role of economic providers to their traditional one of caretaker. There is pressure on women to strive to approximate "super women" status by being glamorous playmates to their husbands or lovers, adoring mothers to their children, gourmet cooks, perfect housewives, and high-powered corporate executives. While this is obviously an unattainable status, achieved only momentarily by actresses in advertisements, it is true that each individual in a society does have many social positions. One can be a wife, mother, lawyer, volunteer fundraiser, daughter, and tennis player. Each status has role relationships attached to it. For example, the role of the mother means that a woman will interact with her children, their friends, perhaps their friends' parents, teachers, sport coaches, and others. This web of relationships makes up social organization at the microlevel.

A person who successfully executes the roles associated with many statuses is described as versatile. Conversely, when an individual engaged in a variety of activities performs some of his obligations less than adequately, you may remark, "He is spreading himself too thin." Often high-school students, eager for

BOX 3.1

CLASSROOM ETIQUETTE OR
HOW TO POSITIVELY INFLUENCE YOUR TEACHER

All members of the College community have an obligation to establish and maintain an environment in which learning can be effected through mutual cooperation, understanding and respect for the rights, privileges and responsibilities of everyone: students, instructional staff and administrative staff.

1. Arrive on Time

Remember it is the teacher's prerogative to deny you access to class if you're late. *If your teacher does allow you to enter late, enter quietly and as unobtrusively as possible.* Do not greet your friends, create a disturbance by noisily shuffling papers or deciding to suddenly move your desk or chair.

2. Adopt a Positive Attitude

Don't start the class by asking these two questions guaranteed to turn the teacher off:
a) "Are we going to do anything important or interesting today?"
b) "What time will we get out?"

3. Use the Teachers as a Valuable Resource

a) Studies indicate that College students, in general, only actually hear 25% of what is being said. So, focus your attention. *Just as you wouldn't engage in noisy "chit-chat" or "cross-talk" during a card game or favourite T.V. program, don't speak while your teacher is speaking.* It's rude and ultimately you are the one that loses out. There's an old saying, "When your mouth is open, your ears are shut."
b) If you are having difficulty understanding something in class—put up your hand or make eye contact with your teacher; *wait* until you're acknowledged. *Don't grunt, groan, shuffle, sigh or make comments to your neighbours.*

4. Be Aware of Your Body Language

You may be communicating a negative message without even realizing it. Sit in your seat correctly, don't put your head down on your desk or read a newspaper or comic book or have your lunch. This behaviour is insulting and is likely to affect your teacher's perception of you and, ultimately, your grade.

5. Be Aware of How You Communicate

Did you know that your tone of voice and facial expression are more important than the words used in speaking to someone?
a) To engage the teacher's attention, make eye contact or begin by saying "Excuse me, may I speak to you for a moment."
b) Choose an appropriate moment. Don't interrupt another person who may be speaking to the teacher. Scheduling an appointment with your teacher is an effective way to ensure that your teacher will have sufficient time to spend with you. Teachers have office hours and are generally very willing to meet with you.
c) Don't start the conversation with an accusation. "I want to know why you gave me this mark." Accept responsibility for what happens to you. Try opening with "I'm confused about how I did so poorly on this test. Could we go over it together?"
d) Make sure you know the difference between aggressive and assertive. Fighting for your rights *does not* include shouting, threatening, or being verbally abusive. Being verballly abusive means saying things like "You can't teach anyway," "You're getting paid to help me," etc. There are means and ways to deal with legitimate problems you may encounter with teachers.

Source: Peggy Vajo-McCoy, Vanier College, Montreal (1992). Reprinted with permission.

independence and spending money, devote more and more time to paid work. Lower marks may well be the result, reflecting the reduced time they have invested in the obligations associated with the role of student.

This situation can also be seen as an example of **role conflict**, a clash between the obligations accruing from two or more roles. The case of the working mother, frequently cited as the classic example, is just one of the many instances of potential role conflict. For example, should Mario stay at the office to finish his departmental report or go home to make himself available to his teenaged son, Tony, who after two years of being uncommunicative is showing signs of wanting to talk to his father? And when will Mario find time to lend support to his wife, who is being driven to distraction by her boss? Should Ivan who spent hours studying for his history final succumb to his best friend's signals for help during the exam and risk jeopardizing his own grade if he's caught cheating? Should Vanessa reprimand Josée for arriving late again for work? It's her task as manager, but Josée is a friend and Vanessa knows she needs the job.

Ascribed and Achieved Statuses

Since status refers to position in the social organization, it can be something that the individual simply has or else it can be "earned" in some way. In all societies, certain statuses are ascribed. An **ascribed status** is based on a characteristic such as gender, race, or religion that is bestowed at birth. Ascribed statuses are difficult if not impossible to alter. One is born male or female into a particular family in a particular country. Some ascribed statuses, such as one's religious status, can be changed, but most remain with the individual for life. Roles, however, even for ascribed statuses, may change. Following the official dismantling of apartheid in South Africa, for example, the roles for blacks, coloureds, and whites are being revised.

Achieved status depends more on individual action and is more amenable to individual control. Education, occupation, and club membership are a few of the many possible examples. Socially undesirable status positions, too, such as drug addict, extortionist, and pimp fall into this category.

Salient Status

As will be obvious by now, every individual holds many statuses. Before you continue reading, make a list of your status positions—simply write down the first five you can think of, in the order they occur to you.

Usually, the first status that you come up with is your **salient** or **master status**, which is the source of your identity. In earlier times, people derived their identities from kinship and regional affiliations. One identified oneself first as a member of a family clan and second as living in a particular village or region. In industrialized societies, the salient status became one that was achieved, particularly for men. When meeting someone new, people tend to ask men not "Who are you?" but rather "What do you do?" Being a wife and mother were, until recently, the salient statuses for most women. While many women are now choosing to define themselves in terms of their occupational status, there is still much social pressure to consider being a wife (girlfriend) and mother as identity-bestowing. The suggestions endlessly offered in magazines and on television for attaining these statuses support the notion that they remain salient.

*Achieved statuses are
amenable to individual
control. Ascribed statuses
are usually bestowed at
birth and are difficult, if
not impossible, to change.*

A. Stawicki/*The Toronto Star.*

Each culture invariably ranks statuses, but what is considered high or low
varies over time and space. Clarke (1981) found that in Canada there has been
a considerable decline in the status of the clergy during the last century.
Evidence of the decline is found in such indices as the proportion of clergy
relative to that of other professionals in the population. Clarke argues that this
reflects the changed orientation of Canadian society, from having been a
predominantly religious one to one that is mainly secular (1981, 215—22). We
shall return to this subject in Chapter 11, "Religion and Secularization."

TYPES OF CULTURES

Culture provides the overarching term to describe the particular way in which
the elements of social organization cohere. If sociologists compare several
cultures, they are likely to find that the elements of social organization in each
one form a particular configuration that permits identification of the *type* of
society. For example, an Israeli kibbutz, in which property is held collectively,

presents quite a different configuration of characteristics than that of a North American community, with its emphasis on private property and individualism.

It is useful to distinguish among types of societies by contrasting their complexity and the ways in which members typically relate to one another. Given the vast array of ways in which the discrete cultural elements can be combined to form different societies, a variety of classification systems is possible. One that we will examine in this chapter is the *Gemeinschaft* and the *Gesellschaft*. These terms, which were used by the German sociologist Ferdinand Tönnies (1855–1936), can be translated respectively as "community" and "society." However, the original German terms are frequently used by sociologists.

RURAL

Tönnies depicted a ***Gemeinschaft*** as a small, homogeneous, mainly rural society. The group has a high degree of self-sufficiency, and the division of labour is simple. The members share values; in Durkheim's terms (see Chapter 1), they are tied by mechanical solidarity. The belief system holds that it is a duty to conform to God's will (however God is conceptualized), and that certain aspects of existence are beyond human understanding and must simply be accepted.

Relationships in this type of small community are close and overlapping. Individuals interact within their economic activities, working cooperatively or exchanging skills and resources; they also pray and play together. Relationships are permeated by both positive and negative emotions; friendships that provide warmth and security may co-exist with intense feuds, such as the famous one between the Montagues and the Capulets, dramatized in *Romeo and Juliet*. Ascribed statuses weigh heavily in determining the functions each member performs. People are expected to behave in accordance with the norms prescribed for their positions. Since expectations are known and clearly understood, individuals can

A Gesellschaft *is a large, heterogeneous society that has been urbanized.*

Ontario Ministry of Transportation.

feel sure of doing the right thing and can predict how others will act. However, there is little tolerance for deviation, and those who do not fit smoothly into their assigned places must face community sanctions. For example, among the Amish, complete ostracism, which they refer to as "shunning," is meted out to those who have severely offended communal standards. The Hutterites are an example of a present-day group that approximates a *Gemeinschaft*.

The polar opposite of the *Gemeinschaft* in Tönnies's schema is the **Gesellschaft.** It is a large, heterogeneous society that has become urbanized (where the bulk of the population has shifted from the countryside to the city). The division of labour is highly specialized, creating interdependence among members; this is organic solidarity in Durkheim's terms. Although the *Gesellschaft*, like any society, has certain overriding values, there is room for a diversity of worldviews. In modern Canadian society, individuals can live together peaceably most of the time even though they hold opposing values on such important issues as capital punishment or the environment.

In the *Gesellschaft*, achieved status is normatively the salient one. Ideally, it matters more what one has achieved by way of education and occupation than whether one was born male or female, Indian or white. The vital question is what one has done. (In practice, of course, one's ascribed characteristics bear on what one is able to do and on the obstacles one must overcome.)

In this kind of society, relationships are typically segmented, which means that one's co-workers or fellow parishioners are not necessarily one's personal friends. The two hundred tenants of a high-rise building live in close proximity, but their contact with each other may be minimal or nonexistent. Emotional involvement is reserved for personal relationships. Minding one's own business, which means not getting entangled in the affairs of outsiders, is positively valued.

In contrast to the high degree of consensus that regulates behaviour in the *Gemeinschaft*, the *Gesellschaft* has no unequivocal prescriptions for what constitutes appropriate behaviour. This uncertainty engenders a high degree of anxiety. A father may agonize over choosing among the roles of being a disciplinarian, an advisor, or a buddy to his children. However, members of such a society have some leeway in what they do and how they do it. They can choose to attend religious services or not, consume alcoholic beverages or abstain, become politically active or remain indifferent to political life.

It is worth noting that the *Gesellschaft* and *Gemeinschaft* types, like many of the constructs of sociological theory, are abstract concepts. In Weber's term, they are **ideal types**, ideas rather than real things. They can be used as measuring devices so that one can examine how actual communities, past and present, conform to or deviate from the model.

SUBCULTURES

By definition, a heterogeneous society contains groups and individuals who engage in a variety of lifestyles and have different sets of goals and priorities. When a group exists within mainstream society but differs from it in patterned ways—for instance, in language, norms, or customs—we describe it as a **subculture**. Sociologists do not clearly agree on the criteria for designating a group as a subculture. However, most

When a group exists within mainstream society but differs from it in patterned ways, sociologists describe it as a subculture.

Ontario Ministry of Transportation.

would categorize an ethnolinguistic group as a subculture. Winnipeggers and Torontonians may refer to certain districts in their cities as "little Italy" or "little Portugal." The implication is that for the immigrants who inhabit these areas, life runs as closely as possible along the lines of the old country.

To the extent that an occupation provides an all-encompassing context for everyday life, it too can be described as a subculture. Examples are the world of the military or that of circus performers. In both cases, members and their families have limited opportunities to interact with outsiders on a continuing basis. Therefore, the development of distinctive ways of living and of looking at the world can proceed relatively unchecked.

The very rich and the very poor have also been described as constituting subcultures. The very rich are not easily accessible for investigation, though some studies have been done. Ferdinand Lundberg, for example, wrote *The Rich and the Super Rich* (1969), and Peter C. Newman did research on the Canadian establishment (1975) in general and on some of its members in particular (1981). The poor have been studied in greater detail. Oscar Lewis (1959) developed the concept of the culture of poverty, based on his research in North American and Latin American slums. He argued that in severely deprived environments, people develop orientations of passivity, fatalism, and a short-term rather than a long-term perspective.[3] Ironically, these very orientations hinder escape from poverty. In Lewis's words:

> Poverty becomes a dynamic factor which affects participation in the larger national culture and creates a sub-culture of its own. One can speak of the culture of the poor, for it has its own modalities and distinctive social and psychological consequences for its members (1959, 2).

Subcultures can be summed up as the collective responses of individuals who share certain values, norms, and behaviour patterns that set them apart from their society at large. A **counterculture** also meets this specification, but its members have joined the group as a form of protest against prevailing societal values and norms.[4] The hippies of the 1960s manifested their dissatisfaction with the existing state of affairs by emphasizing community and hedonism. They ostensibly rejected material possessions, cherished cooperative behaviour and pacifism, and lived for the moment. None of these values or norms were congruent with the materialism and militarism of the United States at that time. Although the term "counterculture" entered the English language in the late 60s with reference to the values and behaviour of this younger generation, it can also be applied to the early Christians of Jewish Jerusalem and, later, of pagan Rome (Yinger, 1982).

CULTURAL CHANGE

In our discussion so far, we have focused primarily on some of the building blocks of culture and on ways in which they are combined into different cultural forms. However, cultures are dynamic systems involved in a continuous process of change. How does change occur?

When the world's means of transportation were rudimentary and travel both cumbersome and hazardous, groups that were off the beaten track lived in relative isolation from each other. Their cultures were slow to change. Other peoples, especially those living near waterways, have had extensive contact with outsiders since antiquity and their cultures are relatively fluid.

Sometimes groups become closed in on themselves because of circumstances. The collapse of the Roman empire, for example, isolated Europe during the so-called dark ages, from about the fifth to the twelfth centuries. Then the crusaders, who set out from Europe to enlighten the "infidels" in the Middle East, were dazzled by the thriving society they found there. They brought back with them a host of innovations, such as new techniques in weaving, dyeing, and metalworking, which then became integrated into the existing European cultures. Slowly, communication and travel both within Europe and with the outside world improved. With the Renaissance and the voyages of discovery, such as those of Christopher Columbus and John Cabot, contact between cultures greatly increased. Voyages to the Americas introduced Europeans to potatoes, tobacco, and corn. Quite rapidly, these items became staples of everyday life. This process is called **cultural diffusion**.

Generally, material items that pass the test of usefulness are accepted more readily than cultural symbols and rituals. Many of North America's native peoples, for example, were using horses, iron tools (including guns), and woven cloth soon after their first contact with Europeans. This century's immigrants to Canada have been quick to adopt cars and labour-saving devices, but some have clung to certain old-country practices, such as those relating to courtship behaviour. In traditional Macedonian families, for instance, a young man brings his girlfriend home to meet his family only after the couple has decided to get married.

With the advent and growth of the mass media, there has been a dramatic speedup in the rate and the extent of cultural diffusion. Coca-Cola and jeans have become part of the youth culture of societies as distant from each other as Russia and Canada.

Cultural diffusion facilitates **acculturation**, the process by which groups or individuals who are in contact exchange cultural traits and acquire new ones. Since Canada is a nation of immigrants, it provides a ready laboratory for observing acculturation. Raymond Breton (1964) has noted that not all immigrant groups become acculturated at the same rate. If they live in ethnic enclaves within which they can worship, shop, and eat, and if they have access to newspapers and other mass media in their native tongue, acculturation is likely to be slow. An example of slow acculturation was relayed to one of the authors by an elderly German professor, when he reminisced about his childhood in Milwaukee in the early 1900s. When he started school, he and his friends knew no English. They picked that up quickly enough, but within earshot of their elders, the children were forbidden, under threat of physical punishment, to speak anything but German. Apparently, the elder generation was anxious to retard acculturation.

Acculturation cannot be staved off permanently or completely, however, unless the group opts for isolation, as do the Hutterites, some Mennonite sects, and ultraorthodox Hasidic Jews. Most children of immigrants go to Canadian schools, learn a new language, and meet youngsters from other groups. Language plays an important part in acculturation because it helps to shape ideas as well as to express them. The more completely the children come to function in the new language, the more removed they become from the culture of their parents. Male immigrants also tend to have at least some contact with the new society at large, even if they work mainly with compatriots. It is the stay-at-home wives who are least likely to be acculturated.

In an encounter between two cultures, which one is more likely to adapt to the other? As we will see in Chapters 6 and 7 on stratification and minority groups, the direction of acculturation is strongly influenced by differences in power. The dominant group has the capacity both to resist change and to impose the group's ways of living and thinking on others. Porter (1965) and others have observed that, in Canada, this has translated into the dominance of Anglo-Saxon ways of seeing and doing things. But this British hegemony is on the wane, proving that acculturation is by no means a one-way street. In our society, the popularity of ethnic restaurants and the burgeoning interest in African and Latin American music show that the host society also adopts cultural traits from incoming groups.

CULTURE LAG

When Comte proposed his law of three stages, he envisioned all sectors of society changing simultaneously, making for a smooth transition. In real life, however, cultural change happens in a piecemeal way at different times and at different rates. More than sixty years ago, Ogburn (1922) noted that material culture, particularly the technological realm, changes more quickly than other elements of social life. It takes time before adjustments are made in these other areas. Ogburn referred to this delay as **culture lag**. This phenomenon is even more common today, given the great explosion of technological advances.[5] Look, for example, at the vast nuclear arms buildup. The lag in developing commensurate control mechanisms may well prove fatal for humanity. Look, too, at automation, which has the potential for increasing productivity and hence overall well-being. But, at the same time, no effective policies have as yet been developed for the redeployment of displaced workers. Computers are changing patterns of work by deskilling certain jobs (such as cashier) and allowing other workers (lawyers) to work from their homes. Leisure activity, for some, now consists of discussions via modem. The consequences of this one technological advance have yet to be measured.

Technology is not the spearhead for change in every instance. Sometimes behaviour changes before institutional support mechanisms have been put in place. For instance, increasing numbers of married women, many of whom are mothers of young children, have entered the labour force, but the availability of good, affordable day care has lagged far behind (Cooke, 1986). In part, this lag can be attributed to the ideology of male dominance discussed above. This notion of a mother's "proper" place allows various levels of government to downplay the urgency for action on day care. But this ideological stance flies in the face of the facts: many women are obliged to work for economic reasons, and others choose to work.

. . . .

OVERVIEW

Culture provides for the meeting of human needs and is a necessity given homo sapiens' biological makeup. Culture is created, learned, sustained, passed on, and changed by people in interaction. This patterned interaction is organized in a relatively stable and predictable system termed social organization. Participation in a culture necessitates sharing its symbols, particularly language. The "oughts" and "ought nots" of conduct form a hierarchy that includes societal values and norms, with norms subdivided into mores, folkways, and laws. Mores are cultural imperatives, often the basis of laws, whereas folkways constitute a code of conduct that is less forcefully sanctioned. Social organization integrates cultural elements. Key to this organization are the twin concepts of status and role. Status defines the rights and obligations expected from incumbents in the position. Role is the behavioural dimension associated with a particular status, which may be ascribed, an accident of birth, or achieved, which means the individual has some control over it. In all groups each individual occupies one status that is considered his or her salient one. In South Africa, for example, racial status still supersedes all others.

Societies like Canada's are large and heterogeneous—it is a *Gesellschaft*, embracing a variety of subcultures, each of which represents a distinctive way of life. Subcultures can form along lines such as age, ethnicity, and occupation. A subculture that constitutes a rebellion against values and norms is called a counterculture.

For a culture to survive, its members must deem it worthy of preservation and transmission. In this sense, ethnocentrism—literally, the assignment of a central place to one's own culture—is a positive force. It becomes negative when people regard their culture as inherently superior and diminish other cultures. To avoid this judgmental stance, one must interpret particular cultural elements in their overall context, the idea behind cultural relativism.

Ideologies, and power and authority, are potent factors in the preservation of culture. However, there are always counteracting forces pressing for change. Prominent among these forces is the process of cultural diffusion, by which artifacts and ways of thinking penetrate an existing culture and become part of it. As this occurs, both old and new cultures undergo modification. When groups are continually exposed to one another, cultural traits are exchanged, resulting in acculturation. Generally, this exchange favours the adoption of the dominant group's ways. Cultural change tends to proceed at different rates in various sectors of a society. Culture lag occurs when one sector, often the technological one, moves ahead before the changes can be effectively integrated with other aspects of social organization.

The process of learning to be a member of a culture is called socialization, which is the subject of the next chapter.

ASSIGNMENTS

1. Television is central in propagating values that serve the interests of powerful groups in society. Watch two programs and identify the cultural values reflected in each. Pay careful attention to the commercials. What kinds of behaviour do they encourage, and whose interests are best served by this behaviour?

2. Every campus has a variety of subcultures. Choose one of these subcultures, such as a political or religious group, and explain the ways in which they are distinctive enough to warrant the label "subculture."

3. Some Canadians accuse the United States of "cultural imperialism," that is, swamping Canadians with American culture. Explain why you think this is or is not a valid charge.

4. Conduct a survey to ascertain the priority of the following values for different groups of individuals: to have a happy marriage; to receive a high income; to travel extensively; to be a good Christian, Jew, Muslim, etc.; to have a stable, assured job; to be a good citizen of the world; to be a good Canadian; to be respected by friends; to have opportunities for creative endeavours; to be famous; to rear outstanding children. How might you explain the similarities and differences in the resulting rankings?

SUGGESTED READINGS

Philippe Garigue, "French-Canadian Kinship and Urban Life," in Marcel Rioux and Yves Martin, eds., *French-Canadian Society*, Vol. I (Toronto, McClelland and Stewart, 1964:123–37). Garigue challenges the widely held notion that the early communities of rural Quebec conformed to the "folk society" model. He analyzes such things as the patterns of settlement, the consequences of large families, inheritance, and the influence of the Roman Catholic Church, and concludes that there is more evidence of a similarity with the sociological features of urban life than had previously been thought.

Edward T. Hall, *The Silent Language* (Garden City, NY: Doubleday & Company, 1959). This classic still provides the reader with an excellent grasp of the notion that culture is pervasive and much more than skin-deep. Examining aspects of non-verbal communication, such as personal space, eye movements, and facial expressions, that many of us take for granted, Hall shows how non-verbal communication "speaks volumes," and describes its eloquence from a cross-cultural perspective.

T. Kroeber, *Ishi in Two Worlds* (Berkeley and Los Angeles: University of California Press, 1962). In August of 1911, the last known survivor of the Yahi tribe walked into a small California town, emaciated and exhausted. The two anthropologists who befriended him named him Ishi, meaning "man" in Yana. Ishi spent his remaining few years in San Francisco, living and working at the museum attached to the University of California. The book is a fascinating account of a culture that is now extinct, and of how its last member experienced modern life.

Neil Postman, *Amusing Ourselves to Death: Public Discourse in the Age of Show Business* (New York: Penguin Books, 1985); and *Technopoly: The Surrender of Culture to Technology* (New York: Alfred A. Knopf, 1992). In these two highly readable books, Postman discusses the impact of technology on American culture. *Amusing Ourselves to Death* is an elaboration of the impact of the television format on our ways of processing information and the repercussions of this change on all social institutions. In *Technopoly*, Postman continues his interesting critique of technology, which he describes as "a particularly dangerous enemy" (p. xii). Although sometimes critical of social science research, Postman offers a worthwhile cautionary tale with insight and humour.

Robert Redfield, *Tepoztlan—A Mexican Village: A Study of Folk Life* (Chicago: University of Chicago Press, 1930); and Oscar Lewis, *Tepoztlan Restudied* (Urbana University of Illinois Press, 1949). Do researchers sometimes find mostly what they set out to look for? To Redfield, the village of Tepoztlan represented the ideal-type "folk society," a cohesive, smoothly functioning, harmonious, *Gemeinschaft*-like community. Less than twenty years later, Oscar Lewis studied the same village, with quite different conclusions. Instead of the cooperation and homogeneity that Redfield described, Lewis saw conflict and heterogeneity. Lewis's study emphasizes the poverty, violence, ill-health, and economic malaise of the community.

Drew Hayden Taylor, *The Bootlegger Blues* (Saskatoon: Fifth House Publishers, 1991). What do you do with 143 cases of beer after a church fundraising effort during a powwow weekend on a Native reserve fails? This is a wonderful, raucous play that was first produced by the Da-Ba-Jeh-Mu-Jig Theatre Group on Manitoulin Island. While Hayden's purpose is to entertain and not to teach, he shows how Native culture has taken on some aspects of white, urban culture (computers, jogging, country-western music), while attempting to preserve its own language, rituals, music, and traditions.

NOTES

1. Definitions of instincts may vary from discipline to discipline. For a psychological/psychoanalytical perspective, definition, and examples, see John Bowlby's *Attachment* (1974). For a biological explanation of social behaviour, see Edward O. Wilson's *Sociobiology: The New Synthesis* (1975). Nonetheless, social scientists agree that while behaviours may be genetically based, humans do not have automatic biological solutions to problems of survival that unfailingly appear, even in suitable environmental conditions. Human behaviour is a complex interaction of genes, culture, experience, and chance.

2. The concept of cultural relativism may appear to be simple, but it is not. The issue of female circumcision in African countries and the extension of this practice to girls from these groups living in Canada has elicited much complex debate. Research is now focusing on this practice worldwide. For a cross-cultural description of female circumcision, see H. Lightfoot-Klein's *Prisoner's of Ritual* (1989). For nonacademic views of the problem, see Ann Louise Bardach's "Tearing Off the Veil" (1993) and Nathalie Silvester's "Can a Genital-Mutilation Fugitive Win Political Asylum?" (1991).

3.   Critics of this formulation counter that, when circumstances change, the attitudes and behaviour of the poor change more readily than the notion of a culture of poverty would suggest.

4.   Ironically, countercultures, conceived in rebellion against community standards, often demand strict conformity to their own standards.

5.   The new reproductive technologies, one of the most recent and potentially most troubling examples of technological development, are discussed in Chapter 12, "Social Change."

Socialization

In the early morning of January 9, 1800, a strange creature appeared out of the woods near the French village of Saint-Sernin, in the district of Aveyron, one hundred and twenty-five kilometres north of the Spanish border. He appeared to be a small boy, but he acted like a wild animal. He was caught digging up vegetables from a tanner's garden, and was soon turned over to a local official who made some notes about him ... his behaviour made it apparent he had been roaming the countryside, apart from civilization, for some time.

Jay Ingram, *Talk, Talk, Talk*

The academic goals of the program are to teach the children that babies go through a combination of biological readiness and interaction with parents and the environment. Students come away with a deep sense of the vital role that parents play in all aspects of the child's development—emotional, physical, verbal, intellectual, etc.—and how parents can either promote or hinder that development. They are made aware of temperamental variations between babies and between parents, and how these variations affect parent–child relationships.

The students also develop emotional and practical skills that are required in child care. They do this through the central component of the program: the baby visits. At the Germantown Friends school, starting in late kindergarten, a parent brings his or her baby or toddler to class once a month. Often the visits start when the mother is pregnant.

Students are instructed to observe what parents bring with them to class: bottles, diapers, toys, favorite blanket or stuffed animal. This gives them a sense of the kind of careful thinking ahead and planning that is required of parents. They also learn by asking questions: "What do you have to take along when you go away for a weekend?" or "Can you ever leave the baby to play alone in her room?"

Myriam Miedzian, *Boys Will Be Boys*

Try the following: Look at the fingernails of your right hand and then, standing up, look at the heel of your right foot. When examining your nails did you hold your hand out in front of you bent upward at a ninety degree angle to your wrist with your fingers straight up or did you curl your fingers in toward your palm, palm facing you? Did you look over your right shoulder to see your heel or did you lift up your foot in front of you and look down? Thirty years ago, in Montreal, ten-year-olds used this test to determine their masculinity and femininity. "Real" girls held their hands up in front of them to view their nails and gazed over their shoulders at their raised heels; "real" boys curled their fingers in, palms up, for nail viewing and raised their heels in front of them to see them. The rules for gender being extremely rigid, any child who "failed" the test was mortified and made sure that he or she learned and practised the proper procedure from then on.

Many people assert that "boys will be boys," making it seem as though masculinity is something natural and inevitable. As the nails-and-heels exercise hints, masculinity and femininity are not inevitable or unproblematic. If that were the case, no one would ever need to worry if they were masculine enough or too feminine.

This illustration of **gender**, the social role assigned to each sex, provides a particular instance of the learning process sociologists term **socialization**, the process through which an individual develops by internalizing the ways of the culture. The process is necessary from two vantage points. Without the initiation of new members, the culture's survival would be at stake and a person would not be whatever is considered human in her culture, as the "wild boy" vignette with which this chapter opens shows. Without being socialized, sociologists say that an infant would not develop a **self**, a conception of who she is, based on the particular combination of physical, psychological, and cultural characteristics that make her unique.

SOCIALIZATION, NATURE, AND NURTURE

To survive and to develop even the most basic of skills, a neonate needs care from other people. This **social interaction** is a fundamental process through which people exchange meanings and have a reciprocal effect on each other by communicating through language, symbols, and gestures. How these social influences transform the biological organism into a functioning human being has long engaged the attention of those who study social life. Have you ever wondered how much you are like your parents or some other family member? Did you ever ask yourself whether you inherited those traits or "picked them up" from these people? Is behaviour as hereditary as physical family resemblance? These questions also puzzle scientists, who would put the question this way: ultimately, how much of "the self" is determined by biology, the endowment with which one begins life, and how much by experience, what one goes through in living? This dispute is known as the "nature/nurture" controversy. Those on the "nature" side of the argument stress the biological bases of behaviour, and those on the "nurture" side of the argument stress the power of experience in determining behaviour.

Incontrovertible evidence of the biological impact on human behaviour, compared to that of the social, is difficult to find. The most effective method for ferreting out the influences of nature and nurture would be to take identical twins who have the same genetic heritage, separate them at birth, and raise each in very different social environments. Similarities manifested by the twins could be attributed to biological factors and differences to social phenomena.

Biological determinists, the "nature" supporters, hold that each person is born with a certain temperament and certain abilities and that these can be changed only within a narrow range—one cannot make a silk purse out of a sow's ear. Logically, this argument assigns socialization a limited role in the development of a human being.

This idea that organisms were given divergent endowments by nature arose from Charles Darwin's *Origin of Species*, which was published in 1859. The book created a sensation, not only because it called into question the biblical doctrine of creation, but also because it drew attention to the human being as a biological organism that shared basic similarities with all other living things. Darwin also talked about the "survival of the fittest," that is, the survival of those organisms able to adapt to changing environmental conditions. At that time, there was an enormous gap between the rich and the poor, with many of the poor living under abysmal conditions. Biological determinism seemed a tidy explanation of such differences, which demonstrates that the assumptions of a theory are often congruous with the beliefs of the particular society. The poor, it was claimed, were obviously less fit. This idea made it perfectly reasonable that Europeans conquer and dominate so-called inferior races and served as a patently useful "scientific" justification for the upsurge in colonialism that took place in the late 1800s.

Arguments containing some of the pernicious assumptions of biological determinism, that the genetic endowment of individuals and of groups of people is the major determinant of how they fare, continue to surface. The "natural inferiority" of certain groups is still used to justify their maltreatment.

Views about the sources of human behaviour tend to oscillate with changes in economic conditions, and these fluctuations affect other areas of the culture. When societies are prospering, the "nurture" adherents seem to prevail and governments are willing and able to invest in creating and maintaining programs for what are seen as socially disadvantaged groups. When times are difficult economically, there is greater support for the idea that human behaviour is predominantly biologically determined, thus the efficacy of social intervention is minimal.

The polar opposite of biological determinism is **environmental determinism** (a view that claims individuals can be shaped and reshaped by their environment); it is situated at the extreme end of the nurture continuum. **Behaviourism** is a psychological theory that reflects the assumptions of environmental determinism. It regards the infant as infinitely plastic, highly susceptible to being moulded to fit desired patterns. (The environmental determinism learning theories developed by behaviourists will be explained in a later section of this chapter.)

The debate between nature and nurture advocates parallels early sociologists' concerns with agency versus constraint—what command do individuals have over their own lives and environments? In much the same way as those advocating the interaction of nature and nurture in socialization, we will claim that people have room to construct their own lives within certain existing parameters. People do not produce the (social) world they inherit, but they do have the power to modify it. We continue with an example of a complicated and much debated socialization process, that of gender, which aptly illustrates the two sides of this debate.

GENDER SOCIALIZATION

It may be surprising to learn that as recently as twenty years ago few introductory texts in sociology made mention of gender. It was taken largely for granted that masculinity was the standard for human behaviour. In recent decades, the resulting imbalance has been debated (as we noted in prior chapters) and is now being addressed. Much of the work was and continues to be carried out by sociologists, usually but not always women, who objected to "the ignore-ance of the female world by male researchers," as sociologist Jesse Bernard put it (1981, 18).

Gender has always been the basic criterion for the division of tasks in a society. Although the division of labour varies widely across cultures, in almost all instances the tasks assigned to men, whatever they might be, are more socially valued than those assigned to women in the same culture. Another constant seems to be that women bear and rear children, although the women who do the rearing need not be the children's biological mothers.

Gender socialization, the preparation of youngsters for the tasks and the values, attitudes, and patterns of behaviour that are deemed desirable for females and males in their respective societies, begins early. The first question parents ask about their newborn, after "Is the baby healthy?" is "Is it a boy or a girl?" For most of the rest of the child's life, the child will be referred to in gendered terms. In some countries during some historical periods, the sex of the child even determined whether the child was allowed to live. Female infanticide was practised in India. In China, rigid birth control policies mean that infant girls may be abandoned, so that the parents can try to have a male child. [1]

The socialization process, as you have seen, ensures that newborns are transformed into functioning members of their culture who, for the most part, know "their place," fitting into the existing structures and providing for their continuity. In North American culture, as in most others, the ideology of male dominance (discussed in the preceding chapter) underlies the gender socialization process. Gender socialization, then, reinforces male dominance in each new generation by assigning not only different but less-valued tasks, roles, behaviours, and personality traits to women. Despite claims that men and women are equal, children are socialized differently and masculinity and femininity, as culturally defined, are still seen as "opposite."

Masculinity and Femininity

The themes that characterize masculinity and femininity are illustrated in a now classic study by Broverman and colleagues (1970). The subjects, mental health clinicians, were asked to rate normal healthy adults, males and females, on a series of personality traits that were defined as opposites, for example, very aggressive or not at all aggressive. The resulting depictions were that normal healthy men were independent, competitive, logical, worldly, dominant, and

BOX 4.1

IT'S A BOY!

She was my friend at school. When she turned 12, her father committed suicide, leaving a note saying that with five daughters approaching adulthood, he couldn't bear the shame of not being able to give them the dowries they needed. He said he hoped his death would raise compassion in the hearts of prospective husbands for his daughters whom he loved deeply.

I remembered this when I met Champa (not her real name), an Asian woman who has been clinically depressed since the birth of her third daughter. She also speaks of suicide and dowries constantly, but on good days she wants to try again because she has heard she can now get "medicine" to have a boy. Champa has written to her abysmally poor parents in India for money—a futile plea.

It costs up to $2,000 for this "medicine" at Britain's only gender clinic, where it is claimed that parents can choose their child's sex before fertilization with a process that involves filtering semen and separating off the Y-chromosome sperm, which produce male children.

The clinic claims a 75-per-cent chance of success—but is this salvation for people like Champa or is it just further exploitation of their pain and vulnerability? There has been much discussion around the ethical and medical aspects of sex pre-selection but the social consequences, particularly in strongly patriarchal communities, have been ignored.

This is what concerns Vibhuti Patel from the Women's University in Bombay and Gautum Appa at the London School of Economics, who have analyzed the effects of existing clinics in India and other countries.

The clinics are franchised by an affluent American, Ron Ericsson, who developed the technique and who also excels at enticing puffery to sell and defend his business. In India in 1986, Ericsson proclaimed that his clinics would help in population control, reduce abortions and enhance a woman's right to choose.

He did confess, however, that in his 46 franchised clinics across Europe, Asia and America, 236 couples had chosen to have boys and 15 had chosen girls. With such

allies, patriarchy is in no danger of extinction.

This, says Vibhuti Patel, reveals the truth behind the rhetoric of these so-called advances in reproductive science: "It is another step in the historical devaluation of women. In some areas of India, people starve or kill their baby daughters. You begin with femicide and then you use science to achieve your aims.

"Already we have such tests as amniocentesis being used to determine sex, leading to the abortion of female fetuses on a massive scale. Now we can go for pre-selection, so we don't have to confront the messy business of guilt and shame. The message is still, 'You are female, you are not welcome.' What we need to eliminate is inequality and not women."

This is not paranoia. Patel and Appa possess alarming statistics to back their views. In South Korea, male births exceed female births by 14 per cent. In one province of China, men between 35 and 40 outnumber women by 10 to one. Interestingly, Ericsson has been a state guest in China.

In India, between 1978 and 1983, 78,000 recorded cases of female abortions took place after sex determination tests and the sex ratio in one area went down in 1981 to 836 females to 1,000 males.

No cause for concern, say the doctors in India who prosper from gender-selection technology. They argue, says Patel, that this is humanitarian work: "There are fewer unwanted children and fewer females means less reproduction. They talk in terms of demand and supply; the scarcity of women will up their status. In fact, it leads to forced polyandry, rape and abduction. Some even say it is better for a female to die as a fetus than suffer as a woman."

There are two reasons why girls on the subcontinent are considered a liability. One is the belief that a girl belongs to the husband's family and is no use to her parents in old age; the second is the burden of providing dowries.

Reported dowry deaths in India have gone up from 358 in 1978 to more than 1,500 in recent years. One of the most successful advertisements put out by gender clinics says, "Spend 500 rupees now to save 50,000 later."

The way to change these attitudes is not to make it easy not to have girls, but to educate the population. And this, according to Patel, is something that women's groups, committed men and even film stars in India have taken on in recent years. "Our movement is fighting to ban sex determination and preselection clinics; in one state this has happened.

"In addition, through rallies, plays and songs, we tell people that women are not a burden. Parents get on the platform and say how their daughters support them. I myself took action after my sister-in-law had an abortion at six months because she knew it was a girl; after my first child, a daughter, was born, I got sterilized to show them."

Nor is all this confined to the subcontinent. The focus is on the ethical debate but what about the social effects of such a service? Champa is a British Asian woman who, like many others, believes her self-worth lies entirely in her ability to produce a son.

This is why Appa is fervently against the gender clinic in Britain: "It is no good wishing patriarchy away, it is deep-rooted in this society. Girls are not wanted and not allowed to flower in many families. What will the effect of this clinic be on our community? We must demarcate this technology as illegal, so that when people do it, they know they are breaking a law."

One Asian woman doctor who agrees with Appa says she sees many women under pressure to produce boys and abort girls. She claims some Asian doctors in Britain are colluding in this.

There is increasing evidence that there is a network of Asian doctors in Britain now performing gender tests and female abortions. For a healthy fee, of course. Of course, gender pre-selection would prevent this kind of activity but it would be continuing the tradition of female devaluation.

That tradition is (slowly) disappearing in the Asian community, according to Hema Devlukia, a health-care worker and mother of two girls. "My husband and I wanted daughters and our families agreed: they think a daughter is yours for life, she cares. A son is yours till he marries, then he changes."

Source: Yasmin Alibhae-Brown, "It's a Boy!" Gazette (Montreal) (3 April 1993), p. B6. Reprinted with permission.

objective—what was labelled the competency cluster of characteristics. Normal healthy women were described by the subjects as emotional, subjective, aware of others' feelings, dependent—the warm-expressiveness cluster of traits. Not only were men and women seen as exhibiting opposite personality characteristics, the traits associated with masculinity were considered to be more socially valued than the feminine ones. Healthy adults, moreover, were identified as healthy males and, again, as the opposite of healthy females. The dilemma for women then becomes being a feminine woman and running the risk of being seen (and treated) as a child or becoming an adult and risking being berated for being masculine.

Currently these definitions are being modified. Women, in increasing numbers, are pursuing, competing for, and succeeding in male-dominated jobs. Men are becoming emotionally attuned to their partners and children. Many researchers in different disciplines, however, will still agree that women are socialized to focus and evaluate themselves in terms of their relationships with others; that men are still socialized to compete; and that competition is undeniably, to many, more worthwhile than sensitivity to others. Exhibit 4.1 lends support to the notion that girls value friendship, being loved, and concern for others more than do boys.

EXHIBIT 4.1

Relational Values and Enjoyment: Females and Males

| | Percent Viewing as "Very Important" | | | |
| | 1992 | | 1984 | |
	F	M	F	M
Highly Value				
Friendship	89%	79%	94%	88%
Being loved	90	68	93	81
Highly Enjoy				
Friendships	96	90	97	94
Brother(s) or sister(s)	58	51	55	52
Mother	70	63	80	76
Father	59	61	69	73
Pet(s)	45	52	—	—

Interpersonal Values: Females and Males

| | Percent Viewing as "Very Important" | | | |
| | 1992 | | 1984 | |
	F	M	F	M
Honesty	82%	56%	90%	80%
Concern for others	75	48	—	—
Forgiveness	71	45	72	62
Politeness	60	46	70	60
Generosity	48	32	—	—

Source: Reginald W. Bibby and Donald C. Posterski, Teen Trends: A Nation in Motion *(Toronto: Stoddart, 1992), 139, 141. Reprinted with permission of Stoddart Publishing, Don Mills, Ontario, Canada.*

Early Gender Socialization

How, then, are these gender patterns recreated? Decades ago, Hartley (1958) studied male socialization and elaborated the difficulties of learning to be masculine in North America. With information garnered from interviews with boys of different ages, she developed a theory of the internalization of male dominance that is part and parcel of learning to be a boy. Her work remains pertinent.

Agents of socialization refer to the people with whom the child interacts in the process of being socialized and to the parts of material culture utilized in the socialization process. Agents of socialization, Hartley said, encourage boys to be masculine from birth. Newborn males are described as active and strong, and those characteristics are encouraged. Rarely though, at any age, are boys explicitly instructed in what masculinity actually entails. **Role models**, those who demonstrate the appropriate attitudes and actions of an occupant of the role, are often lacking, as adult males do not spend much time with children. Their difficulty is compounded because little boys typically spend their days under the jurisdiction of adult women, either at home or at school. Of necessity, then, boys learn their gender role through trial and error. Since being masculine is seen as important, deviations are not easily tolerated and boys are harshly punished when they make a mistake. What boys come to understand, Hartley maintained, is that masculinity is anything that is not feminine, and they strive to exorcise those behaviours in themselves. For guidance, boys rely on each other. This results in an exaggeration of the few traits they know to be masculine—strength, toughness, as demonstrated in athletic prowess, and the absence of overt emotion, or "being cool." The pressure to be masculine and the negative sanctions for feminine behaviour, coupled with the lack of instruction in and absence of appropriate role models, combine to lead boys to internalize the value of male dominance and even to become misogynists, people who hate women.

Early socialization of girls proceeds more smoothly. Restriction and supervision are the bywords of their growing up. Described as cute, soft, and delicate, girls are trained to behave and be obedient. They are considered to be closer to their parents emotionally, more trustworthy, and less aggressive than little boys. Their chores and their play centre on the home and often include taking care of younger children. Those of you with "opposite sex" siblings will have your own examples of these aspects of gender socialization.

According to Deborah Tannen in *You Just Don't Understand*, a study on language differences in adults, gender differences begin early.

> Boys tend to play outside, in large groups that are hierarchically structured. Their groups have a leader who tells others what to do and how to do it, and resists doing what other boys propose. It is by giving orders and making them stick that high status is negotiated. Another way boys achieve status is to take center stage by telling stories and jokes, and by sidetracking or challenging the stories and jokes of others. Boys' games have winners and losers and elaborate systems or rules that are frequently the subjects of arguments. Finally, boys are frequently heard to boast of their skill and argue about who is best at what.
>
> Girls, on the other hand, play in small groups or in pairs; the center of a girl's social life is a best friend. Within the group, intimacy is key: differentiation is measured by relative closeness. In their most frequent games, such as jump rope and hopscotch, everyone gets a turn. Many of their activities (such as playing house) do not have winners or losers. Though some girls are certainly more skilled than others, girls are expected not to boast about it, or show that they think they are better than the others. Girls don't give orders; they express their preferences as suggestions, and suggestions are likely to be accepted ... They don't grab center stage—they don't want it— so they don't challenge each other directly. And much of the time, they simply sit together and talk. Girls are not accustomed to jockeying for status in an obvious way; they are more concerned that they be liked (1990, 43).

Education and Gender

Reinforcing male dominance continues in schools. Although there has been much research on the content of children's textbooks indicating that male achievement is stressed and that few life options are shown for girls, the more subtle and inadvertent processes of teachers' expectations and student–teacher interaction are still being dissected. Recommendations for "girl friendly" education centre on some of the perceived problems. Teachers should be aware of the "silent language" in the classroom, the nonverbal behaviour that can alienate and exclude female students. Teachers often, for example, make eye contact more with their male than with their female students; they nod and gesture more in response to boys' questions and comments; they wait longer for boys than for girls to answer a question before proceeding, which indicates that their expectation that boys will be able to respond are higher than they are for girls. Teachers call on male students directly and by name more than they do female students, and males' comments are given credit and are responded to more extensively than those of females. Teachers are also more likely to coach males, expecting greater improvement from them than from females (Hall, 1982). Box 4.2 highlights the chilly classroom environment female students contend with in science courses.

Adolescence and Gender

For girls the real pressure to be feminine starts around adolescence and, as with boys, the pressure is persistent. Girls may have been allowed a grace period, the tomboy stage (there is no corresponding freedom for boys), in which femininity takes a back seat. However, after that, parental, peer, and media pressure ensure that a girl focuses on her appearance as a critical component of success in adult life. Girls as young as eight diet and may be encouraged to do so. In a survey of young women in Canada, Holmes and Silverman found:

> Almost one in five women list appearance as one of the things they would like to change about themselves or the world. The fact that so many of the young women said they were dissatisfied with an integral part of themselves is disturbing. But in a patriarchal (male-dominated) society which stresses the ideals of feminine beauty and thinness, which places a higher value on beauty for females than for males, and which minimizes the value of women's other qualities, this concern is easily comprehensible (1992, 18).

During adolescence, gender-specific patterns of thinking and acting become solidified. Walshok noted:

> Not only the activities that boys engage in, but also what adolescents value in people and situations, is differentiated along gender lines: girls value physical attractiveness, co-operation, kindness, ability to get along with people, neatness and passivity; boys value strength, competitiveness, toughness, power and drive or aggressiveness. In adolescence, boys and girls begin committing themselves in earnest

to activities and roles that express these socially prescribed and valued characteristics (1981, 88).

According to a participant observation study by Batcher (1987) in a mall situated in a middle-class area of Toronto, girls diminish themselves in order to fit in with groups of other adolescents. In these groups the boys and their relationships with each other are central, the hub of the wheel, with the girls as spokes unconnected to each other and affiliated only via their relationships with particular boys. These girls do not realize that spokes are necessary for keeping a wheel together and do not collaborate to become equal partners in the groups:

> The model of the successful group girl, in fact, conflicts with the model of a successful adult. Talking and thinking about eating less, buying and wearing clothes and doing hair and make-up to be noticed, and getting a protector (boyfriend) may all be considered as clinging to immaturity, not developing to maturity, a state where the body is fully fed, fully grown and the emphasis is on independent accomplishment rather than on being seen (in Nemiroff, 1987, 157).

Sex becomes important during adolescence, particularly for boys. A survey by Bibby and Posterski (1992) indicates that attitudes about casual sexual behaviour have changed little since 1984 and that the gender gap persists. Although males and females are almost equally likely to approve of kissing on the first date, gender differences increase with the level of physical intimacy. In

In adolescent groups, boys and their relationships with each other are central; girls diminish themselves to fit in.

Lawrence Acland.

BOX 4.2

WHY FEWER WOMEN STICK TO SCIENCE COURSES

Astronaut Roberta Bondar may have shown what heights women in science can achieve, but on Earth the "cold environment" of the university science classroom is pushing many females toward other careers.

That's the finding of a study that examined why fewer women than men complete such university science courses as chemistry, physics, and biology, and the reasons why women drop out.

The study, by two sociologists, tracked about 1,200 female students enrolled in science programs at the University of Guelph.

A major goal of the study was to find out why more male than female science students qualified for Canada Scholarships, a federal program that awards $2,000 annually for four years to students who achieve first-class marks in science and engineering. Half the recipients must be women.

In 1988 and 1989, 65 per cent of males with scholarships renewed their grants after their first year, compared with 46 per cent of females.

The main reason cited for non-renewal was inability to retain top marks in the first year of studies, says study co-author Alan Pomfret of the University of Western Ontario in London.

"What we found was that the early drop in marks, for women relative to men, only lasted for the first year and a half or so, and then the women picked up again and their marks began to equal those of the males," Pomfret said in an interview Thursday.

The study, which included questionnaires to the students, suggested several reasons why the females' marks dropped off, said Pomfret, who conducted the study with Guelph professor Sid Gilbert.

Women are often subjected to "overt sexism" from male professors and students, Pomfret said.

He also described the classroom environment as hierarchical, rule-driven and "uncaring, almost."

"Women were less inclined to like or tolerate that kind of setup, relative to males. They found it a less congenial environment for learning." The report also found:

- Good grades in high school, encouragement from teachers and a desire to be self-sufficient are important influences for women in deciding to go into science. Those factors were found less important for most men.

- Female students tended to be oriented to personal relationships, caring for self and others, communication and working in supportive environments. Male students tended to be more self-reliant.

The two authors have made a number of recommendations to help women remain in the field, including: on-campus mentor clubs to offer support; a newsletter, with a focus on coping mechanisms; and follow-up programs, at least for Canada Scholars, to ascertain how students are coping.

Robert Kavanagh, head of scholarship programs at the National Sciences and Engineering Research Council, said women continue to face barriers to studying science.

"Many girls are not brought up to think about the option of a career in science or engineering," Kavanagh said in an interview from Ottawa.

"There are unfortunately, no doubt, still some attitudinal problems within universities, attitudes of male teachers and fellow students," he said. "That's going to take time to change."

The council is encouraging universities to hire more female science instructors, in part to act as role models for woman students. Through its Faculty Awards program, the council provides grant money—almost $50,000 a year for five years—toward salaries and research.

"The object of this is to increase the terribly low percentages of women who are now faculty members in Canadian universities," Kavanagh said.

In engineering schools, only 2 per cent of professors are women, while in physical science—including physics, chemistry and geology—women account for only 6 per cent of instructors.

Source: Sheryl Ubelacker, "Why Fewer Women Stick to Science Courses," Gazette *(Montreal) (1 February 1992), p. A9. Reprinted with permission of The Canadian Press.*

the case of necking, and certainly petting, young females are more inclined than males to say such behaviour is appropriate only after a few dates; and while about 75 percent of males approve of sexual intercourse within a few dates, only 40 percent of females hold this view. Young men, according to Holmes and Silverman (1992), say that more sex and more attractive women would be welcome changes to their lives. For girls, according to the same study, concerns about boyfriends come after relationships with family and friends, and they concentrate on the emotional dynamics of the relationships, not the sexual. Young women do not seem to see themselves as active participants in sex and assign it a lower priority.

The notion of romantic love (discussed further in Chapter 9) plays a part in creating and maintaining these attitudes. Girls are taught by movies, romantic novels, magazines, and song lyrics that romantic love "happens" to females and that they should prepare themselves, via cosmetics and diets if necessary, for being swept off their feet, but they should not take any explicit initiative with the opposite sex. They may have some knowledge of sex but cannot have "gone too far." This prescription to be "good girls," enforced by girls themselves, discourages young women from taking responsibility for their sexuality. Young men are to be more experienced and knowledgeable. It is their role to make the first move and be in control of sexual interaction. Even though romantic love stresses female submission to male control and leaves many young women disappointed, it remains desirable. One possible reason for its success is that it encourages girls to ask for and expect at least some level of emotional attachment from males with whom they are involved, and thereby lessens the pressure for solely sexual activity.

Results of Gender Socialization and Solutions

While these socialization processes are constraining for everyone; it must be remembered that the payoffs for males are greater. In a survey taken by Holmes and Silverman:

> The difference between the sexes on the item ... "I feel good about myself" increases with age. While there is only a difference of 5 percent between the sexes at age 13, that gap widens to 10 percent by age 16. Adolescent men's responses rise slightly with age, while they decrease slightly among young women. Self-esteem decreases over time, as young women gradually become more aware of their status in a society that values them less than their male peers (1992, 12).

These are the microlevel effects of male dominance. Women are not valued as much as men in our culture, even by themselves. When they try to approximate male standards of behaviour, they are often penalized. Early 1970s evidence for this comes from Broverman's research (1970), discussed earlier. The more contemporary Batcher study (1987) highlights the social pressure for girls to fit into the male-controlled group. Clearly, bringing about social change is often a slow and obstacle-ridden process, because one is moving against the tradition. Such tradition is especially hard to break in areas that carry a heavy emotional weight, such as attitudes and expectations pertaining to the relative position of men and women in society. It is important, however, to remember not to reify the social world, that is, to assume it is a set, concrete object. Individual actors do have the choice of challenging or supporting existing frameworks.

Despite its staying power, male dominance is not inevitable. To attain gender equality, some theorists have suggested a two-pronged approach: more men must spend more time raising children and more women must have increased access to socially valued goods—money, power, and prestige—in the workplace. If men, as fathers, would take care of children more, boys would have models and males could learn to be emotive. With shared childrearing, women would be seen as workers on a par with men. Such changes might result in a blending of gender characteristics that would lead to changed perceptions of women and a rejection of the view of feminine virtues as inferior.

It should be noted, however, that many sociologists would argue that modifying socialization practices is insufficient in itself to bring about gender equality. Achieving that would also require fundamental social, economic, and political change, as we hope subsequent chapters will make clear.

Whatever you feel about the socialization processes described above, it must be stressed that if, as an infant, you were left to your own devices, your very ability to survive would be endangered. Examples follow of children, called social isolates, for whom this danger was real.

SOCIAL ISOLATES

Reseachers cannot, nor would they want to, carry out the experiment on separating twins suggested at the beginning of this chapter. There are some cases, however, of children raised with little human contact that can be useful in distinguishing the contributions that culture and biology make to behaviour.

Anna and Isabelle were written about in the 1940s by sociologist Kingsley Davis. In 1937, at the age of 6, a girl named Anna was found in a room in her grandfather's house. Anna was an illegitimate child. Her grandfather was so angered by this evidence of his daughter's sexuality, a violation of the mores of that time, that he refused to have Anna in his house. Various unsuccessful attempts were made to find Anna another place to live, but a lack of financial resources to pay for Anna's care and fear of her father's anger led Anna's mother to relegate Anna to an attic-like room on the second floor of her father's house. Sequestered in the room, she was fed very little food other than cow's milk during her first six years. When found, Anna could not talk, walk, or feed herself even when food was placed in front of her. She did not smile, nor did she show any signs of intelligence. In 1939, Anna was taken to a private home for retarded children. She progressed to being able to walk, tidy and feed herself, understand simple commands, and remember people she had seen. By 1941, she was able to speak at the level of a two-year-old. She died a year later of a type of jaundice.

Another girl, Isabelle, was found in 1938, at $6\frac{1}{2}$ years old. Isabelle, too, was illegitimate and kept in a dark room with her deaf-mute mother. Reports indicate that Isabelle behaved like a wild animal when she was discovered. She gave the impression that she could attain very little. In a training program, however, she rapidly progressed through the normal stages of child development. Eighteen months later she appeared to be a bright, cheerful, and energetic little girl. In 1947, at 14, she participated normally in school activities and passed grade 6.

Many questions arise about such cases. What was the initial state of the two girls at birth? Were they suffering from any congenital physical and/or mental diseases? Were they brain damaged in any way? Did Isabelle benefit and fare better than Anna because she had had human companionship? If Anna had had the same intense training as Isabelle, might she too have progresssed to becoming a normal little girl?

A recent example of another girl, Genie, underlines the detrimental impact of social isolation. Genie was locked in a room by her father from the age of 20 months until she was $13\frac{1}{2}$. She was immobilized, never given solid food, was not dressed, and was not allowed to make any noise. As a result, Genie could not chew or swallow. She didn't react to temperature, and she was nearsighted, able to see only from a distance exactly equivalent to the small distance between the spot where she had been restrained and the wall in front of her. She made no sounds at all. After six years of being cared for, Genie learned to speak in sentences, and managed to go to a special school and forge emotional relationships with others. What is astonishing about Genie is that even her most basic physical abilities were curtailed by her abuse.

What this necessarily anecdotal evidence points to is the fact that humans need a certain amount of sensory stimulation and social interaction to progress normally. Most social scientists will agree that children need consistent and sufficient amounts of attention, stimulation, and affection from caregivers, preferably for at least the first three years of life. Without exposure to socialization of this kind, a child will not approximate the kind of behaviour any culture calls "human."

How does the process of socialization work? How is it that individuals remain individuals as distinctive as a snowflake, while sharing in and adhering to the culture in which they are born? Theoreticians in specific disciplines have varying ideas about what sociologists term the socialization process. Major theories will be examined in the next sections of this chapter.

THEORIES OF SOCIALIZATION

Basic socialization is the process by which a baby is shaped into a member of the group and inducted into the ways and "secrets" of society. The young child is attuned only to his or her own needs; gradually he or she is trained by example and by reward and punishment to conform to the expectations of others. Basic socialization has particularly far-reaching effects because it is carried out on very young children who by nature are physically and mentally helpless. The effects of this early socialization, however, can be overcome, and adults can change.

BEHAVIOURISM: CLASSICAL AND OPERANT CONDITIONING

The Russian physiologist Ivan Pavlov (1849–1936) conducted a number of experiments that powerfully demonstrated the effects of behaviourism. He showed that when a stimulus, such as food, was consistently paired (presented at the same time) with another stimulus, such as the ringing of a bell, a dog

As this seventeenth-century Paris etching shows, there are wide variations, cross-culturally and historically, in how children are reared.

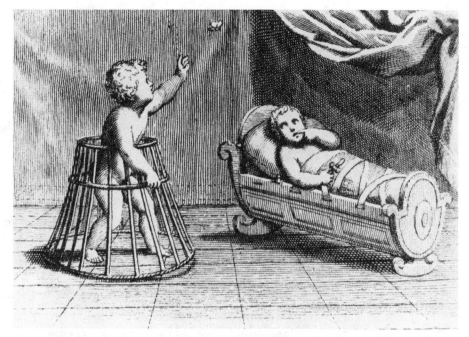

Metropolitan Toronto Reference Library.

would eventually salivate at the sound of the bell, even if the ringing was not accompanied by food. This phenomenon is known as **classical conditioning**. Children learn in the same way: associating two stimuli that coincide. Eventually they respond to either stimulus in the same fashion. If parents start to argue as soon as the child is in bed, the child may associate the fear elicited by the arguing with going to sleep and then act up at bedtime in order to avoid the frightening situation. Behaviourism has many current adherents and many practical applications. It is used in treating alcoholics by pairing alcohol with a substance that induces violent vomiting. The hope is that, in time, the very idea of drinking alcohol will cause revulsion.

Pavlov's work attracted wide attention, and physiologists and psychologists have since experimented with varieties of conditioning processes. The work of B.F. Skinner (1904–1990), in teaching rats to run mazes, is a famous example of **operant conditioning**, in which the desired behaviour is reinforced by rewards, and attempts are made to extinguish unwanted behaviour by punishment. In this case, a rat would be rewarded with a food pellet for choosing the correct turn and punished by an electric shock for going astray.

Clearly, similar ideas are implicit in many current childrearing methods, both at home and at school. The good student is rewarded with a star or a prize (a positive sanction), while the disobedient one is subjected to various forms of punishment (negative sanctions).

Behaviourism relies on a number of basic tenets. One is that observations made by psychologists on (nonhuman) animals can be applied to humans. If certain methods are effective in teaching rats, they should be effective in teaching children. Apart from basic needs, the infant is adaptable, a clean slate.

Another tenet is that since desirable and undesirable behaviour can be respectively reinforced and extinguished, the motives underlying behaviour are unimportant. Behaviourists are not concerned with why Jesse smashes windows but merely with the fact that she does.

Behaviourism also de-emphasizes the significance of heredity and hence dismisses such concepts as the natural inferiority of certain individuals and groups of people, but it replaces biological determinism with environmental (social) determinism, a view that claims individuals are essentially at the mercy of their environment. The assumption underlying environmental determinism has been put to sinister use. For example, trainee guards for Nazi concentration camps were often given a pup. The trainee would care for the dog and spend a great deal of time with it. After six months or so, he would be ordered to kill the animal. Immersion in this brutal training environment was intended to inure recruits to the horrors they would be expected to perpetrate in their work.

Neither biological nor environmental determinism, then, makes allowances for the active, creative dimension of individuals, a product of the dynamic interplay between innate characteristics and social experiences that makes each person distinctive.

THE FREUDIAN VIEW

A psychodynamic perspective of socialization, based largely on clinical observation and focused on the development of various internal characteristics and processes, was provided by Sigmund Freud (1856–1939). Freud's major contribution to thinking about personality (the self) and its development was the notion that human behaviour has unconscious (hidden) meanings. He claimed that the mind is like an iceberg; the tip showing above the water represents the region of consciousness, and the much larger mass below the water level represents the region of unconsciousness. For example, a person who had hypercritical parents might experience lifelong difficulty accepting any criticism, however justified. This idea of a hidden dimension to behaviour was revolutionary in Freud's time, though it is taken for granted today.

Many have contested aspects of Freud's ideas. Chief among them are feminists who question his view of women as defective men. Freud seems to postulate that women, because of their biology, cannot be as moral as men. Their destiny is to be mothers and, indeed, he said, that is what well-adjusted women aspire to. But, rather than entirely dismissing Freud's theory because of its claims of universality, some feminists advise that it be considered an excellent treatise on women's development in male-dominated societies with useful insights on the development of female consciousness in those societies.[2]

Other social scientists question Freud's methodology and sample, arguing that his theories pertain only to a certain historical period and social class. Specifically, they allege that his ideas are culture-bound, being based on data obtained from a skewed sample of upper-middle-class patients in the Vienna of the 1890s and early 1900s. Despite the serious criticisms of Freud's theory, we include discussion of it here because of its enormous impact on our now "common sense" taken-for-granted notions of human behaviour.

Freud hypothesized that the personality is made up of three major systems—the id, the ego, and the superego—and that behaviour is almost always the product of an interaction among the three. The **id** consists of those forces and drives that are inherited (and therefore present from birth). They provide a reservoir of psychic energy that is sexual and aggressive, causing the infant to be impulsive, selfish, and pleasure-seeking. Gradually, the acquisition of culture represses some aspects of the id so that the individual can deal more appropriately with the objective world of reality. What emerges is the **ego**—the "executive of the personality"—whose job it is to mediate, through intellectual and cognitive processes, between the individual's biological requirements and the conditions of the social and physical environment. The **superego**, often referred to as the conscience, is the third system of the personality and the last to develop. The superego's task is the internalization of society's values (morality), which first occurs through the rewards and punishments imposed by the child's family. The superego is oriented to the ideal world, rather than to the actual environment, and pushes the individual to strive for perfection rather than for pleasure.

> Under ordinary circumstances, [the id, the ego, and the superego] do not collide with one another nor do they work at cross purposes. On the contrary, they work together as a team under the administrative leadership of the ego. The personality normally functions as a whole rather than as three separate segments. In a very general way, the id may be thought of as the biological component of personality, the ego as the psychological component, and the superego as the social component (Hall and Lindzey, 1963, 35).

Freud attributed great importance to the early years of infancy and childhood, believing that the child passes through a series of stages. He defined each stage according to the journey of the **libido**—the life-energy, including sexuality, found in all humans—through various zones of the body. At each stage the libido is concentrated or invested in the zone for which the stage is named; the child obtains pleasurable feelings from focusing on that area of the body. If not enough of the libidinal energy is gratified, various personality disorders, often sexual, can occur in later life.

In the oral stage, the first developmental stage, the libido resides in the mouth, affording the child great pleasure through sucking and biting. At around eighteen months of age, the anal stage begins; in it the libido is centred on the bowels. The toilet training that is initiated at this time gives the child the first major experience with the external regulation of a drive. It is at this point that the ego is developing. In the phallic or Oedipal stage, when the child is approximately three years of age, the libido moves to the genital region, leading to the development of gender identity and the appearance of the **Oedipus complex**. At this stage, the child wishes to possess the parent of the opposite sex and to remove the parent of the same sex. The hostility felt toward the parent of the same sex is gradually resolved through a process of identification with that parent and the development of the superego. The mother becomes a role model for girls and the father for boys. If the resolution of this conflict does not ensue, the child may continue to experience difficulties in dealing with relationships in later life. Between the ages of five and twelve, the latency period, children's sexual interests as well as their aggression are assumed to be relatively muted.

The last stage, the genital, begins at puberty, when the individual's narcissism (self-love) expands to include those interests and activities that are characteristic of a mature, reality-oriented, socialized human being. Thus, all five stages contribute to the organization of the personality.

THE SYMBOLIC INTERACTIONIST APPROACH

As noted in Chapter 1, symbolic interactionism is a general perspective on how society functions. Here we are mainly concerned with the explanations this perspective offers concerning the steps by which the individual becomes a member of society.[3]

George Herbert Mead

George Herbert Mead (1863–1931) saw people as different in kind from other species. For him, two factors were crucial in accounting for this difference: language and self-awareness.

Language is an elaborate symbolic code that allows response to symbols rather than to actual stimuli.[4] The words "I am angry" convey a clear message that need not be supplemented by jumping up and down and waving one's fist, though sometimes such behaviour does accompany the words. Self-awareness yields the ability to empathize with others, to put oneself in someone else's shoes. To phrase the matter differently, individuals can become objects to themselves, imagining how others view their behaviour. They can mentally relive situations, savouring a successful performance in a job interview or chastising themselves for having said the wrong thing at the wrong time. They can also fantasize about how they would react in an unusual situation, such as winning an Olympic gold medal, being a famous scientist, or dating a movie idol. The empathy belly, described in Box 4.3, is a good example of taking the role of the other.

Mead's theory of the development of the self proceeds in stages, like that of Freud's, but Mead was concerned in particular with cognitive (intellectual) development—that is, the process by which children learn to place themselves in a social environment and to interpret this environment. The agents of socialization in this theory are the **significant others**, those who are important to the individual at various life stages, such as parents, teachers, and peers.

At birth the infant has no conception of herself as a separate being. In this *imitation stage* the child simply apes the gestures, words, and facial expressions she observes in her environment. During the subsequent *play stage*, at two or three years of age, the child begins to conceive of herself as a separate being and starts to experiment by assuming various roles. "Lucy is a good girl," says the child, displaying her ability to conceive of herself as an object, someone to whom she can respond and evaluate. Children together may play house, successively pretending to be themselves, their parents, and their siblings.

At about the age of five, the child moves to the *game stage* in which she learns to respond to several others at the same time. For example, baseball players must adjust their actions to those of all the other players; each one cannot simply concentrate on what the pitcher is doing. During the game stage the child begins to categorize people and situations, which makes it possible to develop guidelines for behaviour based on situations that have been experienced previously and that are defined as similar. For instance, teacher, police officer, and rabbi may be grouped as "authority figures."

Crucial to the self is the forming of the **generalized other**, an internal monitor of behaviour consisting of the internalized values and norms of the culture as transmitted by the child's socializers. These people pass on the parts of the culture they deem important and relevant to successful functioning in society. The content of what the child absorbs, then, depends on the values of the culture

BOX 4.3

HOW TO MAKE A MAN PREGNANT

The womb compartment is filled with four litres of hot water and two lead weights. It looks and feels like a cross between a flak jacket and Madonna's stage suit. Wearing it for 10 minutes or more can lead to backache, shortness of breath and increased blood pressure. It is a pregnancy simulator for men.

"Take a deep breath in and blow it right out. Now hold onto your bulge while I position your breasts," childbirth educator Kate Dixon tells David, a 29-year-old insurance underwriter. She is transforming him into a pregnant man with the help of an Empathy Belly.

David's heavily pregnant wife Yvonne looks on with evident glee. "I sometimes have to remind the women that we're not looking for revenge," says Ms. Dixon.

There are seven couples gathered in Ms. Dixon's farmhouse in Somerset, in the west of England, for their weekly prenatal class. Ms. Dixon, a 31-year-old mother of three, has used the belly with about 100 couples over the past year.

The Empathy Belly is made of waterproof canvas, weighs 12 kilograms and, according to the manufacturer, enables the wearer to experience more than 20 of the typical symptoms of full pregnancy. The belly was designed to encourage expectant fathers to empathize more deeply with their pregnant partner.

"The first thing men do is have a quick feel of the breasts," Ms. Dixon remarks as David gropes at his new form.

"This is meant to be the baby's head," she says, handing him a bag full of lead beads. "Attach it to the piece of Velcro over your bladder; if it's well positioned, the instant you sit down you should need to go to the lavatory."

Ms. Dixon puts him through a quick routine aimed at demonstrating some of the discomforts of late pregnancy, "Sit down. Now lie down on your back, feel all that weight. Imagine you're in bed, try to turn over." This entails much flailing around on the sofa to the delight of everyone else in the room.

"You've just got settled and you're about to fall asleep but you now need to go to the toilet, so get up." At this point David wipes his brow and says he's feeling a bit hot and breathless.

All but one of the seven men present are eager to try the belly on. There is much ripping of Velcro and struggling in and out of the maternity smock that comes with it, followed by grunting and wallowing on the sofa and prancing up and down stairs. All the men who try it are surprised by the weight.

While instructive on a physical level, the belly is also intended to cater to a psychological need in pregnant men. The brochure that accompanies it cites prospective fathers feelings of "detachment, curiosity, skepticism or frustration," and suggests that they can wear the belly during prenatal classes to "greatly increase their sense of involvement and gut-level awareness."

Research has shown that 10 per cent of men experience physical symptoms during their partner's pregnancy, ranging from abdominal pains and distended stomachs to full-blown sympathetic labour. A further 20 per cent experience feelings of psychological unease.

A label sewn into the belly forbids its use "for frivolous recreational purposes."

"Nobody in my class has ever used it for messing about," says Ms. Dixon. "I certainly have had some real sods in class who have been more gentle with their women after they've worn it."

Source: Emma Brookner, "How to Make a Man Pregnant," The Globe and Mail *(6 February 1993), p. D3. Copyright* © Guardian.

as a whole, particularly on those that are dominant in the specific group or subculture—ethnic, religious, socioeconomic—of which the significant others are members. The child of an orthodox Jewish or Muslim family learns, for example, in whose house he may or may not accept food, and that he must not eat pork.

The self, according to Mead, is made up of separate parts. The *I* is unreasoning, impulsive, and presses for immediate gratification of its wishes; it constitutes the innovative, creative dimension of the individual. For example, even though we are aware of the norms governing situations, we cannot predict exactly how we will behave in a particular context. Sometimes our own behaviour surprises us and we find ourselves questioning "Why on earth did I do that?" The other part of the self, the *me* or the generalized other, represents the aspects of culture absorbed in the course of socialization. Mead's theory gives considerable weight to the importance of culture in socialization. It does not depict the individual as totally constrained by genetic endowment or by social environment; neither does it represent the individual as entirely a creature at the mercy of impulse. The socially created "me" makes possible action that is independent of one's impulses, while the "I" ensures individuality. Mead saw the individual and society as inseparable sides of the same coin. The very notion of what it means to be human presupposes the existence of a social group. Children raised in isolation, without others, as we have seen, lack the attributes associated with humanness.

While the developmental theories of Mead and Freud have some similarities, they are more intriguing for their differences. Freud saw the personality as having three parts that generally operate in concert. At times, however, the id and the superego engage in a power struggle in which the ego—more or less successfully—acts as arbitrator. The id and Mead's I are alike in that both are impulsive and creative, but Freud's id is biologically based, while Mead emphasizes social and cultural factors without reference to the biological. The superego and generalized other are both made up of the values and norms of the culture as transmitted by the socializers. Unlike Freud, Mead theorizes no mediator, akin to the ego, between potentially adversarial elements of the self or personality. Mead saw the individual and society as symbiotic and fused, while Freud emphasized the fundamental conflict between the individual and society, with the energy for social activity obtained at the cost of repressing the urge for constant pleasure.

Charles Horton Cooley

Charles Horton Cooley (1864–1929) was a contemporary of Mead. Indeed, Mead, in developing his ideas about the emergence of the self, made use of many insights Cooley had gleaned from systematic observation of his own children. Cooley also saw the self as a social product that is formed in the process of interaction. He pointed to the emergence of self-perception by referring to the **looking-glass self**, which can be defined as a person's self-evaluation based on his perception of how others see and judge him.

There are three specific steps in this process. First, the individual imagines how he is coming across to others. Then he imagines their assessment of that image, and as a result he evaluates himself. The individual eventually sees himself, overall, as a competent person or a ne'er-do-well, as a worthwhile person or a failure, according to the responses given by significant others. The girl who is frequently told she is clumsy, sloppy, and plain will come to think of herself in those terms. Conversely, good feelings about oneself result from approval and admiration. Since one can only surmise what the other person really feels, misinterpretation is possible and often occurs. For example, parents may withhold praise for fear of making the child conceited, thus conveying a distorted impression of their views. Or they may mention only things that displease them, being too busy to vocalize pleased reactions. Sadly, many people who develop negative self-images in childhood never entirely shed them, even in the face of strong contrary evidence.

Socialization, according to Cooley, typically occurs in groups he labelled "primary." A **primary group** is small; its members are in frequent face-to-face contact and are bound by common values and beliefs. The group is suffused with emotion, which tends to be strong and can run the gamut from love to hate. These groups are also primary in time. Most children's earliest experiences take place in primary family groups, subsequently supplemented by peer groups. Moreover, such groups are primary in importance, because the child forms its basic conceptions of self within them.

Relationships (and groups) can be seen as falling somewhere on a continuum from primary at one extreme to secondary at the other. **Secondary groups** are conceptually distinct from those that are primary. They are not intimate, the persons involved do not see each other in many roles; such is the case with students and teachers, for example. If affect is present, it is related to the task around which the relationship is organized. Indeed, the most important criterion of a secondary relationship is to fulfil some function necessitating that the status rights and obligations of the participants be clearly defined. The uniqueness of the individuals is secondary to the task being performed, in contrast to primary relationships, in which the central focus is the particular individual, who is considered almost irreplaceable. Primary relationships can develop only with persistent face-to-face interaction. This, however, does not guarantee the creation of a primary relationship. Psychotherapists and clients, no matter how long the course of therapy, have a secondary relationship, as the client pays the therapist and the intimacy is not reciprocal: the therapist learns all about the client, but the opposite does not occur. Usually, the development of a primary relationship between client and therapist is even expressly forbidden.

Socialization does not stop when a child has developed a self. New knowledge, skills, attitudes, values, and behaviours are adopted and amalgamated, changing the self, sometimes even radically, over time.

ADULT AND ANTICIPATORY SOCIALIZATION

Socialization, in the form of **adult** or **secondary socialization**, goes on throughout the life cycle. Each new job, a change in marital status or level of education, or new leisure activity necessitates the acquisition of new behaviours and attitudes. This secondary or adult socialization is usually less potent than basic socialization given that adults are more likely to choose new status positions for themselves and have more experience to evaluate what they are learning. As a result, however,

> the self does not develop solely in childhood and reach a final, unchangeable form upon the attainment of adulthood. While the self normally maintains a certain degree of stability and consistency, it nevertheless is constantly subject to modification in its ever changing social environment. The self undergoes a constant process of comparison, assessment and reinterpretation as the individual's statuses and roles change along with related definitions and expectation (Theodorson & Theodorson, 1969).

Often before you enter a new group or assume a new role—for instance, when you become a college student, start a new job, or get married—you undergo a period of preparation for this new role. **Anticipatory socialization** can be defined as the process by which individuals prepare themselves for roles to which they aspire but which they do not yet occupy. It differs from basic socialization in that there is some conscious motivation on the part of the learner or apprentice to acquire the trappings of a given role. In the work world, for example, learning the ropes includes far more than mastering technical skills. Think of the fate of imposters such as "physicians" without actual credentials. Even though they might be able to carry out most technical aspects of the role, they would likely be unmasked eventually by their unfamiliarity with a certain bit of lore. Greenwood has described what is entailed in becoming a professional:

> Mastery of the underlying body of theory and acquisition of technical skills are in themselves insufficient guarantees of professional success. The recruit must also become familiar with and learn to weave his way through the labyrinth of the professional culture. Therefore, the transformation of a neophyte into a professional is essentially an acculturation process wherein he internalizes the social values, the behavior norms, and the symbols of the occupational group (1957, 520).

Secretarial colleges not only teach shorthand, word processing, and bookkeeping, but also alert students to what constitutes suitable modes of dress. Garish clothing and jewellery are definitely out for the aspiring executive secretary. On the factory floor, apprentices learn not only the basics of their trade but also the norms of the group: how much respect to give the shop steward and the boss, how fast to work so as not to incur the wrath of either the group or the manager.

Anticipatory socialization is not confined to the occupational world. A small-town adolescent intent on joining an urban clique prepares himself by adopting the mannerisms, habits, and attitudes of the clique, hoping to become acceptable to its members in the process.

One of the greatest difficulties in being a pioneer stems from an absence of signposts that would familiarize that person with the rights, obligations, expectations, and viewpoints of her social role in the new territory. A male kindergarten teacher or a female welder will likely experience some uncertainty concerning just what to anticipate.

Related to the concept of anticipatory socialization is that of the **reference group**. A reference group provides a model of values, attitudes, and behaviour that one seeks to emulate. In traditional societies, membership groups, both familial and occupational, also serve as reference groups. In our society, which is more fluid, moving to a new neighbourhood or receiving a substantial promotion may mean that a person has selected new "Joneses" to keep up with. In other words, that person has chosen a new reference group.

RESOCIALIZATION

Incorporated into every socialization process are forces of coercion. These influences can be seen in their most extreme form in the case of **resocialization**, which is aimed at stripping the individual of his or her identity or self and replacing it with a new one. The armed services provide a good example. The stripping process that takes place on entry assumes both physical and psychological dimensions. The recruits are issued new clothing, and men must have a regulation haircut. They must learn to adapt their thinking, behaviour, and priorities to conform to army expectations. In his book *Asylums* (1962), Goffman analyzed the ways in which a total institution, such as a mental hospital, concentration camp, prison, boarding school, or convent, seeks to ensure conformity. Goffman categorized as total institutions those that control every aspect of an individual's existence. Box 4.4 on the Lakeview Shock Incarceration Correctional Facility furnishes an excellent description of one such institution.

Certain cults, too, resocialize members who, in many instances, enter the realm of the cult ruler unsuspectingly. The same process of stripping and remoulding may occur and the resulting "cult self" may perceive anyone outside the cult as "wrong" or "evil." When undertaken, the task of dislodging members can become supremely difficult, as the terrible instance of the Branch Davidians highlights. Members were so convinced that David Koresh, their leader, was supreme that they refused to surrender to American legal authorities. In Canada, some of Rock Thériault's followers are waiting for "their leader" to finish the prison sentence (life, with no parole for 10 years) he received for committing murder in order to resume their life with him.[5]

The concept of resocialization provides an example of the way in which the sociological perspective enables one to pinpoint similarities among institutions—boarding schools, monasteries, prisons—that at the same time are strikingly different.

AGENTS OF SOCIALIZATION

Socialization is a process of social interaction carried out by people, agents of socialization, who intentionally and unintentionally transmit aspects of the culture to newborns and neophyte adults (as you learned in the discussion on

BOX 4.4

ASSESSING THE PENAL SHOCK VALUE

For a moment, the granite-faced drill instructor seems to be easing up. "Relax, close your eyes," he intones. "Imagine you're with someone you really love. Think about that person."

Visibly relieved, the 12 nervous young men close their eyes. Since being hustled off the bus into the prison reception centre on this cold, snowy night, they have been ordered around, lined up and yelled at. Something has apparently changed.

They are wrong.

With a deafening clang, the instructor hurls a steel garbage-pail lid onto the stone floor, and this time he is really shouting: "Open your eyes and get your chest out! Time to wake up! Ain't nobody gonna help you from here on in. You got to do it yourself!"

Now the new arrivals look truly scared.

Lakeview Shock Incarceration Correctional Facility lives up to its name: About one-third of those who sign up for its program do not complete it, ending up back in the grim, overflowing prisons that house New York State's 65,000 convicts.

But the instructor was telling only half the story when he said the arrivals were on their own. And six or seven months hence, those who survive the rigours of what appears to be a remarkable success story will look—and probably feel—very different.

If the demands are high, so are the stakes.

New York's Shock program, the biggest of its kind in the world, is aimed at young men and women from 17 to 35, serving their first state prison term for a non-violent offence carrying a minimum term of one to three years. Ninety per cent of the time, that involves drugs. For those who volunteer—and qualify—their prison term is replaced by a radical, six-month program, followed by release on stringent parole.

"Normal jail doesn't work," says Lakeview superintendent Ronald Moscicki, who spent 17 years at the infamous Attica prison, where he was in charge of discipline. "Attica does what it's supposed to do, and it does it well. It keeps the bad guys off the street."

But as every criminologist knows, what the brutal prison culture also does well is foster crime. The underlying premise of Shock is to keep people out of that system, and state-wide recidivism data (there are five Shock institutions in New York, with Lakeview the hub) show that it succeeds...

Coiled razor wire rings the sprawling, 26-hectare complex of modern brick buildings, an hour's drive south of Buffalo on Lake Erie. But for the 700 mostly black or Hispanic Shock participants—at least three-quarters come from the toughest parts of New York City—all resemblance to the conventional prison system ends at the gates.

The biggest contrast perhaps lies in the commitment of the staff, almost all of whom are veterans of the regular system. Their training includes four weeks in which they are put through the same paces as the prisoners.

"I've been in this department for 19 years and this is the first thing I've ever seen that is actually rewarding," Sergeant Ernesto Rivera remarks. (Corrections officers have a ranking system comparable to that of the military.)

"For a lot of these kids [the average age is about 21], this is the first time they've ever been around anybody who even cared what happened to them."

Over a three-day period, a reporter and photographer were permitted to interview and photograph anyone they wished.

The environment is austere, almost monastic. Prisoners have no access to radio, television or newspapers, and essentially no possessions. Instead of pictures, brightly coloured slogans decorate the walls: Pain Is Temporary, Pride Is Forever; People Who Care Don't Let You Off The Hook; Think! The ubiquitous prison mascot is a fierce-looking bulldog in a drill sergeant's hat.

"It's six months, but you can multiply that by three," Captain Cal West says. "Our day here is like three days in a conventional jail."

Prisoners belong to platoons—54-strong for the men, smaller groups for the women—and the same regimen applies to all. Seven days a week, the 16-hour program of work, exercise, drug counselling and education begins with a

5:30 a.m. bugle call, piped through the dormitories' public address system.

"At 5:30 in the morning, I would usually be just pulling the covers up over my head," says 29-year-old Ian Hedge from the Bronx, who if he were not at Lakeview would be serving three to nine years for selling crack cocaine to an undercover policeman.

Thus, the image that lingers is that of boot camp—and that bothers the media-wary staff. Drug and alcohol education is pivotal, with addiction treated as a disease. So is education; on average, prisoners advance by three grades during their six months.

But no one is under any illusion about why they sign up: Under New York's indeterminate sentencing system and punitive drug laws, the alternative to the six months runs as high as life imprisonment.

"None of us are naive," Mr. Moscicki says. "We know why these inmates get in the program. They do it because it's for six months, not because they want to change their lives, or get off drugs. We know that—it's just math—and the inmate thinks, 'What can they do to me for six months? I can stand on my head for six months if I have to.'

"And that's okay with us. You can tell us all you want, but we know the real deal. But what's also clear is that if you come in here with the atttitude '180 days and I'm out of here,' you won't make it. And the inmates will tell you that."

In all areas, the level of expectations is constantly ratcheted up.

Cheryl Clark, chief architect of Shock in New York, said she recently threw out one inmate for writing rap songs about fornicating and fighting when he was supposed to be doing his alcohol and drug abuse homework. "He was three months into the program. I wouldn't have done it if he'd written them in the first month."

Mr. Moscicki says, "I've taken inmates out of the program for taking an extra cookie off the feed-up line. That's a major felony because it's stealing. If he does it in Month 1, that's one thing. If he does it in Month 6, that's a major concern for us."

Nationally, Shock incarceration began gathering pace in the early 1980s. Twenty-three other U.S. states now use it, with the New York program considered the prototype. There appear to be no comparable programs in other countries.

Miss Clark recounts making a presentation to some Correctional Service Canada officers a few years ago. "And they were very opposed to the boot-camp model. They said it was very harsh. My sense was they didn't approve a military model."

The bottom line, she says, is that Shock works.

"We have four-year studies now, and it tells us that consistently we do slightly better than general confinement. And what is also better is that we do it in six months, instead of the average 22 months that a first offender normally serves."

About 29 or 30 per cent of the Shock graduates will reoffend, the studies so far show; among equivalent ex-prisoners of the regular system, the rate is 40 to 50 per cent.

"We have a lot of critics, and some of the things they're correct about," Miss Clark says. "They say things that we would say, such as push-ups don't make you smarter. They will also say, 'You can't just bring in an inmate, scare him and yell at him and have him march around and turn back a better citizen.'

"We agree with that, and that's not what we want to do. We use the vehicle of the military model to teach inmates something about self-discipline and pride.

"Look, we don't want people screaming at inmates about what pieces of dog meat they are. When we started five years ago, that was popularized in the media a lot because there were a lot of Vietnam movies then, things like *Full Metal Jacket*. We're not preparing people for a military career. Basically, what we're trying to do is get young drug offenders back on track...

Given the background of most Shock inmates, however, and the drug-ravaged neighbourhoods to which they will return, the real battle begins on the day of release.

"You're going to run into your old friends and someone is going to say, 'Let's have a taste,'" deputy superintendent Tom Sanders told two proud graduating platoons recently as they prepared to march through Lakeview for the last time.

"And that's when Shock starts."

Source: Timothy Appleby, "Assessing the Penal Shock Value," The Globe and Mail *(19 March 1993), pp. A1–A4. Reprinted with permission.*

gender socialization). The following pages contain a general survey of the themes. More detailed analysis of certain agents of socialization is found in Section 4 on institutions.

THE FAMILY

In our society, it is somewhat taken for granted that early socialization takes place within the **nuclear family**—that is, the father, the mother, and their children, who share the same dwelling. Increasing numbers of children in

In our culture, the biological mother is considered most responsible for child care; in others, wet nurses or collectives of women perform childrearing tasks.

Bodleian Library/Metropolitan Toronto Reference Library.

Canadian society, however, are growing up in families in which there is only one parent, or at least only one biological parent (see Chapter 9). In some other societies, children are brought up in large households that include grandparents, parents, and children, not to mention uncles, aunts, and their children. Such a household is referred to as an **extended family**.

All known societies train their young in the ways of the group, although there are wide variations in what these ways are (cultural content) and in the training methods used (form of socialization). In every society, there is a wide range of methods for moulding a child's behaviour. Children learn by example, imitation, and direct teaching—by being praised when they follow group norms and by being shamed, perhaps by exposure to ridicule, when they deviate from prescribed standards. They also learn from the withdrawal of love and from corporal punishment (as we have already discussed). Many societies, including our own, use a combination of these methods.

Unlike simple societies (*Gemeinschaft*) in which all members substantially share the same values, beliefs, and way of life, complex industrialized societies (*Gesellschaft*) are made up of a variety of subcultures, divided along economic, ethnic, and religious lines. Particular subcultures often favour some methods of childrearing over others. For example, several studies (Bronfenbrenner, 1958; Kohn, 1963) have shown that North American middle-class families state that they disapprove of corporal punishment (even though they may resort to it in practice). On the other hand, working-class families are more likely to affirm that they physically chastise their children, and groups such as the Hutterites see physical punishment as a positive value.

SCHOOLS AND EARLY CHILDHOOD INSTITUTIONS

Parents and parent surrogates, such as babysitters and day-care personnel, are paramount among agents of socialization. In complex societies, institutions have come to play a major role in preparing children to become full-fledged members of society. Day-care centres are becoming more prevalent because of the increase in single-parent families and the growing participation of women in the labour force. In the day-care centre, looking after the child is a paid job, carried out with greater detachment than is usual in a mother–child relationship. Instead of being the main focus, the child is one member of the group. Of course, in a family with many children, the child is also accustomed to being a member of a group.

In Canada, the moralistic conviction that young children should be taken care of by their mothers serves as a barrier to the development of adequate day-care facilities. This is an example of a situation in which the prevailing ideology, that mothers with small children ought to stay at home, is at odds with the practical reality that many must work and that others prefer to do so. Mackay and Clifford have reflected on this dilemma:

> Economic necessity and the demand for equal rights for women have propelled women into the paid workforce. Now that it is more common for mothers to work than stay at home with children, who will look after the children? In contrast with other western industrialized nations, Canada, Britain and the United States have yet

to demonstrate that they really care about childcare; these three countries do not have "family policies" ... Attitudes toward quality of daycare must also change. But first, we will have to change our values. Do we really care more about cleanliness than child development? Have we our priorities in the right order when we pay four times as much for housecleaning as for childcare? In the most formative and impressionable preschool years, do we really want to pay daycare workers one-third the salary received by primary school workers? (1982, 44).

Women's groups have long lobbied for more day-care facilities; government task forces have acknowledged the need for expanded services. Yet the gap persists between the demand for day care and the facilities available. Initiatives by a few private-sector employers have narrowed this gap only marginally, and good private day care is a luxury few can afford.

Even for children whose mothers are not in the work force, the time of leaving the home may come long before the age at which they must start school. Parents may organize play groups or simply trade off on the care of small children to give each other a break. Three- to five-year-olds may attend a nursery school or kindergarten for periods ranging from two hours to all day. In these situations, children are encouraged to share and to become oriented to what other children do. It is often their first experience of being exposed, on a continuing basis, to people outside the immediate family. Thus, teachers and other children become a significant part of the child's environment.

At present, only a minority of Canadian children experience day care and/or nursery school. By contrast, it is obligatory for all children to attend educational institutions from the age of 5 or 6 to 15 or 16—a period of at least ten years, and for many it is longer. Historically, as we will discuss in more detail in Chapter 10, free public education was introduced in the wake of industrialization. It was intended not only to impart basic literary, mathematical, and social skills but also to pass on characteristics suitable for an industrial work force, such as obedience, time-consciousness, neatness, personal hygiene, and tolerance for performing repetitive, routine tasks. Since then, formal education has been greatly expanded, both in duration and in the scope of the curriculum.

When a child goes out from the home—to school or simply to the homes of friends—he finds that things are not always done or thought of in exactly the same way as they are at home. In other words, the child's universe expands—a necessary kind of growth. However, socialization is likely to proceed most smoothly when there is no marked disparity between the values and customs espoused at home and those taught at school. In that event, conflict is minimized, since it becomes quite clear to the child what is considered right and what is considered wrong. Many children, however, cannot make the transition from home to school and home again with ease, at least not until they learn to tailor their behaviour to the specific context. For example, the child reared in a highly disciplined home may experience confusion and feelings of ineptitude in a classroom situation that rewards initiative, innovation, and independent thought.

Ethnic origin is one factor that may differentiate children at school and influence many children's school experience. Social-class background (see Chapter 6, "Social Stratification") can also be a bridge or a barrier between home and school.

PEER GROUPS

A **peer group** consists of individuals who occupy a roughly similar status and who tend to identify with each other. A German proverb states, *"Willst du wissen wer du bist, frag' wer deine Gesellschaft ist"* ("If you want to know who you are, ask who your companions are"). As the child spends more time away from home, children of his or her own age group, as well as older ones, become important role models. In other words, if Johnny's fourth-grade friends are interested in little but hockey, Johnny may quickly abandon his previous interest in gymnastics, which they call sissy, and take up the game even if he doesn't like it much.

As the child reaches adolescence, the peer group becomes markedly more important, touching all areas of life. In a classic study of American high schools (1963), James Coleman found that peer attitudes toward academic achievement profoundly affected whether students put forth their best efforts in academic work or withheld them for fear of being labelled teacher's pets or other, more derogatory terms. The effects of such peer pressure can be lasting indeed because, as we will demonstrate later, educational attainment is crucially linked to occupational and social status and to many other aspects of existence.

Influences that are less permanent, but very strong at the time, are apparent in the tyranny of teenage dress codes, music idols, the use of slang, and the countless fads to which teenagers are prey. Advertisers take advantage of teenagers' susceptibility to peer-group pressure through the use of mass-advertising campaigns. The major objective of such a technique is to establish one brand of sports shoe or soft drink as *the* brand, the use of which will demonstrate conformity and hence not jeopardize one's acceptance by the group.

Sociologists have pointed out that a striking facet of modern North American society is the extent to which age groups are segregated. This segregation is most pronounced throughout the age-graded school system. In human groups generally, homogeneity (sameness) *within* groups enhances the potential for conflict *between* groups. In the case of age groups, the conflict is most evident between teenagers and their elders. For example, parents may strongly disapprove of their teenagers' choice of clothing, hairstyle, and music. School administrators and students may come into conflict over such issues as punctuality and dress code.

It is apparent that the content of the norms, and the means by which they are enforced, may vary in youth subcultures as in other human groups. But the phenomenon of seeking conformity remains constant. Approaching this phenomenon theoretically, Cohen has commented:

> Everyone of us wants to be a member in good standing of some groups and roles. We all want to be recognized and respected as a full-fledged member of some age and sex category ... For every ... role there are certain kinds of action and belief which function, as truly and effectively as do uniforms, insignia and membership cards, as signs of

membership. To the degree that we covet such membership, we are motivated to assume those signs, to incorporate them into our behaviour and frame of reference. Many of our religious beliefs, esthetic standards, norms of speech, political doctrines, and canons of taste and etiquette are so motivated (1963, 56–57).

THE MASS MEDIA

In discussing peer groups, we focused on factors that internally link members of a group, at the same time bringing about differentiation among groups. The mass media provide a powerful countervailing influence to the forces of differentiation. For one thing, they permit mass advertising and programming to millions of people, which tends to bring about a levelling of taste and prefabricated standards of what is desirable. The result of this levelling of taste is often referred to as **popular culture**, the culture of the masses. The term is contrasted with **high culture**, which includes fine arts, classical music, and drama that is patronized and financed by wealthier members of the society.

Mass-media advertising facilitates mass consumption and the spread of popular culture, which creates a superficial sameness. For example, based on the clues afforded by appearance, it would be difficult to make accurate judgments about the income levels of spectators at a movie theatre or a football game.

Mass-media advertisers don't simply sell products; they also promote lifestyles that lead to the consumption of their products. This creates a paradox. On the one hand, the existence of social classes (see Chapter 6, "Social Stratification") is veiled because most Canadians are portrayed as leading quite similar lives. The image is that of the "average Canadian family," or the "average North American teenager." On the other hand, the lifestyles depicted as average can really only be afforded by a small portion of the population. Ironically, then, the majority of people, those who cannot engage in the "average" Canadian lifestyle, are socialized to think of themselves as a deprived minority.

However skewed the mass-media portrayals of "average" lifestyles are, though, the images do accurately reflect and therefore reinforce the extant distribution of power among different groups in the society. For example, seniors, for the most part, aren't represented, and other visible minorities, too, are "symbolically annihilated" (Tuchman, 1979). Since the media, as agents of socialization, contribute to our ideas of what is important, this invisibility reflects and reinforces the low status of these groups. (See Chapters 6 and 7 for more on minority groups.)

The relative powerlessness of women in society is signalled non-verbally in advertisements, as Goffman (1976) explains. Women are shown as submissive, psychologically withdrawn, and, typically, running their hands over, rather than taking hold, of items. Their physical appearance—they are usually slender and almost always shorter than the men they appear with—strengthens this impression of subordination. "The most striking aspect of this body is that it is reminiscent of adolescence; the shape is a version of an immature body ... The practice of shaving under the arms and shaving the legs removes the very evidence that a girl has reached puberty ... It is no coincidence that this sexual ideal is an image which connotes powerlessness" (Coward, 1985, 41). Modelled by excessively thin teenagers, the high fashion industry's most recent look—the waif—is a good example of the phenomenon. Recently advertisers have begun to use smiling male models with their bodies revealed and heads tilted coyly at the camera. This trend of objectifying men is disturbing but less problematic than the same treatment of women, as the weight of the culture is not behind it.

While fashion fluctuates, the message does not vary. No matter how impossible the task, a woman who wants to be admired must at least try to approximate the cultural ideal of the moment even while it works against her. As we have stressed in the section on adolescence and gender in this chapter, the message is potent and is all the more effective for appearing legitimate and natural.[6]

Rock videos furnish an interesting example of how sexual inequality is used to sell merchandise, in this instance tapes, compact discs, and concert tickets. The videos are targetted at a certain segment of the market—young men. To attract their attention, the videos cater to their (heterosexual) fantasies and, therefore, often include females. These women appear, always provocatively, as artists, musicians, audience members, or simply decorations. They are constantly in a state of sexual arousal and so interested in sexual encounters, no matter who the man, that even cursory conversation is an unnecessary prelude. Violence against them is portrayed as being courted (by them) and/or deserved. The camera accentuates the videos' sexual objectification of women: their often segmented bodies are panned close by and carefully; they are filmed in silhouette, shapes with nothing inside.[6]

The popularity of the music channel and of other video programs is evidence that rock videos are pleasurable. The context of the videos obscures

A mass media example of sexual objectification?

Your team won't be taken seriously if it's not wearing adidas.

Liverpool. Germany. Bayern Munich. Glasgow Rangers. If anyone knows how to make a bunch of guys look like pros, we do. Introducing the adidas Team Soccer Program.

Now we can outfit your team with the same high-quality kit the pros wear. From jerseys to shoes, everything has the look and feel of Professional Club equipment. After all, 16 of the last World Cup teams were outfitted from head to toe by adidas. So if you'd like to see what your team could be wearing, call 1-800-665-KICK for a free adidas Team Soccer catalogue and the name of your local Team Soccer retailer. Don't be seen in anything less.

adidas team soccer uniforms.

The gentleman pictured in last month's ad was Adi Dassler, founder of adidas. Congratulations, if you guessed correctly. And many thanks to The Kick of the Canadian National Soccer League for being so immodest on our behalf.

WorldCup **94**

adidas

Adidas Canada.

the objectification of the women in them. Since most people regard popular culture as trivial and are taught not to take it seriously, they remain unaware of the underlying message in much of it. The potentially damaging consequence of watching these videos is that viewers, in the long run, may become inured to real (sexual) violence against women.

Not unexpectedly, the relative importance of agents of socialization has varied, both within particular cultures and among different cultures, at various points in history. We have noted that in Canadian society, the extended family is not as significant an agent of socialization as it tends to be in less industrialized societies. Conversely, the media, and TV in particular, have become increasingly important as socializing agents in our society. Further discussion of some of these agents of socialization can be found in Section 4, which deals with institutions.

. . . .

OVERVIEW

The point of this chapter was to show how the socialization process creates "selves" within a particular cultural framework and to stress the contribution of social interaction to that process. The socialization process determines for individuals who they are—the values they hold dear, the tasks in which they participate, the ways they relate to each other. The actions of these millions of single individuals determine the shape of our society and the lives of those who come after them. Without socialization, one would not have the characteristics we know as human, as the cases of social isolates indicate. Conversely, all varieties of humanity are possible through this process.

In this chapter, gender socialization was used as an example of the socialization process, showing how the cultural values, ideologies, and institutions shape newborns. If the group expects men and women to assume widely different statuses, this difference will be reflected in the attitudes and behaviour they are socialized to acquire. In Canadian culture, despite the progress toward sexual equality, socialization practices still subtly reinforce male dominance.

We examined a number of theories about the process by which the human organism is transformed into a social being. Underlying these explanations are different views of homo sapiens. Biological determinism treats individual development as tightly constrained by genetic endowment. According to environmental (social) determinism, on the other hand, the infant is a clean slate to be written on by environmental influences. Although much of the criticism of Freud's theories is justified, he is still valued as a pioneer in drawing attention to the unconscious motivations that affect behaviour and to the lasting effects of early childhood experience. These effects were also of central concern to sociologists Mead and Cooley. For them, society and the individual are inseparable, and they noted that the very notion of humanity presupposes interaction with others.

Socialization continues throughout the lifespan, and "selves" continue to develop. Anticipatory socialization is the process by which individuals prepare themselves for new roles. Clues about what constitutes acceptable behaviour are gleaned from those who are already members of the group one aspires to join. Resocialization involves being divested of an existing identity and acquiring a new one. The clearest examples occur in extreme circumstances such as prisons or mental hospitals where all aspects of the person's life are subject to control by the same authority.

The main agents of socialization in Canadian society are parents, parent surrogates, peers, teachers, and the media. To the extent that the values transmitted by these various agents are not compatible, the individual being socialized may experience uncertainty and discomfort. On the other hand, such mixed messages may be advantageous in that no particular lifestyle comes to be seen as the only one possible.

ASSIGNMENTS

1. Do a content analysis of a classic children's story such as *Little Red Riding Hood, Cinderella, The Three Little Pigs*, or any other story you remember from your childhood. Explain what you think children learn from this story.

2. If a 14-year-old girl who wanted to become a surgeon asked for your advice about her career choice, what would you tell her? Frame your response in sociological terms.

3. Examine the magazines, videos, television programs, and newspapers you read or watch for gender bias. How are the females and males portrayed? What does this portrayl teach you about your own gender role?

SUGGESTED READINGS

Steve Craig, ed., *Men, Masculinity, and the Media* (New York: Sage Publications, 1992). This series of articles furnishes a detailed and wide-ranging look at men. While it may seem surprising, very few scholars have analyzed the socialization of masculinity *per se*, since men have been viewed as the "norm" and their socialization considered unproblematic. The pluralistic notion of "masculinities" rather than a single encompassing definition of the male gender role is evident in this exploration of masculine images in a variety of media.

Erving Goffman, *Asylums: Essays on the Social Situation of Mental Patients and Other Inmates* (Chicago: Aldine Publishing, 1962). Goffman's interesting analysis is mainly based on participant observation in a state mental hospital, although he also looks at other settings that constitute "total institutions." The book describes what life is like for patients in a total institution, a setting in which every aspect of existence is controlled. Attempts by a patient to resist intensive resocialization and to adhere to behaviour that is appropriate in the outside world are interpreted as symptoms confirming the initial diagnosis of mental illness. Goffman argues that the absolute conformity that is required is likely to make readjustment more difficult when the patient is discharged.

Jack Haas and William Shaffir, "Taking on the Role of Doctor: A Dramaturgical Analysis of Professionalization," in Katherina L.P. Lundy and Barbara Warme, eds., *Work in the Canadian Context: Continuity Despite Change*, 2nd ed. (Toronto: Butterworths, 1986). Using concepts from the theatre and applying them to an innovative Canadian medical school, Haas and Shaffir argue that *performance* is central to becoming a professional, and that professionalism is, in part, a mythic illusion. Learning the role well—that is, taking on a credible identity and knowing how to manipulate the props—is seen to be a difficult and complicated process, one that is necessary if the candidate is finally to succeed in receiving legitimacy as a full-fledged physician.

Michael Ignatieff, *Scar Tissue* (London: Chatto and Windus, 1993). In this novel, we are witness to a kind of socialization in reverse, as a neurological illness slowly erases the habits, attitudes, memories, and intellectual capacities of a mother in a family. In the process, a reconfiguration of family relationships occurs as loving partners become baffled strangers, siblings renegotiate their old roles, children become parents, and parents become children.

Myrna Kostash, *No Kidding: Inside the World of Teenage Girls* (Toronto: McClelland and Stewart, 1987). There are many teenage worlds in Canada, and they mirror the underlying class, ethnic, and racial divisions of the wider society. Kostash documents the 1980s dreams (of economic self-sufficiency, a successful career, a romantic marriage, and children) held by the girls she interviewed, yet makes it clear that these dreams are unrealizable for most in the absence of a fundamental restructuring of Canadian society's economic, political, and social relationships. This book's great strength lies in the riveting words of the girls themselves, as they tell their stories about coming of age in Canada.

Marlene Mackie, *Gender Relations in Canada: Further Explorations* (Markham, Ont.: Butterworths, 1991). This text provides a thorough discussion of all aspects of gender socialization. Mackie stresses the notion that gender is socially constructed and contrasts this with ideological and "commonsense" ideas of female and male differences, and with biological explanations of gender.

NOTES

1. With existing technology, it is possible to ascertain the sex of the child before birth. Some parents very much want that information, but medical personnel may consider it unethical to provide it.

2. For pioneering works, see Juliet Mitchell, *Psychoanalysis and Feminism* (1974) and Jean Baker Miller, ed., *Psychoanalysis and Women* (1973). See also Nancy Chodorow's *The Reproduction of Mothering: Psychoanalysis and the Sociology of Gender* (1978), which synthesizes sociological and psychoanalytic perspectives.

3. The main emphasis of the symbolic interactionist perspective is on the interaction between individual and environment and the symbolic interpretation attached to behaviour at any stage of development. For example, in *The Silent Language* (1959), Edward Hall vividly portrays the differences in meaning attached to time and punctuality in Middle

Eastern and Western society. The symbolic significance of these concepts varies crossculturally.

4. Human beings may not be unique in this respect. Recent research on whales and dolphins indicates that these species may use sophisticated symbolic codes. As yet, scientists have not fully broken these codes; some scholars do not accept their existence.

5. For an investigative report of this cult by journalists, see Paul Kaihla and Ross Laver's *Savage Messiah* (1993).

6. These insights into rock videos come from *Dreamworlds*, a video written, edited, and narrated by Sut Jhally, Associate Professor of Communication at the University of Massachusetts. It is distributed by Kinetic, Inc., Toronto.

CHAPTER FIVE

5

Deviance and Social Control

By Linda B. Deutschmann

WHAT IS DEVIANCE?

Is extramarital sex deviant? Is the recreational use of soft drugs deviant? What kind of evidence do we need in order to agree that, yes, this is deviant, or no, it is not deviant?

Sociologically, **deviance** is best described as a special label put on behaviour (or appearance) that violates a society's salient norms. By **salient norms**, we mean the rules actually in effect, as opposed to those that are "on the books" or that we regard as ideals. The deviant is a person who is not just different: he or she is different in an undesirable way, and significant numbers of people are prepared to say that it matters.

The situation in which a person becomes deviant involves:

1. *Observers* who believe that a particular kind of behaviour or state of being is typical of the person(s) observed.
2. *Standards of judgment,* in the form of images or labels of deviance and respectability.
3. *Application* of these standards to particular people.
4. *Justification* (sometimes implicit) of social control.

Exhibit 5.1 outlines some common pairs of deviant statuses and the normative standards they apparently violate. In each case, the reader can supply columns for "who says so?" and "what is the likely penalty?"

EXHIBIT 5.1

Deviance as the Labelling of Norm Violation

Deviant label	Normative standard
Heretic	Religious orthodoxy (beliefs)
Sinner	Religious regulation (acts)
Traitor	Loyalty
Homosexual	Gender roles
Dangerous driver	Highway Traffic Act
Robber	Criminal Code
Absentee, alcoholic	Reliability, self-control
Slow learner, "egg-head"	Group's desired level of intellectual achievement
Deformed person, freak	Group's definition of desirable physical appearance

WHAT IS SOCIAL CONTROL?

Social control includes all those aspects of social life by which we are enticed, encouraged, or coerced into particular patterns of behaviour, or failing that, isolated from our fellow human beings so that they do not have to deal with our behaviour. Social controls can include the subtle proddings of effective socialization or extend to the most horrifying forms of torture. In the name of social control, people have been burned alive, sterilized, euthanized, given drugs with dangerous side effects, brainwashed, banished, or locked up for years.

Not all violations of stated rules result in social control and the label of deviance. There is a **margin of tolerance**. This margin is usually wider for situations that are further from core values, for people of higher status, and for times of celebration. It is often wider for men than it is for women.

Tolerance for social control is also variable. There is always pressure to increase the control on undesirable behaviour (to treat more kinds of behaviour as deviant), and there is also always pressure to eliminate unnecessary rules and excessive monitoring of the actions of ordinary citizens. Should there be more control on hockey violence? Should police be allowed to install cameras in men's washrooms? How much information about the private citizen should government make available? Should employers be able to demand urine tests? Evgeny Ivanovich Zamyatin's *We* (1924), Aldous Huxley's *Brave New World* (1932), and George Orwell's *1984* (1949) express our abhorrence of total control and domination (Howe, 1963).

Protest at the Glad Day Bookstore in Toronto. Books and magazines destined for bookstores with a homosexual clientele are regularly detained by Canada Customs inspectors, but violent heterosexual material—with women as victims—is regularly admitted.

Fred Lum/ *The Globe and Mail*, Toronto.

BOX 5.1

NINE PLEAD GUILTY TO PUBLIC SEX IN OAKVILLE PARK WASHROOM

Nine of 42 men who appeared in court yesterday pleaded guilty to committing indecent acts in an Oakville park washroom.

The men, from "all walks of life" and ranging in age from 23 to 76, were secretly videotaped on a Halton Region police camera performing acts such as fellatio, masturbation and anal intercourse.

In all, 46 males were charged as a result of the sex crackdown last month, resulting in 61 charges laid. Three men had pleaded guilty prior to yesterday and have already been fined.

After the charges were laid, one of the accused, who had AIDS, committed suicide.

Outside court, one man who was convicted yesterday said he is "living in absolute fear" and hasn't told anyone about the charges.

"Suicide is a real option for me, and of the (charged) at least half are feeling that," the man said in an interview.

Defence lawyers say they don't expect any of the men will be jailed.

Many of the individuals are bisexuals who are married and have children. The majority of the accused had their cases put over to a later date.

The sexual acts they committed are not allowed under the Criminal Code when they take place in public.

Judge William Sharpe of Ontario Court, provincial division, yesterday handed out fines as high as $1,200 and ordered the men to stay away from Shell Park near Lakeshore and Burloak Rds. in Oakville. The park is located near a residential area.

Court was told that on July 15, the Halton police drug and morality bureau installed a video camera above two cubicle toilets in the park for nine days, after receiving complaints from residents.

The park is popular for its walking paths, greenspace and baseball fields, the court also heard.

The video showed men committing sex acts in the washroom stalls.

Defence lawyer Jonathan Marler said he hopes the media don't release the names of the convicted men.

He said the publicity surrounding the case has been "overwhelming," adding that one of his clients just wants to put the situation in the past. He said another man broke down in front of him in one of the interviewing rooms yesterday.

Outside court, one of the accused said his parents are elderly and would be crushed if they found out.

"When I heard my name read out in the courtroom, I thought: 'God, it's over for me.'"

Marler criticized the use of the video surveillance by police.

"If they (police) wanted to stop this, they could have just put signs up saying the washrooms are videotaped," the defence lawyer said outside court.

"In my opinion, it's not an appropriate process for police to put video cameras in washrooms."

He accused the police of using publicity as a weapon to deter the men from using the park washroom for sex. He said homophobia among members of the public is elevating the issue.

But Halton police Sergeant Joe Martin said the park "has been a problem for years."

"The cameras were put there for the purpose of gathering evidence."

Source: Donovan Vincent, "Nine Plead Guilty to Public Sex in Oakville Park Washroom," The Toronto Star *(25 August 1993), A8. Reprinted with permission—The Toronto Star Syndicate.*

DEVIANCE AND HARMFULNESS

Many types of behaviour are considered harmful because they undermine deeply held values and patterns of action, not because they would do direct physical damage to people or things. This is one reason the killing of hundreds of people by unsafe products, by pollution, or by exposure to hazards in the workplace, receives much less attention than does a single murder in the street (Ermann & Lundman, 1978). The gunman is more clearly violating common values and so is more readily labelled deviant than the businessman, who may be negligent about workplace safety, since he is mostly seen as pursuing the relatively acceptable goal of profit-making. As our values change, this situation may change.

THE UNIVERSALITY AND RELATIVITY OF DEVIANCE

Every society has rules that establish that some killing is murder and that some relationships constitute incest. In this sense, deviance is universal. Specific forms of deviance are, however, culturally relative. That is, acts defined as murder (wrongful killing) in one culture may differ from what is called murder in another. "Mercy killing," self-sacrifice, military killing, police work, and the consequences of poor workplace safety may result in deaths that are not called murder.

EXPLAINING DEVIANCE AND CONTROL: THEORIES AND PERSPECTIVES

Some theorists claim that deviance is rooted in single causes such as biological deficiencies, bad parenting, or capitalism. Such explanations are inadequate simplifications. Arson, for example, can intimidate a rival, gain insurance money for a failing business, express psychiatric distress, or be a "bit of fun." No single explanatory theory of arson, or any other form of deviance, is likely to be found. Instead, we have a variety of perspectives that, like different lenses in a microscope, let us see different things.

Over the years, various theories of deviance have been proposed, tested against the evidence, and revised. When a new perspective develops, the process begins again. Older theories often persist alongside the newer, more popular, ones. For example, demonic theory (which is discussed below) can still be found in modern writings (Peck, 1983). You will note, as we go through a brief recounting of the development of theories of deviance, that each theory has implicit policy (control) implications.

DEMONIC THEORY: "THE DEVIL MADE ME DO IT"

The earliest theories blamed deviance on supernatural forces. Curses, spells, possession, enthralment, and other magical forces were thought to make weak people do evil things. Naughty children were sometimes seen as changelings (evil substitutes for human babies stolen in the night). The mentally ill were viewed as possessed by demons or cursed by witches. Deviance was a state to be detected through magical signs, such as seeing how fast a burn would heal (if it festered, you were guilty). It was to be controlled through rituals of exorcism or intense pain aimed at expelling the evil from the body. From about A.D. 1200 to 1700, thousands of "witches" (sometimes virtually all of the women and some of the men from a community) were burned for bringing plagues, droughts, crop failures, and other disasters on their neighbours.

Criminal justice in this period took the form of erratic cruelty (Weisser, 1982). Many people, convicted on the basis of anonymous denunciations, were used to provide ceremonial occasions for expressing social outrage. Elaborate and excruciatingly painful executions, whippings, and mutilations were public. Heads of executed individuals were displayed on city walls, and the bodies of highwaymen were hung in gibbets along the roadway. Such punishment made the community "see" the seriousness of the offence, while it demonstrated the absolute power of the authorities over the lives and bodies of the people. This "justice," however, failed to deter wrongdoing. The presence of pickpockets in the crowds who gathered to see other pickpockets hanged demonstrated the futility of this means of control (Ignatieff, 1978, 21–22).

CLASSICAL THEORY: RATIONAL SELF-INTEREST AND FREE WILL

By the 1700s, the demonic view began to be replaced by the classical view. According to this view, people were rational, pleasure-seeking beings whose deviant behaviour was based on their free will to calculate what they would gain by breaking the rules (Scheleff, 1981; Pfohl, 1985). The solution to this seemed to lie in improving the speed and certainty of punishment and adjusting its severity to a level just sufficient to deter the offender (Beccaria, 1819). Classical theory focused primarily on the criminal justice system, rather than on the control of deviance in general. It led to the establishment of courts of law in which the accused was assumed to be rational unless proven otherwise, and in which carefully graded punishments were applied to specific offences.

Classical approaches were more predictable and less vicious than the demonic ones, but they were not much more effective. Some theorists began to question just how "rational" most deviants were.

EARLY POSITIVISM: SCIENCE AND EXPLANATIONS OF DEVIANCE

How can we explain a person's "choice" to become a cannibalistic homosexual serial killer like Jeffrey Dahmer? Why do some people steal things, only to destroy them or throw them away? Why do people do things that endanger their own lives or the lives of people they care about? Some theorists feel that we do not choose to do these things.

Positivism

In the late 1700s the methods of experimental science (which had made great strides in the study of plants, animals, stars, and chemicals) were applied to the study of human thought and behaviour. This use of science was called positivism. Deviants were not to be seen as morally bad, possessed, or as creatures of free will. They were "sick."

What You Look Like Is What You Are

The earliest "positivist" theories attempted to relate deviance to external bodily features such as the shape of the face (physiognomy), the size and shape of the head (craniometry), or the bumps on the head (phrenology). None of these methods proved to be a reliable method of distinguishing deviant people from normal ones (Gould, 1981).

Atavism: The Ape Among Us

Cesare Lombroso (1835–1909) studied the cadavers of criminals and compared them with normal bodies. Unusually large jaws and cheekbones, abnormal dentition, and long arms and legs with large fingers and toes were among the "signs" of abnormality. For Lombroso (1895, 1918 [1899]) the criminal's body and his or her criminality were signs of atavism, of a genetic throwback to traits characteristic of a more primitive, ferocious stage of human evolution.

Lombroso's critics were quick to point out that the variations he found between prisoners and others might result from the physical effects of prison life, or from the tendency of judges to lock up people who did not seem as civilized as others. Controlled studies of criminals failed to confirm the differences that Lombroso claimed were there (Goring, 1913). Lombroso gradually developed a theory that emphasized an underlying epileptiform characteristic of crime as even more fundamental than atavism. Unfortunately, Lombroso's ideas were sometimes used in the courtroom, so that people who looked "atavistic" or who had epileptic seizures were more likely to be convicted than people who did not (Gould, 1981, 139).

Ernest Hooton, an American follower of Lombroso, extended the theory that criminals were constitutionally inferior. He argued that there was no crime in "savage" human societies, because such flawed individuals could only survive in a modern society, where people misguidedly helped them and allowed them to breed (Hooton, 1939, 388–389). Thus, Hooton argued for the elimination or at least complete separation of the physically, mentally, and morally unfit. Some of Hooton's followers called for sterilization and euthanasia, not only for those who were actually criminal, but also for those who were mentally unfit or physically poor specimens.

Body Shapes and Delinquency

Social scientists such as W.H. Sheldon (1948) worked out a system of body types (see Exhibit 5.2), in which the shape of the body indicates how it will be used. According to this system, mesomorphs (individuals with an athletic build) were overrepresented among juvenile delinquents. Sheldon argued that people with such bodies were more likely to have an imbalance of impulses and impulse controls, and this would lead them to acts of delinquency. Later writers, such as Sheldon Glueck and Eleanor Glueck (1956), argued that the body is not by itself a source of deviance. Thin, short-sighted ectomorphs and round, soft endomorphs, they said, may be motivated to delinquency, but they are much less likely to be recruited by others or convicted if they are accused.

EXHIBIT 5.2

Body Types and Character

	Physical traits	Character traits
Endomorphic	round soft	easy-going sociable indulgent
Mesomorphic	rectangular hard	restless energetic
Ectomorphic	lean fragile	introspective sensitive nervous

The mesomorph is thought to be better adapted to delinquent activities than the soft endomorph or the fragile ectomorph.

Source: Adapted from W.H. Sheldon, Varieties of Delinquent Youth: An Introduction to Constitutional Psychiatry *(New York: Harper and Row, 1948).*

MODERN POSITIVIST THEORIES

XYY

The XYY man has two male (Y) chromosomes rather than one. Although the condition was recognized by the 1920s, it was not linked with deviance until the 1960s, when it was correlated with "supermaleness"—tallness, acne, aggressiveness, skeletal deformities, and mental deficiencies (Jarvik, Klodin, & Matsuyama, 1973). By the 1970s, however, when genetic testing had become easier and more widely used, it was found that few convicted criminals had the extra male chromosome and that many men who did have it remained out of trouble (National Institute of Mental Health, 1970).

This pattern, whereby a biological or physiological cause of some type of deviance is hailed as the latest breakthrough, and then gradually revealed as inadequate or exaggerated, has become a familiar paradigm. Recently, announcements of a gene linked to alcoholism and another to homosexuality seem to be following the same route. People *may* inherit a *predisposition* toward mental illness, violent outbursts, addictive-compulsive behaviour, or (possibly) homosexuality, but they do not always express this predisposition. Social and psychological levels of explanation must also be invoked if we are to answer the question, "why do people behave as they do?"

Arousal Levels

Researchers have recently reported that deviants, particularly those involved in delinquency, are less sensitive to stimuli, such as pain, and have lower arousal rates (as revealed by brain-wave patterns, galvanic skin response, and other physical measures) than are nondeviants. Analysts theorize that this insensitivity may impede socialization in two ways. First, the insensitive individual will be less responsive to threats or promises. Second, their lower arousal rates may be experienced as a craving for danger and excitement. According to this theory, deviants do not learn good behaviour because "normal" socialization does not get through to them, and they seek out stimulation because time goes much more slowly for them than for other people (Lykken, 1982).

But which comes first? Researchers have also shown that people can change their body chemistry by changing their behaviour. Do deviants somehow *become* less sensitive and less easily aroused? Or are these traits inborn?

PSYCHIATRY AND DEVIANCE

The psychoanalytic theories of Sigmund Freud and his followers have had a substantial impact on explanations of deviance. As we discussed in Chapter 4, which focused on socialization, Freudians see each individual as having strong, biologically rooted drives—the id part of the personality. Society, which is represented in the personality by the superego (which develops through socialization), demands that the primitive urges of the id be curbed and channelled. The ego balances these demands and keeps the individual in contact with both inner reality and the reality of the environment. Thus, deviance can be blamed on a particularly strong id (violent behaviour), an overly repressive superego (neurotic behaviour), a weak ego, or a combination of the three. The kind of deviance that is likely to emerge will be symbolically related to the phase (oral, anal, genital, or phallic) in which the unresolved conflicts began. Arrested development in the oral phase, for example, might emerge as alcoholism or excessive smoking. And arrested development is almost always due to a problem within the family.

Psychiatry can be *insightful* or *inciteful* (Samenow, 1984). When deviants gain insight into the way in which their behaviour relates to unmet needs, they can often be helped to find more acceptable ways of meeting these needs. On the other hand, some observers feel psychoanalytic explanations are merely "inciteful" (Samenow, 1984). That is, they give the deviants further excuses for their behaviour, removing the penalty of guilt. It is the fault of society if the culture is too repressive, and the fault of parents if they have not loved well and sensitively. When deviants "use" psychiatry this way, they perceive punishment and exclusion as further persecution and become bitter instead of reformed.

SOCIAL-PSYCHOLOGICAL THEORIES OF DEVIANCE

The Criminal Mind
Prison psychologist Stanton Samenow (1984; Yochelson & Samenow, 1976) argues that the thought processes of criminals are different from those of other people. When ordinary people enter a drug store, they assess how easy it will be to find what they want and pay for it. When criminals enter, they assess how the cash register is protected and where the exits are. They do this automatically, even if they are not currently planning to rob the store. According to Samenow, this type of thinking can be traced to the criminal's earliest childhood, and is just as typical of the drug store robber as it is of the high-level employee who embezzles from his or her company. Samenow has argued that people with criminal minds can be trained to behave normally but will always differ from normal people.

Temperament
There is mounting evidence that temperament (being very active or emotional, or passive and cold) does not change a great deal during an individual's life (Nettler, 1982). The temperament that makes for a successful leader of an urban gang can also make for a successful astronaut. But the person with a temperament that makes risk-taking a pleasure is, it can be argued, more likely to take the risk of breaking the rules. According to this approach, people who are easily aroused by normal levels of stimulation will be more likely to experience reward and punishment, and less likely to seek out extra stimulation in the form of taking risks. They will prefer quiet activities such as reading. People who are *not* easily aroused by normal levels of stimulation may be less sensitive to attempts to train them to behave properly, and may be risk takers because ordinary life seems boring to them. Such people are more likely, according to this theory, to become risk-taking delinquents and criminals (Zukerman, 1983; Mednick & Wolavka, 1980).

SOCIOLOGICAL THEORIES OF DEVIANCE

Functionalism: A Little Deviance Is a Good Thing
Emile Durkheim (1893) argued that anomie occurred when there were unclear guidelines in a fluid society, and that a lot of rule-breaking had a positive function in that it made people decide which rules ought to be supported and

BOX 5.2

FUNCTIONS OF DEVIANCE

1. May cause an unknown or unclear rule to be specifically and clearly stated (aids predictability, planning).

2. May cause a group to unite in support of the value violated (ritual affirmation of values, commitment of members).

3. May cause a group to realize that the rule is a "bad" one (e.g., "test cases").

4. May enhance the value of conformity when others see the deviant suffer punishment.

5. May serve as a scapegoat, for example, when politicians go after delinquency or drug abuse instead of facing problems of upper-level corruption.

6. May serve as an alternative means of obtaining goals such as wealth, power, and recognition (organized crime/antibureaucracy).

7. May act as a tension release at a group or personal level.

which needed to be changed. Many other positive functions of deviance can be noted (see Box 5.2).

Normal levels of deviance tend to make people come together to express their anger and indignation, to take action against an offender, or to force the authorities to do so. Social interaction increases, shared sentiments are confirmed, and common concerns are identified. People increase their sense of belonging, and their solidarity and commitment. They draw clear lines between themselves and outsiders, and become more willing to work for the group and make sacrifices for it. All this usually makes the group stronger. If, in addition, the deviant suffers an unpleasant penalty, the value of conformity is further enhanced.

Durkheim's insight, that a certain level of deviance could be useful to society, informed the work of later functionalists such as Robert Merton. Merton (1957) argued that functions (consequences for the system) are often *latent* (unrecognized, unintended), rather than *manifest* (intended). Consider, for example, the effects of prostitution. The "average citizen" thinks of prostitution as a bad thing, and associates it with many other negative things. Kingsley Davis ([1937] 1961) however, has argued that prostitution has the latent function of maintaining the family. According to Davis, prostitution provides men with a way to have sexual variety, but to do so with women who are ineligible for marriage, so the family is not threatened. Historically, prostitutes have either been highly valued servants of the temple or they have been devalued as fallen women. In either case, they are rarely if ever regarded as marriage partners for respectable men. Davis's unwarranted assumption that men (and not women) are somehow biologically programmed to seek sexual variety can certainly be challenged, but the outline of his theory still holds.

The Morgentaler Case

How would Merton analyze the behaviour of Dr. Henry Morgentaler, who for years operated abortion clinics in defiance of the existing Criminal Code?[1] Dr. Morgentaler challenged the morality of a set of rules that were frequently violated in secret, though officially upheld. He did so flagrantly, deliberately forcing the authorities to recognize what he was doing.

While there is much about the situation that shows the negative side of deviance, there is also a beneficial side, even for those who are in opposition to Dr. Morgentaler. Because of his challenge, citizens learned about the actual effects of the rules and began to concern themselves with these consequences. The battle led to the formation of new rules to clarify the meaning of the law and to establish proper procedures for enforcing all laws.[2] It also led to increased religious solidarity and attention to theology. Ordinary citizens learned a great deal about politics, the law, law enforcement, and citizenship, as well as about abortion. Many people who were normally apathetic were drawn into active participation.

STRAIN THEORIES

Strain theories are those that argue that deviance emerges because society is not perfectly integrated, that some parts of it do not fit well together. Most strain theories maintain that lower-class people feel more strain and that this, therefore, explains why deviance is most often found in the lower classes. Students should be cautious in accepting this idea, however. Research tends to show that upper-class deviance is merely less well known, not less extensive.

Merton's Cultural Goals-Institutional Means Schema

Society provides certain culturally accepted goals, such as a college degree, a car in the driveway, and 2.2 children. It also provides institutionalized means for achieving these goals: study well and work hard. **Anomia**, which is Merton's term for anomie, occurs when the accepted goals are not matched by available means. This idea was developed by Merton (1957) from Durkheim's ideas.

The middle-class child with normal intelligence and a few strings to pull usually has only a reasonable amount of difficulty accomplishing these goals. The disadvantaged child absorbs the same TV version of the good life but may not find an acceptable path to it. Merton set out a paradigm of deviance-producing situations to show that deviance is a product of the social structure, not of individual biology or psychology (see Exhibit 5.3).

- *Innovation.* When an individual accepts the culture's goals but chooses a different means of reaching them, the result is innovation. For example, the embezzler may fully accept the suburban ideal but chooses an illegal way to obtain it.

- *Ritualism.* When the individual loses sight of the goals but systematically goes through the approved means, the result is ritualism. The bureaucrat who makes you fill in twenty forms and then tells you the service you want is unavailable is providing an example of ritualism.

- *Retreatism.* When the individual has neither the cultural goals nor the desire to pursue them, the response is called retreatism. The heroin addict, who seeks the pleasant relief from reality that the drug temporarily provides, may fit this category.

- *Rebellion.* When the individual rejects both the approved goals and means and seeks a new system, the response is called rebellion.

EXHIBIT 5.3

Merton's Paradigm of
Adaptations to Anomia

	Goals	Means
Conformist	+	+
Innovator	+	−
Ritualist	−	+
Retreatist	−	−
Rebel	±	±

Cohen's Counterculture

Where Robert Merton spoke of the individual's structural position, Albert Cohen (1966) emphasized the unequal position of people within the class system. Lower-class boys, according to Cohen, want recognition just as much as middle-class boys, but they are poorly positioned to get it from the schools or employers. Their drive for identity and autonomy leads them to develop an alternative status system in which they can succeed. This alternative system is a **counterculture**, a reversal of the middle-class one. One of its central values is disrespect for property rights. Lower-class girls, he felt, were less motivated toward identity and autonomy, and thus less likely to participate in a counter-culture. His view that boys chase opportunities and girls chase boys is now badly dated.

Cloward and Ohlin: Illegitimate Opportunity

Richard Cloward and Lloyd Ohlin (1960) developed a set of categories similar to Merton's, but included in theirs the possibility of illegitimate opportunities. In their paradigm, the social order offers illegitimate goals as well as legitimate ones. It is possible to succeed in either world. A person may become prime minister or the "boss of all bosses." Or the person may be a loser in both, a double loser, such as the owner of a failing business who sets fire to his factory to get insurance money, but gets caught; or the would-be neighbourhood tough who gets beaten up himself. If the neighbourhood provides more deviant than legitimate opportunities, it may encourage deviant choices (Spergel, 1964).

Walter Miller: Blaming Subcultures

Not all theories that involve subcultures are strain theories. Some subcultural approaches argue that different subcultural groups have different values based on tradition or ethnic backgrounds and that these values may lead them into conflict with the dominant (middle-class) norms of the society.

Walter Miller (1958) argued that the lower class generates "focal concerns" (trouble, toughness, smartness, excitement, autonomy, fate, and hedonism), which make its members more likely to run afoul of the law and other rules. The lower class, in Miller's view, is more likely to show interest in the qualities of a person who can handle trouble, keep a tough image, be smart (street-wise, not academically smart), find or make excitement, and be autonomous. The lower class believes that life's outcome is a matter of fate (not hard work), and that hedonism (immediate gratification) makes sense. In Miller's view, delinquents are not reacting to rejection by the middle class (in the school, for example). Rather, they are acting out lower-class cultural norms.

Differential Association: "It's Normal Practice Around Here!"

Edwin Sutherland (1961) argued that people are not born deviant, and they do not commit deviant acts merely because they are stressed or have easy opportunity. They act as they do because they have *learned* this behaviour in intimate social groups at home, among friends, or at work. Deviant values, said Sutherland, are found in all strata of society, not strictly, nor even predominantly, in the lower classes.

Sutherland maintained that most deviance is learned in small intimate groups that communicate not only attitudes favourable to rule violation, but also techniques and rationalizations for it. The heart of the theory is the idea of **differential association**, according to which a person becomes deviant when the environment to which he or she is exposed provides more definitions favourable to rule violation than definitions favouring conformity. When your mother brags about getting something past the customs officer or the income tax department, you are hearing a "definition" favourable to violation of the law. When your best friend tells you to leave your knife at home because it might get you into "real trouble," you are hearing a definition favourable to conformity. This association with definitions is "differential" in that it may vary by frequency, duration, priority (early or late in life), and intensity. When a person's life includes early, prolonged, and emotional exposure to deviant associations but late, short, and impersonal exposure to conforming associations, the theory predicts that this person will be deviant.

CONFLICT THEORIES

The conflict perspective stresses the role of political power in the rule-making process. There are two main forms of conflict theory: that which is rooted in the works of Karl Marx and is called neo-Marxist conflict theory, and that which is rooted in the work of Max Weber and is usually called "pluralist" or "liberal" conflict theory. Neo-Marxist conflict theorists believe that the power that "counts" in society is really in the hands of one group, the ruling class (to Marx, the owners of the means of production); in contrast, pluralists describe a sharing of power among many competing groups, some of which have a lot of power, and some of which have almost none. In both traditions, deviants are people who have been trapped in the rules made by and for others.

Neo-Marxist Approaches

In neo-Marxist theories, the ruling class comprises the owners of the means of production (mainly white males), who control the political, social, and physical environment for everyone else. According to this theory of history, more and more people fall into the disempowered groups, leaving fewer and fewer people in control. To put off the inevitable overthrow of this progressively more unbalanced social order, the powerful minority at the top must find ever-increasing means for controlling those below them. These controls, which include the rules of welfare agencies as well as overt policing, mean that more and more people are called deviant, receive punishment or therapy, or are controlled by regulatory agencies.

In neo-Marxist conflict theories, therefore, deviance is the result of exploitative regulation, which is masked as benevolent regulation for the society as a whole. These theories have, historically, tended to be *idealistic* in the sense that they have seen deviance as an unreal thing, created by the forces of control. In recent times, some neo-Marxists, calling themselves "left realists" or practitioners of "the new criminology," have attempted to deal with the fact that some deviance, such as rape and robbery, is committed largely by the unprivileged classes on the unprivileged classes, and is very "real."

Many conflict theories express the view that deviance is the result of exploitative regulation by the holders of industrial power or their agents.

Ontario Ministry of the Environment.

Pluralist (Liberal) Conflict Theory

Pluralist forms of conflict theory see the competition for social power as occurring among a variety of groups, which can be divided in many cross-cutting or reinforcing ways: religion, region, age, gender, income, ethnicity, and so on. Each group fights for political power in order to protect or advance its particular interests. As the groups compete, the rules for the society are worked out. More powerful groups can use their power to ensure that they are not subjected to deviance labels, while ensuring that competing groups, or the groups they dislike, are.

Feminist Theories

Feminist theories are conflict theories. They see women as trapped within a social system run by and for men. Women are less likely to be in the public sphere that is dominated by criminal rules, but they are much more affected by myriads of informal rules by which they may be judged deviant (Schur, 1984). Also, women have traditionally been far more likely than men to become ensnared in psychiatric treatment or sidelined because they did not fit the accepted standards of femininity. Some feminist theories follow Marxist lines and argue that women's liberation will be achieved when the systems of oppression for all people are changed. Others are more Weberian, and argue for improving women's ability to compete fairly for privileges in the mainstream.

SYMBOLIC INTERACTION AND LABELLING THEORY

Consider the following statement: "John X is a determined, hard-working, enterprising young man. He is an ex-convict who murdered a former business partner."

Topless protest at the Peace Bridge between Fort Erie in Canada, and Buffalo in the United States. Women protest inequality that is reinforced by the law.

Canapress.

William (Snake) Pulley used tatoos to cover scars from an accident. He attracts attention wherever he goes, and has been banned from a local shopping mall in London, Ontario.

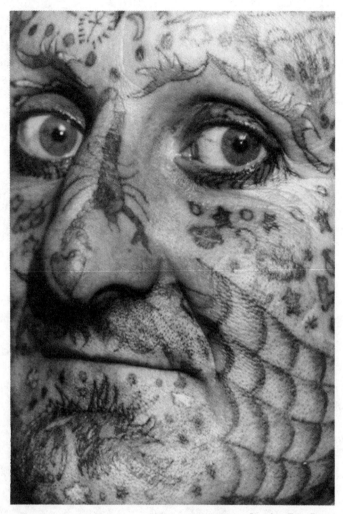

London Free Press.

Would you hire John X? How did "ex-convict" change your impression of John's other qualities? Criminal conviction tends to create a **master status**: everything else you know about the person is reinterpreted in the light of that one piece of information (Hughes, 1945; Becker, 1963, 33). This person is now, and retrospectively, the kind of person who could commit such an act.

The concept of "master status" is drawn from the vocabulary of symbolic interactionism, a theory that stresses the way in which we attribute meaning to our acts and those of others. This theory draws our attention to the processes whereby identities are negotiated. People may present themselves in a deviant or nondeviant way; other people may insist on "seeing" them as deviant or nondeviant. There are patterns in this, such as the master status phenomenon.

Some other commonly used concepts from this perspective and from ethnomethodology (the study of the "methods" whereby people make their meanings) follow.

Identifiers and Disidentifiers

Erving Goffman (1963, 44) introduced the idea of identifiers and disidentifiers. These are signals that people deliberately use to negotiate a position in society. A tattoo, black leather equipment, metallic jewellery, or a certain style of haircut (or the lack of one) can serve as identifiers of a person's preferred self-image. Disidentifiers may be used to disavow such a self-image. The dwarf who wears a beard and carries a cane may be using them to overcome the master-status effect of size (Truzzi, 1971). Youths sometimes take on "adult habits," such as staying out late, in order to disidentify themselves from their pre-adolescent status.

Moral Entrepreneurs

Moral entrepreneurs are people or (more often) organizations that crusade for the establishment and enforcement of definitions of deviance (Becker, 1963). For example, Mothers Against Drunk Drivers (MADD) campaigns for policies that make drunk driving a serious criminal offence and increase the conviction rates for it.

The term "moral entrepreneur" suggests that there is an economic or social stake in the rules that are proposed. The individuals involved may be honestly and deeply committed, but their work also provides them with income, recognition, or other valued results (Tucker, 1992; Lippert, 1990; 1992), and they are not regarded as neutral observers of the facts.

Allowing pornography may harm women. On the other hand, outlawing pornography may encourage other kinds of rule-breaking.

Canapress.

In *Symbolic Crusade*, Joseph Gusfield (1963) interpreted the U.S. temperance (anti-alcohol) movement as an effort by native-born, white, rural, Protestants to preserve their way of life over that of the growing majority of immigrants and urban dwellers. Prohibition in Canada followed the same pattern.[3] In both countries, the banning of alcohol was the result of political pressure exerted by an increasingly unrepresentative minority who still retained, through "old money" and connections, a disproportionate influence over government. Prohibition proved unenforceable. Breaking the law became a source of challenge and amusement. Criminal organizations provided alcohol to the rich and influential, who in turn rewarded and protected their sources. Organized crime became Big Business.

Legislation to make people behave "better" is a gamble. If enough people support it, it becomes legitimate. If it is flouted, it may encourage other kinds of rule-breaking and bring law, and law enforcement, into disrepute.

STIGMA: SOCIAL DISTANCE AND DISHONOUR

The Greek word *stigma* (plural "stigmata") originally referred to a physical sign that marked a "polluted" individual. It was an identifier that warned good citizens to avoid close contact with the person. Cuts or brands were used to identify the bearer as a slave, criminal, traitor, or other kind of unworthy person. Modern signs of stigma still include some kinds of physical differences, but also include less visible characteristics such as a criminal record or a bad reputation.

Stigma has the effect of producing social distance, which is often expressed as physical distance. Some deviants would not be acceptable to us on the same planet (child molesters, for example), while others may be tolerated at work, in the district, or even next door, as long as they do not expect to be welcomed into our personal lives (Bogardus, 1933). Social distance may also be expressed as a lack of empathy or human warmth, if physical closeness cannot be avoided. We may have to share an elevator with someone who disgusts us, but we will act as though he or she were not there.

STIGMA AND THE (SOMETIMES) SELF-FULFILLING PROPHECY

A common, but not inevitable, consequence of stigma is a spiral into increasing deviancy. When a person is convicted (in a real court, or the court of public opinion) his or her options are affected. Some jobs will be unavailable. Some friends and marriage partners will also be unavailable. The individual's sense of self may be shaken. Deviant choices become easier than "straight" ones. The stigmatizing label as "one of them" then becomes the basis for the self-fulfilling prophecy (Merton, 1949, 179–95).

Stigma does not *always* increase deviance. The threat of stigmatization, or the promise of its removal, can be a powerful motivator for change. People who consider themselves overweight sometimes engage in painful and life-threatening measures such as liposuction or stomach by-pass operations in order to meet the cultural demand for slimness. Amateur shoplifters who get caught are usually frightened into quitting, rather than pushed into full-time criminality. Addicts and alcoholics sometimes break out of the downward spiral by becoming "born again" (often through an Alcoholics Anonymous-type, "12-Step Program") into new identities.

Labelling and Secondary Deviance

Edwin Lemert (1951, 1967) was a social interaction theorist who introduced two concepts that underline the way in which the self-fulfilling prophecy works. **Primary deviation** comes from many sources. It is seen as temporary and nonrecurrent, and can even be accidental. Most people do, at one time or another, deviate: they laugh out loud in class or fail to heed a stop sign. Such lapses do not usually produce a deviant identity.

Secondary deviation, on the other hand, is caused by *sustained* societal reaction. The teacher begins to treat you as the class fool, or the court blames you for an accident and you become a criminal. Secondary deviation results from a change in social role (produced by stigma). This role is knowingly (and sometimes willingly) played by the deviant, and may even become part of a deviant self-concept. Frank Tannenbaum observed, in 1938, that part of the solution to juvenile delinquency "is through a refusal to dramatize evil. The less said about it, the better" (1938, 20).

STIGMA AND DEVIANT SUBCULTURES

Stigmatized people who cannot, or do not want to escape from their status, may find acceptance in deviant subcultures. Here their deviant record, appearance, behaviour, or attitude is a kind of membership card. Here they may also find an alternative social system, one that rewards them with respect and support. In comparison to the mainstream, these alternative systems are usually quite limited in their range of positions and paths to upward mobility. Nonetheless, the feeling of being able to "be oneself," without pretense, may make this choice worthwhile, and may help to confirm a "deviant" identity.

CONTROL THEORIES

Control theories ask "why do most people behave so well, at least most of the time?" Control theories trace their roots to Durkheim's concept of anomie and the work of the Chicago School, which blamed deviance on the social disorganization of the rapidly changing urban core. The Chicago theorists thought deviance was caused when immigration and industrialization resulted in disorder that *permitted* deviance to occur (Pfohl, 1985).

Modern social control theory is best represented by the 1960s work of Travis Hirshi. Hirshi (1969) identified four "controls" that create a bond between an individual and the rules of his or her society:

- *Attachment.* Feelings of empathy, sympathy, and sensitivity to the opinion of others. People who are not capable of this are sometimes labelled psychopaths.

- *Commitment.* Investment in the group norms, so that doing things differently would mean sacrificing something of value, such as one's status, job, or reputation.

- *Involvement.* Participation in conventional activities, which leaves little opportunity for deviant ideas or behaviour to flourish.
- *Belief.* Allegiance to the values of the group. When these bonds are strong, they contain and prevent deviance. Society may, however, not provide the environment that supports such bonds.

TECHNIQUES OF NEUTRALIZATION

When bonds exist, deviance may still occur. According to Gresham Sykes and David Matza (1957), deviants reinterpret social reality to exempt themselves from the rules that they have learned to accept. Sykes and Matza (1957) proposed five techniques of neutralization that deviants use to release themselves from compliance with norms. They may sound familiar to the reader.

- *Denial of responsibility.* "I was drunk and upset, and I come from a broken family."
- *Denial of injury.* "I was just borrowing it." "This was just a private quarrel. No harm was done."
- *Denial of victim.* "He was just a bum." "He deserved it."
- *Condemning the condemners.* "Who are you to call me bad? At least I'm not a hypocrite about it."
- *Appeal to higher loyalties.* "A guy has to stand up for his friends." "I stole only for the family."

These techniques permit deviants to engage in rule-breaking behaviour without defining themselves as bad persons. They permit delinquents to commit robbery in the street, and managers to commit fraud in the executive suite, all in more or less good conscience (Matza, 1964, 1969).

EXPLANATIONS OF DEVIANCE: CONFUSION OR CONSOLIDATION?

At this point, you may well feel that we have offered too many tentative explanations for deviance and too few real answers. The integration of all these approaches remains an ideal that is a long way off, but not as far off as it was in the demonic period. In the meantime, we continue to use these theories to guide research, and use the research findings to test the theories. Along the way we learn a great deal about "deviants," about ourselves, and about the society that we live in.

DEVIANCE RESEARCH

The study of deviance has special difficulties. Deviants protect themselves by a wide variety of defensive techniques. They are often skilled manipulators of false fronts, and their communities are often open only to those with deviant credentials and the right identifiers.

Until the late 1960s, most researchers of deviance used statistical information collected by authorities, such as school principals, police, and other public agents. These reports were often limited in their scope, and not at all representative of deviance as a whole.

In 1969, a book by Ned Polsky, *Hustlers, Beats and Others*, helped to initiate a new trend in research. Polsky argued that official statistics are biased and that data obtained from "caught" deviants are not accurate. He saw people caught up in official processes of social control (such as courts or psychiatrists' offices) as being like caged animals in the zoo. They were not representative of the people who had escaped notice. It was better to seek out the deviant in his or her "natural habitat" and study the behaviour in that setting. But this option tends to be time consuming and sometimes risky.

Several alternative approaches exist:

- *Insider reports* are books and articles written by deviants and people who hang out with them.[4] The quality of these reports varies. Some are detailed and insightful descriptions of "the path less travelled." However, the main motivation for many of these writings is access to the mass market. They romanticize, sensationalize, or even advertise. Some are elaborate efforts at self-justification; Mafia bosses, for example, come out looking like responsible, even philanthropic, businessmen.

- *Victimization reports* are data gathered from the potential victims of deviants. They can provide much information about certain kinds of deviance, since most people are willing to answer questions about whether they have been mugged, burglarized, or annoyed by others. They may not be quite so willing, however, to admit that they have been fooled by a confidence artist, or sexually molested by a family member.

- *Self-reports* are anonymous questionnaires used to find out about the kind and amount of deviance within particular groups. A researcher might ask subjects who are drug users, for example, to indicate whether they use particular drugs, how often, and whether they have ever been caught. These questionnaires are usually administered in group contexts (in a school, for example) with elaborate precautions to ensure anonymity. Even so, the questions never ask for details such as "Who is your supplier?"

Self-reports and victim studies have shown that deviance is more common than the official records indicate and that those apprehended are not a representative sample of those who offend.

. . . .

OVERVIEW

Deviance is an integral part of society because it is defined by the salient norms that regulate social life, which, in turn, are based on the core values and beliefs of the society. Deviance is not bad in itself. It is thought of as bad because it challenges the rules. Careful analysis of the actual (not just the intended) consequences of deviance reveals that it may have an important role in creating social cohesion, signalling the problems to be fixed, and helping to adapt the group to social change.

Deviance requires both specific behaviour and a label created for that behaviour by the power system of the society. To explain deviance we must explain not only the actions of the "deviant" but also the actions of those who make and apply deviant labels.

Theories of deviance are numerous. All the disciplines that study human behaviour have contributed to the analysis of deviance. Within each discipline there remains considerable debate over the relative importance of heredity, experience, social structure, and other variables. Each theory carries with it, explicitly or implicitly, a program of social control.

Many questions about the nature of deviance and control remain unanswered. Deviance research presents some special practical and moral challenges. Modern sociologists have given us some stereotype-breaking glimpses of the underworld social order, deviant subcultures, and the perspective of the deviant.

The study of deviants and deviance can help us to understand ourselves, our tolerance, and the ways in which our communities can meet the challenge of integration and regulation while preserving our security and freedom to be "a little bit different."

ASSIGNMENTS

1. Read a novel, an autobiography, or a biography that centres on murder, drug addiction, or some other form of deviance. What theory of deviance does the author use to explain motivation? (How can you recognize this?) To what extent are stereotypes of deviants used to tell the story?

2. Try an experiment such as wearing white gloves everywhere you go for several days. What do people say to you? How do they react? (Do not reveal that this is a school assignment.)

3. Scan your local newspapers for a month. How much space is devoted to deviance? (Count the words, or measure the columns.) What kinds of deviance are found on the front pages? Can you find any reports on "white collar" deviance?

SUGGESTED READINGS

Neil Boyd, *High Society: Legal and Illegal Drugs in Canada* (Toronto: Key Porter Books, 1991). This book argues that the "war against drugs" is not a public health issue, but a moral battle against the use of socially unacceptable substances. It is a sociological account of who uses drugs, why, and with what effects.

June Callwood, *The Sleepwalker: The Trial that Made Canadian Legal History* (Toronto: McClelland-Bantam Seal Books, 1991). In 1987, Ken

Parks drove to his in-laws' home, killed his mother-in-law, and seriously injured his father-in-law. His defense was that he committed the acts while sleepwalking. The book ends before the case was retried, at which time Mr. Parks was found "not guilty by reason of insanity." An honest, but journalistic, account of how the justice system works to decide who is criminally deviant and who is "sick."

Roger Caron, *Go-Boy! The True Story of a Life Behind Bars* (Scarborough, Ont.: Nelson, 1978). A grim story with an apparently "happy" ending, this book offers insight into the factors that make for deviant commitments and the ways in which other commitments can come to replace them. The author has since been charged for his participation in a series of bank robberies.

Michael Harris, *Unholy Orders: Tragedy at Mount Cashel* (Toronto: Penguin Books, 1990). This is an account of sexual abuse at a home for boys run by a lay order of the Catholic brothers. It reveals the nature of the abuse, and why it was difficult to bring the abusers to justice.

Brian Martin, *Never Enough: The Remarkable Frauds of Julius Melnitzer* (Toronto: Stoddart, 1993). An account of "white collar" crime. Reveals deviance-encouraging "weak spots" in the organization of the profession of law, and its integration with banking.

David McClintock, *Indecent Exposure: A True Story of Hollywood and Wall Street* (New York: Dell, 1982). McClintock gives a journalist's account of the story of Cliff Roberston and David Begelman, yet another scenario in which the victim gets blamed and the villain gets promoted. The book provides a clear example of why it is so difficult to nail white-collar criminals and why crime statistics seem to show that the upper classes commit fewer crimes than other groups.

James Miller, *The Passion of Michel Foucault* (New York: Simon and Schuster, 1993). A serious, but readable, book for the student who enjoys thinking about philosophy and sociology. Foucault was a leading intellect in Paris until his death, due to AIDs complications, in 1984. His methods of research included living the "limit experience" in sexual and political extremism. Foucault's work is still considered important in the field of deviance studies and criminology.

Oscar Newman, *Defensible Space: People and Design in the Violent City* (London: Architectural Press, 1972). A pioneering work on the effects of architecture on opportunities for deviance. The hypothesis is that architecture can inspire citizens to defend themselves against crime and deviance. A useful sequel is the same author's *Design Guidelines for Creating Defensible Space* (Washington, D.C.: U.S. Government Printing Office, 1975).

Clifford D. Shearing, ed., *Organizational Police Deviance: Its Structure and Control* (Toronto: Butterworth, 1981). As long as police are recruited from among human beings, the problem of how to control the controllers will exist. This book gives a revealing picture of the organizational reasons for rule-breaking by police officers.

Daniel R. Wolf, *The Rebels: A Brotherhood of Outlaw Bikers* (Toronto: University of Toronto Press, 1991). An ethnographic account of a motorcycle gang by an anthropologist who was accepted into the gang. This book discusses the contexts of the bikers' reality: the club settings, in-group relationships, and the relationships between bikers and women.

NOTES

1. The law that Morgentaler violated has since been declared unconstitutional by the Supreme Court of Canada. The government may eventually try to replace it. At the time of writing, abortion is not illegal in Canada.

2. One change was the so-called Morgentaler amendment, which restricts the power of a court of appeal to change the verdict when a jury has acquitted the accused. The court of appeal may order a retrial but may no longer set aside the jury verdict and substitute a guilty verdict. The change is considered to be an important vindication of the role of the jury, permitting it to modify the application of law when its letter conflicts with substantive justice (see Stuart, 1982).

3. In fact, the differences between the U.S. Volstead Act and the Canada Temperance Act suggest some neat meshing of economic interests. Americans could not legally sell, transport, or manufacture alcoholic beverages, but drinking them was quite legal. Most Canadians were forbidden to drink but could legally manufacture spirits and transport them for sale in some other jurisdictions. Throughout the prohibition years, many, many ships left Atlantic and Great Lakes ports with cargoes of whisky and bills of lading claiming they were bound for Mexico or the West Indies. Remarkably, the trips would take only a few days.

4. Examples include John Dean's *Blind Ambition* (1976) and David McClintock's *Indecent Exposure: A True Story of Hollywood and Wall Street* (1982).

SECTION

THREE

3

....

Power and Social Inequalities

CHAPTER

6

SIX

Social Stratification

Women survived, in Jane Austen's day, by pleasing and charming if they were in the middle classes, and by having a good, strong working back if they were of the peasantry. Writing was, incidentally, one of the very few occupations by which impoverished and helpless females of the gentry could respectably—well, more or less—earn money. To be a governess was another, much fabled, occupation. Beautiful and talented governess, handsome scion of ancient housing, marrying where he loved and not where he ought ... It was a lovely, if desperate, fantasy. (See Elizabeth and Darcy in Pride and Prejudice...)

Fay Weldon, *Letters to Alice on First Reading Jane Austen*

Hierarchy at dinner is usually enforced when a group comes from a mixture of social backgrounds. We hear a good deal about what seems to us the outrageously discriminatory practices at medieval banquets ... Special guests and the hosts of the banquet sat at the raised "high table," upon which stood a huge silver salt cellar, marking the place of the host or of an outstandingly important guest; the other people sat therefore "below the salt," and the further away from it the lower. The high-ups were deliberately given better food, and more of it.

Margaret Visser, *The Rituals of Dinner*

Think of a commonplace situation where you are meeting someone (anyone) for the first time and write down the first five questions you would ask that person other than "How are you?" or "What is your name?" Write down the questions as they come to mind without censoring them. When you are finished, read on.

Canadians like to believe that most of their compatriots are middle class (as the media suggest) and that there is only a sprinkling of others—a very few either wealthy or impoverished people. While this may be the idea that you have, your behaviour, in the form of the questions you listed, may indicate something else. The typical questions that people first ask one another are attempts, unwitting or not, to "place" people in social space, and part of that placement includes where on the social class ladder people stand. Social class is defined by sociologists according to their theoretical perspectives. The definitions, however, incorporate the idea that a **social class** is a large segment of a society made up of people who share a similar position in a hierarchy with respect to money, power, and prestige as determined by level of education and occupation; the members need not have an awareness of their commonality.

Go back to your list of questions. If you are like most students, depending on your age, your list might look like this:

Do you go to school? What program are you in?

Do you work? What kind of work do you do?

Where do you live?

What hobbies do you have?

What are you doing in a place like this?

Each of the questions can be seen as a way of probing for someone's class position. Attending school as a young adult, whether tuition is charged or not, indicates that you and/or your family can afford to forgo the salary you would be earning if you were working. In addition, going to school costs a certain amount of money (for books, transportation, and meals, for example), so not only are you lacking a salary, you are spending money as well. A person's job gives a good idea of that person's income and importance. One's area of residence points to one's position on the social ladder in that most residential areas are homogeneous as to social class; while not everyone in Rosedale, West Vancouver, or Westmount may be wealthy, place of residence gives some clue as to one's social class. People may buy homes in particular areas in order to inform others that they have "arrived." Hobbies or leisure pursuits can require spending a lot of money on equipment (wind surfing), club membership (golf), or clothing (downhill skiing). Playing hockey in the street, basketball in a public gymnasium, and football in a field are not as costly.

The point of the five-question exercise is to stress that although people may espouse very different beliefs, built into the pattern of social organization is **social inequality**, the unequal distribution of opportunities and rewards in a society. Inequality, such as that indicated by the existence of social classes, is something that informs our social interaction and becomes embodied in relationships, as the questions you have made up probably demonstrate.

In this chapter and the next one, "Minorities," the focus will be on inequality and the power—sometimes hidden, sometimes blatant—underpinning social structures. Power, the ability to have dominion over others, even against their wishes, can be derived from achieved or ascribed social statuses, from force, and from charisma. As in complicated woven baskets, the strands of power are often hard to untangle. Threads from different sources may be interwoven into dense patterns, creating systems that change over time and that overlap, compound, amplify, or counteract each other in particular social contexts. The task of sociologists is to explain how power is structured, the process by which power structures work, and the ways the structures are internalized.

SOCIAL STRATIFICATION

Social inequality and **social stratification**, which is the division of the society into strata or horizontal groups, arise from the unequal opportunity to control the acquisition and distribution of **valued goods** in a culture. A valued good must fulfil two criteria: it must be socially scarce and it must be exchanged within the public and not just the private (domestic) sphere. Although activity in each sector has repercussions for activity in the other, the domestic, private realm does not confer power or resources outside the immediate group. It does not translate into public power, prestige, or wealth. Socially valued goods are **material rewards**, such as money and **symbolic rewards**, such as power and prestige.

This distribution and acquisition system, which determines where one is positioned in the hierarchy, perpetuates itself. In this sense, it is more helpful to think of social stratification as a verb, rather than as a noun, since there is not simply a "fixed order" into which human beings are slotted by some "unseen hand." Those at the top, who are garnering the largest amount of valued goods, are able, by virtue of their power, wealth, and/or prestige, to organize the distribution system so that their place is maintained. Via socialization, the distribution rules are perceived by most people as just and "as they should be," thereby solidifying their position. The group's acceptance of the criteria and patterning of rewards can be further reinforced by ideologies, tradition, religion, security forces, or by the state with its ultimate resource, legally sanctioned violence. To the extent that the difference in rewards is a known, shared, and accepted expectation among a significant proportion of the group's members, one can describe the stratification system as institutionalized. Most Canadians expect physicians to earn more than orderlies and agree that they should earn more because of their higher expertise and the greater responsibility they carry.

EXHIBIT 6.1

Life Expectancy by Gender and Neighbourhood, 1986

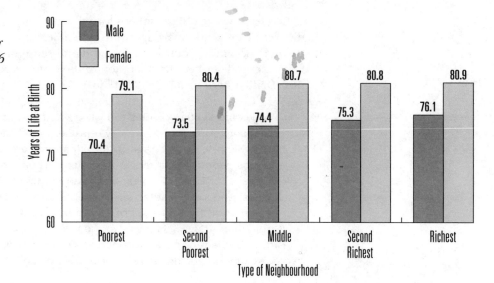

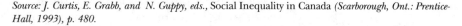

Source: J. Curtis, E. Grabb, and N. Guppy, eds., Social Inequality in Canada *(Scarborough, Ont.: Prentice-Hall, 1993), p. 480.*

A variety of criteria can be used to place individuals in the hierarchy of their society, as long as the criteria for determining placement follow a recognized pattern. Skin colour, gender, number of children (or spouses), occupation, and wealth are a few of the possible criteria.

Where one is situated at the nexus of stratification systems has a profound impact on one's existence. As an example, Exhibit 6.1 illustrates the correlations between the social class of neighbourhoods and mortality for males and females. For each sex, life expectancy is longer for those in richer, rather than poorer, neighbourhoods.

While stratification systems often appear to be immutable, contradictions can become apparent and lead people to protest and even rebel. Social movements for equal rights can arise and reconfigure power arrangements. Sociologists attempt to explain resistance to stratification rules and outcomes as well as offering analyses of conformity. The women's liberation movement, an example of this kind of challenge to the status quo, will be examined in Chapter 12, which focuses on social change.

HISTORICAL AND CULTURAL VARIATIONS IN SOCIAL STRATIFICATION SYSTEMS

CASTE SOCIETIES

India presents a clear example of a society stratified according to **caste**,[1] an inherited social rank that determines its members' lives. One is born into a caste, which is further divided into subcastes, and one lives and dies within the confines of this subcaste.

Status is ascribed. Each subcaste has a monopoly over certain occupations, and members engage in the corresponding lifestyle, the details of which are minutely prescribed. Rigid taboos forbid social interaction between members of different castes; intermarriage with a member of a lower caste results in both partners becoming "outcastes" in the literal sense of the word. Anthropologist Oscar Lewis described the operation of the caste system in Rani Khera, a village near Delhi, where he did field work in 1953:

> The caste system divides the village and weakens the sense of village solidarity. The caste generally represents a distinct ethnic group with its own history, traditions and identifications, and each caste lives in more or less separate quarters in the village. There are separate wells for the Harijans, or Untouchables; dining and smoking between members of higher and lower castes are still taboo; low-caste persons ... will not sit together on the same ... cot with a Jat or Brahman, and when government officials come to the village to explain the new community development projects, the Harijans may attend, but they stay off to one place in the audience and "know their place" (1955, 156).

The tenets of Hinduism furnish the moral sanction for the caste system. The doctrine of continuous reincarnation holds that, provided one conscientiously carries out the duties of one's caste position, one may hope for elevation to a higher caste in a future life. Conversely, failure in one's obligations may result in being reborn in a lower caste or even as an animal. The belief system makes no provision for movement or mobility between castes during one's lifetime, even though exceptional individuals may, in fact, move.

As long as such a system is widely accepted as morally right, it provides stability for the society as a whole. On the other hand, since positions are allocated by ascription, the talents of individuals may not fit the tasks they are called upon to perform. Socialization from birth is an important mechanism in directly preparing people for their future roles. Individuals know what is expected of them; they are not under constant pressure to better themselves, as are members of a society such as Canada's, in which upward mobility is possible and seen as desirable. But people born into occupations for which they have neither interest nor aptitude are likely to become bitter and frustrated.

A caste system suggests a commitment to tradition that makes it difficult to bring about change. An example is the Indian government's continuing battle to curb population growth, a problem shared with many Third World countries. Use of birth control is resisted because it prevents the prestige and security of an old age associated with having many children, especially sons, a preference that adult women have as well. Gender status can be limiting within a caste. Commenting on studies of Indian (caste) society, Caplan notes:

> Although the dominant ideological norms of both Hinduism and Islam can only be followed by the upper castes and classes, women are relegated, ideologically at least, to the domestic sphere—the private rather than the public; the reproductive rather than the productive. Women's work in this sphere, as has been frequently and forcibly pointed out, is not only unpaid, but is usually devalued too (1985, 11).

In placing societies on a continuum from "open" to "closed" according to an individual's ability to move up and down the stratification ladder, a caste society is nearest to the closed pole. But it is not completely static because castes and subcastes are differentiated internally. Some members of the same subcaste may be much better off than others, so that there is some room, at least, to improve one's condition.

ESTATE SOCIETIES

Estate societies were the prevalent form of social organization in Europe in the Middle Ages and until the beginning of the modern era. Membership in an estate was hereditary (and therefore ascribed).[2] The main divisions were the nobility, the clergy, and the peasantry; the peasantry included both free peasants and serfs. The latter were tied to the land and in many respects "belonged" to the landowner, who himself might hold his land through several levels of fealty in the complex web of rights and obligations that constituted the feudal system. Since each estate comprised a variety of occupations and socioeconomic levels, mobility within an estate was easier than mobility between estates. Some premium was placed on individual ingenuity and achievement, however, as demonstrated by the law that a runaway serf who remained undetected for a year and a day was to be set free.

In the later medieval period, more people were attracted to the burghs (towns) that sprang up around castles. Within these burghs arose clusters of artisans, merchants, and professionals. Some of these individuals became wealthy and aspired to partake in the privileges reserved for the nobility.

Members of each estate were governed by different laws, which set out their rights and obligations. These laws, which varied considerably from place to place, impinged on every aspect of daily living. In her work on the fourteenth century, Barbara Tuchman recounts a few of them:

> Proclaimed by criers in the county courts and public assemblies, exact gradations of fabric, color, fur trimming, ornaments, and jewels were laid down for every rank and income level. Bourgeois might be forbidden to own a carriage or wear ermine, and peasants to wear any color but black or brown. Florence allowed doctors and magistrates to share the nobles' privilege of ermine, but ruled out for merchants' wives multicolored, striped, and checked gowns, brocades, figured velvets, and fabrics embroidered in silver and gold (1978, 19).

In estate societies as in caste societies, formal and informal rules regulate the interaction of individuals located in different strata.

Moral justification for the estate system in medieval Europe was provided by the Roman Catholic Church, to which virtually everyone belonged. It taught that God had assigned each person's station on earth, and that everyone had a duty to live within the rights and obligations attached to this station. To the extent that the populace accepted these teachings, the motivation for individuals to seek change in their own condition was minimized.

Moreover, those in power used every means at their disposal to resist changes to a system that granted them such a disproportionate share of societal rewards. Dominant groups generally have the power to block legislative and economic changes that they define as disadvantageous to themselves. They are also able to shape ideologies. In the estate societies of Europe, the belief system stressed the importance both of tradition and of life in the hereafter. Between these poles, the way people existed in the here-and-now was de-emphasized, and change was made difficult. Patriarchy continued to hold sway. This "rule by the father or male head of household" was upheld by law, ideology, and religious and family institutions.

Although the balance of rights and prerogatives clearly favoured the superior group, its members had certain obligations toward inferior groups, as reflected by the term *noblesse oblige* ("privilege entails responsibility"). The nobles had some responsibility for those who lived on their land: to succour orphans, the sick, and the aged; to provide protection from marauders and unfriendly armies; to hold local courts; and to sponsor various publicly used lands and buildings.

CLASS SOCIETIES

The feudal estate system gradually disintegrated because it could not meet the needs of the burgeoning, industrializing society. Two important needs were a labour force that was geographically mobile (able and willing to move where

Class society necessitated a geographically mobile workforce and strictly economic employer–employee relationships.

Ramses Temple.

work opportunities were available) and strictly economic employer–employee relationships, untinged by tradition or sentiment.

By the late eighteenth and early nineteenth centuries—the era when sociology was founded—western society was stratified, as it is today, by classes. In the classic Marxian definition, class membership is based on strictly economic criteria. What class one belongs to is defined by one's relationship to the means of production, in other words, by whether one is an owner or a wage earner. As we have pointed out, in analyzing class membership, sociologists also consider factors such as prestige and lifestyle, as well as attending to how variables like education and attitudes interact with social class.

Membership in a class is not hereditary, though the position held by the family into which one is born significantly affects one's life chances. Insofar as status is predominantly achieved, mobility is possible.[3] Individuals who are exceptionally gifted (and lucky) can indeed go from rags to riches. Professional athletes and movie stars provide outstanding examples. Many well-known political figures—for example, John Diefenbaker, Margaret Thatcher, Brian Mulroney, and Jean Chrétien—had humble beginnings. But numerous studies (Rogoff, 1953; Tepperman, 1975; Warner et al., 1963) have shown that a much more common pattern is one of gradual movement: the able and determined children of working-class parents receive a higher education and become nurses, teachers, or administrators, and sometimes lawyers, architects, or physicians. The movement from manual worker to full professional frequently spans two or more generations.

Not everyone in a **class society** experiences mobility, however, not even in North America, where the ideology assumes a completely open society.

According to the tenets of this system, there is equality of opportunity; whether individuals improve their positions and how far and how fast they move is a function of ability and motivation. This ideology, as was discussed in Chapter 3, ignores structural barriers, such as regional variations in educational and economic opportunities, as well as the effects of the social characteristics of race, ethnicity, and gender.

Because the ideology of the class system is validated by the success of the few, the many who are unable to surmount the obstacles facing them tend to attribute their failure to personal shortcomings. Hence, they are less likely to challenge the prevailing system. Think of a race in which the contestants have different starting points. Theoretically, everyone can reach the finish line, but what entails merely routine effort from the front runners demands extraordinary qualities from those at the back. Thus, the architect's child does not have to sprint as far to the finish line of a law degree as does the labourer's. Yet if the latter does not reach his goal, he may blame himself rather than the conditions of the race.

In industrialized societies, it is assumed that optimum utilization of human resources is a prerequisite for general well-being and progress. Hence, it is seen as crucial that key societal positions be filled by the most able individuals, regardless of their ascribed status. To the extent that this ideal is achieved in practice, our "open" class society offers its members an opportunity to fulfil their potential, thus benefiting themselves and the group as a whole. However, there is a wide gap between what ought to be and what is. An example is provided by a respondent in a study of postwar German immigrants who reported that her father was returning to Germany because "he could not attain the goal he had set himself here. It was just too large" (Lundy, 1972). Recall the discussion in Chapter 4 on the role of the media in fuelling such frustration by bombarding the public with success images.

In class societies, such as Canada and the United States, people are differentiated mainly according to economic criteria. However, there also exist categoric divisions usually associated with caste societies, which cannot be breached by the abilities and efforts of individuals. Historically, and to some extent even today, some of the most important of these divisions have been based chiefly on race. Being nonwhite has meant fewer opportunities on all fronts, a fact of life of which blacks in the American south have been only too aware: "It takes a lot of preparing before you can let a child loose in the white world. If you're black in Louisiana it's like cloudy weather; you just don't see the sun much," a respondent told Robert Coles, a psychiatrist who was doing research on the first black children to attend racially integrated schools (1964, 337).

In Canada, too, nonwhites generally and native peoples in particular have been consistently disadvantaged. Because the majority of native Indians and Inuit live on reserves or in remote communities, many Canadians have been unaware of just how severe these disadvantages are. Doing participant observation research in a northwestern Ontario railway town, Stymeist found:

> The economic and social position of Native people in Crow Lake has not changed significantly over the years. Although greater numbers have settled in town, secured jobs there and intermarried, for most

Historically (and currently) being non-white has meant fewer opportunities on all fronts.

NA. 742.3/Courtesy Glenbow Archives.

Indians Crow Lake is still just a place to trade, to buy automobiles, outboard motors, guns, axes, boats or clothing ... In Crow Lake Indians are still regarded as outsiders, as people who have no real place in the community (1975, 64).

THEORIES OF STRATIFICATION

THE FUNCTIONALIST PERSPECTIVE AND ITS CRITICS

In our discussion of various perspectives within sociology in Chapter 1, we noted that functionalists view society as an integrated system of interdependent parts, which all make some contribution to the workings of the system as a whole. The central question posed by functionalists is, how do societies remain stable and persist over time? What captures their interest is continuity rather than change, and this leads them to concentrate on those mechanisms that achieve consensus, rather than on what provokes conflict.

The functionalist approach to stratification, then, centres on what contribution the universally apparent phenomenon of inequality makes to the maintenance of social order and survival. The crux of their answer is that unequal distribution of income, prestige, and power provides incentives to ensure that people are available to assume society's most vital tasks. Rewards, they argue, are necessary as motivating factors, to bring forth the abilities and the hard work that are required to carry out these tasks. It is assumed that if such rewards were not forthcoming, a pool of talent would not be available, and the appropriate distribution of people in whatever division of labour the social system called for would not occur. According to this view, an individual would hardly be willing to undertake a long and arduous program of medical education without the assurance of ultimately receiving a higher income and higher prestige than, say, a postal clerk.

This view, of which Kingsley Davis (1908–) and Wilbert Moore (1914–) are well-known exponents, has been challenged by those, such as Melvin Tumin (1919–), who argue that many variables are involved in the rankings assigned to individuals in the stratification system, and that there is no strong positive correlation between the rewards of a job and its societal importance (Davis & Moore, 1974; Tumin, 1967). Does society need rock musicians, who receive fame and fortune for the entertainment they provide? Are professional athletes more valuable than farmers? Furthermore, how does one determine the appropriate differential in rewards? To put the question differently, just how much inequality is necessary? For example, should only 20 percent of the Canadian population capture over two-thirds of the wealth generated by the country as a whole?[4]

Some of the criticism levelled at functionalist theory is that the stance appears tautological. With few exceptions, determining which positions are most critical to a society seems to lead back to the positions already highly ranked and well remunerated. The circularity is evident when one looks at gender and work. If women move into work previously staffed by men, their lower gender status diminishes the pay scale, demonstrating that the remuneration for a job cannot only be based on its function. Secretarial work, at the turn of the century, was done by men, partly because the typewriters were too heavy for women to manoeuvre. The occupation became devalued and the work relatively less well paid as the numbers of female clerical workers increased. Examining wage disparities between men and women also highlights the deficiency of the functionalist notion of equality of opportunity (Eisenstein, cited in Hale, 1990).

It is important to note that the functionalist perspective on social stratification emerged in a specific context—the United States—where the ideology of individualism and equality of opportunity stresses the value of ambition and hard work. Such an ideology assumes the absence of a rigid social system in which people are sorted mainly according to ascriptive characteristics, such as race and kinship. The social system is seen, rather, as fluid or open, allowing motivated individuals to acquire those attributes (human capital), such as education, that they need to achieve the best-rewarded positions.[5]

According to functionalism's logic, one attains the position one deserves—hard-working talented individuals succeed; those who are less motivated, capable, or persevering fall short. Conflict theorists, whose ideas are discussed below, argue that the functionalist view serves to legitimize social inequality by providing a rationale for serving and perpetuating the interests of the privileged (Dahrendorf, 1959; Poulantzas, 1978). These critics point out that inequality persists because powerful groups are able to claim the lion's share of rewards, while thwarting any attempts to change the system. The difference between the two schools is clearly a matter of emphasis; neither would argue that there is a perfect fit between talent, effort, and reward. Many theorists, including Lenski (1966), have sought to reconcile the conflict and the functionalist perspectives in order to provide a more comprehensive explanation of the way stratification systems work.

MARX AND THE CONFLICT PERSPECTIVE

In Chapter 1, we described Marx's view of how social change occurs and, specifically, of how societal forms succeed each other. A central theme of Marx's writings was inequality, which he viewed as central to capitalism. The driving force of capitalism is profit. To maximize profit workers must produce more goods for fewer rewards. This must be accomplished, in addition, without mass resistance on the part of the exploited workers in order to avoid the revolution Marx foresaw as inevitable. Some important features of capitalism are:

- The means of production—whatever is used to make the production of goods possible, such as capital (money), workshops, tools, factories—are owned by a relatively small group of entrepreneurs.

- Workers are free to sell their labour to the highest bidder and must be able and willing to move to where work is available. Hence, it is impractical to have slaves, or serfs, or people unwilling to leave the ancestral burial grounds. Wages fluctuate with supply and demand, but are always lower than the value of what the workers produce. This surplus value, or profit, accrues to the capitalists, and continues to augment their economic power.

- The maximization of efficiency and the ever-increasing accumulation of money are important social values. The church preached the New Testament's proverb that said it was easier for a camel to pass through the eye of a needle than for a rich man to get into heaven.[6] Capitalist ideology, by contrast, equates wealth with virtue.

Marx saw society as divided into two main classes. The **bourgeoisie** own and control the means of production. The **proletariat** is made up of landless labourers, who have nothing to sell but their labour. Marx and his friend and collaborator, Frederick Engels (1820–1895), were aware of internal differentiation within these classes, and of the existence of groups that did not fit into either class. However, their main focus was on the relations *between* the two main classes.

For Marx and Engels, the typical mode of production of an era—whether peasant agriculture under feudalism or factory wage labour under capitalism—and the relations of production associated with this mode underlie all other societal institutions. Thus, education, religion, culture, and law are strongly influenced by the nature of the prevailing economic system. Those who control the means of production also control the definition of what is acceptable and unacceptable, moral and immoral, desirable and undesirable. (See Chapter 5 on deviance and social control.)

At the level of the individual, this schema means that economic position is the most fateful factor of one's existence. It influences income and, therefore, where and how one can live, how long one is likely to live, and in what state of health. The head of the household's place in relation to production (that is, whether an owner, a labourer, or a free professional) affects how much and what kind of education the children receive and hence the kind of work that will be open to them.

Belonging to a class does not automatically bestow on its members awareness of their common fate and interests. Marx believed that this awareness was present among the bourgeoisie, who were a relatively small group. Despite internal differences, they were able to present a united front to outsiders and to act in support of their class interests. At first, the workers were not aware of their commonality. However, as they spent long hours herded together in factories and cramped living quarters, and shared the experience of exploitation and similar deprivations, Marx predicted that they, too, would develop consciousness of kind and become a class *for itself*. Over time, members of the proletariat would come to realize that their common interests demanded the overthrow of capitalism, and they would unite to accomplish this.

In the Marxian schema, then, class membership has an objective dimension in that it is determined by one's relationship to the means of production. But it also has a subjective dimension, **class consciousness**, which is the recognition of shared objectives with one's fellow class members, which evolves through similarity of life experience. This recognition spurs action that supports mutual interests.

WEBER'S CRITIQUE OF MARX

It is often said that the writings of Max Weber constitute a dialogue with the ghost of Karl Marx. Since the work of Marx dominated so much of later nineteenth-century thought, it was not surprising that Weber, who was 19 years old when Marx died, felt that the latter's views were something with which he had to contend. His work came to provide a significant critique of Marxian formulations, most notably of Marx's heavy emphasis on economic determinants.

Though Weber conceded that one's role in the marketplace had a fundamental effect on the degree of power one wielded in society, he maintained that this factor was not the sole basis for differentiating people. Weber viewed social power as a multifaceted phenomenon; people are sorted in a hierarchical way, on more criteria than just property, ownership, and wealth. Weber said that social inequality flowed from three interacting factors: class, status, and party.

By **class**, Weber meant essentially what Marx meant by the term: the conditions of life and the social position derived from one's relation to the processes of production in society. Weber did not underrate the significance of wealth in determining what he called the life chances of an individual. In an analysis compatible with Marx's, Weber saw economic position as influencing access to such fateful and socially valued goods as material possessions, education, health, and the opportunity of living a long life in the mainstream of society.

Weber discounted the likelihood of class consciousness, however, claiming that the existence of other sources of social power tended to obscure people's awareness of belonging to an economic interest group. Unless individuals of equal ranking—equal, that is, in wealth and property ownership—recognized their commonality and experienced it as the central feature of their life, he said, they would not tend to pursue class interests per se. Thus, he did not agree with Marx that society would become polarized into the bourgeoisie and the proletariat.

Weber also drew attention to the emergence of a range of middle classes, consisting of people who do not own extensive property but who, unlike the lower classes, have more than mere labour power to sell in the marketplace. These middle-class people may own modest businesses or small farms, or they may have valued skills gained through education and specialized training. (Falling into this latter category are, for example, lawyers, physicians, musicians, and artisans.) Weber argued that Marx's analysis of the class structure failed to place sufficient emphasis on this middle range. Weber's keen interest in bureaucracy as a key feature of modern society led him to recognize that the distribution of people throughout hierarchically ordered administrative systems provides a strong check on the simple dichotomization of classes described by Marx. (It must be remembered that during the half-century separating Marx from Weber, both the number and the size of bureaucracies had grown, creating a large group of people who comprised an intermediate class between the bourgeoisie and the proletariat.)

Weber's most important contribution to the analysis of social stratification, however, lay in his recognition that prestige or social honour—in other words, **status**—is a major source of power and influence. In turn, this power and influence can be used to attain a favourable economic or class position, thus enhancing the life chances of one's descendants. This hereditary transmission of privilege is a powerful factor in channelling social relations and in solidifying the social hierarchy. Weber recognized that class position is a factor in determining the social deference or degradation one receives, but he did not see it as the only determinant. An artist, a university president, a scientist, or a senior government official might not possess much property but could enjoy the same amount of prestige and manifest the same social comportment as the owner of a large firm. By the same token, a group of people from formerly wealthy families might continue to feel superior to a wealthier group whose riches were newly earned.

The third facet of association and social differentiation Weber identified was participation in the political sphere in groupings he referred to as **parties**. Political power constitutes an important basis of command over the resources society values. A political party may represent the interests of a particular class or status group, but this is not inevitably so. One party may draw members from several classes or status groupings.

In brief, Weber's approach to the issue of power was pluralistic in that he saw power deriving from three spheres of social life—class, status, and party. His analyses of social life and of conflict in society, more than those of Marx, took into account the complex matrix in which human interaction unfolds. Although it allowed for a certain predictability within human events, Weber's work did not allow a simplistic scenario of social change. See Gerth and Mills's discussion of Weber's approach in their *From Max Weber: Essays in Sociology* (1946).

GENDER STRATIFICATION

The many references to gender in the text so far have provided glimpses of how male dominance as an ideology works in its interplay with culture and socialization. You have already seen that boys come into the world as the preferred sex and that many more hopes are placed on them than on girls. You have learned that a potential solution to the problem lies in the reciprocal exchange of roles, with men entering the private sphere of childrearing and housework, and women being allowed more access to the public world of work. This section highlights gender as another system of stratification, one that interacts in very complicated ways with the class system. Women have access to fewer of the valued goods, in varying degrees, than men in most countries of the world. Sociologists call this system of male dominance **patriarchy**—a system that handicaps the sex that bears children. A patriarchy is a system of social stratification that ensures that biological sex differences are socially constructed so that men have more power than women. How has this sexual inequality come about and what shape does it now take?

ORIGINS OF MALE DOMINANCE

In this section, two biocultural theories, which were proposed by feminist anthropologists to account for the origins of male dominance, are discussed. Historical and anthropological research suggest that valued and important jobs are allotted to men and that whatever men do is considered positively. Furthermore, it does not matter what the task is—they vary from culture to culture and from era to era. Childrearing is one of the few social functions consistently allotted to the same sex: women. Biological explanations cannot account for these variations. For example, during the Second World War, women's "natural" characteristics of self-sacrifice and caretaking of others were used to encourage their public labour force participation in factories (Mahood, 1993). But, if "nature" were solely responsible for gender there would be little need to discuss it in the social sciences—male and female behaviour would be more fixed and immutable, and the only solution to this "natural" gender inequality would be genetic reconfiguration. Intervention on the social or "nurture" level would be ineffectual. However, since gender is socially constructed, new social relationships are possible.

The nature/culture theory of male dominance, proposed by Ortner (1974), is transhistorical. It does not make reference to a particular point in the history of a particular type of social organization. The theory is as follows. Culture is a way of interpreting, ordering, and making sense of a society's natural and social environment. Ancient Egyptians, for example, in drawing miniature versions of crops and goddesses in their wall paintings, were attempting to control natural events such as fertility and agricultural productivity. Women are aligned with nature because of their biology. Women menstruate, give birth, and lactate, events that to the uninitiated seem magical, uncontrollable, and possibly frightening. Men who seem to have no "natural" connection to these things are aligned with culture, and it follows, then, that it is up to them to exercise some control over women. In our culture we refer to "*Mother* Nature" and try to develop ways of controlling "her" power technologically. Only recently have hurricanes begun to be named after men (for example, Andrew) instead of women; the former practice confirmed this view of nature as female.

Another theory of male dominance (Friedl, 1975) focuses on valued goods and how they came to be controlled by men in hunting and gathering, and horticultural societies. The valued good in hunting and gathering societies was the meat that men obtained when hunting large game. This meat was shared among members of the group. While women may have provided up to 90 percent of the food eaten, including meat in the form of small animals, the only food-acquiring activity they did not participate in was large game hunting. Women, pregnant and/or caring for babies, were seen as not having the capacity to walk long distances for long periods of time, an activity large game hunting necessitates. Women, therefore, stayed closer to the living sites gathering the majority of the foodstuffs. Meat from large game, which was scarce and difficult to trap, was distributed by the men and shared among all members of the group. In this way men could develop alliances and form power bases for managing the society. Women distributed the food they garnered privately to members of their kin group and thus were excluded from the public power-conferring networks.

In horticultural societies, new land for crops was considered the valued good. Clearing this new land for planting might involve warring with enemy groups, and this was done by the males who appropriated the weapons technology. Women, whose childbearing was paramount in the survival of the culture, were considered too valuable to be in such potentially dangerous circumstances. The consequences of this exclusion, however, were that women had little access to the scarce and publicly shared resource of new land and that men dominated the culture (Friedl, 1975).

Joan Huber (1990) carries the theory of control of valued goods forward to account for gender stratification after industrialization by incorporating variables of ecological conditions and population. Declining infant mortality rates decreased the need for numerous births to ensure population replacement. Mass education helped make children less of an economic benefit for elderly parents as the payoff went directly to the educated offspring in the form of wages (Parsons, cited in Huber, 1990). Fewer children, who could be fed with artificial formulas, made women available for labour market participation when necessary. Huber contends that these changes in the birth rate have a positive impact on women's participation in the labour force, potentially increasing their access to public power. Currently, however, raising children limits women's work aspirations. Childcare is still seen as the mother's responsibility and the time spent in "motherwork" curtails women's availability for paid employment. These patterns are very much in flux, but attempts by women to increase their power by having husbands share in the undervalued and unpaid domestic labour are resisted. Men still "help" with the housework and "babysit" their own offspring (Luxton, 1993).

GENDER AND CLASS STRATIFICATION

Statistics Canada reports that in 1991, average earnings were $26,842 for women working full-time, while their male counterparts earned, on average, $38,567; female wages, in other words, were 69.6 percent of male wages.[7] The third annual report by the National Action Committee on the Status of Women argues that this percentage is optimistic: a comparison that includes part-time workers, more than 63 percent of whom are women, supplies the more accurate ratio of women's to men's earnings of 61.5 percent.[8]

Specific explanations for this income gap include the theory that women's "human capital," the qualifications, skills, and experience they bring to the labour market, does not equal men's; that women take more breaks in their work life (presumably to tend children), which leaves them lower on the occupational ladder; and that it is in the interest of employers to squelch rebelliousness among employees by perpetuating a class of low-paid workers (women) as possible replacements for higher-paid (male) workers. One of the most intractable problems seems to be the division of the work world into men's and women's jobs—the pink-collar ghetto versus the blue- and white-collar worlds. The range of choices open to women, although theoretically the same as those open to men, seems to narrow when one looks at actual numbers. "Women do 72 percent of the ten lowest-paying jobs and only one-fifth of the ten highest-paid."[9] Women are concentrated in the fields of clerical, service, and sales work, nursing and related health occupations, and teaching (see Exhibit 6.2.). Although between 1982 and 1989 the number of female managers and administrators more than doubled, the percentage of those in these occupations who are women remains low at 38 percent and accounts for only about 11 percent of employed women. Similarly, the number who are doctors more than doubled, making them 33 percent of all doctors. In the natural sciences, engineering, and math, women progressed from having been 15 percent of the total employed in those fields to now making up to 19 percent of the total (*Canadian Social Trends*, Autumn, 1990).

Women's income is becoming critical for family support despite the widespread and persistent notion that women's place is not in the work force. In Canada, in 1991, the poverty rate for families with two spouses would have more than doubled, going from 9.3 percent to 19.7 percent, if wives in those families had not earned wages (*Poverty Profile Update*, 1993).

Despite the necessity of their paid work, women, in addition, still do most of the work at home. In 1986, women aged 15 and older spent $2\frac{1}{2}$ hours a day on housework; men spent 1 hour. On a typical day, 85 percent of women do housework, compared with 52 percent of men (*Canadian Social Trends*, Spring, 1990). Exhibit 6.3 shows the percentages of women and men who do selected household chores. In all categories more women do the work. Women are over $1\frac{1}{2}$ times as likely to prepare meals; over $2\frac{1}{2}$ times as likely to clean up after meals; and $3\frac{1}{2}$ times more likely to clean the house than men (*Canadian Social Trends*, Spring, 1990).

Partially because paid employment is still not seen as essential for women, their work is devalued and underrewarded. Wolf (1990) has argued provoca-

EXHIBIT 6.2

Employed Women, by Occupational Group, 1982 and 1989

	Total women employed (000s)		Percent of employed women		Percent of employed men	Women as percent of total employment in sector	
	1982	1989	1982	1989	1989	1982	1989
Clerical	1,488	1,680	33.9	30.5	5.9	79.0	80.4
Service	802	938	18.3	17.0	10.3	54.5	56.7
Sales	445	543	10.1	9.9	9.0	39.8	46.4
Nursing/related health occupations	389	472	8.9	8.6	1.2	85.1	85.4
Teaching	248	306	5.7	5.6	2.2	64.3	66.1
Managerial/administrative	262	589	6.0	10.7	13.7	29.2	38.1
Other professionals:							
Social science	82	125	1.9	2.3	1.3	47.5	57.1
Natural science/engineering/mathematics	56	88	1.3	1.6	5.3	14.7	19.2
Diagnostic/treatment health professions	12	25	0.3	0.5	0.7	18.3	33.3
Others	89	135	2.0	2.5	2.8	34.5	41.0
Primary	122	121	2.8	2.2	6.7	19.5	20.5
Processing/machining	85	102	1.9	1.8	7.7	14.1	15.9
Product fabricating/assembling/repairing	193	231	4.4	4.2	11.7	21.2	22.0
Construction	8	16	0.2	0.3	10.4	1.4	2.2
Transportation	24	40	0.5	0.7	6.1	6.0	8.6
Material handling/crafts	77	97	1.8	1.8	4.9	19.5	22.2
Total	4,382	5,508	100.0	100.0	100.0	41.3	44.1

Source: Statistics Canada, Canadian Social Trends *(Autumn, 1990), p. 23. Reproduced by authority of the Minister of Industry 1994.*

tively that women are valued for their physical attractiveness to men, and this concentration of energy, time, and resources on outward appearance diverts them from attaining power. In addition, competitiveness and assertiveness are not viewed as "nice" for women and may even jeopardize their success with men. The demand that women be admired and accepted by men offers a microcosmic example of how women are kept in their place, reinforcing other forms of social inequality. Emotional, psychological, and physical violence against women in the form of sexual harassment on the street or at work, rape, and wife beating also contribute to female subordination.

FEMINIST CRITIQUES: MINGLING STRATIFICATION THEORIES
Feminist sociologists, seeing gender as a hierarchy based on biological sex, were the first to elucidate the problem of introducing gender to conventional sociological theories of power and inequality.

Stratification theories, like many others, have been based on men and on their work lives. Women were not seen to be all that different, if they were "seen"

EXHIBIT 6.3

Primary Responsibility for Work around the House among Couples Aged 15–64 with Children Under Age 19, 1990

Household chore and type of couple	Total[1]	Primary responsibility			
		Wife only	Husband only	Wife and husband equal	Other[2]
Meal preparation					
Dual-earner, both full time	100	72%	13%	12%	2%
Dual-earner, wife part time[3]	100	86	7	6	—
Single-earner, husband full time	100	89	5	5	—
Meal clean-up					
Dual-earner, both full time	100	59	16	15	6
Dual-earner, wife part time[3]	100	72	9	10	3
Single-earner, husband full time	100	78	7	8	3
Cleaning and laundry					
Dual-earner, both full time	100	74	7	13	3
Dual-earner, wife part time[3]	100	86	4	6	—
Single-earner, husband full time	100	86	4	7	—
House maintenance and outside work					
Dual-earner, both full time	100	7	79	4	9
Dual-earner, wife part time[3]	100	9	80	3	6
Single-earner, husband full time	100	8	77	5	9

[1] *May not add to 100 due to rounding and the exclusion of Not Stated.*
[2] *Someone other than the wife or husband has primary responsibility for the chore.*
[3] *In this type of couple, the husband works full time.*

Source: Statistics Canada, 1990 General Social Survey.

at all. Feminist scholarship first focused on married women who were difficult to position in the class system, as their status was connected with that of their hus-band's, the putative breadwinner. Later, increasing numbers of women in the paid labour force, including those who were married and had young children, had to be included in stratification analysis. So did housework. Feminists, however, as we've said, are not all of a piece. In their investigation of women's oppression, some point to the patriarchal system; others see class stratification as central. In this section we have tried to encapsulate the various positions.

In stratification analysis women were not seen to be all that different from men—if they were "seen" at all.

Jake Peters.

Initial attempts to include women in the discussion of power looked at women as a caste, as a class by itself, or as a minority (Eichler, 1973). While each form of analysis had some merit, there were problems with all of them. Unlike caste members, women are not endogamous, with strong rules prohibiting marriage outside the caste—women marry men. Women cannot be seen as a separate class, in which all women hold the same class position. Wage-earning women differ from those who don't earn wages; married female wage earners differ from their nonmarried counterparts; and unpaid "housewives" differ from both. Minority group theory (more of which will be discussed in the next chapter) posits that a particular group is deprived of power by being unfairly treated and consequently comes to define itself negatively. Many of these negative self-conceptions inherent in minority relations are lacking in women. Finding the constructs of class and minority inadequate, Eichler postulated the concept of "personal dependents" to apply to housewives and all women with no independent source of income. Their relationship with their "personal master" is characterized by a lack of group consciousness and identification; gratitude and submission to the master; indirect and manipulative means of control in the absence of real control; and negative self-image.

The concept of class has been expanded to encompass gender, but critics claim this is mere tinkering (Hanmer & Maynard, 1987). Functionalist theory can accommodate women by slotting them on the basis of their paid labour market participation, but this leaves women's work as mothers and houseworkers unaccounted for. Only recently has the unpaid private labour that women perform been acknowledged and made visible (Luxton, 1980). Housework and "motherwork" make a huge contribution to the economy. Statistics Canada has estimated that housework is worth anywhere from 159 billion to 198 billion dollars, or 30 to 40 percent of the gross domestic product.[10] Women socialize their children to accommodate themselves to the vagaries of the economic system; they tend, emotionally and physically, to the needs of their husbands and children, enabling them to be productive in school or on the job; they care for aging and ailing relatives. Galbraith (1973) comments that with the gradual rise of consumption and the loss of personal servants after the Industrial Revolution, "convenient social virtue" became attached to women's work in the home to construct a class of "crypto servants," in other words, wives available democratically to all male members of the population.

How do theorists conflate this nonremunerated labour with the stratification heirarchy? Wives can be seen as serfs and their husbands as feudal lords (Benston, 1990, 292); they can be regarded as cheap labour reimbursed with household spending money (Seaccombe, cited in Hale, 1990); and they can and have been viewed as a reserve army of labour prepared to go in and out of the labour market as the economy necessitates (Armstrong, & Armstrong, 1984). Solutions to this double burden for women involve variations on the ideas of bringing them into the paid public economy with wages for housework (Dalla Costa & James, cited in Hale, 1990), and moving private work in the home into the paid labour force (Benston, cited in Hale, 1990).

Reaching back in history to the initial stages of western civilization can help explicate the ties between sex and class (Muszynski, 1989). Greek men in the Athenian polis or public state forged a social space in which a small handful of them came to be described and treated as citizens with power over women and all other men. This public realm necessitated the creation of an opposing private domain where the basic requirements of living were attended to. Thus, the state and patriarchy arose simultaneously, and the vision of the world as made up of polar opposites, the "bifurcated consciousness," aligned women with the private and natural, resulting in their powerlessness (Smith, 1987). Slaves, the other subjugated group in this society, prepared the field for the modern class divisions of bourgeoisie and proletariat. Other stratification systems, like race (discussed in the next chapter), slid into place with the same apparent ease. This social construction of gender, class, and race, created and sustained in the daily activities of men and women, lies hidden beneath taken-for-granted and conventional claims of the inherent inferiority of the disadvantaged.

GENDER AND POWER—THE EXAMPLE OF RAPE

The idea that rape is about power, not sex, may be familiar to many of you. What you may be unaware of, however, is the radical change in the explanations of rape in the past two decades and the part sociologists played in reframing the debate.

Initial explanations of rape focused on the male perpetrator, in the search for psychopathological causes of what was considered aberrant behaviour. The theoretical spotlight then moved to the victim, searching unsuccessfully for clues in her behaviour and/or personality that provoked the attack. Current research, stimulated in large part by feminist perspectives, is moving to an analysis of patriarchal, social, and cultural forces that allow sexual assault to thrive.

Rape, forced sexual intercourse, lies at the end of the continuum of sexual violence perpetrated by men against women. **Rape** occurs when a woman

> makes it clear, either verbally or non-verbally that she does not want sexual involvement at that time. The man has two choices in responding to this decision. He can accept the woman's feelings and respect her decision, revising his own actions. On the other hand, he can ignore her feelings and her decision and force her to participate. Whether he uses direct or indirect threats; whether he has manipulated her psychologically or physically coerced her, he has assaulted her (Pettifer & Torge, 1982, 30).

As the definition indicates, the intent of the rapist is to ignore the victim's desires and to render her powerless and defenseless. Sex is the vehicle used to humiliate, and control. Claiming that rape is about sex is like describing hitting someone with a frying pan as cooking!

Cultural beliefs about rape are potent contributors to the common view of rapes as rare events carried out by crazy male strangers on women who, in some way, invite and deserve the rape. While incidents of sexual assault are notoriously difficult to measure, the figures cannot be seen to support those claims. Canadian sources indicate that one woman in four is sexually abused by the age of 16 and that two women in three are victims of unwanted sexual acts.[11] Rapes committed by persons unknown to the victims account for only 16 percent of rapes.[12] American data suggest that the actual number of rapes is anywhere from six to ten times higher than estimates show and that women are up to four times more likely to be raped by someone they know than by a stranger (Koss, 1992). One suspected reason for the underreporting is that familiarity with her attacker may lessen a woman's willingness to report the rape.

Brownmiller, in her pioneering work, *Against Our Will* (1975), was the first to catalogue and dissect the rape myths, showing that the crux of rape is power. These myths portray women as inhuman sex objects who are the property of men and have no right to refuse any man's sexual advances. Myths "explain" the assailant—he's driven by lust; is crazy or perverted; is not white; and/or is lower class. Many more pertain to the victim—she deserves to be raped; she provokes the rape; she lies about having been raped; she is (further) sullied by being raped; and she's a "loose woman" to begin with.

These myths themselves function as ideological reinforcements of male dominance by blaming the victims and obscuring the fact that rapists are ordinary men. As a cluster, they reinforce traditional, even stereotypical, female behaviour and fortify the double standard of sexuality that serves to suppress women's freedom and reinforce male privilege and power.

One of the corollaries of male dominance is that men are able to define social phenomena. Such is the case with rape. With the greater power the gender stratification system allows them, men reinforce their superior positions and their spheres of control. Merely linking the terms "masculinity" and "violence," thereby affirming that men are the more violent sex and are more likely to perpetrate violence, causes resistance (Miedzian, 1991). Rape, however, is not gender neutral. Ninety-eight percent of sexual assaults are committed by men; 90 percent of the victims of sexual assault are women and children.[13]

What makes men rape? It is assumed by many that men are biologically geared to be more violent than women because of their sex hormones, androgen in particular. Women, with much lower levels of this substance, will not be as violent. While it may be the case that male hormones provide the biological background for male violence, cultural support in the form of the idea that "boys will be boys" reinforces whatever biological potential exists. Rape is socially determined. The socialization process in early childhood encourages dominance for males and submission for females, thereby preparing the ground. As we have seen, boys are raised to be "in charge" and assertive, at best not to listen to women, and at worst to be misogynists. Think about the epithet "wimp" and what it implies. Rarely is this term used for females. Hetereosexual sexual socialization demands that young males try to get as much sexual experience as possible and that, although "nice" girls will say "no" to sexual overtures, promises of commitment can coax them to overcome their unwillingness. But, instead of being alerted to this danger from the boys they know, young females are mistakenly advised to be wary of male sexual aggression from strangers. They learn that they are responsible for men's sexual behaviour and are the gatekeepers to sexual activity. If men are not attracted to a particular woman, she is told she is not trying hard enough or is not attractive enough. If she is "too" attractive and he is sexually aggressive, it is also her fault. Because women are not the ones in control, focus is put on their ability to avoid rape more than on masculine aggression.

In a recent article, Shotland (1992) formulates a typology of five kinds of date rape that arise at different stages of courtship. Beginning date rapes occur during one of the first dates the couple has. These rapists are characterized as sexually experienced, interested in new sexual involvements, and misogynistic believers in the rape myths. Date rapists who attack after a few dates imagine sexual intent on the part of others when none exists. Correcting the misperception, however, does not stop them. Relational date rape happens when the couple is established but has not had sexual intercourse. These attackers perceive themselves to be less powerful than the women they're with and feel that the situation must be rectified. They view sex and love as synonymous, are sexually conservative, and believe the old-time movie version of rape, that women coerced into sexual activity come to love it. The last two of the five categories attempt to describe rape in sexually active couples; they are distinguished from one another by the presence or absence of battering with the rape. Both types of rapist share patriarchal attitudes. They see women as sexual possessions. Nonbattering rapists seek to regain control by raping. Those who batter in addition to raping use violence as a method of control even in nonsexual situations and employ the violence and sex to humiliate and overpower their partners.

Shotland's study illustrates one of three factors associated with rape: rape-supportive views held by males. These men believe that men should have control in relationships, and that sex is owed them by their partners. They may also be controlling and possessive. They disregard the opinions and feelings of females, and believe both that men are the bosses and women must be submissive.[14]

Internalization of the rape myths may be fostered by mass media that act as agents of socialization for sexual relationships (for example, rock videos, which are discussed in Chapter 4, "Socialization"). Hollywood movies show a rape in one out of eight films, and studies on college students (both male and female) show that portrayals of sexual violence like those in slasher films, fosters callousness toward victims of rape (Linz, Wilson, & Donnerstein, 1992).

Producers of other mass media, too, fall prey to the pervasive and resilient myths. In analyzing newspaper coverage of rape cases, Benedict (1992) shows that the alleged victims are portrayed as either "virgins" or "vamps," depending upon how well their personal characteristics and the process of the rape bring the myths into play. If the victim is young and pretty; knows her attacker; if there is no weapon used in the attack; if the victim and perpetrator are the same race, ethnicity, and class; and if the woman is breaching any traditional female behaviours, she becomes a "vamp" and press coverage becomes biased against her.

Supportive peers are a second contributory factor to rape. Sexually aggressive men believe that physical force is sexually arousing. Their like-thinking peers agree that it's legitimate to get a woman drunk and to use force or verbal threats to coerce her into sex. They believe that women can resist it if they really want to.

Alcohol, the third variable associated with sexual aggression, serves as a disinhibitor. Men who might otherwise feel guilty in raping use alcohol to quell their misgivings. It allows them to plead irresponsibility, a claim that further reinforces the myths.

In 1983, Canadian Criminal Code legislation changed the legal definition of rape, reflecting the reorientation of rape as assault. Instead of being defined as penetration of the penis in the vagina, rape became sexual assault measured by the severity of violence and trauma suffered by the victim. Two sections in the code were designed to combat juridical bias deriving from the myth that women are responsible for being raped, particularly if they are not virgins. These provisions prevented women's sexual history and reputation from being presented as part of the court proceedings in a rape trial. In 1991, one of these sections, dubbed the "rape-shield" provision, was quashed by the Supreme Court, which contended that the rape-shield provision might jeopardize alleged rapists' rights to a fair trial.

The ideology of male dominance has been recognized as a potent contributor to the prevalence of rape in Canada. Material conditions that leave women less economically powerful than men also play a part. More work has to be done on the social level, in order to pinpoint the historical progressions and social contexts that lead to rape. Microlevel research is needed to distinguish male rapists from other males and, without blaming them, to determine dissimilarities, if any, among rape survivors.

OBSCURING INFLUENCES IN MODERN CLASS SOCIETY

Over the last two centuries, industrialization and urbanization have consolidated the hold that economic class maintains as a pre-eminent cause of stratification in North American society. Canadian policies to redistribute income through the taxation and social welfare systems are attempts to reduce inequality and thus to reshape societal stratification. They have been only marginally successful, yet Canadians describe themselves overwhelmingly as middle class. Sociologist W.I. Thomas (1863–1947) noted long ago, "It is not important whether or not the interpretation is correct—if men define situations as real, they are real in their consequences" (Thomas & Swaine, 1928, 572). One important result of Canada's being defined as essentially a middle-class society is the belief by much of the populace that this is in fact the case. The ideology of equal opportunity is so powerful, and the image that Canadians have of themselves as "middle class" is so strong, that the identification by social scientists of inequality of condition, resulting in and arising from inequality of opportunity, makes few dents in these beliefs.

Classes are more than artifacts of definition, since differences in lifestyle, behaviour, and attitude are associated with membership in a class. In the work world, for example, nonverbal communication replicates the gender and class hierarchy on the microlevel of social interaction. Nurses defer to doctors, reveal more personal information about themselves, and are referred to by first names. Doctors are called "Doctor" and treated with great respect (Goffman, 1990). Asymmetrical forms of address are common in other settings as well.

Class boundaries are obscured, however, by factors that cut across class lines and serve to homogenize, at least superficially, the bulk of Canadian society. As was illustrated in Chapter 4, the mass media create mass markets with mass advertising. As early as 1975, Canadian sociologist Wallace Clement explicated the ideology of consumerism, promoted in the mass media, whereby the economic elite consolidated their power over "consumers," in other words, the entire population (Clement, 1975). This ideology functions by selling us solutions to problems that the media advertisers themselves have created. Consumers are led to believe that happiness depends on the supply of goods and services, fostering a similarity of outlook among all (Galbraith, 1973). Energy that might be used to question the status quo is diverted via consumption. The price of this "indoctrination" is subsidized by the consumer, as a large proportion of the price of an item is the cost of the advertising.

The consumption of many goods that are fundamentally alike, if varying in quality, veils class differences. Most of the time, you probably do not encounter people who look vastly different from yourself. In all strata, jeans and running shoes are the uniform of the young. Cheaper versions of high fashion filter down quickly. Within hours of Princess Diana's wedding, Londoners were able to buy facsimiles of her dress. The juxtaposition of obvious, abject poverty and ostentatious wealth is more muted in Canada than, say, in Rio de Janeiro, where shanty towns overlook the luxurious Copacabana Beach. Much of the severe poverty in Canada is hidden in rural areas and remote native reserves. Recently, however, increasing numbers of homeless persons in our cities demonstrate that poverty is a serious problem in Canada. While the poverty rate, the proportion of poor individuals in a particular category, has declined since its peak in the mid-1980s, rates rose again in 1990 with another recession.

Another important levelling influence is mass education (examined in depth in Chapter 10). Except for the relatively small proportion who attend private schools, Canadian children experience prolonged exposure to essentially similar schools. Variations in curricula and in the availability of such facilities as computers and audiovisual equipment are connected with differences in school systems and regions, rather than with class differences. Within schools, students meet youngsters and teachers with social backgrounds different from their own. This homogenization has been weakened by the exodus to the suburbs of the middle class, which has increased residential segregation and reduced opportunities for the mixing of social classes within schools. The controversial bussing program in the United States was designed to counteract the effects of such residential segregation along racial lines. Recently, however, there has been a return of middle-class families to inner-city neighbourhoods, as in Toronto's Cabbagetown and Vancouver's Kitsilano, increasing the chances of "mixed" classrooms.

As we will discuss in greater detail in Chapter 10, "Education: Winning and Losing," students from different class origins do not fare equally in the schools. For the moment, we are emphasizing the commonality of going to school for many years, of being expected to complete specified tasks on time, and of attending assemblies, sports days, and school dances.

SOCIAL MOBILITY: CHANGING PLACES

As we have noted, one of the characteristics that distinguish types of societies is their degree of openness—that is, the extent to which there is movement up and down the hierarchy. Here, we will examine this concept of mobility more closely. First, a cautionary note: conceptions of mobility share the myopia of stratification theories. They have been articulated on the basis of the work lives of (white) men and best reflect that world; other members of the population may not find themselves as well represented.

Vertical mobility refers to movement up and down a hierarchy. Since occupational and social position are closely linked within Canadian society, mobility generally means occupational mobility. Workers who are laid off, whose jobs disappear, as in the fisheries in Newfoundland, usually become downwardly mobile. Those who retrain and subsequently attain higher-level positions are upwardly mobile. For women, mobility has typically come through marriage. The secretary who marries her boss is considered to have moved up. Women, then, derive their status from their husband's as well as from their own independent position in the labour force. In the interplay of derived and independent status, care is usually taken that the husband's position remains paramount—maintaining his "head of the household" status (Eichler, 1973). Women in professional positions may prefer that their salaries be lower than their husbands'.

Vertical mobility can be divided into **intergenerational mobility** (from one generation to the next) and **intragenerational** (career) **mobility** (within one generation). A lawyer whose father was a plumber has experienced intergenerational mobility. If he starts as an associate in a large law firm and becomes a partner, he has also moved up intragenerationally—within his own work life. Intragenerational mobility need not take place within the same occupation. For instance, a nurse may retrain as a lawyer. Intergenerational downward mobility is exhibited by the executive's son who becomes an unskilled cleaner. The teacher who has an alcohol problem, is dismissed, and drifts into casual work is downwardly mobile within her career.

Intergenerational mobility is difficult to measure accurately because the occupational structure itself changes and because the parents and also the child may experience career mobility. Sociologists have traditionally treated movement from blue-collar or farm occupation to white-collar occupation as upward mobility (Rogoff, 1953). This assumption may have to be re-examined in light of the significant income gains made by unionized blue-collar workers and the narrowed scope of the lower-echelon, white-collar labour force, which, significantly, is made up mainly of poorly paid women (Lowe, 1981).

Women, even those in higher positions in the workforce, face problems like sexual harassment that most men do not have to contend with. Their double responsibility for home and work limits the time, crucial for advancement into high-level positions, that they can spend doing work. The after-hours socializing that informally leads to promotions is also less possible, particularly if this socializing occurs in men's locker rooms. If there are few women in the upper reaches of the enterprise, sponsors to pull the employee up may be lacking. Men are more likely to want to sponsor "people like them," in order to continue their line in the organization. Fewer women at the top leads to their being seen, and with this visibility comes the unsolicited spotlight that scrutinizes even their personal relationships (Kanter, 1977).

Horizontal mobility is exhibited when a person moves among jobs that are at roughly the same level. For example, someone in car sales may switch to selling real estate, a bank teller may become a clerk typist, or a nurse may retrain and practise physiotherapy.

Geographic mobility is frequently a necessary condition for moving up. To get a better job—or even any job—people come to North America from Europe and Asia; others move from rural areas to the city, or from one region of the country to another. In Canada since Confederation, this movement has been predominantly westward, from the Atlantic provinces to central and western Canada. During the heady years of the oil boom in the 1970s, Alberta was seen as the promised land.

Structural mobility is brought about by changes in the economy that either facilitate or constrict opportunities for occupational advancement. In industrialized societies, technology helps to eliminate many menial and routine jobs—for example, loading and unloading heavy cargo—and creates a host of new, higher-level ones. When economic activity expands more quickly than the population, structural mobility occurs.

The most recent and dramatic technological developments have been computer-related. Programmers and analysts are needed for this work, as well as technicians to service the sophisticated hardware and software, and all these tasks must be coordinated by skilled personnel. The reliance on computers has led to changes in the nature of certain jobs as well. With computers doing much of the work, as with supermarket cashiers, certain jobs are becoming fragmented, "deskilled" and highly monitored. Others, such as bank tellers and line workers in car assembly plants, are being replaced.

Demographic trends are important here. Historically, industrialization has been accompanied by lower fertility rates, a decrease that has become much sharper with the availability of reliable birth control. Smaller family size has been positively correlated with socioeconomic status. Put simply, those on the top tend to have fewer children than those at the bottom, as noted in the adage "the rich get richer and the poor get children." This has the effect of increasing structural mobility. Tepperman has commented:

> Thus as industrialization adds new occupational positions at the middle and top of the job hierarchy, low fertility at the top diminishes the likelihood that sufficient candidates for such positions will be found in families in the top social classes. Stated otherwise, the ratio of higher born children to higher status jobs declines with industrialization; this means that the likelihood that higher status jobs will be filled by children from lower classes will increase. This phenomenon illustrates the working of a combination of resource mobility—an upgrading of the occupational structure—and demographic mobility—a change from too few higher class children (1975, 38–39).

The shift in available positions pushes the occupational structure upward. At the same time, the insufficient number of offspring produced in the higher classes creates a force that pulls up some well-qualified children from the lower classes. Demographics will work in favour of the younger generation when baby boomers retire in about fifteen years. Jobs will open up in large numbers for those who are then the adults, the members of what's being called "generation X."[15] These predictions, whether or not they prove to be accurate, can be made with some confidence, in that Canada functions in terms of what Turner (1960) calls **contest mobility**, a competition, much like a sporting event, for social rewards as opposed to sponsorship mobility. **Sponsorship mobility** in England, for example, is like a mentoring system in which existing members of the elite choose and recruit newcomers to fill their ranks. (More will be said about this in Chapter 10, "Education: Winning and Losing.")

Mobility rates are based on statistical calculations; they say nothing about the individuals who actually move up and down, those who get better jobs, and those who must make do with worse jobs (or perhaps with no job at all). It cannot be assumed that workers displaced from routine jobs will be capable of obtaining the new jobs. In fact, they may be relegated to the ranks of the marginally employed, or unemployed. In a study of the effect of plant closures on the careers of displaced workers, Grayson (1986) found that a majority of those who did find new jobs experienced deskilling, lower earnings, and greater job insecurity.

Conventional wisdom has long held that getting an education is the most reliable means for getting ahead, but it does not guarantee success. What can be said is that a lack of education is highly correlated with poverty. Remember that correlation does not mean causation but indicates a relationship between variables, in this instance level of education and income. Poor education can be a cause or an effect of poverty. For example, children who are poor may not fare as well in school as their more fortunate classmates if their concentration is hampered by malnourishment. Exhibit 6.4 highlights the differences in poverty rates for various groups that have and do not have high-school diplomas. It shows that differences in education have the greatest impact on unattached women who are under 65 years of age and on couples who are under 65, with or without children. In each of those categories, those without high-school diplomas are twice as likely to be poor as those who graduated. Unattached men under 65 are 67 percent more likely to be poor without high-school credentials. Single mothers are 63 percent more likely to be poor if they don't have a high-school certificate.

While completion of high school important (an increasing percentage of the population is completing high school), the relative advantage of the diploma has diminished. Poverty rates for high-school graduates are 49.1 percent for single mothers, 37.9 percent for older single women, 27.4 percent for younger single women, and 23 percent for younger single men. According to some theorists, the increasing use of credentials as entry to occupations helps keep the existing stratification system in place by seeming to underscore the importance of merit, rather than ascription, in attaining lucrative jobs (Collins, 1979).

Ascription is still potent. Controlling for education (that is, holding that variable constant) shows the effect of gender on income, as illustrated in Exhibit 6.5. The percentages of men's earnings received by women in their jobs range from 56 percent, for those with some secondary education, to 63 percent

EXHIBIT 6.4

Poverty Rates by Family Type and Level of Education, 1990

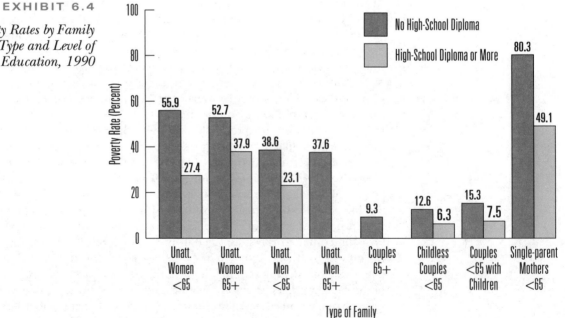

Source: Poverty Profile 1980–1990, *National Council on Welfare (Autumn, 1992).*

for the last three categories. Women with a postsecondary diploma earn, on average, a little more ($505) than men who finish elementary school.

Individual success is strongly influenced by structural conditions. It is a lot easier to get ahead in a period of economic expansion than in a recessionary climate. For example, Harvey and Kalwa (1983) examined the effects of socioeconomic background, educational achievement, and labour market conditions (as indicated by unemployment rates) on the occupational status attainment of five "cohorts" of men and women who graduated from selected Canadian universities between 1960 and 1976.[16] The findings showed that "changing labour market conditions appear to be much more important than the standard socioeconomic and educational attributes" (1983, 446).

We will discuss the effects of other ascribed characteristics on life chances in Chapters 7, "Minorities," and 8, "Work and Its Contexts."

EXHIBIT 6.5

Average Income by Education and Sex, 1991

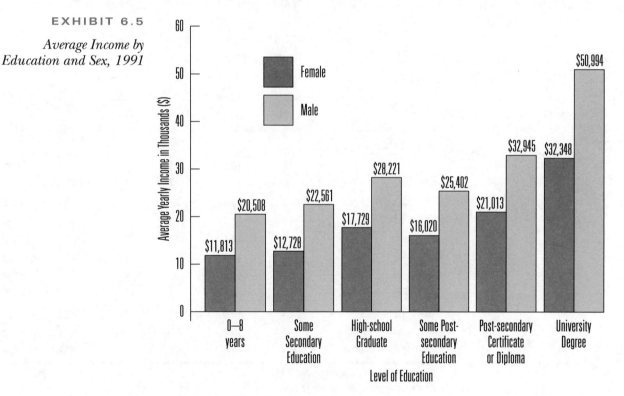

Source: Statistics Canada, Cat. No. 13–207.

STRATIFICATION IN CANADA

Reflective of Canadians' perception of themselves as middle-class is the assumption that Canada is classless. Here again sociologists have found that the suppositions do not fit the reality of social stratification. Stratification is the process of allotting socially valued rewards that produces a structure, a portrait of the results of that allotment. Exhibit 6.6 shows the shares of the national income by quintiles, that is, each 20 percent of the population. The first part of the table shows the highest income for each quintile. The second part of the table shows the relative share of national income for each quintile.

EXHIBIT 6.6

Upper Limits of Income Quintiles of Families and Unattached Individuals and Percentage Distribution of Total Income of Families and Unattached Individuals by Quintiles for Selected Years

Families and unattached individuals

Upper limits—in dollars	1	2	3	4	5*	
1981	10,064	18,570	27,581	38,610		
1982	10,912	19,758	29,256	41,895		
1983	10,648	19,909	30,107	43,810		
1984	11,278	20,554	31,644	45,396		
1985	12,117	21,929	33,507	48,450		
1986	12,697	23,130	35,214	51,024		
1987	13,476	24,349	36,740	53,532		
1988	14,097	25,447	39,000	56,830		
1989	15,497	27,997	41,888	61,100		
1990	15,974	28,638	43,462	63,658		
1991	15,955	28,792	43,573	64,775		
Shares of total income						
1981	4.6	10.9	17.6	25.1	41.7	100
1982	4.6	10.8	17.4	24.9	42.4	100
1983	4.3	10.3	17.1	25.0	43.2	100
1984	4.5	10.4	17.2	25.0	43.0	100
1985	4.6	10.4	17.0	24.9	43.0	100
1986	4.7	10.4	17.0	24.9	43.1	100
1987	4.7	10.4	16.9	24.8	43.2	100
1988	4.6	10.4	16.9	24.9	43.2	100
1989	4.8	10.5	16.9	24.6	43.2	100
1990	4.7	10.4	16.9	24.8	43.3	100
1991	4.7	10.3	16.6	24.7	43.8	100

Source: Statistics Canada, Cat. No. 13-207.
*There is no upper limit for the fifth quintile.

The table attests to income disparity, and shows that over the eleven years highlighted, shares of wealth have remained much the same. The two lowest quintiles received from 14.6 to 15.5 percent of the income in the years from 1981 to 1991. The share for the two richest groups was about two-thirds, ranging from 66.8 to 68.5 percent.

ELITES: GETTING THERE AND STAYING THERE
Wallace Clement (1949–) following in the footsteps of his teacher, John Porter (1921–79), whose pioneering work on Canadian stratification will be discussed

in the next chapter, became interested in the study of elites. An **elite** can be defined as a set of persons who hold the top positions in any institutional hierarchy. Members of the economic elite shared ethnic origins, Porter found, and were from similar class backgrounds, overwhelmingly the upper or middle classes. Many had attended the same private schools and summer camps, and nearly all had been to university. Similarity of background was reinforced by a similarity of lifestyle: membership in private clubs and geographic proximity of both city and vacation homes, respectively. Jointly, these characteristics helped to create a socially homogeneous group, aware of its shared origins and goals. Economic elites hold no monopoly on power—it is also wielded by those at the apex of other societal sectors such as the federal bureaucracy, the universities, the judiciary, organized labour, and the mass media. What is important, Porter said, is that members of these elites have access to each other. Their relations are intermittently marked by conflict, but there is also much cooperation. In his study *The Canadian Corporate Elite* (1975), Clement frequently used Porter's findings as bases for comparison with his own, contributing important dimensions to his mentor's work.

To analyze how much equality of opportunity exists in a society, Clement noted, one must first establish the extent to which there is equality of "condition." As was previously pointed out, according to capitalist ideology, one's condition (that is, position attained and possessions accumulated) is the result of individual ability and effort. Hence, inequality of condition does not run counter to the societal credo. However, Clement and many other analysts hold that inequality of condition necessarily results in unequal opportunities:

> The accumulation of privilege associated with dominant positions affords their incumbents advantages which are transmitted to their kin but not available to other members of society. This is transmitted by differential access to the means of mobility such as private and postsecondary education, inherited wealth, career openings, social contacts and a series of advantages perpetuated through class institutions such as private schools and private clubs. This leads to differential class opportunities in favour of the privileged (1975, 6–7).

Porter's data on the social composition of elite groups supported the existence of such "differential class opportunities." However, major changes had occurred in the interim between the time of Porter's research and that of Clement's. The number of firms had been reduced through mergers and acquisitions, thereby concentrating ownership. Foreign, particularly American, ownership of Canadian firms had become more extensive and more recognizable. The much-publicized "war on poverty" had been launched, and there had been explosive growth in Canadian postsecondary education. How, if at all, did these developments affect recruitment into the elite stratum, and the ways in which elites exercised power?

Clement's three categories of elites serve to remind us that Canada has often been described as a "branch-plant economy":

- *Indigenous elites.* Canadian directors and executives of predominantly Canadian-owned corporations (for example, the chartered banks).

- *Comprador elites.* The upper managers of largely foreign-owned companies in Canada (for example, the top executives of GM Canada).

- *Parasite elites.* Those who govern the foreign-owned multinational corporations from their head offices (example, the Dutch-based management group of Shell Oil).

Since policy is handed down from head offices, comprador elites have administrative rather than policy-making power. This means that outsiders make decisions that vitally affect the Canadian economy and the fate of Canadian workers; this does not necessarily have an adverse effect on the indigenous elite, though, most of whom are concentrated in the commercial sectors of finance, trade, and transportation.

Although conflicts undoubtedly arise, Clement viewed the interests of the indigenous-commercial elite and the parasite-industrial elite groups as inherently compatible and largely harmonious. This view was confirmed by the massive support the business community gave to the 1988 Free Trade Agreement between Canada and the United States (Campbell & Powell, 1989). As Porter put it:

> Whom else would political leaders consult but business leaders, labour leaders, higher bureaucrats, and newspaper proprietors? Sociology often has to deal with obvious facts, and the task here has been to show that within the overall structure of power in society, elite groups coordinate their own activities, and the complex social activities of the institutions they command. A confraternity of power develops among them, and this in turn is reinforced by the establishments of kinship and class (1965, 540–41).

Clement stressed the multiple ties that link those at the top. Shared origins and shared life experiences reinforce the consciousness of commonality. Close-knit groups become resistant to penetration because they fear that outsiders will spoil the cozy, familial atmosphere. The more homogeneous a group, the easier it is for members to predict each other's reactions and the more likely they are to resist change.

We have already quoted Marx's statement that human beings make their own history, though not under conditions of their own choosing. Clement examined the conditions in Canadian society that constrain the history individuals can make for themselves. Powerful interest groups defend structured inequality, and only a few exceptional people are able to breach these defences.

THE POOR—WHO ARE THEY?

The poor are found at the bottom of the stratification ladder.[17] Exhibit 6.7 shows poverty rates for families in the years from 1980 to 1991. (Poverty rates compare the number of poor persons in a particular category, for example, unattached men under 65 years of age, to the total number of people in that category, in this instance, all unattached men under 65 years of age.) These families account for approximately 83 percent of Canada's poor. The remain-

The poor fall at the bottom of the stratification ladder.

Lawrence Acland.

ing 17 percent are made up of less common types of families: siblings living together; married couples with children aged 18 or over who live with them; and single-parent families headed by men.

Women are more likely than men to be poor at some time in their lives, particularly in the later years. The increasing risk of poverty borne by women is a trend referred to as the feminization of poverty. During the 1960s and 1970s, the feminization of poverty escalated. By 1980 it was entrenched and persisted largely unabated through most of the 1980s. It continues into the 1990s.

EXHIBIT 6.7

Poverty Rates for Families

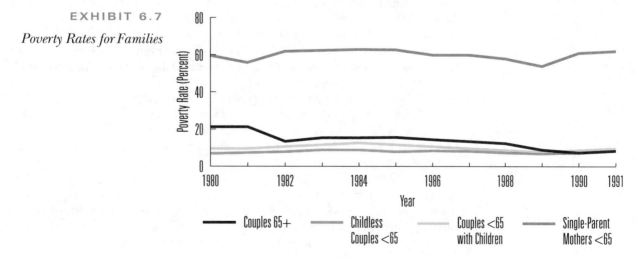

Source: Poverty Profile Update for 1991. *National Council on Welfare (Winter, 1993).*

EXHIBIT 6.8

Poverty Rates for Persons by Age and Sex, 1990

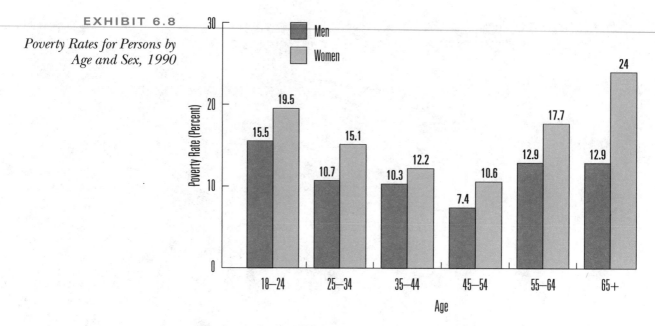

EXHIBIT 6.8

*Poverty Rates for Persons by
Age and Sex, 1990*

Source: Poverty Profile, 1980–1990, *National Council of Welfare (Autumn, 1992).*

As Exhibit 6.8 demonstrates, young women, 18 to 24 years of age, are 25 percent more likely to be poor than their male cohorts. This probability of being poor is consistently higher for women than for men and continues to be so over the life cycle, though their rates fluctuate like a roller coaster. Women are 41 percent more likely than men to be poor between the ages of 25 and 34; 20 percent more likely between 35 and 44; and 37 percent more likely between 55 and 64. Women are also almost twice as likely as men to be poor when they are over 65.

A similar pattern of women and poverty is evident in families. In 1980 the rate of poverty was 46.6 percent for families with female heads who were under the age of 65; this was 5 ³⁄₄ times the rate for families with male heads. By 1987, the rate for families with female heads was still very high, at 40.3 percent or 4.9 times the rate for families with male heads. In 1990, families headed by single mothers faced a 60.6 percent rate of poverty (Welfare Council, 1992). In 1991, it increased again to 61.9 percent (*Poverty Profile Update*, 1993).

Exhibit 6.9 provides comparisons of the incomes of the poor with average incomes. Family types are listed in order of poverty rate, from the highest to lowest. The column at the extreme right shows that single women over 65, single-parent mothers under 65, and single men over 65 come closest to the average income for all the people in their categories, with 66, 60, and 57 percent, respectively. Ranking all the groups by average income (not poverty rate), however, shows that people in those categories have the three lowest average incomes: elderly single women's average income is $17,304; elderly single men's is $20,259; and single mothers' is $22,186. Clearly, the elderly and single mothers are most likely to be poor.

EXHIBIT 6.9

*Incomes of the Poor
Compared to Average
Incomes, 1991*

Family type	Poverty rate	Average income of poor	Average income of all	Income of poor as percentage of all
Single-parent mothers under 65 with children under 18	61.9	$13,382	$22,186	60%
Unattached women 65 and older	47.4	$11,407	$17,304	66%
Unattached women under 65	37.6	$7,753	$22,040	35%
Unattached men 65 and older	33.4	$11,456	$20,259	57%
Unattached men under 65	30.5	$7,787	$26,066	30%
Couples under 65 with children under 18	10.7	$18,626	$59,014	32%
Childless couples under 65	9.3	$11,402	$52,873	22%
Couples 65 and older	9	$16,549	$35,553	47%

Source: Poverty Profile Update for 1991, *National Council of Welfare (Winter, 1993).*

Conceptually, poverty can be characterized in absolute terms (those of absolute deprivation): does the individual have enough on which to subsist—to obtain the basic necessities of life, such as food, clothing, and shelter? Poverty can also be seen in relative terms (those of relative deprivation): does the individual's economic well-being fall short of community standards? In this sense of the term, one asks how the person or family fares in relation to others in society. Those who are poor by relative standards tend to be those who, because of low education and lack of job opportunities, cannot participate fully in community life.

Changing the government guidelines that regulate the income cutoff lines for determining who is poor can expand or contract the number of poor in the population in a moment. Defining poverty then becomes part of the wielding of power. Massive government debt and a severe recession have challenged governments. One response has been to ponder cutting social programs to economize. Will advocacy groups for the poor succeed in ensuring that government assistance is forthcoming, or will government proposals, most recently one that would radically reduce the number of Canadians who would be considered poor, leave fewer with aid? Clearly, changing criteria can alter people's lives in very dramatic ways. Cutoff rates vary according to size of family and size of community, as can be seen in Exhibit 6.10.

Contrary to popular belief, most poor people do work. As Exhibit 6.11 illustrates, two-thirds of poor family heads and three-quarters of poor unattached people worked on either full- or part-time basis in 1990.

The working poor are concentrated in the most precarious and vulnerable sectors of the economy, where employment is irregular, low paying, and lacking in fringe benefits. Ross comments:

As the National Council on Welfare concluded, "It is not their ages, education or geographic distribution that distinguish low-income workers. The single common factor which sets the working poor

Family size	Community Size				
	Cities iof 500,000+	100,000– 499,999	30,000– 99,999	Less than 30,000	Rural areas
1	$ 15,509	$ 13,621	$ 13,307	$ 12,131	$ 10,558
2	21,022	18,465	18,038	16,443	14,313
3	26,721	23,470	22,928	20,900	18,193
4	30,767	27,021	26,398	24,065	20,945
5	33,615	29,524	28,842	26,292	22,885
6	36,488	32,045	31,306	28,538	24,840
7+	39,244	34,469	33,674	30,697	26,717

*Based on inflation of 2.2 percent as forecast in the 1992 budget speech.

Source: Poverty Profile Update for 1991, *National Council on Welfare (Winter, 1993)*.

apart as a group within our society is their jobs." Not only do the wage-earning poor hold low-paying jobs and suffer more and longer spells of unemployment, but they also tend to have hard, dirty, boring and low-prestige jobs with little or no chance for advancement. These jobs in most instances do not represent the career and income opportunities that play such a central economic and social role in the lives of most Canadians. They are simply dead-end jobs that barely permit the holder to scratch out a living (1981, 23).

The problem of income security has been persistent throughout Canadian history, especially since industrialization increased the concentration of people in urban centres (see Herbert Brown Ames's *The City Below the Hill* [1972]). Although Canadians have now achieved one of the highest standards of living in the world, many of its citizens live at the margins of society. Since the Second World War, a complex structure of social welfare programs has been created, entitling Canada to be referred to as a welfare state.

Despite the responsibility for social security that Canadians have assigned to government at both the federal and provincial levels, and despite large infusions of money into programs designed to bring about income redistribution, income disparities have not, in fact, been substantially reduced. Disparities persist among classes, among regions of the country, among sectors of the economy, and among age, gender, and ethnic groups. In his analysis of the redistributive role played by the Canadian state, Banting notes that it has been a modest one, below the norm for industrialized countries and "representing a restrained response to the social insecurities of industrial life" (1987, 311).

Regional Disparity

In addition to the social categories of age and sex, Canada's poor can be located geographically. Canada's unique geographical, natural resource, and population variations have led to differential economic conditions, creating what has been labelled regional disparity or regional inequality. In defining a region,

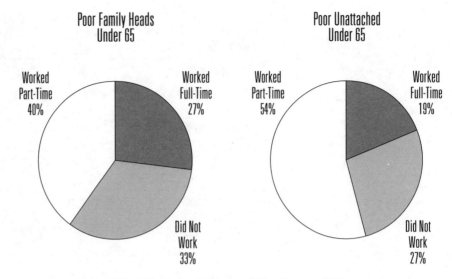

Source: Poverty Profile 1980–1990, *National Council on Welfare (Autumn, 1992).*

EXHIBIT 6.11
Work Activity by Family Heads and Unattached People, 1990

Poor Family Heads Under 65

Worked Part-Time 40%

Worked Full-Time 27%

Did Not Work 33%

Poor Unattached Under 65

Worked Part-Time 54%

Worked Full-Time 19%

Did Not Work 27%

provinces, being major administrative and political units, are usually, though not always, the unit of analysis with inequality measured in economic terms. Exhibit 6.12 shows that Newfoundland, Quebec, Manitoba, and Saskatchewan have poverty rates higher than the overall Canadian rate.

Three major approaches have been used to explain this regional inequality (Wien cited in Curtis, Grabb, & Guppy, 1993). One, the staples theory focuses on indigenous raw or partially processed materials. If marketable in other areas, these resources can become the mainstay of the economy fostering growth. But market fluctuations and disruption in the demand for the product can have dire consequences. Newfoundland's and the Atlantic provinces' reliance on the fishing industry and the depletion of the fish stocks demonstrates the biggest potential hazard of staple reliance.

The developmental model was first advanced in analyzing Latin American countries. Modernization was seen to flow from large urban industrialized centres to smaller less-developed areas that would model themselves after these urban economies. This might mean the establishment of large well-equipped factories, mass communcation, and transportation.

The last approach emphasizes the exploitation of a particular region on the part of and for the benefit of others, typically multinational corporations in large urban areas. In Canada, the "core" is in large urban areas with "satellites" in the North, the West, and in the Atlantic provinces. Underdevelopment, according to this thesis, is a result of the appropriation of cheap raw and semi-processed materials from satellite areas to the core where these are manufactured, processed, and then returned for sale to their original source at a highly inflated cost. The approach can be applied to countries as well: Canada, for example can be seen as the exploited satellite to the core of the United States.

EXHIBIT 6.12

*Measures of Regional
Inequality in Canada, by
Province*

Province	Personal income per capita 1990	Unemployment rate 1991	Poverty rate 1990
Newfoundland	15 846	18.4	15.6
Prince Edward Island	16 316	16.8	12.5
Nova Scotia	18 151	12.0	13.4
New Brunswick	17 060	12.7	14.3
Quebec	20 567	11.9	18.0
Ontario	25 151	9.6	11.7
Manitoba	19 250	8.8	17.8
Saskatchewan	17 784	7.4	16.6
Alberta	21 972	8.2	15.4
British Columbia	22 437	9.9	14.6
Canada	22 184	10.3	14.6
Disparity ratio (highest/lowest)	1.59	2.48	1.53

Source: N. Curtis, E. Grabb, and N. Guppy, Social Inequality in Canada *(Toronto: Prentice-Hall, 1993).*

Government policies can and have been used to develop a depressed area by helping inhabitants retrain, by funding the infrastructure, like schools and transportation, and by supporting local industries with tax breaks. Transfer payments from the federal to provincial accounts, in the form of unemployment insurance, family allowance, and old age pensions, also provide financial assistance. While these cash infusions have narrowed the gap between regions, they do not promote the growth of the regional economies themselves. Instead, they redistribute money made elsewhere (Wien, cited in Curtis et al., 1993).

The Stigma of Poverty

One of the many costs of poverty is that it imposes on individuals a significant **stigma**—a social mark of unworthiness or discredit—that affects their social identity. As Goffman has observed:

> Our society appears to have several basic types of stigma. There are "tribal" stigmas, arising from unapproved racial, national, and religious affiliations. There are the stigmas attached to physical handicap, including—to stretch the term—those associated with the undesirable characteristics of female sex and old age. And there are stigmas pertaining to what is somehow seen as a decay of moral responsibility, including those persons who are unemployed or who have a known record of alcoholism, addiction, sexual deviation, penal servitude, or who have been committed to a mental hospital (1962, 196).

The poor are a powerless group of people whose participation in the social, economic, and political life of the country is low, and whose life chances are severely restricted. Capitalist ideology promotes the view that failing is a symptom of individual inadequacy (lack of ambition, unwillingness to adapt to market conditions, and a weak character or laziness). The internalization of this character sketch combined with structural disadvantages of being poor in the first place makes it difficult, if not impossible, for most people to break out of the cycle of poverty, and it becomes a condition that is then perpetuated from one generation to the next (see Ryan, 1972).

We have stressed that people start the social race at different points on the track. Thus, the social system does not merely have winners and losers—it helps to create them. However, the blame-the-victim approach, which has influenced Canadian public policy toward the poor, presumes that individuals are personally responsible for success or failure; the policy thus seeks to change the behaviour of individuals rather than attempting to find long-term solutions in the social structure itself. Assistance to the poor is delivered on a short-term, crisis basis, and programs are designed not only to encourage self-reliance and hard work but also to discourage dependence and lack of effort. Canadian society attaches a heavy stigma to being poor and dependent but, as we have noted, cannot seem to find an effective way to reduce poverty and dependence.

. . . .

OVERVIEW

In this chapter, we have examined society's sorting of people into levels or strata that bring with them unequal rewards. Those in the higher strata obtain both higher material and symbolic rewards. Societies differ in the amount of movement permitted. Caste and estate societies are more or less closed: status is ascribed; movement between levels is difficult, and interaction among individuals situated at different levels is regulated by social norms.

A class society is more open. An individual's class position is claimed to be determined by achievement. However, even in open class societies, substantial gender inequality manifests itself, at the extreme, in violence against women. In addition, particular regions and racial or ethnic groups are consistently overrepresented in such indices of disadvantage as minimal education, poor health, and marginal employment. Such overrepresentation demonstrates that inequality cannot be satisfactorily explained by individual attributes. Despite an ideology that proclaims equal opportunity for those of equal ability and that rejects the notion of a frozen hierarchy, considerable structural inequality exists in Canada.

Social thinkers substantially agree that some type of inequality exists in virtually every society. Disagreement centres on the causes and consequences of this inequality. Marx's analysis centred on economic inequality: how it is created and preserved, and how it affects the lives of individuals. Weber acknowledged the importance of economic factors but expanded his focus to the social and political dimensions of inequality. In this sense, Weber's is a pluralistic approach to the study of stratification. Some feminist scholars attribute gender inequality to patriarchy, while others give more attention to the ways in which women's subordination serves the interests of capitalism.

Is inequality necessary? What purpose does it serve? To Marx, the function of inequality was clear: it serves the interests of the dominant group. To structural functionalists such as Davis and Moore, unequal rewards benefit the society as a whole by providing able individuals with incentives to make the efforts required for performing society's vital tasks. Feminists note that it is men who occupy the upper echelons and, therefore, reap the rewards.

Until empirical research was conducted, the notion prevailed that class differences did not exist in the new world. Studies have challenged the myths that class is not a significant variable in these societies, and that rapid upward mobility can be easily achieved.

Class differences are obscured by levelling influences that make for superficial similarities among people and create the impression of a common lifestyle. The widespread acceptance of this view discourages the emergence of class consciousness and makes conflict less apparent.

Even though mobility is hampered in modern class societies, it does occur. The mobility of the few keeps alive faith in mobility for all. How much mobility takes place is influenced by such macrofactors as the expansion or contraction of the economy, and technological advances that reorder the occupational structure. Personal attributes do play a part in determining who will move up or down and who will remain stationary. In all instances, however, mobility is constrained or facilitated by structural conditions beyond the individual's control.

ASSIGNMENTS

1. Chart your family tree as far back as you can go. See what, if any, patterns of mobility you can identify between and within generations. Explain your findings in sociological terms. For example, a skilled tradesman coming from Europe may have to start work as a labourer in Canada because his formal qualifications are not recognized here (downward mobility).

2. What would a day spent in upper-class activities be like? List these activities and try to determine the origin of your notion that such things are upper class. You may have actually engaged in such activities, or you may have derived your notion that such activities are upper class from television programs or from magazines and books.

3. Select a religious group that is unfamiliar to you (for example, Jehovah's Witness or Hare Krishna). Do some library research to learn about the group, and then attend one of its services. Be alert to the rituals, and listen carefully to the points stressed in any sermon or impromptu speech. Can you establish the social class membership of the participants? What prevents or enables you to do so? How did you try to measure social class? What sociological explanations might there be for differences, if any, in the social class membership of particular religious groups?

SUGGESTED READINGS

James Curtis, Edward Grabb, and Neil Guppy, eds., *Social Inequality in Canada: Patterns, Problems, Policies* (Scarborough, Ont.: Prentice-Hall, 1993).This is a comprehensive investigation of various patterns of social inequality in Canada and of the ideologies that help to create and sustain them. The contributors also examine the consequences of particular achieved and ascribed statuses on a number of ranking systems. This book is valuable to those interested in the area of stratification and power, and to those who may plan to continue on in sociology.

Kingsley Davis and Wilbert E. Moore, "Some Principles of Stratification," *American Sociological Review* 10 (1945):242–49. This classic paper outlines a functionalist approach to social stratification. Davis and Moore argue that it is necessary for society to have a differential reward system (for example, more rewards for doctors than for janitors) in order to ensure that those jobs that are most difficult and most important get filled. Without such inducements, so the argument goes, the tasks needed to keep society functioning would not get performed. Equality of opportunity is the other side of the coin: everyone must be able to compete for the rewards, so that merit, rather than inherited advantage, will determine who obtains them. For a critique of this approach, see Melvin Tumin, "Some Principles of Stratification: A Critical Analysis," *American Sociological Review* 18:387–93.

Alfred Hunter, *Class Tells* (Toronto: Butterworths, 1981). Hunter provides an informative discussion of the causes and manifestations of social inequality in Canada. He traces the development of the Canadian class structure, and examines the relationship between class membership and power. He also looks at the extent to which Canadians are aware of the existence and the consequences of stratification.

Elliot Liebow, *Tell Them Who I Am: The Lives of Homeless Women* (Glencoe, Ill.: Free Press, 1993). Liebow investigates the routines of homeless women to find out how they meet their needs, such as food, shelter, storage, companionship, and religious comfort. The book dispels many misconceptions, showing that there are many routes to homelessness and that it does not always constitute a retreat from society.

Leonard Marsh, *Canadians In and Out of Work: A Survey of Economic Classes and their Relation to the Labour Market* (Toronto: Canadian Scholars' Press, [1940] 1993). Pre-dating John Porter's *The Vertical Mosaic* by 25 years, Marsh's research on stratification in Canada is an overlooked wealth of information and may be considered the first major quantitative study of Canada's national class structure. Marsh based his analysis on a truly national sample, the 1933 census data, and was innovative in including gender in his analysis. In his writings, he also considered the implications of his findings for public policy.

Karl Marx, *The Communist Manifesto* (New York: Modern Library, 1932; first published in 1848). This famous manifesto was written on the eve of the 1848 revolutions against the oppressive regimes that held most of Europe in thrall. The revolutions failed, but *The Communist Manifesto* survived, a superb example of polemical writing. The ideas expressed in it have given impetus to several revolutions in the present century. Marx briefly traces the evolution of the bourgeoisie into the dominant class and spells out, with remarkable accuracy, the trend toward large, multinational enterprises. For other writings of Marx, see Tom Bottomore's edited collection, *Karl Marx: Selected Writings in Sociology and Social Philosophy* (London: Watts, 1956).

Richard Sennett and Jonathan Cobb, *The Hidden Injuries of Class* (New York: Random House, 1972). This study is based on in-depth interviews with blue-collar workers during the early 1970s. The respondents offer poignant testimony to the ways in which the disjunction between the ideology of equal opportunity and the reality of structured inequality are experienced by those who perceive themselves as not having "made it."

NOTES

1. The Indian government has outlawed many aspects of the caste system. However, much of it persists in some rural areas—a good example of society's simply ignoring laws it does not agree with, as well as of the fact that it is the group, not some outside authority, that sets the criteria for stratification.

2. "Estate" comes from the Old French *estat*, which was derived from the Latin *status*. The word is still current in the phrase "the fourth estate" as a name for the press.

3. One of the chief developments of the modern class system has been its increased emphasis on achieved status. In the nineteenth century, as we see in the novels of Jane Austen, for example, the newly rich, especially those who made money in less acceptable occupations such as "trade" (merchandising), were of lower status than those whose wealth came from inherited land or even those from the professions.

4. Based on Statistics Canada, Cat. No. 13–207, 1991.

5. Many people, including blacks, Hispanics, and native peoples, would challenge the actuality of this ideal. But few would deny that this is the ideal, and that many Americans believe it to be at least partially true.

6. Most biblical scholars say that this reference is not to a literal needle but to a very low gate to the city of Jerusalem. A camel could go through it, but only with great difficulty.

7. *Gazette* (Montreal), February 8, 1993, C1–C4.

8. *The Globe and Mail*, July 16, 1993, A4.

9. *Gazette* (Montreal), July 16, 1993.

10. *Gazette* (Montreal), May 3, 1993, D5.

11. National Clearinghouse on Family Violence, Health and Welfare Canada, Cat. No. H 72–22/9–1993E.

12. Juristat Service Bulletin, Canadian Centre for Justice Statistics, Statistics Canada, Vol. 12, No. 6 (March 1992).

13. From a brief on Bill C-49 by the National Action Committee on the Status of Women, May 14, 1992.

14. See *Canadian Council on Social Development*, Vol. 9, No. 4 (Winter 1992).

15. For more information on generation X, see Douglas Coupland's *Generation X: Tales from an Accelerated Culture* (New York: St. Martin's Press, 1991).

16. A cohort is a group of people who share some statistical characteristic or set of characteristics, age and/or sex, for example, in a demographic study. One might speak of the cohort of Canadians born in 1972 or the cohort of North American women born between 1945 and 1949.

17. The poor can be considered a minority group. The concept is explained in Chapter 7. Essentially, groups that have little power can be seen as minorities, no matter how many people are in the group.

Minorities

> *On Curriculum Night when I was introducing myself to the community, I looked out and there was national dress from around the world and every colour of the rainbow. You know, to me, that's what Canada should look like. It was such a wonderful experience.*

Ms. Ohlke, staff member, Kingsview Village Junior School, Etobicoke, Ontario

> *Official multiculturalism and the lack of self-confidence it betrays can only result in Canada becoming a diffuse conglomeration of all the world's cultures, suffering all the feuds and foibles of other lands and other times, losing our own identity as Canadians. Is that what we really want?*

Inge Cumberland, Mississauga, Ontario

This chapter, like the last, is about power and how that is affected by being a member of a minority group. Generalizations about groups of people ignore individual differences but provide the basis for the ways in which individual members of the group are perceived and treated. Often, in contrast to the attitude expressed by Ms. Ohlke in the first passage above, minorities are seen negatively. In a recent study called "Who Gets the Work?" (described in more detail in the section titled "A Vertical Mosaic" in this chapter) sociologists Henry and Ginzberg (1993) documented the existence of racial discrimination in employment practices in Toronto. Qualified applicants were less likely to be offered jobs if they were black or belonged to certain ethnic groups than was the case if they were white (Curtis, Grabb, and Guppy, 1993).

Historically, sociologists have focused on racial and ethnic minorities, groups that are still of particular interest in pluralistic societies like Canada and the United States. Although in Canada, relationships among ethnic groups—specifically between the French and the English—have been pivotal, we examine race first because the minority status of those belonging to other races is visible and permanent (at least in the short run and in the absence of continuing intermarriage), and because they have suffered the most severe discrimination.

In addition, we look at some groups you may not have thought of as minorities. Children, the aged, the disabled, and homosexuals are social categories that have been subjected to varying degrees of discrimination. Human rights legislation, and events such as the Year of the Child and the Year of the Disabled, have been designed to address the inequalities that people in such categories experience. Accordingly, in this chapter we will widen our scope beyond race and ethnic groups to include a discussion of the aged and a brief report on homosexuals. (For a discussion of other groups that fit the definition of minority [alcoholics, disabled], see Kallen [1989].) Women, too, can be conceptualized as a minority. How is that possible given that women make up approximately 51 percent of the population? The sociological definition of "minority" stresses the (lack of) power of the group.

DEFINING MINORITIES

In defining a **minority**, we have made use of Kallen's concept (1982, 109–10), according to which a minority is a social category, within a society:

- that is defined by the majority as incompetent, inferior, abnormal, and/or dangerous;
- whose members experience categorical and systemic discrimination, that is, members of minorities are restricted on the basis of their group, not personal attributes, and the barriers they confront are embedded in the way institutions and organizations are structured;
- whose members are to some degree denied political, economic, and/or social power, human dignity, and fundamental human rights; and
- that comes to occupy a disadvantaged and stigmatized position in society.

Notice the differences between this sociological definition and conventional usage. In the latter, "minority group" describes a group that is numerically smaller than another group. For instance, a political party that is a minority in Parliament is one that has fewer seats than some other party. The sociological definition we are using makes no reference to numbers; rather, it draws attention to the relative standing of different groups and the ways in which they interact. The very concept of a minority group that is discriminated against implies the existence of another group or groups that enjoy disproportionate power and access to valued goods and services. Such a **majority** or **dominant group** may be a small numerical minority, as is the case with whites in South Africa.

Power is central to an understanding of majority/minority relationships. According to Kallen, the majority exercises "the greatest degree of political, economic, and social power in the society and [is] able to control the life destinies of minorities" (1982, 110). This ability of the majority to define laws, values, and informal norms leads the minority to experience some degree of "oppression (denial of political power), neglect (denial of economic power), and/or discrimination (denial of social power and human dignity)" (1982, 1).

Once the minority status of a group becomes entrenched in the social structure, the ability of the group's members to manipulate their own fate is constrained. If the group's access to educational and occupational opportunities is restricted, individuals find it very difficult to get ahead. Moreover, minority status may set in motion a **self-fulfilling prophecy**, which is:

> a belief regarding a social situation, which, because one believes it and one acts upon it, actually manifests itself as truth, further strengthening the belief. If, for example, an outgroup is believed to be hostile, and if people act as though it were hostile, the outgroup will most likely show hostility in response (Theodorson & Theodorson, 1969, 375).

Minority group members may come to believe that their group is unworthy, and this lack of confidence in the possibility of success may hamper an individual's aspirations and ability to achieve. One of the first steps in organizing to protest minority status is a rejection and reformulation of these negative assessments (Kallen, 1989). The sixties rallying cry "Black is beautiful" was one attempt to reverse the (internalized) negative image of black Americans.

PREJUDICE, STEREOTYPES, AND DISCRIMINATION

Often members of minority groups are treated with prejudice and discriminated against. Biased attitudes and a negative or hostile evaluation constitute **prejudice** (literally "pre-judgement" of) against a group of people (Berry, 1991). Prejudice renders the world more predictable and less anxiety-provoking by allowing one easily to sort friend from foe (Sniderman et al., 1993). Prejudice can also be normative and conventional—that is, having no underlying hostility or harmful intent (Berry, 1991). Ng (1987, 101) calls this "commonsense sexism and racism, those unintentional and unconscious acts which result in the silencing, exclusion, subordination, and exploitation of minority group members." A recent study of anti-Semitism illustrates the phenomenon. Interviewing a representative sample of Canadians, sociologists found that Quebeckers are more ethnocentric and anti-semitic than other Canadians (Sniderman et al., 1993). They are more inclined to disagree with positive characteristics attributed to Jews and agree with negative ones. Other groups, too, that appear to stand out by resisting absorption into French culture are described negatively. Anti-semitism and ethnocentrism, researchers explain, are unintended consequences of Quebeckers' strong emphasis on conformity as a value and on the ensuing norms requiring people to fit into groups.

Prejudice is based on **stereotypes**, overgeneralizations about other groups of people based on the human tendency to simplify the world. These "mental cartoons are formed by generalizing too much or exaggerating people's characteristics on the basis of too little information" (Hale, 1990, 579). "Stereotyping is not 'bad' in its own right, but acquires a negative connotation when it denies a person his or her right to equal treatment on the basis of personal merits and credentials" (Fleras and Elliott, 1992, 318). Stereotypes are resilient as they are emotionally held and any evidence negating the stereotype is seen as the exception that proves the rule.

It should be noted that, theoretically, prejudice and stereotypes can be positive or negative. An example of a positive stereotype is the perception of the Dutch as being extremely careful about cleanliness (hence the brand of scouring powder called Dutch Cleanser). The point of the stereotype, however, even if positive, is to set the group members apart as being "unlike us," and this may diminish acceptance by other groups of the individuals in that group.

Attitudes that involve stereotypes often lead to behaviour that involves **discrimination**, "the maltreatment of minorities on the basis of colour, sex, disability, or other attributes" (Fleras and Elliott, 1992, 314).

Today, at least in North America, it is no longer socially acceptable to declare prejudicial sentiments publicly, much less officially, nor to act openly on them.[1] Because biased attitudes and behaviour have, therefore, tended to go underground, it is important to recognize the ways in which they persist and continue to shape the experiences of groups and their individual members.

Prejudice is based on stereotypes, that is, overgeneralizations about other groups of people based on the human tendency to simplify the world.

Roger Hallet/ *The Globe and Mail*, Toronto.

THE SOCIAL SIGNIFICANCE OF RACE

Conventionally, the term **race** denotes people who share physical characteristics, such as skin and eye pigmentation. Many physical scientists voice serious doubts as to whether the concept as a biological and physiological determination is a useful device for classifying human beings. There are no pure races: physical racial characteristics glide imperceptibly from one category to another.[2]

Sociologists and other social scientists point out, however, that scientific validity aside, people do use race as a major criterion for sorting people. The significance of race is social even though it is based on perceived physical differences, as in the study on employment we cited at the beginning of the chapter.

Membership in a particular racial group can affect every aspect of an individual's life. Being a native Indian in Ontario meant, until the 1950s, that one could not buy liquor in a liquor store. Native peoples who wanted to drink had to do so in hotels during licensed hours. Hence, any who became intoxicated did so in public view and were likely to come to the attention of the police, thus inflating statistics on Indian drunkenness. Before civil rights legislation took effect in the 1960s, blacks in the American south had to learn the locations of "colored" washrooms on venturing into a strange city. As recently as 1980, Hershel Walker could not attend a banquet celebrating his Georgia high school's football championship, even though he was the team's star, because the local country club did not admit blacks. **Racism**, which is discrimination on the basis of race, of a Canadian variety was depicted in a cartoon when Ben Johnson lost his Olympic Gold Medal for using steroids in 1988. The cartoon's three successive captions read: "Canadian Wins Gold Medal," "Jamaican Canadian Accused of Steroid Use," and finally, "Jamaican Stripped of Gold Medal" (cited in Goyder, 1990, 107). The nineties have found overtly racist white supremacist groups, like the Heritage Front in Canada, trying new techniques to recruit adherents. Soliciting is done in schools, rock concerts are arranged, television coverage is sought, and a magazine is published. Although their rhetoric may have softened, their racist, right-wing message, that whites are discriminated against because Jews and blacks have too much power, has not changed.

By definition, racial groups constitute visible minorities. Therefore, their differences from the majority group cannot disappear, even if the minority-group member is prepared to assimilate into the dominant culture. Talking about this dilemma, David Suzuki likened his own Japanese-Canadian group to

The Lieutenant Governor of Manitoba. Members of visible minorities cannot disappear even if they are prepared to assimilate.

CF Photo/Master Corporal J.P. Forget.

bananas, "yellow on the outside, but white on the inside." In other words, members of a racial minority may act and think like the dominant group, but they remain physically different.

All races are represented in Canadian society today: native peoples, orientals, and blacks. Each is sharply subdivided along tribal or national (ethnic) lines, but other people often see only the physical characteristics of race and do not realize the difference between, say, Chinese and Koreans or Haitians and Jamaicans.

During the 1970s and 1980s, when changes were made in immigration laws, the percentage of nonwhite immigration increased markedly. Herberg comments on such changes in immigration patterns:

> If one uses a rather restrictive definition of "visible minorities" as including only Asians and Blacks (the number and proportion of immigrant Indians and Inuit to Canada have been infinitesimal), then visible minorities represented less than 1% of immigrants before 1960 and only about 13% in the 1960s. In the decade 1971–1980, however, they made up about 41% of all immigrants here. If, moreover, the definition of visible minority is expanded to include Filipinos, Lebanese, and Central and South Americans—as many of these peoples perceive themselves to be in Canada and as many "white" Canadians declare them to be—then the visible minorities made up 54% of immigrants to Canada in the period 1971–1980. Immigration to Canada, then, has become increasingly variegated in the post-war era (1989, 72).

Exhibit 7.1 pictures immigration from pre-1961 to 1991 and illustrates the increase in visible minority immigrants.

EXHIBIT 7.1

Immigrant Population by Place of Birth and Period of Immigration, 1991

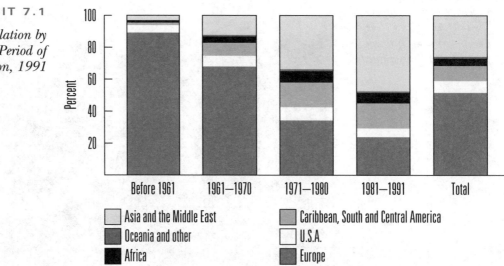

Source: Statistics Canada, Canadian Social Trends *(Summer, 1993). Reproduced by authority of the Minister of Industry 1994.*

Recent statistics indicate that immigrants who arrived in the decade between 1981 and 1991 were more likely to be Asian and Middle Eastern. These groups represented almost one-half of all immigrants. Asian countries accounted for six of the ten most common birthplaces cited by recent arrivals (Badets, 1993).

KINDS OF RACE RELATIONS

Paternalism and Competition

Pierre Van den Berghe (1967) has posited two models of race relations: paternalism, typical of the *Gemeinschaft*, and competition, typical of the *Gesellschaft* .

Paternalistic race relations are typical of, but not limited to, pre-industrial societies. Dominant and inferior groups live in close proximity, but interaction between them is ritualized. Rules spelling out appropriate behaviour for each group are generally understood. Only menial tasks are allocated to the inferior group. The colour line is impenetrable, except to those whose physical characteristics allow them to "pass." (Since women from the minority race are deemed sexually available to dominant men, the number of individuals who can "pass" increases over time.)

Members of the dominant group view minority individuals as immature, irresponsible, and impetuous, as children who need the guidance of a father. Like well-behaved children, docile minority-group members are rewarded with kindness and little treats. The movie *Gone with the Wind* depicts an idealized picture of a society based on paternalistic race relations. The minority group's acquiescence to their depressed status reduces overt conflict. Paternalism is not a thing of the past; it continues to play an important part in majority/minority relations today. Consider the way the elderly are treated. Similarly, a paternalistic view of native peoples is embedded in Canadian public policy.

Competitive race relations are more typical of modern industrialized societies. Because such systems of competition depend on utilizing talent within the society, race can no longer be the exclusive determinant of the individual's place in the division of labour (although it continues to affect one's position). The rules for intergroup relations become fuzzy. Informal mixing is minimized by spatial segregation—for example, black ghettos, whites-only neighbourhoods, and Chinatowns. Dominant-group members view minority individuals with hostility rather than with condescending tolerance, because they are now seen as competitors for such valued goods as education and jobs.

Thus, a continuing struggle is waged between the dominant group, which seeks to defend its privileges, and the minority, which wants its piece of the pie. "Our time has come" was the banner cry of Jesse Jackson, a black candidate for the 1984 Democratic nomination for president of the United States. In 1988, when Jackson again ran for the nomination, that time still had not been reached.

While constructed for race relations, these models can be used to analyze relations among minority and majority groups in general. Women can be seen as immature, requiring paternalistic care, or as dangerous competitors in a depressed economic climate. Similar analogies can be developed for members of the different ethnic groups discussed in the next section.

ETHNIC GROUPS

Race, as we have noted, refers to a way of classifying human beings according to physical characteristics. In contrast, **ethnicity** distinguishes various cultural categories. Fleras and Elliott define an ethnic group as "a social classification in which a particular group of people define themselves as a distinctive category on the basis of an identification that is felt with a particular set of customs, and language, religion, nationality, and homeland" (1992, 315).

In other words, the members of an ethnic group share cultural attributes. These similarities are apparent to others in the society and serve as a basis for categorizing the individuals as belonging to a particular group. For instance, if you see a man in a broad-rimmed, black hat driving a horse and buggy, you will likely put him under the rubric of Mennonite (and thereby engage in a form— sometimes a useful one—of stereotyping). Equally important is the subjective dimension of ethnicity. Members of an ethnic group may conceive of themselves as being alike and identify with each other: "We Greeks [or Jews or Québécois] must stick together."

This ethnic cohesion that sustains the subculture is related to the length of time immigrants are in Canada, the prevalence of their ethnic organizations and institutions, government policy, and the economic success of ethnic group members (Goyder, 1990, 102). New immigrants who find a welcoming ethnic community that can provide religious, economic, and cultural organizations will affiliate with their compatriots. Breton (1964), studying ethnic groups in Montreal, found a correlation between what he called the "institutional completeness" of an ethnic community, that is, the organizational support the group could provide for its members, and the amount of interaction individuals had with other members of their ethnic community. Groups providing high institutional completeness accounted for 89 percent of relations; medium-support groups accounted for 54 percent of relations, and low-support groups had 21 percent of their relations within the group. Indeed, the main function of ethnic associations, such as language schools, social clubs, and publications, is to preserve group traditions while strengthening members' identification with them. Economic success, however, can mitigate against ethnic identification, as Makabe (cited in Goyder, 1990) found in a case study of Japanese Canadians. Only 11 percent of second-generation Japanese white-collar workers in the sample identified with the Japanese Canadian community, compared with 45 percent of their blue-collar compatriots. Government policies, covered in the next section, can also foster the maintenance of immigrant subcultures.[3]

MULTICULTURALISM—THE CANADIAN OPTION

Canada is a nation of immigrants. At several times in our history, authorities have deliberately recruited immigrants for economic reasons. Even at other times, there has been a steady enough influx of people who, fleeing political strife, persecution, or economic hardship, have sought entry to this country. But immigration to Canada has never been open to everyone. Using various criteria, officials have selected candidates based on their presumed ability to blend into the mainstream of Canadian society. In the days of New France, colonists had to be Roman Catholics (a requirement that prevented the entrance of Huguenots, even when these French Protestants were tolerated in France). For many years, Orientals, East Indians, blacks, and sometimes Jews were deemed undesirable.[4]

Many immigrants to Canada are refugees fleeing political strife, persecution, and/or economic hardship.

UNHCR/22029/05.1992/A. Hollman/UN Photo.

Given Canada's large number of immigrants, how newcomers become **acculturated** is a major social concern. On the macrolevel, acculturation is "culture change resulting from contact between members of two autonomous cultural groups" (Redfield et al., cited in Berry, 1991). Although, in principle, acculturation can be mutual, in reality power affects the process, producing more change and accommodation in the less powerful group.

Berry (1991) contends that two issues concerning acculturation must be addressed: cultural maintenance of the incoming ethnic group and the contact of that group with the host society. These factors are also pertinent to microlevel analysis of individual members of the immigrant group.

Exhibit 7.2 translates Berry's two issues into two questions. Answering "yes" to both of them leads to integration. Group identity is nourished and the group becomes one of the identifiable pieces of the puzzle comprising the larger society—the idea behind the Canadian government policy of multiculturalism, which was adopted in 1971. The aim of the policy, in line with the integration model, is fourfold: to encourage ethnic groups to maintain their identities; to foster harmony and tolerance among groups; to bolster group interaction, and to encourage the learning of a common official language.

EXHIBIT 7.2

*Four Modes of
Acculturation as a
Function of Two Issues*

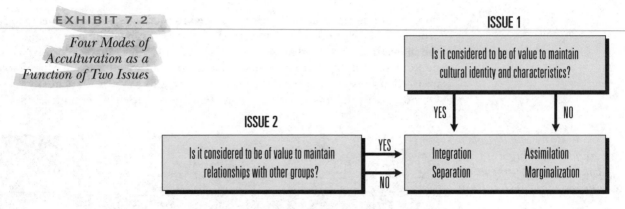

EXHIBIT 7.2

*Four Modes of
Acculturation as a
Function of Two Issues*

Source: J.W. Berry, Working Paper 24, "Sociopsychological Costs and Benefits of Multiculturalism," Economic Council of Canada, 1991, 11.

Separation occurs when immigrant groups decide to keep their ethnic identity and have minimal contact with other groups. If this process is controlled by the dominant group, whereby the members of the immigrant group are "kept in their place," segregation results. Segregation is especially likely if the group members are seen as "dangerous."

Assimilation leads to the loss of ethnic identity and the merging of the group with the larger society. This corresponds to the American "melting pot" idea. Again, this can be enforced by the dominant society, or it can be voluntary. Marginalization is the last outcome. In that event, individuals have little group connection, having lost their ethnic identity; but they have also not been assimilated, which leaves them perched on the fringes of the culture (Berry, 1991). Many of Canada's native peoples, having lost their traditional ways of living, find themselves in this position.

A VERTICAL MOSAIC

John Porter (1921–1979), in a major work (1965) that made extensive use of statistical data on such factors as education, occupation, and income, showed how stratification was manifested in Canadian society. He found a great deal of evidence that contradicted the image of Canada as a classless society or one that was essentially middle-class, without the extremes of poverty or wealth (as did Clement after him, discussed in the previous chapter on stratification).

Porter gave his book the title *The Vertical Mosaic* because, he argued, while Canada may be a mosaic, a patterned combination of small pieces, the parts that constitute it do not enjoy equality. Economic position (class) and ethnicity have a significant relationship. The decennial censuses from 1931 to 1961 consistently revealed those of British origin to be overrepresented at the top of the occupational and income hierarchies, whereas native peoples were grossly overrepresented at the bottom. The other groups forming the ethnic mosaic ranged between these poles. Drawing on Blishen's analysis of the 1951 census data, Porter commented:

> Within the total occupational system the vertical mosaic can be
> summed up as follows: "... the proportion of British in each class
> generally increases from the lowest to the highest class whereas the

Separation occurs when groups keep their identity and have minimal contact with other groups.

Lubavitch Centre/Toronto.

reverse is true for the French. The Jewish group follows a pattern similar to that of the British whereas all other origins follow the French pattern" (1965, 90).

Uncovering the extent and the form of inequality in Canada was a major focus of Porter's enquiry. A second, related objective was to examine the structure of power. Porter defined power as "the recognized right to make effective decisions on behalf of a group of people" (1965, 201). Who exercised power, what was the composition of the elite (power-holding) groups, and how did they interact with one another?

The economic elite, which Porter defined as individuals who held directorships in one or more corporations employing at least 500 people, was dominated by those of British origin. Francophones constituted a mere 6.7 percent of this group, and "ethnic groups of neither British nor French origin, which made up about one-fifth of the general population, were hardly represented at all" (1965, 286).

Overall, Porter found strong relationships between ethnicity, class, and power in Canadian society. He predicted that these links would persist and that the "historical pattern of class and ethnicity will be perpetuated as long as ethnic differentiation is so highly valued" (1965, 558).

Porter provided a fresh way of looking at stratification in Canada. In the 1950s and 1960s, the functionalist perspective, in which society was seen as a smoothly operating system of interlocking parts, was especially prominent. Social scientists focused on the bright side by writing about opportunity and mobility. Porter, however, shifted attention to the roadblocks that stood in the way of mobility. He pointed to the wasted potential of those who did not manage to get ahead because they were born in the wrong province or had the wrong class or ethnic background. Porter's work has spurred continuing research into the issues of power and inequality in Canadian society.

More recent research has not found contemporary support for the existence of a British elite in Canada or for the thesis that ethnic affiliation limits mobility for immigrants from European countries, but visible minorities, including women and Aboriginals, may still be penalized (Agocs & Boyd, 1993; CRSA, 1992). Using quasi-experimental techniques, Henry and Ginzberg (1993) examined racism in the labour market in Toronto. Two questions were considered: did black and white applicants receive the same number of job offers when seeking employment in person, and were they treated in a similar fashion on the telephone when attempting to arrange for interviews? Answers to both indicated racial discrimination. White people were offered jobs three times more often than blacks when the jobs were solicited in person. The numbers of calls necessary to obtain job interviews increased for callers with discernible accents—Italian and Slavic—and when the discernible accents were tied to being those of nonwhite— Jamaican and Pakistani people.

Exhibit 7.3 explains other discriminatory practices in the workplace that may prevent success for minority group members, including women.

EXHIBIT 7.3

Forms of Discrimination

	Unequal Treatment	Adverse impact (systemic)	Failure to accommodate diversity
Employment systems	Refusal to hire or promote qualified members of a racial minority; Different hiring procedures are used for women and men, and women are not hired	Selection criteria disproportionately screen out minorities or women and are not job-related	Employer refuses to seek solutions when job requirements conflict with family or religious requirements
Workplace climate	Sexual or racial harassment; Assignment of roles in social situations based on stereotypes	Business decisions are made in male sports settings (e.g., golf)	Diverse languages or customs are not accepted in social situations

Source: Carol Agocs and Monica Boyd, "The Candian Ethnic Mosaic Recast for the 1990s." In J. Curtis, E. Grabb, and N. Guppy, Social Inequality in Canada *(Toronto: Prentice-Hall, 1993), p. 342.*

THE IMPACT OF GENDER

As with stratification analyses, researchers are now highlighting previously hidden aspects of gender that intersect with ethnicity and race. Recent controversies concern refugee claimants. The Geneva Convention defines a **refugee**, in part, as someone with a well-founded fear of persecution on the basis of race, religion, nationality, membership in a particular social group, or political opinion. In 1991, a Saudi woman applied for refugee status in Canada, saying she had been stoned and beaten for refusing to wear a veil and for protesting discriminatory laws against women in her native country. After much public pressure, the government admitted her on compassionate and humanitarian grounds. Her admission was erroneously interpreted as a change in government policy regarding gender-based claims, but her case has led to the drafting of new guidelines that will make it easier for women to claim refugee status on the basis of gender persecution.[5]

Gender and wealth intersect when wealthy Chinese women migrate to Canada as family class immigrants with their husbands who qualify for entry because of the capital they plan to invest in Canada. At the other end of the socioeconomic scale are Caribbean black women who enter Canada temporarily as domestics and nannies.[6]

Exploring the situation of female immigrants in Canada, Ng (1988) focuses on the social processes that (re)create the vertical mosaic, including gender. In her study of a nonprofit employment agency that specifically serves immigrant women, Ng found that job counsellors inadvertently support the hierarchies of gender, ethnicity, and class by matching immigrant women with the minimum wage, low-skilled, monotonous jobs that have traditionally been filled by immigrant women in Canada. Being pegged as "immigrant woman" generates certain consequences, including almost guaranteeing low status for the women themselves and solidifying the category of immigrant women workers for the labour market.

Exhibit 7.4 shows the immigrant incomes by gender and period of immigration.

Since the sixties, wages for all immigrants have declined. The data show that the women remained disadvantaged and, unlike the men, did not come to earn wages similar to those of native-born Canadians of the same sex. Note, too, that all the men, whatever their origin, earned more than the women.

The impact of gender, class, and ethnicity is vividly illustrated in Box 7.1. Because of their status as immigrants, these women find themselves even more isolated than Canadian women in violent homes.

Canada's aboriginal women are also familiar with beatings and discrimination. A 1989 report cites the figure of 80 percent of Indian women as survivors of violence.[7] Prior to 1985, Indian women were stripped of their Indian status if they married non-Indian men, which did not happen to Indian men who married non-Indian women. Bill C-31, designed to correct this injustice, has not proved effective, since individual bands have the power to decide if these women can return to the fold even though the federal government has reinstated them.[8]

NATIVE PEOPLES

Canada's native peoples are the Inuit, the Indians, and the Métis.[9] Because these racial minorities differ so much, umbrella terms such as "native peoples" impose an artificial similarity on quite diverse cultural and linguistic entities. Almost the only thing that Baffin Island Inuit share with members of the Six Nations Reserve near Brantford, Ontario, is that their ancestors inhabited this country long before those of white Canadians. The terms "native peoples," "First Nations," and "aboriginals" are used merely for ease; they do not imply uniformity on all dimensions.

Initially, relations between Europeans and native Indians after the arrival of the Europeans in North America were largely peaceful, aside from those times

EXHIBIT 7.4

Income of Immigrants by Gender and Period of Immigration

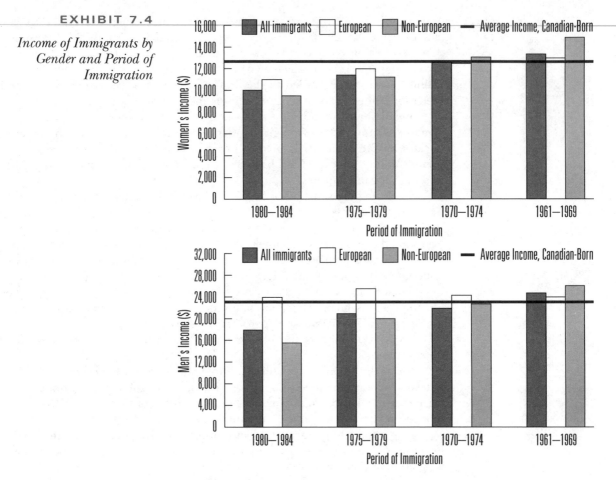

Source: A. Fleras and J.L. Elliott, Multiculturalism in Canada *(Toronto: Nelson Canada, 1992), p. 47.*

when Europeans took sides in Indian tribal hostilities. Peace was advantageous to the Europeans, who drew on the Indians' valuable expertise in hunting and trapping animals, the furs of which were in great demand in Europe. Systematic oppression of natives became widespread, however, as European settlement expanded. The Indians inhabited vast lands that the whites coveted. Because native Indians had no conception of private ownership of land, they often did not understand that in signing treaties they were giving up their land forever. Land that Indians did not give up peacefully was taken from them by force. Frequently, it was deemed most efficient simply to kill those native Indians whose territory was desired:

> By 1800 the Beothuk population of Newfoundland had reached a critical point. Increased settlement had upset the delicate balance of their nomadic way of life and they were being indiscriminately slaughtered by the whites and their Micmac fur-trade allies, who were encroaching on Beothuk territory. Evidence suggests that at about this time three or four hundred Beothuk were herded onto a point of land near their favourite sealing-site and shot down like deer (Such, 1973, vii).

BOX 7.1

WOMEN CROSS CULTURAL BOUNDARIES TO DEAL WITH CONJUGAL VIOLENCE

Heading home after a day huddled over a factory sewing machine, the Sri Lankan immigrant starts her second shift: getting dinner, dealing with the children's homework, the housework and the fact that her husband expects to be waited on and hits her when he's not.

Coming to terms with a new life in a new place with a new culture and a new way of doing virtually everything is stressful, says Sherine Xavier, a community worker at the South Asian Women's Centre who came here from Sri Lanka in 1987.

"There is pressure on both parties," she says.

Sometimes, she says, men relieve that pressure at home. With their wives as targets. Of course that wouldn't wash in Sri Lanka, where someone is always watching. Men live with their wives' families, members of the extended family are everywhere and everyone minds everyone else's business, Xavier explained. And if you have to answer to other people, you think twice before you wallop your wife.

Back home in Sri Lanka, women stay at home and look after the children. Men are the breadwinners. When they come here, often the women have to go to work outside the home. Traditional as they might be, the men don't have a problem with their wives being in the work force, Xavier says. But then they want them to come home and be homemakers again.

Few immigrant women report domestic violence. Socially and culturally conditioned to believe that breaking their silence is betraying a family secret or a community trust, they suffered silently. Until recently.

"We were taught your family problems stay between the walls," says the 26-year-old Xavier, who works mainly with the Sri Lankan community. "It is not something that has been discussed publicly until now, but at least now it is being recognized."

Slowly, women are venturing out into existing women's networks and shelters and building their own. And next Sunday, Nov. 29, a conference on family violence in ethnocultural communities will be held at Concordia

University, bringing together women from the Italian, black, Greek and South Asian communities...

"An ethnic woman often feels she has nowhere to turn. She can't go to her own community and there is the shame and the fear of going elsewhere. So where does she go? Some of the women leaders in ethnocultural communities are beginning slowly to come out and speak about it."

It's the first time in Quebec that a conference of this scale is taking place, says Peluso, a research fellow at Concordia's Simone de Beauvoir Institute.

No one is saying that conjugal violence is any worse in black or Greek or South Asian families than it is in the mainstream community—a landmark 1980 federally funded study estimates that one woman in 10 in this country is abused—but cultural factors do influence how the problem is confronted or, as has often been the case, not confronted.

Women in the cultural communities, says Peluso, have been taught not to criticize men in their own community—lest the men be further discriminated against, or the women be accused of castigating the entire community.

Silence of communities

To Fabienne Pierre-Jacques, a member of the Collective of Black Women of Montreal, the issue is not the silence of women but the silence of communities she believes should be dealing with the problem more openly. "At a community level, I think there exists a certain silence about it. We're not making it a priority, as an issue."

In the face of family violence in the ethno-cultural communities, the silence of government and social agencies is deafening, organizers of the Concordia conference contend. Mainstream social-service centres and CLSCs don't keep data on family violence and, as a rule, don't provide relevant information to the people who need it, says Peluso.

To Omaira Falcon, a worker at Secours aux Femmes, a Montreal emergency shelter for immigrant women and their children, it's not so much that immigrant women are less willing to speak out on conjugal violence.

They just know less about their rights and local community resources than Quebec women do.

If there is a crucial role for the community centres run by the cultural communities, Falcon says, it is to inform.

She told of one Middle Eastern woman who learned about Secours aux Femmes only when she had been in Montreal for a year. And she heard it was a place for women without children. So she left without her children at first, although she was able, with the help of shelter workers, to return later to collect them.

But not all women get to community centres. Many are isolated. Often, of course, the women who are targets of abuse cannot speak French or English. Or they have no network of friends or family in which to confide. Or, in the case of immigrant women sponsored by their husbands, the legal rights of these women to remain in this country might rest with their abusers.

The goal of such centres as the South Asian Women's Centre is to help women adapt and integrate. Community workers strive hard to build a relationship of trust with the women. "It takes a lot for them to come out with it," says Xavier.

A lot of pressure
Certainly it is easier to leave once you know what your rights are, says Falcon of Secours aux Femmes.

Yet, even armed with that information, immigrant women feel a lot of pressure from a lot of places—their children, their parents and even the church: pastors have been known to call the shelter where Falcon works to ask women not to leave home.

For many women, much of their identity and sense of identification comes from being married—even if it's to someone who assaults them, says Falcon.

"Women are concerned about being badly thought of if they come forward, because as far as they are concerned responsibility for the marriage rests with them. If a marriage fails, the woman is guilty," she says.

In the end, nearly half the women who come to the shelter eventually do leave their abusers for good—about the same proportion as in other shelters. It's just that they often take a longer route...

As difficult as it is to adapt and integrate in a new country and culture, it is that much more difficult, of course, when your husband has no interest in your doing either.

"Is it in the husband's interest to have his wife adapt? Not really. I see it as a way to keep her under his thumb," says Falcon. "Often he already thinks women here in this country are too liberated."

One possible way
Some women believe one possible way to draw more women away from the tinderboxes their homes have become is to make shelters culturally appropriate places...

In theory at least, cultural communities are in an ideal position to set up alternatives to the traditional social-service network. They're sensitive to issues that a mainstream agency might not be and will make a commitment to a community-based system.

On the other hand, women who live in small, close-knit communities might hesitate to go to a shelter where they would not be anonymous.

What's important, women in the field agree, is that more women learn that there are options.

Source: Susan Schwartz, "Somewhere to turn," Gazette (Montreal) (23 November 1992). p. F1. Reprinted with permission.

Gradually, but inexorably, the Indians were pushed onto reserves, most of which did not permit self-sufficiency but at least provided escape from imminent starvation. The natural resources of the land had been depleted, often by needless waste, as in the case of the Plains buffalo herds. Other employment opportunities were minimal, because many of the reserves were in remote areas far from industrial activity and also because most Indians lacked the education, training, and skills needed in the society Canada was becoming.

In brief, Canada has no reason to feel proud of its record in dealing with the Indians or other native peoples. They fared poorly in the past; their present situation is scarcely better. As Canadians have plunged into native peoples' traditional territory, regarding its riches as a prime opportunity for economic growth (in fact, as the "last frontier"), the foundations of native cultures have been undermined by the increased contact with whites, the depletion of their resources, and the disruption of traditional pursuits. Grescoe describes the appalling health conditions among native Canadians:

> The wretched physical and mental health of Native Canadians is a national disgrace. Native deaths come quicker. The infant-mortality rate among Canadian Indians and Inuit is four times the national average, and the average age of death for Indians, 42.4 years, is nearly 24 years younger than that of the general population. Among native people between the ages of 20 and 39, death by violence (homicide, suicide, and accidents) is almost four times more common than among whites. And the brief lives they lead are far less healthy. Tuberculosis, supposedly under control, has had a slight resurgence in the North and is still seen in the South: ten new cases of TB appeared last year among the four hundred residents of the house-poor, pollution rich Stoney Creek reserve near Vanderhoof, British Columbia (1987, 127–28).

Cultures can be regarded as patterns of living designed to allow group survival in a particular environment. When the environment changes as drastically as it did for native Canadians, many of these patterns become irrelevant, if not maladaptive. Hunting lore may be painstakingly passed on to one's son, but what use is it when the herds to be hunted have been decimated, and when survival depends on welfare doled out by strangers? The result can only be Durkheim's anomie: internalized values and norms are no longer effective for dealing with the realities of existence. For instance, Chance noted that the Inuit of North Alaska who were engaged in wage labour soon realized that:

> Their success on the job depends largely on individual rather than cooperative effort and, as such, conflicts with much of their past experience and cultural outlook (1966, 76).

The manifestations of anomie among native peoples form a litany of woes: a high incidence of drunkenness, fatalism, family violence, and suicide, to name only a few. In urban environments, native peoples are strikingly overrepresented among prisoners, welfare recipients, and the homeless.

Along with cultural dislocation, most native Indians face substandard "shelter," on and off reserves. Writing in the late 1970s, Krauter and Davis noted:

> Indian families working for ranchers often live in shacks on the property. Those who are transient labourers in the larger cities usually find housing in slum areas because either landlords will not rent to them elsewhere or they can afford no better. The situation is particularly acute in western urban centres (1978, 20).

Things are hardly better for the Métis, who continue to exist on the social and economic fringes of western communities. Howard Adams has described what it was like growing up as a Métis in Saskatchewan during the Second World War:

> Although the majority of the population were Métis—French and Cree —not a single business was owned or operated by us. We remained the casual and unskilled labourers, the depressed and powerless people. The hotel, garage, store, lumberyard, and cafe were all run by white Frenchmen. A few Anglo-Saxons ran other small businesses and had importance and power in the community quite out of proportion to their small numbers. Dotted along the back roads were more halfbreed shacks, log and mud houses used as permanent dwellings throughout the year, built to accommodate large families and withstand the severe sub-zero Saskatchewan winters (1979, 23).

Canadian government policy with regard to native peoples has never been clearcut. On the one hand, the reserve system was used to deal with the Indian "problem," presumably in the hope that problems that were made "invisible" would disappear permanently. (The Inuit were already "invisible," since there were relatively few of them and they lived in remote northern areas.) On the other hand, there was the desire to assimilate the native peoples into Canadian society. An important means to this end was residential schools, operated by Christian denominations but supported by government funding. In a case study of one such institution, *The School at Mopass* (1967), King found that the school sought to strip students of their traditional ways but did not provide them with the social and academic attributes to succeed in mainstream society.

> The fact that children always wait for directives, even in the most routine situations, is somehow not connected by Whitemen with the fact that these children are never encouraged to make personal decisions or choices among real alternatives. It is taken as prima facie evidence that directives are needed. "They're only children; even their parents are just like children in so many ways ... " is a common theme. "You have to tell them what is right." Over a period of many days, such directives constitute the totality of verbal communication from most adults to the children (1967, 75–76).

In other words, the view of Indian children (and of Indians generally) as needing constant, detailed directions meant they were given little opportunity to use their own initiative. Hence, self-direction remained unpractised. The prophecy that Indians could not act autonomously thus became self-fulfilling.

Today such attitudes are being challenged by increasingly militant native peoples. The example of the civil rights movement and of the new phase of the women's liberation movement during the 1960s sparked the mobilization of other minority groups no longer willing to accept inferior status. One important consequence is that native Canadians are much less accepting of the dominant group's definition of various situations. Native rights movements are seeking a rebirth of aboriginal cultures. They are facilitating this change by taking control of their schools, by insisting on self-administration of government funds allocated to them, and by pressing for cash settlements, which they claim to be due under various treaties. Furthermore, native peoples are questioning whether industrial and technological development of the north would really be to their benefit in the long run. They are also asserting the right to reclaim land in some areas of Canada—for example, the Haida in British Columbia and the Inuit in Labrador.

In the 1970s, the quest for new sources of energy fostered pressure for the construction of a pipeline to transport Arctic gas southward. For the first time since colonization, native peoples, in collaboration with environmental conservationists, were able to exert effective counterpressure. The result was the appointment of the Berger Commission, and the landmark report it produced, entitled *Northern Frontier: Northern Homeland* (Berger, 1977). Although its chief recommendation—that no construction be started for ten years—was ignored, the hearings themselves achieved a breakthrough in race relations in Canada. Indians and Inuit were able to voice their concerns in their own languages and in their own communities, to whites in positions of authority who were willing to listen. (This is the kind of approach described in Chapter 2, in the section called "Feminist Approaches to Sociology.")

As is often the case with groups categorized under a broad label, native peoples are divided by the conflicting goals of subgroups. Yet, they have a strong and growing awareness of their shared identity and common interests as a minority group. Self-assertion has reversed their former invisibility. Native peoples remain a discriminated-against minority, but they are no longer a passive one. However, as Ponting points out, their ability to command resources and to force change is extremely limited. In view of the Canadian state's reluctance to accede to rapid change, Ponting predicts that native peoples will resort increasingly to such tactics as civil disobedience, international embarrassment, and a selective use of the courts (1988, 640).

The most recent event of this kind occurred in Kanesatake in the spring of 1990 when Mohawks blocked a road to the town of Oka in Quebec, protesting a proposed extension of a municipal golf course on sacred Indian burial grounds (Lorimer & McNulty, 1991). In July, the Sûreté du Québec (the provincial police), called in by the Oka mayor, attacked; in the resulting stand-off one officer was killed. Increasing their defiance, the Mohawks barricaded one end of a major bridge to the island of Montreal, cutting off a suburb and causing immense daily traffic pile-ups. Over the summer, the hostility of the suburb's residents increased, and Mohawk vehicles were stoned crossing the bridge into the city. The Canadian army was called in by the province as negotiations remained stalled. With the army attempting to tear down the barricades, producing the much publicized press photo of an Indian and soldier confronting each other, face to face, some Mohawks retreated to a drug and alcohol treatment centre on the reserve. Finally, in September, the Mohawks surrendered. At issue in the conflict was jurisdiction over land and ultimately the status of First Nations, which became a major point of discussion in the failed constitutional proposal, the Charlottetown Accord.

Another highly publicized snapshot of reserve life came in the form of a 1993 *Globe and Mail* article. The picture was of Davis Inlet, Labrador—known as

Native people remain a discriminated-against minority but, as the stand-off at Oka showed, many are beginning to fight back.

Lawrence Acland.

Utshimasits to the inhabitants. With caribou herds in decline, the Innu were convinced by their missionary priest and the government to move into houses on an island in Davis Inlet. Having lost their traditional ways of life, these Indians became marginalized, one of the consequences of acculturation discussed at the beginning of this chapter. Marginalization, like anomie, leads to social and psychological distress that is revealed in alcoholism, drug abuse, suicide, and violence. The shocking poverty and squalor of the community prompted attention. A number of children found sniffing gasoline fumes were exported to treatment centres in the south. Some of them progressed well, but aid for the whole community and promised resettlement have yet to be realized. Until twenty-six years ago, the Innu had been nomadic subsistence hunters of caribou. Box 7.2 gives an idea of Innu life during that period.

BOX 7.2

BYGONE LIFE: A LOOK BACK AT DAVIS INLET

Davis Inlet was a stop on my clinic run between Nain and Hopedale. It was 1965, and I was temporarily in charge of the Grenfell Association's beat that covered northern Labrador. Our base was North West River at the head of Hamilton Inlet, which looks on the map like the mouth of the dog that is Labrador. Once a month I did clinics at each of the coastal communities, flying with Hector Baikie, pilot of the hospital's Beaver, on floats or skis.

Davis Inlet was one of the prettiest settlements on the coast and my favourite place to stay over, partly because of the gentle Innu people who lived there, partly because of the prospect of stimulating discussions with Father Frank Pieters, the Oblate priest who ran the Catholic mission.

When the plane touched down in front of the community, most of the village people would rush down the hill and through the foreshore ice to garner news from up and down the coast.

Those were the days before the community was moved to an island 16 kilometres down the bay, which was said to provide better moorage for the supply boats. There were few permanent buildings in Davis Inlet, just the mission that acted as church, meeting hall, clinic and rectory, Chief Joe Rich's house, a small Hudson's Bay store, and a few family cabins.

Most of the Innu, Indians of the Naskaupi tribe, lived in tents scattered among the trees that led away into the inhospitable interior of Labrador.

Their wall tents were hung from spruce frames. Inside, a woodstove kept a constant temperature in the small space for an entire family. Every few days the women would lay a new spruce-bough carpet and then the whole tent smelled sweetly of resin. It was soft to walk on and squeaky clean.

We had to choose our dates carefully for the Davis Inlet clinic because soon after freeze-up most of the Innu families disappeared into the bush until Christmas, when they returned to stay for a couple of weeks before moving off again. They lived nomadically, travelling between trapping and hunting grounds according to the abundance of game.

Just after New Year I arrived there by dog team from the North on my run down the coast. Following the tradition of Grenfell doctors, I was trying to visit all the people who were habitually shut in for the duration of the winter.

We had set off from Nain with Bob Voisey driving a team of 17 dogs. At Shango, we were stormbound for a day, but when it cleared, Ben Pardy drove a dozen dogs on to Davis Inlet.

I visited every tent in the village, accompanied by Father Pieters, who carried my doctor's black bag. From reading the *Merck Manual of Diagnosis and Therapy*, he had gleaned a working knowledge of medicine, and did all the clinic work in between visits from nurses and doctors.

We watched the Innu families getting ready to go back into the bush. They wrapped all their gear in a light canvas travelling tent laid out on the sledge and then parcelled and lashed it with rope. Alongside the rifle, babies were put on top of the load, in spaces made by drawing apart the canvas. Mothers expressed breast milk into small deerskin bags in which the baby sucked, drawing milk through the pores in the skin. This way they did not need to stop for feeding when on the move.

They would travel all day without taking a break, trotting beside the sledge that was pulled by only one or two dogs to make travel in the woods easier. If caught out in severe weather, they would camp out, wrapped in a single blanket lying on a thin layer of spruce boughs.

Doing my clinic rounds with Father Pieters, I observed that the families who had spent the previous months in the bush were significantly healthier than families who, for whatever reason, had remained in Davis Inlet. In the woods they survived well on what they caught with gun, fishing line, snare wire and traps, together with some flour and a few extra staples.

I spent an afternoon with Chief Joe Rich on his trapline. He was too old to go on long trips but he kept active close to home. He was still a master in the bush, where we walked on round, bear-paw snowshoes, tending and setting his traps.

In the evenings, Father Pieters and I sat at his dinner table and put the world to rights late into the night. He would thump the table to drive home his argument or punctuate excited outbursts with loud guffaws. We did another clinic in the morning and then I left to continue my journey south to Hopedale with an Innu dog driver, Chenis, and John Edmunds.

I am reluctant to paint an idyllic picture of Davis Inlet as some Labradorian Utopia. But it was evident to me then, nearly 30 years ago, that the Innu thrived in their desolate mountains and forests, where they were masters of survival.

When I was with them in their environment—and I rather fancied myself as a mountaineer and outdoorsman—I was helpless as a babe in arms, and humbled by it. I just did not have the skills to let me travel through that inclement land alone, and my Innu companions commanded my most profound respect.

I believe this vignette of a bygone life is significant today because our national failure to respect the Innu, and legions of other native groups, is at the root of their present sadness. We all have fragile egos, and when they are ruthlessly crushed by lack of opportunity, poverty and their successors, alcohol and drugs, a culture is destroyed.

Back in those days, a pulp mill was proposed. But it never materialized, because of lack of cash, as with other schemes designed to enable the Innu to remain on the land and follow a way of life in which they thrived.

The Innu cannot return to an earlier era. But anything must be better than the way successive governments have hived off the problems of dealing with native groups that do not fit neatly into the molds created for them.

With imagination, it must be possible to divert part of the vast sums of money set aside for relocating these people into helping them establish programs that would allow them to pursue the lives in which they excel.

They should not need to compete with our foreign ways, which have brought them, over the generations, nothing but heartache and misery.

Source: Peter Steele, "Bygone life: a look back at Davis Inlet," The Globe and Mail (19 February 1993). Reproduced with permission.

In some areas of the country there is optimism. In late 1992, a referendum in the eastern Arctic created Nunavut Territory, which is to become self-governing by the local Inuit in 1999. In British Columbia, the Gitksan and Wet'suwet'en Indians won a major victory in the area of land claims. The British Columbia Court of Appeal granted them rights, although not ownership, over an immense area (58,000 square kilometres) in the northwest of the province. The case overturned an earlier judgment that was described as racist and ethnocentric in its description of the lives of the Gitksan and Wet'suwet'en as "nasty, brutish and short." The case, too, provides a precedent in ruling that pre-Confederation laws did not extinguish aboriginal rights to land in British Columbia.[10]

Another Royal Commission report tackling options for native self-government is due in 1994. This will be added to the list of over thirty government-sponsored studies of Canada's first peoples done in the last twenty-five years.

ORIENTALS

Historically, relations between whites and Orientals in Canada have clearly fallen into the competitive model of race relations (refer back to the section on

Saila, Pitaloosie, *Mother's Lullaby*/INAC.

paternalism and competition in this chapter). The dominant group used its political and economic power to retain lucrative and prestigious activities for itself. Opposition to such a monopoly was minimized because of widespread prejudice based on negative stereotypes. Hence, for many whites, attitudes of prejudice against Orientals were consonant with discriminatory behaviour. Illustration can be provided with a brief history of the experience of Canada's two main Oriental immigrant groups, the Chinese and the Japanese.

THE CHINESE

The first Chinese are believed to have come to Canada during the Fraser River gold rush of the 1850s. In 1871 when the province of British Columbia was established, Chinese men were hired as domestics, in laundries and in the salmon canneries, since there were not enough women available to do the "women's work." Royal Commissions of 1885 and 1902 referred to these men as a "feminine race," underscoring their lack of power. When the Canadian Pacific started construction of the trans-Canada railway, it petitioned the federal government to import the labour needed to work in the unpopulated west. The result was that about 17,000 Chinese were brought to Canada. By permitting only males to come and making it clear that relationships with white women would be punished severely, the government constantly reiterated that their stay was meant to be temporary. However, because they received only meagre wages, most of which had to be used to pay for food and board, many of these workers had insufficient savings to pay the return fare to China when the railroad was completed; nor could they afford to bring over wives and children from China. The Canadian Pacific Railway and the federal government were unwilling to pay

Petitioned for workers by Canadian Pacific, the Canadian government imported almost 17,000 Chinese men to build the trans-Canada railway.

CAM TEEDON S.A.C. RECRUITS.

I wuv to wide the wailway!

1773/Vancouver Public Library.

the return fares, though reduced rates were available and men over the age of 60 were transported at government expense.

Most of the Chinese remained in the vicinity of Vancouver, where they formed a pool of cheap labour. In the absence of government programs, such as unemployment insurance or welfare, they had to accept whatever wages employers chose to offer. The Chinese were, therefore, regarded as unfair competition by white workers, who reacted vehemently. In 1878, the whites formed the Workingman's Protective Association, and, in a related move, "respectable" citizens united against "the oriental threat" and succeeded in having a $10 annual cue tax levied on every Chinese male over the age of 18 who wore long hair. Soon the federal government, too, responded to anti-Chinese feeling by imposing a head tax of $500 on every Chinese person who entered Canada, resulting in the admittance of many more Chinese men than women.

Although these taxes escalated steadily, they did not manage to halt Chinese immigration. The Chinese Immigration Act of 1923, however, did stop immigration. Meanwhile, Orientals, both Chinese and Japanese, had been barred from voting in provincial and municipal elections in the western provinces. In 1919, this ban was extended to federal elections on the basis that anyone barred from voting in provincial elections because of race should not be allowed to vote at the federal level either.

Disenfranchisement affected employment opportunities. In British Columbia, for example, Orientals could not obtain a licence to sell liquor, or to practise law or pharmacy, because entrance to these professions was limited to those who would be eligible to vote when they attained the age of majority. The Japanese were excluded from teaching in British Columbia, and Orientals could not perform work under public works contracts (Krauter & Davis, 1978).

Such blatant discrimination is no longer legal in Canada, and the emphasis in immigration legislation has shifted from racial and national origins to the educational and occupational qualifications of applicants. Many Chinese have taken advantage of the more liberal immigration policies instituted in 1967. Once in Canada, they have tended to do extremely well in the educational system. Their educational achievement is reflected in a changing occupational distribution, with more Chinese in administrative and professional positions. This does not mean that prejudice has disappeared.[11] It does mean that Chinese Canadians, both immigrant and Canadian-born, are now able to fight discrimination more effectively than they could in the past.

Recent Chinese immigrants have gravitated to Vancouver, Montreal, and Toronto, but the biggest impact has been in British Columbia's lower mainland, where Chinese people make up 32.1 percent of all new immigrants to Vancouver. Many have come under the business-class program that promises landed immigrant status to those willing and able to invest enough money ($250,000 to $350,000) in Canada. Chinese immigrants have spurred economic growth in the West and have generally been welcomed. Only rarely has anti-Chinese sentiment been blatant. In 1992, graffiti expressing these feelings appeared on overpasses in Vancouver, and some residents complained about their razing of old homes for new, larger ones (Fennell, 1993). Of course, not all Chinese immigrants are wealthy, and those who are continue to experience systemic discrimination. Those from mainland China, particularly the women, find themselves working in sweatshops for meagre wages and struggling hard to stay afloat.

THE JAPANESE

For much of their history in Canada, which began in about 1885, the Japanese were subject to somewhat less discrimination than the Chinese, in part because there were fewer Japanese and in part because they were represented in this country by articulate organizations. They also enjoyed some protection from the Japanese government. This situation changed drastically with the outbreak of the Second World War, particularly following the Japanese attack on the American navy base at Pearl Harbor and the occupation of Hong Kong (in which a large number of Canadians were taken prisoner).

Almost all the Japanese in Canada had settled on the West Coast. In 1942, most Canadian residents of Japanese origin, regardless of citizenship or place of birth, were removed to camps in the Canadian interior, some as far east as Ontario. There they spent the rest of the war. In *Obasan*, Joy Kogawa (1981) has hauntingly portrayed the experiences of the members of one family torn from their home and separated from each other.

Depriving citizens of all legal rights was officially justified on the basis of national security. However, longstanding prejudice against the Japanese and their "clannish, foreign ways" had prepared the ground for general acceptance of such action. It is also significant that by 1942 many Japanese had established successful market gardening and fishing enterprises, the forced sales of which, it is said, benefited white business people.

The experiences of 1942 and 1945 changed the settlement patterns of Japanese Canadians. Many did not return to the West Coast, and they have avoided clustering in cities in which they have settled. Those born since the war have rates of outmarriage so high as to threaten the survival of the Japanese as a distinct group in Canadian society; that few Japanese have immigrated to Canada since 1945 increases this likelihood.

In many ways, the Japanese have fared well in Canada since the war. The Brazilians have a saying that "money blanches"—dark-skinned individuals become quite acceptable if they are rich enough. A somewhat similar process has been the case for the Japanese people in Canada: their image has been enhanced by Japan's spectacular economic success in recent decades. Japan is now a major player in the world economy and one of Canada's important trading partners; the establishment of subsidiaries of Japanese corporations in the West is eagerly pursued. On the other hand, the ability of Japanese industry to outperform North American firms has heightened economic competition and, with it, awareness of the "we/they" dichotomy.

BLACKS

In the United States, relations between blacks and whites have been one of the most explosive issues in its history. From its very inception as a nation, the United States has had to try and reconcile, on the one hand, an ideology that proclaimed everyone to be entitled to life, liberty, and the pursuit of happiness with the reality of slavery, followed by gross, often legally entrenched discrimination against blacks. In a monumental study, Gunnar Myrdal (1944) labelled this problem *An American Dilemma.*

In Canada, this dilemma was mitigated by the small number of blacks within its borders. Slavery existed here, but it never became widespread, in large part because there was no plantation agriculture suited for slave labour. Furthermore, the harsh climate made it expensive to house, feed, and clothe slaves. Canada was still a relatively unpopulated, undeveloped area when the British Parliament passed the Emancipation Act of 1833, abolishing slavery.

During the Revolutionary War of 1775–1783 and again in the war of 1812–1814, the British promised to free any slaves who escaped from the United States and went to Canada. These refugees and those who came later by way of the Freedom Railway certainly desired political freedom, but they also needed economic opportunities, which proved sparse. As Krauter and Davis noted, speaking about the pattern of land grants in Nova Scotia:

> Certainly, in every instance where acreage was granted to both Black and white settlers, Blacks received less. For example, while Blacks were given one-acre lots in Digby, whites were granted from one-hundred to four-hundred acre lots throughout Annapolis County. Moreover, only Blacks who settled in Chedabucto Bay or in Preston township were not completely segregated. Most of the Black settlements eventually failed; as a result many former slaves, now freed in Canada, continued to work as hired or indentured servants (1978, 42).

During the 1840s and 1850s, American abolitionists organized the above-mentioned Freedom Railway to help slaves escape, and blacks clustered at its terminal points in Canada. Sizable settlements were established near Chatham, Ontario, and in Nova Scotia. The most famous was Africville, which was a part of Halifax. This community existed for more than one hundred years, until it was demolished in the 1960s as part of an urban renewal plan. By that time, Africville had become a notorious slum.

The story of Africville is an apt example of a self-fulfilling prophecy. Because blacks were negatively stereotyped, their community was last in line for services from the city. Africville never obtained water or sewage systems, its roads were not paved, and its snow and garbage removal were inadequate. Small wonder, then, that it deteriorated, allowing white Haligonians to cluck their tongues and deplore "the way these people live."

Substandard housing, an inferior and segregated education system, and hence, lack of access to good jobs kept most Africville residents tangled in a web of deprivation. In turn, this deprivation made it very difficult to mount an effective campaign for positive change. Clairmont and Magill wrote that:

> Africville residents were always poor. The historical pattern was that the males worked as labourers on the docks or in small industries and businesses near Africville, and the females worked in low-paid service jobs as domestics in homes or in nearby institutions. Africville residents of Halifax had been petitioning the City for services available to other residents of Halifax since the middle of the nineteenth century, but successes were few (1974, 62).

Blacks in Canada remained small in number until well past the Second World War. With liberalization of the Immigration Act in 1967, however, numerous West Indians began to arrive. Since then, problems in the Caribbean such as poverty, unemployment, political unrest, and the lack of opportunities for advancement have remained powerful "push forces" for West Indian emigration.

Most West Indian immigrants to Canada have settled in large, urban centres; the majority settle in Toronto. The 1986 census showed 106,040 individuals living in the area who had come from the Caribbean and Bermuda. Many, possessing limited education and few occupational skills, were forced to take whatever menial jobs were available. Most also encountered prejudice and discrimination. Of those who came with expertise, and intellectual and creative skills, many have successfully established themselves in Canadian society, even though they too have suffered discrimination.

RACIAL MINORITIES IN CANADA TODAY

Since 1967, changes in immigration legislation have resulted in a significant increase in visible minorities in Canada generally. In addition to the Chinese and blacks, recent immigrants have included diverse East Indians, such as Pakistanis and Indian nationals, as well as Koreans and Vietnamese (some of whom came as "boat people" in the late 1970s). The East Indian group was swelled by an influx of refugees from Uganda following President Amin's expulsion of Asians from that country in 1971.

As visible minorities have increased numerically, so have incidents of discrimination, harassment, and outright violence. The Toronto subway, for example, has been the scene of a number of attacks on East Indians. These attacks became sufficiently serious to arouse public concern and spurred the appointment of a task force to study race relations in Metropolitan Toronto. Its findings, reported in 1977, were in line with those of many other studies of racial interaction in North American cities. The initiators of physical attacks against minority group members tend to be young, male, uneducated, and frequently unemployed. The victims perceive the police as not particularly helpful. The researchers described what happens when the police are called following an incident of vandalism:

> When the police arrive at his home, the complainant, because of his fear and anxiety, is often highly excited. The only organization to which he can turn for help is the police. He demands action—the police must do something. At the same time the policeman is exceedingly frustrated. There are no leads to follow and he knows that there is little he can do. He must cope with the very excited civilian who may be extremely critical of him. The consequence is a loss of confidence in the police by the minority on the one hand, and the reinforcement of the police stereotype image of the South Asian as demanding and with high expectations (Task Force on Human Relations, 1977, 133–34).

Today, more than fifteen years after this study was conducted, relations between law enforcement agencies and visible minority groups continue to be problematic. Recent riots in Toronto in the aftermath of the Rodney King attack and rebellion in Los Angeles in 1992 offer visible proof that race relations have not vastly improved.

No institution is immune to racism in a racist society. Thus, schools often become vehicles that transmit racism to the next generation. The Task Force on Human Relations also found that many children spoke of nonwhite immigrants as being "dirty" and "smelly" and as "taking away our jobs" (1977, 174). Nonwhite parents perceived the schools as "de-motivating" their children by channeling them into vocational rather than academic streams, thus depriving them of opportunities for upward mobility.

That many Canadians believed race relations to be unsatisfactory was reflected by the establishment in 1983, by the federal government, of a committee under the chairmanship of Bob Daudlin, that would conduct a nationwide investigation into race relations, and provide recommendations for improving relations between nonwhite and white Canadians.

In its 1984 report, *Equality Now*, the committee noted a connection between the depressed economy and curtailed opportunities for visible minorities. This is a particular instance of a general phenomenon. When economic conditions deteriorate, discrimination against minorities increases as the groups in power make every effort to conserve scarce opportunities for themselves. Since power in Canada is overwhelmingly wielded by whites, visible minorities are given short shrift.

Minorities also furnish ready scapegoats for majority members who suffer economic and social dislocation. This phenomenon is not new. For instance, around the turn of the century, lynchings of blacks in the American south fluctuated with the price of cotton, which was the mainstay of the southern economy. When cotton prices were low, the number of lynchings increased as people vented their frustration and helplessness against the even more helpless blacks. Across Canada, the Daudlin committee rediscovered discrimination against nonwhites:

> Visible minorities encounter a variety of systemic discriminatory practices in the workplace. Minority workers are denied access to employment by such recruitment, "Canadian experience" criteria and culturally biased testing procedures and interviews. Barriers also exist for advancement and promotion through relegation of the minority persons to low status and low income positions, through seniority policies, and through limited exposure to new job openings (1984, 33).

On the positive side, the researchers noted several initiatives aimed at remedying this situation. Examples were special programs instituted by Nova, An Alberta Corporation, as well as by Hydro Quebec, at its James Bay project, to train native peoples for skilled positions.

This overview of the experiences of some visible minority groups in Canada leads us to conclude that physical attributes, which in themselves have no effect on an individual's character or competence, have had far-reaching negative consequences. Reaction to physical differences is exacerbated by cultural differences, another characteristic of racial minorities. The fact that discriminatory attitudes and practices are defined as a social problem, that is, a state of affairs deemed to be in need of change, inspires some hope that the vicious circle of prejudice will be broken. In the mid-1980s, the Commission on Equality made recommendations for modifying institutional practices both to prevent the multiple disadvantages experienced by racial and other minority groups and to compensate for the disadvantages they have faced in the past. This two-pronged strategy of prevention and remedy is referred to as "**affirmative action**" (Abella, 1984) and became law, as the *Employment Equity Act*, in 1986. (Employment equity provisions are entrenched in the Canadian Charter of Rights and Freedoms, as well.) While the concept is gaining acceptance, and is legally mandated, implementation remains highly controversial.

Another tactic to prevent racism and ethnocentrism from rooting is contained in a new Ontario law, according to which, by 1995, all school boards are mandated to bring in policies to modify curricula, testing practices, and hiring to reflect the growing diversity of the population. This diversity is obvious in the following example. In the 1974 Grade 6 class at Kingsview Village Junior School in Etobicoke, Ontario, there were no black faces; however, the 1991 graduating class shows only seven students who were not from visible minorities. The local high school, with a population of just 1,200, includes students from 57 countries.[12]

Exhibit 7.5 shows the current and projected percentage of visible minority members in selected Canadian cities. The percentage of visible minorities in Toronto will rise from 25.2 percent in 1991 to 44.6 percent in 2001. According to the demographer responsible for the data in this table, John Samuel, by the year 2001 Canada's percentage of visible minorities will reach 17.7 percent, an increase of 8.1 percent from 1991.

EXHIBIT 7.5

Visible Minorities in Urban Centres

	1991	Percent	2001	Percent
Toronto	961,000	25.2	2.11 mil	44.6
Vancouver	378,000	23.8	830,000	39.3
Edmonton	119,000	14.1	260,000	25.0
Calgary	119,000	16.0	260,000	25.0
Winnipeg	80,000	12.2	147,000	20.6
Montreal	336,000	10.8	737,000	19.9
Ottawa-Hull	83,000	9.3	182,000	16.0
Halifax	26,000	8.2	57,000	13.5
Canada	2.58 mil	9.6	5.68 mil	17.7

Source: John Samuel, Gazette (Montreal) (14 June 1993). Reprinted with permission.

In the year 2001, visible minorities will make up 17.7 percent of the population in Canadian cities.

Zoran Milich.

FRENCH/ENGLISH RELATIONS IN CANADA

When the British North America Act was signed in 1867, the Canadian Constitution remained in Britain. Following several unsuccessful attempts, it was patrioted to Canada in 1982, but Quebec refused to be a signatory. The stalemate continued until the 1987 Meech Lake Accord, which would have restored Quebec to the constitutional fold and recognized it as a distinct society within Canada. The Accord was to be ratified by each province no later than June 1990. If a consensus was not achieved, the agreement was to become null and void. (In the United States, the Equal Rights Amendment that guaranteed women and other minority groups certain rights "died" when it was not ratified by two-thirds of the fifty states within the stipulated time period.) The next attempt at including Quebec in the constitution was the Charlottetown Accord, which was preceded by numerous travelling panels and hearings in an attempt to consult "regular" Canadians. In a nation-wide referendum this package, too, was rejected.

How did one Canadian province come to see itself as a "distinct society"? History books have often referred to the French and the English as Canada's "founding races." This is an error, since French and English share membership in the Caucasoid race. However, they are (at least technically) distinct ethnic groups, since they differ in language, in traditions, and frequently in religion. The French are overwhelmingly Roman Catholic, whereas most early British settlers belonged to Protestant denominations.

The complexities of French/English relations within Canada are clearly beyond the scope of this book, but some historical background can aid in an understanding of ethnic relations between the two groups in present-day Canadian society. Following the signing of the Treaty of Paris in 1763, most members of the French elite returned to France. The bulk of the population, heavily concentrated in Quebec, carried on their agricultural way of life. Their linguistic and religious rights were guaranteed by the 1774 Quebec Act and eventually entrenched in the British North America Act in 1867.

Members of the clergy were an active force in government. The local parish was, in fact, the basic social-political, as well as religious, unit. The importance of family, land, and church was proclaimed from the pulpit and emphasized in the schools, which were controlled by the Catholic Church (a control that was not completely relinquished until 1964).

As early as the 1830s, high birth rates among the Québécois meant that not everyone could continue working the land. Thus, the children of the habitants had to migrate. During the nineteenth and early twentieth centuries, some were able to duplicate their way of life on Quebec's frontiers—the Gaspé, Lac St-Jean, the Laurentians—and some took up land in the West. Others had to adapt to a more industrialized life in cities and towns dominated by the English: Montreal, Quebec, and other Canadian cities; the burgeoning northern communities of Ontario, such as Sudbury and Timmins; and the factory towns of New England. For most of the migrants to urban areas, the move meant accepting minority status.

John Porter (1965) has argued that the British charter group encouraged the maintenance of ethnic boundaries because they helped the group itself remain dominant. This argument is relevant to the French/English question. While the French tilled the land, went to church, and produced children, most of whom received only minimal education, the British group was consolidating its economic power in the industrialized society Canada was becoming. French workers were integrated at the lowest rungs, and a confluence of external and internal obstacles kept them from going up the ladder. For most, moving up meant having to give up the mother tongue as well as values that placed domestic loyalties ahead of occupational advancement. Discrimination by the British, based on negative stereotypes of French workers and on the wish to monopolize desirable positions, was an important external factor. In a study of Cantonville, a Quebec textile town, Everett Hughes perceptively analyzed this phenomenon:

> When the subject of French foremen is raised, the answers come in stereotypes, of which these are the common ones: "The French have to be told what to do and therefore cannot be trusted with jobs requiring initiative and the meeting of crises" ... "They are so jealous of one another that they do not yield to the authority of one of their own number" ... These clichés become painfully familiar to anyone who talks about this problem in Quebec ... It is evident that those who have the power to appoint foremen in Cantonville think that ethnic differences are significant and that the English are superior (1971, 55–56).

Hughes's observations on language in a predominantly French community are also instructive:

> The executive and technical language of industry in our community is English. Since, in addition, the persons in authority are English, it is but natural that English should percolate downward among the French workers. The pressure is on the subordinate, whose mother-tongue is French, rather than upon the superior, whose language is English (1971, 82).

This pattern is typical. Where ethnic groups coexist in a society, the language of the superior group becomes the dominant one. In the polyglot Austro-Hungarian empire, Poles, Czechs, and Hungarians who wanted to get ahead had to learn German. Knowledge of English was mandatory for ambitious Indians and Africans living under colonial rule; by contrast, many British administrators did not speak a native language.

During the 1950s and 1960s, life changed among the Québécois. They remained attached to their language and to other aspects of their culture, but a world view emerged that focused on individual success rather than on traditional values. This altered orientation in Quebec manifested itself in many ways. Control of education passed from the Catholic Church to the Quebec government. More francophones attended institutions of higher learning. Higher education veered from its classical bent (geared to turning out lawyers, physicians, and theologians) to a more technical one. Members of the emerging stratum were educated, eager for achievement, and aware of the disadvantages francophones suffered in the labour market. They wanted to change this state of affairs, to be "masters in their own house." Their increasing refusal to accept minority status, combined with a determination to preserve French culture, created pressure for greater bilingualism both in the federal government and throughout Canada, so that francophones outside Quebec would be able to conduct official business in their own language.[13]

Meanwhile, fears had arisen about the survival of French culture in Quebec itself. Since the British conquest, Canada's francophone population had hovered at about 30 percent of the total, even though the French-speaking group had been relying on natural increases to maintain its numbers. The percentage remained constant; the strong tendency of immigrants to opt for English was balanced by the high francophone birth rate—and because its birth rate was very high—the well-known "revenge of the cradle." In the 1960s, however, the francophone birth rate dipped sharply as reliable birth-control methods became readily available and Québécois women, less obedient to the dictates of the Catholic Church, became eager to use them.

Moreover, Montreal became home to more and more immigrants with each postwar decade. A majority chose acculturation into the anglophone group, thus inspiring fear among the francophones that even their own members might receive the message that their children's route to advancement lay in anglicization.

In response to these fears, Quebec passed successively more stringent language laws, aimed at giving primacy to the French language and at forcing immigrants to adopt French rather than English. Ironically, Quebec's insistence on becoming a unilingual francophone province has made anglophones in the province fear becoming a minority that is discriminated against on the basis of language. When Quebec passed its Charter of the French Language, one section of that mandated that "public signs and posters and commercial advertising shall be solely in French," anglophones sought a court declaration against these restrictions for the reason that they violated the Canadian Charter of Rights and Freedoms and Quebec's own Charter of Human Rights and Freedoms.

The Supreme Court of Canada, in its decision rendered on December 15, 1988, held that Quebec's "sign-law" was a breach of its own Charter of Human Rights and Freedoms. The Court found that the "freedom of expression" guaranteed by Quebec's human rights Charter included the right to express oneself in the language of one's choice since language is one of the means by which a group is able to express its cultural identity. The Court further decided that commercial, free speech is to be accorded the same constitutional safeguards as political speech because commercial speech "serves individual and societal values in a free and democratic society." Following this reasoning, the Supreme Court struck down Quebec's "sign law." Within a week, the Quebec government responded by passing new legislation that also placed restrictions on the use of languages other than French on public signs. The government shielded this new law from court scrutiny by stating that the new law would operate notwithstanding the protections of Quebec's Charter of Human Rights and Freedoms and those of the Canadian Charter. The Canadian Charter allows a government to opt out of the enshrined guarantees merely by expressly stating that it is doing so. The Quebec government chose to

The depth of emotion that surrounds language rights in Canada attests to the widespread awareness of their importance.

Seneca College.

exercise this option with respect to the "sign law" legislation. In the spring of 1993 the provision in Bill 178 for excluding English from commercial signs was abandoned. Public opinion, a ruling by a United Nations Human Rights Commission that the law broached civil rights, and a changed political climate contributed to the decision.

The Quebec language conflict turns on the notion of individual versus collective rights. To ensure its vitality, many francophones believe that their culture and language need legal protection. The argument is that Quebec anglophones, as part of the continent's vast majority of English speakers, are not at risk of assimilation so their individual rights must bow to the needs of the francophone collectivity. For anglophones in Quebec, francophones are the majority supporting French language and culture at the expense of minority language rights. Concern for collective rights surface when a group sees itself as endangered. For Quebeckers, part of the issue is defining the minority—is it francophones in North America or anglophones within Quebec?

THE IMPORTANCE OF LANGUAGE

Why all the commotion over language? Language is often the issue that reflects more fundamental disputes over power. Debates over language, rather than power per se, are easier to articulate and comprehend. Often, subordinate groups will champion the use of their own language to express their discontent. Since language reflects and structures reality, the language of the dominant group, they feel, cannot be used to accurately describe their plight or to formulate their demands for change. Language, then, has consequences for political, economic, and social control.

The vitality of a language is essential for the survival of a culture. It indicates the unique status of the group, its difference from other cultures, and contributes to group and individual identity. Traditions and group history are transmitted from one generation to the next through language. Canada's aboriginal peoples worry about the loss of indigenous languages that express personal and collective identity.

Language affects a group's access to economic power. Legal measures to change the language of work in Quebec increased the economic power of francophones in Quebec although, to date, they continue to be underrepresented in the upper levels of Canadian corporations.

Language is also a variable in political power and participation. One can't be heard if one does not speak the language. Conversely, discussing which language should be heard can be a forceful strategy for political mobilization.

Language functions as one of the principal ingredients in the quality of life; it is not just a medium of expressing oneself but also, as Bill 101 calls it, a medium for living—at home, on the job, in recreation. The individual's whole identity is wrapped up in it.

The depth of emotion that surrounds language rights in Canada attests to the widespread awareness of their importance. The struggle is by no means evident only in this country. It is being waged in Belgium between the Flemish and the economically dominant, French-speaking Walloons. There is agitation for broader usage of Welsh in Wales and of Gaelic in Scotland. Minority groups are increasingly aware that protection of language, economic well-being, and cultural survival are interrelated.

EUROPEAN IMMIGRANTS IN CANADA

Even though powerful push factors, such as poverty and political oppression, may encourage people to leave their home countries, immigrants are a self-selected group. They must mobilize the physical and psychological resources to leave everything that is familiar and to begin a new life. One can argue that immigrants to North America are advantaged in the sense of possessing favourable personal qualities—determination, motivation, and a desire for success by dint of hard work. They are also disadvantaged, however. They discover that immigrants who have come before them have taken the desirable work, and with it the better housing, and higher education for their children. The history of immigrant groups in North America is a story of discrimination, deprivation, and exploitation. Parillo describes their plight at the turn of the century:

> As unskilled workers, most found employment in the low-status manual labor jobs in the factories, mines, needle trades, and construction. At that time the worker had no voice in working conditions, for labor unions had not yet become effective. The fourteen-hour day, six-day week for low wages was common. There were no vacations, sick pay, or pension plans. Child labor was the norm, and entire families often worked to provide family income. Lighting, ventilation and heating were poor; in the factories, moving pieces of machinery were dangerously

exposed. There was no workers' compensation if, as was likely, someone was injured on the job. A worker who objected was likely to be fired and blacklisted (1980, 156).

Yet, for the descendants of many immigrants, the story had a happy ending in that they were able to triumph over obstacles and become "full-fledged," even influential, Canadians and Americans. Here we must note a significant difference between visible minorities and others. In the absence of continuing intermarriage, racial characteristics are permanent and trigger prejudice and discrimination. Members of European ethnic groups are gradually absorbed into the mainstream of society and are able to become more or less equal participants. The Irish are an example of a group that experienced severe discrimination when large numbers arrived, virtually destitute, in the wake of the famines of the 1840s. "No Irish need apply" proclaimed notices on job postings in Protestant-dominated Toronto. Although some anti-Irish prejudice was evident in Ontario until the 1950s, being of Irish ancestry today has little direct impact on one's life chances.

In the United States, the thrust has always been toward rapid assimilation (as mentioned in the previous section on multiculturalism), producing the melting pot in which the constituent parts blend into a new amalgam. The immigrants (or at least their children) were to shed their distinguishing characteristics and become "real," not hyphenated, Americans. (One reason for pushing assimilation was the need for patriotic citizens, given the many armed conflicts in which the United States has been involved during its relatively brief history.) In practice, ethnic groups have not disappeared in the United States. Cities such as Chicago, Philadelphia, and Buffalo have large, active ethnic communities. Social scientists—for example, Michael Novak in *The Rise and Fall of the Unmeltable Ethnics* (1971)—have argued that the melting is by no means total. Indeed, during the last two decades, there has been a revival of ethnic consciousness.

In Canada, large-scale immigration took place later than in the United States, and immigrants were ranked and granted entrance in accordance with their perceived ability to assimilate. Those from Britain were deemed most desirable, followed by Germans and Scandinavians. Writing in 1909, J.S. Woodsworth categorized Germans as being, on the whole, "among our best immigrants" (1972, 84). Scandinavians were similarly described:

> Taken all in all there is no class of immigrants that are as certain of making their way in the Canadian West as the people of the peninsula of Scandinavia. Accustomed to the rigors of a northern climate, cleanblooded, thrifty, ambitious and hard-working, they will be certain of success in this pioneer country, where the strong, not the weak, are wanted (1972 [1909], 77).

Woodsworth was not equally sanguine about all immigrant groups. Some had worrisome tendencies toward "clustering":

> Not only are they less open to Canadian ideas, but, closely united, they can control the entire community. The social, the educational, the

religious, the political life is dominated by alien ideas. It would seem a wise policy to scatter the foreign communities among the Canadians, in this way facilitating the process of assimilation (1972 [1909], 234).

It should be remembered that Woodsworth, who was the founder of the Cooperative Commonwealth Federation (CCF), was considered at the time to be an enlightened, concerned Canadian, not a racist bigot.

Apart from admitting some immigrants more readily than others, Canada has never pursued assimilation with the zeal exhibited by the United States. As already noted, Porter (1965) argued that the British charter group encouraged the maintenance of ethnic boundaries because they helped the group itself to remain dominant. However, it is really only since the end of the Second World War that Canada has espoused a policy of deliberate multiculturalism, the promotion of a cultural mosaic in which the constituent parts remain visible and distinct. From a practical standpoint, the vast number of immigrants who arrived over a relatively short period of time in the postwar era could not be assimilated. As Reitz explained, other factors also contributed to the new orientation:

> The ideology of multiculturalism has evolved in Canada at a time of increased tension between the dominant linguistic communities, English and French. Following the post-World War II Quiet Revolution in Quebec, the federal government tried to improve English–French relations by setting up a Commission on Bilingualism and Biculturalism in 1963. At this time, pressure grew to recognize "the cultural contribution of other ethnic groups" (1980, 10).

Multiculturalism has positive as well as negative consequences for members of ethnic groups. Socialization to the values and norms of the ethnic community allows individuals to feel secure as part of a "we-group." However, the individual continues to be an outsider in the society at large, a situation that can entail heavy social and psychological costs. Rayfield focused on some of these costs in a study that entailed participant observation of women in an English-language school:

> As her children progress in the Canadian school system, they soon speak only English to each other at home. When spoken to in Italian they answer in English. Maria feels this as a rejection of her as a mother, sometimes even as a deliberate rejection. She feels that the children do not want her to know what they are talking about. This is another vicious circle. The more isolated the mother is from the world outside her family, the less the children are able to communicate with her. Even if they speak the same language, they feel they have nothing to talk about. So the children, who might have been a contact between the mother and the outside world, involving her through the school and their friends in a wide network of associations, have just the opposite effect. They increase her diffidence about venturing outside the social world of the family at the same time as they break communication within the family network.

Canadian-born children of immigrants may also face difficulties as they attempt to reconcile the differences between the values and practices of the home and those they encounter at school and in other social institutions.

On the positive side, as Reitz's study of ten ethnic groups in five large Canadian cities showed, ethnic communities provide economic opportunities that may not be readily available within the larger society. This is especially important for the minimally educated. In Reitz's words:

> Having a good education is completely unrelated to income mobility in the minority setting. The irrelevance of education in such settings may be attributed to the job involved—expertise provided by the school system may be unnecessary to effective job performance. To be productive in such jobs, knowledge of the ethnic language and the ability to maintain relationships with other ethnic members as coworkers or as customers, clients and suppliers, may be more important than education (1980, 164).

Anderson made similar points in her study of Portuguese immigrants, specifically noting the role of ethnic networks in securing employment for compatriots:

> Networks function to allow the possibility of job mobility for persons in our society who might not otherwise risk career or geographical changes. They enable the persons to "try out" for different jobs, in situations where they are assured assistance in learning new skills and role requirements in a congenial and supportive atmosphere. The employer can locate new employees rapidly and with minimal expense and trouble, by merely asking his present employees if they know of suitable workers. He is thus assured of a reasonably congenial work group who will exert peer group pressure for adequate job performance. New immigrants experience a cushioning effect by working among kin and friends, so that the adverse effects of culture shock are minimized (1981, 331).

Once again, it is important to remember the wide variations concealed by umbrella terms such as "ethnic groups" and "immigrants." However, a general discussion of race and ethnic relations is essential because it provides insight into the dynamics of power in society. A large sociological literature addresses the history, problems, and current position of specific ethnic groups.[14]

THE AGED

In the normal course of events, most North Americans can anticipate being old before they die. How then is it appropriate to discuss the aged as a sociological minority?

There is little consensus in the sociological literature as to the validity of such a label. On the one hand, the aged are highly visible, are stereotyped by other groups, and experience powerlessness, prejudice, and discrimination. They are excluded from most occupations, and if they work, they tend to receive lower-than-average pay. They are often segregated both socially and physically. They typically respond to their subordinate status with defensiveness and negative self-concepts. On the other hand, the aged are not socially organized as an independently functioning subgroup. Rather, they are engaged, through family ties, with other age groups. They exhibit wide diversity in socioeconomic status, state of health, degree of participation in mainstream life, amount of prestige traditionally bestowed on them in their own ethnic communities, and the degree to which they experience discrimination and loss of dignity.

In our opinion, the arguments that favour viewing the aged group as a minority are more compelling than those against. Diversity need not keep social scientists from exploring what individuals have in common. The minority perspective sensitizes people to many aspects of life for the aged in Canadian society that might otherwise be overlooked.

AN AGING SOCIETY

The study of aging as an area of enquiry is referred to as gerontology, a field that brings together the perspectives of a wide variety of disciplines, such as economics, demography, political economy, epidemiology, and sociology. It is also receiving growing attention from applied disciplines, such as nursing, medicine, social work, health administration, and health planning. The fact that the first Canadian text (Marshall) devoted to the social aspects of aging was published in 1980 points to the very recent nature of the interest in this field.

The area has considerable importance in Canada today because the country has, in recent years, become an aging society, with a striking increase in the number and proportion of older people. Historically, high birth rates, declining rates of infant and child mortality, and the large influxes of immigrants made the average age of the population relatively low. It is estimated that by the year 2036, people aged 65 and over will constitute approximately 25 percent of the total population, compared with 10 percent in 1981 (Statistics Canada, 1992).

This upward shift in the proportion of the population over the age of 65 raises concerns for policymakers. How does society plan to cope with the financial implications of having a large group of people who no longer support themselves through working? How will social and economic necessities be made available? Alterations in the age structure of society also raise questions for social scientists about changing patterns of social interaction and shifting balances of power. Some analysts predict that, as the enormous baby-boom cohort ages, Canadian society will experience heightened intergenerational conflict. The ability to plan is, at present, severely hampered by the dearth of scientific knowledge available on all aspects of aging.

THE AGED IN CANADA TODAY

Some statistical data are available on aged Canadians today. Their economic situation, as a group, is not enviable. Relative to that of other Canadians, the income of people aged 65 and over has improved since the early 1970s, a change that can be largely attributed to the growth of the Canada and Quebec Pension Plans. However, as Exhibit 7.6 shows, unattached elderly people have

EXHIBIT 7.6

Incidence of Low Income by Family Type, 1980–1990

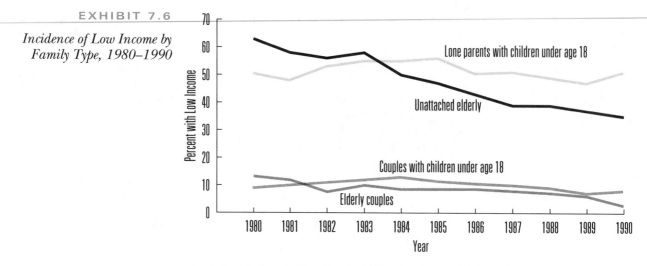

Source: Statistics Canada, Canadian Social Trends *(Summer, 1992), 13. Reproduced by authority of the Minister of Industry 1994.*

low incomes. In 1990, 35 percent of unattached seniors had low incomes; for senior couples the rate was just 4 percent.

Exhibit 7.7 shows the poverty rates for unattached people 65 and over. While the rate has dropped for both men and women, the gender gap persists. Seventy-nine percent of women 65 and older have incomes that are less than $15,000 per year, compared with 47 percent of men (Canadian Woman Studies, Winter, 1992).

The issue of security in old age should be seen in relation to "lifetime earnings." Thus, the problem of income for elderly persons begins long before they reach old age. Since the risk of poverty is strongly linked to labour-force attachment, it is not surprising that elderly women bear the highest risk. The price of never having worked, or of having worked intermittently in low-paying jobs that did not entail pension benefits, is one that becomes particularly heavy for women in their later years. Foreign-born elderly women bear the brunt of their immigrant status in addition to age and sex. They are more likely to have worked in the shadow economy, which does not confer legitimate status, to have worked in the home, or not to have been in the country long enough to qualify for government benefits; therefore, these women tend to be among the most vulnerable.[15]

We have already explored the ways in which poverty itself confers minority status on individuals; one of these, as mentioned, is a drastic reduction in social participation. For the aged, this reduced participation is further exaggerated by their forced departure from the labour force, by lack of access to transportation, and by physical infirmities that restrict their activities. At the same time, the rate of institutionalization of the elderly in Canada is one of the highest in all industrialized countries. Schwenger (1974) has pointed to a pronounced tendency in Canada to institutionalize people, such as criminals and invalids, who do not fit the societal norms.

THE STIGMA OF AGING

It is widely recognized that the aged are subject to considerable stigmatization in a youth-oriented society. Posner has argued that this is especially true for

EXHIBIT 7.7

*Poverty Rates for Unattached
People 65 and Older*

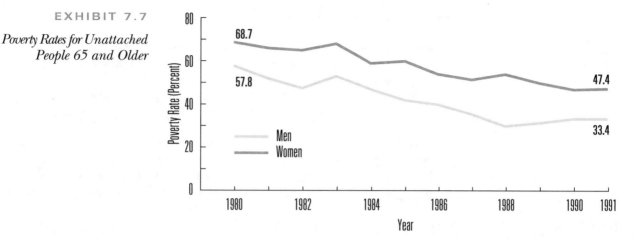

EXHIBIT 7.7

*Poverty Rates for Unattached
People 65 and Older*

Source: Poverty Profile Update for 1991, *National Council of Welfare (Winter, 1993), 19.*

aged women, who experience what she calls the "double whammy" of being both old and female, two attributes that are socially depreciated (1980, 80). The negative stereotypes of the elderly increase social isolation, causing individuals to confine their contacts to a shrinking pool of age peers, and to avoid contact with the majority.

> Old people even look repulsive to the young. This revulsion is heightened when intimate physical contact is required. This may affect an old person's chances for something as fundamental as life itself. One intern in the emergency ward of one of the hospitals which Sudnow studied indicated that he could not stand to give mouth-to-mouth resuscitation to an old woman who came in and was later pronounced dead. On a less dramatic basis, consider the difficulty in getting people to care for old people who have lost the ability to control their urination and defecation (Jarvis, 1972, 620).

The physical changes that accompany aging are perceived negatively, particularly for women, in a society that extols youth, beauty, and physical vigour to such an extent as to devote whole industries to the promotion, display, and perpetuation of these qualities.

Becker described a master status (salient status) as that status of a given person that overrides this person's other statuses in determining how other people treat the person (1963, 33). Typical social interaction with the elderly demonstrates that age itself confers the master status, leading to the attribution of a great many other characteristics that make up the stereotype. Have you ever found yourself raising your voice when talking to an old person, on the assumption that he or she is hard of hearing? Or described your grandmother as "amazing" or "cute" because she is able to make witty observations, contradicting the image of the old as confused or senile? Have you assumed physical frailty in the absence of evidence? Have you ever challenged the assumption that it is delightful for you to have a late Sunday breakfast in your dressing gown but only sensible that the elderly in nursing homes should dress before being served an early breakfast? These are not frivolous questions. One of the greatest risks involved in the aging process is that the elderly themselves will consent to the stereotype and, unnecessarily, begin to confirm it with their own behaviour. The self-fulfilling prophecy may thus launch an irreversible downward spiral.

New social definitions of the elderly are popping up to supplant these depressing visions. The General Social Survey, first conducted in 1985 to gather data on social trends, includes a representative sample of older Canadians. The findings challenge the popular belief about the dependency of old people. High levels of well-being, measured by health, happiness, and satisfaction with most aspects of life were reported by the elderly. Exhibit 7.8 gives these data.

EXHIBIT 7.8
Self-reported Health and Happiness Status of Canadians Aged 55 and Over, 1985 and 1990

	Men		Women	
	1985	1990	1985	1990
Health status				
Excellent	25%	32%	23%	27%
Good	42	46	44	48
Fair	23	17	26	19
Poor	9	4	7	6
Not stated	1	1	1	1
Happiness status				
Very happy	46%	56%	45%	49%
Somewhat happy	48	39	49	43
Somewhat unhappy	4	2	5	5
Very unhappy	1	1	1	1
No opinion, not stated	1	3	1	2

Source: Statistics Canada, Canadian Social Trends *(Summer, 1992), 17. Reproduced by authority of the Minister of Industry 1994.*

In both 1985 and 1990 over 90 percent of Canadians over 55 reported being happy or very happy. This happiness may be correlated with family relations. Only 2 percent of the males and 1 percent of the females who were very happy reported discontent with families. For the very unhappy, 23 percent of men and 27 percent of women were dissatisfied with their relations with their families (*Canadian Social Trends*, Summer, 1992). While happiness, however, did not depend entirely on income, only 4 percent of very happy men and 9 percent of very happy women had incomes under $10,000 (*Canadian Social Trends*, Summer, 1992)

The survey also found that seniors are self-reliant, receiving little unpaid help from people outside their household except for transportation. In

Definitions of old age are changing.

R. Lautens/ *The Toronto Star.*

addition, women care for aging husbands and tend to elderly relatives. Men may help financially. This research points to a future dilemma for the society. How will the elderly and sick be cared for without the large population of middle-aged and older women who now freely take on that responsibility?

HOMOSEXUALS

The Stonewall Riots in Manhattan, provoked by a police raid on the Stonewall Inn, a Greenwich Village gay bar, in 1969, are credited by many with launching the gay liberation movement. Twenty-five years later, scientists are cautiously heralding the discovery of a "gay gene" (see Box 7.3) that they think may be responsible for homosexuality.

BOX 7.3

DECODING THE "GAY GENE"

On July 16, U.S. scientists announced that they may have located a region in the body's DNA that contains a gene or genes related to homosexuality. Since then, *Globe and Mail* readers have posed many follow-up questions about the implications of the findings.

Q: Why were scientists connected with a body called the National Institutes of Health looking for a gene in the first place? Homosexuality isn't a disease.

A: The genesis of the research was an effort to understand why gay men with AIDS often come down with Kaposi's sarcoma—a form of skin cancer. Non-gay people with AIDS hardly ever exhibit this particular manifestation of the disease. Some scientists thought there might be a genetic explanation for the anomaly.

Q. Why didn't the study look at lesbians?

A: Another part of the same study is doing just that.

Q: Why the search for a homosexuality gene and not one for heterosexuality?

A: There are two responses to this. With somewhere between 50,000 and 100,000 genes in the body, and with little more than 3,000 having been identified, discovering what an individual gene does requires scientists to sift through a very large DNA haystack.

The classic way scientists narrow their search is by identifying smaller populations who carry a slightly mutated copy of the gene. The question they then ask is: What gene-form do these people, and only these people, carry?

Thus, because there are many fewer gays than heterosexuals, it should in theory be relatively easier to find a gene for homosexuality than one for heterosexuality.

However, this explanation implies a linkage that does not exist. A "gay gene" would not be carried by gay people alone. If a gene for homosexuality exists (and the "if" must be continually stressed), all humans would carry it. The variation in homosexuals would be

some small chemical rearrangement in that gene that made it operate in a somewhat different manner. It is also possible—and again one must be very cautious because we haven't found anything yet—that what will be found is a gene or genes that control sexuality in general. Thus, it is conceivable that the "gay gene" is really the sexuality gene.

However, the whole issue may turn out to be one of those smaller-boxes-in-bigger-boxes puzzles. Psychologist Sandra Witelson of McMaster University points out that what the U.S. geneticists might have turned up is a gene that produces an ancillary condition—left-handedness for example—often associated with homosexuality.

Q: Isn't this just Nazi-style genetics, and didn't we see how superficial and stupid a science it was then? Isn't trying to associate genes with behaviour like the work of 19th-century phrenologists who claimed they could identify personality traits from bumps on people's heads?

A: No. This is not history repeating itself, and modern genetics is not a jumped-up pseudoscience. What should be understood is that the "genetics" of the Nazis—and other eugenicists who wanted to improve the human race by eliminating those with "bad" genes—was a farce. Not one gene had yet been discovered in the Nazi era. Without a gene, and without a known population of people who could be proved to carry one of its mutations, behavioural genetics was turned into dumb statistics.

When eugenicists found some statistical expression of a complicated human behaviour—say IQ scores and intelligence—they imputed an entirely genetic basis to it. This was analysis on the level of, "Poor people don't take as many baths as rich people, so maybe they carry a gene for dirtiness." Eugenicists now appear to be scientific ignoramuses.

Today, we are discovering real genes and real functions. With this should come a truer understanding of how genes physically operate and interact. However, whatever the connections are, they are likely to be almost impossibly complicated.

Genes will likely influence the operations of other genes in a sort of cascade effect. Already there is evidence that a form of "genetic buffering" exists that results in some people carrying a disease mutation without suffering from the illness it encodes for.

Beyond this, what the "new genetics" should do is make traditional categories of bigotry meaningless. No matter what their skin colour or ethnic origin or sexual orientation, your brothers and sisters and friends and lovers will undoubtedly carry what society at any given time may choose to define as "bad genes." Similarly, many of the hated "others" will carry "good genes."

Thus, the truths of a genetics that actually has genes to study would seem to be the exact reverse of Nazi eugenics ideology. Our early exploration of DNA has already made two things clear: Nobody is perfect. And nobody is pure.

Q: Are people going to use the new genetics to discriminate against gays? Will people be forced to have tests to see if they carry the mutant gene? Will some people abort fetuses in the womb if screening tests say the child is carrying the "gay" mutation?

A: The authors of the original paper piously hope not. "We believe that it would be fundamentally unethical to use such information to try to assess or alter a person's current or future sexual orientation, either heterosexual or homosexual, or other normal attributes of human behaviour. Rather, scientists, educators, policy-makers and the public should work together to ensure that such research is used to benefit all members of society."

If the "gay gene" is found, experience shows that screening tests will soon follow and tell parents whether their unborn child carries the mutant gene. Against this background, a cynical geneticist has suggested that the moment a "gay gene" is actually found, all homosexuals will turn into right-to-lifers.

Perhaps the truth is that it is precisely here, where old communal hatreds and a truly new genetic knowledge intersect, that we will see just how wise the 21st century is going to be. Nothing is good or evil but thinking makes it so.

Source: Stephen Strauss, "Decoding the 'Gay Gene,'" The Globe and Mail (5 August 1993), A9. Reprinted with permission.

Whatever the causes of their preference for same sex partners, gays are marching in large numbers in Gay Pride parades across North America and are demanding they be treated fairly, legally, socially, and economically.

Quebec, in the 1977 amendment to its Charter of Human Rights, was the first (and only) province to include sexual orientation as prohibited grounds for discrimination. Canada's Charter of Rights and Freedoms does not include homosexuality specifically, but the list is not exhaustive and does not preclude it. Despite the AIDS epidemic that fuelled **homophobia**, that is fear and hatred of homosexuals, the nineties have seen progress for gay people. In 1992, the Ontario Court of Appeal decided that the Canadian Human Rights Act would in future be read as if it prohibited discrimination on the basis of sexual orientation (Robertson, 1992). In that same year, the Canadian Armed Forces stopped using sexual orientation as grounds for restricting enlistment and promotion. In 1993, a decision under the Ontario Human Rights Code required a private health insurance company to extend benefits to a lesbian's partner. Ontario legislation requiring employers to extend spousal benefits to same-sex couples was forecast for the spring of 1993.

Changes, like the ones described above, in the minority status of homosexuals start with the process of "coming out of the closet" (a term also referred to as "coming out"), discussed by Kallen (1989) in describing minority protest movements. (Homosexuals fit the sociological and the numerical definition of minorities.) Coming out represents attempts by members of a stigmatized minority to stop hiding and to proclaim their rightful place in the society. The initial step is to label group members in positive rather than negative terms. Reappropriating the power to name themselves has led to the changes in terminology from "faggot" and "dyke," associated with unnatural, immoral, or "sick" behaviour, to "gay" and "lesbian," representing legitimate, alternative ways of living. The terms themselves are not at issue: the power to make a label adhere is crucial. The second stage of collective action is to establish organizations that can mobilize minority members. In becoming activists, gays have taken what Kallen (1979) calls the revitalization rather than contention option. Revitalization, instead of calling for individual rights, claims cultural equality for the group, so that homosexuality would be recognized and protected as a bona fide lifestyle. Using Breton's construct of institutional completeness (mentioned in the section on ethnic groups at the beginning of this chapter), Kallen argues that homosexuals have enough political, economic, educational, and religious institutions to function as a nonethnic subculture and supports their desire for collective rights.

The contention option demands individual rights for stigmatized minority group members to enable these members to integrate into the larger society. Organizations for disabled people have followed this route, which is based on the principle of normalization. According to this approach, individuals will be able, given sufficient legal and social protection, to overcome barriers associated with their handicaps and to make their own way.

. . . .

OVERVIEW

In looking at stratification in Chapter 6, we noted that inequality cannot be adequately explained in terms of individual differences; rather, one must take into account structural factors that create and perpetuate social inequality. In this chapter, we have investigated the significance of minority status for the individual's life chances and position in society.

Traditionally, the term "minority" has been used to describe racial and ethnic groups. The dimensions of the definition we use permit us to include, under this umbrella term, other groups that experience prejudice and discrimination. The aged, like women and homosexuals, are found in all class strata. However, these collectivities are often categorized on the basis of one negative characteristic, such as being female in a male-dominated society, or being old or physically impaired in a culture that extols youth and physical perfection. These negative categorizations give rise to discriminatory treatment that impedes access to political, economic, and social power. Lack of such power entails a disadvantaged position in society.

In recent history, developments within society have made it easier for certain minority groups to secure more equitable treatment. They have become more aware of their rights and are determined to continue fighting for them. For the struggle to succeed, however, the dominant group must be willing to acknowledge minority rights. Experience has shown that acknowledgment of these rights, and the action to back it up, are more easily obtained in good economic times than in bad.

ASSIGNMENTS

1. The sociological perspective permits us to discern similarities among groups that are ostensibly not similar at all. Using such a perspective, discuss two of the following in terms of minority status: children, the physically disabled, and former inmates of prisons.

2. Over a two-week period, make a file of newspaper clippings on the topic of native peoples. Review Chapters 3, 6, and 7 on culture, stratification, and minorities, and analyze the information you have collected in the light of the conceptual material discussed in each of these chapters.

3. Minority groups do not necessarily accept discrimination passively. For example, in recent years a number of homosexual and lesbian groups have emerged to represent their interests. Their efforts have met with some success: Gay Pride parades in major Canadian cities attract large numbers of participants and supporters; and legislation is being changed to accommodate same-sex sexual relationships.

    Do some research on one or more of these groups. Use the library as a resource. If such a group is active in your community, speak to some of the people associated with it. Find out how they got involved, how the group is organized, what its objectives are, and how members go about achieving those objectives. Compare your information with the concepts discussed in this chapter.

4. Using the definitions in this chapter, discuss the ways in which women can be seen as minority group members and ways in which the concept is inadequate in explaining the social position of women.

SUGGESTED READINGS

Janet Mancini Billson, "Interlocking Identities: Gender, Ethnicity and Power in the Canadian Context," *International Journal of Canadian Studies* 3:50–66, 1991. Billson's research is based on the assumption that both gender and ethnicity must be understood as variables that interact to produce multiple oppressions in Canadian society. Her data are gathered from interviews with individual women, and groups of women, in a wide range of racial and ethnic communities: Jamaican, Aboriginal, Inuit, Chinese, Ukrainian, and Mennonite. Cultural messages that mandate passivity and obedience in interpersonal relationships, she says, tend also to be reflected in passivity and obedience in the public sphere. Billson argues that greater equality can only be achieved by changing societal institutions, not merely individuals.

David Freeman, *Creeps* (Toronto: University of Toronto Press, 1972). This play centres on a sheltered workshop where disabled people are employed to do repetitious, simple tasks at token wages, ostensibly to be kept occupied and to be able to feel useful. That they feel diminished, exploited, and restless, yet fearful of the outside world, which some of them nevertheless dream of entering, becomes evident as the obstacles to their leaving the workshop become clear. The play illustrates particularly well the concept of the self-fulfilling prophecy.

Edward N. Herberg, *Ethnic Groups in Canada: Adaptations and Transitions* (Scarborough, Ont.: Nelson, 1989). Herberg provides an admirably thorough historical picture of ethnic, racial, and religious groups in Canada. Drawing heavily on census data from 1871 to 1981, and on other published survey results, he examines three things in particular: how Canada has changed ethnically over time; changes in the numbers and the distribution of specific ethno-racial-religious groups; and how these groups, with respect to their social organization and cultural practices, have adapted to Canadian society. See especially Chapter 9, "Institutional Completeness," for a dimension of ethnic solidarity based on the extent to which ethnic groups in a particular locale have developed their own religious, educational, economic, social and recreational, media, cultural, and political institutions.

Thomson Highway, *The Rez Sisters* (Saskatoon: Fifth House Publishers, 1988); and *Dry Lips Oughta Move to Kapuskasing* (Saskatoon: Fifth House Publishers, 1988). There has been an explosion of Native theatre in North America in the past ten years, as Native playwrights seek to recoup their cultural and spiritual heritage and to give expression to the contemporary situation of their people. These plays often emerge through a lengthy process that involves use of the oral tradition, some collective writing, improvisation, "workshopping" on the reserves, first urban appearances in centres such as the Native Earth Performing Arts Inc. in Toronto, and then performances in large theatres considered to be "mainstream." Highway is a full-blooded Cree from northern Manitoba who has won international acclaim for his work. These two comedies contain both hilarious and horrific episodes, as well as rendering beautifully the sheer banality and boredom of life in isolated communities. See also the Fall 1991 issue of the *Canadian Theatre Review*, Vol. 68, for an interesting overview of the renaissance in Native arts in the Americas that has occurred 500 years after the fateful voyage of Columbus.

Joy Kogawa, *Obasan* (Toronto: Lester and Orpen Dennys, 1981). Kogawa was a child of six in 1942 when Japanese Canadians were summarily removed from their homes on the west coast and located in camps in the interior of British Columbia. Many had been born in Canada; they were punished not for anything they had done, but for their racial origin. By telescoping a shabby chapter in Canadian history into an account of one family, Kogawa allows us to experience this outrage vicariously. In September 1988, when former prime minister Brian Mulroney extended a formal apology to the Japanese-Canadian community and announced a lump-sum payment of compensation, Kogawa was among those invited to the ceremony.

David Malouf, *Remembering Babylon* (Toronto: Alfred A. Knopf Canada, 1993). How long does it take settlers to absorb a new place into their consciousness even as they attempt to fill that place with their own meanings? This question is probed in Malouf's powerful story about an encounter in the mid-1800s between a group of insecure white settlers in Australia and a young white man who, having been cast ashore in a shipwreck at the age of thirteen, has lived for sixteen years among the aboriginal people. To the settlers, the man represents the threat of a people who have occupied the land for 40,000 years. For him, the dilemma is one of reconciling his experience of the two drastically different cultures.

Roxanna Ng, "Teaching Against the Grain: Contradictions for Minority Teachers," in Jane Gaskell and Arlen Tigar McLaren, eds., *Women and Education*, 2nd ed. (Calgary: Destselig Enterprises, Limited, 1991), 99–115. Perhaps you will be able to relate your own experiences in the classroom to what Ng has to say. She argues that sexism and racism are systems of oppression that come to be reflected in all of those little unintended and unconscious acts that result in the further silencing, exclusion, and subordination of minority group members. Ng writes as a middle-class woman and a member of a racial minority group who has felt her own authority undermined in her role as a professor. She explores how a critical feminist pedagogy can help to eradicate the insidious effects of racism and sexism both in and out of the classroom.

NOTES

1. For example, the title of Agatha Christie's *The Little Nigger Boys* was changed to *Ten Little Indians* to eliminate the pejorative reference to black people.

2. For further discussion of this topic, see David R. Hughes's "Introduction" in Kallen (1982).

3. For a sociological history of other groups, see Fretz (1989) on the Mennonite and Amish community in the Waterloo area. See also Baar's (1983) study of Mennonites in the Niagara region.

4. Sociologists wage an interesting but as yet inconclusive debate about whether people act first and then develop attitudes to fit the action or whether actions follow from attitudes. In this case, the question is whether discrimination follows from prejudice or whether prejudice is developed to justify discriminatory behaviour.

5. *The Globe and Mail*, February 5, 1991.

6. For a history of women emigrating to Canada from the Caribbean to be domestic workers, see Calliste (1989).

7. *Gazette* (Montreal), May 28, 1993.

8. Ibid.

9. The Métis are descendants of European fur traders and Indian women. They emerged as a distinct and self-conscious group on the Prairies at about the beginning of the nineteenth century. Their culture combines

native and Euro-Canadian values and norms; for example, although most are Catholic, they retain many spiritual beliefs and customs of their Plains Indian ancestors. And, although most speak English, they also use a distinctive Métis language that combines Cree and English words in a French base.

10. *The Globe and Mail*, June 26, 1993.

11. For a well-documented study of the effects of institutional racism, see Li's *The Chinese in Canada* (1988).

12. *The Globe and Mail*, November 28, 1992.

13. The 1985 Supreme Court of Canada order that Manitoba render all statutes and government documents in both French and English started with the 1976 complaint of Georges Forest that his $5 parking ticket was printed only in English.

14. For studies of a wide variety of racial and ethnic groups, see *Generations: A History of Canada's People*, a series under the general editorship of Jean Burnet and Howard Palmer (1988).

15. For a detailed analysis of the sources of public and private income for the aged in Canada, see Lindsay and Donald (1988).

C H A P T E R

8

E I G H T

Work and Its Contexts

The variety of jobs covered in the employment opportunities section in any major Canadian newspaper reflects the highly specialized division of labour in Canadian society. The **division of labour** refers to the differentiation of tasks in the production of goods and services, and to the bases on which these tasks are allocated to individuals and groups. These bases vary among societies; some societies use caste, for example, others use race or gender, and in some the main criteria are training and expertise.

How work is divided in a society is an important indicator of its stage of development. An "advanced" society is usually seen as one that has access to sophisticated technology, whose division of labour is complex, and whose workforce is relatively well educated. Experts—individuals who have knowledge that is typically acquired during long years of formal training—are deemed vital to the continuing well-being and development of society. Experts are generally highly rewarded, both in terms of material rewards (in our society, pay and perquisites [perks] that have a monetary value) and in terms of symbolic rewards (such as power and prestige). Workers who possess few or only simple skills are the most easily replaceable individuals and usually receive the fewest rewards.

The same work is not equally valued in all societies or within the same society at different times. For example, in the eighteenth and early nineteenth centuries, hospital nursing was a lowly occupation, performed for a pittance by the lowest-class women, who were often untrained and regarded as little better than prostitutes. Today nursing is a profession whose practice requires considerable postsecondary education at the college or university level. The work is integral to the operation of modern hospitals, and the occupation has become a "traditional" one for women of all classes who meet the educational requirements. Nurses today argue that "respectability" is small compensation for the subordinate place that nursing occupies in the patriarchal medical hierarchy of hospitals.

The central place that work now holds in our lives makes it difficult to appreciate that the view of work itself has varied over time and space. For example, many societies, including those of the Western world, have for much of their history regarded work, especially manual labour, as a punishment for some sin committed by the individual or by humanity in general. (Think of the story of Adam and Eve.) Therefore, not having to work, especially not having to perform manual labour, became a sign of high status.

In this chapter, we will examine work in relation to a number of contexts. These contexts are located at different levels of abstraction and, insofar as it is possible to do so in a logical way, we will move from the macrosociological to the microsociological level of analysis. Thus, we begin with the broad contexts of industrialization, capitalism, bureaucratization, and patriarchy, and conclude with a discussion of work in the context of specific occupations.

HISTORICAL CHANGES IN THE DIVISION OF LABOUR

In considering culture in Chapter 3, we discussed simple and complex societies, the *Gemeinschaft* and the *Gesellschaft*, and described some basic differences between them. Here, it is useful to examine very briefly the transformation from simple to complex societies and the corresponding changes that occurred in the division of labour.

PRIMITIVE SOCIETIES

Since the earliest societies left no written records, little evidence of the ways in which they functioned exists. So, anthropologists speculate backward from the primitive societies studied in the nineteenth and early twentieth centuries, as well as from the few that exist today (for example, the tribe discovered in a Philippine jungle in the late 1970s).

Primitive societies are assumed to have been hunting and gathering societies in which:

- The division of labour was minimal, except for the gender division necessitated by the demands of pregnancy, lactation, and care of young children. Women tended to be confined to working near their home. Everyone was more or less equal and did similar work, limited only by the biological factors of extreme youth or age, and illness.

- Nobody was totally free from physical labour. Those who had special talents, perhaps as healers or magicians, practised them in addition to their daily tasks; hence, these "specialists" were not radically different from everyone else. Using modern terminology, we would say that they were "moonlighting."

- The minimal technology available did not allow the production of a surplus; therefore, the group was always on the edge of survival. A sudden change in the climatic pattern, leading to extreme drought or flooding, might bring widespread disaster and even destruction of the group.

ANTIQUITY

Eventually, the domestication of animals and the development of rudimentary technology increased food production. When it was more or less possible to predict a surplus, some people could be excused from food procurement for more specialized tasks. The earliest indications of a priesthood come from naturally fertile areas, such as Egypt, Mesopotamia, and parts of Central America.

The Old Testament chronicles the shift from a transient to a sedentary, agricultural society in which land and property (primarily livestock) were valuable assets. These assets had to be defended, so warriors became important—and another stage in task specialization was accomplished.

Many of the material and intellectual breakthroughs of the ancient world were made possible by the enslavement and forced labour of conquered peoples. Achievements during the "golden age" of Greece were facilitated by the presence of a large helot (slave) population, which freed the (male) citizen class from physical labour. The higher prestige accorded to mental work is a carry-over from that time. In Greece, mental effort was not regarded as work at all, but rather as intellectual exercise. As Krause notes, increasing division of labour was accompanied by increasing social differentiation:

> The primary mark of the citizen was his leisure. Choice of vocation—the division of labor in the citizen elite—was by talent and by intrinsic interest of the citizen. One did what could gain the most honor in the contest system of social competition for prestige. Another main function of the citizens was to fight in the army. Slaves were prohibited from fighting because of the risk of desertion and because of the honor-bestowing functions of battle, an opportunity that could not be offered to slaves (1971, 14–5).

At the bottom were the slaves, forced to perform the hardest and most dangerous tasks, for example, rowing galleys and digging in the salt mines. The group of free citizens consisted of patricians and plebeians. The latter, artisans and tradespeople, performed relatively mundane jobs. In contrast, the patricians possessed specialized knowledge; they were the warriors, the statesmen, and the philosophers. For an insightful and readable account, see Bowra's *The Greek Experience* (1985).

In the Roman empire, disparities between patricians and plebeians were maintained and even widened. However, in that large, far-flung empire, there was a continuous need for able soldiers and administrators. Although the constraints on mobility were greater than those of today, those plebeians, or even slaves, who were competent and lucky could move up by capitalizing on their special skills. Exceptional individuals, such as Julius Caesar, could rise from obscurity and go very far, very fast. Carcopino (1962) provides a vivid description of life in Rome when that city was the centre of the ancient world.

THE MEDIEVAL WORLD, THE RENAISSANCE, AND THE REFORMATION

As the Roman empire disintegrated, a process that culminated in about A.D. 400, the dark ages descended on Europe. The loss of much effective government and trade meant that a great deal of effort again had to be devoted to just staying alive—producing food, clothing, and shelter, and then staving off people who threatened to take these necessities away. The division of labour did not vanish, but it became broader, and other skills became important. Literacy all but disappeared, even among the aristocracy. It remained alive, however, in the church, whose monasteries became the protectors and producers of intellectual work for most of the next thousand years.

In the face of continuing warfare and raiding, successful warriors became highly valued. They were rewarded by grants of land from kings and overlords, who were themselves unable to provide much protection for the people on their land. Note that the people who lived on the land "came with it," as it were. They became serfs, obligated to render services to the landholder in return for his protection. Soon, the lord not only became entitled to most of the products of the serfs' labour but also acquired rights over their persons. Serfs were forced to accompany their lord on campaigns, could not leave the land on their own volition, and could be beaten. Serfdom persisted for a long time, especially in eastern Europe and Russia.

Society was overwhelmingly rural, with just incidental towns. Slowly, this state of affairs changed as burghs (villages) sprang up outside the manors or castles, although the burghs remained close to them for protection. At first these settlements grew slowly, but a number of developments helped to accelerate their growth. In these rudimentary cities, groups of artisans, merchants, and professionals began to congregate in order to pool their knowledge and to exchange skills. Once more, the division of labour became more complex.

These developments received an unanticipated boost from the crusades, a series of expeditions organized between 1096 and 1291 to conquer the holy places of Christianity and, at least theoretically, to free them from "infidel" rule. The societies of the Middle East were thriving at the time, and the crusaders marvelled at the techniques for weaving, dyeing, and painting, and at the vigour of the cultural and intellectual life they encountered. They brought back much new knowledge, including a rediscovery of Greek learning, which had been lost in the West.

Meanwhile, the gradual growth of towns and the increase in trade were disrupting feudal society. Warfare, which inspired technological innovation, was still common, but raiding was better controlled and systems of government more extensive. Travel was safer and thus more frequent. Universities had been created. Members of the aristocracy and even some merchants had amassed vast fortunes, and a few were willing to sponsor artists and scholars. As the "new" learning spread through the upper and artisan classes, the interplay of these significant changes gave rise ultimately to the Renaissance era, literally a "rebirth" of enquiry, of learning, and of experimentation with new ideas and techniques. A spirit of discovery was kindled, which led some individuals to search for new continents and others to re-examine physical phenomena, questioning traditional explanations.

The supremacy of the Catholic Church was undermined by the Protestant Reformation, which began in the early fifteenth century. As we shall see in Chapter 11, "Religion and Secularization," the Reformation had important consequences in terms of ushering in another new era.

What happens when old and new social orders collide? Medieval Catholicism had generally viewed the world as a vale of tears that one had to traverse en route to everlasting salvation in the hereafter. Much of Protestantism considered the world to be the Lord's vineyard, where one must work as hard as possible for His greater glory. Work, then, became a "positive good" rather than a necessity for survival.

THE INDUSTRIAL REVOLUTION

Over the next three hundred to four hundred years, the feudal order was shattered; by the beginning of the 1700s, the Industrial Revolution had begun, gathering momentum during the 1800s. In its wake came rapid **urbanization**, the shift of the population from the countryside to the cities.[1]

The revolution was really an evolution in that the progression was gradual. At first, artisans working in their own homes or shops were responsible for the entire manufacturing process, whether their products were cloth, furniture, or wagon wheels. The artisans bought the necessary materials, made the articles, and sold them to purchasers. Gradually, intermediaries entered this sequence: they supplied the raw materials, provided exact specifications for the articles to be produced, and handled the sale of them. They became the entrepreneurs— the owners and controllers of the means of production.

With the growth of population and the improvement of facilities for exporting goods, the volume of business increased, and it became more economical to move production into centralized premises owned by the entrepreneurs. Workers were provided with tools and paid a wage based either on the number of articles produced or on the number of hours worked. Gathering workers into the same premises facilitated control over them and made it possible to fragment tasks. No longer did a worker produce a finished article. Each performed one operation and passed the article to the next person, who took the product one stage further toward completion. By the mid-1800s, the transformation of independent artisans into factory labourers was in full swing. Anthony has noted that in the *Inquiry into the Nature and Causes of the Wealth of Nations*, which was written in 1776 but is still regarded as seminal in economic thought, Adam Smith dwelt on the increased productivity attainable by task specialization:

> The detailed division of labour is carried to its highest point in industrial production, says Smith. It is a most important principle because it explains and is required by increases in productive capacity ... it combines three advantages. It leads to an increase in the dexterity of workmen, it leads to the saving of time by avoiding the workers having to move from one place to another, and it leads to the development of machines "which facilitate and abridge labour" (1977, 54).

A less rosy picture emerges when factory work is examined from the viewpoint of those recruited into it:

> Hard and fast rules replaced the freedom of the small workshops. Work started, meals were eaten and work stopped at fixed hours, notified by the ringing of a bell. Within the factory each had his allotted place and his strictly defined and invariable duty. Everyone had to work steadily and without stopping, under the vigilant eye of a foreman who secured obedience by means of fines or dismissals, and sometimes by more brutal forms of coercion (Mantoux, 1961, 375).

Once production had been broken into simple, repetitive components, it did not take employers long to establish that many tasks could be performed by women and children.[2] They could be paid much less—after all, they were supplementary wage earners, while it was men who earned the "family wage," one that was intended to suffice for the family's needs. Also, women and children tended to be more docile than men. Moreover, before public schools were established, employers could rationalize that they were keeping children off the streets by putting them to work.

At first no legislation regulated wages, hours of work, or working conditions. In Britain, there was bitter opposition to the 1833 Factories Regulation Act, which prohibited the employment of children under the age of 9 in textile mills and limited those under the age of 11 to nine hours of work per day (Anthony, 1977, 58). Disabling accidents were common, but no compensation was available, except from unusually charitable employers.

The appalling conditions experienced by the working class, including its children, eventually aroused the concern of social reformers.

C56705/NAC.

The appalling condition of the working class spurred self-help in the form of attempts at unionization; it also aroused the concern of reformers, including some members of the clergy. By a slow and piecemeal process, developments such as universal education, full enfranchisement, the right to collective bargaining, and technologically induced increases in productivity led to better pay and working conditions.

The shift from preindustrial to capitalist modes of production, and its far-reaching impact on how people work and live, is a fascinating story. There is a voluminous literature on the subject; we recommend Beaud (1983), and Miller and Form (1980).

So far, we have provided a historical overview of the division of labour in the Western world, and have drawn the rough contours of the present-day situation. We now proceed with a brief examination of the theoretical contributions made by analysts of society to the study of work, work contexts, and work relationships.

As we have noted in previous chapters, Durkheim, Marx, and Weber adopted a broad perspective that encompassed the way the division of labour influences and is influenced by the overall structure of society. However, none lost sight of how individuals' lives are affected by their economic placement.

INDUSTRIALIZATION AND INTERDEPENDENCE: FUNCTIONALIST PERSPECTIVES

Durkheim described the new order that emerged with industrialization as a state of organic solidarity, in which many specialized economic, political, and cultural institutions provided a very different, and fragmented, context for social life in rapidly expanding urban centres. Individuals, in turn, were obliged to rely on each other for the goods and services that they could no longer provide for themselves. For example, the carpenter has need of the physician, the physician needs the carpenter, and both need the factory worker to produce clothing. Recognition of interdependence would ultimately serve as a kind of social cement, generating the tolerance needed to avert the societal conflicts that could be occasioned by differences in such things as occupation, ethnicity, race, religion, and education. This new state of affairs was strikingly different from the way of life that Durkheim described as being characterized by **mechanical solidarity**, a state in which individuals living in small, homogeneous communities experienced a social order that was cemented by shared values and beliefs.

Although Durkheim was well aware that the increasing differentiation of work in modern society could be a source of isolation and alienation for people, he had great hope for the sense of community and the normative consensus that professional and other occupational associations could provide. As a substitute for the diffuse bonds that made traditional groups cohere, these would bring together people with common work, common lifestyles, and, presumably, common values. The division of labour, in other words, both because of interdependence and because of occupational solidarity, could be a unifying force in society rather than a disruptive one. Durkheim recommended the abolition of inherited privileges as means of access to occupational positions, so that there would be what we now call **equality of opportunity**.

Subsequent thinkers in the functionalist tradition have tended to be as sanguine as Durkheim about the positive consequences that industrialization could have for society. Talcott Parsons (1951) was interested in the nature of relationships that participation in industrial society requires. He contrasted the kinds of relationships characteristic of primary groups and of secondary groups (see again the discussion of Cooley in Chapter 4) and described these differences in terms of what he called **pattern variables**, opposites that represent different patterns in which people typically relate to one another in specific situations (see Exhibit 8.1).

EXHIBIT 8.1

The Pattern Variables of Relationships

In primary groups	In secondary groups
ascription	achievement
affectivity	affective neutrality
diffuseness	specificity
particularism	universalism
collectivity orientation	self-orientation

Parsons was influenced by Weber as well as by Durkheim, as we will see in our discussion of bureaucracy. The pattern variables reflect the assumption that, within modern society generally, and in the work context in particular, impersonal relationships prevail:

- *Ascription—achievement.* Achievement is the normative determinant for hiring and promotion in a bureaucracy. It is also the underlying premise of human rights legislation and fair employment standards. To the extent that ascription (*who* you are) supersedes achievement (*what* you are) in deciding the individual's fate at work, the situation deviates from bureaucratic norms. Today it also often deviates from societal norms as expressed in law. Canadians who believe they have been discriminated against on the basis of ascriptive factors such as race or gender can seek redress from the human rights commission or labour relations board in their jurisdiction.

- *Affectivity—affective neutrality.* "Affective" means that which pertains to the emotions. Superiors and subordinates, officials and clients, and physicians and patients, for instance, relate to one another in an affectively neutral manner. Emotion is not supposed to enter these relationships.

- *Diffuseness—specificity.* Work relationships are circumscribed in the bureaucracy; they do not spill over into one's total existence. A subordinate's private life is of no concern to his or her superior, unless it impinges on job performance. Teacher/student interaction is centred on academic issues. To some extent, the concept of specificity is captured by the aphorism "business and pleasure don't mix."

- *Particularism—universalism.* Individuals are treated in accordance with general, universal criteria. All students follow the same procedure at registration. You do not pluck your niece from the line-up and allow her to proceed ahead of everyone else. Likewise, the rest of the staff are likely to resent a secretary's enjoyment of special privileges because of a particularistic relationship with the boss. The concept of equality before the law embodies universalism.

- *Collectivity orientation—self-orientation.* In Parsons's scheme, self-orientation is normative in the *Gesellschaft*.[3] In other words, it is accepted that individuals consider their own interests ahead of the group's, just as a business puts profit-making ahead of community concerns. However, the self-orientation that is expected both in society generally and in business does not apply in the ideal public bureaucracy, or in the interaction between professionals and their clients. The interests of the clients, the "collectivity," are expected to take precedence. Revenue Canada personnel are supposed to search for tax overpayments with the same zeal they devote to finding shortfalls, even though the latter may be of greater help in career advancement. Dentists are not supposed to recommend root canal treatment because they are in need of cash.

Parsons formulated each pair of variables as dichotomous and mutually exclusive. In practice, it is useful to think of each set as a continuum, with interaction tending to fall toward one or the other pole. Typically, the relationship between customer and salesperson is specific, oriented to concluding a commercial transaction. However, if the same customer has repeated contact with the same salesperson, elements of diffuseness are likely to arise. Thus, the two may exchange information about their work, families, and hobbies. Can you think of examples from your own experience? Many studies have demonstrated that primary groups develop in the midst of vast, bureaucratic organizations. Within these groups, relationships are personal or, in Parsonian terms, diffuse, affective, and particularistic, more like family relationships.

It is a very short step, in the functionalist approach, from identifying these different patterns of social attitudes and behaviour to seeing them as "natural" and inevitable. As we shall argue in the Chapter 9, which discusses families, the sharp separation between the public world of work and the private world of the family, accepted so readily, places a heavy burden on both spheres and serves as a conservative force in maintaining the status quo.

CAPITALISM AND THE ASYMMETRICAL RELATIONS OF PRODUCTION: THE MARXIST FOCUS

Marx was a **materialist** in that he regarded the economy as the substructure, or base, for all other societal spheres, such as law, education, and religion.[4] In the first volume of *Capital* ([1867] 1976), he defined capitalism as a commodity-producing society in which the principal means of production are owned by one class, the bourgeoisie, and in which the individual's labour power is also a commodity that is bought and sold. The essential features of capitalism are the following: (1) it expands continuously through accumulation via the concentration of capital; (2) it takes advantage of advances in technology to intensify work processes; (3) in its development, it is subject to cycles of prosperity and depression; and (4) the divergent interests of the bourgeoisie (the owners) and the proletariat (the workers) become increasingly pronounced, leading to major class conflict (Bottomore, 1993, 60–63).

The profits of the owners, as we noted in Chapter 1, are based on surplus value, that is, the difference between the wage paid to the worker and the profit that the owner earns in the market on what the worker has produced, after other costs (such as those for machinery) have been deducted. Individual capitalists can increase their surplus value in several ways. They can extend the length of the working day; they can manipulate wages and prices in a variety of combinations such that profits improve; or, they can introduce labour-saving technology so that the worker's output is increased.

Capitalism, according to Marx, contains a number of contradictions that would eventually lead to its destruction if the spiral was not interrupted by a revolution of the labouring class. (He predicted that such a revolution would occur.) What are these contradictions? Expanding production means that more goods flood the market, and, through competition, prices are lowered, bringing less profit. This impels the owners to attempt to exploit workers even more, by paying them less. However, when workers earn less, or are fired, they lose their capacity to purchase goods, and this reduction in consumption also affects profits. Marx predicted that the lines of conflict between owners and workers would harden, and that, eventually, the resistance of workers to exploitation would ultimately result in their gaining control over the means of production.

To say the least, this is a drastically simplified version of Marx's arguments, but we hope it is sufficient for you to appreciate that work in the context of capitalism, as conceived by Marx, involved issues of power and inherent class struggle. This is in stark contrast to the functionalist preoccupation with differentiation, complementarity, and consensus.

Marx's discussion of **alienation**, another word for which is "estrangement," is relevant to our focus on work in this chapter (see Bottomore, 1956). He argued that in performing repetitive, meaningless tasks to earn a survival wage, workers become estranged on several levels:

- Working on the employer's property, using the employer's raw materials and tools, and performing partial operations rather than turning out a completed article result in the *product* of the worker's labour being alienated from him or her.

- The wages the employer pays represent only a fraction of the value the worker produces. The more money employers make, the more their power increases. Since Marx saw capitalists and workers as irreconcilable enemies, he assumed the employers would use this increased power to oppress the workers yet further. Thus, the very products of the workers' labours are turned against them as an alien force of oppression.

- By using their hands to perform tasks that do not engage their hearts or brains, workers become alienated from themselves.

- Each person is a "species-being," a member of the human species. Hence, anyone alienated from himself or herself becomes, by extension, alienated from humanity as a whole.

Marx first wrote about alienation in the 1840s, a time when the excesses of the Industrial Revolution weighed heavily on British workers. Oppression of workers continued for an extended period. The New England textile industry in the early 1900s provides an apt example:

> Everywhere, men, women and children were fixed to the fast pace of the machines, until they too seemed just pieces of machinery, anonymous, uniform, and interchangeable in the tiring din (Gambino, 1981, 199).

Though wages and working conditions have improved since that time, there has been little abatement in the alienation that results from those routine, monotonous jobs, which are the lot of textile-mill operators, workers on assembly lines or video-display terminals (VDTs), as well as many others. The pivotal role of work in society and in the lives of individuals is reflected in social scientists' continuing interest in the alienation engendered by work (Blauner, 1964; Rinehart, 1987), and in the impact of this alienation on other areas of life.

Critics of Marx have pointed to what they consider evidence that his predictions were incorrect. Writing in a different period, Marx did not anticipate the effect that "shareholder" capitalism would have in mitigating the concentration of capital. The rise of a large middle class was also not foreseen as a phenomenon substantially moderating the class polarization that Marx described. The worst effects of capitalism, critics also point out, have been softened by social welfare policies adopted by the state, by the unionization of workers, and

*Marx said that by using
their hands to perform tasks
that do not engage their
hearts or brains, workers
became alienated from
themselves.*

28901–1/McCord Museum of Canadian History/Notman Photographic Archives.

by democratic politics. Some Marxist theorists, however, argue that the ultimate "crisis of capitalism" has only been postponed, because of the West's capacity to exploit the Third World, thereby avoiding the most flagrant and dangerous (to capitalism) forms of exploitation in our own society.

Marx's own writings have engendered many different perspectives in what can be called the Marxist tradition, but we cannot even begin to capture the scope of the debates in one brief chapter. Let us turn, instead, to a more specific focus, that of the Canadian political economy.

WORK AND THE POLITICAL ECONOMY OF CANADA

A political economy perspective is a critical, interdisciplinary approach to understanding society in terms of the complex relationships between the economy and politics. In one of its influential forms, as we shall see, it draws heavily on Marxist theory.

An early interpretation of Canadian economic history, referred to as the **staples thesis**, stressed the importance of geography, natural resources, and technology in shaping the Canadian economy. A staples approach (Innis, 1970) pointed to the flow of unprocessed raw materials such as fur, fish, timber, wheat, and oil, from **hinterland** (resource-producing) regions to metropolitan centres (manufacturing and financial centres) or **metropoles**, and the reverse flow of capital and manufactured goods. Innis viewed Canada as a "hard frontier" that could not be developed by individual initiative alone. Vast amounts of capital, corporate forms of business enterprise, and the support of the state were required to make the most of Canada's rich endowment of natural resources (Clark, 1968, 232).

In the international context, theorists, such as Frank (1979), studied the exploitative nature of the relationship between Third World countries (hinterlands) and the developed nations (metropoles). Their approach was called "dependency theory," since it stressed the downward spiral of dependence, underdevelopment, and impoverishment in which resource-producing regions are caught.

Dependency theory appealed to Canadian scholars, since it appeared to be useful in explaining the underdeveloped nature of the Canadian economy as a whole, in relation to centres of dominance first in France, then Britain, and, finally, the United States. As "hewers of wood" and "drawers of water," Canadians had failed to develop a strong manufacturing base, had had to rely on imported technology, and had become a "branch plant economy," with major decisions being made in the head offices located in another country (Levitt, 1970). Levitt referred to Canada as "the world's richest underdeveloped economy" (1970, 25). Dependency theorists argued that retarded development is not the only possible negative result of our lopsided integration with a foreign economy. We can also go backwards, and become de-industrialized when foreign companies face dire straits or discover cheaper labour opportunities, and decide to move their operations elsewhere (Laxer, 1973).

It may be helpful at this point to refer back to the discussion of Clement's typology of elites in Chapter 6, the chapter on stratification. Clement argued that the route to underdevelopment was smoothed by the compatibility between the interests of indigenous and foreign elite interests in Canada.

The hinterland–metropole paradigm was also seen to be useful in explaining the uneven nature of economic development *within* Canada, as seen in the strong disparities in work opportunities from region to region. Resource-producing regions such as the Prairie provinces exist in a position of heavy dependence on metropolitan centres, such as Toronto, where there is a concentration of financial institutions and manufacturing enterprises. The paradigm can be applied to an even narrower level of analysis, that is, within a single region. Northern Ontario, for example, exists in an asymmetrical relationship with southern Ontario, with economic power being concentrated in the latter.

Dependency theory has come under attack in recent years, on a number of grounds that challenge the view of Canada as a victim of external forces. Critics point out that, with the growth of multinational corporations and the new ease in transportation and communication that technology has made possible, all industrial countries, not just Canada, are seeing the locus of production move to other countries where labour is cheaper. The dependency perspective is also said to underestimate both the involvement of early

Canadian capitalists in industrial projects, such as the building of railroads, and the resilience of the contemporary manufacturing sector, which has been abetted by government policies that make manufacturing more competitive.

While Clement had stressed the "confraternity" formed by business and state elites, Ornstein (1986) found that the extent to which the two spheres interlock is not enough to make plausible a view of the state as being completely under the thumb of business interests. Carroll (1986) has emphasized that, despite a great deal of foreign investment in Canada, Canadian capitalists have also engaged in "economic imperialism," actively investing in ventures outside of Canada.

These arguments suggest that the Canadian economy is not an aberration, but rather, one that is subject to the crises of restructuring being faced by all industrialized economies as the barriers to the flow of capital and goods throughout the world are increasingly eliminated, and as production becomes increasingly internationalized. We will examine the process of restructuring later on in this chapter, since it is having a profound effect on the world of work. First, however, we turn to other theoretical approaches to the study of work and its relation to society.

THE IRON CAGE OF BUREAUCRACY

Think about your activities over the last couple of days. How many involved organizations, directly or indirectly? Make a list of these organizations. (Remember that even solitary pursuits such as reading a book or watching television depend on organizations that publish books and beam television programs into your home.)

As Canadians, all of us live in an organizational society. Most Canadians are born in an organization, are educated in organizations, are likely to work in an organization, and die in an organization. Even religious, political, and leisure activities are carried out in organizations (stepdance groups, bowling centres, duplicate bridge clubs, environmental lobby groups). From cradle to grave, organizations are prominently featured in our existence, shaping more of our attitudes and behaviour than we may realize.

Weber was interested in the kinds of organizations best suited to the administration and coordination of an increasingly complex division of labour. For him, bureaucracy represented the epitome of rationality and efficiency (also the hallmarks of industrial capitalism), and he saw it coming to dominate, and dehumanize, society in all spheres. It was not a form of organization that originated with industrialization, but as capitalism matured, it came to be the defining characteristic of workplace organization.

In the Western world before the Industrial Revolution, "going to work," as we have noted, was a rare practice. The majority of people lived and worked on the land. For many tradespeople, the workplace and their living quarters were the same location, and apprentices frequently boarded with the artisan's family. Industrialization changed all that, though in the beginning workshops and factories tended to be small. Both Marx and Weber accurately foresaw that the multitude of small enterprises would be diminished through bankruptcies, mergers, and takeovers, and that the search for greater efficiency would lead to the corporate giants that dominate the business world today. Growth in the private sector has been accompanied by rapid expansion of the public sector, namely government and related agencies.

Whether public or private, large organizations take the form of **bureaucracies**, the root words of which may be translated as, "government by offices." From his research on earlier societies, Weber observed that their organizations shared certain characteristics. From these common features, Weber drew up a model of an ideal bureaucracy—a theoretical measuring stick that would be free from the distortions that occur in the actual functioning of real-world bureaucracies. It has the following key characteristics.

- Members are recruited on the basis of competence, usually attested to by formal qualifications. Thus, a hospital cannot hire a nurse who does not have the requisite credentials (B.Sc.N., R.N., or R.N.A.). Promotion is based on merit. Frequently, further training and examinations are required, as it is for teachers aspiring to become vice-principals or principals. In other words, achievement, rather than ascription, is the determinant for recruitment and promotion.
- The organization is arranged according to hierarchical principles. The incumbent of each office knows where he or she fits in the chain of command. Positions and their relationships to each other are set out in the organization chart.
- Each office carries with it rights and obligations. In theory, it is immaterial what individual occupies it. Rules set out the mandate for the office of police inspector or vice-president of marketing, not for Marion Carter or Pierre Lachance.
- Authority, too, inheres in the office, not in the incumbent, and in the technical competence that the office presumes.
- The official carries out duties without "anger or passion." Faced with an abusive motorist, the police officer is not expected to counter with verbal or physical abuse.
- Rules and administrative decisions are recorded in writing. Files are an integral part of bureaucratic organization because they can be consulted for guidance on precedents.

Weber believed that bureaucracy was the optimal form of organization because it provided:

- *Specialization*. Individuals are slotted into a division of labour in accordance with their skills and expertise.
- *Predictability*. Each individual is constrained by the mandate of the office and bound by precedent.
- *Impersonality*. Decisions are made on the basis of objective criteria, rather than personal whim.

In practice, of course, bureaucracies deviate from the ideal, and much research has been devoted to demonstrating the ways in which this is so. Who one knows may be more important in getting a job than what one knows; evaluating merit is a subjective exercise, and the predilections of a particular official may have an impact on decisions. Separation of jurisdictions leads to buck passing, the claim that "this is not my department." Emphasis on predictability tends to stifle experimentation, and impersonality engenders depersonalization, thereby reducing people to ciphers.

Marxist critics of Weber have argued that he paid too much attention to efficiency in his ideal-type bureaucracy, and too little attention to power. Bureaucracy is above all a means of exercising *control* over both its employees and its clients. Because bureaucratic organizations have become such a pervasive feature of our society, and because the "ideology of efficiency" is so taken for granted, the dimension of control, or discipline, tends to go largely unrecognized. (See Box 8.1 for an example of the control exercised over telemarketers.)

BOX 8.1

TELEMARKETERS GET NO RESPECT

Bev DeMille is having a bad night. The 51-year-old telemarketer has made 14 phone calls on her shift but has sold just one magazine renewal. "Come on, computer, move it," she says, waiting for the next beep in her headset and the next name to flash on her screen.

Around her, co-workers tethered to their desks by telephone cords gesture as they speak and signal supervisors to listen to the "confirmation" of a sale. A young supervisor, half Ms. DeMille's age, reprimands her. "You're low, girl—one in 14."

Ms. DeMille knows that the pressure goes with the job. Working for nine other employers during her 10 years in telemarketing, she has seen co-workers take tranquilizers to relieve stress and she has seen people fired for missing sales targets.

That strain is felt by many among an estimated three million to four million U.S. telephone sales representatives, 70 per cent of whom are women, according to Telemarketing Magazine. One worker is likely to talk with hundreds of indifferent or hostile customers daily, while being monitored by supervisors who insist that sales reps remain cheerful and stick to their scripted message.

Under the circumstances, workers burn out quickly and feel unappreciated. Management, powerless to relieve the monotony, must cope with disloyalty and high turnover.

Tough work, but this sort of job is among the largest segments of the U.S. work force. Ralph Whitehead, a professor at the University of Massachusetts at Amherst who writes about work trends, calls these people "new-collar workers." They now make up nearly 40 per cent of workers born after 1945. Some are salespeople or data processors, some work in finance or government. What they have in common is computers or telephones. They do blue-collar jobs in a white-collar world.

The new-collar workers spend their days not in factories but in air-conditioned offices. Unlike professionals and executives who enjoy some variety in their work, they are stuck doing limited, repetitive tasks, with little time for camaraderie and next to no chance for advancement.

"There's a tremendous amount of stress, work pressure and performance pressure," says Michael Smith, a professor of industrial engineering at the University of Wisconsin at Madison. "They're turn-of-the-century factory workers, but they're educated and they have technology."

Tens of thousands of telemarketers do their jobs from Omaha, the industry's hub. Restless in their careers, telemarketers here, as elsewhere, feel capable of doing more than their work allows them to do. And that inevitably creates tension.

Next to the Goodyear dealership on Omaha's west side, the small, brick office that houses a branch of DialAmerica Marketing Inc. gives little hint of the frenzy inside, where 325 telemarketers work in three shifts: 8 a.m. to noon, noon to 4 p.m., 5 to 9:30 p.m. The evening shift—the company's busiest—is about to begin.

"Let's do it," a supervisor says as the clock strikes 5 p.m. and the automatic dialing machine begins placing calls. Supervisors—one for every eight reps—pace about, eavesdropping on calls with cordless phones, logging sales on a big blackboard and coaching callers.

As the shift drags on, the room heats up from all the bodies here—about 50 of them—some standing as they speak into their headsets. It sounds like a cocktail party, with none of the laughter or clinking of glasses. On each screen, an electronic message reminds workers: "Our first job—happy customers."

Each rep will make at least 100 calls in a typical shift, pitching magazine subscription renewals or trying to get lapsed subscribers to re-order.

The company does this work for a number of well-known publications. In a typical shift, a rep will speak to the person he or she is trying to reach about half the time and will "convert" about 15 per cent of those who hear the phone presentation.

Reps, who earn commissions based on the number of sales and on the presumed difficulty of selling a particular magazine, have no say in what they are pitching and to whom. The automated dialing system installed last year takes care of all that.

For the first hour of the shift, Myan Jencks is lucky. One of her first calls is to a Mrs. Zwifelhofer, reached on her garden telephone in Wisconsin. "I've been asked to call you personally and offer you the absolute lowest renewal rate," Ms. Jencks begins, reciting the memorized script.

When Mrs. Zwifelhofer says no, Ms. Jencks tries another tack that begins: "I can certainly appreciate how you feel, but. . ."

Mrs. Zwifelhofer is coming around. "You drive a hard bargain," she says. A little more cajoling and Ms. Jencks draws a reluctant "alrighty" out of Mrs. Zwifelhofer.

Ms. Jencks has logged eight sales in the first 35 minutes—twice as high as anybody else's count. But, just then, the supervisor announces that a different magazine is to be pitched by everybody in her group and Ms. Jencks sees her luck change. Names of the magazines can't be mentioned here, a condition DialAmerica insisted on in providing *The Wall Street Journal* access to its sales floor.

An irate woman in Iowa demands to be taken off the calling list, which DialAmerica and other telemarketers are obliged to do. Ms. Jencks wakes up one prospective customer, reaches another who doesn't speak English and a third who can no longer see well enough to read magazines.

One thing that keeps sales reps on their toes is the knowledge that supervisors, company executives or clients may well be listening in.

In a conference room overlooking the sales area, supervisor Alan Drain uses a speakerphone to review one of his new reps, Kathy Boelter. He feels Ms. Boelter's presentation is too quick and eager. When she makes a sale, she sounds surprised. Mr. Drain calls her in. "You're working too hard—you've got to slow down," he tells her.

"Kathy will make it," Mr. Drain confides after she leaves the room. He punches in another number on the phone and produces the halting, timid voice of another new rep. She stutters and surrenders quickly. "She's not long for telemarketing," Mr. Drain says.

A chart on the wall provides a constant measure of performance. It lists everybody's guaranteed pay for the previous week—currently $7.50 (U.S.) an hour—and their actual pay from commissions. The best anybody is doing is to make $13 an hour. Those whose work does not justify the guarantee are on "wage makeup," the company's way of saying that they are not pulling their weight. Too many weeks of that and they are out of a job.

Source: The Globe and Mail *(11 September 1993), B1. Reprinted with permission.*

Other critics have emphasized that the notion of bureaucracy reifies, or gives a separate life to, what is actually the sum of individual human actions that daily give shape to the workings of organizations. Bureaucracy, from this perspective, is not a "thing" into which people are slotted and to which they are compelled to conform; rather, it is a way of rationalizing what people actually do in organizations, so that the participants themselves come to believe that they are merely carrying out proper and eminently reasonable procedures.

Though Weber was well aware of both the "irrational" and the dark side of bureaucracy, he was unable to conceive of an alternative form of organization that could effectively cope with large-scale administration and coordination. For him, it was an "iron cage" that could not be escaped.

SCIENTIFIC MANAGEMENT

Scientific management represented an attempt to impose the principles of capitalism and bureaucratic organization on factory production in order to increase its efficiency. Devising effective means for improving labour productivity became a major concern for entrepreneurs, as the coercion of workers had to be tempered in the face of union pressure, increasing public awareness of working conditions, and government legislation. Also, employers had made large capital investments in machinery and wanted to maximize returns on these investments. The **scientific management** approach, spearheaded by F.W. Taylor (1856–1915), was based on the premise that the interests of workers and employers can be reconciled if pay is tied to productivity. Taylor has been called the father of the assembly line because his time-and-motion engineers observed factory tasks with a view to breaking them down to their simplest components. Taylor recommended that each individual execute only one or two subtasks, become highly proficient at them, and be rewarded on a piecework basis. Thus, he said, workers would be able to increase their earnings and the organization would enjoy greater productivity and higher profits (Taylor, 1919).

Implicit in Taylor's notions of scientific management was the goal of being able to employ workers of minimal intelligence and ability (Ritzer, 1993, 3). Mechanical robots would have been preferable, but they were not available at that time. Taylor's view of the ideal worker is expressed in the following passage:

> Now one of the very first requirements for a man who is fit to handle pig iron as a regular occupation is that he shall be so stupid and so phlegmatic that he more nearly resembles in his mental make-up the ox than any other type. The man who is mentally alert and intelligent is for this very reason entirely unsuited to what would, for him, be the grinding monotony of work of this character. Therefore the workman who is best suited to handling pig iron is unable to understand the real science of doing this class of work. He is so stupid that the word "percentage" has no meaning to him, and he must consequently be trained by a man more intelligent than himself into the habit of working in accordance with the laws of this science before he can be successful ([1919] 1947, 59).

Taylor and his colleagues considered workers to be motivated solely by economic rewards. They ignored the fact that work also meets social needs and that people do not want to spend their days pitted in relentless competition against their co-workers. Scientific management methods did enhance productivity but not to the extent that had been anticipated.

THE HUMAN RELATIONS SCHOOL

During the First World War, as is generally the case in times of labour shortage, employers had to make concessions to workers, and unions were thus able to entrench their position. With the return of the veterans after the end of the war, the balance of power shifted as, once again, there were more workers than available jobs. Even so, employers were anxious not to provoke overt industrial conflict.[5] In part as a response to the limited success of the scientific management approach, Elton Mayo (1880–1949) and his colleagues at Harvard University developed the **human relations school**, which focused on developing better human relations within industry. The hope was that providing more pleasant surroundings and getting workers involved in decisions about their hours of work and fringe benefits would counteract the alienation engendered by doing intrinsically meaningless work in large, impersonal organizations. Lower turnover rates, less absenteeism, and less industrial sabotage—and, therefore, higher productivity—would be the concrete manifestation of happier workers (Mayo, 1945).

At the Hawthorne plant of Western Electric, a study, discussed previously in Chapter 2, based on the assumptions of the human relations perspective, was to become a classic. The initial study, carried out in the 1920s, considered the impact that changes in lighting were having on the productivity of a group of female mica splitters. To their surprise, the researchers found that, regardless of whether they increased or decreased the lighting, output rose. The same pattern was observed when they tried other variations, such as introducing coffee breaks, lengthening or shortening them, or removing them altogether. The conclusion was that the workers were reacting positively to having attention focused on them.

A small group of workers who assembled telephone sets were also observed on a long-term basis. The researchers found that the workers evolved their own norms, which frequently ran counter to the official ones, and enforced them with positive and negative sanctions. For instance, the group set its own output quotas. Workers who continually exceeded the quotas, thus showing up everyone else, were labelled "rate busters"; consistent underproducers were known as "chisellers." If individuals persisted in violating group norms, they were ostracized by fellow workers. The findings furnished empirical support for Durkheim's argument that working together gives rise to shared values (Roethlisberger & Dixon, 1939).

The Hawthorne experiments, while resulting in influential prescriptions about how to manage workers, have been re-evaluated in subsequent research, with mixed conclusions. Carey (1967) argued that economic incentives and coercive supervision were better able to explain the increases in output than was the attention management gave to human relations. Gillespie (1991) shows that the researchers manufactured a coherent version of the findings, even though the results were often inconclusive and sometimes even contradictory. The research itself became part of the process, so that the workers used the very fact of being studied to further their own interests (that is, to increase output when rewards were present). In his reanalysis of the Hawthorne data, Jones (1990) concurs with the original researchers' interpretation that the human relations management style did shape the response of the workers. Acker and Houten (1974) examine the gendered nature of the Hawthorne experiments (a dimension ignored by the experimenters themselves) and note that the men (who were in the bank wiring room) and the women (who were in the relay assembly test room) were treated very differently. The authors conclude that it was the cumulative effect of coercion, paternalistic treatment, and special rewards that resulted in the latter's increase in productivity.

In the account we have just given of the Hawthorne experiments, you have an example of how a sociological study can have a long-term effect both on policies in the organizational world and on subsequent academic research. Clearly, the Hawthorne experiments have not lost their fascination.

The primary goal of both the scientific management and human relations approaches was increased productivity. This does not mean that no importance was attached to the benefits workers would receive. Indeed, both approaches sought to demonstrate that management and labour were partners rather than adversaries. Also, both focused on organizational analysis, examining how various characteristics of the work setting affected worker output and morale.

The premises of both approaches are evident in today's work settings. Braverman (1974) has argued that Taylor's principles of subdividing and deskilling work have moved from the factory to many other workplaces, notably the office. The decline in status and the increasing regimentation of white-collar workers were addressed by C.W. Mills in his important work, *White Collar* (1956). Suggestion boxes, workers' membership on some corporate committees, participatory management, flexible hours, company picnics and other amenities, and the redesign of jobs to expand workers' responsibilities represent today's human relations emphasis. Another strategy has been to institute stock purchasing plans that allow workers to buy company shares through payroll deductions. It is hoped that ownership will give workers a direct stake in higher productivity and higher profits.

OUTSIDE BUREAUCRACY: GOING IT ALONE

Although modern North American society has been aptly described as an organizational society, not everyone works in a bureaucratic setting. Here we examine only two alternative work settings.

Small Business

Relatively small businesses continue to exist, despite the predominance of large corporations. Small firms are likely to provide a more personal work atmosphere for employees. On the negative side, however, such firms are highly vulnerable to economic fluctuations and have high mortality rates. They tend to exist in what is often called the **peripheral economy** where their workers have less job security, lower earnings, and fewer fringe benefits than employees of large firms.

The dream of being independent persists among many people. The few small entrepreneurs who attain success help to sustain the belief that it can be realized with perseverance, hard work, and a little bit of luck. Ironically, the dream is particularly strong among those who are least equipped for success (see the discussion of Tanner's high-school dropouts in Chapter 10, "Education: Winning and Losing"). Using findings from a study of Ontario industrial workers, Knight noted:

> We find that expectations for self-employment are greatest among
> the older workers, among those with the least education, and among

those with the least resources and opportunities to become successfully mobile by commencing and pursuing a bureaucratic or professional career (1981, 287).

A further irony is that many small businesses, such as convenience stores and gas stations, are now franchise operations. Although they ostensibly provide opportunity for independent entrepreneurship, what can be sold, at what price, during what periods, and often in what manner is stipulated by the franchiser, who typically operates in a highly bureaucratic manner.

Often a small business, whether franchised or independent, is run by a whole family, who must work long hours for relatively low returns. Nevertheless, there is less regimentation and more autonomy than is afforded to those who work in the lower echelons of large corporations, and this will likely be of great importance to the kind of person who aspires to be his or her own boss.

Work in labour-intensive family enterprises can be different for women and for men. Phizachlea (1990) points out that women in these settings may be subject to a double set of patriarchal mechanisms, operating both in their work for the firm and in the domestic sphere where they continue to take sole responsibility.

Solo Practice

Professionals are another occupational group often thought of as working in solo work settings, free of bureaucratic constraints. Many professionals (especially dentists) do continue to be in practice by themselves or to work in small partnerships, but, as Hall has noted:

> The country doctor heeding the call of the sick or working in his laboratory, the individual lawyer searching for support for his client's position, or the architect developing original and controversial designs have been discussed and celebrated in fact and fiction. Although central to many conceptualizations of professional work, this type of setting is in actuality a disappearing phenomenon (1975, 82).

Solo practice affords autonomy, but in the case of lawyers, engineers, or architects, it generally entails exclusion from large projects. Clearly, an undertaking like the West Edmonton Mall required the resources of large engineering and architectural firms. Major corporations use large law firms that have access to an array of legal specialists. In studying solo lawyers, Carlin (1962) found that their work is for the most part routine and professionally unchallenging, though it may be lucrative financially. Hall commented:

> These lawyers tend to deny their low status by stressing their independence and the fact that they are in the general practice of all facets of the law. The feeling of autonomy, however, does not overcome the fact that these lawyers also feel insignificant in the overall structure and are frustrated because their high ambitions have not been realized, even though they are professionals (1975, 87).

Our two brief examples indicate that, while there is life outside of bureaucracy, there are prices to be paid for pursuing it.

WORK, CAPITALISM, AND PATRIARCHY: FEMINIST CONTRIBUTIONS

A far-reaching change in this century has been in the labour force participation of women. This change has occurred for many reasons, including economic need, the encouragement provided by the women's movement, and the availability of reliable birth control methods and household conveniences.

As Exhibit 8.2 shows, the increase in women's participation has risen steadily from 1901 to 1991, with one major leap occurring in the 1960s; 1980 was a benchmark year, the first time a majority of Canadian women constituted part of the officially defined labour force (Krahn & Lowe, 1993, 63). As of 1991, 58.2 percent of Canadian women worked for pay.

EXHIBIT 8.2

Labour Force Participation Rates by Gender, Canada, 1901–1991

Year	Both Sexes	Female	Male
1901	53.0%	16.1%	87.8%
1911	57.4	18.6	90.6
1921	56.2	19.9	89.8
1931	55.9	21.8	87.2
1941	55.2	22.9	85.6
1951	54.3	24.2	84.1
1961	55.1	29.1	80.8
1971	58.0	39.9	75.4
1976	60.0	45.0	75.5
1981	64.8	51.8	78.3
1986	65.7	55.1	76.7
1991	66.3	58.2	74.8

Newfoundland included, beginning in 1951.

Sources: 1901–81 from Chen and Regan (1985:135); 1986 from Statistics Canada, The Labour Force *(Cat. No. 71-001, 84, December 1986); 1991 from Statistics Canada,* Labour Force Annual Averages, *1991 (Cat. No. 71-220, 8-2). Reproduced with permission of the Minister of Industry, Science, and Technology 1994.*

Marriage is no longer a significant factor in keeping women from paid work. In 1991, 73.3 percent of married women age 15 to 24 years of age, and 76.8 percent of those aged 25 to 44 were in the labour force (Statistics Canada, 1992). But what about the presence of children? As Exhibit 8.3 shows, having children, like marriage, is not generally a significant factor in inhibiting women's labour force participation, although it is something of a barrier when the children are under the age of 3. While 76.2 percent of women with children under 15 years of age work for pay, only 61.5 percent of women with children under 3 do so. Still, the latter figure is extraordinarily high when compared with earlier periods.

Despite the dramatic increase in women's participation rates, little has changed in the nature of women's paid work. While some have been successful in entering male strongholds, most women remain concentrated in low-status,

EXHIBIT 8.3

Women's Labour Force Participation Rate, by Age of Youngest Child, 1976 and 1991, Canada

Age of Youngest Child	1976	1991
Less than 3 years	31.7%	61.5%
3 to 5 years	40.9	68.2
6 to 15 years	50.1	76.2
Total, with a child 16 years and under	43.0	70.2

Source: 1976: Statistics Canada, Labour Force Survey, *unpublished data. 1991: Statistics Canada,* Labour Force Annual Averages, *1991, Section B18, Table 8, Cat. No. 71-220. Reproduced by authority of the Minister of Industry 1994.*

low-paying, and often insecure jobs that are characterized as "women's work." The fact that the labour force is segregated by gender has made it easier to maintain low wages for women, just as assumptions about the "family wage" (earned by men) and the economic dependence of women have also been used to justify pay inequalities. As Exhibit 8.4 shows, women who worked full-time earned on average 67.6 percent of what men earned in 1990. The exhibit shows variations by age, education, and marital status. For university-educated women, the wage gap is smaller than for others. It is also much smaller for single women, and for young women.

To document inequalities in labour force participation, with regard to occupational status and in wages earned, is one thing; to explain them is another. This is one of the major tasks that feminist scholars have set themselves.

Feminist studies of women and work have burgeoned since the 1960s, and have extended in a number of different directions in the quest for explanations of women's subordination in both the public sphere of paid work and the private sphere of the family (see Armstrong & Armstrong [1990] for a good overview of feminist contributions to theory; see Chapter 9 on families in this book for a more lengthy discussion). While there has been a great deal of lively debate, almost all agree that the role of women in the labour force cannot be understood without examining it in relation to their role in the home. Put dif-

EXHIBIT 8.4

The Wage Gap

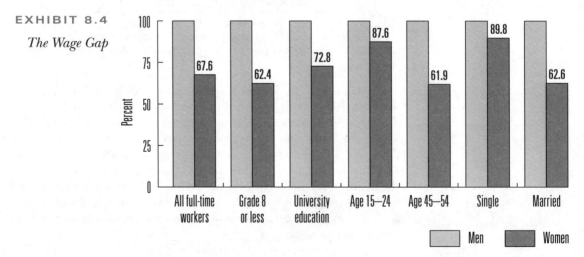

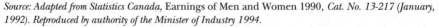

Source: Adapted from Statistics Canada, Earnings of Men and Women 1990, *Cat. No. 13-217 (January, 1992). Reproduced by authority of the Minister of Industry 1994.*

ferently, one must examine women's *productive* roles (their paid work) in relation to their *reproductive* roles, for it is in the family that they reproduce the labour force's next generation of workers, by having and rearing children, at the same time as they "reproduce" labour power on a daily basis by taking care of male workers. The responsibility for these tasks has had profound effects on their participation in paid work. We shall examine the interplay between women's paid and unpaid work at some length in Chapter 9.

MIDDLE-CLASS PROBLEMS: THE GLASS SLIPPER, THE GLASS CEILING, AND THE GLASS ESCALATOR

It should not surprise us, perhaps, that the problems confronting middle-class women who wanted to work were to receive considerable attention from middle-class feminist academics and activists.

Although Perrault's Cinderella story was written in the seventeenth century, it is not without relevance to contemporary life. The "glass slipper solution"— marriage, or being rescued by the prince—is not unique to middle-class women.

While women have succeeded in entering some male strongholds, they are unlikely to rise to the top positions.

Police Cummunaute Urbaine de Montreal.

However, it is perhaps all the more striking when such women choose it, since they are doing so despite the advantages of socialization and formal education that would encourage them to aspire higher, and would presumably give them more opportunities to succeed. Yet, even they face daunting obstacles in a male work world, often causing them to elect a form of retreat.

In 1975 women constituted an unprecedented 10 percent of the students in the Harvard MBA program. Gallese (1985) interviewed the female graduates from 1981–1983 to discover what had attracted them to the program, how they felt about their experiences in it, and to what degree their aspirations and expectations had been realized. Gallese found that even these elite women were neither as ambitious or successful as men with the same backgrounds. Nevertheless, they appeared satisfied that they had attended the Harvard Business School.

A recent task force, set up by the Canadian Bar Association, showed that women are leaving the legal profession at a much faster rate than men, because their firms make no accommodation to their childrearing obligations. In Washington, D.C., a Lawyers-at-Home Forum was established by the Women's Bar Association to help women who had left their practices to become full-time mothers. Since a large percentage of these women who had left their jobs wanted to keep in touch with the profession, the Forum took on the task of touting the benefits of hiring women lawyers on a part-time basis. Professional women are more likely than other women to have the opportunity to negotiate good part-time positions of the kind described in the sections below on part-time work and job sharing. Female physicians may choose to work on a schedule of reduced hours in what is still referred to as a "full-time career," in order to be able to carry out their childrearing responsibilities.

Some middle-class women choose not to work for pay, but build "careers" around voluntary work. Sociologist Cynthia Fuchs Epstein worked for three years as a writer and research assistant for the program director of Hadassah, the women's Zionist organization that raises millions of dollars annually for hospitals and training programs. Epstein describes the women she encountered in the organization:

> I learned a great deal about myth and reality there. The women at the top were high-powered executive types. They came in early in the morning and left late at night; they vied for power and control of the organization; they had strong ambitions as well. Although they were described by the Census Bureau and themselves as housewives since they did not work for money, they were as involved and active as any IBM executive (1990, 355).

Studies of exceptions to sex segregation in the workforce have tended to focus on the experience of women in male-dominated occupations. For women executives, their ascent in the organizational hierarchy tends to be limited by a "glass ceiling," invisible and unacknowledged, that prevents them from reaching the top positions. However, some attention is also now being paid to what happens to men when they undertake "women's work." The "glass escalator" is a term used by Williams (1992) to describe the structural advantages men experience in the feminized professions that propel them to the top. She examines men in nursing, elementary school teaching, librarianship, and social work, all of which are occupations that have been identified as women's work in the twentieth century. Williams shows that even in these professions, many of the better-paid and more prestigious positions come to be defined as male specialties. Men's gender difference confers on them a positive advantage rather than being, as is the case with women in male-dominated occupations, a liability.

Whereas males are no more free from stereotyping than females, Williams finds that those applied to men are not sufficiently bothersome to outweigh the advantages they receive. As one teacher told Williams:

> As a man, you're teaching with all women, and that can be hard sometimes. Just because of the stereotypes, you know. I'm real into computers ... and all the time people are calling me to fix their computer. Or if somebody gets a flat tire, they come and get me. I mean, there are just a lot of stereotypes. Not that I mind doing any of those things, but it's ... you know, it just kind of bugs me that it is a stereotype, "A man should do that." Or if their kids have a lot of discipline problems, that kiddo's in your room. Or if there are kids that don't have a father in their home, that kid's in your room. Hell, nowadays that'd be half the school in my room (laughs). But you know, all the time I hear from the principal or from other teachers, "Well, this child really needs a man ... a male role model" (laughs). So there are a lot of stereotypes that ... men kind of get stuck with (1992, 260).

Williams's respondents were more concerned about the stereotypes held by members of the public than by colleagues. Male elementary school teachers, for example, felt susceptible to suspicions of having pedophiliac tendencies. Williams concludes that, when men face discrimination because of being in female professions, it tends to come from outside the profession rather than, as is the case with women, from inside. Men on the inside are more likely to be carried upwards in the organization on the glass escalator which, like the glass ceiling, is translucent and operates without official recognition.

William Goode (1991), who also shows a penchant for metaphor, has noted that, when women begin to establish a sizable presence in occupations that have traditionally been male domains, they are "rising on an elevator in a crumbling building." In other words, the status of the occupation itself becomes downgraded as it becomes feminized. While the women in it receive higher rewards than they would in more lowly occupations, they receive lower rewards than men once did in the same occupation. One example is the profession of medicine in the former Soviet Union after the country had sustained heavy Second World War losses and needed women just to keep things running (Giele, 1992, 11). Even in this situation, female doctors were less likely to be chosen for leadership positions; they earned lower wages than men and, as women came to be numerically predominant, they found themselves in a profession that was heading into a status decline (Lapidus, 1992). In Canada, between 1981 and 1986, women came to account for over half of the labour force in pharmacy. By 1991, almost 56 percent of all pharmacists were women. Likewise, between 1986 and 1991, there was a 38 percent increase in the number of female dispensing opticians, which meant that by 1991 more women than men were in this occupation (Statistics Canada, 1993). These two examples should offer interesting opportunities for the study of occupational change in relation to gender.

BROADENING THE FOCUS

In their research on women and work, feminists have by no means only paid attention to the dilemmas of the middle class. Excellent studies have been carried out on working-class communities (see, for example, Luxton, 1980; Connelly & MacDonald, 1983), while others have looked at women in low-paid, exploitative jobs, for example, in the garment industry (Gannage, 1986). Accompanying the documentation of women's participation in a broad range of occupations has been a vigorous and controversial effort to theorize about women's work.

Some explanations for women's subordination in the labour force have focused on the characteristics and attitudes of the women themselves that have kept them from succeeding in the work world. Feminists have sought to expose the "biologistic" assumptions that stress the "natural" role of women in the bearing and raising of children, primary activities that these theorists maintain have prevented women from participating in paid work in anything more than a secondary way. Others have stressed the differences in the socialization of males and females that have led to their having different aspirations, as well as varying personality characteristics. Here, the problem is one of ideas and beliefs: we must change the culture, the argument goes, and this will change the way women see themselves in relation to the division of labour.

Marxist feminists have sought to explain women's position in the labour market in terms of the needs of capitalism for a cheap and flexible labour supply. Since women have not been seen to have to earn a family wage, but only to supplement one, they could be paid less than men and could work intermittently. Some have argued that women thus serve as a "reserve army of labour" that can be drawn into jobs, particularly part-time jobs, when needed and can simply be let go when the economy is in decline.

Radical feminists argue that patriarchy, a system in which men subject women to exploitation and domination, is the most fundamental form of domination. This approach stresses that it is men, rather than the capitalist system per se, who benefit from women's domestic labour. In fact, men also stand to be disadvantaged by capitalism's use of women as cheap labour, since it is a way of undercutting wages. This is why, it is argued, men have tried to keep women out of the labour market, and to control them when they do work.

Feminist research has provided an increasingly rich picture of the ways in which women experience both their paid and their unpaid work. It has also contributed to our understanding of the constraints within which women make their choices about working, working part-time, or not working, and the costs and benefits attached to each set of choices (Duffy et al., 1989; Duffy & Pupo, 1992).

Most recently, feminist research has broadened its purview to include a consideration of the ways in which ethnicity and race interact with gender to produce multiple oppressions (see, for example, Ng, 1988; Billson, 1991). Through an in-depth examination of the counselling process in a community employment agency that provided placement services for nonanglophone and

Feminist research has contributed to our understanding of the constraints within which women make their choices about working full-time, part-time, or not at all.

black women, Ng revealed the subtle mechanisms that ensured the placement of these women in the lowest echelons of the labour market.

Since feminists are committed to getting rid of inequalities in the workplace as well as studying them, they have been actively engaged in lobbying for (and sometimes winning) such things as pay equity, affirmative action, policies dealing with sexual harassment, and so on. However, not all women benefit equally from such gains. As Armstrong and Armstrong note, " ... to the extent that legislation and other policies have been successful in altering women's condition, they have often served to increase divisions between women rather than to reallocate power or pay between women and men" (1990, 8). For a thorough, readable, and balanced discussion of the issue of pay equity, we recommend Cuneo (1990).

GENDERING THE ANALYSIS OF ORGANIZATIONS

Until 1974, the analysis of organizations was virtually sex-blind. Given what we have said about the pervasiveness of organizations in modern society, this is a serious defect. Feminist analyses of work emerged much earlier than feminist analyses of organizations.

Acker and Houten, in a seminal article (1974), argued that, whenever organizational analysts recognized sex differences in organizational behaviour, they attributed it to sex-role socialization and to the different roles that males and females play *outside* of organizations. Acker and Houten emphasized the importance of the sex–power difference in organizations (that is, the fact that men generally wield more power than women) and called for attention to be given to the ways in which women are recruited into organizational roles that require passivity and compliance, and are then subjected to mechanisms of control that keep them in positions subordinate to men. In support of their argument, they reanalyzed two classic organizational studies, one of which was the Hawthorne studies, which we have already discussed, to show that attention to the sex–power difference between the sexes requires an entirely different interpretation of the data.

In *Men and Women of the Corporation* (1977), Kanter demonstrated that there are few women in management positions and that even when women do attain such heights, their positions often carry less discretionary and decision-making powers than comparable positions occupied by men. These power disparities, and the inconsequentiality of women's presence at the top, Kanter says, send messages to both male and female employees about their relative worth in the organization. Women's upward paths are blocked, and they must tailor their aspirations accordingly.

Despite a handful of early studies, the feminist critique of organizational theory only gathered momentum during the past decade. The same tendency to reify, that is, to accept as a reality rather than an abstraction, the concept of bureaucracy, which was mentioned above, has also turned the workers in abstract organizations into abstract workers. Acker puts it this way:

> A job exists separate from those who fill it, as a position in the hierarchy of an organizational chart. It is a reified, objective category. But the abstract job must contain the assumption of an abstract worker if it is to be more than a set of tasks written on a piece of paper. Such a worker has no obligations outside the demands of the job, which is a bounded, abstract entity. To fit such demands, the abstract worker does not eat, urinate, or procreate, for these activities are not part of the job. Indeed, the abstract worker has no body and thus no gender ... Real jobs and real workers are, of course, deeply gendered and embodied. The abstract worker transformed into a concrete worker turns out to be a man whose work is his life and whose wife takes care of everything else. Thus the concept of a job is gendered, in spite of its presentation as gender neutral, because only a male worker can begin to meet its implicit demands (1992, 257).

The organizational literature produced since the early 1980s has explored a number of interesting aspects of the gendering of organizations, including sexual harassment (Guteck, 1985), the de-eroticization of workplaces (Burrell, 1992), organizational culture, and the gendered nature of state bureaucracy (Grant & Tancred, 1992). Organizations provide a promising site for excavating the hidden processes of control over women, processes that are hidden precisely because of the ostensibly gender-neutral concepts of bureaucracy and the abstract worker.

THE POST-INDUSTRIAL TRANSITION: SECTORAL CONTEXTS

An important feature of countries undergoing industrialization has been the continuing shift in labour force distribution (the proportion of people engaged in various kinds of work).[6] As is evident from the Canadian data in Exhibit 8.5, this shift has occurred from the primary sector (agriculture, fishing, mining) to the secondary sector (manufacturing) and, most recently, to the tertiary sector (services). The decline in the primary sector is especially striking. In 1891, this group constituted 49 percent of the labour force; by 1991, it had shrunk to 6 percent.

In contrast, the percentage of workers employed in the service sector has more than doubled in the same period, now standing at over 70 percent. In fact, nearly 90 percent of net employment creation in the past forty years has taken place in the service sector (Economic Council of Canada, 1991, 1). This is one of the defining characteristics of what has been called the "post-industrial era." Is the growth in this sector likely to continue? What is the quality of the jobs that have been created? Do the widespread applications of high technology mean that workers must be more skilled, or less skilled? A broader question, to which we shall turn shortly, is, are we witnessing the transition to a new kind of society?

EXHIBIT 8.5

Sectoral Distribution of the Canadian Labour Force, 1891, 1951, 1991

	1891	1951	1991
Primary Sector[1]	49%	22%	6%
Secondary Sector[2]	20	31	23
Tertiary Sector[3]	31	47	71

[1] Primary sector includes agriculture, mining, forestry, and other resource extraction industries.
[2] Secondary sector refers to manufacturing and construction.
[3] Tertiary sector refers to the service sector, and includes, among other things, the finance, education, retail trade, government (public administration), and health service sectors.

Source: Krahn and Lowe, Work, Industry and Canadian Society *(Scarborough, Ont.: Nelson Canada, 1993), p. 68.*

Even while production in the primary and secondary sectors has expanded (Krahn & Lowe, 1993, 68), the figures in Exhibit 8.5 reveal that this expansion has not generated a higher demand for employees. For example, the mechanization of agricultural work has led to larger farms, but fewer of them. Likewise, the introduction of robotics and microelectronics has increased productivity without creating a concomitant increase in jobs. On the other hand, services have tended to be more labour-intensive.

The demand for services has increased for a number of reasons: higher incomes and more leisure time have given rise to greater demand for such things as recreational services and food services. The state's enlarged role in providing educational and social services, and in funding health services, has also contributed to the growth of the service sector (Krahn & Lowe, 1993, 68–69). Further, the manufacturing sector relies heavily on distributive and business services, even while it employs fewer people in the manufacturing process itself (Myles, 1993, 127).

In its report, *Good Jobs, Bad Jobs: Employment in the Service Economy*, the Economic Council of Canada makes a distinction among dynamic services (for example, transportation, communications, finance, insurance, and business services), traditional services (such as retail trade, accommodation and food, and personal services like haircutting and recreation), and nonmarket services (which include education, health, social services, and public administration). Each of these areas has its own special characteristics and employment patterns, making it foolish to attempt to make generalizations about "services" per se.

During the 1950s and 1960s it was the nonmarket services that grew fastest. More recently, dynamic services have seen the greatest expansion (Krahn, 1992).

The trend that is creating consternation is the polarization between high-skilled, well-paid service jobs (the "good jobs"), chiefly in the dynamic and non-market service subsectors, and the low-skilled, poorly paid jobs (the "bad jobs") in the traditional subsector. It is in the latter that part-time jobs are concentrated, and also it is here that we find women overrepresented. Moreover, despite the assumption that services are more "footloose" than manufacturing or resource-based activities and can therefore serve to generate work in deprived regions, the dynamic services are concentrated in metropolitan centres. This means that the post-industrial economy may actually contribute to regional disparities, and to uneven economic opportunities within regions.

DESKILLING OR UPGRADING?

In *The Coming of Post-Industrial Society*, Daniel Bell (1973) described an industrial economy as one in which there is a polarization of skills between a small, elite group of managers and engineers, and a large mass of unskilled and semi-skilled machine operatives. He argued that, with the advent of the information technologies and the replacement of labour-intensive production work by high-tech production systems, the need has grown for a well-trained and highly skilled labour force both to produce information and to manipulate it. This will lead to a social structure that has an entirely different shape.

Bell envisaged the expansion of an educated, well-rewarded population of knowledge-workers, and the eventual elimination of disaffecting, mind-numbing work. In his scenario, the fruits of economic growth that would accompany this transformation would be widely distributed, and there would be greater political and institutional harmony.

Harry Braverman's vision was quite the opposite. In his influential book, *Labor and Monopoly Capital: The Degradation of Work in the Twentieth Century* (1974), he argued that technological innovation was being introduced in ways that robbed workers of their skills (that is, "deskilled" them), so that employers would remain even more firmly in control of the labour process. In his view, the "lower-level occupations" would expand, chiefly in clerical, sales, and service work, and even the middle-level jobs would ultimately become proletarianized. Braverman pointed out that there was a progressively weakening relationship between educational credentials and the way jobs are actually performed; the majority of jobs, he said, could be mastered in two to twelve weeks, a drastic change from the length of time it used to take to master a craft.

The debates over the nature of post-industrial society began in the 1970s and continue to this day. Myles (1988) argues that it is simplistic to see the main issue as one of inevitable "deskilling" or "upgrading." There is some evidence of a polarized labour market for skills, he claims, but not Braverman's split between professionals/managers and the mass blue- and white-collar occupations: "Rather, the polarization is within these 'mass' occupations, between high and low skill clerical workers, high and low skill blue collar workers, high and low skill sales workers and the like" (1993, 126). Will this polarization become even more pronounced, making societal cleavages worse? Or, can it be avoided?

Myles argues that outcomes are largely a matter of political choices. If public policy encourages "flexible" (that is, cheap, dispensable) labour markets at the bottom of the wage structure, of the kind we describe in our section on part-time work below, and if there is a policy of restraint in providing public services (a source of good jobs), then the wide split in job opportunities will continue. There are, however, alternative choices. In Sweden, for example, wage policies have the effect of putting low-wage employers out of business, and the welfare state apparatus itself also discourages low-wage, unskilled service industries. This combination of factors serves to direct investment toward the upper part of the wage and skill ladder, rather than toward its bottom.

THE CONTEXT OF TIME: ALTERNATIVE WORK PATTERNS

Despite some indications, particularly from opinion polls, that a small fissure in the work ethic is beginning to appear, and despite those who herald the coming of a "leisure society," workplaces are still "greedy" localities. With earnings eroded by inflation, many workers have to scramble harder just to stay afloat. Some attempt this by working overtime, some by holding more than one job. Others are working longer hours without extra pay, out of the fear that they might lose their jobs.

However, the standard Monday-to-Friday, 9-to-5 structure in the world of work does not suit the needs and preferences of everyone, and some who want conventional work patterns are unable to obtain them. Here we examine several alternative patterns of labour force participation.

PART-TIME WORK

The part-time labour force has grown at a dramatic pace in the past twenty years and has finally outstripped the growth in full-time workers. The number of part-time workers in Canada has increased at an average annual rate of 7 percent since 1953. This figure is more than three times the growth rate of the full-time labour force (Coates, 1986, 6). In 1993, part-time workers constituted 17.7 percent of all workers, up from 15.4 percent in 1990.

Through better statistical monitoring and research, we are obtaining an increasingly clear picture of the extent of part-time jobs, their sectoral and occupational distribution, their nature, and the characteristics of part-time workers. Many questions, however, remain. How have economic, social, and political forces interacted to produce so many marginal, low-paid jobs, with few or no fringe benefits, no security, and with little chance for advancement? What are the forces that determine who will hold these jobs? Why are women, and racial and ethnic minorities, overrepresented among part-time workers? Over 70 percent of part-time workers are women (Duffy & Pupo, 1992, 41). If these jobs were to be improved, would the part-time work force look different? These are some of the questions that social scientists interested in part-time work are beginning to address.

Part-time work has a number of advantages for persons at certain stages of the life cycle. It permits individuals to earn money and, at the same time, allows them the freedom to study or retrain, to meet domestic commitments, to phase into retirement, or to supplement income in old age. In other words, it is a form of employment that offers flexibility to the worker.

But what are the costs of this flexibility? Part-time jobs are concentrated in service industries. These jobs are traditionally, as mentioned above, characterized by low pay, few or no fringe benefits, little job security, and few opportunities for advancement. The advantages for employers are clear. For one thing, parcelling out work in this way permits firms like banks, department stores, and fast food chains to extend hours of business at less cost. For another, it is far cheaper for employers to create several part-time jobs than one full-time position that would both require a more costly benefit package and not be as easy to dispense with if the needs of the organization changed. Universities and colleges, for example, use part-time instructors for these kinds of reasons.

Do individuals choose part-time work to suit their own needs? The majority of part-time workers are classified as voluntary, and one can only speculate about the extent to which their numbers would swell if the disadvantages and risks of part-time employment were reduced. However, there has been a disturbing growth in the proportion of part-time workers who have taken their jobs on an *involuntary* basis, that is, because they cannot obtain full-time work. These workers are often referred to as the "hidden unemployed" or the "underemployed," and they account for almost all of the growth in part-time employment in recent years (Tilly, 1990).

In modern society, time is a commodity: we talk about "saving," "spending," "losing," and "wasting" time. Therefore, the term *part-time* is not a neutral one; rather, it carries the negative connotations of lack of ambition and weak commitment. It also suggests that the incumbent of a part-time job is merely working for

Part-time jobs bring low pay, few or no fringe benefits, no security, and little chance for advancement. However, for young people, they provide an opportunity to work while pursuing an education.

Cedarbrae High School.

"pin money," as a supplement to other income. These assumptions are questionable in view of the expanding number of involuntary part-time workers, the insufficiency of family incomes, the growth of female-headed, lone-parent families, the failure of social security to provide adequately for those with disabilities, and the economic vulnerability of increasing numbers of women at all stages of their lives. It has become clear that employment is no less central to the lives of part-time workers than it is to full-time workers (Warme et al., 1992, 3).

Unions have played a role in shaping part-time work, both by commission and omission, that is, by the policies they have adopted and those they have eschewed. Rates of unionization are considerably lower for part-time than for full-time workers. In their examination of the ambivalence that Canadian unions display toward part-time workers, Pupo and Duffy observe that:

> Labour negotiators inconsistently bargain away, bargain about, and bargain on behalf of, part-timers. Some identify part-time work as women's work and dismiss the possibility of organizing part-timers, because of inaccurate ideas about women's interest in unions or about the temporariness of these jobs. Others point to the difficulties and expense involved in organizing part-timers. As a result of such misperceptions, scarce resources, and an historical tradition of protecting men's full-time jobs and upholding the traditional ideology of the family wage, often at the expense of women's jobs, part-time workers' needs are not usually placed foremost on the bargaining table (1992, 108–109).

However, since employers are unlikely to retreat from their attempts to create a more flexible work force, and since this trend will increasingly affect men as well as women, it is in the long-term interests of unions to gain some control over how flexible working patterns are introduced, how they are used, and how they are compensated (Ellis, 1988).

Despite the argument that part-time work brings clearer advantages to employers than to employees, there are now some interesting "pockets of innovation" that can benefit both constituencies. We are referring to some of the new forms of part-time work, what Kahne (1985, 1992) calls the "new concept arrangements," such as job sharing, permanent part-time work, and phased-in retirement. These types are usually characterized by better pay, greater job security, negotiated rather than imposed schedules, and prorated fringe benefits. However, only a small fraction of the part-time workforce is engaged in these more inviting positions.

JOB SHARING

Job sharing is a work arrangement engaged in voluntarily by employees who seek the flexibility that working fewer hours than they would if full-time gives them. Under such an arrangement, two workers fill an equivalent full-time position and receive partial pay and benefits (for instance, pensions). Job sharers may divide the working hours in a number of ways; for example, they may each work $2\frac{1}{2}$ days per week, or they may each work a full week on alternate weeks. Such scheduling provides them with more leisure time, more time for domestic commitments, or time to upgrade their education.

Job sharing provides an opportunity for women to maintain their skills, contacts, and career prospects during the period in their lives when childrearing responsibilities are heaviest. Although no statistics are available on the extent of job sharing in Canada, Wallace found that job sharers tend to be women with post-secondary education and young children at home (Wallace, 1983). For employers, the main advantage is that they obtain the skills and commitment of two employees for the price of one. However, it is more expensive to fill a position with job sharers than with part-time workers, because of the costs of pro-rated benefits and the full-time salary that is divided between the job sharers.

Interestingly, job sharing first emerged at the initiative of professional and managerial women who, given their valued skills, were in a better position than lower-level workers to negotiate with their employers.

HOMEWORK

Working in one's home is a way for women with young children, or disabled persons, or older workers, to have paid employment without the requirement of "going to work." Homework can provide an opportunity for increased control over one's life, and the flexibility to integrate work with other activities. Sewing on a piecework basis is one example. Traditionally, homeworkers have been almost exclusively women (Huws, 1984); however, it can scarcely be said that they have gained "increased control." The price for working at home has generally been lower pay than office or factory-based work, no benefits, no

Working at home provides many women with the opportunity to juggle paid work and family responsibilities. However, it has its disadvantages, such as isolation from fellow workers.

Sue Dobson.

assurance of a steady flow of work, lack of union protection, and extreme isolation. In the clothing industry, there is a long history of using a flexible work force by means of homeworking, and this employment strategy continues to this day. (For a good analysis of the risks and problems faced by women in this industry, see Johnson & Johnson [1982] and Leach [1993]).

The "new homeworkers" in Huws's British study (1984) were chiefly engaged in word processing. Huws found that there are advantages and disadvantages to homework for both employers and employees. On the positive side, employers cited increased productivity, lower overhead, and flexibility. Furthermore, the new technologies themselves allowed management to monitor a remote workforce. On the other hand, employers complained of higher administrative costs and the problem of a less committed workforce. As with traditional homeworkers, the new homeworkers saw the flexibility to juggle work and family responsibilities as a major advantage. On the negative side, homeworkers found pay rates lower than for similar on-site work, felt they had no promotion prospects, and complained of isolation as the chief drawback.

In his book *The Condition of Postmodernity*, David Harvey (1989) stresses the regressive side of the new/old labour processes that technological advances permit. New production technologies and new coordinating forms of organization, he says, "have permitted the revival of domestic, familial, and paternalistic labour systems. The revival of the sweatshops in New York and Los Angeles, of homework and 'telecommuting', as well as the burgeoning growth of informal sector labour practices throughout the advanced capitalist world, does indeed represent a rather sobering vision of capitalism's supposedly progressive history" (1989, 187). It should be noted, however, that "telecommuting" is not confined to lower-level workers. Box 8.2 profiles a female bank vice-president who works at home two days a week.

In the future, it is likely that the demand for alternative work patterns will increase. Technological advances and the capitalist push for economy are likely to ensure that the supply of such work is also likely to increase. However, the search for a convergence, or "fit," between the needs of workers and those of employers is a process that will no doubt entail heightened conflict over the ways that the costs and benefits of these work options are to be distributed.

UNEMPLOYMENT: WHEN TIME HANGS HEAVIEST

Marx argued that capitalism would be plagued by recurring boom and bust cycles, and that the bust part of the cycle would produce massive unemployment. The Depression of the 1930s, in which millions of unemployed roamed the continent in search of work, any work, demonstrated the accuracy of these predictions. One consequence was that governments felt compelled to create minimal safety nets for these contingencies, such as unemployment insurance. These measures acknowledged that unemployment was a public issue, not merely the result of personal fecklessness—but their design was also based on the assumption that unemployment was a temporary condition (Drummond, 1986; Struthers, 1983).

However, it has become clear that some unemployment is a permanent feature of industrial society. This is due to such structural factors as technological displacement (for example, by robotics), corporate consolidation, and, in

BOX 8.2

TALES FROM THE "TELECOMMUTING" FRONT.
LISTEN. YOU MIGHT BE NEXT.

Virginia R. Coffey, a vice president at Bankers Trust, shares her office two days a week with a 4-year-old and an 18-month-old. Working out of her Brooklyn house, she is at one moment handling the accounts of banks in Australia and New Zealand, and at the next moment attending to the needs of her two children. "At the office, I have one function," she said. "At home, I'm a mommy and a banker." It is, to say the least, "a wearing situation."

Some of her colleagues are skeptical about her working at home the past four years; they "think it's a bunch of malarkey," Ms. Coffey said.

But not her boss at Bankers Trust, Richard W. Upton. He says Ms. Coffey is more productive than many employees who are in the office full time. "It works because you have a mature and responsible individual," Mr. Upton said.

It has been more than a decade since American workers, helped by advances in computers and telecommunications, began going downstairs instead of downtown. There are about 6.6 million such "telecommuters"— employees of businesses or government agencies working part or full time at home instead of at the office—nationwide last year, up 20 percent from 1991, according to Link Resources, a New York market research firm. And they're growing in number faster than any other kind of home worker. Still, the telecommuters represent only about a sixth of the 39 million Americans who worked at home last year. Among the rest, 11.7 million were part-time self-employed, 12.1 million ran a business full time from home and 8.6 million took work home from the office after-hours.

With the number of telecommuters expected to rise sharply, the experiences of pioneers like Ms. Coffey and her employer can be instructive.

From an employer's standpoint, working from home has proved a winner. The 10 supervisors interviewed for this article all reported either an increase in the employee's productivity or no change; none saw a decrease. Several recent studies in government and business have also found higher productivity. The gains were attributed primarily to fewer interruptions by co-workers, meaning better concentration on the task at hand.

Employers also said an offer to work at home allowed them to retain and recruit valuable employees, and sometimes to make double use of desks at headquarters, meaning lower overhead for office space.

On the other hand, an employee's absence from the office can mean delays in urgent work and meetings. And the arrangement can be a fiasco if the employee has children who are unattended, or if the employee doesn't have the discipline to work without continuous supervision.

From the employees' standpoint, telecommuting has proved a mixed blessing but one they would not relinquish. Telecommuters say they miss the social contact. Then there is the compulsion to work at all hours, because the office is right there, and the sense that they are captives to the job even at home. At the same time, some telecommuters expressed fear that their absence from the office might lead co-workers to think they're goofing off, and bosses to forget them for promotions.

Still, all telecommuters pointed to the many benefits. Those with children mentioned the value of spending more time with them. Those who had endured long commutes talked of the time saved. They were pleased about saving money they would have spent on transportation, business clothes and meals.

While telecommuting has grown in the past several years, it is still insignificant compared with what is soon to come, for a number of reasons.

Advances in technology are making remote offices not only possible but appealing. Personal computers, facsimile machines and cellular phones grow more powerful and cheaper; new hardware and software that seamlessly connect home PC's and office networks allow a "virtual office" almost anywhere.

As the decade progresses, telecommuting will also be propelled by environmental demands. The Federal Clean Air Act amendments of 1990 mandate that businesses with

100 or more employees in urban areas seemed to have certain air-quality problems reduce the use of cars by employees. Some companies in New Jersey, Connecticut and Texas are expected to begin implementing their plans next year, with those in eight other states, including New York, Pennsylvania and California, expected to comply by 1996. Telecommuting would be a good solution, said Thomas E. Miller, vice president of home office research for Link Resources.

Another trend points to increased reliance on telecommuters: the use of part-time and contract workers, many of them not covered by benefit plans, as companies shrink their "core" work forces to cut costs.

Most telecommuters, about 5.1 million, were white-collar workers, Mr. Miller said. More men (3.5 million) than women (3.1 million) telecommuted last year.

"Small businesses lead in adoption of telecommuting," Mr. Miller said, "because they're less procedure-bound than bigger organizations." But he added that bigger companies are discovering telecommuting as an outgrowth of streamlining. Among the big businesses that have embraced tele-commuting are Bankers Trust, American Express Travel Related Services, the Travelers Companies, Sears Roebuck and Tele-Communications, Inc.

Source: Robert E. Calem, "Working at Home, for Better or Worse," The New York Times (18 April 1993). Copyright © 1993 by The New York Times Company. Reprinted by permission.

the era of a global economy, the exporting of jobs to countries where wages are lower (think of how many clothing items are manufactured in Southeast Asia).[7]

Unemployment has beome a chronic feature of the lives of some individuals, and is more pronounced in some social groups than in others. Even in boom times, workers who are minimally educated, old, or living in depressed regions (for instance, Atlantic Canada) can be found in the ranks of the chronic (hard-core) unemployed. They are then subjected to the deprivations that accompany this status—poverty, loss of self-esteem, and estrangement. Burman explores the perspectives and problems of the unemployed in his study *Killing Time: Losing Ground* (1988). In a clock-oriented society, when the day and the week lose the punctuation that a job provides, the result can be profound disorientation.

THE SORTING PROCESS: WHO DOES WHAT?

What are the formal and informal criteria that determine who gets to do what? Before the Industrial Revolution, occupational inheritance was the norm. The sons of farmers farmed, those of blacksmiths ended up in the smithy. A daughter who was not entirely occupied with household tasks and child care might help in her father's, then in her husband's, business. Changes in the occupational structure and the broader availability of education have been important factors in changing this pattern.

Modern North American ideology proclaims that work is allocated to individuals on the basis of their competence and achievements. However, as we saw in the chapter on stratification, changes in the level of work performed by different generations of the same family have been less dramatic than the myth of continuous upward mobility would lead us to expect.

To some extent, occupational mobility is inhibited because the sorting process begins long before the work is allocated. Recruits are selected, and select themselves, for the preparation necessary to assume certain occupational roles. Ascription still plays a role in the allocation of tasks and in the definition of the kind of person suitable for performing certain work. Thus, categorization still has important consequences for steering individuals into some types of work while excluding them from others. Once this sorting process is in existence, it operates on many levels. It comes to be perpetuated by socialization, which urges a particular level of expectation, and by vocational preparation consistent with the anticipated status. Individuals thus raised are not likely to challenge the legitimacy of the sorting process, and they are also unlikely to test the strength of the barriers (Lundy & Warme, 1986, 207).

A combination of socialization, socioeconomic class, education, gender, membership in an ethnic or racial group, and personal characteristics influences what kind of work a person will do. (Of course, chance also plays a part.) A girl from a struggling Greek immigrant family may excel at science, but even if financial assistance for university is available to her, it is unlikely that she will pursue the advanced studies that would lead to a high-level scientific career.[8] If she obtains post-secondary education at all, she is apt to choose the shorter training necessary to become a laboratory technician, or she may perhaps become a science teacher. The likelihood of becoming a scientist is much greater for a male who has this level of intellectual endowment and whose father is an executive in a large corporation.

From a logical perspective, membership in a racial group should not be relevant to one's placement in the division of labour. In fact, however, race does exert an influence. Henry and Ginzberg (1985), as noted in Chapter 7, provided empirical evidence to show that nonwhites had disproportionate difficulty in finding work in Toronto.

THE LANGUAGE OF THE WORKPLACE

The language in which work is conducted is a feature of the work setting that is often taken for granted. Yet it brings severe economic and political disadvantages to those who must learn to function in a language other than their own. This is why struggles over language rights have been so persistent in a great many countries, including Belgium, Switzerland, and Canada. For the majority of the Quebec labour force, French has been the native tongue. However, for over a century, those who sought advancement found it necessary to learn English in an economy dominated provincially, nationally, and internationally by anglophones.

In the course of the Quiet Revolution in the 1960s, the Quebec educational system, especially the post-secondary sector, underwent substantial expansion. The new cadres of educated francophones found their career opportunities blocked by the pre-eminence of English in corporate and government bureaucracies (Beattie, 1975; Guindon, 1978). The language of the work milieu became a significant aspect of the more general language issue, which was tied to the preservation of culture.

The official Languages Act of 1969 represented an attempt, at the federal level, to ensure equality for the French and English languages. As the Royal

Commission on Bilingualism and Biculturalism noted about the importance of bilingualism in institutions:

> It is important to understand the difference between individual and institutional bilingualism. A bilingual institution is not necessarily an institution made up of bilingual individuals; it may also be one that contains groups of unilingual persons working in their own language, as well as a number of bilingual individuals. An institution is bilingual not solely because individuals speaking two languages are involved in it, but also because members of both language groups and cultures are able to work and participate in their own language at all levels of the institution (1969, 113–14).

Quebec francophones have insisted, however, that the only solution to their marginalization in the provincial economy lay in making French the sole official language of the province.

THE OCCUPATIONAL HIERARCHY

An occupation's place on the occupational hierarchy is affected by many variables. Generally, lengthy education and training yield high rewards. Sociologists want to know how high, and here they encounter a problem. Material rewards—pay and fringe benefits—are quantified and thus easy to measure. But how are such symbolic rewards as power and prestige factored in?

One way is to determine the relative standing of a number of occupations. One of the earliest and best-known studies was that conducted by the National Opinion Research Centre (NORC) in 1947. A sample of almost 3,000 people from across the United States was asked to rank 90 occupations on a five-point scale, ranging from "excellent" to "poor."[9] The respondents ranked justices of the U.S. Supreme Court first. Professionals such as physicians, architects, and ministers were all placed in the top quarter, while taxi drivers, waiters, and street sweepers were in the lowest. (No predominantly female occupation, such as nursing or secretarial work, was in the list of occupations.)

When the study was replicated in 1972, the rank order of occupations remained substantially unchanged. Interestingly, studies in other countries, including Third World countries, produced similar rankings, especially with regard to professional and white-collar occupations. A notable exception is the relatively low rank accorded to physicians in the Soviet Union. One can speculate that the numerical dominance of women among Russian physicians (referred to previously in this chapter) has lowered the group's prestige.

In 1967, Pineo and Porter published the results of their study on occupational prestige in Canada, the first such national study undertaken in this country. It was also designed so that rigorous U.S./Canadian comparisons could be made. Canadian and American prestige rankings showed no major differences. Professional and executive occupations received the highest scores, and unskilled work was at the bottom.[10]

In 1967, Blishen and McRoberts published a socioeconomic index for occupations in Canada, in which occupations of the male labour force were rated using a combination of three variables: education, income, and prestige ranking. Among five hundred occupational titles, "administrators, medicine, and health" was first, followed by "nuclear engineers" and then "dentists." "Newsboys" ranked 497th, while "locomotive engineers and firemen" and "photographers and cameramen" were in the upper half at 209th and 175th, respectively.

Blishen, in collaboration with Carroll and Moore, revised the index using 1981 data. The revised index takes into account socioeconomic scores, education (job preparation), income levels, and gender composition for census occupations. However, the authors caution that the index is most applicable when access to data is limited to occupational titles and when one is seeking a rather simple way of locating individuals in the Canadian occupational hierarchy at a specific point in time. Used alone, it does little to advance our understanding of structured inequality (1987, 473).

PROFESSIONS AND POWER

Law, medicine, social work, teaching, and nursing are some of the occupations considered to be professions, and the first two represent what can be called "classic" professions. By this we mean that they conform most closely to the ideal type of profession. According to this ideal type, practitioners have specialized expertise, based on extensive formal training, which gives them power to make decisions that affect their clients significantly. Many modern analysts, such as Freidson (1986) have argued that professionals are vital to the knowledge industry, which forms a linchpin of modern societies. Hence, professionals have power within society generally, on the basis of their monopoly over an area of knowledge. The credentials of individual practitioners signify that they have mastered this knowledge and can be admitted to the profession by the "gatekeepers."

Autonomy (literally, "self-regulation") is a jealously guarded privilege of professional groups, though it is realized in varying degrees. The elementary school teacher has less autonomy than the university professor over course content and teaching methods. The physician is more autonomous than the social worker in developing a plan of action for a client.

Professional autonomy is crucially affected by the work setting. The majority of teachers, librarians, and nurses, as well as increasing numbers of engineers, pharmacists, and architects, work in organizations in which they are subject to the bureaucratic authority of superiors who may not be professionals or of the same profession. Although, as we noted earlier, the professional in a solo practice is becoming rare; physicians and lawyers may work in relatively small partnerships in which hierarchical distinctions are downplayed. Alternatively, they may work in "professional" organizations, such as hospitals or large law firms, in which the practitioner is subject to administrative authority in such matters as scheduling operating time, in the case of doctors, but is autonomous in making professional decisions regarding the handling of a case.

Members of most professions are generously rewarded in terms of the "three Ps"—pay, power, and prestige. However, the rewards received by members of professions as a whole vary considerably, and variations also exist within each professional group. Certainly, the Wall Street lawyers studied by Smigel (1964) had far more power and prestige than Carlin's (1962) solo practitioners. More recently, a study of the legal profession in Toronto found that the profession is "stratified by classes that are defined in terms of power relations" (Hagan, Huster, & Parker, 1988, 50).

The professional community seeks to ensure that its members adhere to normative ethical and performance standards. As we mentioned in our discussion of the pattern variables, professionals are expected to put client (collectivity) interest ahead of self-interest. This apparent self-denial, coupled with specialized expertise, legitimates the high rewards most professionals enjoy. As Goode notes:

> The advantages enjoyed by professionals thus rest on evaluations made by the larger society, for the professional community could not grant these advantages to itself. That is, they represent structured relations between the larger society and the professional community (1957, 196).

A CLOSER LOOK AT OCCUPATIONS

E.C. Hughes (1887–1981) and his colleagues and students at the University of Chicago carried out detailed analyses of occupational worlds (for example, those of waitresses, janitors, jazz musicians, and physicians), focusing on what people actually do in carrying out their jobs and how they feel about these activities. Hughes (1958) contended that the limits of an occupation can never be assumed but, rather, must be discovered or "mapped out." To achieve this, the researchers engaged in as much participant observation as was feasible, as Reiter (1991) did in her study of Burger King workers.

Hughes observed that occupations tend to contain both prestigious and demeaning elements, and he observed that members dwell on the prestigious ones. For example, in interviewing apartment janitors, Gold (1964) was able to elicit only with difficulty that they had to sort and separate tenants' garbage for appropriate disposal. Analogously, Lundy (1977) found in her study of executive secretaries that they emphasized activities such as scheduling meetings and preparing background material, rather than tasks such as taking dictation and typing, which were categorized as mundane.

Members of the Chicago School also did a great deal of research on adult socialization—that is, on the ways in which individuals are prepared to assume occupational, especially professional, roles. A well-known study of this type is *Boys in White* (Becker et al., 1961), which traces the transformation of medical students into full-fledged physicians. Through professional socialization, the aspiring practitioners gain confidence in their own competence and convey this to "legitimating audiences"—namely, superiors, colleagues, and patients. Stebbins (1987) provides us with a more recent, and Canadian, example of this kind of analytical orientation, in his study of football players (see this chapter's Suggested Readings).

Perhaps the list of questions in Box 8.3 will be of some use to you when you contemplate pursuing a specific occupation.

BOX 8.3

CHECKLIST FOR THE ANALYSIS OF AN OCCUPATION

- What type of occupation is it? What is the broader category (or categories) to which it belongs (e.g., profession; service occupation)?

- How does the occupation rank in prestige? What kinds of social rewards does it receive? What kind of lifestyle does it tend to be associated with?

- What kinds of skills are required? How are the skills—and the "appropriate" occupational attitudes—acquired (e.g., on-the-job training; trade schools; university education)?

- What are the components of the self-image that emerges during the socialization process? Does that socialization process tend to be short or long?

- How are people recruited to this occupation; in other words, who, theoretically and in fact, has access to the occupation? What is the ratio of women to men? In what proportion are ethnic and racial minorities represented?

- What kinds of groups protect and advance the interests of the occupation? Is there a well-developed sense of occupational community?

- How is the occupation structured? On what basis is prestige allocated within it? What is the division of labour (e.g., specialization) within the occupation? Are men and women distributed differently among the positions within the occupation?

- Is there a typical career line associated with the occupation? What kind of mobility is possible, and what is typical?

- What is the nature of the typical work setting (e.g., large organization, clinic, small firm, solo practice, freelance)? Is more than one setting common (say, private practice office and a hospital)? In what ways does the setting influence the occupation?

- What is the nature of the occupation's relationship to other groups in society (related occupations, government, pressure groups)? Over what issues has conflict occurred, and how has conflict been expressed?

- How have the nature of the occupation and the functions it performs for society changed over time?

OVERVIEW

We have briefly traced the route by which the division of labour in our society has reached its present complexity. The centrality of work to societal functioning and its impact on the individual were recognized by early sociologists. Marx, Weber, and Durkheim focused primarily on the macrosociological level but did not overlook the significance for the individual worker of occupying a specific position in the division of labour.

When unionization and government regulation of employment made workers somewhat less exploitable, employers attempted to find incentives for enhancing productivity and worker morale. The scientific management and human relations schools provided different approaches to this quest. Both schools remain influential today. Under Hughes, the Chicago School pioneered in-depth exploration of individual occupations, a focus that continues to inform research.

Who gets to do what is affected by a combination of many factors. The societal ideology of equal opportunity for those of equal ability is confounded by the ongoing significance of ascriptive characteristics, such as sex, race, and ethnicity. Feminists have been concerned with identifying the complex relationship between women's productive and reproductive roles, a relationship that re-enforces their subordination both in the family and in the world of work.

Changes in the nature of work have been accompanied by changes in the contexts in which work is performed. The number of small enterprises and solo practices has declined. Although the ideal bureaucracy described by Weber does not exist in practice, more and more work is carried out in bureaucratic settings. Such organizations seek to make task performance rational, predictable, efficient, and impersonal. These features have come to be seen as characterizing interaction in modern society generally and in the workplace specifically. However, more traditionally patterned relationships continue to prevail in the world of small business.

The prestige rankings of occupations have remained remarkably stable since social scientists started to measure them over fifty years ago. Furthermore, rankings are similar across industrialized countries generally. These patterns of stability and similarity reflect the extent to which advanced societies depend on expertise.

White-collar occupations continue to enjoy greater prestige than blue-collar ones, even in the face of the former's declining relative earnings. In part, this may be a continuation of traditional values according to which manual work is devalued and assigned to low-status groups.

ASSIGNMENTS

1. Discuss the advantages and disadvantages of part-time work. As resources, you might use the discussion of alternative work patterns in this chapter, as well as one or more of the following books listed in the references at the back of the text: Duffy and Pupo's *Part-Time Paradox: Connecting Gender, Work, and Family* (1989); Reiter's *Making Fast Food: From the Frying Pan into the Fryer* (1991); and Ritzer's *The McDonaldization of Society* (1993).

2. Select an occupation and analyze it in terms of at least six of the questions listed in Box 8.3 in this chapter.

3. Have you ever had a job that was "alienating" in the Marxist sense of the term? If so, describe the job and your reactions to it. Were your reactions typical of those of other workers in the same position? What impact did the job have on other areas of your life?

SUGGESTED READINGS

Horatio Alger, Jr., *Silas Snobden's Office Boy* (New York: Doubleday, 1973; first published in *Argosy*, 1889–90). In the late 1800s, Horatio Alger was a prolific writer whose books were eagerly awaited. Their plots ran along similar lines: after a series of adventures, the poor, honest, hard-working hero emerged triumphant and on the road to riches. Frank Manton, Silas Snobden's office boy, is no exception. Alger's message, which has been incorporated into modern ideology, is clear: virtue and personal effort lead to occupational success. It is the message of industry leaders like Lee Iacocca today.

Pat Armstrong and Hugh Armstrong, *Theorizing Women's Work* (Toronto: Garamond Press, 1990). The Armstrongs examine the wide-ranging contributions that feminists in English Canada have made to the understanding of women's work. The authors raise important questions about the failure to bring about fundamental alterations in the nature of women's work, despite the dramatic increase in their labour force participation and their success in winning favourable legislation on many fronts. The book offers a clear analysis of the difficulties involved in building adequate theories at different levels of abstraction, in developing adequate methodologies, and in establishing links between theory and practice in order to bring about social change.

Patrick Burman, *Killing Time, Losing Ground: Experiences of Unemployment* (Toronto: Wall and Thompson, 1988). In his sensitive analysis of the personal costs of unemployment, Burman explores the many meanings that holding a job has for individuals in a consumption-oriented society. What rewards, in addition to the obvious economic ones, are lost when people lose their job? What happens to their sense of time? What happens to their social relationships? In his introduction to the book, James Rhinehart remarks on the irony that a study of unemployment reveals so much about employment, and tells us why "a job, any job, is better than no job at all."

Ann Duffy and Norene Pupo, *Part-Time Paradox: Connecting Gender, Work and Family* (Toronto: McClelland and Stewart Inc., 1992). The authors bring together the various theoretical perspectives that have been used in the study of work in general, and weigh their relevance for the study of part-time employment and its relation to women's family roles. The book is enriched by their own qualitative research on seventy female part-timers. The voices of the women themselves provide solid bases for the authors' broader investigation at the macrosociological level, and are not merely "added on" to embellish the text.

Lawrence Felt and Peter Sinclair, "'Everybody Does It': Unpaid Work in a Rural Peripheral Region," in *Work, Employment & Society* 6 (1992): 43-64. Work that takes place in what is referred to as the "hidden economy" may involve illegal activities (for example, prostitution and drug trafficking) or legal work that is performed for cash or in exchange for other services, but which does not appear in official statistics. The little research that exists suggests that this type of work is fairly common, both in cities and in rural areas. This is a very interesting article about unpaid work in rural Newfoundland.

Franz Kafka, *The Trial* (London: Penguin Books, [1925] 1953). The dark and irrational side of bureaucracy is brought into stark relief in the nightmarish experience of Kafka's copy clerk, who finds himself accused of an unidentified crime. The rabbit warren of offices and corridors he confronts, and the meaningless maze of rules and procedures he encounters, epitomize the cumbersome social organization at the end of the Austro-Hungarian monarchy. However, the frustrations and anxieties they arouse have a contemporary ring.

Robert A. Stebbins, *Canadian Football: The View From the Helmet* (London, Ont.: Centre for Social and Humanistic Studies, 1987). Basing his study on observation and interviews, Stebbins examines the fascinating inside world of Canadian football, from the actor's perspective, at both the amateur and professional levels. Both kinds of player are undoubtedly engaged in "work," but a career in professional sports is of particular interest because it entails the special problems of an early decline not common in other occupations.

Studs Terkel, *Working* (New York: Avon Books, 1972). Terkel, who speaks almost entirely in the voices of the people he interviews, sought out workers in a vast range of jobs across America. He invited them to describe the way they experience their work, their frustrations, disappointments, and satisfactions, and how the daily job affects the meaning of their lives. The overwhelming impression is one of emptiness, boredom, unfulfilled dreams, and a sense of waste. As one respondent stated, "I think most of us are looking for a calling, not a job. Most of us, like the assembly line worker, have jobs that are too small for our spirit. Jobs are not big enough for people." The book is worth skimming as a richly detailed chronicle of the way in which a variety of people spend the major portion of daily life.

NOTES

1. It should be noted that the dates cited refer to developments in Britain, where the Industrial Revolution had its start. Some parts of Europe, as well as the United States and Canada, reached similar stages of industrialization somewhat later.

2. The idea did not lack precedents; women and children had previously worked in cottage industries.

3. We described the distinction between a *Gesellschaft* and a *Gemeinschaft* in Chapter 3. Primary-group settings are typical of the *Gemeinschaft*, while secondary-group settings are a distinctive feature of the *Gesellschaft*.

4. In contrast, an idealist regards a society's values, beliefs, and attitudes—its ideas—as the substructure.

5. In fact, the period immediately after the war was one of bloody confrontation, of which the 1919 Winnipeg General Strike is an example.

6. As defined by Statistics Canada, the labour force includes the residents of all Canadian provinces (but not the territories) who are age 15 or older; are not members of the armed forces, inmates of an

institution, or residents of an Indian reserve; and are either employed or unemployed. An unemployed person is one who is without work but available for it and who has actively looked for work in the past four weeks, has been on layoff for less than 26 weeks, or has a job due to start within four weeks.

7. National unemployment rates are calculated by dividing the number of persons out of work and seeking work by the total number of labour-force participants (including the unemployed). These rates conceal variations among regions of the country, among occupational groups and industrial sectors, among age groups, and between gender groups (for a fuller discussion, see Gonick, 1978; Krahn and Lowe, 1993).

8. Individuals have, however, done just that, so "unlikely" does not mean "impossible." But, we are discussing statistical probabilities rather than individual biographies.

9. "The final rankings were obtained by a scoring system that gave an occupation that received 100 percent excellent a score of 100, and those that were unanimously rated as poor a score of 20. None achieved unanimity, of course" (Hall, 1975, 246).

10. For example, the mean score for 21 professional titles was 72.04; 15 titles for proprietors, managers, and officials in large organizations showed a mean score of 70.42; 18 titles of unskilled work produced a mean score of 23.46 (Pineo & Porter, 1967, 35). The scoring was much like that of the 1962 NORC study, whose design Pineo and Porter adapted. (The mean score is simply the arithmetic average of a group of scores.)

SECTION

4

FOUR

· · · · · · · · · · · · · · · · · · ·

Social

Institutions

CHAPTER NINE

"The Family" and Families: A Heavy Freight

Here is the house. It is green and white. It has a red door. It is very pretty. Here is the family. Mother, Father, Dick and Jane live in the green-and-white house. They are very happy. See Jane. She has a red dress. She wants to play. Who will play with Jane? See the cat. It goes meow-meow. Come and play. Come play with Jane. The kitten will not play. See Mother. Mother is very nice. Mother, will you play with Jane? Mother laughs. Laugh, Mother, laugh. See Father. He is big and strong. Father, will you play with Jane? Father is smiling. Smile, Father, smile. See the dog. Bowwow goes the dog. Do you want to play with Jane? See the dog run. Run, dog, run. Look, look. Here comes a friend. The friend will play with Jane. They will play a good game. Play, Jane, play.

Here is the house it is green and white it has a red door it is very pretty here is the family mother father dick and jane live in the green-and-white house they are very happy see jane she has a red dress she wants to play who will play with jane see the cat it goes meow-meow come and play come play with jane the kitten will not play see mother mother is very nice mother will you play with jane mother laughs laugh mother laugh see father he is big and strong father will you play with jane father is smiling smile father smile see the dog bowwow goes the dog do you want to play with jane see the dog run run dog run look look here comes a friend the friend will play with jane they will play a good game play jane play

Hereisthehouseitisgreenandwhiteithasareddooritisveryprettyhereisthefamily motherfatherdickandjaneliveinthegreenandwhitehousetheyareveryhappysee janeshehasareddressshewantstoplaywhowillplaywithjaneseethecatitgoes meowmeowcomeandplaycomeplaywithjanethekittenwillnotplayseemother motherisverynicemotherwillyouplaywithjanemotherlaughslaughmotherlaugh seefatherheisbigandstrongfatherwillyouplaywithjanefatherissmilingsmilefather smileseethedogbowwowgoesthedogdoyouwanttoplaywithjaneseethedogrun rundogrunlooklookherecomesafriendthefriendwillplaywithjanetheywillplaya goodgameplayjaneplay

Thus begins Toni Morrison's novel *The Bluest Eye* (1972) about a black child who longs for blue eyes and all the things that blue eyes represent in her imagination: predictability, order, niceness, fun, and a high pitch of cosiness. The excerpt is both a bitter parody of school readers that were found in North

American classrooms until not long ago, and an ideological portrait that has served dominant societal interests, shaped the aspirations of individuals, and expelled from the charmed circle of Mother, Father, Dick, and Jane all those whose own living arrangements have not conformed. Morrison's portrait progressively collapses, until the words of the third paragraph, rushing forward, become indistinguishable and impossible to read without tremendous effort. Speaking sociologically, we could say that much has had to come unravelled in the old ways of thinking about the family before a more realistic and less prescriptive set of patterns could begin to emerge.

In the title of this chapter, we have made a distinction between "the family" and families, for they are very different things. The model of "the family" that has been dominant in sociology until very recently is inappropriate when applied to the reality of how Canadians organize their private and domestic lives today (Eichler, 1988; Mandell & Duffy, 1988; La Novara, 1993). It is even inappropriate, we are beginning to learn, when applied to the reality of family arrangements of the past. It is an ideological construct that asserts how families *should* be, rather than recognizing them as they really are: diverse, rapidly changing, resilient, and full of contradictions, both responding to and influencing the transformations occurring in society at large. To say that the ideology is misleading, however, is not to say that it does not continue to exert a powerful influence on people's expectations, on the political activities of interest groups, and on those corporate and governmental policies that affect the constraints and opportunities faced by various types of families.

Why the term "a heavy freight"? You will see throughout the chapter that it has multiple applications. For most individuals, family life is the repository of our most tenaciously held hopes for nurturance, security, and intimacy—a heavy freight indeed. Despite evidence that these hopes are often thwarted, the vast majority of Canadians marry or remarry, and have children.

Industrialized societies such as Canada's are characterized by a sharp, though necessarily illusory, separation between the private and the public sphere, with family life firmly entrenched in the former. At one and the same time, this separation places heavy burdens on private life and divests the public realm of much of what could be called its "humanity," robbing it of its potential to provide, in Luxton's words, "community-based love and caring" (1988, 255). If we look exclusively to our family to satisfy our most human desires, we are more likely to accept that the world outside the door remain instrumental, amoral, and "heartless" (Lasch, 1977). This very acceptance means that life outside the door also must carry a heavy freight. As Barrett and McIntosh (1982, 78) have put it, "The family sucks the juice out of everything around it, leaving other institutions stunted and distorted." Sennett (1970) has also deplored the "brutality" of the modern family, a brutality that lies in its insularity and exclusivity.

Within families, it is women who work for pay while continuing to be responsible for household work, childrearing, and the care of the elderly, that carry the heaviest freight. As for children, although there is widespread disagreement concerning how their needs are best met, there is also increasing agreement with the view that too many of them are currently receiving short shrift (Hewlett, 1991).

The family as an institution is an arena of virulent public debate. Interest groups that mobilize under the "pro-family" banner see themselves as bearers of the traditional values needed to save society—*their* society—from disintegration, just as they oppose measures to relieve the burdens carried by actual families. Abortion, divorce, homosexual relationships, the labour force participation of women, welfare, feminism, and day care are some of the things that are alleged to be undermining the institution of the family and, hence, to be destroying the very fabric of society.

THE SEARCH FOR A DEFINITION

Is it possible to study family life in our own society when, as Rapp (1992, 50) has noted, we are all "participant observers"? As you saw in Chapter 2, "Sociologists at Work," participant observation has both strengths and weaknesses. Thus, while our own experience as family members may sensitize us to the many nuances of family interaction, this degree of detail might elude us were we attempting to study, for example, how an Inuit cooperative works. Our very participation also arms us with untested assumptions (the things we take for granted) that deprive us of the curiosity and detachment needed to turn these assumptions into questions.

In ordinary speech, we use the term "family" in a variety of ways. If you were to hear any of the following remarks, you would grasp immediately what was intended in each instance:

> I have to be careful what I eat, because obesity runs in my mother's family.
>
> Those "National Geographic" programs on TV are good family entertainment.
>
> The family always has to rent a place for special occasions, because there are so many of us.
>
> Our rabbi keeps saying that the family is in crisis.
>
> We've had a family cottage near Sault Ste. Marie since the 1930s.
>
> Just because my dad's living with someone now, we're supposed to be an instant family. Ha!
>
> My grandmother said that she moved to a home for the aged because she didn't want to be a burden on the family.
>
> We're all family here at Taco Bell.
>
> I heard that Steven Spielberg said his family was too young to see *Jurassic Park*.
>
> In *my* family there aren't going to be any ridiculous curfews!

Can all of these usages be captured in a single definition? And even if they could, would such a definition be of any use? Definitions work in two directions: they are important for what they include and for what they exclude. For example, they determine who is counted and who is not counted in forming statistical pictures; they determine who is eligible for certain state or corporate benefits and who is ineligible; and they also affect who receives social approval and who is stigmatized as "deviant" or "problematic."

Using his analysis of approximately five hundred societies, Robert Murdock attempted to provide a definition of the family that would be universal across time and place. His definition exerted an enormous influence for several decades:

> The family is a social group characterized by common residence, economic cooperation, and reproduction. It includes adults of both sexes, at least two of whom maintain a socially approved sexual relationship, and one or more children, own or adopted, of the sexually cohabiting adults (1949, 1).

If we applied this definition to Canadian society, it would include common-law couples, but would exclude many other contemporary arrangements, some of which will be examined later in the chapter.

A number of definitions of the family exist for specific purposes. In 1991, the Canadian census defined the family as "a now-married couple (with or without never-married sons or daughters of either or both spouses), a couple living common-law (with or without sons or daughters of either or both partners), or a lone parent of any marital status with at least one never-married son or daughter living in the same dwelling." An "economic" family is given a much broader definition: "two or more persons who live in the same dwelling and are related to each other by blood, marriage or adoption." Comparing the two definitions, you can see, for instance, that two or more adult siblings living together would be counted as an economic family, but they would not be included among census families.

Stack (1974, 31), in writing about black families who live in poverty, chose to define family as:

> the smallest, organized, durable network of kin and non-kin who interact daily, providing domestic needs of children and assuring their survival. The family network is diffused over several kin-based households ... An arbitrary imposition of widely accepted definitions of the family, the nuclear family, or the matrilocal family, blocks the way to understanding how people in the Flats describe and order their world.

Going even further, others have proposed that the kinship-based approach to the family should be discarded altogether and replaced with the simple notion of "living together" (Ball, 1974, 35).

DIMENSIONS OF FAMILY LIFE

Eichler (1988, ch. 2), like others, rejects the quest for an all-encompassing definition as something necessary for research. She proposes, instead, that what ought to be conceptualized and investigated are the *dimensions* of family life. The major dimensions that she identifies are procreation, socialization, sexual

EXHIBIT 9.1   *Dimensions of Familial Interaction*

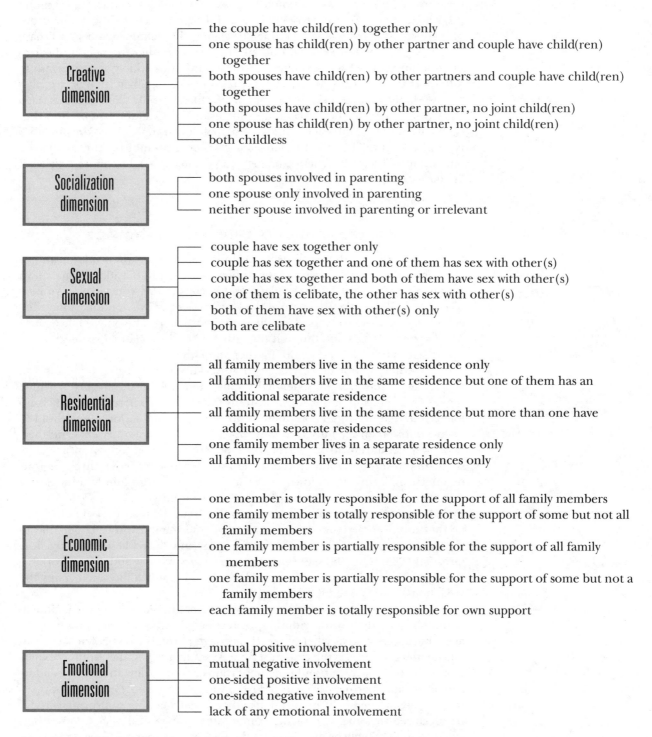

Creative dimension
- the couple have child(ren) together only
- one spouse has child(ren) by other partner and couple have child(ren) together
- both spouses have child(ren) by other partners and couple have child(ren) together
- both spouses have child(ren) by other partner, no joint child(ren)
- one spouse has child(ren) by other partner, no joint child(ren)
- both childless

Socialization dimension
- both spouses involved in parenting
- one spouse only involved in parenting
- neither spouse involved in parenting or irrelevant

Sexual dimension
- couple have sex together only
- couple has sex together and one of them has sex with other(s)
- couple has sex together and both of them have sex with other(s)
- one of them is celibate, the other has sex with other(s)
- both of them have sex with other(s) only
- both are celibate

Residential dimension
- all family members live in the same residence only
- all family members live in the same residence but one of them has an additional separate residence
- all family members live in the same residence but more than one have additional separate residences
- one family member lives in a separate residence only
- all family members live in separate residences only

Economic dimension
- one member is totally responsible for the support of all family members
- one family member is totally responsible for the support of some but not all family members
- one family member is partially responsible for the support of all family members
- one family member is partially responsible for the support of some but not a family members
- each family member is totally responsible for own support

Emotional dimension
- mutual positive involvement
- mutual negative involvement
- one-sided positive involvement
- one-sided negative involvement
- lack of any emotional involvement

Source: Margrit Eichler, Families in Canada Today: Recent Changes and Their Policy Consequences *(Toronto: Gage, 1988), 8–9.*

interaction, residential interaction, economic cooperation, and emotional relations. Within each dimension, there is a range of possibilities (see Exhibit 9.1, which lists the possible types of interactions, presented in descending order of intensity). We cannot assume, Eichler claims, that family members will have an intense degree of interaction on all dimensions; rather, we need to bear in mind a range of behavioural alternatives that may vary widely as a response to different circumstances. When married persons live together (that is, are high on the dimension of residence), and have children only from this marriage (that is, are high in the procreation dimension), we cannot assume that they both have sex only with each other (the sexual dimension) or that one member is totally responsible for the support of family members (the economic dimension). Using this schema, one is in a position to explore more fully what families actually do.

PATTERNS OF KINSHIP AND MARRIAGE

Familiarity with a rather technical vocabulary is helpful when one examines marriage customs and kinship patterns both within, and outside of, one's own society. **Kinship** refers to those relations that constitute a constellation of people related either by common ancestry, by marriage, or by adoption. A **matrilineal society** traces kin relationships through the mother's line only, while a **patrilineal society** traces them through the father. Ours is a **bilateral society**, for we regard as kin the relatives of both mother and father.

Whether or not more than two generations of kin live together (an arrangement known as an **extended family**) depends on the means by which the family obtains its sustenance. In industrial societies, where the family is no longer the unit of production, there is no economic reason for a household to include more than the **nuclear family**, which would consist of parents and their dependent children. In fact, a small family core is an advantage in a society requiring a mobile labour force. It is more feasible to move three or four people from Truro to Kelowna than to relocate a large family unit. Social historians now tell us that, even when households in nineteenth-century Canada contained more people than they do today, the reason was not likely to be that they were extended families. Rather, the numbers were larger due to the transitory presence of boarders, domestics, and "hired hands" (Darroch & Ornstein, 1984; Nett, 1981). Because life expectancy was low and infant mortality was high, it was uncommon for grandparents and grandchildren to occupy the same household at one time.

Marriage patterns vary among societies. A **marriage** is a socially legitimated union, intended to be enduring, of two people who assume certain rights and obligations vis-à-vis each other. If marriage partners must be chosen from outside the group, as is the case in several Australian tribes, the group is **exogamous**. Most ethnic, racial, and religious groups in our society strive to be **endogamous**—that is, partners are selected from within the group. Generally, outmarriage is discouraged because of the likelihood that a couple's offspring will not be socialized into the ways of the community. Roman Catholics try to ensure against this possibility by insisting that the Catholic partner in a mixed marriage undertake to raise the children within the church. Orthodox Jewish rabbis refuse to marry mixed couples unless the gentile formally converts. Families often encourage children of marriageable age to date within their own ethnic group and socioeconomic class. Marriage across racial lines was illegal in South Africa until 1985.

Power relationships are inherent in the family setting. Being located on home territory gives obvious advantages to one partner. In Western societies today, a young couple generally moves into their own apartment or house; in other words, their residence is **neolocal** (literally, "at a new place"). A shortage of housing or funds may force newlyweds to live with parents or other relatives, but most people view this as an undesirable and thus temporary arrangement.

If extended families are typical in a society, residence for newlyweds may be **patrilocal**—that is, the couple lives with the groom's family. This is the traditional practice in rural India. Quite often, the native villages of the bride and groom are relatively far apart, given limited transportation facilities, and ritual forbids the bride's family from visiting her in her in-laws' house. Hence, the new wife is at the mercy of her husband and his family. Awareness of this situation is symbolized by a wedding custom: "they [the groom and his men] ultimately carry off the bride to their own village, she weeps, clutches her brothers and screams that she is dead" (Marriott, 1969, 176). Other societies practice **matrilocal** arrangements, that is, a couple may move in with the bride's kin.

In addition to the variations in kinship patterns just noted, there are differences in the number of spouses to whom an individual can be married at the same time. In Western society, **monogamy**, marriage between one man and one woman, is the rule. The practice of one man having several wives is known as **polygyny**. Polygyny is permitted in many societies today, especially in Arab and African countries, but only a fraction of the population opt for it. By contrast, **polyandry**, the practice of one woman having several husbands, is rare. Anthropologists have discovered only three or four such groups; one of them is the Toada of southern India.

Polygyny and polyandry are the two types of **polygamy**, the practice of being married to more than one person at the same time. It is illegal in Western societies; an individual who is a partner in two or more marriages at the same time is committing bigamy.

THEORETICAL APPROACHES TO STUDYING FAMILIES

Earlier, we noted that the family as an institution is the focus of public controversy. It has also become the subject of academic controversy, with the functionalist approach that has dominated the field for so many years now facing strong challenges.

THE FUNCTIONALIST PERSPECTIVE

In Chapter 1, we saw that functionalism conceives of society as a dynamic system, like an organism or complex machine, that is composed of many interrelated parts. The parts, or subsystems, perform particular functions for the system as a whole. When change occurs, mechanisms come into play that incorporate the change in such a way that the equilibrium of the total system is not destroyed.

In assigning central importance to the family as a social institution (or subsystem), functionalists have contributed in many ways to our understanding of how families operate internally, and how the institution interacts both with other institutions and with society as a whole. However, they have also encouraged the error of bestowing universality, and hence the assumption of "inevitability," on what we know to be only one of many family forms, the one now conjured up by the very term "the family." What began as a model for purposes of analysis turned prescriptive, reflecting a powerful ideology that influenced scholarly and popular thinking alike. As Kingsley Davis observed over forty years ago, "Most social research into the family has had an immediate moral purpose—to eliminate deviations like divorce, desertion, illegitimacy and adultery—rather than a desire to understand the fundamental nature of social institutions" (1948, 393). With some exceptions, only recently has sociological investigation left the moral high ground and begun to document the forms and workings of families in all their rich diversity.

While it cannot be said that functionalists have not been interested in change (see Goode, 1963), their emphasis has been on the changing ways in which the family meets its basic functions. Murdock (1949, 10) claimed that the family universally fulfilled four functions that were vital to the survival of society: the sexual, the economic, the reproductive, and the educational. Without provision for these, he argued, society would become extinct, culture would come to an end, and life itself would cease to exist. In focusing on how these functions are fulfilled, the functionalist perspective has revealed more about continuity than about change.

Margrit Eichler (1988, chs. 1–4) has spelled out at length the constrictions and distortions imposed on the study of the family by the functionalist approach. She identifies four major biases that have permeated the literature: the monolithic bias, the conservative bias, the sexist bias, and the microstructural bias. As we shall see, a monolithic bias emphasizes uniformity and universality in studying the structure and functions of the family. A conservative bias is revealed in the propensity to use analytic frameworks that either ignore or underestimate the significance of recent changes, to turn a blind eye to the ugly side of family life, and to view children as passive family members. The sexist bias obscures the fact that husbands and wives, fathers and mothers, have different experiences of family life. The microstructural bias leads to a concentration on interpersonal relationships, instead of locating families in legal, economic, social, and cultural frameworks. In the micro-structural approach, psychological and social-psychological variables receive attention to the neglect of structural variables such as the economy and government policies. The influence of these four biases will become clearer as we proceed through the chapter. For the time being, we will concentrate on the monolithic bias.

The Nuclear Family as Monolith

A monolith is an immovable, unalterable, unitary structure. It is interesting that the word also carries the connotation of a monument, shrine, or testimonial.

When we say that the functionalist approach has a monolithic bias, we mean, as noted above, that it claims universality for one particular family form and sees this form as, if not "inevitable," then at least as highly desirable. Put somewhat differently, we can say that the model of the nuclear family has come to be a testimonial or tribute to Mother, Father, Dick, and Jane, whom we know to be middle-class, white, and in possession of those blue eyes so coveted by Morrison's

The functionalist model of the family is a tribute to Mother, Father, Dick, and Jane.

G&M, 149560–S/City of Toronto Archives.

black child. In the monolithic approach, the following assumptions are made: a married couple will want to have children together; when there are children, both parents will be involved in the socialization process, though in fundamentally different ways; neither husband nor wife will engage in sexual relations with other people; all members of the family will inhabit one residence; and, the father will be the primary breadwinner.

It is known, of course, that a multitude of different family forms have always existed in other societies, and that new forms are emerging in industrial societies today. However, they tend to be treated as exceptional cases. Ruth Benedict (1934) observed an interesting pattern of authority among the Dobu of New Guinea, where spouses had to be selected from outside of one's own village. The couple was required to spend alternate years in the husband's and the wife's villages, so that "Each alternate year one spouse has the backing of his own group and commands the situation. The alternate year, the same spouse is a tolerated alien who must efface himself from the owners of his spouse's village" (1934, 126). Among the Nayar of India, until this century, a child's biological father was socially irrelevant, and children might not know the identity of their father (Gough, 1952).

The socialization practices of many Hutterite communities do not rely exclusively on the basic family unit to provide early nurturance and training. Children sleep in their parents' residence, but from the age of two they are cared for, taught, and disciplined in groups. The main thrust of their socialization is that the group takes precedence over the individual and that the Hutterite way of life requires unquestioning acceptance. Hoesterel and Huntington have summarized the philosophy that underpins this way of life as follows:

> The community is more important than the individual and governs the activity of the individual, and the corporate group has the power to exclude and to punish, to forgive and to readmit. The German teacher is charged with the formal instruction of the young and he is their primary disciplinarian. The father, as head of the family, supports the discipline of the colony, and the colony can require him to punish his own child in the presence of the group. The older person is required to correct the younger, regardless of his relation to the offender, and self-assertion by the individual against the group is not permitted. The duties of each person are assigned by the community, and tasks may not be chosen or positions aspired to by the individual (1967, 12).

The agricultural communes of Israel, the kibbutzim, provide another well-known example of communal childrearing. Wide variations in practice exist today, and most features of the family are now present in the kibbutzim (Etzioni, 1993; Spiro, 1960). In the classic instance, however, children are cared for in child-care centres and spend only a few hours per day visiting their parents. These parents are not personally responsible either for the material well-being or the socialization of the children.

We do not, however, have to turn to other cultures for examples that contradict the monolithic model of the family. The model emerged within North American society itself, and can be challenged in this context alone. The

BOX 9.1

THE 1950S SAW THE ZENITH OF THE TRADITIONAL FAMILY MODEL

The relief people were at our house one afternoon when I came home from school. They told Dad he had been reported for living in common-law with Sarah, and along with all the other reports they had received over the years they would have to do something this time. Dad didn't speak for a long time. Finally he said, "If Sarah leaves, will you help me with an allowance of some kind, so I can stay home? I don't want Maria quitting school." The man answered, "No, I'm sorry, Mr. Campbell. We can only help widows. You're healthy and you can work. You'll have to marry this woman or we'll just have to take the kids."

Dad and I sat down for the first time in months and talked without getting mad at each other. I told him that he could either marry Sarah or I could quit school—anything so we would not get sent to an orphanage. He told me not to worry, that we'd work something out.

The next day Sarah said she was leaving us, that Dad really didn't want to marry her and that she and the kids were getting too attached to each other. She said she'd stay until school was finished in June so I could finish grade eight. That was the most I had ever heard her say at one time.

June came and Sarah left us. Daddy seemed to be in a daze after that, and although he worked, he was very depressed. I asked him why he wouldn't marry Sarah. He said that he couldn't, that Mom was the only woman he had ever loved. Nothing more was ever said, and again the responsibility for the family was left to me.

Jamie and I had long talks those first few weeks about what we would do. Bob was going to visit a sister in Blue River, so Jamie decided he would go to British Columbia with him and look for work. He could make nearly four hundred dollars a month out there, and we couldn't live on what he and Dad made at home.

Dad said nothing when Jamie told him he was leaving and I doubt if he even heard him.

Jamie was fourteen years old. He got a job as section man on the railroad and, true to his word, he sent money home each month. He didn't make four hundred but it was still a fortune to us. I got a job as a clerk in a store and Dolores looked after the house. Then the relief people came again and said they were going to put us in three separate homes.

Daddy just didn't seem to understand what was happening to us and I was sick with fear. The relief man said I was too young to look after all of us, so I wrote Jamie that night and asked him to come home. He arrived a week later and we tried to make plans. We talked of moving to B.C., but we had no money to go anywhere. There was only one alternative. I would have to get married. Then they wouldn't be able to say I was too young to care for a family. I thought of Smoky, but knew he had nothing, and we had to find someone who wanted to take over a large family and could afford to support all of us.

I found my man a couple of weeks later. He came into the store one evening and spent nearly an hour talking to me. I could tell by his expensive clothes and new car that he could afford to keep us all. He was originally from Saskatchewan but lived in Vancouver. He had just come back to sell the farm left to him by his parents.

Darrel and I became engaged on the first of October. Daddy tried to talk me out of it, saying that if I was going to marry, to marry Smoky because he loved me and was one of my own people. He said that I might never have much, but at least I would be happy. When I refused to change my mind, Dad answered, "I won't give you my permission to get married. You're under age." So I told him the only thing I knew which would make him change his mind. I lied and said, "I'm going to have a baby. You have to let me." That was it. I was married on October 27th, 1955. I had a husband and I could keep my brothers and sisters. I was fifteen years old.

Source: Excerpted from Maria Campbell, Halfbreed *(Halifax: Goodread Biographies, 1973), 118–120.*

nuclear family of husband, wife, and biological children now represents only a minority of family structures in Canada. As noted earlier, definitions are important for what they exclude. This one of the nuclear family dismisses the reality of many other arrangements that the participants themselves think of as families. For example, it excludes the following: lone-parent families; homosexual couples who may or may not have children living with them; **reconstituted families**, where one or both spouses has remarried and where one or both spouses may have biological children living in a different household; and unmarried siblings who live together and pool their resources. The excerpt from Maria Campbell's autobiography (Box 9.1), describing her decision to marry, illustrates the consequences such exclusions can have.

Nevertheless, the nuclear family is the core unit of the functionalist approach. Biological imperatives are seen to provide the basis of such a unit: the sexual drive, the drive to reproduce, and the need to transform the "raw material" of the infant into a functioning social being. While there is great variation among cultures in the length of time it takes to achieve this transformation, in industrial societies the dependency extends through childhood, adolescence, and, sometimes, into young adulthood.

The monolithic model posits a clear division of labour based on sex differences. Women are seen to be the ones "naturally intended" to raise children, because only they are capable of giving birth and of nursing babies. Males, due to their greater strength and "natural aggressiveness," are viewed as biologically predisposed to see to the family's material needs and protection.

Functionalists such as Parsons (1951) have argued that the division of labour between men and women is necessary in modern societies because the family sphere and the world of work have become strictly differentiated and specialized. This differentiation is based on two opposite types of orientation (review the pattern variables on pages 243–244 in Chapter 8). Parsons argued that the family, as the quintessential primary group, is based on ascription as the determinant of membership, on emotional bonds, on diffuse obligations among family members, and on particularistic values that ensure that each member is accepted as unique rather than being judged by impersonal criteria. In other words, at home you can be "yourself." The separation of home and work, says Parsons, has reduced the tasks assigned to families, while intensifying the tasks that remain. The family is thus left with two principal functions: (1) the socialization of children, and (2) the emotional support of family members.

The family itself, as we have noted, is a system that must be maintained in a state of equilibrium. Parsons and Bales (1956) have offered a view of how the sex-specific division of labour ensures the smooth functioning of the family. In his research on small groups, Bales observed that it is typical of such groups to develop two types of leaders: (1) the **instrumental leader**, who sees to it that the necessary tasks are accomplished, and (2) the **expressive leader**, who, through encouragement and nurturance, sees to it that tensions are resolved. Within the family, this division of labour generally means that it is the man who, by working outside the home, provides the material resources needed by the group and makes the decisions regarding their allocation. Since it is he who travels between the home and the external world, he is the family's emissary to society at large; when at home, he represents the world to the family, preparing children to assume their adult roles. The woman, then, takes on the expressive tasks, re-enforcing cultural values and playing peacemaker. Here is the familiar picture of father as breadwinner and authority, and mother as "the angel of the hearth."

MARXIST AND FEMINIST PERSPECTIVES

In his wide-ranging *The Origins of the Family: Private Property and the State*, Engels ([1884] 1986) provided the basis for a materialist explanation of the family. Engels was concerned with specific historical patterns, and identified the origins of the oppression of women in the monogamous, patriarchal family that developed with the emergence of private property. Using historical and (somewhat questionable) anthropological evidence, he sought to establish that the form of the family had varied over time and place as a result of changes in the mode of production. In primitive societies, he speculated, family life was based on group marriage, both men and women enjoyed sexual freedom, and descent was reckoned through the easily demonstrated relation between mother and child. This state of affairs was eroded by two developments. First, a shift from being societies based on hunting and gathering to those relying on the more stationary activities of herding and agriculture occurred, permitting men to gain control over property. The second development was the emergence of an awareness of the male role in conception; this meant that, if women's sexual activities were strictly controlled, men could identify their own children. The conjunction of these two developments led to a form of marriage based on strict monogamy for women, so that a man's property would not be passed on to another man's son. The male partner, on the other hand, retained his sexual freedom. The women he consorted with were marginalized as prostitutes.

Engels recognized that this development entailed dire consequences for women; in fact, he referred to it as "the historical defeat of the female sex." He noted, "The man took command in the home also; the woman was degraded and reduced to servitude; she became the slave of his lust and a mere instrument for the production of children. This degraded position of the woman … has gradually been palliated and glossed over, and sometimes clothed in a milder form; in no sense has it been abolished" ([1884] 1986, 87). Engels saw only two ways that male dominance could cease. Families could become egalitarian if poverty existed to the extent that there was no property for men to pass on. Or, they could become egalitarian if property were held communally and if women participated in productive work. The socialist state would then take over the work usually carried out in the home.

To explain women's subordination, O'Brien (1981) turned Engels's argument on its head. It is the female act of reproduction that led to male initiatives to control private property, she argued, rather than the reverse. Men are alienated from their seed after conception occurs, and thus are driven to engage in a continuing struggle to establish power over women. O'Brien identified only two periods of significant historical change regarding reproductive activities: (1) the discovery of physiological paternity, and (2) the much more recent changes brought about by the development of reproductive technologies. Her critics have pointed out that this is essentially a static and biologistic interpretation that fails to explain how the subordination of women is established and why it increased under capitalism (Armstrong & Armstrong, 1990). Unlike Engels's theory, O'Brien's theory does not permit a solution based on the collective ownership of the means of production and on women's equal employment. Her theory predicts that, even without private property, men will attempt to exercise control over the reproductive powers of women.

While debate over the origins of patriarchy and property accumulation may seem terribly abstract and irrelevant, they have served to stimulate research on the complex relationship between production and reproduction. They have also promoted interest in the socially constructed aspects of human biology.

In two influential papers, Dorothy Smith (1977, 1983) has examined how the changing forms of property ownership that evolved in conjunction with the development of Canadian capitalism served to restructure the relations between husbands and wives. In the pioneer years, property was shared, husband and wife worked together to meet their needs for survival, and no rigid evaluative distinctions were made between productive and domestic work. This is not to say there was no division of labour, but that there was a fundamental "rough-and-ready equality" in spousal contributions and, hence, in spousal relations.

When a cash economy emerged, and money was needed for mortgages and bank loans, there was an erosion of this equality because only men had the legal right to hold property, incur debt, and extend credit. Wives continued to work as they had always done, but this denial of economic power left them fully dependent on their mates.

With the transition to corporate capitalism, the split between the private and the public realm became even more pronounced (see Chapter 8, "Work and Its Contexts"). For families, as we have seen, this generally meant that men went out to work for wages, while women were confined to tasks that were performed in the home and, importantly, were not defined as work. In this arrangement is the division of labour that functionalists defined as universal. Marxists, however, have argued that it is not universal, but specifically tied to a stage in the development of capitalism. Further, Marxist feminists argue that the functions performed by women in the home are not separate from the capitalist enterprise; on the contrary, they are an integral and vital part of it (Smith, 1977). Women meet the physical and psychological needs of men on a daily basis so that the men can perform their labour. Women also produce and raise the next generation of workers. From this perspective, one could say that the corporation "contracts out" this work to women, but does not pay for it (Hale, 1990, 338).

The question then becomes, how does this interplay between home and paid work create and sustain those features of society that come to be described as the "class structure"? When the question is formulated in this way, it is consonant with an approach that views the class structure not as a hierarchy that is "out there" and into which people are slotted, but rather as a changing constellation of processes through which human beings both respond to external constraints and actively participate in shaping their own destinies. Smith's analysis does not ignore differences between working-class and middle-class families. The work of working-class women centres on meeting the needs of the members of their households; middle-class women, on the other hand, are oriented to meeting the values and standards of their social class. Middle-class women, then, also perform unpaid labour that serves capitalist interests. They do this, for example, by taking on the household and childrearing work so that men can devote more time to their careers. They create a family image that conforms to what is required for the "organization man" (Whyte, 1956). They also raise their children with the values that they will need to pursue careers.

Harrison and Laliberté (1991), in their ongoing study of military wives, claim that these women represent an extreme case of the problematic relations between home and work. They confront an extra layer of ideology—the combat ideology—that endows the traditional support of their husbands' work with a "noble purpose." The cultivation of hostility toward women is one of the ways in which the military apparatus encourages the male bonding deemed so essential to the solidarity of combat units. The segregation of military men from wives and children in the early career stages, and segregation from the community (achieved through the practice of moving personnel every few years) also contribute to male solidarity. This has important consequences for the life of the military wife, who operates much of the time as a lone parent and who, in any case, tends to take on sole responsibility for running the household. She is, however, encouraged in every way to define her existence vicariously, that is, in terms of her husband's career. This means that she is expected to relate to other women in accordance with their husbands', and her husband's, rank. The military organization actively works to help wives develop a point of view that defines their lives as glamorous, adventurous, flexible, and exciting. Harrison and Laliberté note, "The military definition of a feminist is a 'strong woman' who cheerfully foregoes the opportunity for a career and cheerfully supports, with scarcely any support system, the unpaid labour of housework, childcare, and setting up households in new locations" (1991, 9).

Feminist scholars have raised useful questions about the nature of family boundaries. As Thorne (1992, 5) contends, " ... there are close and sometimes combustible connections between the internal life of families and the organization of paid work, state-organized welfare and legal systems, schools, day-care centers, and other institutions." By broadening their focus, they have also increased our understanding of the significance of domestic labour.

Domestic Labour

The interaction of constraint and human agency is central to Meg Luxton's groundbreaking study (1980) of the domestic work performed by three generations of working-class women in Flin Flon, Manitoba. Luxton uses the term "domestic labour" in a broad sense, to encompass four distinct, but interrelated work processes:

- looking after the daily needs of those adult family members who work for wages (this may include herself, her husband, and adult children), so that their capacity to labour is "reproduced" or renewed;

- bearing children and looking after them;

- performing the myriad household tasks, such as meal preparation and cleaning; and

- transforming the wages brought to the household into goods and services for household consumption.

To this list we could add the "kin work" that involves maintaining kin contact *across households*, since, as di Leonardo (1992) concludes, this contact also fulfils cultural expectations of a satisfying family life. Based on her research of Italian-American families in northern California, di Leonardo argues that maintaining a sense of family involves time and skill, and is primarily the responsibility of women.

It is commonly thought that, since technology has permitted the production of so many goods for use in locations outside the home, domestic labour has been concomitantly reduced. One of Luxton's respondents disputes this view:

> Sure things are easier today. Modern houses are much easier to keep up. No one's denying that. But the same is true of mining. Mining today with power drills and trains and all that is much easier than mining was in my grandfather's day. But no one ever says that modern mining isn't work anymore. So the people who say housework isn't full time, demanding, hard work are full of it. All that proves is they don't know what housework is really about (1980, 20).

Luxton's meticulous analysis of the complex connections among the components of domestic labour shows it to be arduous, recurrent, and fragmented. One of the strengths of her study is that she does not describe the women as victims. Although their room for manoeuvring is constrained by circumstances over which they have little direct control, they actively structure family life, manipulating circumstances, challenging ideologies, resisting "inevitabilities," and struggling to improve the quality of their lives.

Luxton returned to Flin Flon five years after she had carried out the first study and discovered that some important changes in the division of labour

Middle-aged women are sometimes referred to as the "sandwich generation," since they are likely to take prime responsibility for childrearing and for looking after aging kin.

Baycrest Centre for Geriatric Care.

were beginning to occur (1983). She was able to interview 49 of the original 52 third-generation women, and found that most now had paid jobs. Whether they had wanted to make this change or would have preferred staying at home, they were beginning to change their identification of themselves as primarily house-wives. When asked for their views about who should be responsible for the domestic labour, they gave three types of response, which Luxton categorized as follows: (1) separate spheres and hierarchical relations (the conservative view); (2) separate spheres and cooperative relations (a "different but equal" perspec-tive); and (3) shared spheres and changed relations (a feminist perspective). Family tensions were likely to be high when husbands and wives fell into differ-ent categories.

Luxton's examination of time budgets for these households showed a rather impressive increase in the average amount of time men spent on domestic labour. Women's time spent in this way, however, had decreased very little. In 1981, they were still spending on average the equivalent of at least one-half day per week more than men on domestic labour. Luxton also found that considerable tension was generated by the change in the women's attitudes and the insignificant shift in responsibility from women to men. Her descriptions of the power struggles between husbands and wives over the redistribution of domestic labour are vivid. Some of the women were reluctant to relinquish power within the household, especially if they were not compensated for this loss by gains secured elsewhere, such as in their paid work.

Like Luxton's research, Arlie Hochschild's study (1989) of the division of domestic labour in two-income families combines a microstructural and macrostructural approach, placing close observation of what goes on within families in the wider social, economic, and political context. It is women, she says, who work the "second shift," taking on what she calculates to be tanta-mount to an extra month of work per year. She reports that "These women talked about sleep the way a hungry person talks about food" (1989, 9). While some aspired to be the "superwoman" of the magazine ads, most found the glamorous image preposterous. As one working mother of two said, "Ha! they've got to be *kidding* about her. Look at me, hair a mess, nails jagged, twenty pounds overweight. Mornings, I'm getting my kids dressed, the dog fed, the lunches made, the shopping list done. That lady's got a maid" (1989, 1). Preposterous or not, the image provides a standard by which performances are measured, even by the women themselves.

One of the ways in which the discrepancies between the wives' and the husbands' contributions to domestic labour are handled is through the devel-opment of what Hochschild calls "family myths." What might a family myth look like? Hochschild provides the example of a myth created by a couple, Nancy and Evan Holt, in a marriage that was on the brink of divorce because of Nancy's push for a more egalitarian distribution of responsibilities. Finally choosing marital stability over equality, Nancy resolved the tensions by convinc-ing herself that it was fair for her to do the "upstairs" (living room, dining room, kitchen, two bedrooms, and two bathrooms), while Evan did the "down-stairs" (the garage, which was a place both for storage and for Evan's hobbies). Both husband and wife described this division as a "sharing arrangement." Hochschild notes, "For purposes of accommodating the second shift, then, the

Holts' garage was elevated to the full moral and practical equivalent of the rest of the house" (1989, 43). The family myth, an architectural, and gendered, solution that required much more accommodation from Nancy than from Evan, succeeded in smoothing over tensions, and reduced the threat of family breakdown.

Dividing the work in one way or another does not always eliminate tensions, however, because domestic work is a forum for each person's ideas about gender and marriage, and these ideas tend to carry a heavy emotional freight. When one husband cooks dinner, his wife sees it as a demonstration of love; when another does it, his wife feels guilty because she feels she is not protecting time that he needs for his career. When one husband makes the sauce for the pasta, his wife experiences it as a criticism of her own sauce-making abilities; when another roasts the chicken, he sees it as helping his wife with "her" work (Hochschild, 1989, 188). This kind of tug-of-war should not be viewed, however, as simply a matter of individual psychology. It represents in microcosm the deep contradictions experienced by families in the face of societal change.

Melody Hessing (1993) has taken another tack, beginning with the office rather than with the home. She examines the strategies developed by female employees in order to combine their dual responsibilities of paid employment and domestic work. The subjects of her study include secretaries, administrative assistants and technicians employed by a technical college on the West Coast of Canada. Hessing looks at the intricate and resourceful ways in which these women plan, supervise, accomplish, and assess their double workload, and her analysis helps to extend our understanding of what constitutes work. She finds that, in spite of the structural constraints of inflexible, low-status clerical work and the ceaseless requirements of their households, the women develop notions of autonomy and choice as a means of integrating their two workplaces.

Studies such as those we have just mentioned show that women's lives have changed more quickly than men's, and that the gap is a source of stresses and strains for both sexes. Why should men change when they reap benefits? As Hamilton (1988, 5) notes, "If your mother has always washed your clothes, cooked your meals, and generally cleaned up after you, do you think it likely that one day you would throw up your hands in horror and insist on developing a more equitable division of labour? We should not be surprised that the motivation for examining these practices came not from men, but from women." Luxton (1983) points out that there is very little social and material support from the outside for either men or women who want to establish more egalitarian arrangements. It is in converting these stresses and strains from private troubles to public issues, as we shall see in Chapter 12, "Social Change," that the feminist movement has sought to provide an agenda for change.

RECONSTRUCTING MOTHERHOOD

The division that Western thought has made between nature and culture, and between the biological and social realms, has meant that women have been consigned to the private world of the family on the basis of their unique capacity to give birth. It is far from obvious, however, how the biology of procreation gave rise to the historical institutionalization of motherhood. In the contemporary Western world, an elaborate ideology of motherhood has evolved, and this has served to cement the monolithic model of the family. In the traditional view, as we have seen, it is the mother who possesses not only the more obvious biological traits but also those "soft" expressive qualities needed for the nurturing of children.

Indeed, it is not just that children are seen to need mothers. As Veevers points out, the motherhood mystique also incorporates the belief that women need children. They need them in order to achieve "emotional maturity, psychological stability, and the demonstration of femininity" (1973, 182). Women who elect *not* to have children are, by implication, doomed to a life of immaturity and instability, and can never be truly feminine. Such is the power of this ideology that infertile women are often stigmatized and, internalizing society's judgment, come to perceive themselves as failures (Rehner, 1989). It is possible for women who cannot bear children to turn to adoption. Williams (1990) has found that some women turn to in vitro fertilization (see the section on reproductive technologies in Chapter 12) even after they have already adopted a child, in order to obtain the social rewards of biological motherhood. Society not only defines pregnancy, childbirth, and breastfeeding as proof of femininity, but also assigns a high value to genetic continuity.

The cult of motherhood, however, is full of contradictions. On the one hand, there is the image of the asexual, self-sacrificing saint, who submerges her identity in devotion to the child. On the other hand, we have the image of the all-powerful, insatiable, and destructive mother (see Wylie's *Generation of Vipers*, 1942) from whose control children must be wrested by experts and public institutions if they are to become capable of functioning competently in industrial society.

As we have seen, many women themselves feel contradictory pulls between the life lived within the family and the life lived in the labour force. One of the women interviewed by Luxton remarked about her children, "I love them more than life itself, and I wish they'd go away forever" (1980, 86). Maroney (1985, 49), citing Radl, provides another quotation that expresses the dilemma: "I hate motherhood, but I love my kids." At a time when women increasingly have to work for pay, or choose to work, yet when child care and other family supports are so difficult to come by, one need not resort to psychological explanations to understand this ambivalence.

The feminist critique of motherhood, in its ongoing attempts to sort out the historical, social, biological, and psychological components of maternity, has not developed in a simple and linear way. The "maternal feminists" of the late nineteenth and early twentieth centuries sought to bring about reforms that would improve the conditions of family life and extend maternal nurturance to the wider society, but they did not dispute the view that motherhood was a woman's natural vocation. In the second wave of feminism, which began in the 1960s, that vocation itself came to be challenged as women began to identify the negative, constraining nature of traditional arrangements. It was argued that women should have the option *not* to bear children, should have access to safe contraception and abortion, and should be able to obtain high-quality child care if they worked outside the home.[1] Feminists also began to analyze childbearing and childrearing as forms of work that can be alienating and exploitative.

Some feminists argued that women should be freed from both biological and social motherhood, since they were the sources of their oppression by men. The most extreme antimaternalist position was taken by Firestone (1971), who argued that women should give up childbearing altogether, in favour of reproduction carried out in laboratories. Firestone believed that if reproduction could take place without the direct involvement of women, they would be more free to pursue other activities that would bring them greater equality with men.

As the image of the traditional family began to crumble, feminists began to identify the positive aspects of alternative family forms. Afro-American scholars, challenging the stereotypes of "the mammy, the matriarch, and the welfare mother," began to describe complicated patterns of fluid networks that are sometimes formed among biological mothers ("bloodmothers") and other women ("othermothers") who share their childrearing responsibilities (Collins, 1992). These women-centred networks extend beyond the boundaries of real kin, and include "fictive kin" (Stack, 1974). As bell hooks has noted:

> This form of parenting is revolutionary in this [American] society because it takes place in opposition to the idea that parents, especially mothers, should be the only childrearers ... This kind of responsibility for child care can happen in small community settings where people know and trust one another. It cannot happen in those settings if parents regard children as their "property," their possession (1984, 144).

Maroney (1985) traces the recent emergence of a positive re-evaluation of motherhood among feminists. She claims that the women's movement faces the vexing dilemma of validating the mothering work that women do, while at the same time challenging the ideological—and patriarchal—glorification of the role. As Chodorow and Contratto (1992, 19) have observed, "Feminist writing now recognizes that many women, including feminists, want to have children and experience mothering as a rich and complex endeavour."

RECONSTRUCTING FATHERHOOD

Because the primary role of men, as breadwinners, has been located outside of the family, very little research attention has been given to the subject of fatherhood. Gibbs (1993, 31) quotes an observation made by the sociologist who directs the National Survey of Families and Households at the University of Wisconsin: "There's no interest in fathers at all. It's a non-existent category. It's the ignored half of the family."

Some evidence, however, indicates that this neglect is coming to an end. Articles on the "new father" are beginning to appear in the press and in magazines, and a trickle of studies is making its way into the academic literature. These studies follow on the heels of a much larger literature devoted to the changing roles of women. Until recently, research has been guided by the assumption that it is only women who experience role conflict with respect to work and family. Eichler (1988, 91) cites this focus as an example of the sexist bias in family research, claiming that if sociologists look for, and expect to find, role conflicts among women, it is not surprising that these conflicts are found more than among men. However, if we assume that men and women jointly construct their positions in the family, it is reasonable to expect that men, too, are being caught up in conflicts and contradictions, as the reconstruction of motherhood and fatherhood proceeds (see, for example, Stebbins, 1988).

Work organizations place a high value on the "family man," since he is viewed as a more reliable worker who, with his economic responsibilities, is in greater need of promotions and raises. Yet, organizational policies rarely address the family roles of men. Provisions for paternity leave are not widespread. As we saw in the chapter on work, opportunities for working reduced hours are also rare, unless one is willing to pay high costs in terms of career advancement. Furthermore, even when male workers are in a position of relative autonomy, few work places provide an environment where men are comfortable taking time off to perform family tasks. One executive who took advantage of his company's paternity leave plan reported:

> My boss made me pay a price for it. He was very generous with the time, but he never let me forget it. Every six seconds he reminded me what a great guy he was and that I owed him really, really big. You don't get a lot of points at the office for wanting to have a healthy family life (Gibbs, 1993, 33).

Men who wish to play a greater role as fathers may also face obstacles within their own families. Some talk about their wife's reluctance to relinquish maternal authority, or about her perfectionist standards in insisting on the "one best way" to parent. The father's lack of "insider knowledge" can lead to situations like this: "Dad is putting the baby to bed. He's holding his seven-month old on his shoulders and walking around in circles. Mom comes in and says, 'She likes it better when you just lay her down on her stomach and rub her back'" (Gibbs, 1993, 34). Dad, of course, feels frustrated that Mom is undermining his way of doing things, which he thinks works perfectly well.

The role of father as assistant-mother is one that some men resent. Others choose to distance themselves from the mothering role even as they help out, describing themselves as "babysitting" their own children (Luxton, 1983). As the discussion over egalitarian parenting evolves, there seem to be two themes emerging: (1) fathering as something different-but-equal; and (2) the interchangeability of maternal and paternal contributions. The first, which bears a strong resemblance to the traditional instrumental/expressive perspective, sees fathers as having a unique role to play in disciplining, in encouraging initiative and risk-taking, in teaching practical skills, and so on. The second sees fathers as equally capable of providing emotional nurturance. The men's liberation movement, still in its early stages, has leaned toward the second perspective, protesting both the prevailing stereotypes of masculinity and the confinement of men in the world of work and public activity.

In his study of historical changes in attitudes toward fatherhood, Griswold (1993) describes the difficulties faced by certain ethnic immigrant fathers in adjusting their paternal roles after they come to America. Other studies show that the "masculinity crisis" precipitated by changing gender roles is particularly felt by working-class men who have already experienced the erosion of their breadwinner role (Segal, 1990; Stacey, 1992). It is they who are most likely to cling to their patriarchal role within the family. In his long-term study of a working-class neighbourhood in downtown Toronto, Crysdale (1991) assessed the gains and losses experienced by families in a period of rapid social change. He found that "low status and scarce resources leave little room for manoeuvering. Because most workers do not enjoy intrinsic satisfaction or prestige at work, they place more stock in a positive image of self in marriage and at home" (1991, 131). This need to protect their image renders them immune to the potential pleasures of a reconstructed form of fatherhood.

"EVEN SOCIOLOGISTS FALL IN LOVE": BEYOND THE ROMANTIC LOVE COMPLEX

We have borrowed our heading from Jackson (1993), who says that an exploration of the ways in which the emotions, and love in particular, are culturally constructed and subjectively experienced have escaped serious scrutiny by sociologists. Like the word "family," one uses the word "love" in a host of ways. You might say that you love pizza, love your parrot, love your motorcycle, love your parents, and even—is it too much to hope?—love sociology. But you mean something very different when you say that you have "fallen in love" with someone. Can one talk in sociological terms about something so mysterious, indefinable, and irrational? Eichler (1981, 206) complained that what we have had in male-dominated sociology is a sociology about "rational men" rather than about "sentient persons."

Social scientists have, however, given some attention to what constitutes the basis of marriage partner selection. The notion that it is love that determines and legitimates the choice of a mate is a modern phenomenon. Sociologists speak about the "romantic love complex" because they have found that, in reality, many other factors enter into the choice of a marriage partner. As Berger notes:

> In Western countries, and especially in America, it is assumed that men and women marry because they are in love. There is a broadly based popular mythology about the character of love as a violent, irresistible emotion that strikes where it will, a mystery that is the goal of most young people and often of the not-so-young as well. As soon as one investigates, however, which people actually marry each other, one finds that the lightning-shaft of Cupid seems to be guided rather strongly within very definite channels of class, income, education, racial and religious background (1963, 35).

Jackson argues that, since emotions are not observable phenomena, they can only be studied through the discourses of our culture, that is, through the ways in which people write and talk about them. One way of talking about love is, as Berger described it above, "the lightning-shaft of Cupid" that strikes from out of the blue. Sarsby (1983) has noted that this is a curious basis for lifelong marriage, since it can easily pose a threat to monogamy. Is there likely to be only one bolt from the blue? And doesn't a lifelong commitment need to rely on something different from the bolt that was seen to have initiated the relationship? Yet, love stories in which individuals see themselves as one of the characters abound in our culture, and Jackson claims that they help people to make sense of their own emotions. These love stories are found in novels, plays, movies, poems, operas, and popular songs. Jackson argues, moreover, that we are not merely passive recipients of cultural representations of love, as some would have it, but that we are active creators of our own stories and our own emotions, continuously constructing and reconstructing our own biographies.

Jackson cites Davies's study (1989) of Australian preschool children as evidence that even the very young learn the romantic conventions, and show dismay when these conventions are flouted. Davies found that, when presented with a feminist fairy tale in which the self-reliant princess rejects the prince, neither the boys nor the girls were pleased. Even though the girls admired the resourcefulness and the independent spirit of the princess more than the boys did, they still expressed disappointment that the story lacked a conventional conclusion.

As Berger notes " … the lightning-shaft of Cupid seems to be guided rather strongly within very definite channels of class, income, education, racial and religious background."

Courtesy Japanese Information Centre.

Gender has a role to play here, for it may be that males and females are susceptible to different cultural messages concerning love, and that they take on very different roles with respect to the emotions. Rubin, in her book *Intimate Strangers: Men and Women Together* (1983), makes the case that different societal expectations for men and women inhibit the development of real intimacy. Hochschild (1975) argues that "emotion work" is the most invisible kind of domestic labour. Emotional life is largely regulated by what she calls "feeling rules," which prescribe how people *ought* to feel in situations. It is women, she says, who engage in "emotion work" to try to display the appropriate emotion or to influence the way others feel. The fact that this task is left to women has been attributed, as we saw in the section on fatherhood, to men's greater engagement with the public sphere. A recent spate of literature has defined this difference as a deficit in men, which they have to overcome in order to be fully human (see, for example, Bly, 1990; Tanner, 1990).

Duncombe and Marsden (1993) explore three basic questions in their research on gender differences with respect to the emotions. First, are men and women equally susceptible to the discourses of love and intimacy? Second, do they handle such emotions similarly in the context of intimate relationships? Finally, how do partners in long-term relationships negotiate the transition from the first phase of being "in love" to the stage of a less heady, but more stable, "companionate love"? Their research, still in its early stages, promises an alternative to the deterministic perspective, which views individuals as passive (or exploited) consumers of the ideology of romantic love. As they note, "For although romantic imagery may often disguise exploitation, people experience feelings of love as powerfully 'real' in ways which have very real consequences for their lives" (1993, 237).

Their findings, which reveal that there are substantial gender differences, lead them to speculate that women's demands for reciprocity in the sphere of intimacy may constitute a new frontier in the struggle for gender equality.

Hamilton (1990), in looking at the "politics of intimacy," puzzles over what happened to the optimism of feminists in the late sixties and early seventies about the possibility of shedding the yoke of monogamy within the nuclear family, and of establishing more communal and less restricted identities and relationships. Identifying a decline in the progressive politics of intimate life since that time, despite an evident loosening of sexual mores, she asks:

> Did our trenchant critique of family, of marriage, of monogamy, presuppose the evolution of autonomous individuals who could retain their autonomy as they wove in and out of relationships? ... Did we understand that with love came the ongoing need to negotiate the parameters of autonomy and dependence, and that, for most of us, most of the time, this would be a "painful paradox"? (1990, 87).

That these questions are only beginning to be asked suggests that the achievements of feminists in challenging the monolithic concept of the family and the ideology of romantic love have not yet provided an understanding of people's emotions as authentic and consequential.

TRENDS IN CANADIAN FAMILY LIFE

MARRIAGE, DIVORCE, REMARRIAGE

The 1991 census shows that, at 77 percent, the vast majority of Canadian families consist of married couples (see Exhibits 9.2, 9.3, and 9.4; in Exhibit 9.4, notice some of the more pronounced differences among the provinces with respect to family structures). However, attitudes toward marriage have changed profoundly. The change is reflected in the increasing number of divorces, in the greater number of people who are forming common-law unions, and in the later age at which people are marrying.

EXHIBIT 9.2

Family Structure, Canada, 1991

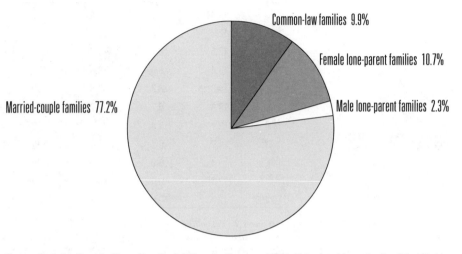

Source: Statistics Canada, Canadian Social Trends *(Summer, 1993). Reproduced by authority of the Minister of Industry 1994.*

EXHIBIT 9.3

Distribution of Families, by Structure, 1981 and 1991

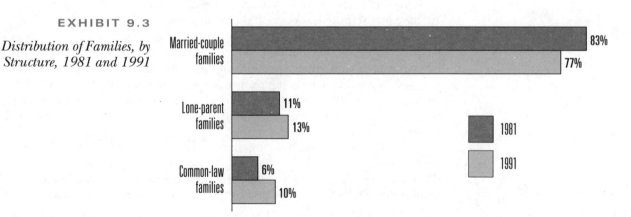

Source: Statistics Canada, Canadian Social Trends *(Summer, 1993). Reproduced by authority of the Minister of Industry 1994.*

Both males and females are choosing to marry at a later age. In 1971, the average age at first marriage was 22.1 for women, while in 1990 it was 26. The portion of women who married before the age of 25 having first lived common-law rose from 25 percent for those born between 1936 and 1945 to 70 percent for those born during the 1960s. For men, the average age at first marriage was 24.9 in 1971, and 27.9 in 1990 (Statistics Canada, 1992). At the end of the last century, the average age at marriage in Canada was also relatively high, and a large part of the population did not marry at all. For those, however, who reached the age of

EXHIBIT 9.4

*Family Structure, by
Province, 1991*

	Families					Average family size	Families without children at home
	Lone-parent %	Common-law %	Married-couple %	Total[1]	Number		%
Nfld.	11.9	6.6	81.4	100	150,715	3.3	25.1
P.E.I.	12.9	5.9	81.1	100	33,895	3.2	30.3
N.S.	13.5	8.2	78.2	100	244,615	3.1	33.8
N.B.	13.4	8.0	78.6	100	198,010	3.1	31.9
Que.	14.3	16.3	69.4	100	1,883,230	3.0	34.1
Ont.	12.6	6.7	80.7	100	2,726,740	3.1	35.0
Man.	13.1	7.4	79.4	100	285,935	3.1	35.8
Sask.	11.7	6.9	81.4	100	257,555	3.2	36.7
Alta.	12.4	8.9	78.6	100	667,985	3.1	34.4
B.C.	12.1	9.6	78.3	100	887,660	3.0	40.3
Canada[1]	12.9	9.8	77.2	100	7,356,170	3.1	35.1

[1] *Includes the Yukon and Northwest Territories.*
Source: Statistics Canada, Canadian Social Trends *(Summer, 1993). Reproduced by authority of the Ministry of Industry 1994.*

20 at the end of the Second World War, marriage was early and almost universal. We have now returned to a period of late and nonuniversal marriages.

Today, many marriages do not last long enough for couples to raise families. Those unions that do produce children are producing fewer of them, leaving women with greater portions of their lives to spend after their children have left home. Since people now live longer, and since the life expectancy of women considerably exceeds that of men, women now spend a greater portion of their lives neither within the family into which they were born nor in the family they created through marrying.

All of these changes have important implications for Canadian society and for Canadian social policy. The complexion of family life today is drastically different from that which characterized the zenith of the traditional nuclear family in the 1950s, and which coincided with the postwar baby boom.

DIVORCE

Divorce is the legal procedure by which a marriage is terminated. Most demographers estimate that newly married couples face a 40-percent risk of divorce. This prognosis reflects a tremendous societal change in the past twenty-five years. It tells us very little about changes in marital happiness, but a great deal about a transformation in the attitude toward the concept of marriage as a lifelong commitment, "for better or for worse."

Before the 1960s, there were few divorces, and the legal procedures for divorce were costly and difficult. Adultery constituted the sole ground for divorce, except in Nova Scotia where cruelty was also taken into consideration. Accessibility to the courts was not uniform; Ontario did not have the authority to establish its own divorce court until 1930. Prince Edward Island acquired the right in 1945,

EXHIBIT 9.5

Divorces per 100,000 Population

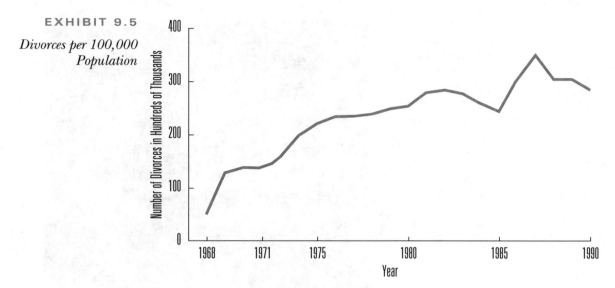

Source: Statistics Canada, Cat. Nos. 82-0035S and 84-205. Reproduced by authority of the Minister of Industry 1994.

and Quebec and Newfoundland followed, though not until 1968. Before the right was acquired, citizens of these provinces were obliged to apply to the federal government in Ottawa, which was a strong economic deterrent for many.

In Canada, two major reforms occurred to remove many of the obstacles to divorce. The Divorce Act, 1968, provided new legal grounds for marriage breakdown. To adultery were added the grounds of physical and mental cruelty, desertion, and separation for not less than three years. As Exhibit 9.5 shows, there was a sharp rise in divorce following the enactment of this legislation. A further easing of restrictions came with the Divorce Act of 1985. Note from Exhibit 9.5 that this legislation gave rise to another major increase. Divorce may now be granted for one of three reasons: (1) mental or physical cruelty; (2) adultery; (3) and twelve months of separation. The last of these represents abandonment of the notion of fault and replacement of it with the simple ground of marriage breakdown. That the "faults" of cruelty and adultery continued to be valid represented a compromise between those who maintained that reform would undermine the sanctity of the traditional family and those who favoured the elimination of the obstacles that make divorce an adversarial process.

The 1985 legislation also addressed the matter of custody of children. It permitted joint custody, but stressed that arrangements for custody and access should provide children, when it was considered to be in their best interests, maximum access to both parents. In the majority of American states, joint custody is now mandatory. Proposals to institute it in some of the other states are being hotly debated. Critics argue that it does nothing to ensure the full involvement of both parents in the nurturing of their children, imposes greater economic risks on mothers, and permits fathers to exercise greater control over both the children and their mothers, even when they choose not to be involved in the nurturing of the children on an ongoing basis. In some Canadian cities, a United Family Court has been set up to unify all jurisdictions dealing with divorce and to assess the best arrangements for the children.

Joint-custody arrangements permit parents maximum access to their children, but do not guarantee that fathers will be involved in the nurturing of their children.

Courtesy Parents Without Partners.

The Canadian legislation of 1985 abandoned the idea that, just by having been married, a woman is entitled to economic support from her ex-spouse. Any support that is granted is regarded as short-term, enabling the woman to become economically self-sufficient as soon as possible (for example, by pursuing some sort of occupational training).

Is this self-sufficiency usually achieved? Hochschild (1989, 250) argues that most women, on leaving a marriage, face "an apparently 'autonomous' and 'free' form of inequality. There is a great deal of evidence that, following divorce, most women experience a drastic reduction in their standard of living, while men experience a moderate-to-considerable improvement in theirs. Using longitudinal data to examine the economic well-being of men, women, and children before, during, and after marital breakdown, Finnie (1993) found that, even three years after divorce, a woman's income remains markedly below its pre-divorce level, as well as below the current level of the ex-husband's income. He argues that, since men have, on average, a positive economic incentive to divorce while women have an economic disincentive, the threshold level of discontent necessary to trigger divorce is lower for men than women. Men thus tend to have more bargaining power within marriages, while women may be obliged to make more concessions. In other words, the very prospect of divorce, considering its economic consequences, can exert a powerful influence on what goes on within marriages (1993, 229).

What about the children? About half of all Canadian divorces involve dependent children. Certainly, insofar as they participate in the economic fate of their mothers, as most do, they face a reduction in their standard of living. The literature addressing the psychological effects of divorce on children does not permit a conclusive picture (Richardson, 1988), although some findings present a rather bleak picture (Wallerstein & Blakeslee, 1989). Children are confronted with a more complicated set of familial relationships after divorce, especially in the event of the remarriage of one or both parents. New marriage partners may bring children from a previous marriage into the household, and then the couple may have one or more children of their own. Research on families created by remarriage is meagre, and, as Eichler (1988, 265) points out, we have scarcely begun even to develop a vocabulary to describe all the various relationships that may come into existence through remarriage.

LONE-PARENT FAMILIES

Lone parenthood is not a new phenomenon in Canada. As Exhibit 9.6 shows, over 12 percent of all families in 1941 were headed by a lone parent, and in 1991 the proportion, at 13 percent, was scarcely higher. However, the exhibit also reveals a decline until the mid-1960s, followed by a considerable rise to its present level. We must look to the reasons for lone parenthood to explain this

EXHIBIT 9.6

Lone-Parent Families as a Percentage of all Families, 1941–1991

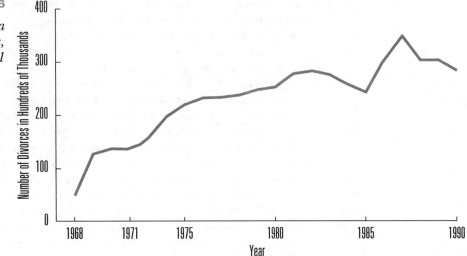

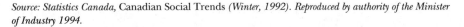

Source: Statistics Canada, Canadian Social Trends *(Winter, 1992). Reproduced by authority of the Minister of Industry 1994.*

pattern. In earlier years, the death of a spouse was the most common reason. In addition, life expectancies for parents were lower, and the risks associated with childbirth were greater. The death of fathers in the Second World War also contributed to the 1941 level.

Today, lone parenthood is most likely to occur because of divorce or separation, with mothers usually living with the children. A relatively large portion of today's lone mothers, especially those in the younger age ranges, have never been married. In 1991, 19 percent of lone-parent families were headed by females who had never been married, compared with 11 percent in 1981 (Statistics Canada, 1992). Williams (1990, 551) reports that almost 90 percent of unwed mothers in Ontario now keep their babies.

The vast majority of lone-parent families, 82 percent in 1991, are headed by females. This phenomenon has contributed to the feminization of poverty and to the high incidence of poverty among Canadian children. During the 1980s, over half of lone mothers were living below the poverty line, and most of these women received government transfer payments as their principal source of income (Odekirk & Lochhead, 1992, 18). When compared to their male counterparts, female lone parents tend to be younger, have less formal education, and are raising younger children. Most also have less formal education and are younger than wives in two-parent families. They are not, however, a homogeneous group. While over one-third of them in 1991 had not completed high school, almost one-third had graduated from community college or university. It is this latter group, of course, that has the best job prospects. Nevertheless, their labour force participation is considerably lower than it is for wives in two-parent families (Devereaux & Lindsay, 1993).

COHABITATION

Cohabitation is an arrangement in which two people live together without making the explicit legal commitment that marriage involves. This does not mean that the relationship does not have some aspects that are legally binding. A common-law partnership of more than three years' duration entails support obligations in the event that the arrangement is dissolved, although there is wide variation in the rights to support from province to province. Separation does not, however, require the sharing of community property.

The reported number of common-law families has risen sharply in recent years. The 1991 census data show that common-law families now represent 10 percent of all families (see Exhibit 9.4 for sharp interprovincial differences), an increase of 4 percent since 1981 (La Novara, 1993). The prevalence of common-law unions is highest, by far, in Quebec, and lowest in Prince Edward Island. More than half of common-law spouses are between 20 and 34 years of age, and the majority of these have never been married. However, in older age groups, divorced persons and, to a lesser extent, widowed persons, are also increasingly choosing to cohabit instead of marrying again or living alone.

Cohabitation cannot be viewed simply as a rejection of marriage. Some research done in the 1980s shows that over 40 percent of all couples who ultimately married had lived together first (Bumpass & Sweet, 1988; Burch, 1985). The likelihood of marriage increases considerably when a common-law couple has a child.

The gay liberation movement is encouraging challenges to official definitions of the family in Canadian society.

Jake Peters.

SAME-SEX FAMILIES

As you saw in the chapter on minorities, the gay liberation movement is posing increasing challenges to the legal, social, and economic barriers that homosexuals experience in a heterosexual society. It is not surprising that some of the most fiercely contested issues have to do with interpretations of the term "family," and that the debates have generated a great deal of moral heat.

In her article "We Are Family," Karen Andrews (1989) describes her attempt to obtain spousal benefits for her lesbian partner when the latter decided to leave her job and return to school on a full-time basis. Andrews was encouraged by the fact that her employer, the Toronto Public Library, was already providing benefits for persons in other types of non-traditional relationships. She says, "There was, however, a lot to consider. Would I suffer at work by admitting to my lesbian family? Would we find our lives spread across the pages of *The Toronto Star*? Would we get a brick through our window? Would Mary's daughters object? Would custody be contested?" (1989, 18). Despite these apprehensions, she embarked on what proved to be a lengthy, costly, and complicated battle.

Andrews v. Ontario (Ministry of Health) was one of the earliest cases in Ontario to address the question of whether the term "spouse" includes same-sex couples. The court ruled that "spouse," undefined in legislation, always refers to a person of the opposite sex. This was an important ruling, since it has been calculated that, in Ontario alone, the word is used in over seventy legal statutes (Robertson, 1992).

The federal Old Age Security Act has provisions for spousal pension benefits in instances where one of the spouses is over 65, the other is between 60 and 64, and the income of the couple is less than a specified amount. Heterosexual

BOX 9.2

CHALLENGING OLD DEFINITIONS

According to F.H. Kim Krenz, same-sex unions can't be compared to marriage between a man and a woman because the latter bond is "the closest approach to divinity of which human beings are capable" (letter —Jan 19).

The power to create another human being puts such a relationship on a higher plane. This is a new one to me: I've often heard the argument that heterosexuality is natural but never that it's quasi-divine! What of married couples who cannot or do not wish to procreate? Are they less close to the divine? One can imagine a sort of medieval hierarchy of angels with married procreating heterosexuals at the summit, nearest to the divine radiance, followed by unmarried procreating heterosexuals, closeted procreating homosexuals, married but nonprocreating heterosexuals, unmarried childless heterosexuals and finally, in deepest darkness and furthest from the divine presence, us poor same-sex types.

The rationales for special status which some heterosexuals manage to concoct for themselves are sometimes quite amusing. But why do they need to feel superior in the first place?

Brian Mossop, Toronto

Source: Globe and Mail *(27 January 1993).*

As a married heterosexual, Don Ewing doesn't believe his state is "in any way affected by the new connotation" of marriage (letter—Jan. 6). With identical credentials, but perhaps more information about what many in the homosexual community mean by the term "marriage," I beg to differ. In the Mossop case, at present being deliberated by the Supreme Court of Canada, Brian Mossop and his lover, Ken Popert, are seeking family status, although Mr. Popert has said: "I am in a web of relationships, but there is no centre and no boundaries. It's not structured and institutionalized, the way the family is. Each person can feel at the centre of it—because in fact it has no centre" (How Gay Society Is Blazing A Trail For The Future — June 27, 1992). In its intervention on Mr. Mossop's behalf Equality for Gays and Lesbians Everywhere (EGALE) argued that a family is whatever the participants choose to

define as family even if there is no co-habitation. It doesn't take much imagination to see what legal, economic and emotional chaos such state-sanctioned models will loose on society.

The bureaucracies alone, which will be needed to administer the public and private-sector benefits to the multitude of individuals involved in these ever-changing, more-for-less partnerships will cost us all millions each year. Those who are committed to the sacrifice of sustaining the traditional model of family life will pay heavily for the short-term choices of their neighbours. Tragically, those who will pay the greatest cost are the children caught in the mutating "circles of love" in which they are involved.

The state has recognized the valuable contributions of children and the stability which the biological family provides by according it certain benefits. When such benefits are given to all and sundry, regardless of their willingness to live in committed, long-term relationships with obligations to future generations, the duties and sacrifices of marriage and family are devalued to the detriment of all.

Judy Anderson, National President
Real Women, Toronto

Source: Globe and Mail *(27 January 1993).*

I am persuaded by Brian Mossop's letter (Jan. 27) that same-sex marriages have the same claim to legitimacy as heterosexual unions. Traditional marriage is attractive to same-sex partners for a variety of reasons, not the least of which are financial and legal. Love and affection, and the respect bestowed upon individuals within the marriage bond by society plays a role. But we can leave that aside for the moment because their effects are more emotional than practical. If people of the same or opposite sex could choose to live together and be married whether they are sexually involved with each other or merely sharing the same digs, there would be a potentially enormous enlargement of the number of families requiring financial and legal adjustment. Matters of inheritance, property ownership, sickness and family leave, insurance, pensions, medical and dental benefits, tax status and special treatment of many other kinds would, in suddenly accruing to millions more of us, require expensive change. Almost everyone would choose to benefit from the preferences granted traditional families. It is this matter rather than all moralistic and supposedly "religious" argumentation that underlies the present public rejection of homosexual marriage. A simple solution would be to remove all marriage benefits from everyone, including tax preferences. Then every person may live with any other person as he or she chooses, with a marriage certificate or without. Married and

unmarried would enjoy equality. It will then prove interesting to see how many persons sharing accommodation will choose to solemnize their relationships before clerical persons or judges when the financial benefits of doing so differ by not a single iota from those enjoyed by people in "common law" or "no-law" relationships. Not to say that marriage won't continue to be popular. Almost everyone enjoys a good cry at a wedding. Some of us might even wish to shed a tear for lost financial advantage.

Norman Klenman, Ganges, B.C.

Source: Globe and Mail *(3 February 1993).*

couples who have lived together for a year or more are entitled to these benefits. When a gay couple who had lived together more than forty years was denied access to the benefits, they launched a challenge under the Canadian Charter of Rights and Freedoms, alleging discrimination on the basis of sexual orientation. The Federal Court heard the case in 1991, and ruled against their claim.

The letters to the editor in Box 9.2 were occasioned by the case of a federal civil servant, Brian Mossop, who was denied bereavement leave to attend the funeral of the father of his homosexual partner, a case that went before the Supreme Court of Canada. There is no doubt that such challenges to laws and administrative rules are only just beginning, and that the complicated issues surrounding the status of same-sex families will increasingly come to be aired. For an interesting discussion of these issues, see Weston's paper "The Politics of Gay Families" (1992).

THE NOT-SO-EMPTY NEST

Shawn Baldwin, 28, single and recently laid off from his job as a carpenter, didn't spend a lot time poring over the classifieds looking for a cheaper place to live. He didn't agonize over how to come up with first and last month's rent. He simply took out an old key, still attached to his Mickey Mouse key chain, and stuck this note on the refrigerator: SURPRISE — I'M MOVING BACK. WHAT'S FOR DINNER?

The refrigerator belongs to his parents, Al and Judy of Etobicoke, who concede they were taken aback at first. "Kids grow up and then they leave ... Isn't that what happens?" asks Judy, remembering Shawn packing for his first apartment at age 24, a stereo under one arm, his worn teddy bear under the other. He had a good job and a girlfriend, prospects, she thought, of an imminent marriage, buying a home and settling down with a couple of kids of his own (*Toronto Star*, 1991).

Although Shawn, in moving back home, is not typical of the majority of young adults, he may represent a short-term trend that some social scientists claim is worth keeping an eye on (Boyd & Pryor, 1990; Schnaiberg & Goldenberg,

1989). He is what has been called a "returning young adult." Along with young adults who simply remain at home, for whatever reasons, instead of moving out in the first place, returning young adults belong to a group that Schnaiberg and Goldenberg (1989) call "incompletely-launched young adults." In Canada, in 1971, about one-quarter of unmarried women and one-third of unmarried men between the ages of 20 and 29 lived at home. By 1986, the figures had risen to 40 percent of unmarried women and 50 percent of men in this age group. Percentages in the United States are somewhat higher.

Schnaiberg and Goldenberg argue that young people who do not make a smooth transition to young adulthood, by becoming economically independent, living away from home, and launching careers, violate the norms of socially appropriate behaviour that emerged in the expansive period following the Second World War. This era saw a growth in opportunities for bureaucratic–professional employment, as well the emergence of an ideology of intensive parenting (as promulgated by experts like Benjamin Spock). The goal of intensive parenting was to prepare children, emotionally and socially, for independence in a young adulthood that would see them establishing nuclear families of their own. If this goal was achieved, parents could feel that their heavy financial and emotional investment in their children had been worthwhile, and that their "success" as parents had been validated. Further, the proper launching of their children would leave them free to pursue their own fulfilment rather than wringing their hands over the "empty nest."[2]

In recent years, however, these expectations have been thwarted, as opportunities for education and careers have contracted in a harsh economic climate. The return of young adults to the home can create tough problems of adjustment for all parties. Tensions are particularly likely to arise over the allocation of family resources and the establishment of a division of labour.

FAMILY VIOLENCE

Despite the traditional view that the home is a place in which people can look for nurturance, security, and intimacy, it can be an extremely dangerous place for some family members. In this section, we examine two forms of violence in the family: wife abuse and child abuse.

WIFE ABUSE

Domestic violence, spousal abuse, wife abuse, wife-beating, and wife assault are terms that may seem simple at first, but they are labels used either to obscure or illuminate the social problem of violence in marriages. The designations "domestic violence" and "spousal abuse" cloak the gender stratification problem; the last three appellations make gender evident but hide the range and types of abuse. Of all of these terms, "wife assault" is most apt since "the victim is almost always the woman; she is usually living in a marital or marital-type relationship with her assailant; and the violence against her, i.e., the assault, can take many forms (battering, intimidation, sexual abuse, confinement) and constitutes an assault to her entire person, not only to her physical body" (Frankel-Howard, 1989, 57). Men do suffer abuse from their partners, but not to the same extent as women and, in most instances, with less-severe consequences when it comes to physical violence. A 150-pound female, five feet five inches tall, hitting a male does not have the same impact as the reverse. When women do commit violence against men, it is usually provoked, a defensive response on the part of the women (DeKeseredy & Hinch, 1991, 11).

Even the label of wife assault, however, shifts attention to the woman rather than the perpetrator. As in rape cases, answers are sought in the behaviour of the targets, not the attackers (Pahl cited in Frankel-Howard, 1989, 69).

Reliable statistics on wife assault are difficult to obtain. Many women internalize the commonplace view that they deserve to be abused and that they are at fault for provoking their partner's actions, and so they do not report the abuse. Other women consider the abuse a private problem and do not see police or outside intervention as helpful. Some women want to protect the batterer. Women may not perceive the violence as battering or they may think that violence is a normal, though abhorrent, part of an intimate relationship. Batterers often excuse or justify their assaults, so the data cannot be counted on to provide reliable information (Dutton, 1988). What the data do show is that in 1980, one in ten Canadian women married or with a live-in lover was battered; in 1985 the proportion rose to one in eight, or at least one million women (MacLeod cited in DeKeseredy & Hinch, 1991, 14).

Statistics indicate that wife assault cannot be seen only from a psychological or social-psychological perspective that concentrates on the individual personality characteristics of one or both parties involved. Attributing the violence to personal pathology allows us to avoid perplexing questions like why batterers typically do not hurt people other than their wives (and often their children) and why they do not do them greater harm than they do. Contrary to the psychological theory that these are sick men out of control, the men rarely accidentally kill their wives. Their physical violence, in fact, seems calculated not to be lethal. Sociological theories that locate the problem in the social stratification patterns and gender power relationships are more effective in explaining the patterned variety of this abuse. (For a detailed account on the many sociological theories, see Frankel-Howard [1989].) One plausible hypothesis is that these men, lacking control in the public sphere, take control in their private households by demeaning and attacking their partners. They may batter because they have the power to do so. They may claim the privilege of the head of the household, with their homes as their castles and their partners as belongings. The violence, possibly learned in their family of origin, proves effective and solidifies their hold over their private realm.

Who are the attackers? Initial research showed that men from any social strata or occupation could be the batterers. While it remains that abusers do come from all occupational groups, more recent studies (DeKeseredy & Hinch, 1991, 28) have pinpointed consistent risk-markers: youth, low income, divorce or separation, providing substantiation for the hypothesis that power is at the core of the problem. The Canadian Urban Victimization Survey supports this finding. Women in low-income households experienced the highest rate of assault (*Canadian Social Trends*, Spring, 1988). The following less-reliable risk markers of abusers are also correlated with power: low educational attainment, low occupational status, and unemployment (DeKeseredy & Hinch, 1991).

Studies show that women are battered an average of 35 times before they seek help. Why do they stay? According to Lips (1991), women find it too difficult to leave their homes and partners because of a combination of the effects of the abuse on their self-confidence and their perceived absence of other alternatives. Cultural notions of intimate relationships also play their part. Women are socialized to believe that the emotional aspects of marriage, or relationships, are their responsibility. Divorce may be seen as wrong or a failure on their part if they believe it is the lot of the woman to change her name and stick with her man no matter what. Women often have fewer resources, financially, occupationally, and socially, that allow them to leave, and they are reluctant to have the drop in their standard of living adversely affect their children. Women are also at the greatest risk of being killed when they leave.

The interpersonal dynamics in abusive relationships is another factor that encourages women to stay. A predictable cycle of violence features a tension-building phase and a violent crescendo followed by a "honeymoon" period. During this honeymoon stage, the man is loving, contrite, apologetic, remorseful, solicitous—in short, the husband his wife wants him to be. This glimpse of what is possible offers hope to the woman of long-term improvement.

Many people assume that only certain women are prone to becoming involved in abusive relationships. Research has not supplied corroborating evidence. As of now, no characteristics of the victim have been found to be totally reliable indicators or predictors of violence in relationships. As Hotaling and Sugarman (1986, 120) note, searching for clues in women's behaviour, attitudes, personality, or demographics is "futile." They add that "what is surprising is the enormous effort to explain male behaviour by examining characteristics of women."

We think it is important that these women, the targets of abuse, not be seen or labelled as victims but as survivors. The courage they demonstrate in living lives that appear normal to the outside observer is a testament to their strength and their ability to cope under devastating circumstances.

THE ABUSE OF CHILDREN

The abuse of children has received growing public and scholarly attention over the past twenty-five years. We have no way of knowing that the incidence of such abuse has increased; the most that can be said is that there is now much greater awareness of it as a social problem, and that more cases are being reported. Despite a recent spate of statistical and clinical studies and a buzz of media attention, silence remains a continuing problem in dealing with child abuse in a culture that clings to the notion that the home is a private sphere. The reticence to interfere with what goes on in other people's homes is in direct conflict with the principle that the protection of those who cannot protect themselves is a collective responsibility.

The public protection of children became a matter of law in a sensational case in the state of New York, in 1871, when a child named Mary Ellen was discovered badly beaten, undernourished, and chained to her bed. The discovery was reported to the Society for the Prevention of Cruelty to Animals, since there was no law governing the safety of children. Shortly after, the Society for the Prevention of Cruelty to Children was founded in New York City, followed by the establishment of child protection agencies in Britain and

Canada. Today, Children's Aid Societies are charged with carrying out this protective function, and there have been many attempts to strengthen clauses in provincial acts that pertain to the mandatory reporting of abuse.

Studies show that abusive parents come from a cross-section of society, from all socioeconomic levels, religious affiliations, and racial and ethnic groups. It may occur disproportionately more often in homes where parents have the fewest "buffers" such as steady employment, adequate income, personal gratifications, access to periodic relief from child-care duties, and a history of not having received decent parenting themselves (Warme & Thomas, 1978). It should be noted, however, that those parents who have the most "buffers" also have more "screens," that is, more effective ways of shielding abusive practices from public scrutiny.

In the search for an explanation of child abuse, a wide variety of theories have been developed (for a brief overview of these theories, see Drakich & Guberman [1988]). Physical violence and sexual abuse constitute one end of a spectrum that includes such behaviour as physical neglect, psychological abuse, and emotional deprivation. When these forms of abuse are included in our frame of reference, it is clear that the problem of even identifying the maltreatment of children is a monumental one.

Certainly, there is no society-wide consensus on what constitute acceptable parameters in disciplining children. Is a severe spanking acceptable? What about a shaking? Or a slap? A strapping, perhaps at school? How about the arm pulling you can see in any shopping mall? Or, is physical punishment unacceptable in any form? Lenton (1990) argues that violence against children can be viewed as an extension of socially acceptable punishment patterns in over 90 percent of cases. In her research, she compared groups of parents who discipline their children through pro-active teaching, and those who employ a reactive, violent disciplinary style. She argues that parents' own socialization experiences exert a strong influence on the tendency to discipline through teaching, whereas factors related to the distribution of power in the family and in society at large are the chief causes of electing to use a reactive, violent style.

Sexual abuse is another form of aggression against children, and it, too, has been widely documented in recent years (Badgley, 1984; Rogers, 1990). Since estimates regarding its incidence depend, of course, on how it is defined and measured, there is controversy over the extent to which it exists in Canada. Few would doubt, however, that it is a problem of worrying proportions. The acknowledgment of sexual abuse as a public problem has encouraged many people to break their silence about their own past experiences and, in some cases, to bring charges against their abusers. Some have had what are called "recovered memories." For example, after forty years of "forgetting," novelist Sylvia Fraser remembered her experiences of being sexually abused by her father throughout childhood and adolescence. Out of this recovered memory she wrote *My Father's House: A Memoir of Incest and Healing* (1988).

In 1992, an organization called the False Memory Syndrome Foundation was established in Philadelphia, and it has since established a branch in Canada. Its adherents include: mental-health experts who allege that many memories of abuse are prompted by poorly trained or biased therapists; memory experts, who stress the fine line between memory and suggestion; and, not surprisingly, people who have been accused of abuse and protest their innocence.

False Memory Syndrome, however, is controversial, and many dispute its authenticity. Critics say that adherents are hiding a political agenda under the guise of medical terminology, as the term "syndrome" is a misnomer and has yet to be substantiated. While some survivor's "memories" are undoubtedly false or even fabricated, critics dispute the notion that it is a widespread phenomenon, and see the movement as a way for alleged abusers to silence and/or discredit their accusers. For an excellent discussion of the aftermath of trauma, see Herman (1992).

. . . .

OVERVIEW

The search for an all-encompassing definition of the family is an exercise in futility. It is more useful to think about what families actually do, and what they actually look like, than to measure them against a single model. The functionalist model of the family that prevailed in sociology until very recently is inappropriate when applied to the reality of how families organize their private and domestic lives today. It is also inappropriate when applied to the past. However, it reflects a powerful ideology that serves dominant societal interests, shapes the expectations of individuals, and punishes those who do not conform.

The distinction between the public and private spheres in industrialized societies places a heavy burden of expectation on family life and, at the same time, divests the public world of some of its "humanity." Marxist and feminist scholars, in tracing the complex interconnections between paid labour and unpaid domestic labour, have shown that the separation is more apparent and real.

Women's lives have changed much more rapidly than men's, and the gap is a source of family tension. A perspective that views motherhood, fatherhood, and childhood as social constructions is helpful in studying the ways in which family roles are renegotiated.

Despite predictions of its imminent demise, the institution of the family in Canada has shown no signs of withering away. In its versatility, it continues both to reflect and to shape changing societal values.

ASSIGNMENTS

1. Analyze your immediate family in terms of the dimensions of the familial interaction outlined by Margrit Eichler (see Exhibit 9.1). How does the pattern you describe conform to the monolithic model of the family? If it deviates from the model, can you identify any social costs that your family pays for non-conformity?

2. Read Marabel Morgan's *The Total Woman* (Markham: Simon and Schuster, 1973) and write a response to it from a feminist perspective.

3. Can you identify any "family myths" that may be maintained in your own family? Does one have to do with the division of labour? Whose interests are best served by these myths? Who bears the costs for perpetuating them?

4. Interview six fathers who you think are participating in what we have termed a "reconstructed" form of fatherhood. What role conflicts do they experience? How do they attempt to resolve these conflicts? What types of resistance do they encounter both inside and outside of the family?

SUGGESTED READINGS

David Bakan, *Slaughter of the Innocents: A Study of the Battered Child Phenomenon* (Toronto: CBC Learning Systems, 1971). In a sensitive and sweeping analysis of child abuse, Bakan argues that infanticide has, historically, served the function (as have plagues and wars) of population control. The twists and turns his argument takes will surprise you, as well as his provocative analyses of some of the hateful messages embedded in the seemingly benign lullabies and stories that adults pass on to children.

Margrit Eichler, *Families in Canada Today: Recent Changes and their Policy Consequences*, 2nd ed. (Toronto: Gage, 1988). Eichler provides a wealth of Canadian data about Canadian families and shrewd analysis of the trends that these data reveal. She discusses the biases that have dominated the family literature, preventing recognition of change and diversity and hindering the development of effective and equitable social policies.

William Goode, *World Revolution and Family Patterns* (Glencoe: Free Press, 1970). Using a functionalist perspective, Goode has done a lot of cross-cultural research on families. He has been particularly interested in the impact that the modern forces of industrialization and urbanization have had on family arrangements.

Arlie Hochschild, with Anne Machung, *The Second Shift* (New York: Avon Books, 1989). On the basis of close observation, Hochschild sketches a delicately nuanced portrait of men and women doing battle, negotiating, compromising, winning, and losing, in the face of the demands of jobs, marriage, and childrearing. She argues that it is primarily women, in embracing the "second shift," who have absorbed the speedup in work and family life. Perhaps most interesting of all is her analysis of the subtle ways in which women develop and encourage family myths to disguise, even from themselves, the fact that the ideal and the real are out of whack.

David Leavitt, *A Place I've Never Been* (New York: Penguin Books, 1990). In ten short stories, Leavitt weaves a seamless web of relationships that includes parents, children, homosexual and heterosexual lovers, and friends. Leavitt shows that the gratifications, disappointments, banalities, and responsibilities of intimate relationships are not the sole preserve of "conventional" families.

Meg Luxton, *More Than a Labour of Love: Three Generations of Women's Work in the Home* (Toronto: The Women's Press, 1980). Written from a Marxist-feminist perspective, Luxton's oft-cited study focuses on working-class women in the mining town of Flin Flon, Manitoba. Luxton describes in compelling detail the work that is hidden in the home, and analyzes how both paid and unpaid work are central to the economy of industrial capitalism. Her women are portrayed as active agents, struggling to create, resist, and modify their circumstances.

Jane Rule, *Memory Board* (Toronto: Macmillan of Canada, 1987). Rule's wonderful novel describes the relationship of two women in their sixties who have lived together throughout their adult lives. One of them is struggling with progressively severe deficits in the functioning of her memory. The "memory board" of the title is an ingenious device created by her partner to help her cope.

Barrie Thorne, and Marilyn Yalom, eds., *Rethinking the Family: Some Feminist Questions*, 2nd ed. (Boston: Northeastern University Press, 1992). This excellent collection of papers broadens the discussion of family life considerably. The book emphasizes the complexities and contradictions that appear when gender, class, race, and sexual orientation are taken seriously as dimensions of analysis. For somewhat differing perspectives on fatherhood and male participation in family life, see the papers by Goode, Lacqueur, and Ruddick.

Utne Reader, May/June 1993. This magazine brings together excerpts from news reports, journal and magazine articles, and books, and draws them from a wide spectrum of opinions. This particular issue is devoted to the question, "Who Cares About Kids?" Among the contributors are sociologist Amitai Etzioni and journalist Susan Faludi. Read the contrasting views regarding the effects of day care on children, paying attention to how these views have been derived, and form your own opinions.

NOTES

1. It should be noted here that the concept of "choice" with respect to childbearing has a double-edged nature. McDaniel (1988) argues that, although the reproductive technologies (which we shall discuss in Chapter 12, "Social Change") now make it seem plausible that motherhood is a deliberate choice, a "choice" framework of analysis contains numerous contradictions. Some women lack access to contraception or abortion, and unwanted pregnancies continue to be high. Other women experience motherhood by coercion rather than by choice, in marriages where reproduction is traded off for economic support. At the same time, if childbearing is seen in the choice framework, it becomes easier to make the case that women who have chosen to have children should stay home to raise them.

2. Studies report that husbands and wives tend to experience a higher degree of marital satisfaction after their children have left the home (Skolnick, 1983).

Education: Winning and Losing

There was always someone trying to interfere with your reading. At school, where it all began, it was as though they'd showed you you had a magic wand but then grudged you the use of it. They even tried to stop you from reading ahead of the class in the textbooks. And they spoiled the textbooks by insisting you had to LEARN from them. What distrust of school-learning I learned from those countless short-term memory hurdles over the unmemorable and now unremembered. As for real books, there was hardly anything to read in the schools I went to. At most you might have a few volumes in the classroom. I remember the anxious fervour with which I dreamed of "passing" to a classroom that actually contained such a library, how I worried I wouldn't be considered "smart enough" according to the mysterious standards of teachers, to whom my sloppiness and poor penmanship and general unruliness clearly represented a serious failure of intelligence. And when I did get there I found the books surrounded by rules about when you could or could not get to look at them.

Adele Wiseman, *Memoirs of a Book-Molesting Childhood and other Essays*

I don't much like looking back at what happened to me at school. It seems to me that the only thing I enjoyed was playing hooky and running away. One of the difficult things I had to cope with was something called "time". The teacher would talk about wasting "time". I didn't know what that meant, I didn't know how you could waste "time". She'd read us a story in school and then she'd say we've lost all that "time", so now we have to hurry and make it up. I couldn't figure out what that meant, either. There were all kinds of things about time that really bewildered me. I did not understand what all this clock watching was about, because in our community we ate when we were hungry and slept when we felt tired. We did not do things on any kind of schedule, yet that never presented a problem. The things that were necessary always got done.

Wilfred Pelletier, *For every North American Indian who begins to disappear, I also disappear*

After two years at another university, I dropped out for a year and worked. At first, I thought it was just great—I don't have to study, I don't have to write exams—but by the end of the year I was so glad to be going back to school. I thought, I don't want to do this for the rest of my life, working at these dead-end jobs for minimum wage. Well, just a little over. So it is sort of disillusioning. I have a lot of career-oriented experience for the job I would like to get, in journalism. But I can't get a job in journalism because there just aren't any.

Amy Wilson (aged 24), *Maclean's* interview

The liberal vision that shaped the establishment of mass education in the industrialized nations was that of a "prosperous democracy" based on equality and efficiency. The young would receive both a moral and a practical education that would prepare them, according to their abilities, for participation in citizenship and for participation in an increasingly differentiated labour force. But are equality and efficiency compatible goals? How equality should be interpreted and pursued in the educational system, the priority which should be given to it or to efficiency, and the extent to which either can been achieved via education are matters of ongoing debate.

By international standards, Canadians enjoy a level of educational attainment second only to that of Americans, and the education sector itself employs approximately 7 percent of the total work force (Economic Council of Canada, 1992, 2, 40). In most countries, fewer females than males complete secondary school, and fewer participate in higher education. This is no longer the case in Canada at the secondary school and university undergraduate levels. A growing senior population is also flocking to educational institutions. Yet, despite massive growth, and despite heady periods of educational reform aimed at promoting greater equality, it is generally agreed that the education system's contribution to reducing social disparities in Canadian society has been disappointing, even dismal. Those currently concerned with Canada's economic performance also argue that the system is not meeting economic needs, and urge reforms that would provide a better fit between education and the labour market. Those who have these concerns point to the waste represented by high drop-out rates, underachievement in the areas of science and technology, and the irrelevance of the curriculum. See Box 10.1 for a discussion of how an extension of the school day might affect efficiency and equality.

BOX 10.1

SHOULD WE HAVE YEAR-ROUND SCHOOLS?

In any debate about school reform, parents and business leaders inevitably call for a longer school year. We can't improve academic achievement, the argument goes, if our school year averages only 190 days, compared to 200 to 240 days in Europe and Japan.

The case for a longer school year rests partly on the gap between the instruction time that our schools claim to offer and the days they actually deliver. For example, a 1992 New Brunswick commission on education reported that the schools in that province rarely honoured their mandate of 182 days. Test schedules, professional development days, winter storms and other events reduced the average school year to an "unsatisfactory" 161 days.

Although extending the school year may sound like a quick way to foster better learning, the solution is simplistic. At issue is not just the number of days spent in school, but the length of the school day, the actual hours spent learning and the quality of teaching.

What really sets Japanese schools apart from ours is not their vaunted 240-day school year—which, like Canada's, is whittled away by school trips and other non-academic events. Japanese schools generally have a longer day, from 8 A.M. to 4 P.M., with six 50-minute periods for junior high school and 45-minute classes for elementary students. Even more important is the rigour of Japanese teaching. Japanese pupils concentrate on 80 percent of their lessons because teachers are well prepared, engage the whole class and allow nothing to interfere with the lesson. No hard data yet exists for Canadian schools, but the same study showed that U.S. children barely focus on their work for half of their lessons because of constant interruptions, idle chitchat and "child-centred" instruction in which the teacher tries to give individual attention to 32 students rather than absorb the whole class in the lesson.

Child-centred teaching and disruptive school routines erode learning time in Canada, too, to judge from hundreds of letters I receive from teachers every year. A disgruntled high school teacher in Scarborough, Ont., recently sent me a typical list of time-stealers. They included 45-minute periods set aside for club meetings, library research, and extra help (rarely requested)—all activities that could have been scheduled after school, Then, there were 75-minute lunches, spares, sports events and special assemblies.

Once teachers actually get to class, they are often greeted by no more than half the students, while the rest are away on field trips, working in a local business as part of a cooperative education program or just playing hooky. There's nothing inherently wrong with field trips and job training, of course, but activities like these claim too much of the school day. In turn, teachers may lose a school day a month to work-related stress, administrative hassles and "professional development."

The Scarborough teacher calculated that, as a high school student 30 years ago, she had nine 38-minute periods each day totaling 342 minutes, while today's students get only three or four 75-minute periods for a paltry total of between 225 and 300 minutes. "This gap, to my mind, amounts almost to a fraud," she wrote. "The only glaring problem with lessons given to most Ontario students is their infrequency."

Given such a common scenario, a hasty extension of the school year would likely gain nothing but more days filled with "nonsense, trivia and truancy." Educators must start with more basic reforms that improve the quality of teaching and increase the number of hours spent learning academic skills. Along the way, they should pare down the schools' crowded social curriculum—the spate of new programs on parenting, AIDS, drug education and the like. Every time an interest group gives the schools another noble mission, teachers lose time for reading, math or history. The lamentable result is that harried and exhausted teachers try to do too much—and often do it poorly—instead of trying to teach a few things well.

While a longer year is no panacea, it makes sense for one group of schools—those near low-cost or subsidized housing. Many of the children in these schools are always playing catch-up because they come from homes where learning is not valued. Many studies have shown that a longer school year with shorter breaks helps these students retain what they've learned.

These children and others could benefit from the Japanese approach to school vacations. Our three-month-long summer holidays were originally designed so children could help on farms in a rural economy, now rapidly shrinking. Once summer is over, many invariably need a couple of months of study and review before they're back at the level they'd reached the previous June. Although Japanese schools also have three months of holidays a year, vacation time is interspersed between three terms of three months each so that it's less disruptive to learning. For students needing extra help, most schools are open half-days on Saturdays.

Is extending the school year a good idea? For schools serving disadvantaged children, yes—provided teachers make wise use of the additional hours. But generally speaking, this reform belongs at the bottom of school boards' priority lists. Until Canadian educatiors and parents have done their homework on how local schools now use the day and to what end, then extending the school year may simply add more trips to the zoo.

Source: Andrew Nikiforuk, "Should We Have Year-Round Schools?" Chatelaine (May 1993), 38. Reprinted with permission.

HISTORICAL OVERVIEW

That one can speak of a historical view of education signifies that in the distant past some individuals were able to record in writing what happened during their lifetimes, how people felt about these events, and what mysteries of the universe they sought to unravel. Today we have such records from many parts of the world. In the West, the earliest come mainly from ancient Greece. There, as in most societies, organized learning was mainly a privilege of the elite, furnishing opportunities for intellectual play as well as supplying practical benefits. The academies of Plato and Aristotle provided a forum in which Greece's brightest and wealthiest young men could engage in stimulating discourse on the nature of humankind and the workings of society. The perception of intellectual pursuits as desirable filtered down to other members of society, and some determined individuals of the less privileged classes managed to improve their social position by becoming literate and proficient at mathematics.

Thus, even 2,000 years ago, education provided an avenue for upward mobility. However, literacy, the ability to read and write, remained a scarce and precious commodity for centuries. In the Roman empire, slaves who had the skill before being captured, or who contrived to acquire it later, worked as scribes and bookkeepers. Their importance to their masters often enabled them to accumulate enough money to buy freedom.

With the disintegration of the Roman empire, western Europe moved into the dark ages, a period during which the vast majority of the population was illiterate. Learning became the purview of the Catholic Church, which supplied the clerks needed by the aristocracy for written communication, records, and bookkeeping.[1] The focus of education was mainly on religious issues, though secular enquiry was kept alive by exceptional individuals who managed to stay in touch with each other, eventually through the late medieval world's centres of learning, such as those in Paris and Padua. In a culture that made far less distinction than ours between religious and worldly matters, theologians and philosophers tackled problems that today would be considered as falling in the realm of physical or social science. Albertus Magnus (1206?–1280) and Roger Bacon (1214–1294), both of whom helped to advance the scientific method, were churchmen who wrote on philosophy as well as on theology. Such enquiry blossomed and expanded as the Renaissance began, sparking a new zest for intellectual discovery and for physical exploration of the universe.

Among some Protestant groups that emerged from the Reformation, literacy became highly valued because it enabled people to read religious texts without a priestly intermediary. Interestingly, education acquired for such a noneconomic motive has historically bestowed material as well as intrinsic rewards. For example, widespread literacy among Quakers, at a time when this was a rare accomplishment, contributed to the group's importance in the North Atlantic trade. Somewhat analogously, Jews have reaped economic benefits through the ages from skills that were developed initially as a prerequisite for study of the Talmud.

In the Western nations, the beginning of mass public education roughly coincided with the latter stages of the Industrial Revolution. More sophisticated machinery and the growth of enterprises necessitated written communication and hence a literate work force. Labour laws delaying the age at which children could start work and reducing the length of their work day created the need for a caretaking service, a function that education continues to perform today. In many cases, church-sponsored schools preceded or co-existed with schools funded from the public purse.

Meanwhile, the Napoleonic Wars (1795–1815) and the American Revolution (1776–1783) had spurred the emergence of modern nationalism and the large-scale use of citizen armies to replace hired mercenaries. In public schools, nationalistic feelings could be inculcated and reinforced by such rituals as raising the flag, singing the national anthem, and learning a glorious version of the nation's history.

In the United States, the schools became important vehicles for assimilating children from different ethnic backgrounds into the mainstream culture of the society. By the same token, depriving any group of education was a means of ensuring its continuing subordination. During the period before the American Civil War (1861–1865), it was an offence in many parts of the country to teach slaves to read and write. Providing an inferior education was also a means to ensure subordination. Coleman describes some of the differences between the early British and American systems of education:

> The emergence of public-tax supported education was not solely a function of industrial development. It was also a function of the class structure in the society. In the United States, without a strong traditional class structure, universal education in publicly-supported free schools became widespread in the early nineteenth century; in England, the "voluntary" schools, run and organized by churches with some instances of state support, were not supplemented by a state-supported system until the Education Act of 1870. Even more, the character of educational opportunity reflected the class structure. In the United States, the public schools quickly became the common schools, attended by representatives of all classes; these schools

provided a common educational experience for most American
children—excluding only those upper-class children in private
schools, those poor who went to no schools and Indians and
Southern Negroes who were without schools. In England, however,
the class system directly manifested itself through the schools. The
state-supported, or "board schools" as they were called, became the
schools of the laboring lower classes with a sharply different
curriculum from those voluntary schools which served the middle
and upper classes (1968, 10).

Egerton Ryerson was Superintendent of Education in Upper Canada from
1844 to 1876, and is regarded as the father of Ontario's public school system.
Free, compulsory education was established in that province in 1871. Ryerson
described the important role of education in terms of building character and of
elevating students to a higher moral plane. By inculcating and rewarding such
qualities as punctuality, neatness, obedience, and tolerance for monotonous
tasks, the schools would serve to prepare the young for life in the labour force.
This socializing function was deemed crucial because of the fear that these
virtues would not be transmitted by the working-class family, given that parents
had to work long hours and children largely had to fend for themselves. (See
Prentice [1977] for a close examination of the attitudes that influenced the
Ontario public school system in its early years.)

Even when legislation made school attendance mandatory, not all
children attended, some went only sporadically, and the vast majority left at the
minimum age of fourteen or fifteen. Only following the Second World War did
attendance up to the minimum legal age become firmly established. Protracted
participation in secondary schooling, and certainly in university education, was
the prerogative of a privileged few.

It was in the decade of the 1960s that the massive expansion of the
Canadian educational system occurred. Public expenditure on education
increased by 67 percent over that of the previous decade (O'Connor, 1989, 136)
and schools strained to accommodate the influx of students. New universities
and community colleges proliferated across the country. In the school systems,
old facilities were expanded and new ones were built. Expansion was accompanied by sweeping reforms, designed to improve the quality of education and to
make it more equitable. The early streaming of students into pre-university and
vocational educational programs was abandoned, choices concerning credits
and courses were increased, and uniform testing was replaced, in many
instances, by a more individualized form of evaluation. The horizons seemed
limitless. As the Ontario Hall-Dennis Report of 1968 put it:

They [the students] must be made to feel that the world is waiting
for their sunrise, and that their education heralds the rebirth of an
"Age of Wonder." Then surely, the children of tomorrow will be more
flexible, more adventurous, more daring and courageous than we
are. Each will have learned, with Don Quixote, in *Man of La Mancha*:
To dream the impossible dream ... (Ontario Provincial Commission on
Aims and Objectives of Education, 1968, 9).

The vision of the 1960s was not based merely on the liberating potential that education has for individuals. It also assumed that the expansion of education would have direct salutary effects on the economy. As Pike notes, " ... it melded a materialistic message with the moral tenets of the liberal notion of equality of educational opportunity. Educational reforms designed to widen educational opportunities and overcome social barriers to scholastic achievement were supported because they were socially just *and* because they would lead to the more economically productive use of human resources" (1988, 267).

From the perspective of the 1990s, the 1960s stand out not as the beginning of a continuous upward swing (except in enrolments) but, rather, as a heyday that would be starkly different from the difficult times that ensued. Himmelfarb and Richardson (1991, 352) describe the aftermath as follows: "The 1960s, then, were indeed an exciting time to be a student, teacher or administrator. By the early 1970s, the 'party' seemed to have come to an end. And like all 'good binges,' the morning after was a time for sober recrimination and for facing the inevitable mess."

Educational reforms are a source of controversy in Canada today. Manisha Bharita, the first student appointed to a Royal Commission, is a member of the Ontario Royal Commission on Education.

Frank Gunn/ *The Globe and Mail,* Toronto.

Since that time, enrolments have increased; the enrolment of women in particular, has increased dramatically. In addition, educational reforms have continued to be implemented, and there is little doubt that education retains its central importance for Canadians. However, some would argue that the vision of education as a means of bringing about greater social equality in Canada has become pinched. Now, attention tends to centre on questions about the efficacy of the educational system in meeting the needs of the economy. Many educators and social scientists, however, continue to puzzle over the problem of the persistence of inequality (see, for example, Wotherspoon, 1987).

THEORETICAL APPROACHES TO THE STUDY OF EDUCATION

While it is generally recognized that children do not benefit equally from schooling, explanations of why this is so vary considerably, depending on the theoretical perspective used. The functionalist and Marxist perspectives are essentially deterministic and mechanistic explanations of the role of education in relation to social inequality, but they differ in their basic assumptions. Symbolic interactionists, ethnomethodologists, and others working in the interpretive tradition have sought to examine more closely those microlevel processes that lead, albeit unwittingly, to unequal outcomes. In this view, social actors in the educational system (students, teachers, administrators, policymakers) are not shaped exclusively by structural forces beyond their control, but become "active sense makers, choosing among alternatives in often contradictory circumstances" (Mehan, 1992). Finally, different strands of feminist scholarship have examined the gender biases in the content and organization of education that affect women as teachers, as students, and as parents, and that influence what is defined as legitimate knowledge.

THE FUNCTIONALIST PERSPECTIVE: SCHOOLS AS THE LOCUS OF EQUAL OPPORTUNITY

In the functionalist model of society as a social system, education as an institution is second only to the family in importance. As we have seen in the previous chapter, the socialization of the young was the primary responsibility of the family in pre-industrial times. Children learned in the family setting those skills and values that they would need in their adult roles outside of the home. As the nature of work was transformed, new values and competencies had to be acquired. While family relations were based on ascription, warmth, diffuse obligations, and particularistic values, the workplace called for relations based on achievement, impersonality, specific obligations, and universal values. Formal education, then, would provide the bridge between the two spheres. It would also serve to sift and sort the young on the basis of merit, that is, on their abilities and efforts. In other words, all would have an equal opportunity, through schooling, to develop their potential. This would increase the likelihood that society would be **meritocratic** (Young, 1958), that is, that social rewards would be distributed according to individual achievement rather than say, on the basis of inherited wealth or membership in the dominant ethnic group. In this way, top positions would be filled by "the brightest and the best," regardless of their social origins. Moving upwards in the social hierarchy, in other words, would be a matter of contest mobility rather than sponsored mobility.

Parsons (1951, ch. 6) is very explicit about the ways in which education serves this bridging function between the family and the labour force. Children, he says, need to be gradually emancipated from their strong attachment to their mothers. When they enter school, they first come into the care of women who are similar to, but different from, the mother. Parsons says, "The fact of being a woman and of having a kindly, protective attitude toward the children is the most important similarity. A woman can by and large permit herself greater tenderness and solicitude than can a man" (1951, 241). While acknowledging that the predominance of women teachers in the early grades may have something to do with the fact that they can be obtained for less pay than men of comparable levels of training and competence would receive, Parsons attributes a positive function to having female, rather than male, teachers, since they are more like mothers. He also goes so far as to claim that what might seem like an "irrational prejudice" against married female teachers is not so irrational after all, since spinsterhood makes them less like the mother. This discriminatory practice, too, has a function! The teacher is also unlike the mother in that she cannot devote her attention exclusively to one child: she is responsible for twenty or so children who are approximately the same age and thus in greater competition with each other than siblings at home would be. There are also limits to her involvement with the children, since it is confined to the hours of the school day. She will accustom them to being judged in accordance with standards of achievement, and these standards become more explicit as the child proceeds through the age-graded school system.

Attachment to a single teacher is not enough, however, to wean the child from the home. Thus, in the later grades, students have a different teacher for each subject throughout the day. "This," says Parsons, "is another big step toward the acquisition of universalistic orientations, in that the focus is on competence in the subject matter rather than the more diffuse, general, and hence parent-like superior knowledge and standing of the teacher" (1951, 242). Significantly, teachers at this later stage are likely to be men, who better represent the values and commitments necessary for the (male) students to make the transition to the world of work. Since female students are destined for adult roles in the family sphere, they experience tensions in nonsegregated classrooms.

Parsons thus attributes functional significance to the minutest details of the organization of schooling.[2] The implication is that things are as they are because the proper functioning of the wider social system requires it. The minutiae of the classroom mesh to the benefit of the individual, the educational system, and the society in which this system is embedded. Changes, such as having male teachers instead of females in the lower grades, would upset this delicate balance.

In brief, according to Parsons, education performs several functions:

- It encourages homogeneity and creates a shared cultural identity.

- It provides caretaking services (when one talks about the utility of keeping young adults in school when jobs are scarce, this caretaking function is sometimes referred to as "warehousing").

- Through selective reward and punishment, it reinforces traits needed in an industrial workforce.

- It provides training in the specific skills and knowledge required for occupational roles.

- It measures the performance of students by universal standards, so that they can be directed toward occupational roles on the basis of merit.

- By emphasizing merit, it legitimates the unequal distribution of rewards in society, and socializes students to accept this principle of allocation.

Family Background, Aspirations, and Achievement

In the functionalist perspective, inequality results from the fact that the aptitudes and motivations of individuals differ. If success is to be attributed to ability and/or effort, failure must be seen as resulting from a lack of ability, or insufficient effort. Responsibility thus lies with the individual rather than with the system. Sennett and Cobb describe what a terrible burden this responsibility can be:

> Since the teacher appears to him as passive, is it not his own fault if he fails to catch the teacher's attention? The system must work, for the child can see that a few are chosen—but not he. Could he have paid more attention, worked harder? He wants and needs friends; since he cannot read the teacher's mind, how can he know that forming friendships based on 'hanging around,' mutual defense, and breaking small rules, reinforces the teacher's belief that he hasn't much intellectual ability? Before the passive judge, some people make it, while the teacher tolerates *him* impersonally—that is what he knows. All the burden of the situation seems on him, there is nothing in this passive, judgmental authority that he feels he can fight (1973, 88–89).

Education and Status Attainment

In the United States, nation-wide surveys on status attainment established quite definitively that family background played a key role in achievement at school (Blau & Duncan, 1967; Coleman et al., 1966; Jencks et al., 1972). The research of Jencks and his colleagues, however, cast doubt on whether education had as much influence as had been believed on subsequent success in the work world. "Luck," they argued, also plays a role, and we should not pin such high hopes on schooling. Yet, in a later publication, Jencks et al. (1979) looked again at the determinants of economic success, and concluded that luck was a slim factor; the kind of family one had *did* put a heavy stamp on the individual's fate in school and on economic prospects. Similar evidence was found in Canada (Anisef, 1973–1974; Anisef, Paasche, & Turrittin, 1980). Breton (1972) looked at students whose ability test scores placed them in the bottom third of their cohorts. Of those from upper-class families, 72 percent were in academic programs, compared with 38 percent of those from lower-class families.

A study by Wright (1970) was sparked by a brief presented to the Toronto Board of Education by a group of mothers from a public-housing development. The mothers had asked the board why so many of their children were being placed in vocational rather than academic classes. In April 1970, the 106,921 students who were in the school system were surveyed to determine whether a student's place of birth, mother tongue, and the occupation of the head of the household in which he or she resided affected placement. No clear relationship emerged between those students who were foreign born or whose mother tongue was not English and placement. However, the occupation of the head of the household was strongly related to placement, especially at the secondary school level. Only 0.5 percent of the children of "accountants, engineers, lawyers, etc." were in special vocational classes; 89.7 percent were in five-year academic programs. For the children of "labourers, taxi drivers, etc.," the respective proportions were 9 and 46.5 percent. Students whose parents were on public assistance fared worst: 28.6 percent were in vocational classes and only 21.4 percent in five-year academic programs. Wright summarized the findings:

> The pattern of results is easy to describe in terms of occupation. Starting with the categories "Unemployed" and "Welfare," then "Housewife" (mother only) and from there moving on an occupational scale from labourer to professional, there is a steady change in the proportions found by grade, programme and special class, the children of professionals being the most likely to be found in 5-year programmes and the least likely to be average or in a special class (1970, 49).

In a panel study of Ontario students who graduated from grade 12 in 1973, Anisef, Paasche, and Turrittin (1980) commented on the importance of the high school program in post-secondary achievement. Of the respondents who had been in academic high school programs, 40 percent graduated from university, compared with 4.1 percent of students who had been in commercial programs and 7.4 percent of those who had been in technical and vocational programs. The findings for the whole of Ontario were consonant with those cited earlier for Toronto: "Respondents who chose academic programmes were disproportionately selected from upper middle class sectors of Ontario society" (1980, 65).

Functionalists stress the importance of socialization on the educational achievement of young people.

Guy Dixon.

Porter, Porter, and Blishen (1982) wanted to investigate the relationship between the family backgrounds of students and their aspirations to study at the university level. Beginning their research in 1971, they conducted a large-scale survey of Ontario students in grades 8, 10, and 12. To measure the social class background of the students, they used the students' fathers' occupations. They found a direct relationship between the fathers' occupational status and the aspiration of the students to complete grade 13 and enter university. Only 46 percent of students whose fathers had unskilled jobs planned to attend university, while 76 percent of students whose fathers were in the professional category intended to do so. Porter and his colleagues administered an intelligence test to the students to measure their mental ability, and found that the variations in student aspirations could not be explained solely by variations in ability; their fathers' occupational statuses had much more explanatory power. Girls in grade 12 had aspirations equal to or higher than boys only among middle- and low-ability students within the upper-middle class. In all other categories, their aspirations were lower.

Porter and his colleagues also found other factors to be associated with aspirations to attend university. Students from urban areas were more likely than students from rural areas to want to attend university. A greater proportion of Jewish students aspired to graduate from university than Catholics and Protestants, while a marginally greater proportion of Protestants than Catholics held those aspirations.

To explain why so many high-ability students reject the idea of university (a finding not consistent with meritocratic assumptions), the researchers turned to the symbolic interactionist notions of socialization and self-concept (review the discussions of Cooley and Mead in Chapter 4). This approach stresses the importance of the family in shaping the child's development. Families in different social classes provide children with different beliefs about what they can achieve, regardless of their innate abilities. With a series of questions designed to measure self-concept and to determine whom the students regarded as significant others, the researchers found that girls perceived their own abilities as lower even though they consistently obtained higher grade-point averages than boys in every category of mental ability. This is a reflection of their socialization and of the expectations that parents hold for their futures.

If the researchers' emphasis on family socialization is warranted, we must conclude that important changes in attitudes about the appropriateness of education for girls have occurred since these data were collected. The enrolment of women in higher education has soared since that time (see Exhibit 10.1) in both absolute and relative terms. Has their socialization been different, or have they simply managed to overcome it?

MARXIST PERSPECTIVES: SCHOOLS AS AGENTS OF CAPITALIST SOCIETY

Scholars working in the Marxist tradition completely reject explanations for inequality that have to do with the aspirations and abilities of individuals. Rather, they locate the source of inequality in the capitalist mode of production. In this view, schools merely reproduce the social division of labour, preparing children for a place in the class structure that is predetermined by

EXHIBIT 10.1

*Bachelor and First
Professional Degrees
Awarded by Year and Sex,
1920–1990*

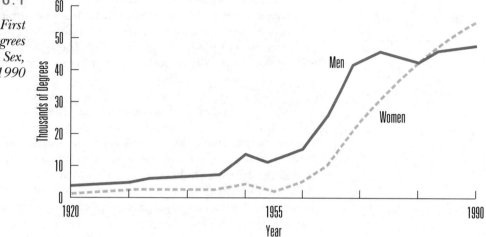

Source: Statistics Canada, Cat. Nos. 81–568, 81-569, 81-204.

their family origins. As the principal exponents of this approach in the United States, Bowles and Gintis (1976) exerted a major influence on educational research for over a decade. They argued that there is a fundamental incompatibility between the needs of a democracy for an enlightened citizenry that is committed to the preservation of individual rights and the protection of minorities, and the capitalist economy's need for a highly differentiated, and unequal, work force. The education system is caught up in this dilemma. Bowles and Gintis argue that it is impossible for schools to promote individual growth and social equality and at the same time prepare the majority to fit into alienating and unequal roles when they leave school. Since the majority of jobs actually require very little skill and intelligence, ambition and talent can be handicaps. What, then, are schools to do?

According to Bowles and Gintis, schools resolve this dilemma by imitating the structure of authority in the workplace, and, at the same time, emphasizing competition and continuous sorting on the basis of achievement, so that outcomes will be seen to be fair. They trace a structural correspondence between relationships in the school system (for example, between teachers and administrators, teachers and students, and among students) and the relationships (for example, supervisor/worker) encountered in the work-place. The result is a picture of the school as a factory.

For the stability of society, schools use a variety of strategies to reconcile students to their fate so that their expectations become aligned with their achievements:

> By rendering the outcome (educational attainment) dependent not only on ability but also on motivation, drive to achieve, perseverance and sacrifice, the status allocation mechanism acquires heightened legitimacy. Moreover, such personal attributes are tested and developed over a long period of time, underlining the apparent objectivity and achievement orientation of the stratification system ... Frequent failures play an important role in gradually bringing a

student's aspirations into line with his or her probable career opportunities. By the time most students terminate schooling, they have been put down enough to convince them of their inability to succeed at the next highest level. Through competition, success, and defeat in the classroom, students are reconciled to their social positions (1976, 106).

The needs of the economy have not, however, been static. Bowles and Gintis describe the changes that have occurred in the development of education, and argue that these changes are a direct reflection of changes occasioned by the development of capitalism. For example, the expansion of higher education in the 1960s, including the establishment of community colleges, came as a response to capitalism's need for a large corps of white-collar workers at what Bowles and Gintis call the subprofessional level: lower-level supervisors, legal and medical paraprofessionals, and so on. As a surplus of people with bachelor's degrees and subprofessional qualifications was produced, employers could keep salaries to a minimum level. Credentials thus came to be cheapened, and one had to pursue a still higher degree, in order to gain an advantage in the job market: this trend is known as credentialism.

Cultural Capital

The concept of cultural capital, introduced by Bourdieu (1977) provides a subtler explanation of the relationship between economic structures and schooling. **Cultural capital** can be defined as that configuration of formal and informal knowledge and social skills that enables people to cope with their environment. It is transmitted in the family to children, and determines their success or failure in school. Imagine, for example, a child bringing home an assignment that asks for a report on dinosaurs. Middle-class parents in an urban setting might take the child to a museum; even in a small town, such parents would likely steer the child to the research section of the library, or haul out the family encyclopedia. Minimally educated parents might be equally anxious for the child to do well, but lack both an awareness of what resources are available and the facility to use them. Thus, for the lower-class child to produce an assignment as good as that of the middle-class child likely requires greater ability or a higher level of motivation.

Several of the teachers interviewed by Hall and Carlton in their study of Albertown (an alias) spoke in this vein:

> There's a small minority, about twenty per cent ... no matter what you do it is negated outside school. From Kindergarten on we give them special attention, but there's only about a five per cent result ... Kids reflect the attitudes of the parents; they don't want to be at school; see the school as a hindrance ... authoritarian figures putting restrictions on them (1977, 48–49).

One teacher noted, "Parents care, but are ill-equipped."

Preparation for the labour force begins as soon as children enter school. Martell (1974) argues that the notion of allowing children to achieve their full potential is spurious in an educational system that is based on labelling and

*The "cultural capital"
acquired by middle-class
children in their family life
enables them to do better
than others at school.*

Visitors in the Henry Moore Sculpture Centre,
Art Gallery of Ontario, Toronto.

streaming, since it slots them into predetermined places. In an earlier publication, he describes how the social status quo is maintained:

> How, then, do our schools prepare kids to fit into these various levels
> of working-class and middle-class employment? Primarily, it seems
> to me, the job is done by setting up a social system within the
> schools, in which the social relationships the kids experience are the
> same they will later experience in factories and offices. This
> transplanted social system in the schools is there when the kids
> arrive. In order to survive in it, the kids have to fit in (and are fitted in)
> to that level of the system for which their already developed public
> character has prepared them. That is, by the time they reach school,

they already have a way of living within the society as they
experience it, and that way of living or behaving—including forms of
resistance, acquiescence and local community life—is appropriate to
a certain stream or grouping within the social system (1974, 18).

Using survey data, Persell et al. (1992) argue that cultural capital does not
work in the same way for males and females. The latter need *more* of it in order
to achieve success commensurate to that of men. They provide evidence that
attendance at elite private boarding schools minimizes the gendered pathways
to the best colleges and universities.

Radical Reform?

A logical conclusion of the deterministic view, according to which schools
merely replicate the social structure, is that educational reform alone is
impotent to bring about greater social equality. From this perspective, reform is
only a matter of tinkering; real change can only come about by changing the
wider economy in which schools are embedded, and this would necessitate the
dismantling of the corporate capitalist system.

Ivan Illich, however, thinks reform is both possible and desirable. In his book
Deschooling Society (1971), he proposes a vision of learning that is participatory,
decentralized, and liberated. He argues that credentialism produces a "ladder that
has no top," leaving behind those with lesser credentials or no credentials at all.
Furthermore, the education system produces people with an inordinate respect
for expertise and a mistrust of their own experience. Illich proposes that more
effective learning could take place outside of schools, through more direct
observation of people who are actually exercising the skills one wants to acquire.
Individuals should therefore take responsibility for their own learning.

Paulo Freire developed his proposals for educational reform in the process
of examining the problem of illiteracy in the slums of Brazil. Learning, he
argues, is an oppressive, alienating, and meaningless exercise if it is removed
from the experiences of those wanting to learn. The model of "student as empty
receptacle" creates students who are apathetic and passive. Freire insists that students need to be engaged in acts of questioning that bring to bear on problems
the wealth of experience that they have gained in their daily lives. Only in this
way can education empower them to bring about change. Although his focus
was on basic literacy and the condition of the poor in the Third World, Freire's
analysis made a great deal of sense to those involved in literacy campaigns in
industrialized nations as well.

THE SOCIAL CONSTRUCTION OF INEQUALITY

The major criticism of the Marxist approach in the variants just discussed is that,
in its emphasis on structural factors and its reduction of human actors to passive
role players (or bearers of a bundle of cultural capital), it neglects those microlevel processes through which the young receive, interpret, and then act in accordance with, the class-based messages that permeate their education. Critics argue
that the **hidden curriculum** of the schools, by which the appropriate values and
attitudes necessary for adaptation to the social status quo is transmitted, is largely
unintended and unrecognized. It becomes important, then, to identify how these

processes work in particular contexts (Mehan, 1992). Mehan points out that ethnographic research in the sociology of education has a long and impressive tradition beginning with Willard Waller's classic, *The Sociology of Teaching* (1932), and extending, in the Chicago School (discussed in Chapter 8), through to Becker's studies of Chicago School teachers (1952, 1953) and Jackson's descriptions of classroom life (1967). This approach was eclipsed by the large-scale quantitative studies of the relationship between family background and scholastic achievement or occupational success carried out by researchers like Jencks and Coleman. By the mid-1970s it was time, Mehan says, to go back and look at the internal life of schools in order to understand inequality. Subsequent research has shown, he claims, that "When the black box of schools is opened to careful observation, one finds that schools are relatively autonomous institutions, responding to community interests and practical circumstances that are not automatically related to the economic demands of capitalism" (1992, 16). The school's contribution to inequality can be found, he argues, in the mundane, routine, and repetitive work that educators engage in as they conduct lessons, administer tests, and attend meetings: "Students' intelligence, their access to educational curricula, their scholastic achievement, steps on their career ladders, their school identities, and their opinions later in life are assembled from such practices" (1992, 16). Close examination of these practices is one of a number of contributions that feminist scholars have made to the sociology of education.

GENETIC EXPLANATIONS OF SOCIAL INEQUALITY

A social Darwinist has a simple explanation: through biological selection, the "fittest" have attained an advantaged socioeconomic position. Their superior qualities are genetically transmitted to their offspring and manifest themselves in high academic performance.

Such an argument seems dubious if only because it cannot be tested empirically. As discussed in Chapter 4, "Socialization," there is no way of completely separating the respective impact of nature and nurture. No achievement tests exist for newborn babies, and those performed on very young children have proved to be quite unreliable because children mature at different rates. In any case, the performance of even a one-year-old is a function of both native endowment and environment. As studies of institutionalized children have shown, lack of attention, stimulation, and love retards physical and mental development (Bowlby, 1951).

The nature/nurture argument has received prominence in the controversies surrounding the validity and usefulness of IQ tests (for a review of some of the arguments, see Aronowitz [1976] and Karier [1972]). The Standford-Binet test designed by Lewis Terman was based on his conviction that people found their place in the social order on the basis of heredity and not social environment. Terman claimed:

> Preliminary investigations indicate that an IQ below 70 rarely permits anything better than unskilled labor; that the range from 70 to 80 is preeminently that of semi-skilled labor, from 80 to 100 that of the skilled or ordinary clerical labor, and from 100 to 110 or 115 that of the semi-professional pursuits; and that above all these are the grades of intelligence which permit one to enter the professions or

the larger fields of business. Intelligence tests can tell us whether a child's native brightness corresponds more nearly to the median of (1) the professional classes, (2) those in the semi-professional pursuits, (3) ordinary skilled workers, (4) semi-skilled workers, or (5) unskilled laborers. This information will be of great value in planning the education of a particular child and also in planning the differentiated curriculum here recommended (1923, 27–28).

The pernicious implications of these assumptions are not difficult to recognize. Paradoxically, it is the liberal commitment to meritocracy that has encouraged the persistence of testing and sorting. Even in the 1960s, and 1970s, and beyond, scholars such as Jensen (1969) and Herrnstein (1969) promoted the idea that there is a close correlation between heredity and intelligence, and that blacks are demonstrably inferior when measured by IQ tests. Aronowitz (1972, 38) insists that the impact of Jensen and Herrnstein must be seen in the context of shrinking employment opportunities and the strengthening of the hierarchical division of labour. He argues that their theories emanate from the same sources as arguments for such things as the "instinctual" basis of aggression, and for the chromosomal basis of criminality.

It is a premise of democracy that intellectual endowment is randomly distributed in the population, regardless of race, gender, or class. In our view, no scientific evidence exists to contradict this assumption.

FEMINIST PERSPECTIVES

Education has been of particular interest to feminists for a number of reasons. For one thing, it is women who have had the primary responsibility for children in the family, and thus have had closer contact with their schooling. Second, teaching as an occupation has had a high proportion of women, and is a "female occupation" at the elementary school level. Third, education offers hope as a route to eliminating gender inequality (Gaskell & Tigar McLaren, 1991, 2). Before inequality can be removed, however, it must be identified and understood in all its complexity. Education is not only a solution, it is part of the problem; since the young spend an enormous amount of time in their formative years being socialized in schools, it is there that the ideologies of masculinity and femininity become entrenched. These ideologies also influence what areas of study are pursued by males and females. The latter tend to be concentrated in the traditional areas of study that equip them for "female" jobs that are less well paid and less prestigious.

Feminist scholarship on education has not been disinterested; rather, it has been "engaged," seeking concrete ways to bring about greater gender equality in education. It also reflects a variety of theoretical perspectives and methodologies. Feminists working in the liberal tradition have directed their attention to the creation of equal opportunities and, in that more females are now found at all levels of the education system, they can be said to have been successful. Feminists in the Marxist tradition have maintained that schools reflect the gendered and class-based nature of the capitalist economy, and therefore more attention must be paid to the links between education and production. Radical feminists, on the other hand, have devoted attention to the hidden curriculum (mentioned earlier) that presents a male, or androcentric, view of the world. Women, they suggest, have different ways of knowing and of learning, and cannot find their voice in a patriarchal educational setting. Finally, feminists of colour have challenged the suggestion that there is only one "female experience" and reproach the feminist enterprise for using a model based on white, middle-class women instead of taking into account class, racial, and ethnic differences (Abbott & Wallace, 1990; Wolfe, 1991).

Sex-Role Socialization: Difference Is Bad

Gaskell and Tigar McLaren (1991) identify four phases in the development of feminist approaches to education. The first phase, spurred by the 1970 report of the Royal Commission on the Status of Women, emphasized the detrimental nature of sex-role socialization. Dick and Jane of the school readers and the school classroom do not do the same things. Dick plays boisterous boys' games, likes adventure stories, is good at math, works the classroom projector, and so on. Jane plays quietly with the girls, likes fairy tales, finds math difficult, and cleans the blackboard brushes. In the readers, Father is a truck driver, doctor, or businessman, while Mother tends the home. If she works, she is a teacher, secretary, or nurse. These stereotypes, which permeate both the curriculum and classroom practices, it was argued, become self-fulfilling prophecies. The answer was to change self-concepts by changing the images presented in the texts, and to change school practices by changing the organization of the classroom, the curriculum, the staffroom, and the playground. Many of the stereotypes began to be eliminated from the reading material; the home economics/industrial shop division was dismantled, at least in some schools; and segregated playgrounds and staffrooms were no longer the norm. You can see that the focus here was on modifying the behaviour and attitudes of individuals. It is a focus that remains, for example, in contemporary attempts to interest "clever" girls in science and technology (Mahood, 1993).

Revaluing the Feminine: Difference Is Good

In the second phase, the development of an infrastructure for feminist research (the establishment of journals, women's studies programs, feminist associations, etc.) gave a boost to studies of gender inequality in education. In this phase, the focus turned away from the how-can-a-woman-be-more-like-a-man question, and asked, "What are the positive ways in which women are different?" If their best qualities are their abilities in nurturance, sociability, intuition, and interdependence, how can these be made to work for them in the educational process? Some argued that this could only be achieved by single-sex schooling; others maintained that the incorporation of "female" qualities into education would benefit both sexes.

The Social Construction of Knowledge

In the third phase identified by Gaskell and Tigar McClaren, the nature of knowledge itself was brought into question. Traditional scholarship was challenged for being "malestream" (O'Brien, 1981), that is, shaped by male experience, and not the objective, value-free inquiry it purported to be (you might find it useful here to review the arguments in Chapter 2, "Sociologists at

Work"). In the previous chapter, we discussed the biases that Eichler claims lead to sexist research because they are based on unexamined assumptions about masculinity and femininity. In the study of education, these unexamined assumptions can be seen, for example, in the status attainment research that we described earlier in this chapter. The model of direct links between educational achievement and employment status cannot explain why it is that the academic credentials of women do not lead to the occupational success achieved by men. It does not explain, for instance, why men ride the glass elevator to the top positions in the education hierarchy.

Bringing in Diversity

The most recent phase in feminist research on education stems from the recognition that sexism is not the only bias from which scholarship suffers. If the female experience is to be taken into account, the question to be asked is, "What female experience?" (Gaskell & McClaren 1991, 9). This question calls for an examination of the ways in which variables such as race, ethnicity, class, age, and sexual orientation interact with gender to form the experiences of girls and women in the education system. Class analysis has proceeded more quickly in Canada than has analysis of other dimensions. Ng (1989) claims that, at best, women of colour have been "tokenized," that is, added on to other feminist considerations only as a sign of concern. The acknowledgment and appreciation of difference poses many challenges to educational research and to the practices of education itself. In this perspective, a curriculum is required that does not glorify whiteness and marginalize minorities as "the Other." Mukherjee (1989) argues that many course offerings at Canadian universities render people of colour almost illiterate (the self-fulfilling prophecy at work) when they try to relate their own experience to what they are required to learn.

It is estimated that, by the year 2000, 70 percent of students in Toronto will have as their mother tongue a language other than English.[3] In a poll conducted in 1993, 81 percent of Ontario respondents reported that they were somewhat or very concerned about racism in the schools.[4] Clearly, the school system faces formidable problems, and a radical transformation of the curriculum alone, while important, is not sufficient to tackle them. Explanations and solutions must also be sought in the social and economic structures in which education is embedded.

EDUCATION PAYS

Early status attainment research established conclusively that education pays, and this finding has not been refuted (see Exhibits 6.4 and 6.5 in Chapter 6 "Stratification"). There is not, however, a simple one-to-one relationship between education and occupational success. The same education, for example, does not reward men and women equally, nor does it reward dominant and minority groups of other kinds equally. The search for explanations of inequality has caused researchers to examine education as both a cause and an effect—or, in methodological terms, as an independent or dependent variable.

Whether a sociologist treats education as cause or effect depends on the conceptual framework adopted. As we have seen, for example, Porter and his colleagues (1982) viewed socioeconomic position as the independent (causal) variable that influences how much education (dependent variable) one is likely to receive. Anisef and colleagues treat education as a dependent variable in relation to geographic location, finding that:

> The overall rate of post-secondary experience was found to vary by as much as 21% (highest in Toronto and lowest in small towns and rural areas). Insofar as a majority of young persons must expect to leave home to enrol in post-secondary institutions, and insofar as rural areas are disproportionately populated by lower socioeconomic families, rural people suffer a double hardship in terms of gaining access to and financing their post-secondary education. In terms of occupational consequences, our analysis suggests greater job opportunities exist for city people than for rural people, and that the former group held down relatively more prestigious jobs (1980, 383–84).

Numerous studies have treated education as an independent variable, affecting, for example, attitudes toward minority groups, childrearing practices, and degrees of political participation. Exhibit 10.2 shows the level of education as an independent variable affecting the unemployment rate of individuals. It is clear that, the higher the education, the less the risk of unemployment. Hunter and Leiper (1993) demonstrate the enormous importance that educational certificates, rather than simply years spent in education, have for income, while Anisef and colleagues (1992) argue that the quality of education, as measured by graduation from either university or community college, also has an important effect on occupational attainment.

EXHIBIT 10.2 *Canadians' Unemployment Rates by Educational Attainment, 1975–1992*

	1975	1976	1977	1978	1979	1980	1981	1982	1983	1984	1985	1986	1987	1988	1989	1990	1991	1992
Total labour force	6.9	7.1	8.1	8.3	7.4	7.5	7.5	11.0	11.9	12.4	12.2	10.7	10.6	8.9	8.4	8.1	10.3	11.3
0–8 years schooling	8.2	7.9	9.4	9.6	8.8	9.0	9.1	13.3	13.5	15.1	15.1	13.7	14.0	12.5	12.6	12.5	15.4	16.0
High school	8.0	8.2	9.3	9.4	8.4	8.6	8.7	12.7	13.9	14.5	14.5	12.9	12.7	10.8	10.0	7.7	15.3	10.9
Some postsecondary education	6.4	6.4	7.5	7.8	6.6	6.4	6.7	10.0	11.7	12.6	11.0	9.5	9.7	7.7	8.3	8.0	10.3	11.4
Postsecondary certificate or diploma	4.3	5.2	5.3	5.8	5.1	5.0	4.9	7.5	8.9	9.2	8.7	7.2	7.2	6.3	5.8	6.3	8.2	9.3
University degree	3.0	3.2	3.4	3.8	3.2	3.1	3.2	4.9	5.2	4.3	5.3	4.8	4.5	4.1	4.0	3.7	4.9	5.5

Sources: Statistics Canada (1984c, table 8), and The Labour Force *(71-001) to Jan. 1989 (table 5). For 1990, 1991: Statistics Canada,* Labour Force Annual Averages, 1991. *Cat. No. 71-220 (February, 1992). For 1992:* Labour Force Annual Averages, 1992. *Statistics Canada Cat. No. 71-220 (1993).*

Exhibit 10.3 shows that in the vicious circle that entraps the poor, education serves as both an independent and a dependent variable. It performs similar functions in perpetuating affluence. In our society, these circles are neither closed nor inevitable because both downward and upward mobility can occur intergenerationally. For many individuals, education has paved the way for upward mobility. How the downward cycle can be penetrated for greater numbers of people, and for specific groups of people, is an important question for sociologists, educators, and policy makers.

EXHIBIT 10.3

The Circular Relationship between Education and Economic Status

THE EDUCATION SYSTEM IN CANADA

The structure of the education system and the manner in which it operates are closely intertwined. Under Canada's federal political system, the provinces are responsible for education, a matter deemed rather unimportant when the British North America Act was drafted. School boards act under provincial or territorial guidelines. Hence, when we talk about "Canadian" schools, we are, in fact, referring to schools directed by the appropriate ministries or departments of the ten provinces and two territories, and by a large number of school boards. Private schools may operate in any province and grant diplomas provided they meet the regulations and standards set by the province or territory. They are independent of the public system, are managed privately by an individual association or corporation, and charge fees, but they usually closely follow the curriculum and diploma requirements of the relevant department or ministry of education.

Through the Department of Indian Affairs and Northern Development (DIAND), the federal government is responsible for the education of status Indian and Inuit children. Every province except Newfoundland has federal schools, and they are operated either by DIAND or by Indian bands or tribal councils. As well, the federal government may pay for the education of native children in provincial schools. The issue of native education is currently in flux, as native peoples are seeking greater control over the location of schools, the language of instruction, and the content of the curriculum.

The main sources for financing secondary and elementary schools are provincial funds and municipal property taxes, so that there are pronounced differences throughout the country in resources for education. Each ministry of education, headed by an elected politician, sets educational goals in light of the province's overall priorities and the resources available to meet them. Translating these goals into action is left to the bureaucratic officials (civil servants) of the ministries concerned. General policies are handed down by the ministries and form the basis for adaptations made by local school board officials, who are elected, appointed, or both, depending on the jurisdiction; their decisions are implemented by hired administrators, including school principals. Within provincial guidelines, most school boards have a fair degree of autonomy. For example, the trustees of the Etobicoke Board of Education may decide to increase local taxes in order to continue remedial programs no longer funded by the province of Ontario. The Board's authority, however, is limited. In 1985, British Columbia required its local boards to reduce their budgets and removed the trustees of two school districts that refused. For an interesting analysis of the evolution of the Canadian educational system, along with comparisons of this system with that in the United States (which is less centralized) and those of western Europe and Japan, see Pike (1988).

CONFESSIONAL SCHOOLS

The intricacies of the Canadian educational system are made even more complex by the existence in some provinces of publicly supported separate school systems—usually Roman Catholic—and the practice in others of providing public funds for private schools. This support of confessional education has existed in Canada since the nineteenth century. It reflects the belief that religion and education are inseparable and that the state has a responsibility to foster, insofar as possible, a harmonious relationship between them.

The British North America Act (now incorporated in the Constitution Act of 1982) guaranteed separate, publicly funded Protestant and Catholic school systems in Ontario and Quebec. Ontario's Protestant system became its present public system. Provincial funding for its Catholic system was extended in the mid-1960s, from having been to the end of elementary school, to the end of grade 10 (roughly, the official school leaving age of 16), and, in June 1984, to the end of high school. Both enlargements caused considerable public discussion.

Bernard Shapiro, in The Report of the Commission on Private Schools in Ontario, documents the protests, including court proceedings, that have been launched by the Associated Hebrew Schools and other religious schools against discriminatory funding. He notes that "While the Jewish population rejected the Christian hue of the public schools, and Catholics revolted against a perceived Protestant bias, more fundamentalist Christian groups charged that the public school system had become too secular. They wanted schooling for their children firmly grounded in fundamentalist Christian values" (1985, 201).

Some people believe continuation of tax-supported confessional schools fans prejudice, retards the assimilation of cultural groups whose religious identity is strong, and is expensive because of duplicated services. Supporters invoke Canada's multicultural tradition, pointing out that, historically, separate schools have protected minorities in some provinces, and claim that competing systems spur each other to better performance.[5]

THE LANGUAGE OF INSTRUCTION ISSUE

In provinces such as Quebec, New Brunswick, Nova Scotia, Ontario, and Manitoba, the alternatives in public schooling are also cut along language lines. Historically, most francophone schools were Catholic and most anglophone schools Protestant (an exception was the Catholic schools in Ontario, partly created to serve Irish immigrants and guaranteed in the British North America Act as a tradeoff for the guarantee of anglophone Protestant schools in Quebec). Historically, too, the question of the language of instruction has been a contentious one in Canada. Manitoba, for instance, joined Confederation as a bilingual province, with guarantees for both English- and French-language schools, but in 1890, after two decades of controversy, the government set English as the sole language of instruction.[6]

Today the situation is more complex, but the question of the language of instruction still creates storms. As we noted in the chapter on minorities, parts of Quebec's series of language laws have been aimed at reducing the number of children, especially immigrant children, eligible for the English-language schools. Ontario boards, public and separate (Catholic), offer French schools "where numbers warrant"; the interpretation of that phrase and demands for separate (francophone) facilities as well as curricula have split several communities and have given rise to litigation. Controversy has also erupted in some New Brunswick and Nova Scotia communities. On the other hand, in recent years, French immersion classes have proved enormously popular with middle-class anglophone families, even in such nonfrancophone cities as Calgary and Vancouver.

The vehemence with which people fight for and against schools that are confessional and/or taught in a minority language suggests they well understand that schools are engaged in passing on values (Olson & Burns, 1983).

In Chapter 6, we discussed the systemic discrimination experienced by native peoples. The methods used to acculturate native children by means of the educational system is a good example of systemic discrimination. One of the most effective ways of stripping the children of their native culture was to prevent them from speaking their own language at school. They received severe corporal punishment for doing so, even in the playground. Students who attended residential schools entered a foreign environment that extended beyond the hours of instruction; they were required to abandon their native language altogether. Not surprisingly, they were ill-equipped to function in their native language upon returning to their communities. (For a discussion of native education, see Assembly of First Nations [1988].)

EDUCATION FOR EXCEPTIONAL CHILDREN

The situation of exceptional children highlights both the fatefulness of where one grows up and the limitations of public education. Mass education systems are primarily geared to educating the average child. Schools in regions low in funds or numbers have fewer facilities to diagnose and teach gifted children or children with learning disabilities, emotional disorders, and physical or mental disabilities.

Efforts are made to help many of these children. Ontario's Bill 82, passed in 1982, required that each child be provided with an adequate education, regardless of exceptional qualities. This well-intentioned law ignores two problems. First, "adequacy" may be defined differently by varying interest groups—for example, by the parents of a multi-disabled student and by the local school board. Second, even minimal implementation requires the availability of a cadre of experts, such as psychologists, psychometrists, social workers, and special teachers. Hence the program is bound to be more manageable and more accessible in Toronto, Hamilton, and Ottawa than in remote northern communities.

In the less populous and poorer provinces, exceptional children are unlikely to do well. For instance, a child with a reading disability may be labelled "retarded." Such a classification can set in motion a self-fulfilling prophecy: teachers gear down their expectations and efforts, and the child comes to think of himself or herself as dull and performs accordingly. However, it must be remembered that we are talking about probability: a learning-disabled child may not be diagnosed in a highly sophisticated school system, whereas such a disability may be noticed by an alert teacher in a small country school.

INDEPENDENT SCHOOLS

Expensive private or independent schools have traditionally catered to a minuscule proportion of the Canadian population, yet they have played an important part in shaping our country in their role of socializing the future members of its elite. For, as Porter (1965), Clement (1975), and numerous other analysts of Canadian society have pointed out: private school graduates are overrepresented in this country's key economic, professional, and political positions.

In his review of the history of private schools in Ontario, Stamp (1984) identified three periods of private schooling: 1) 1780–1850, schools of necessity; 2) 1850–1900, schools of privilege; and 3) 1960–1980, schools of protest. While privilege remains a feature of many contemporary independent schools, protest has undoubtedly contributed to their expansion in recent years.

During recent years, enrolment in private schools has grown significantly, even as the overall school-age population has decreased. From 1982/83 to 1992/93, enrolment increased by 15 percent, while that of the public schools increased by only 5 percent (DeMont, 1993). Ontario witnessed a 17 percent jump in private school enrolment between 1988 and 1993, a period when public school enrolment increased by only 8 percent (Daly, 1993).

Several factors have contributed to this development. In the 1960s and 1970s, the American civil rights movement, the women's liberation movement, and the student movement both reflected and heightened the urge to cast off traditional restraints. As we have noted, "open" schools became geared to providing "self-actualization" for the individual student, rather than adhering to standard curricula. Discipline became more relaxed, and teachers assumed the guise of "resource persons" rather than authority figures. Parents who were dissatisfied with the education their children were receiving as a result of these changes and who could afford to do so opted to send their children to those independent schools that were slower to institute such changes, in part because these schools had to be responsive to the generally conservative leanings of their boards of governors.[7]

In the 1990s, parents choosing to send their children to independent schools stress such advantages as codes of behaviour, mandatory core subjects, enforcement of compulsory attendance, uniforms, small-sized classrooms, and, above all, the strong emphasis on academic achievement that often means better labour market opportunities (Crawford, 1993). The growing concern about violence in large urban and suburban public schools may be another explanation for the increase in private school enrolment. In one survey of delegates from women's guilds attached to thirteen independent schools in Ontario, all the respondents listed academic achievement as a prime reason for sending their children to such schools. The belief that independent schools enforced stricter behavioural standards and were "character-building" also ranked as important motives. Almost 40 percent of the respondents reported no prior association with a private school among their immediate kin. The push of dissatisfaction with public education and the perceived advantages of private schools had induced them to enrol their children in the latter (Lundy, 1982).

Some American findings have shown that private and religious schools are more successful in increasing student achievement. Likewise, in Quebec, where private school enrolment as a percentage of total enrolment remains the highest in Canada, achievement in the public system is consistently lower than in the private schools (Economic Council of Canada, 1992, 13). These findings must be interpreted with caution, however, given the incontrovertible evidence concerning the impact of family background on students' academic performance, which is a good example of advantages compounding advantages.

In Minnesota, a voucher-type arrangement has been established that allows entire schools to opt out of the public system and apply directly to the state for funding. Alberta, British Columbia, and Manitoba currently have legislation in place to provide public funding to independent schools, giving parents greater freedom to choose schools outside of the public system. Some explicit differentiation exists within the public school system itself. In certain places, what have been called "magnet schools" within the public school system itself have taken on some of the elite features of independent schools. Metropolitan Toronto, for example, has public schools that specialize in such things as the arts, or space science. West Humber Collegiate chose to distinguish itself from others by becoming "green," that is, developing a focus on environmental issues. The school reports that, since the inception of its specialized orientation, absenteeism and vandalism have markedly decreased, and the honour roll has expanded.

How Much Choice?

Arguments for granting parents and children greater freedom to choose from all the schools within the public system are frequently advanced, and critics are quick to point out the dangers of such a market-based proposal. How would it influence equality of opportunity and equality of condition? Box 10.2 provides a list of some of the advantages and disadvantages of this freedom, as perceived by the Economic Council of Canada, and raises questions about the viability of allowing greater choice.

POST-SECONDARY EDUCATION

In our discussion of the functions education performs for society, we noted that it creates, maintains, and expands the pool of expertise on which the society can draw. As Canadian society has become more highly industrialized and urbanized, an increased percentage of the labour force has moved to the professional, technical, and administrative sectors. This shift has occurred in

BOX 10.2

CHOOSING THE SCHOOL OF ONE'S PREFERENCE

In many countries, there is increasing support for allowing students and parents to choose their school within the public system. A payment from the appropriate educational authority, determined by a formula, would allow the student to attend the school of choice. The school would be free to spend the resulting budget as it pleases. Such a system would attempt to simulate the behaviour of the market in an industry presently characterized as quasi-monopolistic.

Advantages

- Parents and students could express their preference and their view of the quality of schools.
- Currently, such preferences are expressed by well-to-do parents who choose to buy or rent housing in areas with good schools or send their children to private schools. The proposed system would extend this freedom of choice to the less well-off.
- It would force the good schools to maintain—and the less good ones, to upgrade—the quality of instruction.
- It would encourage schools to develop a set of values—the school ethos—conducive to learning.

Disadvantages

- Good schools would attract strong students—and weak schools, the weaker students—hereby widening disparities in school quality.

- Areas with a low tax base could not compete for resources, unless given additional funds by the financing authorities.
- It is the weak student who needs the most resources.
- The community ties fostered by the common school would be loosened.

Problems

- In case of freedom of choice, should the payment follow the child to private schools?
- If a school proves particularly popular, will the central authorities provide the funds needed for expansion? Conversely, will the authorities allow particularly weak schools to go bankrupt?
- Will the authorities allow new schools to enter the system?
- Is there much justification for freedom of choice if a commom curriculum is imposed?
- Can decentralized schools operate in a freedom-of-choice environment as long as the salaries of teachers are set by collective bargaining, involving a strongly centralized union?
- Unless a central authority provides the correct information, how could parents make an appropriate choice among schools?
- Should schools that take less-able or socially disadvantaged children receive higher payments?

Source: Economic Council of Canada, A Lot to Learn: Education and Training in Canada *(Ottawa: Minister of Supply and Service Canada, 1992).*

conjunction with the explosive growth of post-secondary institutions since the end of the Second World War.

The growth was fuelled by the confluence of several trends. Economists and social scientists were calling for investment in human resources to ensure continued prosperity and technological advancement. The baby boom cohorts were passing through the school system, looking to further education as a means to the good life. The federal and provincial governments, riding a buoyant economy, made available scholarships, student grants, and loans to broaden access to post-secondary education. As noted earlier, they also provided capital funding for colleges and new universities, and increased operating grants. Academics were recruited from the United States and Britain to staff the expanded system.

EXHIBIT 10.5

Full-Time Post-Secondary Enrolment, Canada, by Level, 1951–52 to 1991–92

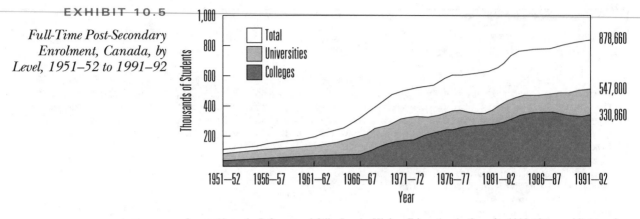

Source: Alexander D. Gregor and Gilles Jasmin, Higher Education in Canada, 1992 *(Ottawa: Minister of Supply and Services Canada, 1992).*

Exhibit 10.5 shows the upward swing in enrolments that persisted even after the baby boom generation had passed through the system.

In 1961, 7.5 percent of Canadians aged 18 to 24 were enrolled in university programs; among females, the percentage was 3.9, compared with 11.2 percent among males. By 1982, overall participation had increased to 12.8 percent, and the difference between males and females had shrunk to two percentage points—13.8 compared with 11.8 percent (Council of Ontario Universities, 1983). Much of the overall increase, then, is the result of the much higher participation of women. As Exhibit 10.6 shows, the numbers of women as a proportion of students enrolled in post-secondary education at the college level have exceeded those of men since 1975. At the undergraduate university level, the proportion was greater than that of men by 1990. It is only at the M.A. and Ph.D. levels of study that they remain a minority. In 1990, 46 percent of masters' degrees and 31 percent of doctoral degrees were awarded to women (Guppy & Arai, 1993).

Part-time students, too, have played a large part in bolstering university enrolments. Between 1962–63 and 1982–83, their number increased from 11,904 to 87,155—a rise of 632.1 percent. During the same period, full-time enrolment increased by 447.9 percent (Statistics Canada, 1984). In 1987, overall part-time enrolment was 286,207, with the overwhelming majority of these students at the undergraduate level. Part-time students now constitute 37 percent of the population enrolled in post-secondary education at both the university and community college levels (Statistics Canada, 1992). Shorter working hours, smaller families, awareness of the importance of advanced education, and the desire to utilize opportunities that may not have been previously open to individuals jointly created this trend.

It is important to remember that broad-range statistics, such as those documenting changes in overall university enrolment, may conceal important information about the groups that comprise the total. In this case, the new constituencies of women and part-time students account for a significant proportion of increased university enrolment; full-time male enrolment has increased only slightly.

EXHIBIT 10.6

Full-Time Post-Secondary Enrolment, Canada, by Level and Sex, 1975–1990

Number of Full-Time Students

	College Level*	Undergraduates	Master's	Doctorate
FEMALES				
1975	114,011	139,987	7,385	2,215
1980	133,008	155,554	10,292	2,975
1985	165,654	201,623	13,857	4,476
1990	176,380	244,946	16,133	6,322
MALES				
1975	112,150	188,837	16,158	7,055
1980	127,753	182,398	15,510	6,972
1985	156,558	210,794	18,087	9,025
1990	148,170	220,146	19,527	12,041

Proportion of Female Students

	College Level*	Undergraduates	Master's	Doctorate
1975	50.4%	42.6%	31.4%	23.9%
1980	51.0	46.0	39.9	29.9
1985	51.4	48.9	43.4	33.2
1990	54.3	52.7	45.2	34.4

*College enrolment data not available by sex for 1975.
Data are for that of 1976.

Source: Statistics Canada. Special tabulations produced for the Department of the Secretary of State of Canada. Profile of Higher Education in Canada, *1990 edition*, Table 107.

One of the fundamental goals of universities is to promote free enquiry. As they have become more vulnerable due to tighter government purses, and as governments have increasingly looked to them for solutions to problems in the economy, their links with the corporate sector have increased. Critics such as Newson and Buchbinder (1988) argue that this growing service orientation poses threats to free enquiry and jeopardizes the important scientific norm of openness. In the competitive world of corporations, the findings generated by research that has been sponsored are viewed as precious private property, and thus are likely to be shielded from the scientific community in general.

Faith in the economic credo that "more is better" can also give priority to the development of technologies that have an immediate application, thus setting the research agendas of universities in the direction of applied, rather than basic, science. Levin and Dennison show that community colleges are also becoming more entrepreneurial in the context of increased direction from government and reduced fiscal support. Their examination of changes in the direction taken by community colleges (which, it must be emphasized, are not a homogeneous group), leads them to conclude that, "rather than being driven by a desire to raise the quality of college education or ... by a commitment to improve teaching, changes brought about by the various adaptations seem to be the products of economic necessity ..." (1989, 54).

ILLITERACY AND ITS COSTS

How serious a problem is illiteracy in Canada today? The widely publicized Southam Literacy Report of 1987 brought the bad news that 24 percent of the population over 18 years of age is illiterate. The researchers used the term "illiterate" to refer to two types of people: (1) basic illiterates, that is, adult Canadians who can barely read and write; and (2) functional illiterates, that is, those whose writing and numeracy skills are insufficient to get by in everyday life. The portion of respondents that fell into the first category was 8 percent, while 16 percent were found to be functionally illiterate. Respondents had to give correct answers to eight of the ten questions to be categorized as literate, with "correctness" determined by a panel of jurors. The items ranged from reading instructions on a cough syrup bottle to answering a question on the Charter of Rights and Freedoms.

Education is the most important factor affecting literacy, but it does not guarantee it. As might be expected, the survey showed that the incidence of illiteracy decreases as the level of schooling increases: 55 percent for those with no secondary school education, 24 percent for high-school drop-outs, 17 percent for high-school graduates, and 8 percent for university graduates. Contrary to expectation, however, Canadians in the 21-to-25-year-old age bracket per-

Illiteracy is a serious problem in Canada today, and brings both tangible and intangible penalties to those who are illiterate.

Frontier College.

form at a slightly lower level than Americans in the same age group who responded to the same survey, developed in the United States by the National Assessment for Educational Progress.

Poverty and illiteracy are closely linked. People with literacy problems are twice as likely as other adults to be unemployed, and are much more likely to be receiving social assistance. Many find it difficult to gain entry to job-training programs because of their deficiencies (National Anti-Poverty Organization, 1992).

The Statistics Canada Survey of Literary Skills of 1989 confirmed this grim picture, finding that approximately 38 percent of Canadians cannot meet everyday reading demands. More than 28 percent of the youngest group surveyed, who were aged 16 to 24, fell below the everyday reading level, while 44 percent could not meet the numeracy requirements (Economic Council of Canada, 1992). The council warned:

> If these figures do not improve, our school system will produce well over *one million* new functional illiterates over the next 10 years. This is a most alarming prospect, and the *first priority* must be to prevent it. It is unacceptable that after nine years of schooling and at the age when they are legally able to enter the labour force, so many Canadians cannot meet the very modest requirements of the Statistics Canada survey (1992, 8).

The costs of illiteracy can be assessed both for the society (untapped potential, less accumulation of cultural capital, lowered productivity) and for those who are illiterate. Modern societies are oriented to written communications of many kinds, from highway signs to government forms, so illiteracy entails both tangible and intangible penalties for the collectivity and for the individual. In the United States, concerns about literacy arose when it was discovered that nearly one quarter of American soldiers lacked sufficient literacy and numeracy skills. The inference was also made that a large proportion of the American public would thus be immune to the propaganda broadcast by newspapers and billboards.

For the individual who is illiterate, how can he or she find and keep a job, and how much is the job likely to pay? How does one fill out the form for a tax credit? Feelings of isolation, shame, and inadequacy make acknowledgment of illiteracy difficult and the possibility of help remote. Among immigrants, women who are homebound or work in immigrant job ghettos often have the fewest opportunities to learn English, let alone to acquire literacy skills in the language. The journal *Canadian Woman Studies* devoted one of its issues to the topic of women and literacy (see the Suggested Readings). Many of the articles emphasize the important consequences that the acquisition of literacy can have for women, enabling them to acquire self-esteem, to leave abusive relationships, and to find better work.

DROPPING OUT

While dropping out of school occurs far less frequently now than it did earlier in this century, its occurrence today occasions greater alarm. It is estimated that approximately one-third of Canadian students presently do not complete high school. A 1991 survey, based on self-reporting, found that Quebec had the highest rate of school leaving, while Alberta and Saskatchewan had the lowest (Statistics Canada, 1991). Concern about this phenomenon arises on at least three counts. First, the social and economic costs are perceived to be great. High drop-out rates signify a waste of human capital. Second, it has been well documented that the personal costs are substantial, since dropping out is a route to dead-end jobs and unemployment. Exhibit 10.3 shows the powerful effect that level of education has on unemployment. Early leavers are likely to be the most disadvantaged segment of the youth population (Ashton & Lowe, 1991). In addition, drop-outs are seen to be rejecting the North American norm of contest mobility. The fact that those who leave school prematurely are overwhelmingly from lower socioeconomic backgrounds draws attention to the weaknesses of a system that emphasizes mass participation and purports to be meritocratic (Tanner, 1990, 109).

As the drop-out levels created increasing alarm throughout the 1980s, the search was on for explanations (Radwanski, 1987). Did the fault lie with the educational system itself or the backgrounds of those who left it? And if the background variables could be identified, what were the processes by which they actually came to be translated into drop-out rates? In Britain, where the concerns were also great, Willis (1978) studied the culture of "the lads" in working-class schools to explain their resistance to schooling, and their rejection of the norms of achievement and mobility. His research was a departure from the classical Marxist position in that he did not merely take it for granted that their material existence inevitably imposed failure on them. Using a qualitative methodology, he sought to document the processes by which they actively participated in creating and sustaining a subculture that runs counter to the values represented by education. Why did they choose to leave school for low-paying, unskilled jobs when school would seem to offer them the opportunity to do better? Did the failure lie with the teachers? Willis found his answer in the machismo, the sexist attitude that they brought with them to school from their working-class background, one that prized physical strength and manual labour, and despised book learning as effete and useless. Rejection of schooling, to them, represented a positive choice, not failure, since it promised autonomy and the freedom so lacking in the controlling and alienating environment of the school.

Willis's study inspired other research on working-class counterculture and its relation to school resistance. Subsequent findings suggest that the world of working-class adolescents is much more pluralistic than Willis supposes, and that, even in Britain, the world he described is becoming obsolete due to the massive decline in manual jobs in the manufacturing sector. Taking Willis's study as a point of departure, Tanner (1991) investigated the views of school and work held by drop-outs from high schools in Edmonton. He found that the young people he interviewed, while having rejected school, had not rejected the advantages that schooling brings.[8] Tanner argues that the label "drop-out" conceals basic similarities in values between those who stay in school and those who do not. The Canadian students had only abandoned a particular school experience; they had not given up on the work ethic and on their occupational ambitions. They also had not discarded the belief that upward mobility is both possible and desirable.

The Edmonton students had varied motives for dropping out, but the reasons given as most important had little to do with their family and community backgrounds. Their quarrel was with the schools themselves. Some, who had been performing poorly, were encouraged by school counsellors to leave. Some had negative experiences with teachers. Others, like Crysdale's (1991) students in a Toronto working-class neighbourhood, could not see the relevance of the curriculum as preparation for their future participation in the workforce, and chafed under the restrictive and authoritarian structure of the classroom. There were students who felt out of place in the peer culture of their school. One female respondent explained why she had left an affluent and prestigious school:

> Ah, 'cause I wasn't enjoying myself, I wasn't having fun there, I didn't really fit into that kind of group 'cause at 'Mac' people were one way or the other. The major people that I knew there were very rich and very full of themselves. If you weren't part of this group and didn't know these people, they wouldn't speak to you. They're all snobs, I was shocked because they were all so snotty. There's just no way you can get in with them unless all of a sudden you come into a lot of money. They judge you by what you wear and how you talk and what your parents do for a living and I felt I didn't have to justify myself to anyone. I didn't appreciate them at all (Tanner, 1991, 86).

After dropping out, however, the experience of unemployment and of miserable jobs induced a large portion of these young people to re-evaluate the advantages of an education. Almost 70 percent of them expressed a wish to seek further education, although many made it clear that they would look for an alternative to high school, such as trade-related training, correspondence courses, or vocational colleges.

The School Leavers Survey conducted by Statistics Canada in 1991 (Gilbert et al., 1993) was an attempt to untangle the economic, social, cultural, and personal factors that may contribute to dropping out of school. It also compared the labour market experiences and quality of life of school leavers with those who had completed high school. The survey found that approximately one in five respondents of both sexes cited "boredom" as the most important reason for leaving school. However, there were also some gender differences. Only one in ten females reported "preferring work to school" as the most important reason for leaving, while one-quarter of the males gave this reason. Females more often cited "problems with school work" (12.5 percent) and "pregnancy/marriage" (9 percent). Over 31 percent of drop-outs reported having had averages of A or B while in secondary school; approximately 10 percent reported Ds or Fs. An interesting finding that calls for further exploration was that many drop-outs reported having failed a grade in elementary school. Did they drop out because they were then labelled as "poor achievers" in their subsequent years of schooling, or did they leave because they themselves carried with them a debilitating lack of self-esteem?

These studies suggest that school experience is an important mediating factor between socioeconomic background and educational outcome, and that we need to know a great deal more about what transpires in school itself. Why do some flee the system, while 70 percent do not, even though almost all subscribe to the idea that education is of crucial importance to a satisfactory life?

TRANSITIONS: EDUCATION, TRAINING, AND EMPLOYMENT

Unlike countries such as Germany, Japan, and Sweden, Canada does not provide a structured transition from school to work, with straightforward paths from educational programs in the schools to niches in the occupational order. In Canada, the transition tends to be a haphazard and highly individualized process (Jones et al., 1990), one that can be prolonged and circuitous. It is too simplistic, then, to think in terms of a linear school-to-work model in Canada: to speak of "transitions" instead of "the transition" is more apt.

Thomas (1993) argues that a great many contemporary realities have to be ignored if we focus only on the passage from formal, full-time schooling to full-time employment. There is an ever-increasing flow of traffic back and forth between educational and vocational programs and the labour market, and, in a growing proportion of cases, work and study are taking place concurrently, for example in co-op programs. As well, learning takes place in a variety of contexts that do not fall under the heading "formal education." "Informal learning," for example, describes all of those self-directed activities that we undertake outside of the authority or requirements of any educational institution. In between, there is "nonformal learning," referring to all of the other educational activities carried out by any social agency, and offered mainly to adults on a part-time basis (Livingstone, 1993). Livingstone notes that the distinctions between these three types of learning are becoming blurred:

> Self-directed learning projects increasingly involve standardized packages of learning materials designed and sold by large corporations. Both high school and post-secondary formal educational institutions are more attentive to mature part-time credit students who are the major growth potential in their enrolments. From the vantage points of both independent adult learners and formal education authorities, there is clearly a growing attraction to rely on expanding non-formal programs to address lifelong learning needs (1993, 93).

A flexible culture of "lifelong learning" requires that bridges be built among the various types of learning described above. Thomas (1993) argues that ways must be found to give recognition to uncredentialed learning, so that people can move more easily into formal programs. How does one assess the value of uncredentialed learning, and does its acceptance pose serious threats to academic standards? These are questions that are now being pursued in research, for example, at the Ontario Institute for Studies in Education.

While Canada has a strong "education culture," it lacks a strong "training culture." Historically, Canada has relied heavily on immigration to fulfil its skilled labour force needs. The absence of an apprenticeship system as the main form of occupational socialization has meant that vocational education

While Canada has a strong "education culture," it lacks a strong "training culture." However, increasing numbers of people must be retrained if they are to keep their job or find another one.

Courtesy International Business Machines Corporation.

has been incorporated into the curriculum and organization of the educational system, particularly in high schools and the community colleges (see Ashton & Lowe [1992] for an interesting comparison of the situations in Canada and Great Britain). For one thing, vocational training is held in low esteem by parents and students alike. While every province except Newfoundland has vocational training at the secondary school level, only 10 percent of students are enrolled in them (Economic Council of Canada, 1992, 18). The private sector takes very little responsibility for training that is not of the brief, on-the-job sort to prepare workers to carry out specific tasks. Private industry in the United States spends roughly twice that of Canadian industry on training. The Japanese investment is over five times that of Canada's, and Germany spends almost eight times more (Government of Canada, 1991, 6).

A patchwork of government training programs has emerged as short-term ad hoc responses to crises in the economy rather than being conceived as attempts to structure training opportunities in a systematic way. Access to the programs that do exist has been shown to disadvantage women, native peoples, older workers, and ethnic minorities, the very people who are most in need of them. One recent report noted:

> Many undereducated individuals are excluded not by formal entrance requirements, but by training program tendencies to "cream"—to select the "best" candidates so that programs can demonstrate high success. This particularly applies to courses of short duration. One social service job-training referral manual we saw, for instance, suggested that referrals would be successful if the referee had at

least a Grade 10-level education and only a small family (National Anti-Poverty Organization, 1992, 84).

It is sometimes also the case that courses do not coincide with the needs of the community in which they are given. For example, in Arviat, in the Northwest Territories, carpentry training courses were offered in the summer, which is the only time seasonal work is available, and ended in November, when there is little opportunity for employment. Costs are another barrier. For many people, attending courses involves extra expenses such as transportation and child-care costs. Often, training allowances are so low that lone mothers may fare better on social assistance. This is especially true if, by taking the training, they risk losing the dental and drug benefits provided under social assistance programs (National Anti-Poverty Organization, 1992, 85).

The changing demographic situation, with fewer young people entering the labour market (see Exhibit 10.7), means that youths will not by themselves be able to provide the economy with the skills that are required. Therefore, there will be an increasing need for people in the workforce to be retrained.

EXHIBIT 10.7

Youth (Aged 15–24) Share of the Labour Force, 1966–2000

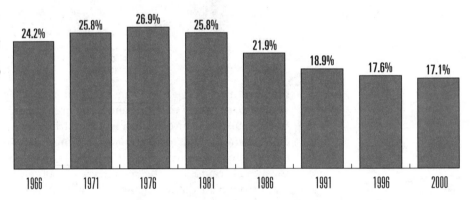

Source: Statistics Canada, Historical Labour Force Statistics *(1988) and* Employment and Immigration Canada *(1989). Reproduced by authority of the Minister of Industry 1994.*

What kind of training will they need? What will employers want? The answer is not clear. Jackson (1988) found that the private sector frequently calls for workers who have a more general than specific education, along with human relations skills, communication skills, and good problem solving abilities. On the other hand, when they are asked to describe the skills they demand for a specific position, they generally fall back on the very specific, often low-level, competencies that the job description sets out. These mixed messages from industry—the emphasis on general education, on the one hand, and the actual underutilization of skills on the other—make it difficult for individuals to make sensible decisions about education and training, and means that planning at the institutional level occurs in a context of ambiguity (The Centre for Policy Studies in Education, University of British Columbia, 1993).

. . . .

OVERVIEW

The establishment of mass compulsory education was envisaged as a means of ensuring a "prosperous democracy" by preparing the young for citizenship and for participation in a differentiated and hierarchical labour force. Equal opportunity would be provided so that individuals could develop their full potential and compete for the privileges that society had to offer. Education would also serve to reduce social inequality.

Among the industrialized nations, Canadians enjoy a level of educational attainment second only to that of Americans. However, it is clear that children do not benefit equally from schooling. Class, gender, ethnicity, and geographical location exert an influence on the kind of educational experience individuals will have, and on what credentials they will obtain. Different theoretical perspectives can prompt very different explanations as to why this is so.

Functionalists tend to accept that equal opportunity exists. Unequal outcomes can generally be explained by the different kinds of socialization processes that children experience at home. Thus, they come to school differently motivated and differently equipped to benefit from their education.

In the Marxist perspective, the education system has no autonomy; rather, it changes and expands in response to the changing needs of the capitalist economy. Marxists argue that there is a fundamental contradiction between the goal of developing each student's potential and the goal of preparing students for the labour market. The ideology of equal opportunity serves to legitimate the sorting and selecting in which schools engage, and masks the fact that unequal schooling is provided. A logical conclusion of the mechanistic view that schools merely replicate the existing social structure is that educational reform alone is impotent to bring about greater social equality.

Ethnographic research, with its close scrutiny of the internal life of schools, helps us to understand those processes, often banal, routine, and unrecognized, by which the education system perpetuates inequality. In this approach, social actors in the education system are not at the mercy of forces beyond their control. Feminist scholars have also been closely examining classroom practices in order to gain more understanding of the ways in which the ideologies of masculinity and femininity become entrenched. Feminists argue that education can be a transformative experience only if students are helped to develop their critical skills so that they can reflect on, and challenge, prevailing social relations.

In Canada, the organization of education is decentralized and complex; there are also pronounced regional disparities in the degree of resources. The transition from school to employment is unstructured, haphazard, and circuitous. Canada does not have a strong training culture. Demographic change, technological change, and the rapid transformation of work require that more emphasis be placed on lifelong learning and multiple transitions.

ASSIGNMENTS

1. Read Benjamin Levin's article, "Low Tuition Fees are Not the Answer," in *Policy Options* 13(1992):7, 10–12. Using one or more of the theoretical approaches discussed in this chapter, evaluate his argument that low tuition fees do not increase accessibility and that higher fees would not decrease it. Do you agree with his solutions to the problems of accessibility?

2. Using Andrew Nikiforuk's article (see Box 10.1) and some of the concepts discussed in this chapter, make a case for or against extending the school year in Canada.

3. Make a case for or against single-sex classrooms. You might start with Linda Eyre's paper, "Gender Relations in the Classrooms: A Fresh Look at Coeducation," in Gaskell and Tigar McLaren (1991, 119–219).

SUGGESTED READINGS

Paul Anisef and Paul Axelrod, eds., *Transitions, Schooling and Employment in Canada* (Toronto: Thompson Educational Publishing, 1993). Here you will find very recent Canadian research that examines the complex linkages between the educational system and the labour market. How does the transition from school to work typically occur in Canada? The papers present a picture of multiple transitions that vary substantially for different categories of people. Such factors as ethnicity, region, and rural/urban location have an impact on students' aspirations, on their experiences and, most definitely, on their opportunities.

Canadian Woman Studies/les cahiers de la femme, *Women and Literacy* (vol. 9, nos. 3 and 4, Fall/Winter 1988). This issue will give you an understanding of the experiences of women, in various parts of the world, who are disadvantaged by their inability to read and write. The articles also describe some of the imaginative programs, often linked to other services, that have been designed to help women acquire the literacy skills they need for a more independent life. Many programs in Canada have been influenced by the writings of Paulo Freire, and by work carried out in the Third World, such as the Nicaraguan literacy crusade.

Commission on Excellence in Education, *To Live and Learn: The Challenge of Education and Training* (Fredericton: Government of New Brunswick, 1993). This report is a good example of the ways in which the role of education and training is being defined in specific provincial contexts. The report encompasses all forms of learning: the institutional and extramural schools, colleges and universities, and also literacy programs, labour-market training, and other forms of lifelong learning. Is it possible to build a coherent system that will serve the needs of individuals and also the provincial economy? If you are more interested in the West, see, for example, the Manitoba Department of Education and Training's, *Partners in Skills Development: The Report of the Skills Training Advisory Committee*

(Winnipeg: Department of Education and Training, 1990), or, by the Province of British Columbia, *A Legacy for Learners* (Victoria: Province of British Columbia, 1988).

Paulo Freire, *Pedagogy of the Oppressed* (Harmondsworth: Penguin Books, 1972). This is a classic argument for education as a subversive activity (as opposed to that which merely transmits information and established values). On the basis of his experience in Latin America, Freire urges that the aim of a liberating education be to create an awareness of selfhood and the capacity to view critically the social context of one's life. How else can one contemplate conditions of oppression? "Problem-posing education does not and cannot serve the interests of the oppressor. No oppressive order could permit the oppressed to begin to question: Why?"

Jane Gaskell and Arlene Tigar McLaren, eds., *Women and Education*, 2nd ed. (Calgary: Detselig Enterprises Limited, 1991). The contributors to this volume share a concern with the experiences of women as students, teachers, and mothers, and a commitment to changes in education that will bring about greater equality for women. Collectively, they provide a feminist critique of such things as the educational establishment, the gendered nature of the curriculum, the social construction of knowledge, gender relations in the classroom, and the position of women in training programs. The book is a fine example of the diversity of methodological and theoretical approaches that have allowed feminist scholars to open up new avenues of research.

Ivan Illich, *Deschooling Society* (New York: Harper and Row, 1971). Focusing on education, Illich argues that in all areas of life, individuals in modern Western societies are in danger of being swallowed up by institutions that keep growing in size and number. In his view, a great deal of learning could be acquired more cheaply and more effectively outside formal educational institutions. He also warns against the "hidden curriculum" of schools, which imbues students with conservative worldviews that entrench opposition to fundamental change. For a Marxist critique of Illich's views, see Herbert Gintis, "Towards a Political Economy of Education: A Radical Critique of Ivan Illich's *Deschooling Society*," *Harvard Educational Review* 42 (1972):1.

P. McLaren, *Cries from the Corridor* (Toronto: Methuen, 1980). The highrise dwellings along Toronto's Jane/Finch corridor contain large numbers of polyglot, low-income, and often single-parent families. In this book, McLaren describes his three-year experience as a teacher in one of the area's junior high schools, where he found that the lesson plans advocated in teachers' college did not spark the interest of streetwise kids who were his students, and who frequently came to school hungry and who might be ignored, neglected, or abused at home. The book is a plea for adapting schools to the needs of children, rather than trying to squeeze children into prefabricated slots.

Randle Nelsen, *Miseducating*: *Death of the Sensible* (Kingston, Ont.: Cedarcreek Publications, 1991). Although Nelsen pays some attention to all levels of schooling, his radical critique of education is primarily directed at what goes on in universities. He argues that the myth of the "ivory tower" obscures the close connections that have been forged between educational institutions and the power structures of society; at the same time, education *is* isolated in what he calls a "bureaucratized professionalism," far removed from that which makes sense to people in the course of their daily lives. The pedagogy he proposes aims to transform learning situations by encouraging more of the relations characteristic of primary groups and small communities, so that the gulf between professional and nonprofessional expertise can be bridged.

NOTES

1. Note that the word "clerk" is derived from "cleric."

2. For an elaboration of the analysis just discussed, see Parsons's essay "The School Class as a Social System" (1951).

3. *Toronto Star*, June 3, 1993.

4. *Toronto Star*, June 4, 1993.

5. Although the rules vary from jurisdiction to jurisdiction, a determined parent can often find ways to transfer children from one system to another, no matter what the family's religious preference.

6. Until well after the Second World War, however, some schools in francophone districts continued to provide instruction in both languages, hiding the French textbooks when provincial school inspectors were expected.

7. By contrast, some private schools pride themselves on their innovative and flexible curricula.

8. In their Project Teen Canada 92 survey, Bibby and Posterski also found a discrepancy between attitudes toward schools and recognition of the importance of education. While only 23 percent of the young people surveyed said they liked high school "very much," 41 percent saw it as "very important" for their later lives. "Pressure at school" was cited as a source of anxiety by 72 percent of them (1992, ch. 6).

Religion and Secularization

Scientists can send cameras and detection equipment through space to inspect the planets for signs of life, but they cannot send probes to test for life after death.

Rodney Stark, *Sociology*

When I went to the moon, I was as pragmatic a scientist-engineer as any of my colleagues. I'd spent more than a quarter of a century learning the rational-objective-experimental approach to dealing with the universe. But [during the Apollo 14 mission] ... I underwent a religiouslike peak experience, in which the presence of divinity became almost palpable, and I knew *that life in the universe was not just an accident based on random processes. This knowledge, which came directly, intuitively, was not a matter of logical abstraction. It was deduced not from information perceptible by the sensory organs. The realization was subjective, but it was knowledge every bit as real and compelling as the objective data the navigational program or the communications system was based on.*

Edgar D. Mitchell[1]

Each of the societal institutions we have so far examined has revealed paradoxes. For example, the family is the archetypal primary group, but for most people, it also provides an introduction to unequal power distribution, in this case among family members. Formal education can be viewed as a vehicle for reducing inequality, but the greater opportunities for advanced education enjoyed by the children of the privileged consolidate their advantaged position.

Religion also presents contradictions. It is both a very public and an intensely private thing. On the one hand, in particular circumstances, it has served to maintain, and perhaps to create, social inequality. On the other hand, it is a great leveller, providing a meeting ground for the uncertainties people share in the face of human mortality. Why do humans exist? Why is there suffering? What awaits individuals when they die? What is the basis for hope? The answers to questions of such magnitude are a matter of faith, not of scientific certitude.

Religion has traditionally provided the moral consensus necessary for social cohesion. Yet, it has also justified the persecution of minority groups, those considered "outsiders," from the early Christians who lived during the days of the Roman empire, to Jews and Protestants during the Inquisition, and to those of the Baha'i faith in the Middle East today. Religion has been a source of both continuity and change. Historically, it has played an important part in legitimating and supporting existing social orders. The doctrine that kings were God's anointed on earth and, therefore, ruled by divine right meant that insubordination to the king was the same as insubordination to God. Hence, civil disobedience was a very serious offence. On the other hand, the growing conviction among clergy and laity that the corruption of the medieval church, which this identification of king and deity led to, violated "true" religion and spurred the Protestant Reformation, which resulted in fundamental societal change. Religion has been used throughout the centuries to justify political and cultural colonization, such as western Europe's takeover of the Americas and the Arabs' sweep of the Middle East, northern Africa, and the Iberian Peninsula in the seventh and eighth centuries.

Religious fervour has fuelled conflicts, such as the English Civil War (1642–1646) and the Thirty Years' War (1618–1648) and continues to set people against each other today, in India as in Northern Ireland. At the same time, in an increasingly secular age, we are witnessing an astonishing array of new forms of religious expression and the resurgence of religious themes in social movements concerned with issues such as peace, human rights, and the protection of the environment.

There is evidence that, at least since the days of the Neanderthals, religion has been an enduring institution in all societies. However, there are vast differences in the forms of religious expression, in the substantive content of belief systems, in the social organization of religious communities, and in the relationships of religious groups to each other and to other societal institutions. Since sociologists have no more purchase on answers to questions of ultimate meaning than anyone else, they must be content with exploring these, and other, social dimensions.

RELIGION AND EARLY SOCIOLOGICAL THOUGHT

Given the important role played by religion, it is hardly surprising that early sociologists made it an object of study.[2] In the following pages, we will provide a brief overview of the ways Durkheim, Marx, and Weber looked at religion.

RELIGION AND SOCIAL COHESION

As we noted in Chapter 1, Durkheim was a functionalist in that he analyzed practices and institutions by looking at the functions they perform for the group. In his final major work, *The Elementary Forms of Religious Life* ([1912] 1954), he addressed the role of religion in human society. Because religion is known to be present in virtually all human societies, he argued, it must serve a key function in maintaining the social order. It cannot be based merely on illusion or superstition, or it would not persist in the face of the many "factual" claims made against it by science and technology.

Durkheim studied what he believed to be one of the most simple varieties of religion, the totemism found among the aboriginal peoples of Australia. There, the clans that constituted tribes were considered equal, and this equality was reflected in their religion. Although each clan had a different **totem** (an ordinary object that serves as a sacred symbol for the collectivity), all totems enjoyed equal status. By providing common sacred symbols, Durkheim argued, religion affirms the unity of the group and helps to maintain group boundaries. The emphasis on religious prescriptions and taboos sharpens the distinctions between the sacred and the profane (i.e., worldly) spheres.

The **sacred** sphere pertains to those objects and activities to which supernatural significance are attributed; that is, they are seen to be governed by a power that is outside of, and greater than, human beings. The realm of the **profane**, in contrast, is seen to be devoid of supernatural significance, not governed by a power that lies beyond human beings.

In his comparison of major religions, Durkheim shows that, while they differ markedly in terms of their beliefs and practices, they each provide for their members a set of shared beliefs and collective rituals. The root of the word "religion" is *ligio*, which means "I tie" (a cognate word is *liga*ment, which is tissue that ties muscle to bone). Durkheim's definition emphasized the tying aspect of religion:

> A religion is a unified system of beliefs and practices relative to sacred things, that is to say, things set apart and forbidden—beliefs and practices which unite, in one single moral community called a Church, all those who adhere to them ([1912] 1954, 47).

Durkheim noted that objects are inherently neither sacred nor profane. Sacredness is bestowed on them only when they are given ritual significance in group worship. The cow is sacred to Hindus but not to Christians or Moslems; a wafer of bread becomes sacred to many Christians as a symbol of Christ's body. Possession and commonality of sacred symbols are reinforced by **positive rituals**—occasions when group members gather to reaffirm their commonality, thus strengthening mechanical solidarity. Confirmation, the Hindu initiation rite,[3] and the pilgrimage to Mecca are examples of positive rituals. If such ritual occasions are no longer observed, the cohesiveness of the group and the individual's adherence to it are weakened. Therefore, most religions insist on some minimal participation and attendance. For instance, a Roman Catholic must take communion at least once a year.

Disintegrative tendencies were prevalent in nineteenth-century Europe. Durkheim realized that the old social regulators—custom, tradition, and religion—had become weakened. Insofar as the stability of the social order depended on these regulators, the social scientist's task was to find alternative foundations. Durkheim (1961) envisioned a rationally based humanistic ethic that would replace religiously based ones. In his words: "We must discover the rational substitutes for these religious notions that for a long time have served as the vehicle for the most essential moral ideas" (1961, 9).

In many ways, the modern "isms"—nationalism, communism, and fascism—have assumed religious significance. Indeed, the official opposition to

Durkheim emphasized the "binding" function performed by religion in providing a set of shared beliefs and collective rituals.

Anglican Diocese of Toronto, Archives.

traditional religion in the former Soviet Union could be seen as an attempt to eliminate all other faiths but communism. Bellah (1970) argued that the Americans had developed a "civil religion" made up of beliefs, symbols, and rituals that sanctified the American way of life and construed any other way as immoral. This is an explicit application of Durkheim's view that, through religion, society worships itself.

As we have seen, Durkheim's concern was not with how individuals experience religion but, rather, with the transcendence of self that occurs through participation in religious activities with others. By contrast, Yinger (1954) defined religion in terms of the function it provides for the individual: "a system of beliefs and practices by which people struggle with the ultimate problems of life" (1954, 358).

The satisfaction of individual needs is only one of the tasks attributed to religion by scholars who have continued to take the functionalist approach. The argument is that, whether religion is central to a society or not, it meets certain needs, both for the group and for individuals:

1. It enhances solidarity among the members of the group and supports the group's values and norms. At the microlevel, this effect is expressed by the aphorism "a family that prays together, stays together." Even in societies in which several religious groups co-exist, religion, in general, buttresses such institutions as the family and the law. Acts that are deemed undesirable, even if they do not contravene formal laws, are defined as sins. To the extent that individuals identify with a religion, its ethical content may keep them from engaging in such antisocial acts. In this way, social control is reinforced. Because societies depend

on their members' willing cooperation, such reinforcement is especially important, since it is primarily based on internalized values, rather than on external surveillance.

2. Membership in a religious group may be an integral part of individual identity. The relative importance of such membership depends on structural as well as individual variables. One structural variable is the centrality of religion in a particular society at a particular time. For the early Christians or the Huguenots of sixteenth-century France, religion was a crucial aspect of identity, since membership in these forbidden groups exposed one to the risk of torture and death. For many people in Canada today, even for those who are regular churchgoers, religion has far less impact on identity.

   Another such structural variable is the nature of the religious group itself. For the Hutterite or the Hassidic Jew, every facet of life is pervaded by religion. Distinctive clothing is a public manifestation of membership in the religious group, so the first identifier others recognize in such an individual is a religious one.

   Membership in such an all-embracing group permits little variation in personal commitment. Those who do not conform are expelled. Many other religious communities, however, permit differences in the extent to which religion impinges on personal identity. A man who attends church only for christenings, weddings, and funerals may identify himself as an engineer, a husband, a father, a Canadian, and a resident of Charlottetown before considering that he is a member of the United Church.

3. Religion provides explanations for the mysteries encountered in human existence, thus making the world more comprehensible. Often, deities or supernatural beings are endowed with human characteristics. For example, the Bible describes God's anger at the corruption of the people of Sodom and Gomorrah as if it were a father's anger toward his wayward children.

   Religion is an approach to understanding the world that requires the individual to accept certain phenomena on faith. By contrast, science seeks understanding through empirical verification. In today's secular societies, scientific activities are carried out for the most part without regard to their compatibility with faith. The late medieval and early Puritan scientists, far from treating science and religion as incompatible, saw their efforts as leading to a clearer understanding of the Lord's creation. In a study of science in seventeenth-century England, Merton quoted the physicist Robert Boyle, who left in his will the following message for the Fellows of the Royal Society:

> Wishing them also a happy success in their laudable attempts, to discover the true Nature of the Works of God; and praying that they and all other Searchers into Physical Truths, may cordially refer their Attainments to the Glory of the Great Author of Nature, and to the Comfort of Mankind" (Boyle, cited in Merton, 1968, 630).

4. The prescriptions ("thou shall") and proscriptions ("thou shall not") that underpin religion's social control provide the individual with a guide for everyday conduct. Opinions, attitudes, and actions can be justified in terms of the religious code, which establishes what is right and what is wrong. For example, a devout Catholic physician categorically excludes performing an abortion unless the pregnant woman's life is in dire peril.

5. Practical conditions change, but certain aspects of human existence do not. Everyone in every age must cope with fear and anxiety and with the inevitability of death. The belief of many religions in a life after death, in which present injustices will be corrected, makes bearable what otherwise would not be. Acceptance "that the Lord giveth and the Lord taketh away" affirms that there are happenings in the universe that are beyond human understanding but also holds out hope of an eventual reunion with loved ones.

     The persistence of religion in societies in which it is suppressed or discouraged by the state seems to indicate that it meets fundamental human needs that are not fully met by such secular belief systems as communism.

This list of the functions performed by religion is by no means exhaustive, but it is argued that these functions do meet *universal* needs of groups and individuals.

RELIGION AS THE "OPIATE OF THE MASSES"

Critics of the functionalist approach have argued that, whereas it may have been true that the small-scale societies studied by Durkheim were characterized by an extremely high level of cohesion, the same is not true for modern industrialized societies that exhibit an unequal distribution of power and social rewards. In such societies, religion has tended to serve the interests of the dominant class.

Consonant with his conception of the economy as the substructure of other societal institutions, Marx viewed established religion as legitimating a given social system. Like Durkheim, then, he recognized religion as providing a basis for social stability. However, for Marx, this stability obscured the opposing interests of those who ruled and those who were ruled. By teaching that acceptance of one's earthly fate and faithful performance of religious obligations are pleasing to God and conducive to eternal salvation, religion helps to contain potentially explosive forces. For the oppressed masses, religion becomes an "opiate" that assuages present deprivations with visions of future happiness, rendering people passive and disinclined to challenge the social order.

The view that religion is instrumental in promoting passivity is one shared by many—though not all—modern social scientists. For example, Glenn (1964) described how, for most of their history, the churches attended by blacks in the American south have served to pacify their flocks:

> The emotionalism and the strong otherworldly orientation of this traditional religion of American Negroes have made the Negroes' subordinate status more bearable. The religious services have

provided tension release, excitement and escape in an existence characterized by hardship, drudgery and vicissitudes of various kinds. The focus upon the afterlife has promised the Negro "pie in the sky by and by when you die" and has had a soporific and diversionary influence. This type of Negro religion has not encouraged efforts for the improvement of the status of the Negro in the here and now and has tended to reconcile him to an inferior status. From emancipation almost to the present, the Negro church was the main influence in orienting Negroes to the dominant white population, and there is almost unanimity among scholars of American race relations that the overall influence of the church has been more toward acquiescence and docility than toward rebelliousness and protest (1964, 629).

In his study of the textile mills that existed in North Carolina in the late nineteenth century, Pope (1942) showed how the managers and owners extended support to the local churches as a means of discouraging workers from unionizing or rebelling against their working conditions.

In the short run, such psychic relief may facilitate survival in a dehumanizing environment. Like a narcotic, religion eases the pain but does not remove its cause. In the long run, accommodation retards the struggle for change.

RELIGION AS AN AGENT OF CHANGE

Central to Weber's view of religion were two aspects of his overall theoretical stance. First, he insisted that phenomena be viewed in their historical context. Thus, he believed it essential to examine the parts played by specific religions in given societies at specific times. In this respect, Weber followed in the tradition of Marx and the school of German historical scholarship. Second, one of Weber's prime concerns was to understand the effect people's ideas had on their actions.

In tracing the rise of capitalism in England, Marx focused on the confluence of economic factors without analyzing the values underlying the behaviour that had propelled individuals to transform what had been a feudal society to one that was capitalist. Weber, on the other hand, rejected the notion that ideas are a simple reflection of material interests. He undertook a series of comparative, historical studies to determine how religious ideas had influenced earlier civilizations that had developed in relative isolation from each other, and how they were related to the rise of capitalism in western Europe.

Weber argued that, although many material preconditions for the development of capitalism had been present in India and China, Hinduism and Confucianism did not provide values supportive of its development. By contrast, ascetic Protestantism, specifically Calvinism, had an *elective affinity*, that is, a close compatibility, with a capitalistic economic orientation.

Calvinist doctrine espoused hard work in this world, "the Lord's vineyard," but it condemned luxury and any "indulgence of the flesh." Since the money earned with all this hard work could not be spent, it was reinvested, promoting technological innovation that led to greater productivity and thus freed funds for more research, further innovation, and growing productivity, in an endless, upward spiral.

In *The Protestant Ethic and the Spirit of Capitalism* (1958), Weber did not posit that Protestantism had caused capitalism, but he did address the vital role religion had played in its emergence. As Hansen notes:

> The Protestant Ethic discouraged consumption, especially of luxuries; at the same time, it unloosed the impulse to acquire. The great campaigns of the devout against the temptations of the flesh and indulgence were struggles as well against irrational spending and for rational saving. Thus capital accumulates through a compulsion to save. And from accumulated capital and the impulse to accumulate more, production escalates higher and higher. Capitalism flourishes (1976, 157).

Religious values that help to undermine one social order may provide moral justification for a succeeding one. As we have noted, ascetic Protestantism emphasized relentless labour and self-denial for the greater glory of God. The material success that ensued from this combination came to be seen as a sign of divine approval. By extension, poverty became a symbol of having failed to please God. This view served as a justification for treating the destitute punitively. In this sense, religious ideology came to be used to legitimate economic distinctions that arose under capitalism. As Birnbaum observes:

> In his later years [Weber] discussed the class basis of religion in the following terms. Religions of privileged, ruling strata emphasize this-worldly values. Members of such strata feel intrinsically worthy because of their present social positions, and their religious beliefs justify the social system that allowed them such elevation. Members of underprivileged and oppressed strata, far from feeling worthy in terms of what they are, emphasize the importance of what they will become. They emphasize otherworldly values, and their religions depict a future salvation entailing a radical transformation of society's present relationships (1953, 133).

In America, Puritanism as an organized religious influence had almost disappeared by the end of the eighteenth century. However, its tenets found their secularized embodiment in the injunctions of moralist Benjamin Franklin. He, too, equated wealth with virtue: "Industry multiplied by Frugality gives the product Wealth, which equals Virtue" (cited in Karier, 1976). Since wealth is essential to capitalist society, Franklin argued that begging was to be shunned and poverty despised. His moral maxims, such as "Time is money," appeared both in popular adult literature and in children's readers, and are familiar to us today.

ORGANIZED RELIGION AND SOCIAL CONCERNS

Historically, religious groups have helped to bring about social reform through their charitable work with the poor, the orphaned, the aged, and those disadvantaged in other ways. Religious organizations have not only provided immediate relief to the needy, but, by publicizing their plight, these groups have also aroused public concern and influenced social-welfare policies.[4] The reformist call of people associated with religious groups has often had more weight because it has invoked the higher values espoused in the society at large.

In present-day Canadian society, for example, the Jewish community is very active in the provision of social services, mainly (but by no means exclusively) to its own members. Survivors of the Holocaust and, more recently, immigrants from the former Soviet Union and from Middle Eastern countries have been assisted in becoming established, both economically and socially.

In considering the role religion has played in the process of change, it should be noted that by reducing the worst excesses of deprivation and injustice, religiously sponsored charities and reform organizations have indirectly helped to maintain a given social order by reducing pressure for revolutionary change.

The Social Gospel movement, influenced by both British and American examples, emerged in Canada in the 1890s when a number of younger Protestant laypersons and ministers, principally Methodists, Presbyterians, and Anglicans, began to argue that the church had to abandon its otherworldly orientation in favour of an active involvement in social reform. They drew attention to problems of the new industrial age, such as the health and housing of the poor, the needs of children, and the destitution of immigrants to Canada, and attracted followers from farmers' movements as well as labour reform movements. While the Social Gospel cause had conservative, middle-of-the-road, and radical adherents and, so, could have been rendered ineffectual from its diffuseness, it did succeed in influencing the development of Canadian social policy (Guest, 1980, 31–32). For example, the Lord's Day Act, enacted in 1906, restricted weekly hours of labour by granting workers Sundays off. Although the movement had run out of steam by the 1920s, it left a legacy in the political sphere with the formation of the Co-operative Commonwealth Federation in the early 1930s (the CCF party was later to become the New Democratic Party). The first leader of the CCF, J.S. Woodsworth, was a former adherent of the Social Gospel movement, and Tommy Douglas, the leader of the first provincial CCF government to assume power, was a Baptist minister. As Woodcock notes, this electoral victory was to usher in an era "when political and social issues would be constantly intermingled" (1988, 347).

The co-existence in mainstream Protestant denominations of support for the status quo through an emphasis on individualism and the promotion of change through a social gospel is also found in Catholicism. Drawing on Marxism, liberation theology, for example, strikes the radical note, calling for contemporary theology to be directed away from its traditional, individualistic focus and toward an emphasis on the social dimension of the Christian message. The Latin American version of liberation theology sprang from a combination of detailed documentation of forms of oppression, and the sociological and political analyses of these forms. Theologians transformed the term "structures of oppression" into "structures of sin." Since the Catholic Church has become compromised through its identification with the ruling class, say the liberation theologists, it must now embrace the "option for the poor," standing, like God, on the side of the poor in their struggle for social and spiritual liberation (McHugh, 1993, 337). While traditional theology gave primacy to theoretical

The Lord's Day Act of 1906 restricted weekly hours of labour by granting workers Sunday off. The issue of Sunday shopping is a source of controversy in the 1990s.

Hudson's Bay Company.

knowledge, liberation theology stresses action, or *praxis*. This action necessarily has a political nature, but it is shaped by deep religious experiences.

In Canada, the Roman Catholic Church, our largest religious organization and traditionally extremely conservative, has become increasingly involved in promoting social and political reform in recent years. A nascent sympathy for social justice causes was evident in English-Canadian Catholic support for the CCF in its early years. The Atlantic Canadian Antigonish Movement, in its promotion of consumer and producer co-ops in the Depression years and in the 1940s, is another early example, as is the radicalism of Catholic cells in Quebec during the 1960s. However, it was only in the 1970s that the elaboration of a program for social justice emerged at the national level, with the Canadian Conference of Catholic Bishops issuing strong indictments of the status quo (Hewitt, 1991). Recent examples of their explicitly critical statements, prepared by the Episcopal Commission for Social Affairs, are "Ethical Reflections on the Economic Crisis" (1987) and "Free Trade: At What Cost?" (1987). The Commission has an action orientation, engaging in social research, education, and outreach to organizations such as labour organizations, women's groups, and ecumenical organizations (Hewitt, 1991, 307).

SECULARIZATION, REVIVAL, AND INNOVATION

SACRED TO SECULAR

In Chapter 2, we noted that western societies have moved from the small, homogeneous *Gemeinschaft* to the large, heterogeneous *Gesellschaft*. One aspect of this transformation is a change from a mostly sacred orientation to one that is predominantly worldly (one that does not resort to supernatural explanations and in which religious beliefs and practices lose their influence on society). This process is generally described as **secularization**, and it tends to go hand in hand with the processes of industrialization and urbanization. Societies develop a more complex division of labour, and institutions emerge that take over the functions once performed by religion. For example, physicians assume the healing function that used to be performed by priests; scientists assume the task of interpreting natural phenomena. At the same time, morality (for example, "love thy neighbour") comes to be expressed and pursued in humanistic, rather than religious, terms. A "decent society" is seen to be possible without the integrating force of religious commitment and religious authority. Patriotism, or commitment to country, becomes one of the substitute integrating forces to provide social cohesion (Bellah, 1970). In a sacred society, there is much concern with the supernatural, and events are explained in terms of the prevailing belief system, the tenets of which cannot be questioned. Similarly, social relationships, as between ruler and ruled, or parents and children, tend to be viewed as absolute and unchallengeable. In a secular society, the supernatural is accorded far less importance; primary values are rational and utilitarian, and change and innovation are a matter of routine. The sacred orientation that prevailed in Europe during the Middle Ages meant that virtually all issues sooner or later came within the jurisdiction of the Roman Catholic Church.

Galileo's (1564–1642) claim that the earth was just one of the planets that revolved around the sun was treated, not as an empirical observation to be confirmed or denied by further research, but as a heresy that cast God's word into doubt. In Bertolt Brecht's dramatization of the episode in his play *Galileo*, one of the astronomer's accusers captures the presumed threat:

> They make heaven and earth no longer exist. No earth, for it is a star in heaven. No heaven, for it is many earths. There is no longer any difference between above and below—between the eternal and the mortal. We know we die. Now they tell us heaven will die too. It is written—there are stars, sun, moon and the earth below. But that man says the earth is a star! There are only stars! We will live to see the day when these heretics say—there are no men and animals, there are only animals, man is an animal ([1939] 1981, 39).

The minor ups and downs of daily life were also subject to sacred interpretation. In societies such as that of seventeenth-century England, misfortunes might be blamed on witches:

> It was dangerous, if you were an old woman, a beggar perhaps, of disagreeable appearance, to curse your uncharitable or unkind neighbour, or even to allow your lips and what Hannah Woolley called "that slippery glib member the tongue" to move in some possible version of a curse. For then if your neighbour suffered a loss, grief or other form of injury, you might be suspected of having caused it ... with the aid of the devil. It would be suggested either

that he had brought about the injury himself or that he had endowed
you, as his partner, with the powers to do so (Fraser, 1984, 104).

A sacred orientation held sway in rural Quebec until well into the twentieth century. The power of the Catholic Church was reinforced by its control
over the educational system and by the ethnic and religious homogeneity of the
population. Loyalty to the church was not cross-cut by other institutional loyalties, and local priests felt free to tell their parishioners what was acceptable and
unacceptable in many realms, as is evident in Hughes's excerpt from a sermon
delivered by a curé in the 1930s:

> There were races last Sunday, and there are races announced for next
> Sunday. I speak to you as Catholics. Not as to Protestants, or people
> of other religions, who can discuss, each for himself, what his minister
> says. I am not discussing. I am telling you, as your pastor and rightful
> moral leader and guide, the will of your Infallible Church. God reveals
> to His Church His Will; and His rightful representative, the Pope, and
> your bishop, and finally we, your pastors, tell you. God's
> representatives know these moral questions better than you do; it is
> their rightful prerogative, and it is for you to listen ... So, dust is blowing
> over the fields of the western provinces. [5] Generally, such things are
> the just punishment of God. Your children will beg their bread—if they
> do not live and practice what God wills (1971, 100–101).

In a secular society, there is supposed to be clear separation between
church and state. What individuals believe and whether they belong to a formal
religion or engage in religious practices are matters that do not affect their
status as citizens. In fact, questions pertaining to religious affiliation have had
to be removed from government and employment forms as contravening
human rights legislation.

At times, the separation has been breached, as was clear in the case of John
Scopes, a Tennessee schoolteacher who had been teaching Darwin's theory of
evolution, which holds that, over a very long time, the human species evolved from
a lower animal species. In 1925, Scopes was accused of violating a state statute that
made it unlawful to teach any theory that denies the story of the creation of man
as taught in the Bible, and to teach instead that man has evolved from a lower
order of animals. In a much-publicized "monkey" trial, Scopes was convicted of the
charge and fined $100, but the conviction was reversed on a technicality in order
to prevent an appeal against the law from being brought to the U.S. Supreme
Court. Not until 1968 did the Court strike down the Tennessee law, and similar
laws in Arkansas and Mississippi, on the grounds that they violated the U.S.
constitutional principle of the separation between church and state.

The Scopes trial represented the clash of two world views concerning: (1)
the context of "truth," and (2) the appropriate process by which "truth" was to
be determined. As Postman notes:

> These "fundamentalists" were neither ignorant nor indifferent to the
> benefits of science and technology. They had automobiles and elec-

tricity and machine-made clothing. They used telegraphy and radio, and among their number were men who could be called reputable scientists. They were eager to share in the largesse of the American technocracy ... What wounded them was the assault that science made on the ancient story from which their sense of moral order sprang. They lost, and lost badly ... The battle settled the issue, once and for all: in defining truth, the great narrative of inductive science takes precedence over the great narrative of Genesis, and those who do not agree must remain in an intellectual backwater (1993, 51–52).

It is interesting that with the recent resurgence of a conservative world view, creationists (those who insist on the literal truth of the biblical account of creation) have made a strong comeback, particularly in the United States but also in Canada.

What that relationship between church and state should be is an issue that is still very much alive. For a discussion of the interaction of politics and religion in many countries, see Shupe and Hadden (1988).

CHURCH AND SECT

Christianity is the overwhelmingly dominant religion in Canada. According to the 1991 census, more than 82 percent of the Canadian population belong to one of the Christian denominations (see Exhibit 11.1). This apparent homogeneity conceals great diversity, especially in the Protestant category, which subsumes such mainstream denominations as Anglicans and Presbyterians, as well as smaller groups, such as the Society of Friends (Quakers) and the Christadelphians.

One of the distinctions commonly made in studying religious organizations is between church and sect. In his book *The Social Sources of Denominationalism*, H. Richard Niebuhr (1929) set out to explain why it was that Christians had formed so many denominations instead of having only one. He found part of the answer in Max Weber's conceptual distinctions between church and sect. **Churches** have a bureaucratized structure, a hierarchy of authority, and a professional priesthood. Services are conducted by the minister or priest in a ritualized manner, with congregational participation at prescribed intervals, as in the singing of hymns and the interjection of an "amen." The prayers are quite formal, addressed to a distant deity. **Sects** are loosely organized, nonhierarchical, and rely more on lay persons for leadership. They are less intellectual in their teachings, encourage emotionalism and private mystical experiences, have a "familiar" relationship with the deity, and prefer informality and spontaneity in prayer.

Niebuhr also drew on a conflict perspective to explain the differences between church and sect. He observed that a major difference between church and sect is in the social-class base of the membership. Class conflict, then, is at the root of the denominational splits in Christianity. Members of churches tend to be from the middle and upper classes, or to have aspirations for upward mobility. As their members become more affluent, churches develop a

EXHIBIT 11.1

Canadians by Religious
Preference, 1981, 1991

	1981		1991	
	Number	% of Total	Number	% of Total
Catholic	11,402,605	47.35	12,335,255	45.70
Protestant	9,914,580	41.17	9,780,710	36.23
Eastern Orthodox	361,560	1.50	387,395	1.44
Eastern non-Christian	305,890	1.27	747,455	2.77
Jewish	296,425	1.23	318,070	1.18
Parareligious	13,450	0.05	28,155	0.10
No religious affiliation	1,783,530	7.40	3,386,365	12.54

NOTE: Any of the religions listed in the table could be separately disaggregated. A number of the denominations or religions listed under "Protestant" could possibly be otherwise classified. The Eastern Orthodox group subsumes the Greek Orthodox group and a number of National Orthodox groups, such as Antiochian Christian, Armenian, Romanian, Russian, Serbian, Ukrainian, and Orthodox, n.o.s. Historically, the terms Greek Orthodox and Eastern Orthodox are considered to be equivalent, but the latter term is used in the 1981 Census only to indicate the presence of responses to the religion question where Greek Orthodox was either not indicated or was overwritten by a more specific National Orthodox Church group. The Jewish main group is the only group that does not contain subgroups. The Eastern non-Christian main group is composed of Baha'i, Buddhist, Hindu, Islam and Sikh, as well as Confucian, Taoist, and other Eastern non-Christian. The parareligious group is the smallest of all of the main groups and contains religions such as Fourth Way, New Thought-Unity-Metaphysical and Theosophical groups. Finally, the last main group is "no religious affiliation," which combines agnostics, atheists, "no religion," and "other nonreligious."

Source: 1981 data: Statistics Canada, Cat. No. 92–912, National Theories, Population: Religion, *Vol. 1, Table 1, 1983.*
1991 data: Statistics Canada, Cat. No. 93–319, Religions in Canada, *Table 1, 1993.*
Reprinted by authority of the Minister of Industry 1994.

comfortable relationship with society. This greatly reduces their capacity to appeal to the poor—the "socially disinherited" who, by virtue of their marginality, are more oriented to the rewards promised in the life that awaits them after death. Their solution lies in breaking away from churches and forming their own organizations (sects). By strict adherence to group norms, sect members can feel part of the elect, who may be poor in material goods but are rich in spirit:

> Because the sect is lower class, its appeal rests on providing an exclusive fellowship of the elect for those who are denied access elsewhere and on supplying an ideology of escape and other-worldly salvation for those who find this world oppressive. Much of the sect's emphasis on doctrinal purity and the total ideology is designed to provide a new framework for self-evaluation for those who are evaluated so demeaningly by prevailing standards (Demerath & Hammond, 1969, 71).

Niebuhr proposed that a dynamic cycle existed: sects would eventually become denominations; these denominations would again fail to satisfy the needs of the less well-off, and this dissatisfaction would lead to the formation of new sects.

Demerath and Hammond (1969) have argued that because the sect provides the salient status for many of its members, they are willing to let it influence every aspect of their lives. A Jehovah's Witness accepts the group's ban on smoking, drinking, receiving blood transfusions, and celebrating birthdays, even the birth of Christ (Christmas).

S.D. Clark was one of the founders of sociology in English Canada. Clark was concerned with how the social disorganization of "frontiers" in Canada affected religious organization. In frontier areas, people felt alienated from the established religious organizations, and formed their own sects. However, in time, as their social position improved, their clergy became more educated; at the same time, the frontier became more like the established regions, and the sectarian orientation lost much of its appeal. In *Church and Sect in Canada*, Clark (1948) showed, for example, that with the growth of towns and the expansion of trade in the early 1800s, the Baptist restrictions on private conduct became irksome and thus unacceptable to many adherents in the Maritimes; the result was "increasing defection of Baptists to religious denominations commanding greater prestige and making fewer demands with respect to private conduct" (1948, 244). For many middle-class people, religion is one of several statuses, and the church must, therefore, permit the individual some leeway in everyday life.

Clark has also outlined differences in the ways church and sect relate to the larger society:

> The church seeks the accommodation of religious organization to the community; the welfare of society is something for which it feels responsible. The sect emphasizes the exclusiveness of religious organization; the worldly society is something evil, of no concern to the spiritually minded. While no sharp line can be drawn between the two forms of religious organization (the church always contains some of the attributes of the sect while the sect is never "pure," completely otherworldly in character), within the church the spirit of accommodation tends to dominate, within the sect the spirit of separation. It is the difference in outlook, in attitude of mind, which is so important in setting the one off from the other (1948, xii).

Johnson (1963) refined Niebuhr's typology by focusing on the dimension of tension in the relationship between religious groups and society. A church, he argues, lives with a low degree of tension; put differently, one can say that it exhibits a high degree of accommodation to society. The clergy are, for example, less likely to demonstrate against pornography or commit acts of civil disobedience. Sects, on the other hand, exhibit a high degree of tension in their relationship with society. In fact, their norms and values have sometimes been so contrary to dominant cultural values that they have been persecuted.

The process of sect formation has, as we have seen, been viewed as a response to the process of secularization. Sects represent an attempt to *revive*

Sects encourage informality and spontaneity in prayer, and attempt to revive the original meanings on which the establishment of now-worldly churches was based.

Lawrence Acland.

the original meanings on which the establishment of churches was based. But is secularization ultimately an irreversible force? Many have argued that it is, and that it can only lead to the demise of religion in an age so dominated by science and technology. How, then, can we explain the emergence of so many new religious, and quasi-religious, movements?

The work of Stark and Bainbridge has provided a new perspective in the sociology of religion. They have argued that secularization is a *self-limiting process*, that it leads, not to irreligion, but to a pronounced shift in the sources of religion. Revival (the formation of sects) is only one type of response to secularization. A very different response is the formation of **cults**, religious groups that break entirely with conventional beliefs and practices. Their characteristics are so different, in fact, that they do not lie on the same continuum as churches and sects.

CULT FORMATION: RELIGIOUS INNOVATION

Cults can be innovative in a given context either because they represent a faith imported from elsewhere (for example, Eastern religions in Canada) or because they embody new religious insights. All religions find their beginnings in cult movements. This is true of Christianity, Islam, Buddhism, and other major faiths, although it is something present-day believers are mostly unaware of. One of the reasons, perhaps, that the film *The Last Temptation of Christ* provoked angry public demonstrations in some places is that, in its representation of Jesus and "his band of crazies," it vividly portrayed the cult nature of the origins of Christianity. The term "cult" carries negative connotations in modern societies. Sensational media representations of cults, which give them publicity far out of proportion to their small numbers, serve to heighten this negative view. Newspaper headlines such as "Stalking Fundamentalist Cults on Campus" and "Cults Engaging in Campus Soul-Snatching, Opponents Say" are not rare.[6]

Cults lack structure and have loosely defined memberships. In contrast to most other religious groups, a cult is something no one is born into. It is usually headed by a **charismatic leader**, an individual whose claim to authority is based on personal qualities, rather than on her or his position in an organization. Cults tend to be fugitive things, that is, rarely lasting long, at least in their original form.

Stark and Bainbridge have done a great deal of work in the sociology of religion, both in formulating theories and in doing empirical research. In *The Future Of Religion* (1985), they hypothesized that the formation of sects would occur where church membership is still strong. On the other hand, cult membership would be high where conventional churches are weak, since cults represent a radical alternative to established churches. Findings on the correlation between church membership and the prevalence of sects and cults strongly supported their hypotheses. The ratios of cult membership to church membership are highest on the Pacific Coast, second highest in the Rocky Mountain region, and far weaker than either of these in the East.

Although Stark and Bainbridge examined whether the negative correlation between the strength of conventional religious traditions and the presence of cults holds for Canada as well as for the United States, they did not use Canadian census data to test their hypothesis. Nock (1987) replicated this part of their study using 1981 Canadian census data. His findings confirmed a high correlation between "irreligion" (expressed in the census as "no religious preference") and "cult receptivity." The latter ranges from a high in British Columbia to a low in Quebec and Newfoundland. Nock concluded that "the hypothesis that cults benefit from irreligion and apostasy from the conventional religions seems to be strongly sustained" (1987, 519).

Findings regarding "sect receptivity" are not as clear-cut. Whether this receptivity coincides with a high or low degree of irreligion varies with the nature of the sect. Nock commented:

> This part of the study is as yet tentative and incomplete. However, it does seem that the areas of greatest strength for Evangelical conversionist sects are much more widely dispersed across the general population than for cults. However, revolutionist sects, at least in Canada, tend to vary positively with cults and regions of high irreligion. This is a distinction which should be looked into more closely in the context of the United States (1987, 523).

In 1972, Campbell observed that the cult was the "Cinderella" of the family of terms in the taxonomy of religious collectivities, and that they had received little research attention. This is no longer the case. In fact, the study of cults has in many ways revived the study of religion (Robbins, 1988). Robbins says that the proliferation of exotic and esoteric cults has somewhat "anthropologised" the sociology of religion in the sense that their cultures have been the object of

Some cult movements, like Hare Krishna, provide converts with a total way of life.

Hare Krishna Temple/Toronto.

close analysis (1993, 191). Many cults emerged from the psychedelic drug culture of the 1960s. Today, the average convert is unusually well educated, with excellent career potential. It is not only the young, however, for whom cults hold appeal. "New Age" groups appear increasingly to appeal primarily to middle-aged adults (Robbins, 1988, 10).

Stark and Bainbridge (1983) propose a typology of cults. An **audience cult** is the most diffuse and least organized kind; they do not require serious commitment from their members who may, for example, gather occasionally to hear a lecture. In a **client cult**, the relationship between those who promote the cult and those who partake in it is like the relationship between therapists and patients, or consultants and clients (in fact, many therapies have cult-like characteristics). The third kind, which Stark and Bainbridge (1983) call **cult movements**, are "fully fledged religious organizations which attempt to satisfy all the religious needs of converts. Dual membership with any other faith is out. Attempts to cause social change, by converting others to membership, become central to the group agenda" (1983, 16). Some cult movements, such as the Unification Church and Hare Krishna, function much like conventional sects.

The study of new religious movements has created linkages between the sociology of religion and other areas of sociological study, such as medical sociology (via the study of alternative healing systems), the sociology of social movements, and the organization-environment perspective in the sociology of organizations. There is an increasing theoretical emphasis on power in the sociology of religion, arising both from the controversies concerning "mind control" and the observed potency of cults with respect to identity transformation, social control, and healing (Robbins, 1993, 194).

THE SLEEPING GIANT?

In his book *Fragmented Gods: The Poverty and Potential of Religion in Canada* (1987), Bibby argues that Canadian churches are like enormous multinational enterprises, engaged in an unending battle for shares of the Canadian religious marketplace. To succeed, they provide what people want: self-help groups, aerobics classes, popular liturgies, and so on. Consumer culture, he says, has given rise to consumer religion, a condition in which the church offers a little bit of everything. As a result, people have a fragmented relationship with religious bodies, still using them for special "rites of passage" such as baptisms, weddings and funerals, and otherwise receiving little from them that they cannot find in the secular culture. If this continues, Bibby predicts, the decline of the mainline churches is inevitable. However, he finds significance in the fact that the majority of Canadians do not actually desert their religious groups.

Exhibit 11.2 shows the results of a large Canadian poll taken in 1993. People who were polled were asked to compare their religious affiliation in childhood with their present situation. You will note that the largest falling away among the major denominations occurred in the Roman Catholic group, while the largest

EXHIBIT 11.2

Breaking Away

When Canadians compare their religious affiliations as children to their current associations, the fastest growing denomination is "none."

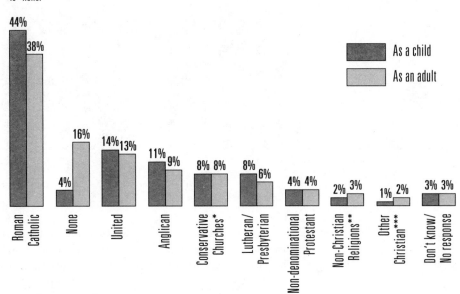

* includes Baptist, Church of Nazarene, Pentecostal, Apostolic, Mennonite, Canadian Reformed, Church of Jesus Christ of Latter-day Saints (Mormon), Seventh-day Adventist, Brethren, Plymouth Brethren, Salvation Army, Alliance, Evangelical, Methodist, Congregationalist, Wesleyan, Gospel, Worldwide Church of God, Church of Christ, born again Christian, Christian Reformed

** includes Jewish, Islamic, Hindu, Buddhist, New Age, Sikh, Spiritualist, Soka Gakki International, North American native religion, Theosophical Society, paganism, Baha'i, humanist, agnostic, Wicca, Lemurian, New Thought Movement

*** includes Orthodox, Unitarian, Jehovah's Witness, Christadelphian, Christian Scientist, Church of Scientology

Source: "The Religion Poll" (Angus Reid for George Rawlyk). Table published in Maclean's *(12 April 1993), 37. Reprinted with permission.*

change occurred in the group declaring no affiliation. The 1991 census data show that the number of persons reporting "no religion" increased by 90 percent from 1981. In the same decade, sects, cults, and various religions characterized as "para-religious groups," grew by 109 percent, although they still only account for 0.1 percent of the Canadian population (Statistics Canada, 1993).

As Exhibit 11.3 shows, there are strong regional variations in "religiosity" as measured by attending religious services on a weekly basis, praying daily, and reading the Bible or other religious writings. In all instances, it is highest in the Atlantic provinces. For Canada as a whole, the results show that considerably less than one-third of Canadians now engage in these activities.

EXHIBIT 11.3

Prayer, Attendance, and Reading: Regional Differences

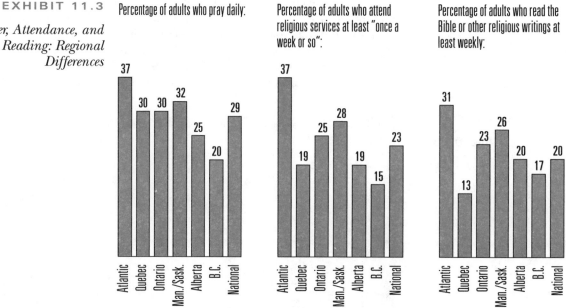

Percentage of adults who pray daily:

Percentage of adults who attend religious services at least "once a week or so":

Percentage of adults who read the Bible or other religious writings at least weekly:

Source: "The Religion Poll" (Angus Reid for George Rawlyk). Published in Maclean's *(12 April 1993), 37. Reprinted with permission.*

Bibby (1990, 192–99) argues that religion is still a powerful, but latent, force in Canadian culture, and that it is a force that the churches can tap. These organizations still command large resources, and they are still in a position to respond to the spiritual hunger that people experience. In other words, he is arguing that revival through sect formation and innovation through cult formation are not the only possible responses to secularization; rather, the churches themselves can pull up their socks and become reinvigorated.

RELIGION AND STATUS

Weber maintained that religious values influence economic conduct, as in the relationship he posited between the Protestant work ethic and the emergence of capitalism. Here, then, religion is treated as an independent (causal) variable. On the other hand, Weber also noted that members of the privileged strata tend to belong to religions that stress the values of this world, an emphasis that is useful in consolidating their position. Membership in a religious group is, therefore, a dependent variable, influenced by socio-economic status.[7]

In his study of the corporate elite, Porter (1965) noted the overrepresentation of Anglicans and Presbyterians and the underrepresentation of Catholics in this group in modern Canada.[8] Supporting data from the 1981 and 1991 censuses show the differences in educational attainment among the members of various religious groups (see Exhibit 11.4) Such statistical information does not tell us to what extent religious values influence educational attainment or whether people with given levels of education are attracted to particular religious groups. Since the majority of people are born into a religion, we can speculate that the reverse frequently occurs, that is, that religious values affect educational attainment. However, since religion may be either an ascribed or an achieved characteristic, it may be that individuals are attracted to different religions as they become more highly educated, or they may abandon religion altogether. Interestingly, the proportion of university graduates among those reporting affiliation with a para-religious group is second only to their proportion in the Jewish group. The proportion reporting no religious preference is third.

EXHIBIT 11.4

Highest Level of Schooling Attained by Canadians of Various Religious Affiliations, 1991 Census

	Total Population age 25–44 years	Less than Grade 9	Secondary School Certificate	Some Post-Secondary Education	University Degree
Anglican	691,930	3.76%	33.38%	46.0%	17.30%
Baptist	212,480	4.13	35.14	45.78	14.95
Pentecostal	143,775	7.30	38.41	46.50	7.81
Salvation Army	35,930	12.60	42.40	38.70	6.40
Roman Catholic	4,222,520	6.43	36.26	42.90	14.40
Jewish	96.860	0.8	13.90	33.30	52.10
Para-religious Groups	12,390	5.60	20.10	52.30	22.10
No Religious Preference	1,311,145	3.76	34.30	42.28	19.65

Source: Religions in Canada, *Statistics Canada Catalogue 93–319, 1993. Table 5. Reprinted by authority of the Minister of Industry 1994.*

Tomes (1985) used 1981 census data on native-born males aged 25 to 64 who were working in 1980 to examine the relationship between religion and earnings. He focused specifically on Jews and found that, on average, they earned 12.7 percent more than Protestants. However, as he noted, Jews are overwhelmingly urban: "95 percent live in Canada's 13 largest cities, and 70 percent in the two largest ones: Toronto and Montreal" (1985, 247). Hence, to some degree, he hypothesized, Jews' higher earnings reflect the higher wages available in urban centres. When he compared urban Jews with urban Protestants, the earning differential in favour of Jews declined to 7.25 percent, which was "equivalent to the payoff from 1.8 years of schooling" (1985, 247). As we noted in Exhibit 11.4, Jews as a group have the highest level of education among the Canadian population.

Hitherto, research on the association between religion and earnings has focused on males. Tomes made a preliminary examination of women workers and found that figures for them demonstrated the converse of his findings for males: on average, Jewish women earn less than Protestant or Catholic women (1985, 249). Again, we remind you that significant variations occur *within* groups: that the *average* earnings of Jews are higher does not mean that there are no poor Jews or that a given Jewish male earns more than a Protestant or Catholic male.

WOMEN, FEMINISM, AND RELIGION

The analysis of women's roles within religious organizations, and the feminist critique of religion are both of relatively recent origin. The myths of primitive matriarchy and the role of the mother goddess in certain cultures in the distant past notwithstanding, women have historically met with a deeply entrenched patriarchal order in the religious realm. From St. Augustine to Thomas Aquinas to Martin Luther and beyond, one can put together a very long list of explicit antifeminist positions taken by religious leaders. We shall not rehearse the list here, except to note that quotations such as "Women, do you not know that you are Eve? You are the devil's gateway" are not difficult to come by. Arguably, Jesus was an exception in this regard: he had women friends and seemed to treat women with great respect.

The persecution and killing of women as witches was carried out for several centuries on the basis of the crassest superstitions about the malevolent powers of women; yet it was sanctioned, and even inspired, by male religious leaders. It was those women who did not fit the stereotype of the compliant, silent, nurturing female, and who ventured into the public sphere, who were at greatest risk of torture and death. Arthur Miller, whose play *The Crucible* dealt with the Salem witchcraft trials in Puritan New England in the late 1600s, referred to that period as "one of the strangest and most awful chapters in human history." It is vividly portrayed in the CBC production, *The Burning Times*.

Women, of course, did find vocations within the Roman Catholic Church, but in strictly subordinate positions. In *Taking the Veil: An Alternative to Marriage, Motherhood and Spinsterhood in Quebec, 1840–1920*, Danylewycz (1987) provides an excellent study of the religious vocation for women, and of life in the cloister.

As Box 11.1 shows, many nuns in Canada today are playing active roles in ministering to parishes, due to the dearth of priests, but they are still barred from such priestly activities as celebrating mass, hearing confessions, and performing marriages. It is only in recent years that, in the Roman Catholic Church as in other Christian denominations, the obstacles to equality for women have begun to be challenged.

Several important victories have been won, though often after bitter struggles. There is still resistance however, when women attempt to exercise the rights that they have been granted. Admission to the clergy has not been easily won, and in most instances when women have been accepted, they have found

Admission to the clergy has not been easily won by women and is fiercely resisted in many denominations.

Reuters/Bettman.

themselves in small and unimportant parishes, or in minor administrative positions. In 1944, Li Tim of Hong Kong was ordained, becoming the first female Anglican priest; she later resigned under pressure. During the period from 1948 to 1974, women won the right to be ordained in the African Methodist Episcopal Church, the Methodist and Presbyterian denominations in the United States, and the American and Swedish Lutheran churches. The first female rabbi in the United States was appointed in 1972. In 1975, the Anglican Church of Canada moved to allow women priests, and in the autumn of 1993, appointed its first woman bishop. It is the United Church of Canada, however, that has led the way, first in ordaining women to the ministry and then in selecting a woman as head of the Church in 1980. There are now three female bishops in the Episcopal Church in the United States.

Despite these precedents, however, the proposal to permit the ordination of women in the Church of England unleashed a furor in 1992, and the right was won by only a tiny margin of votes. During the debate, one of the bishops, who opposed the legislation, said "We are asking to push down one of the walls that holds the very house together." On the other hand, the Bishop of Durham queried, "Is it not shameful to be quarrelling as we are about women in the church when the world is torn by poverty, strife and lostness? ... Is it not disgraceful that we have so little faith in the Catholicity of Christ's incarnation for all ... that we confine that sacrament to men's hands? Surely women's hands are as human and as able to be hallowed by God's grace and calling" (cited in Hinds, 1992). Traditionalists argued that if a bishop were to ordain a woman, he would break the sacred chain in the powers that have been handed down from priest to priest throughout the centuries, which had begun with Jesus and his Twelve Disciples. Some of the opposition was based on the fact that the acceptance of women priests would erect a major barrier to union between the Church of England and the Roman Catholic Church, since the latter has so resolutely opposed the ordination of women. With the outcome of the vote, the Vatican announced in April 1993 that lay members and clergy of the church of England would be accepted into the Catholic Church if they so wished.

The rights of women have been central to the controversies that have beset the Roman Catholic Church in recent years (see Boxes 11.1 and 11.2)

BOX 11.1

NUNS ADMINISTERING TO MORE PRIESTLESS PARISHES IN CANADA

A growing number of Catholic nuns are administering "priestless" parishes to fill the vacuum caused by a continued shortage of priests.

Statistics from the Canadian Conference of Catholic Bishops show that of 5,323 parishes, 171 are in "the care" of nuns.

While the numbers of parishes grew by 58 between 1991 and 1992, fewer have diocesan or religious priests as full-time pastors and more are administered by nuns, male deacons or lay people.

There are 18 parishes administered by nuns in Ontario, 70 in Quebec, 61 in the western region, and 22 in the Atlantic region. Most are in rural and remote areas. There are no such parishes in the Toronto archdiocese, which comprises more than 1.2 million Catholics and has 212 parishes.

Besides taking care of day-to-day parish activities, the nuns lead prayer and communion services, visit the sick and prepare people for the reception of the sacraments. But they do not celebrate mass nor perform other specific duties of an ordained priest such as hearing confession, performing marriages or anointing the sick.

Where possible, a priest goes into the parish, usually once a week, to celebrate mass and administer the sacraments.

Sister Marie Tremblay of the Catholic Network for Women's Equality, which espouses women's ordination, says the statistics could suggest a positive trend.

"It may be a transitory process that is necessary before full recognition is given to something more inclusive," she said.

The bishop's conference acknowledges that one of the challenges facing the church is encouraging more men into priesthood to ensure a "pastoral presence" in every parish.

There were almost 12 million Catholics in Canada at the end of 1992, reflecting a 1 per cent increase over a year earlier.

However, the number of diocesan priests at the end of 1992 was 6,502, down 97 from 1991. The number had dropped by almost 1,000 since 1977. Candidates for the diocesan priesthood declined from 547 to 482 in 1991–92.

Source: The Toronto Star *(19 June 1993), F14. Reprinted with permission—The Toronto Star Syndicate.*

BOX 11.2

"EXTREME FORM" OF FEMINISM DRAWS WARNING FROM POPE

The Pope warned U.S. bishops yesterday about Roman Catholics practising nature worship and pagan rituals after coming under the influence of radical feminism.

Addressing bishops from the U.S. East Coast, the Pope said such practices are the result of an "extreme form" of feminism entering the Roman Catholic Church.

Prefacing his remarks by saying the strength of the parish system in the United States has been weakened by modern living, the Pope said the dangers of radical feminism go far beyond the push for the ordination of women to the priesthood.

"In its extreme form, it is the Christian faith itself which is in danger of being undermined," he said. "Sometimes forms of nature worship and the celebration of myths and symbols take the place of the worship of the God revealed in Jesus Christ."

The Pope warned in particular about nuns performing these rituals, which frequently pay homage to the goddess Earth.

"Unfortunately, this kind of feminism is being encouraged by some people in the church, including religious women whose beliefs, attitudes and behaviour no longer correspond to what the gospel and the church teach," he said.

He told the bishops it is their job to challenge such people to a dialogue about women's expectations in the Roman Catholic Church, which teaches that the priesthood is reserved for men since Christ chose only men as his apostles.

A recent survey showed more than two-thirds of U.S. church members think women should be allowed to become priests.

Source: The Globe and Mail *(4 July 1993).*

particularly since the Second Vatican Council emphasized the equality of the sexes and the importance of the laity. There has been open agitation for the ordination of women, and a majority of American Catholics now favour such a move (Ostling, 1992). Pressures to liberalize the Catholic position, however, have made few inroads, and have met opposition from vocal antifeminist groups such as Women for Faith and Family.

Feminist scholars have emphasized that the symbolic systems, language, and social organization of religion have been the creations of men and serve to legitimate a patriarchal social order. Women have been excluded by the very vocabulary of the faith. It is interesting that, in North American Indian languages such as Cree and Ojibway, there is no gender, and thus Nanabush, the pivotal mythological ("Trickster") figure, is neither exclusively male or female, but is both simultaneously. Daly (1978) has argued that women should take the radical position of leaving the established Christian churches, and find their own language and value system in the ancient religions of womankind.

THE MASS MEDIA AND RELIGION

When future historians focus on the second half of the twentieth century, a phenomenon that will undoubtedly attract their attention is the intrusion of the mass media into all areas of life, even the spiritual. In his book *The T.V. Ritual: Worship at the Video Altar*, Goethals (1981, 134) cites Margaret Mead's comment that "TV more than any other medium gives models to the American people—models for life as it is, or should, or can be lived." Religion concerns itself with how life "should be lived," and the way for spreading the religious message through television was paved by a long history of using radio broadcasting.[9] Furthermore, there is a strong tradition of evangelical revivals in North America.[10] The Methodist movement in the eighteenth century and the urban revivals led by the Salvation Army at the turn of this century are examples. It is hardly surprising, therefore, that evangelical denominations are using the mass media to promote modern revivals and that TV religion has a strongly evangelical flavour. What is new is the medium; the message has been stated many times before.

Oral Roberts, a prominent electronic minister, has explained why he decided to use television as his pulpit:

> The previous twenty years God had said, "Go into all the world and preach the Gospel to every creature" . . . Now as I struggled with this great need, deep inside I heard God say: "GO INTO EVERYMAN'S WORLD" . . . Well, I didn't know how so I said, "How God?" In my heart God spoke: "Do it through weekly and quarterly television programs" (1974, 91).

Roberts's claim of personal communion with God, by extension, renders his pronouncements unchallengeable.

Sociologists want to find out what electronic religion offers that large numbers of people need and seem unable to find in conventional religious institutions. Hendricks pinpointed one area: "In an impersonalized world where people are reduced to numbers, where life seems part of a programmed assembly line, the electronic church offers 'someone up there who likes you,' and who will do special things for you" (1984, 64).

Traditionally, evangelical religion has appealed most strongly to those whose critical skills have not been developed by higher education, and to disadvantaged groups generally. The minimally educated and those trapped in monotonous work are most apt to perceive themselves as faceless numbers and to be attracted to the apparent intimacy of TV religion. Quebedeaux places the blame on the churches themselves:

> Too many of the local churches and their ministers across our nation don't really care. In particular, they don't care about the very people—the elderly, the infirm, the socially retarded, the "unappealing" who most often have to turn to media religion with their unfilled needs and unhealed hurts (1982, 170).

Hadden and Swann (1981, 6), in their study of television evangelists, found that the audience for syndicated religious broadcasts increased from about ten million in 1970 to over twenty million a decade later. A Canadian survey, conducted in 1993, found that the national faith network, Vision TV, is

BOX 11.3

LOGGING ON TO GOD

The prayers came from around North America, from California and Florida and Ontario. Translated into digitalized code, they zipped along telephone lines to a computer in Louisville, Ky. Then they made their way to Champaign, Ill., where Bill Capel received them.

Mr. Capel, a ruling elder at McKinley Presbyterian Church, had been "flaming"—computer jargon for going into an uncontrollable rage—after hearing a comment on the Ecunet religious computer network. Someone had expressed regret that the word "gay" had been co-opted by the homosexual community. Mr. Capel, who was coming to grips with his own homosexuality, says he "went ballistic."

Hiding behind the pseudonym "Alan Turing" (the name of the great British homosexual mathematician and computer pioneer), he flamed so brightly that some Ecunet subscribers feared he was suicidal. Prayers were clearly called for—and prayers were logged, in electronic form, on the computer for Mr. Capel to read. "A lot of people started ministering to me," he says. "Over a year and a half, I worked through my anger. Finally, I put 'Alan Turing' away."

Mr. Capel is just one parishioner in a new kind of church—an electronic church. The congregation is drawn from all over the world and from different denominations, and even if its members never meet, they feel a sense of community sometimes even more powerful than the one they have at their local church.

Linked by modems connected to a central computer, church-workers and lay people from dozens of denominations exchange messages, news, opinions, jokes and theological musings in both private and public sessions.

Ecunet, which was born 10 years ago, contains two gigabytes of computer memory running on a fast desk-top computer at the Presbyterian Church's U.S. national office in Louisville. Today, more than 20 Christian denominations take an active part in Ecunet.

Members have written notes in 3,649 different "meetings" or "conferences" (both terms mean subject areas) and can read more than 160,000 notes left by others. About 300 meetings are active during any given week, says Rev. Merril Cook, who heads the stewardship and communications ministry for the Presbyterian Church (U.S.A.) and acts as a system operator of Ecunet. As well, there are dozens of invitation-only meetings for special subjects.

Meetings can be denominational: The United Church of Canada has its UCCAN conference, Catholics have Fishnet, Presbyterians have PCNET and the Anglicans and Episcopalians have Quest International. But anyone can join in.

Ecumenical conferences are also available, on such subjects as hymnology, native ministers, men sexually abused as boys, the art of church administration, liturgies, black studies, religious jokes, homosexual ordination, sermon ideas and even discussion groups dedicated to the spiritual implications of *Star Trek*, *Northern Exposure* and *Quantum Leap*.

Rev. David Shearman, a United Church minister in Peterborough, Ont., and an Ecunet system operator, calls the network "cyberspace," where "time, distance and geography mean nothing." He compares its appeal to a giant cocktail party. "We're in a large room which is getting bigger and bigger by the second, and the number of con-versations is multiplying, and you're eavesdropping," he says.

"It's possible to handle as many as 400 conversations at once."

Some members use the network to communicate vital information. Last fall, for example, Mr. Shearman posted exhaustive daily news summaries of events at the United Church general meeting in Fredericton, N.B.

Rev. Ian MacKenzie, a United Church minister working in northern British Columbia, is hooked up via the computer in Louisville with remote native members of his congregation so he can help organize treaty negotiations with the federal government.

Rev. Peter Chynoweth, whose congregation in Bonnyville, Alta., is far from any other United congregation, finds Ecunet the only way of maintaining constant contact with his United Church colleagues.

Ecunet started almost by chance in 1984.

Rev. David Lockhead and Rev. Gordon Laird, United Church ministers in B.C., pioneered a system at about the same time that some members of the Presbyterian Church (U.S.A.) started communication in a separate conference on the U.S. Compuserve network; the United Church of Christ started one as well. Soon they discovered one another. Serious networking started with 25 members in 1986. Today, with 2,000 members, Ecunet is the largest North American religion-only electronic church...

Canada Remote Systems, a giant Mississauga-based bulletin board with 10,000 subscribers, dedicates nine of its 5,000 conferences to religion. These include a newswire for religion stories, a Scientology section and a largely Anglican-based meeting that originates in Australia.

Demand for electronic networking is still growing. In 1990, David Keating, a computer consultant, founded a religion-only system based in Stirling, Ont., called TELOS. He counted about 200 religious networks across North America, and still believes there is room for his own. TELOS, which stands for The EcumenicaL On-line System, has about 200 members, and attracts people "who call out of interest and have no theological background."

Mr. Keating hopes to start an on-line job-opportunity search for missionaries and an information resource for people searching for religious texts.

For religious people, the attraction of computers is the ability to communicate with members of other churches, says Ecunet's unofficial historian Debra Farrington, who works in the Graduate Theological Union Bookstore in Berkeley, Calif. "It levels the hierarchical structure of the church," she says. "People will discuss things they wouldn't dare discuss anywhere else."...

Moreover, users of religious networks can work in anonymity. Rev. Hal Stockert, a part-Siberian and part-Sioux Byzantine-Catholic priest in upstate New York, is a classic case of different persona. A former nuclear physicist, Father Stockert, 67, chose the name "Avatar" as his Ecunet identification. A computer junkie for many years, he had played a variety of role-playing science-fiction games on early bulletin boards with SF writer Paul Anderson. "Avatar" grew out of one of those games.

...Father Stockert sees a lot of good coming out of the exchanges of opinion and theology. "The moderator on Ecunet is God," he says simply.

Source: Jack Kapica, "Logging on to God," The Globe and Mail (27 February 1993). Reprinted with permission.

watched for at least some time each week in over 25 percent of the six million Canadian homes that receive it by cable (Nemeth et al., 1993).

TV evangelism is big business in Canada and the United States. For instance, Mironowicz (1985, 11) reported that official tax receipts were issued for donations received from Canadians in the following amounts:

Worldwide Sect of God (1983)	$12,171,230
100 Huntley Street (1984)	11,660,127
Rev. Humbard Associates (1985)	1,886,824

Mironowicz said that many of these donations came from people who had to deprive themselves of basic necessities in order to send money. Tischler (1993, 283), using 1987 U.S. government statistics, notes that the average American weekly viewer of religious television is over 50 years of age, female, Baptist, not a high-school graduate, lives in the South, and is likely to donate more than $300 per year to the television ministry.

Well-publicized revelations of corruption and hypocrisy on the part of some TV evangelists has not seemed to affect the popularity of electronic religion. Jim and Tammy Bakker were found guilty of diverting funds from the PTL (Praise the Lord) Foundation for personal use. Jimmy Swaggart, who publicly proclaimed the virtues of chastity and a "clean" life, was found to be consorting with prostitutes.

It would seem that the weakening of communal and family ties and the anonymity of working in large organizations and living in cities have left a void in the lives of many. For some, it is being filled by TV religion, and they are willing to spend scant material resources to feel part of a caring, spiritual community.

. . . .

OVERVIEW

The role of religion in society contains many paradoxes. It has frequently acted as a pacifier, the function on which Marx focused when he called it the opiate of the people. On the other hand, religious fervour has been the wellspring of revolutionary change and the rationale for many colonial conquests. Religious groups have relieved the misery of individuals and have often been in the vanguard of social reform. However, such reform activities have not led to a restructuring of the social order and have often helped to buttress the status quo.

Each of sociology's founders addressed the role of religion in society. Marx recognized the function it performs in maintaining stability. Durkheim, too, focused on the contribution religion makes to social order by bolstering cohesion among group members. However, while ties are strengthened among members within the group, differences among religious groups are sharpened and aggression against members of other groups are often justified. Weber drew attention to the part religious values have played in generating or discouraging societal change.

One aspect of the transformation from *Gemeinschaft* to *Gesellschaft* has been a shift from a religious (sacred) to a secular orientation. In the latter view, the mysteries of the world can eventually be unravelled by rational analysis and scientific investigation. Another notable characteristic of a secular society is increased separation between church and state. Secularization is a powerful counterforce to the force of religion in modern society, and the interaction between the two sets of forces is a matter for sociological study.

Although significant variations exist among individual Christian denominations, they can be ordered into typologies that differentiate them along several dimensions. One influential typology identifies cult, sect, and church. The formation of cults and sects can be seen as responses to the process of secularization.

Even though church membership is declining, major religious denominations have proved resilient over long periods of time. Can they remain relevant in a secular age?

Women have faced a deeply entrenched patriarchal order in the religious realm. Feminists have posed challenges to the symbolic systems, language, and social organization of religion. Established churches are facing increasing pressure to change their practices, and some victories have been won.

By building on the tradition of evangelism, TV religion has become an influential presence on the religious scene. Electronic religion has an especially strong appeal for those who, for one reason or another, find themselves outside of the social mainstream.

ASSIGNMENTS

1. Select a religious group with which you are not familiar. Investigate and report on its membership, beliefs, practices, and organization. Where would it fit in terms of the typologies we have discussed in this chapter? Would you say that it exhibits secularizing trends, or that it actively resists them?

2. Have a look at the trend report in *Current Sociology* on "Cults, Converts and Charisma: The Sociology of New Religious Movements" by Thomas Robbins (see the Suggested Readings). What are some of the difficulties involved in studying cults? Are there ethical problems? What criticisms have been made against some of the cult studies?

3. In *Nostalgia for the Absolute* (Toronto: CBC Publications, 1974), originally a series of CBC radio broadcasts, George Steiner argues that the decay of Christian theology and dogma has left a vast emptiness that "modern mythologies" have attempted to fill. Choose one of the mythologies that he discusses and analyze it from a functionalist perspective.

SUGGESTED READINGS

David Bergen, *Sitting Opposite My Brother* (Winnipeg: Turnstone Press, 1993). Bergen is one of a striking number of writers to emerge from the cluster of Mennonite towns south of Winnipeg in the past ten years. In this small collection of short stories, he examines the dilemmas and the moral compromises of Mennonite men who no longer stand under the protection of the closed, rural communities where faith and ethnicity lent coherence to experience. In the secular world in which they find themselves, they carry with them disturbing residues of their upbringing, so that they encounter not freedom, but a paralyzing ambiguity.

Margaret Craven, *I Heard the Owl Call My Name* (New York: Dell Publishing, 1973). In this gentle novel set in British Columbia, a young Anglican clergyman goes to minister to an Indian village that does not welcome his notions of what is best for native peoples. Ultimately, persuasion works in the other direction, and he slowly develops a deep appreciation of their interpretation of what is important.

Leon Festinger, Henry W. Riecken, and Stanley Schachter, *When Prophecy Fails* (New York: Harper and Row, 1956). This is a participant-observer study of a small group that formed in the mid-1950s around a middle-aged woman who had received an urgent message from extra-terrestrial beings that the earth would be destroyed on December 21, 1955. Only the righteous would be rescued, by flying saucers. The research provoked criticism on ethical and methodological grounds. It was conducted with neither the consent nor the knowledge of the persons studied, and the researchers' own participation may have reinforced the beliefs of the members of the group. This work is a good example of the problems of conducting research as discussed in Chapter 2, "Sociologists at Work."

Edmund Gosse, *Father and Son* (Harmondsworth: Penguin, 1979). First published in 1907, this is the fascinating account of a lonely childhood stamped by the religious fanaticism of an unbending Plymouth Brethren faith. It is also Gosse's account of the relationship with his father, a well-known natural scientist who lost all professional respectability by his implausible attempts to reconcile the religious doctrine of creation with the theory of natural selection promulgated by his colleague and friend, Charles Darwin. Gosse describes the relationship between father and son as a "struggle between two temperaments, two consciences and almost two epochs. Of the two human beings here described, one was born to fly backward, the other could not help being carried forward."

Malcolm X, with Alex Haley, *The Autobiography of Malcolm X* (Harmondsworth: Penguin Books Ltd., 1968). From ghetto hustler to prison convict to national spokesman for Elijah Muhammad's Black Muslim sect to a new self as El-Hajj Malik El-Shabazz, after conversion to the "true" religion of Islam, Malcolm X lived many lives before his murder in 1965. With its spartan discipline, its demonization of whites, and its rejection of the route taken by Christian leader Martin Luther King, the separatist Nation of Islam helped to either radicalize or alienate some of the most disaffected segments of the black community in the United States during a turbulent period. The successive personal transformations of Malcolm X reveal much about the role religion can play in the political sphere.

Thomas Robbins, "Cults, Converts and Charisma: The Sociology of New Religious Movements," (*Current Sociology* 1988, 36), p. 1. This is a "trend report" of the *Journal of the International Sociological Association*, dealing with the period from the late 1960s to the late 1980s during which new religious movements flourished in North America and western Europe. Robbins provides a wide-ranging description and analysis of the response of sociologists and other social scientists to this development, and gives an interesting account of the movements themselves, the social contexts in which they occurred, and the theoretical and methodological controversies they have given rise to among those who have sought to study them.

Rodney Stark and William Sims Bainbridge, *The Future of Religion: Secularization, Revival and Cult Formation* (Berkeley, Calif.: University of California Press, 1985). The authors' innovative work has contributed to reducing the marginal status of the sociology of religion as a subdiscipline within sociology. In this influential and controversial book, Stark and Bainbridge argue that the tendency of established churches to identify with dominant secular cultures weakens their ability to generate effective religious rewards. Sects and cults provide very different responses to this vacuum, but both provide evidence that the process of secularization has not extinguished the religious impulse. It is worth paying particular attention to the imaginative ways in which the authors collect their data and make use of them to identify patterns of religious attitudes and behaviour.

NOTES

1. This quotation is from astronaut Edgar D. Mitchell's article, "Outer Space to Inner Space: an Astronaut's Odyssey," in *Saturday Review*, February 22, 1975.

2. Comte did not systematically address the question of religion; however, in his later, eccentric years, he founded the "religion of humanity" and made himself its "pope" (Coser, 1977, 38–39).

3. The Hindu initiation rite, conducted by the guru (teacher and divine inspirer), permits the individual to create a link between his or her inner self and the universe.

4. For example, the Moral and Reform Council of Canada, an interfaith council of churches at the turn of the century, evolved to become the Social Service Council of Canada in 1913.

5. Dust storms devastated agriculture on the prairies during the 1930s. They are explained here as God's punishment for people's neglect of religious obligations.

6. *Globe and Mail*, July 21, 1993.

7. Education, occupation, and income are the variables most frequently used to calculate socioeconomic status.

8. Specifically, 25.5 percent of the economic elite were Anglicans, a group that constituted 14.7 percent of all Canadians. The respective representations of Presbyterians and Catholics in the elite were 11.3 and 10 percent, compared with a representation in the overall population of 8.6 and 43 percent (1965, 289–90).

9. In fact, radio preaching changed politics in western Canada in the 1930s. William Aberhart, founder of the Social Credit party, blended religion and economic doctrine in radio sermons that swept the party to power in Alberta in 1935.

10. Garrett defines "evangelical" as a theological stance that claims: (1) the complete reliability and formal authority of scripture in matters of faith and practice; (2) the necessity of *personal* faith in Jesus Christ as saviour from sin and consequent commitment to him as Lord; and (3) the urgency of actively seeking the conversion of sinners to Christ (1983, 61).

. . . .

Social Change

Social Change

Both continuity and change are fundamental, constant features of human society, and the study of social life must seek to account for both. History reveals both much stability and repetition in the way human beings have arranged their lives, and it also reveals many discontinuities and drastic alterations. In every chapter of this book, we have pointed to changes in Canadian society. Yet it can be argued that Canadian society has persisted, over time, in a remarkably stable, orderly way with few alterations to its structure. Both perspectives are true.

The dynamic perspective we have taken throughout the book has led us to identify the ways in which societies, cultures, stratification systems, belief systems, social groups, and institutions have undergone transformation—sometimes suddenly because of crisis or innovation, and sometimes incrementally, over a long period of time.

Although change is the hallmark of today's world, it is not new. It is unlikely that preliterate peoples lived fixed, placid lives, free from dislocation and upheaval. What is peculiar to the twentieth century, and particularly to the past few decades is the scale, the diversity, and the dizzying pace of change. Furthermore, to a greater extent than ever before, change has become institutionalized, with many societal resources devoted to forecasting behaviour, predicting outcomes, and developing policies for *planned* change.

Do people welcome change or fear it? Habit and custom exert a powerful influence, and novelty is not always welcomed. Nisbet observed:

> Most of us do everything we can, of course, to shore up the old ways. Such is the shock of enforced social change that most people will often employ what the nineteenth-century English philosopher called "fictions." No matter how extreme the need for change in our old ways, we adopt, in effect, verbal, legal, religious, or other fictions through which we convince ourselves that change of behaviour is not needed, that the old and cherished, if properly understood, can continue despite all overt evidence of its unsuitability. Much of the world's literature consists, basically, of justifications and rationalizations of practices that have become obsolete or even injurious... Few of us are altogether immune to the practice of creating fictions, by which we so often prop up what should be dismantled (1970, 317–18).[1]

Prizing what is familiar and unchanging is bolstered by the assumption that stable conditions are necessary for the human spirit to thrive and achieve its potential. "For how but in order and ceremony," asked William Butler Yeats, "can beauty and truth be born?" Yet we know that some of the most creative periods in history have occurred when migrations, conquests, and expanded trading patterns gave rise to the collision of ideologies, value systems, and social structures.

You are living at the end of a century that has been described as "one of the most violent in human history" (Outhwaite & Bottomore, 1993, xiv), despite the faith in progress that characterized its beginning. Consider the span of your own life to date. If you were born in the Western world, you have probably experienced a rather stable existence. And yet the world, and the society, you inhabit is shifting in an astonishing variety of ways. In this chapter, we first examine attempts that have been made on the part of social scientists to make theoretical sense out of the phenomenon of change. We then turn to an examination of several major areas of change in modern society. The changes we have chosen to explore—out of the nearly endless list of possibilities—are among those bringing fundamental alterations to Canadian society, particularly society as you are likely to encounter it.

THEORIES OF CHANGE

Ordinary speech is full of garden-variety theories of change, which generally fall into two categories: the optimistic ("every day, in every way, we're getting better and better") and the pessimistic ("the world is going to the dogs"). Where some see growth and progress, others see decay and loss. Still others liken changing features of social life to features of the human life cycle (witness, for example, the use of phrases like "the birth of a new era" and "worn-out ideas") or of perpetual cycles ("what goes around comes around"). Some question whether things really change at all ("the more things change, the more they stay the same").

These ordinary notions are reflected in the scholarly works of a number of early social theorists. As we have noted in other chapters, these theorists made ambitious historical analyses of society (or civilization) as a whole, rather than examining only a specific social group or institution. They sought to explain society in terms of what had occurred in the past, yet, as Harding notes (1992, 312), " ... unlike many of today's sociologists, they were personally, politically, and intellectually in touch with the great epochal transformations facing them in their times." As you saw in Chapter 1, it was concern with these transformations that laid the groundwork for sociology as it is known today.

The Greeks and Romans saw social, physical, and biological reality in terms of relentless, continuous change, and they were preoccupied with questions about origins, stages of growth, causes, and purposes. Christianity adopted the same metaphor of growth but shifted it to the realm of the sacred: the universe, created by God, was unfolding according to divine purpose. The Renaissance, the Enlightenment, and especially the nineteenth-century contributions to modern science did nothing to dispel this analogy between the social world and the ever-evolving world of nature. The analogy has come, in fact, to have a deep influence on present-day functionalist theory in sociology.

CYCLICAL CHANGE

Ibn Khaldun ([1377] 1967) was perhaps the first theorist of social change to describe change in terms of cycles. His analysis was based on his observations of Arab societies in late fourteenth-century North Africa. What he saw was a fluid, but patterned, ordering, of two kinds of societies: (1) nomadic herding societies, displaying strong social solidarity, and (2) urban societies, characterized by a weak degree of solidarity. He postulated that a cycle of change occurred, in which the herding society conquered the fragmented urban one and established a new social order. Eventually this new society would also deteriorate due to decreasing social solidarity, and thus would be susceptible to conquest by another herding society.

Oswald Spengler (1880–1936) viewed the history of civilization as proceeding in cycles, analogous to the development of the single organism: birth, childhood, maturity, senescence (old age), and death. The end of each cycle returned a culture to its beginnings. For Spengler, Western civilization had passed its stage of maturity and was well into its phase of decline and inevitable death. This, too, had been the fate of the great civilizations of Babylon, Egypt, Greece, and Rome.

British historian Arnold Toynbee (1889–1975) explained the rise and fall of civilizations in terms of the notions of challenge and response. Every society, he said, confronts major challenges from its natural and social environments. If it faces limited natural resources or warlike neighbours, for example, it is challenged to fashion a response through innovation. When the responses are adequate, that is, when the society is capable of changing, it can grow and thrive; otherwise, it is doomed to decline. In his twelve-volume *Study of History*, Toynbee attempted to show that only 21 societies had ever succeeded in becoming real civilizations, and that they resembled one another in their patterns of growth and decay.

Pitirim Sorokin (1889–1968), writing just before the outbreak of the Second World War, was another theorist who conceived of change in terms of social cycles. Society, he argued, moves between two extreme types of culture, the *ideational* and the *sensate*. In the ideational phase, of which the medieval period is the best example, strong spiritual values give meaning to life and lend coherence to social organization. The sensate phase is shaped by what is immediately apparent through the senses, and is characterized by materialistic values. In such a society, people emphasize self-expression and the gratification of immediate physical needs. Occasionally, an intermediate point between these two extremes is reached (what Sorokin calls the "idealist point"), permitting sensate and ideational values to co-exist harmoniously.

While cyclical theories, like other ambitious abstractions can be admired for their sweeping horizons, they leave little room for human manoeuvring: the cycles have a life of their own and thus are seen as constituting an "irresistible force" in human affairs. Such theories have perhaps had a seductive kind of surface plausibility because they are analogous to the pattern of growth and decay inherent in the human life cycle, with mortality the inevitable outcome for both. Cyclical theories provide an essentially pessimistic perspective on social change, in contrast to the views of the evolutionary theorists whose work we shall turn to next.

LINEAR PROGRESS: EVOLUTIONARY THEORIES

In Chapter 1, we referred briefly to Comte's Law of Three Stages, explicated in his *Course of Positive Philosophy*. Comte viewed society as ascending in a linear fashion from the theological to the metaphysical to the "positive" (scientific) stage, with each stage exhibiting greater complexity. In the first stage, thinking is shaped by the belief in supernatural entities, with all of nature being endowed with religious significance. In the metaphysical stage, explanations are couched in terms of abstract forces. The third stage, the most highly evolved, would be characterized by a mode of enquiry that regarded social life in the same way as nature was regarded, that is, subject to identifiable and invariable "laws" that could be discovered through the exercise of reason. Understanding the laws of social life would, he argued, make it possible "for man to influence the course of his own civilization" (1877, 572). This was the task he set for sociology.

Comte's was an optimistic view. So, too, was that of Herbert Spencer (1820–1903). Each phase of social growth or evolution, Spencer argued, was marked by increasing complexity, greater differentiation among functions, greater interdependence among society's various parts, and a higher level of moral development. He envisaged this evolutionary process as leading to a more rational, humane, and orderly universe. Consequently, Spencer was opposed to collective action (such as state education and state medicine), which he felt would interfere with natural processes and artificially preserve society's weakest members. Ironically, a faith in the "naturalness" of social processes also provided justification for social interference in the form, for example, of Western colonialism, which entailed the economic, political, and social domination of "less fit" societies.

As we noted in our discussion of Darwin's theory of evolution (1859) in Chapter 4, viewing human beings as subject to the biological law of survival of the fittest (a term that Spencer explicitly applied to human evolution in society) has consequences for the ways in which social phenomena are explained. One can, for example, rationalize differences between the rich and the poor, the successful and the unsuccessful, and the powerful and the weak, on the basis of the notion that the poor, the unsuccessful, and the weak are less fit than the others. A belief in biological determinism, or social Darwinism, does not promote the view that the structure of society can—or should—be purposefully changed.

Evolutionary theory has managed to survive a great variety of attacks and to retain a place in social thought. After the Second World War, it took on new forms, appearing in conceptions of modernization, development and underdevelopment, and, more recently, in theories of the development of moral reasoning and human thinking as a whole (Outhwaite & Bottomore, 1993, xv).

CHANGE THROUGH CONFLICT

Marx's theory of history was also evolutionary, but it specified a mechanism, that of class conflict, by means of which social change occurs. Change, according to Marx, results from the tensions, or contradictory forces that develop in every social system. Thus, as we noted, one reason the feudal system collapsed was that the emerging capitalist mode of production, abetted by technological developments, required a labour forced that was not tied to the land so that the productive potential of human beings could be realized.

Marx viewed the events of each historical epoch as hinging upon the struggle between a dominant group and exploited groups for a share of societal rewards. The power of the dominant group, he argued, stems from its control over the means of producing the goods and services society requires. The ultimate struggle in the capitalist system would occur between owners (the bourgeoisie) and workers (the proletariat). Radical intellectuals would have a role to play in helping to educate working people so that the latter would understand their oppression and come to see the possibilities for bringing about change that would be in their own interest. The confrontation, which would result in the triumph of the proletariat, would lead ultimately to a classless society that would be free from conflict. Despite his insistence on the necessity and inevitability of revolution, Marx offered an essentially optimistic view of social change.

Critics of Marx have noted that he failed to foresee the capacity of capitalism to absorb opposition in a variety of ways. What about the legalization of unions, collective bargaining, and strikes? What about the emergence of political parties, bent on reform, that would take into account the needs and interests of the underprivileged? Marx also did not foresee that the state would be assigned responsibility for regulating some of the activities of corporations in the interests of consumers and employees.

Modern conflict theorists look at change as the struggle between groups with a vested interest in the existing order and those who challenge that order. For instance, corporations seek to continue to minimize expenditures on pollution control, while environmentalists assert the priority of protection over profit.

Ralf Dahrendorf (1959) has argued that conflict theory provides the most useful paradigm for analyzing forces of interruption and change. Unlike Marx, he claimed that conflict is present in both capitalist and socialist societies, and that it does not only revolve around issues of class. Cleavages that cut across social classes can occur on the basis of religious beliefs, for example. Thus, people who are antagonists in one sphere may be allies in another. Alliances, then, may temper the likelihood of full-blown conflict. On the other hand, one particular line of cleavage may become salient, in specific historical circumstances.

Dahrendorf insisted that conflict can be a positive thing:

> The clash of values and interests, the tension between what is and what some groups feel ought to be, the conflict between vested interests, and new strata and groups demanding their share of power, wealth and status, have been productive of vitality; note for example the contrast between the "frozen world" of the Middle Ages and the burst of creativity that accompanied the thaw that set in with the Renaissance (1973, 68).

At a less general level, Dahrendorf noted, such a view raises doubts about the human relations school approach (which we discussed in Chapter 8), with its emphasis on palliative gestures to workers in the interests of harmony. If a social system fails to allow for the open expression of conflict, the likelihood of violent eruption is increased.

THE CUMULATIVE WEIGHT OF HUMAN ACTION

Weber challenged Marx's preoccupation with economic factors, arguing that, in the case of capitalism, economic changes were preceded by changes in the value system of Western society. Thus, he gave the Protestant ethic, which was expressed in Calvinism, a central place in his explanation of the emergence of capitalism. As we have emphasized, Weber did not ignore the importance of economic factors; rather, he insisted on a broader view that took into account the interplay of many factors. In this insistence, exemplified in his own work, he has been influential in helping sociology to reject narrow, deterministic explanations.

Weber viewed cultural change as a process of ever-increasing rationalization—for example, in the transition from magic to science and in the transfer of work from a primary-group setting to that of a large, impersonal bureaucracy. He was firmly opposed to any view of social change that hypothesized the existence of an inevitable social force. Rather, he believed that a great many individuals must make a great many decisions. Think of the dramatic decline in the Quebec birth rate. By itself, the availability of reliable birth control methods could not have produced this change. Instead, many women, for various reasons, had to decide to practise birth control. Cumulatively, such decisions lead to social change.

HOW IS STABILITY ACHIEVED?

In Chapter 1, we explained that present-day functionalist theory is rooted in the tradition of Durkheim, who was greatly concerned with the problem of social order. You will recall that his concept of organic solidarity describes a group that has both a high degree of social differentiation (manifested in a highly specialized division of labour) and a high degree of interdependence.

Here, the metaphor of society as a complex organism is clear. In such a differentiated system, the various parts must perform their functions properly if society as a whole is to operate coherently. Likewise, a change in one part has consequences for other parts as well as for the whole. Thus, if one identifies a change in some aspect of social life—say, a change in the way work is performed—one can be alert to any resulting adjustments and transformations in other aspects of society. However, Durkheim strictly rejected evolutionary theory that posited stages through which society *must* pass: "The stages that humanity traverses successively do not engender one another" ([1895] (1950), 117). In other words, chronology does not imply causation.

Modern functionalism, too, rejects sweeping evolutionary notions. Its analytical focus is on the consequences, rather than the causes, of sets of social arrangements. In the chapter on the family, for example, we examined arguments that maintained that the nuclear family emerged as a response to the needs of industrial society. Like Durkheim, modern functionalists treat society as a system of interdependent parts. Central to this view is the concept of equilibrium. To maintain continuity and balance in society, certain "functional requisites" must be met. For example, the young must be socialized to accept the moral precepts necessary for their adult roles in society. In Chapter 10, "Education: Winning and Losing," we noted the view that schools socialize children to accept middle-class values, such as deferred gratification, competitiveness, and verbal rather than physical proficiency. Another functionalist view, outlined in Chapter 6, "Stratification," argues that rewards (e.g., pay, power, and prestige) must be distributed unevenly to ensure that society's most important tasks are accomplished. You will note that the "effects" that we have cited as examples are assumed to be positive.

Any model encourages certain questions and discourages others. An equilibrium (functionalist) model invites the question, "How do things persist?" while inhibiting the question, "How do things change?" Observed change is interpreted as an occurrence that will require complementary changes in the system as a whole in order to re-establish equilibrium. Society as a whole thus is seen to change on an incremental basis. When a mobile labour force, for example, is required by an industrializing society, functionalists seek to identify the new arrangements (functional alternatives) developed to perform the functions that the relatively immobile extended family used to fulfil.

Wilbert Moore (1974) has advocated the view of society as a "tension-management system," a model that encourages the identification of tensions likely to produce change. The participation of women in the labour force, for example, produces tensions between their domestic roles and their work roles. This alerts the sociologist to the possibility that changes are likely to occur, though it does not predict *what* changes. One possible outcome is the reorganization of the division of labour within the home. Another is the reorganization of work itself, to accommodate female participation in a way that allows women to continue to take responsibility for domestic tasks.

MODERNIZATION

Modernization refers to the process of economic, social, and cultural change that traditional, undeveloped societies undergo as they move toward industrialization. Modernization theory has its roots in evolutionary theory; it assumes that different societies develop in similar ways, though at different times. In other words, it places greater emphasis on what societies have in common than on how they differ. For example, as technological change spreads throughout the world, a certain homogenization of attitudes, values, and behaviour ensues. With his pattern variables, which we examined in the chapters on work and on the family, Parsons attempted to capture in ideal–typical categories the different types of relationships and orientations characteristic of the beginning (the traditional) and the end-point (the modern) of this change. Implied in Parson's model is that cultural and structural changes must occur in traditional societies in order for them to enter into the process of modernization. During this process, the pattern variables of achievement, affective neutrality, specificity in role obligations, universalism, and self-orientation will become more salient as these societies adapt to modern influences and relinquish their emphasis on ascription, affective ties, particularistic loyalties, diffuse role obligations, and orientation to the collectivity. Kinship systems will thus become less central, and bureaucratic structures will exercise a dominant influence.

Inkeles and Smith (1974) studied the processes of modernization in six developing countries: Argentina, Chile, East Pakistan, India, Israel, and Nigeria. They found that education in all of these countries had a liberating influence on many individuals, as did exposure to work in modern organizations such as factories. Through these experiences, people became less fearful of novelty, less

convention-bound, and more confident and pro-active, because they believed
that they had the capacity to effect change both in their own lives and in their
society. This picture is quite different from the dislocation and disorientation
documented by researchers whose interest is in the negative effects of the
imposition of Western agendas on non-Western societies.

WORLD-SYSTEM THEORY

World-system theory provides a conflict approach to social change, essentially
using a Marxist model of class analysis but applying it on a global scale. Its
leading exponent is Immanuel Wallerstein. Although Wallerstein (1974)
studied the emergence of the capitalist system as a world-economy in the
sixteenth century, his main interest is in contemporary developments. In an
integrated world-economy, he argues, advantage to some states is obtained only
at the disadvantage to others. The advantaged, or "core," nation-states exploit
those states that are on the periphery. For example, core countries benefit from
the flow of raw materials from underdeveloped (peripheral) countries and
send them their manufactured goods, leading to the further deterioration of
the latter. Foreign firms and investors control the economic and political
decisions affecting peripheral nations, and they make those decisions in terms
of their own interests.

It is this asymmetry in relationships, rather than the traditional, "backward" attitudes of local peoples, that leads to the greater impoverishment of
societies that were once self-sustaining. Thus, rather than the eventual homogenization of societies, as modernization theory predicts, world-system theory predicts an increasing polarization between the "haves" and the "have-nots."

Some evidence of this polarization is provided by Trainer (1990), who
argues that economic growth in the core countries has failed to improve the
material living standards of the underdeveloped nations' poor majorities, and,
in fact, has significantly reduced these standards for overwhelming numbers of
people. Trainer claims that the problem is not lack of development *per se* but
rather is *inappropriate* development that is not in the best interests of local
economies.

Critics of this perspective argue that it fails to take into account factors
that are internal to core and peripheral nations, such as the nature of social
classes and the level of education. As a result, it cannot explain differences in
the development of various economies in the Third World. Why is it, for example, that the economy of South Korea has made such strides, while others have
fallen further behind? Why hasn't Canada lagged behind with many other
countries that are mainly producers of raw materials? Why have some peripheral countries been able to adopt, and benefit from, new technologies while others have not?

TECHNOLOGY AND CHANGE

The simplest definition of **technology** is "applied science." It refers to all the
problem-solving activities that human beings have developed to cope with their

environment. Technology is not simply artifacts or "products"; it is a *system* that entails far more than the sum of its individual material components, for it involves "organization, procedures, symbols, new words, equations, and, most of all, a mindset" (Franklin, 1990, 12). Franklin points out that our language is ill suited for describing the complexity of technological interactions among the various components of technology: "How does one speak about something that is both fish and water, means as well as end?" (1990, 15).

When technology is conceived of as human practices (Boulding, 1969), we are able to see that it involves much more than the neutral, straightforward application of "expert knowledge." Here indeed is fertile ground for sociological study: the notion of technical expertise itself is opened up for examination and its social, cultural, and political dimensions can be examined. Ursula Franklin (1990) gives the rather simple example of the building of bridges and underpasses, utterly familiar aspects of our modern landscape. Franklin argues that many of the political decisions about provision for the public infrastructure (for example, drinking water, sanitation, and roads) are made at a technical level, without public input and scrutiny, but these decisions have major social consequences since they affect different segments of the population unequally. She cites the example of the design of the bridges and underpasses of the New York state parkways, carried out under Robert Moses:

> These bridges and underpasses are quite low, intentionally specified by Moses to allow only private cars to pass. All those who travelled by bus because they were poor or black or both were barred from the use and enjoyment of the parkland and its "public amenities" by the technical design of the bridges. Even at the time of Robert Moses, a political statement of the form "We don't want them blacks in our parks" would have been unacceptable in New York State. But a technological expression of the same prejudice appeared to be all right. Of course, to the public the intent of the design became evident only after it was executed—and then the bridges were there (1990, 71).

Here, then, are "invisible" features of bridges and underpasses, which themselves are such tangible, visible features of highway systems, easily recognized on detailed maps. What about "electronic highways" these new networks of communication that extend invisibly over much vaster spaces? How can we develop cognitive maps, or mental pictures, of them so that we can appreciate their reach and the intricacies of their routes? And what are their hidden social, cultural, and political dimensions?

Technology is as old as human history, and each major new technological discovery means far-reaching changes in the way social life is organized. Marx recognized this when he wrote, "The hand mill gives you a society with feudal lords, the steam mill a society with industrial capitalists" (1847). Marx was interested in the consequences of the rapid advance of technology for the future of capitalism, a subject he addressed in *Grundrisse* ([1857–58] 1973). He saw the social processes that are set in motion by technology as intimately bound up with the class struggle, and, hence, saw these processes contributing to the ultimate revolution that would result in a classless society.

Alexis de Toqueville, a French aristocrat who visited the United States in 1831, described what he called the "ethos" (what Franklin, quoted earlier, calls the "mindset") that made the New World so predisposed to technological innovation:

> The American lives in a land of wonders ... everything around him is in constant movement, and every movement seems an advance. Consequently in his mind the idea of newness is closely linked with that of improvement. Nowhere does he see any limit placed by nature to human endeavour; in his eyes something that does not exist is just something that has not been tried ([1835–40] 1969, 404).

One of the wonders of the nineteenth century was the telegraph, the development of which permitted what newspapers of the time called "the annihilation of space." For the first time, transportation and communication became uncoupled, meaning that the barrier to the movement of information had suddenly dropped. This not only had enormous social, economic, and political consequences, but also transformed the character of information itself. As Postman notes:

> Prior to the telegraph, information could be moved only as fast as a train could travel: about thirty-five miles per hour. Prior to the telegraph, information was sought as part of the process of understanding and solving particular problems. Prior to the telegraph, information tended to be of local interest ... telegraphy created the idea of context-free information—that is, the idea that the value of information need not be tied to any function it might serve in social and political decision-making and action. The telegraph made information into a commodity, a "thing" that could be bought and sold irrespective of its uses or meaning (1993, 67–68).

Francis Bacon (1561–1626), a great propagandist for science, had long before celebrated the connections among science, progress, and power in human society. In *Novum Organum* (1960), he looked at three discoveries that were recent in his time, namely, printing, gunpowder, and the magnet. He adjudged them to have changed the "whole face and state of things throughout the world; the first in literature, the second in warfare, the third in navigation; whence have followed innumerable changes; insomuch that no empire, no sect, no star seems to have exerted greater power and influence in human affairs than these changes" ([1620] 1960, 118). One need not, however, subscribe to the reductionist notion of **technological determinism**, that is, the idea that social change is a direct outcome of technological change, in order to acknowledge the importance of major breakthroughs such as the telegraph and the computer in helping to re-shape social life.

The technological advances that have occurred in the twentieth century have been greeted with both enthusiasm and alarm. Positive assessments (consonant with theories of "progress") stress their contributions to such things as economic growth through more rational and efficient forms of production, the elimination of degrading and alienating work, the alleviation of poverty, improvements in health, the expansion of leisure time, and the breaking down of geographic, temporal, and cultural barriers (Bell, 1973; Toffler, 1980). Critics brood on the unanticipated consequences of technological change, such as destruction of the natural environment, cultural dislocation, the displacement of workers, iatrogenic (physician-induced) illness, and the psychological assault of constant, rapid change (Roszak, 1986; Winner, 1989).

The Chicago World's Fair, which attracted 39 million visitors, was dedicated to the worship of science and technology.

Collection Centre Canadien d'Architecture/
Canadian Centre for Architecture, Montreal.

A functionalist might be interested, for instance, in identifying the adaptations that social institutions such as the family and the education system make when a new technology is introduced. What disturbances and adjustments must occur before the culture, scrambling to catch up, succeeds in absorbing the innovation? A conflict approach to technological change encourages a different set of questions. How will the costs and benefits be distributed? Will some social cleavages be eliminated and new ones created, or will the existing lines of cleavage be reinforced?

THE MICROCHIP REVOLUTION

When the first computer was built in 1946, it filled a large room. It weighed 30 tons and had 19,000 vacuum tubes, but possessed a very limited capacity. The subsequent development of the tiny silicon chip, known as the microchip, constitutes one of the most important technological changes in modern society.

It is impossible to imagine all the potential applications of this technology. Yet it is certain that such applications are uniting the globe in a single complex economic system, radically shifting the level at which decision making takes place. What this will mean for existing cultures and political systems is an important question.

We are only beginning to grasp the implications that computer technology has for work in all sectors of the economy (see Menzies, 1989). How will it affect both the quantity and the quality of work? Computer systems will provide a substitute not only for routine tasks now performed by factory and office workers, but also for some of the complicated, decision-making responsibilities of professionals. In other words, jobs at all levels of the occupational structure are threatened. Many jobs, for example, low-level secretarial jobs, are becoming even more routinized. At the same time, like other technological breakthroughs, computers are also contributing to the creation of interesting jobs, as was mentioned in our discussion of the debates concerning deskilling and upgrading in the chapter on work.

In that chapter, we also discussed the issue of control of the workforce, a goal that computers facilitate through their capacity to provide mechanized surveillance. Machines can monitor a typist's speed, how many calls an operator is handling, or how steadily a checkout clerk is working. These practices, an aspect of what Franklin (1990) calls "prescriptive technologies" have brought loud protests from unions, who say they dehumanize the workplace in the interests of raising productivity. They can also track an individual's movements away from any particular "work post." Franklin gives the example of the new "smart" buildings, whose occupants must carry a special card with a barcode that allows them access to certain areas of the building and excludes them from others. The computer provides what Wanner calls "the digitalized footprints of social transactions" (cited in Franklin, 1990, 25), traces that reveal where individuals spend their time. Technological control over working populations, of course, is not a new phenomenon. The technological practices of ancient Egypt or the Roman empire, elaborated in huge bureaucracies, also exercised strict control over workers.

Robots are a good example of a technological innovation that has both beneficial and threatening effects. Robots can be programmed to perform delicate microsurgical procedures, and they can manipulate heavy machinery. They can shear sheep, harvest grain, and pick fruit. They can operate in environments hazardous to humans, such as the ocean bed, outer space, and nuclear or chemical plants. They provide an opportunity to conserve energy, since they require less lighting than humans and have no need of costly amenities such as air-conditioning. Moveover, they can work around the clock. Their major application so far has been in the industrial sector, where they have relieved humans of mind-numbing, monotonous work at the same time as they have relieved many of them of their jobs entirely. Robots have, since they were introduced, replaced tens of thousands of autoworkers, bringing obvious

BOX 12.1

COMPUTER THAT CAN READ MINDS IS NEAR

It sounds like the ultimate in chilling Big Brother technology: scientists in Japan are close to developing a computer that can read your mind. Researchers at Fujitsu, Japan's largest personal computer manufacturer and parent company of Britain's ICL, announced last week that they are training a computer to pick up specific patterns of thoughts in the brain.

It means computers could be operated without tapping at a keyboard or even speaking a word. The secret is what the researches call "silent speech." Simply thinking a word such as "yes" or "no" generates a distinctive pattern of brain waves that the Fujitsu team had detected with stick-on electrodes.

They are developing supersensitive devices called Squids (Superconducting Quantam Interference Device) contained in a space age helmet, which pick up the "silent speech" by remote control. The team is trying to programme a computer to recognise thought commands such as "up" and "down" so that a cursor can be moved simply by thinking about it.

Michael Beirne, of Fujitsu in Tokyo, explained that Squids are so ultra-sensitive they can pick up even the tiniest electrical signals from a distance. "Potentially a person could sit in front of a Squid-operated computer without having to wear a helmet. Our goal is to create an intuitive computer that can pick up your thoughts even as you walk around a room."

British scientists welcomed the concept of thought-driven computers. Dr. Andrew Ioannides, co-director of the Open University's biomagnetism research group, believes the Japanese discovery marks a significant phase in the interaction between humans and machines. "I firmly believe that what the Japanese are trying to do is possible. It will revolutionise the way we perceive machines. Once we start playing with these ideas we will rapidly need to develop new concepts," he said.

There are many beneficial effects of this advance: the Japanese project could form the basis for research into medical disorders, say British doctors, as it promises to lead to a greater understanding of the workings of the brain. Ioannides believes it could lead to early diagnosis and eventual cures for such mental disorders as schizophrenia and Alzheimer's disease.

Squid-based computers would be of particular benefit to handicapped people who cannot move or speak, such as Stephen Hawking, the Cambridge professor of physics who, due to motor neurone disease, is confined to a wheelchair and unable to move or talk. A Squid computer would allow him to communicate far more easily than at present.

In military use, fighter pilots may be able to direct and fire missiles faster, gaining critical microseconds over their opponents. In psychological research, Squids might detect if a person is inclined towards criminal behaviour because mental imbalance leaves a characteristic pattern of brain waves.

But there is a darker side to all this. For the moment it will be a challenge just to recognise the thoughts "yes" or "no" from brain waves, let alone understand complex thoughts. Comprehending the connection between a particular thought and the voltages emitted by brain cells is still in its infancy.

However, potential misuse for such a system is already causing concern. Squid technology with computer thought recognition may one day lead to invasions of people's privacy such as the deciphering of dreams and unwarranted detection of thoughts. "It's like Pandora's box," said Andy Puddelhalt of Liberty, the British civil rights organisation. "You can't stop the clock. Only a general right to privacy in law can give people protection against the misuse of equipment such as this."

Source: Christopher Lloyd, "Computer that Can Read Minds Is Near," Sunday Times *(13 March 1993).*

economic advantages to employers. In 1986, the hourly cost of labour in the U.S. auto industry was around $24, including benefits. One robot, replacing several workers, cost only $6 to operate (Krahn & Lowe, 1993, 46). Their potential use in the service sector, for example, in commercial cleaning or in the fast food industry, is also great.

The fifth-generation computer behaves in ways that have long been said to reflect intelligence; it can understand something of the world around it and can use this understanding to reason, deduce, estimate, and plan. Such a computer gathers information about its environment through vision, speech recognition, touch, and manipulation, as well as through more conventional devices such as typewriters, touch-sensitive screens, and magnetic tape. It stores, organizes, and integrates data along with other general knowledge in its memory bank. Then, it uses all the pertinent information to arrive at a solution to a problem. What it replaces is not human muscle but, rather, many functions of the human brain. One such computer devises methods for a robot to move objects around in a room; another is able to identify problems in train locomotives, and repair them; a third, appropriately named PUFF, can diagnose lung problems and make treatment recommendations. An awesome type of artificial intelligence computer system, Eliza, attempts psychologically therapeutic discussions with human beings.

VIRTUAL REALITY

Virtual reality is a reality created by electronic sensors and computer-generated images, with which one can have the sense of participating in fabricated events. It was originally developed to train astronauts, but quickly found a civilian role in the form of high-tech video games. A player of such games may wear a helmet with a pair of miniature televisions aimed at the eyes to produce a three-dimensional image. When you turn your head, the perspective changes just as if you were actually in the artificially created setting. The helmet serves to shut out the outside world, so that the user (a term, critics are quick to point out, that suggests the addictive quality of such experiences) steps, magically, into a "virtual" world. In some situations a sensor-laden glove gives the user the opportunity to have the sense of grasping and moving the objects on display. Or, the users can wear a full bodysuit filled with sensors.

This technology has the potential for many practical applications. As a tool in professional training, for example, it permits physicians to rehearse complex, high-risk operations without endangering an actual patient. Business can use it to design and promote products; consumers will be able to go wandering through the "hypermall" and then order items electronically (Engelhard, 1989). A virtual reality fighter-plane cockpit gives pilots the opportunity to operate simulated aircraft with natural eye and hand movements. In the realm of education, the possibilities are enormous. One can browse through a museum like the Louvre, or study hieroglyphics in the dark passageways of an Egyptian temple. Persons with disabilities will be able to have experiences, and to take on jobs, otherwise denied them.

Critics point out that the possibilities that virtual reality present may not be purely beneficial, and worry that solitary immersion in artificial environments, dissolving the boundaries between the human and the mechanical, will make us

Critics of virtual reality worry that solitary immersion in artificial environments will make us less fully social in a society that is already atomized.

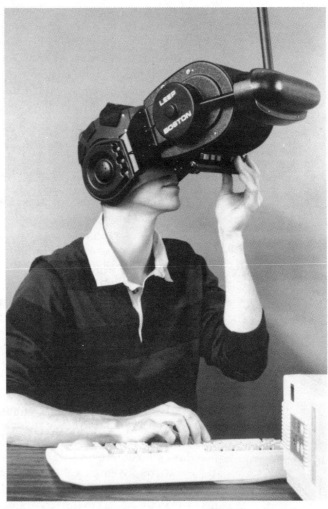

Ulrich Figge/Leep Systems.

less fully social in a society that is already atomized. Fitting (1991, 300) argues that the future portrayed in cyberpunk fiction, such as the works of William Gibson (see the Suggested Readings list at the end of this chapter) is not so much about what lies in store for us as it is an expression of the deep anxieties many people feel about their encounters with technology in the present.

PRIVACY: A PUBLIC ISSUE IN THE INFORMATION AGE

The proliferation of computer-related technologies has transformed our capacity to obtain, store, manipulate, and communicate information. Information has thus become a highly valued commodity. This means that where one stands with respect to its flow is critical. For example, if a large corporation has the means to be the first to discover that government is planning to spend money on the expansion of transportation services in the north, that firm has an advantage over its competitors.

It is also true that the capacity to produce information has outstripped the ability to control it, especially since computer technology now permits not only the formation of data banks but also data linkage (the mingling and manipulation of information from a variety of data sources). An astonishingly thorough profile of an individual can be created from various sources of partial information.

In the *Gemeinschaft*, sustained interaction with a relatively small group of people meant that everyone knew everyone else's business. It is unlikely that privacy was ever a consideration. The emergence of the *Gesellschaft* brought greater anonymity and the ability to keep the various spheres of one's life separate from each other. Privacy has thus come to be valued as a basic right and one worth protecting. Placing privacy in jeopardy is a significant threat in the information age.[2]

The notion of privacy of information is based on the assumption that all information about you belongs, in a very basic way, to *you*. You can choose to disclose it or to keep it secret, as you see fit. The key to effectively maintaining the right to privacy rests with the individual's ability to control the circulation of information relating to himself or herself, an ability necessary for maintaining social relationships and for retaining personal freedom.

Think of a "zone of privacy" surrounding a person as resembling the plastic bubble built for the child whose own immune system could not protect him from infection. An important question is just how large this zone should be. There is always a tension between what is necessary for individual well-being and what is in the best interests of the social collectivity. In any democratic society, the balance achieved is never frozen in a once-and-for-all state, but is constantly being negotiated as issues arise. Developing an abstract notion of what is the optimum size for a privacy zone, however, is a very different thing from putting it into practice. A sociological perspective invites us to examine how the "right to privacy" is applied differently to different groups. Poor people have a much smaller zone of privacy than those who are well off. As consumers, they are more likely to buy on credit, and are therefore more subject to the scrutiny that obtaining credit entails. Similarly, as citizens, they are more reliant on welfare and social services, and therefore more subject to intrusive bureaucratic procedures.

The technological ability to handle vast amounts of information is already available to governments and large organizations in the private sector. As this technology is being produced more and more cheaply, it is also becoming available to small organizations, public and private, and to households. Widened access to information confers many advantages, but it also entails greater and greater risks to privacy.

As we have noted, information is a valued commodity. For example, it has commercial value for a variety of firms. Manufacturers who want to target their advertising effectively find it useful to gather information about your tastes and buying habits. Credit bureaus gather data to prepare reports on where you are employed, where you live, and how quickly you pay your bills; they then sell this information to firms that make decisions about applications for such things as credit, insurance, jobs, or rental dwellings. The files these agencies prepare may be large and contain an assemblage of both facts and opinions (including possibly, your neighbours' opinions of your general character), and the file can provide the basis for rejection of your application for credit.

Some of this information has, of course, always been collected, but the process was previously more laborious. What has made it easier is in the exponential increase in banks of available information and the concomitant decrease in the cost of gathering data. Firms that once would have found the cost of obtaining such information prohibitive can do so for a pittance today.

People have a right to know what is in their own files, but many do not ask. Few complain to government consumer bureaus about violations of their rights. In addition, a confusing mass of government regulations addresses this type of activity. Thus, regulatory confusion and lack of public awareness have combined to permit the marketing of information in what has been called an open season on privacy.

The use of information about individuals is not confined to potential retailers of goods and services. Firms also gather detailed information about their own employees in the interests of bureaucratic efficiency. For example, managers may be in a hurry to identify, among their employees, those who have specific skills. However, in the process of seeking that information in the records, they may also obtain access to information concerning such things as an employee's financial condition, insurance-policy beneficiaries, state of health, and so on. Such information, even if seen inadvertently, may affect decisions with regard to promotion or firing. Is this, then, an invasion of the privacy of employees?

Cheaper production techniques are now making computer technology increasingly available to the individual consumer. This availability has a number of implications for the issue of privacy. Vast amounts of information already enter the home through three major points of intrusion: the mail slot, the telephone, and the television set. A new electronic marvel is on the horizon: two-way interactive television, creating the possibility of a great deal of personal information *leaving* the home. Via this two-way set, you can be enticed to provide information about your opinions on every possible subject, including your political preferences. The apparatus creates the possibility of public-opinion polling on an unprecedented scale. Although the validity of such polling is highly questionable, it gives the illusion of scientific legitimacy. What kinds of decisions will such polls serve to justify? In addition, interactive television can compile enormous amounts of data on your consumer habits, since you will be able to order goods as they are being displayed on your screen. Because it will involve the use of credit cards, it will increase the points of access to information on your finances (and, of course, encourage purchasing on credit).

Proponents of interactive television point to its unquestionable convenience and claim that financial privacy will be respected. However, the ethics of computer use in the private sector have not yet been clearly articulated. In fact, the area of computer crime has only recently begun to be studied, and very few legislative recommendations have resulted. Since the technology itself is in such a constant state of change, it is difficult for society to anticipate the possibilities for using these systems in ways that harm others and infringe on privacy. Over ten years ago, a group of adolescents from a New York private school attempted to tap into 21 Canadian data systems as a lark. They succeeded in entering the data banks of Bell Canada, Canada Cement La Farge, Honeywell, Concordia University, the Universities of Toronto, Alberta, and

Waterloo, and two federal government bureaus, and they destroyed the files of two firms. This incident is only one of many that have raised concerns about the vulnerability of data banks to intrusion, whether done by caprice or by serious intent.

With the coming of the Second World War, the federal government assumed vast responsibilities for economic planning under its constitutional mandate to maintain "peace, order and good government." By the end of that period, the notion that government activity is a positive thing had become entrenched in the national psyche. The consequence of this notion has been burgeoning public-service bureaucracies to accommodate new regulatory functions and to pursue the task of providing a more uniform standard of well-being for Canadians across the country.

Obviously, the more citizens ask government to do for them, the more it needs to know about them. Thus, it has become the largest repository of information about individual Canadians. Decisions crucial to individuals are made on the basis of this information. Who, for instance, is entitled to a disability pension or qualifies for unemployment insurance? The question of who has access to the information collected by government, especially that which falls into such areas as health, education, employment, social services, and law enforcement and corrections, is an important one. Government *routinely* collects and stores data on individuals in order to carry out its normal, socially approved functions. Yet one must ask to what extent the government's need to know infringes on the individual's right to privacy. Further, how is the right of the individual, or the public at large, to know what the government is doing to be weighed against the government's need for secrecy in some of its affairs?

Paradoxically, one can say that privacy itself has finally become a public issue. This development is of very recent origin. In the past fifteen years or so, a number of North American and European jurisdictions have adopted privacy-protection laws. In the spring of 1983, the Canadian government passed Bill C-43, known as the Privacy Act.[3] It defines a zone of privacy for individuals in two major ways: (1) it sets out conditions for the collection, storage, and disposal of personal information, and (2) it provides a code for the use and the disclosure of the information. The act also requires that the Index of Personal Information, in which approximately 1500 federal data banks are currently listed, be available to the public and be housed in such places as libraries, government information offices, and post offices. You can ask to see the information collected about yourself, and you can appeal to the federal courts if access is denied. Furthermore, personal data can only be disclosed to someone else with your permission.

The legislation does, then, make an attempt to safeguard privacy. However, there are significant loopholes, since a substantial number of data banks are exempt from access. If you are alleged to have engaged in activities defined as potentially harmful to the national welfare, you can be denied access to your file.

A watchdog function is performed by the privacy commissioner, whose task is to ensure that the federal government does not collect more information about individual citizens than is practically necessary. In his 1993 report, the commissioner claimed that a major threat to privacy is now being posed by the new, powerful information technologies. The federal government may soon set up electronic "information kiosks" or Infocentres, which would allow individuals to inquire about government services, check Employment Canada's job listings, apply for government programs, and so on. To gain access, they would need personal identification numbers, as well as photograph and fingerprint identification. The privacy commissioner warns that this could lead to the merging of all government databases into a mammoth unitary system that would be capable of providing extraordinarily detailed files on individuals.

Even in the information age, Canadians tend to possess only a vague notion of what is involved in the issue of privacy, and they are less vigilant about its protection than are Americans or Europeans. The commissioner claims that a "technological trance" inures people to the gradual loss of individual rights. The report of the first national survey of Canadians' views about privacy, entitled *Privacy Revealed*, was released in the spring of 1993. Very few of those surveyed had ever heard of a privacy act or a privacy commissioner. However, 60 percent felt they have less privacy than they did a decade ago, 52 percent expressed "extreme concern" about their privacy, and 54 percent were extremely concerned about the linking of personal information from one electronic data base to another. Only 26 percent felt that self-regulation by business (the current situation) with respect to the protection of privacy is acceptable (Privacy Commissioner, 1993, 27–28). The first legislation to regulate private sector collection, use, and disclosure of client and employee personal data was introduced by the Quebec government in 1992.

THE BIOTECHNOLOGICAL REVOLUTION

The technological applications of the biological sciences are referred to as **biotechnology**. This field involves the altering of phenomena in the natural world and the creation of new combinations of "building blocks." The interdisciplinary science base of biotechnology includes chemical and biological engineering, microbiology, applied genetics, molecular biology, biochemistry, toxicology, forest and foods chemistry, physiology, and parasitology.

The use of bacteria to transform natural substances is an endeavour with an ancient history, dating from the first making of fermented drinks, cheese, and yogurt. People have used biological processes for thousands of years to make such things as foods, dyes, drugs, and fuels. High technology builds on these techniques but permits them to be carried out in ways previously unimagined.

When food production is fundamentally transformed, this development entails other types of changes; although it is not always possible to know in advance what they will be. Substitutes for human milk can now be produced in enormous quantities. What will this mean for infant nutrition and the traditional cultural patterns of child care? New sweeteners, such as high-fructose corn syrup and aspartame, are now being manufactured. What will be the effect on sugar economies? In the plant world, research is leading to new hybrids such as triticale, a cross between wheat and rye. How will the availability of grains that can grow in salty soils change the traditional uses of land areas? Shiva (1988) describes the effects of imported Western agricultural technology on the economies of developing countries. While scientists claim success for the hybrid crops that require enormous amounts of pesticides and fertilizer, many are not as sanguine about the results. Fausto-Sterling, in discussing Shiva's findings, explains:

> Middle-level farmers have become wealthier and crops can be exported to North Atlantic countries. But from the point of view of people who previously lived by subsistence farming, the results have been a disaster. Their food supply has been cut off, the ecology has been altered, often producing flooding or drought and women especially have been displaced as economic providers and as a repository of empirical knowledge about native varieties of plants and less ecologically destructive systems of sustainable agriculture. Western technology has worked for some people and seems painfully unnatural for others (1993, 22).

If one attempts to study the effects of technology importation at the level of analysis posited by the modernization thesis, or by world-system theory, one might miss the various effects that technology has on different segments of the society in question.

Waste material, including human sewage, is being used as a food source for bacteria, producing compact forms of protein-rich substances that are edible when mixed with plasticizers, flavourings, binding agents, preservatives, and dyes. A process has been developed that can transform forestry waste, sawdust, wood chips, and twigs into a basic food substance. Factories using such processes will replace land as the site of production—with a transfer of capital from land and agricultural labour to chemical plants. Social changes are inevitable when patterns of food production change so radically, a phenomenon we have already seen with the mechanization of farming.

Biotechnology is also affecting the world of medicine. For example, medical substances that can be extracted, at great expense, from human or mammalian organs (insulin for diabetes, interferon for cancer research) can now be made more cheaply from bacteria. Genetic engineering can also increase the yields of antibiotics from the moulds that produce them. Society has much to gain from these advances. But will the commercial push of pharmaceutical companies serve not only to meet the demand for new wonder drugs but also to create such a demand? The social consequences have yet to be explored.

Animal genetic engineering is another area of biotechnology that is making headway. For instance, the international trade in frozen cow embryos, which can be implanted in other cows, is now worth millions of dollars. At first, it was only possible to combine organisms within the same species or closely related species. Now experimentation is leading to both the mixing of genes, such as those of rabbits and mice, and of putting human genes into bacteria. As Yoxen notes:

> In a mere seven or eight years biotechnology has grown from being an esoteric research topic of university scientists into the foundations of a new industrial movement, a new wave of

investment, commercialization and production... This is not just a change of technique, it is a new way of seeing. It is now possible to think of making organisms to a specification to carry out particular industrial tasks ... The living world can now be viewed as a vast organic Lego kit inviting combinations, hybridization and continual rebuilding. Life is manipulability (1983, 15).

What are the invisible dimensions of the new biotechnologies? (Recall our discussion of bridges and underpasses.) It is not scientific answers to research questions that are invisible, for they are made public. It is the *import of the questions* that is invisible if the public does not have the vocabulary, in the broadest sense, to enter the conversation. An increasing number of scholars are attempting to broaden the conversation about genetic research. David Suzuki, a Canadian geneticist, has been concerned with making visible the "mindset," the belief in human perfectibility (an evolutionary and social Darwinist assumption) that underpins genetic research. The Nazi race purification programs, he says, seemed to represent the application of some of the most "progressive" ideas in science, applying studies of the inheritance of physical characteristics carried out on fruitflies and corn plants to the inheritance of intelligence and behaviour in people (1988). Suzuki and Knudtson (1992) make the argument that the search for gene therapies (cures for human illnesses, or "defects," involving the manipulation of a person's genetic makeup) that is now under way on a massive scale presents unknown risks for future generations. Therefore, they claim, this tinkering should not be carried out without the consent of all members of society. In other words, genetic "cures" are a social, not an individual, issue.

Richard Lewontin, an American scientist, has been a leading adversary of sociobiology, which asserts that certain social behaviours can be transmitted genetically from one generation to the next, and which subscribes to Darwin's theory of evolution as it is interpreted by contemporary biologists. Lewontin (1991) has sought to expose, and discredit, the ideological predispositions that influence genetic research and that lead us to believe that it is not only possible, but desirable, to be able to frame solely in biological terms what it is that makes us human. The Human Genome Project and its international counterpart, the Human Genome Organization (HUGO), together make up an administrative and financial organization created to facilitate cooperative research aimed at mapping out the biological makeup of human beings. The clue to our makeup is thought to be found in the molecule, found in every cell of the body, that is called DNA (deoxyribonucleic acid).[5] The attempt to decipher the genetic code has been likened to the medieval search for the Holy Grail (Kevles & Hood, 1993). The project aims at more than a description of our makeup: it seeks ultimately to establish the causes or the biological sources of our behaviour, and that is a giant leap of faith. Lewontin explains the implications of making such a leap. He recounts that, when the editor of the prestigious journal *Science* was asked why the funds dedicated to the Human Genome Project should not be given to the homeless instead, he replied, "What these people don't realize is that the homeless are impaired ... Indeed, no group will benefit more from the application of human genetics" (1993, 38). Lewontin points out that there are visions of genes for alcoholism, unemployment, domestic and social violence, and drug addiction, and observes:

> What we had previously imagined to be messy moral, political, and economic issues turn out, after all, to be simply a matter of an occasional nucleotide substitution. While the notion that the war on drugs will be won by genetic engineering belongs to Cloud Cuckoo Land, it is a manifestation of a serious ideology that is continuous with the eugenics of an earlier time (1993, 38).[6]

What does it mean to say that unemployment lies in the genes? The geneticist might argue that it means that there is a biological flaw or discrepancy that renders the individual unable to function normally. The hope, then, would be that the flaw could be identified and a gene therapy provided. Someone with a sociological perspective might position the problem very differently, arguing as follows: information about the DNA of prospective employees is extremely useful to employers. First, since employers provide health insurance to employees either directly or through the payment of premiums to insurance companies, they can reduce their wage bill by only hiring workers with the most positive health prognoses (such prognoses would be provided by genetic analysis). Second, if there are certain hazards in the workplace to which a prospective employee could be sensitive, the employer would choose not to hire such a person. In other words, rather than taking responsibility for eliminating workplace hazards, employers would be able to choose their workers more carefully. Hence, the individual who is shown to have a health problem or a susceptibility incompatible with the environment of the workplace might be refused the job, and indeed end up unemployed (Lewontin, 1993, 38).

NEW REPRODUCTIVE TECHNOLOGIES

In Chapter 9, "'The Family' and Families: A Heavy Freight," we noted that many sociologists argue that it is simplistic to view human reproduction mainly in biological terms. The recent development of extraordinarily complex and expensive new reproductive technologies, which can both facilitate conception and monitor pregnancy, has made the social nature of reproduction patently clear.[7] We have, however, barely begun to formulate the economic, legal, ethical, and political questions that their existence raises. As O'Brien has noted:

> ... the immense expansion of the possibility of male control of women's fertility, or the abolition of women in the creation of a technological womb, is such that we have to think of a politics of reproduction. We must also abandon the notion of childbearing as "essentially" biological. It has in fact, never been that (1987, 6).

In earlier times, a decision to control fertility probably meant a decision to practice sexual abstinence or to abort a fetus. Neither practice waited on the development of sophisticated technology. It cannot be assumed, however, that these options were unproblematic for women. Abstinence was subject to marital

For some women, reproductive technology offer their only hope for becoming mothers

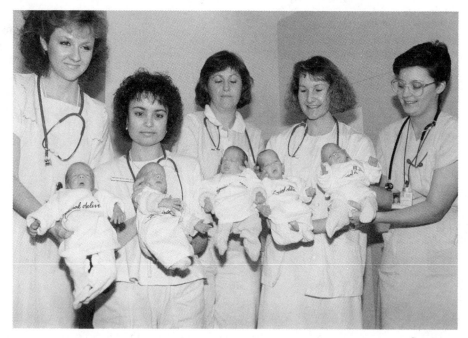

Canapress.

politics, and abortion involved grave physical risks. Childbearing itself was risky for women, and maternal mortality was common. When medical advances reduced the risks of giving birth, death rates from abortion remained high, since most women who elected to have abortions were obliged to resort to illegal and unsafe measures.

Arguments for birth control and family planning were made in Britain and North America in the latter part of the nineteenth century, and some of the debates over this issue had class and racial overtones (there was, for example, an organization in Britain called the Society for Constructive Birth Control and Racial Progress). As McLaren and Tigar McLaren (1986, 64) point out, the popularization of birth control in Canada represented a curious amalgam of ideas. While it championed the idea of the emancipation of women, the assumption persisted that women would remain in the home. Similarly, while it promoted the freedom of individuals to determine their own family size, it also sought to curb uncontrolled reproduction on the part of undesirables such as criminals and alcoholics.

It was not, however, until the second half of this century that the development of birth control techniques such as the birth control pill, intrauterine devices (IUDs), and safer procedures for sterilization and abortion resulted in a major transformation in the process of reproduction. The consequences for women were mixed, for it became clear that reproductive technologies were anything but gender-neutral. While they expanded women's options, they created risks that women were scarcely in a position to assess. IUDs and the pill were developed by male researchers, promoted by pharmaceutical companies, and usually prescribed by male physicians. While these developments were welcomed by women, it is now known that both IUDs particularly the Dalkon shield, and birth control pills, when taken over a long period of time, pose substantial dangers to women.

As with the prevention of pregnancy, pregnancy itself can be examined in terms of the politics of reproduction. One of the reproductive technologies now being hotly debated, artificial insemination by donor (AID), is not new. It involves the fertilization of an egg without sexual intercourse. This is customarily, but not always, done with a syringe. The first reported case of artificial insemination involving humans occurred in 1884 in the United States, without the woman's knowledge (chloroform had been administered) or consent (Corea, 1988, 12). Eichler (1988, 253–54) lists five possible motivations for seeking AID today.

1. Most commonly, it is a way for a couple to have a child when the husband is sterile.

2. A woman may want to have a child without wanting to be involved with a man.

3. A widow may want to have a child by means of the sperm of her deceased husband.

4. A couple may want to improve the family's "genetic stock" by using the sperm of someone with characteristics that they admire. This was the rationale for the establishment, in the United States, of a sperm bank of Nobel Prize winners and other distinguished males.

5. In a new type of AID, when the female partner is sterile, a couple may enter a pre-conception contract with a woman (a "surrogate") who agrees to bear a child for the couple and is then inseminated with the man's sperm. At birth, the child is then adopted by the couple.

All five of these categories give rise to a host of difficult questions. For excellent discussions of the issues involved, see Eichler (1988, 280–310; McDaniel 1988a, 175–206). One question pertains to the child's right to know about his or her genetic heritage. At present, Sweden is the only country that guarantees this right to an artificially conceived child.

The second category mentioned above may include single women and lesbians. With donor semen, it is not difficult for women to inseminate themselves. A group of women in Windsor, Ontario, founded the first Canadian women's artificial insemination service in 1982. The service has been severely criticized by medical professionals, since it exists outside of the profession's control. Brodribb (1986, 415) cites one physician's reaction: "It's another women's self-help group taking medicine out of the hands of the physician." Brodribb argues that the practice of self-insemination poses a threat to "the family" and to men, and therefore, not surprisingly, is at risk of being criminalized.[8]

Most artificial insemination technologies are being institutionalized. The reasoning behind this seems to be that as long as the technologies remain under the control of the medical and legal establishments, they are far less likely to pose threats to the monolithic model of the family. Decisions are highly influenced by the medical profession, since physicians and hospital policy-making bodies serve as gate-keepers to determine who has access to the procedures. Women who wish to take advantage of the new procedures thus experience a loss of control. McDaniel (1988b, 10) notes that decisions about eligibility for these procedures are made by doctors as medical decisions (just as decisions about bridges and underpasses are cast as technical decisions), but that they are "often not made on medical grounds at all but on social ones such as the women's marital status and lifestyle … "

Category 5 on Eichler's list also raises a multitude of questions regarding the rights of all players in a surrogacy arrangement and can be particularly problematic regarding the rights of the woman who carries the child to whom she has made a genetic contribution. What if, after giving birth, she decides she wants to keep the child (as occurred in the famous Baby M)? To what extent can her behaviour be controlled while she is carrying the child? Has she agreed to bear the child because she is poor and needs the money? That destitute and powerless women may be exploited by this technological process is not merely an abstract possibility: the widespread existence of exploitation in such cases has already been well documented. Woliver (1991, 485) argues that reproductive technologies, when used for contraception, sex-selective abortions, and sterilization have already "seriously violated the rights, dignity and indigenous cultures of poor women the world over while failing to address the underlying poverty and inequalities in their societies." It is clear that any attempt to explain the use of reproductive technologies as one of individual choice is seriously limiting, since such an approach neglects the importance of macrosociological factors that help to structure these choices.

In vitro fertilization (IVF) is a sophisticated and very expensive method of artificial insemination in which the male sperm and the female ovum are united outside of a living body, and the resulting embryo is then implanted into a woman's uterus. Preparation for this expensive and usually unsuccessful procedure (the failure rate is 80%) requires that the recipient, before undergoing surgery, take powerful fertility drugs, which have potentially dangerous side effects. Since nothing is yet known about the possible long-term effects of these drugs on the health of children who are born in this way, and on the mothers themselves, critics claim that it is immoral to engage in this type of human experimentation, and call for a moratorium on IVF treatment. The testimony of infertile women themselves who have undergone this long, stressful, and dangerous procedure (often more than once, and without success in the vast majority of cases) is very mixed. Some claim that, once the decision is made to undergo treatment, the patient becomes subject to a medical process that takes on a momentum that is almost impossible to halt. The *how* of a successful pregnancy becomes paramount, and there is no opportunity to pause and reconsider *why* (Rehner, 1989).

On the other hand, Cameron (1990), argues that infertility is a physical problem and should be fixed the same way that physicians fix problems with kidneys and livers. Women with a reproductive disability can only exercise a right of choice with respect to bearing children by seeking medical intervention. A moratorium on IVF would deny them this right. After studying the physical and emotional price paid by women who have undergone IVF, Williams (1989) concludes that the public attention given to "happy endings" obscures the harsh reality of the typical IVF experience. Many groups and individuals who presented briefs to Canada's Royal Commission on New Reproductive Technologies (established in 1989 and embroiled in controversy almost from the beginning) urged that a moratorium, or temporary ban, be placed on the production of test tube babies, until more is known about the risks involved. This approach is advocated by both feminist and so-called pro-family antifeminist, women's groups.

The idea that the woman who produces the ovum for fertilization is the same woman who will carry the fetus in her womb is not inherent in the IVF technology, nor is the idea that the male who produces the sperm is the "social" father of the child who is born. The technology allows for sperm to be supplied by any male donor, and for a "surrogate mother" to provide the womb but not the gentetic material (that is, the ovum). An astonishing array of social relationships can emerge from the combinations that the technology permits. One result is that three distinct types of mothering may be involved in the conceiving, bearing, and raising of a single child (Eichler, 1988, 1). One can speak of genetic motherhood (the supplier), uterine motherhood (the carrier), and social motherhood (pertaining to the one who takes responsibility for the child after it is born). By the same token, as we have noted, the donor father may be a male other than the one who will be the social father. This web of relationships raises an incredible number of legal, moral, and social issues that are only beginning to be addressed. Sociologists are interested, for example, in what assumptions about the nature of the family as a social institution serve as the basis for making legal determinations regarding "property rights" and responsibilities with respect to the child that is born. If a surrogate is hired to provide the womb, does she have any rights?

In 1993 a new chapter in creating human life may have begun. A researcher reported to the American Fertility Society that he had succeeded in cloning human embryos, that is, splitting the embryo into two or more identical parts. Although the method employed is not a new technique—it is already used to clone animal embryos—its application to human embryos opens a Pandora's box of ethical and legal questions. Writing in the *New York Times*, October 24, 1993, Gina Kolata described several uses to which the technique could be put. One possibility is that it would allow parents to save identical copies of embryos, so that if their child ever needed an organ transplant, the mother could give birth to the child's identical twin, who could then contribute an organ to the twin who needed it. Or, parents could keep a frozen embryo as a backup: in case their child died, they could have the perfect replacement.

Who Will Manage Technological Change?

Who will control the development and deployment of all of these new technologies? When decisions are left to the market, control is in the hands of giant corporations—for example, chemical, oil, food, seed, and pharmaceutical companies—which are propelled by the profit motive. Are such decisions too important to be left to commerce? In the case of the new reproductive technologies, we have seen the risks posed to women when control lies in the hands of the medical profession.

It is often said that technological change is sweeping over us like a relentless tidal wave. This fatalistic view implies that nothing that can be done about it and obscures the fact that the impact of technology will differ from one society to another and from one societal sector to another. In fact, as we have stressed throughout our discussion of technological change, both the development and the implementation of technologies is fundamentally a social process. Computer technology permits both increased centralization of decision making and greater decentralization. It can increase social isolation, or it can help to knit previously isolated persons into the community. The mere existence of the technology tells us nothing about which of the possibilities will occur; in fact, at any given time in a particular society, one can likely identify developments in both directions. Likewise, biotechnological developments can make a tremendous contribution toward improving health in the general population, even as they raise the spectre of negative consequences that we cannot yet fully imagine for the well-being of future generations. The new reproductive technologies can be liberating for women, increasing their reproductive choices, or they can contribute to the further subordination of women.

Should the harnessing of technological change in order to serve carefully articulated societal goals command greater pubic attention? Should the distribution of the costs and benefits of change be left to the market, or should they be determined in the political arena? What Yoxen had to say about the biotechnological revolution can be applied to technological change in general:

> New technologies, processes and products have to be dreamt, argued, battled, willed, cajoled and negotiated into existence. They arise through endless rounds of conjecture, experiment, persuasion, appraisal and promotion. They emerge from chains of activity, in which at many points their form and existence is in jeopardy. There is no unstoppable process that brings invention to the market. If this view is correct, then the scale, pace and social impact of the biotechnological revolution must be open to negotiation. There must be alternative pathways (1983, 29).

This stance supports the Weberian view that change is the product of human decision making. It also reflects the modern view that change can be planned and, perhaps, controlled in accordance with negotiated priorities. Our examination of social movements in the following section shows that human beings do indeed attempt to initiate, temper, or reverse social change.

SOCIAL MOVEMENTS

The antinuclear, environmental, pro-life, and feminist movements are only a few examples of social movements with which you are no doubt familiar. A **social movement** can be defined as "a conscious, collective, organized attempt" to bring about some form of social change (Wilson, 1973, 8), to protect the status quo, or to restore society to a previous state. In the first instance, we would be speaking of either a revolutionary or a reform-oriented social movement. In the second instance, we would say that the social movement is conservative. The third kind, the social movement that seeks the restoration of a previous order, can be termed reactionary.

A host of new social movements, such as the environmental movement, have emerged since the 1960s.

Western Canada Wilderness Committee.

There is a vast literature on social movements, and we shall not attempt to review it here. Carroll (1993, 310) notes that the increased theoretical sophistication of this area of research reflects the fact that, since the 1960s, social movements have become more and more central to the events and practices that are shaping our times, "whether they take the form of micro-political challenges to domination in everyday life or supranational resistance to state violence and capitalist globalization."

While discontent about some major aspect of society is necessary for a social movement to emerge, discontent alone is not sufficient to produce a movement. Proponents of a collective action approach to social movements argue that, at any time, there is likely to be enough discontent in any society to justify social unrest, and that what needs explaining is why and how that discontent comes to be expressed in a social movement. According to this perspective, the ability to mobilize resources is the key to understanding how social movements emerge. Until this mobilization occurs, the people experiencing discontent are merely an amorphous, unorganized collectivity.

By resources, we mean such things as an ideology, effective leadership, connections to influential individuals and groups, public support, funding, networks of communication, and networks of cooperative relationships. Collective action theorists seek to identify the cleavages in society that set people at odds with one another, and those factors that integrate them or link them together. An understanding of both cleavage and integration, it is argued, is necessary for an understanding of how particular social movements emerge (Clark, 1986, 368). In a comparison of nationalist movements in Quebec and the collective action in which native peoples have engaged, Clark notes that the former have been more vital and effective than the latter. This cannot be explained merely in terms of cleavage for, while the cleavage between French Canadians and the rest of the populace is great, it is less pronounced than that between native peoples and other Canadians. Shouldn't stronger collective action, then, emerge among native peoples than among French Canadians? Clark looks for the answer in factors of integration within each of the two groups. Native peoples are far less integrated than French Canadians. As we saw in the chapter on minorities, native peoples are divided by geography, language, and culture. They are also separated by administrative distinctions; they are designated as treaty or nontreaty Indians, for example, and as status or nonstatus Indians. When to these distinctions are added organizational weaknesses that discourage integration, such as the lack of material resources and a small pool from which educated leadership can be drawn, the barriers to collective action are clear. It is only recently that some of the barriers have been reduced, leading to a stronger organizational base for collective action, and a greater sense of collective identity. As Clark notes, an attempt to explain native activism or the lack of it in terms of its discontent alone would fail, because the discontent was there long before, and collective action did not emerge until recently (1986, 376–78).

WOMEN'S MOVEMENTS

Women's movements are not a new phenomenon. There are (often scant) records of them in most periods of documented history, and they have emerged in all regions of the world. For example, the Koran (the book of writings accepted by Muslims as revelations made to Mohammad by Allah) refers to an organized uprising of women in South Arabia who objected to Mohammad's injunction that women should not engage in trading. The history of colonial Latin America contains accounts of women mobilizing to defend their economic interests. In eighteenth-century France, some of the women's associations that had already been formed participated in the French Revolution. Women's movements developed in the revolutionary upheavals of the 1840s in Europe, and a women's rights newspaper, *Les Voix des Femmes*, was founded in France.

Also, in the nineteenth century, women in many regions of the world began to organize in order to protest against inequalities based on sex, and to demand legal reforms that would enable them to participate in the public sphere. Some of their initiatives were taken in association with political parties, and some with broader movements promoting social change. It was at this time that the term "feminist" was adopted by women's rights campaigners in North America and Europe, as well as in countries such as Japan, Russia, Argentina, Turkey, India, and the Philippines (Molyneux, 1993, 712–13). Although these separate movements had diverse goals and strategies, they shared a commitment to opposing the oppression of women in its many forms. They pursued this aim from many different vantage points. As Molyneux notes:

> Some, like the Persian Women's Society of 1911, confronted entrenched religious laws and attitudes; others worked within the context of liberal states for greater legal equality and the vote; and still others linked their struggle for equality with socialist revolution. In the less developed regions of the world such as Turkey, India, China and Egypt, feminist associations saw their interests represented within the project of a modernizing nationalism, while others remained independent from political parties, committed to a more radical interpretation of women's liberation, one which went beyond equal rights to embrace questions of sexuality and interpersonal relations (1993, 713).

It is difficult now, perhaps, to imagine that in many countries women were not legally considered "persons" with the right to own property and to vote. In the late 1800s, the British jurist William Blackstone ruled that "women become incorporated and consolidated with their husband," and thus, "a man cannot grant anything to his wife for the grant would be to suppose her separate existence" (Gavron, 1966). The quest for the right to vote (suffrage) was a driving force in bringing women together. In the United States, this quest was spurred by the participation of women in the movement against slavery, and by the determination to have the consumption of alcohol prohibited. The latter was also a motivation for demands for the vote among Canadian women. The first Canadian suffrage organization was founded in Toronto in 1876 by Dr. Emily Howard Stowe. The first woman to practise medicine in Canada, Dr. Stowe was initially obliged to go to the United States to obtain a medical degree that was refused her in Canada. It was not until 1918 that the federal franchise was granted to all women. By 1922, women had obtained the vote at the provincial level throughout English Canada, but in Quebec that did not occur until 1940.[9]

What is known as the "first wave" of feminism, which drew its momentum from countless voluntary associations, also centred on women's issues such as pregnancy rights, education, and economic independence. We have seen in previous chapters that there are different currents of feminist thought and, thus, different prescriptions for change. The question of what "equality" means, a question that divided the movement from its inception, is still a matter of debate. Does the route to equality lie in equal opportunities? Or, does equality mean taking difference into account? If so, does the attainment of equality between women and men wait on a major restructuring of economic and social institutions that will improve the quality of life for both groups? Equal-rights feminism, focusing on suffrage and property laws, was a forerunner of the liberal feminism of today with its concern for equality of opportunity. (Recall our discussion of this perspective in the chapter on education.) Similarly, the early concerns and strategies of socialist and trade-union women have had an influence on the politics of present-day socialist feminists. Women who were socialists, representing the interests of working women and leery of associating themselves with the women's movement, were concerned with the economic inequalities engendered by capitalism, and saw suffrage as useful only if it could help to secure broader social and economic reforms (Adamson et al., 1988, 33–35).

The perspective of radical feminists today reflects the influence of the early maternal feminists, whose ideology of female difference and female superiority explicitly linked biology and morality (Adamson et al., 1988, 30–31). Lady Aberdeen of the National Council of Women of Canada explained the "mission" of the maternal feminists in the following way:

> But in the meantime, how can we best describe this woman's mission in a word? Can we not best describe it as "mothering" in one sense or another? We are not all called upon to be mothers of little children, but every woman is called upon to "mother" in some way or another; and it is impossible to be in this country, even for a little while, and not be impressed with a sense of what a great work of "mothering" is in a special sense committed to the women of Canada (cited in Adamson et al., 1988, 31).

Lady Aberdeen's use of the singular noun "woman" in speaking of mission is not accidental, for the maternal–feminist model was a unitary one. It emphasized the biological imperatives that govern the female role and that make a woman fundamentally different from a man. In this view, it is the capacity for mothering that makes a woman an ideal reformer and a protector of public morality. As we noted in Chapter 9, it is a view that does not call for a radical restructuring of societal institutions. Women's participation in the public sphere was construed as an extension of their traditional role in the family.

The "second wave" of feminism emerged in the late 1960s, in a climate of confrontation that included student radicalism and the American civil rights movement. Just as the suffrage issue provided an integrating force for the women of diverse persuasions who were active in the first wave, so also did the campaign for free abortion on demand become a focal point for the mobilization of women in the second phase. The Abortion Caravan that crossed Canada in 1970, made a problem, long hidden as the "grubby little secret" of individual women, highly visible and defined it as a public issue. The abortion issue also raised the larger question of control of women's bodies by the state and by the medical profession. It should be noted, however, that although the issue served as a powerful unifying factor in the women's movement, it also produced disagreement among women, who supported either pro-choice or pro-life positions. This cleavage was to become grist for the mill in the emergence of the countermovement that we shall examine in the next section of this chapter.

Calls for the establishment of a Royal Commission on the Status of Women came, in the late sixties, from already-established women's organizations who were experienced in lobbying governments and had faith in the state's capacity to bring about social change. The commission was established in 1967, and submitted its report in 1970. The process involved in the commission's investigations, encouraging women's groups to take positions, air grievances, and make recommendations, served as a spur to the feminist movement, just as the highly publicized report itself helped to identify problems and provide an agenda for strategies to improve the position of women. An umbrella organization for women's groups, the National Action Committee on the Status of Women (NAC) was founded in 1973, and now has over 500 member groups. The assembly of women who attended the meeting at which NAC was formed included representatives of groups ranging from the Communist Party to the Imperial Order of Daughters of the Empire (Vickers, 1992, 42). The proclamation of 1975 as International Women's Year was another watershed for institutionalized feminism, and resulted in government funding for women's activities. This move was viewed with suspicion by some feminists, who spoke of the dangers of "token gestures" and of co-optation; the creation of links between women's groups and male-dominated power structures, they argued, would deflect women from a commitment to bringing about fundamental change in social structures. You will recall the argument in Chapter 8, "Work and Its Contexts," that the way in which women's interests came to be pursued in state bureaucracies actually served to marginalize these interests (Grant & Tancred, 1992).

We have said that forces of integration, such as communication networks, are important if discontent is to find expression in a social movement. Two types of networks played a strong role in the feminist movement. At the institutional level, as Adamson et al. note,

> ... it is made up of hundreds of groups: some small, some large, some focused on single issues, some with a complex and wide-ranging political perspective. Some organize around legislative issues, some provide services, others focus on organizing women into unions. The constituency of some organizations is homogeneous: immigrant women, lesbians, women of colour, business and professional women, women in trades. Others have a heterogeneous constituency and focus on specific issues such as day care, or on supporting a political perspective, as does the women's committee of the New Democratic Party (NDP). Some are based in large institutions like universities and government ministries; some are located in small communities (1988, 8).

With such diversity, a strong ideology was needed for a social movement to be sustained. The feminist rallying cries of "the personal is political" and "sisterhood is powerful" helped to serve this function. Existing women's organizations began to transform and strengthen their agendas by clarifying their goals with respect to social change. Canadian farm women, who had begun to develop a rich web of organizations since the late 1800s, became more politically active (Hundertmark, 1985). One initiative was to develop ways of making their contributions to farmwork more visible by changing the conception of work so that their contribution

Wives Supporting the Strike, a Sudbury group that had mobilized to help the men in their strike against Inco, linked up with the women's movement to march in the 1979 International Women's Day demonstration in Toronto.

Frank Rooney.

would be accounted for by the census of agriculture. They also were encouraged to lobby governments concerning such things as rural child care facilities, rural transportation, and measures to deal with various social and economic aspects of the "farm crisis," including increased farm bankruptcies and cutbacks in rural social services (Shortall, 1993).

At the grassroots level, the consciousness-raising groups that sprang up in the early days of the movement gave organizational expression to the idea that the personal is political (we have mentioned this idea before, and in different words throughout the book, in speaking about how private troubles may come to be seen as public issues). These groups provided an opportunity for articulating, validating, and reinterpreting private experiences, and were highly influential in politicizing and activating group members. Belonging to such a group often gave women the courage not only to move into the political sphere, but also to challenge traditional patterns in their own daily lives. Further, and broader, channels of discussion and communication were opened up with the establishment of collectives, women's caucuses, women's centres, shelters, feminist bookstores and presses, feminist journals, and women's studies programs in universities.

The feminist movement got under way and gathered steam through the efforts of white, middle-class, well-educated, and often young, women. Organizations of "other" women, such as black, native, working-class, and lesbian women, remained marginal. Eventually, however, the movement was obliged to recognize the racism, ageism, and heterosexism that permeated its ranks (Adamson et al., 1988, 260). This recognition, and the building of bridges to groups of women that struggle with other forms of oppression in addition to sexism is a process that is just beginning. A more pluralistic notion of feminism is also required if feminism is to be effective at the international level, since the preoccupation of Western feminists with sexual equality seems less urgent to women who situate their activities within a context of overwhelming poverty, political strife, and problems of modernization.

The women's movement has been instrumental in bringing about substantial changes in legislation, attitudes, and public consciousness. Banting has noted that it "has created a powerful political constituency with a commitment to social intervention in a variety of forms ..." (1987, 318). However, as the stubborn persistence of social inequalities that we have discussed throughout the book indicates, one should not overestimate what has been accomplished. To speak of having reached a "post-feminist" era in which the need for feminism is obsolete, as some do, is surely premature. The sobering findings of Sidel's (1990) study of young American women show that a young woman today may feel that she is free to "do it all" and "have it all" (the New American Dreamers); she may feel that she will need to work but will still maintain a strong, primary commitment to a traditional role in the family (the Neotraditionalists); or, she may see few choices or options for the future at all (the Outsiders). What is striking is that, in each case she feels she is, as the title of Sidel's book suggests, *On Her Own: Growing Up in the Shadow of the American Dream* (1990). It is a deep irony that this sense of self-reliance has perhaps emerged both in spite of, and because of, the women's movement.

COUNTERMOVEMENTS

It is common for social movements to be accompanied by "anti" or countermovements that organize in opposition to the changes that the social movements advocate. Mottl (1980, 620) adapts Wilson's definition of a social movement to define a **countermovement** as "a conscious, collective, organized attempt to resist or reverse social change." Gale (1986, 209) argues that the ideology of the countermovement takes shape as the social movement grows. A sort of dialectical, or back-and-forth, relationship emerges between the opposing movements in a way that brings changes to both. Turner and Killian (1972) argue that if a conflict is prolonged, a pattern of interdependence emerges in which both sides continuously adjust their programs, ideologies, and strategies to take into account the programs, ideologies, and strategies of the other. As a result, the initial social movement is nudged in the direction of moderation. The interaction between feminist movements and antifeminist movements provides an example of this process (Erwin 1993; Conelly & Christiansen-Ruffman, 1977).

Anti-Feminist Countermovements

The social movement that eventuated in the vote for women spawned organized opposition along the way, and many antisuffragists were women. Both sides argued that the other side did not represent the "true interests" of women. Those who opposed the vote for women argued that it would be redundant, or unnecessary, for women to vote, since their interests were perfectly well represented by their husbands. One antisuffragist gave the following advice to women: "Raise good and able men and in one generation the world will be governed by good and able men" (Arnold, cited in Marshall, 1984, 349). Political activity, it was argued in the publication *Anti-Suffragist* (1911, 7), would strain the delicate female reproductive organs, "making [women] childless or mothers of a weak-kneed race." Arguments against suffrage for women rested firmly on the idea that it posed a threat to the traditional family and to the traditional destiny of women. There was a willingness to believe in this threat because of the numerous other progressive movements that existed at the beginning of the twentieth century. In Canada, a full-fledged antisuffragist movement did not emerge, perhaps because proponents of suffrage reasoned that extending the vote to women who were mainly Christian and conservative would help to reduce the threat posed to the status quo by the suspect politics and religions of new immigrants (Steuter, 1992, 292). What was common to the American and Canadian situations, however, was that the significance of the vote was interpreted in the light of what it would mean for the family.

This same concern for the traditional, patriarchal family has also galvanized opposition to the contemporary women's movement, this time both in Canada and the United States. While the groups involved identify themselves as "pro-family," they are actually firm believers in only one version of the family, what we have referred to as the monolithic, patriarchal model of the family. In their perspective, those who do not subscribe to this model—that is, those who accept a diversity of family forms—are "anti-family" and pose a serious threat to society.

In the United States, opposition forces mobilized against the proposed Equal Rights Amendment to the American constitution in the early 1980s, which would have made all sex-based distinctions in the laws and activities of all levels of government unconstitutional. By the late 1960s and early 1970s, women who had not gone out to work were finding that they had to explain that they were "just a housewife" and this constituted a serious "pay cut" in their social prestige (Mansbridge, 1986, 108). If economic independence could be achieved by working women, what did this mean for women who stayed at home and were dependent on their husbands? Clearly, their own economic security was threatened if men did not have a sacred obligation to take care of their families. This reasoning also required opposition to any measures that smacked of the welfare state, and thus, antifeminists gained strength from an ideological alliance with other rightist, or politically conservative, groups. By the same token, they were immeasurably strengthened by the compatibility of their interests with those of fundamentalist religious groups, groups to which many antifeminists belonged. These religious groups provided a network of communication that was invaluable to the growth of antifeminism as a social movement, just as the religious groups to which William Aberhart was able to appeal via his radio broadcasts in the 1930s in Alberta helped the Social Credit Party to achieve power there in 1935.

The feminist proposal that women should have free access to safe abortions was also construed as a potentially lethal blow to the traditional family. Again, the interests of American antifeminists coincided with those of religious groups who interpreted abortion as wrongful interference with God's plan.

Religion has also played a role in the mobilization of pro-family, antifeminist forces in Canada. The largest and most visible of the pro-family groups is an organization called R.E.A.L. Women (whose acronym stands for the slogan

Realistic, Equal and Active for Life). With its roots in the anti-abortion move-ment, it was established in Toronto in 1983, taking as its motto, "Women's rights, but not at the expense of human rights." Fundamentalist and Catholic churches have provided substantial financial support to the organization, as well as office space, equipment, and free advertising in religious publications (Erwin, 1988). It has also received funding from the Secretary of State's Women's Program and has succeeded in gaining considerable media attention. In addition to abortion, R.E.A.L. Women has opposed no-fault divorce, univer-sal child care, sex education, affirmative action, and pay equity; it has also taken a firm stand against gay and lesbian rights. One of their pamphlets likened homosexuals to "bikers such as Hell's Angels" (Eichler, 1988, 416). On eco-nomic issues, its leadership has endorsed neoconservative positions, such as cut-backs in social services, taken by groups that constitute what has been called the New Right (Hannant, 1988).[10]

Ironically, it is both the successes *and* the failures of the feminist move-ment that have attracted adherents to the countermovement. Their success in widening women's choices with respect to work and family life have had the unintended consequence of encouraging an image of "the feminist" to which many women cannot relate: young, white, urban, career-oriented, competitive with men, and uninterested in children. At the same time, feminism has failed to "deliver the goods" in bringing about substantial changes in the structure of society, so that "freedom" and "equality" still connote, for many women, being free to work in low-paying, segregated jobs, often with children and without the assistance of a male partner. This, too, is a prospect (or a reality) that many women find oppressive.

In recent years, the pro-family movement has tempered its antifeminist rhetoric, taking care not to suggest that every woman should be in the home. It, too, talks about "choice" and "equality." In acknowledging that women should have choices about working or staying at home, it has adopted the most moderate elements of the feminist position, leaving the feminist movement to be seen to be identified with a more "extreme" anti-family stance. In doing this, it hopes to be more acceptable to a broader constituency of women. Publicly, it has also stopped framing its opposition in fundamentalist religious terms. Feminists, on the other hand, have diverted considerable energy to countering the criticisms of pro-family groups. Dubinsky (1987, 7) notes that feminists in government agencies have reported that more and more of their time is taken up with justifying actions or decisions that might provoke pro-family groups. As Luker (1984) notes in her analysis of the conflict between the pro-choice movement and the pro-life countermovement in the United States, both sides, paradoxically, contribute to making the countermovement seem more powerful and successful than it really is. Thus, both contribute to a self-fulfilling prophecy, arousing even greater interest in the countermovement among uncommitted women, the general public, and legislators.

Although feminists themselves first drew attention to the social value of women's work in the home, some now argue that the threat posed by the countermovement is one that needs to be addressed. But in what way? Can the women's movement afford not to respond to the anti-family caricatures drawn by such groups as R.E.A.L. women? If they do respond, do they risk meeting the countermovement on some middle ground, compromising their commitment to bringing about far-reaching social change?

. . . .

OVERVIEW

A major theme of this book is the co-existence of continuity and change in society. In areas such as socialization, the division of labour, the distribution of societal rewards, and the relationships between minority and dominant groups, we have noted that the thrust for change has usually clashed with the weight of tradition, inertia, and the interests of groups intent on maintaining things as they are. What distinguishes change in the modern world is its accelerating pace and its magnitude, facilitated by a rapidly expanding knowledge base, a heavy investment in technological innovation, and an increasing emphasis on rational decision-making that is oriented to planned change.

In this chapter, we have reviewed cyclical, evolutionary, and conflict theories of change. Most sociologists today study change from a functionalist or a conflict perspective. While functionalists are primarily interested in the mechanisms of adjustment that contribute to social stability, conflict theorists focus on the opposition between groups that seek to maintain their position of dominance and groups attempting to change their condition.

Technological innovation is a major agent of social change, although how technology is developed, received, and deployed can vary markedly among societies. Technology is much more than the sum of material artifacts; it comprises a *system* of knowledge, artifacts, organization, human practices, and attitudes. We have examined the nature and implications of the microchip revolution and the far-reaching developments in biotechnology, including the new reproductive technologies. Whose interests are served by these developments, and how is technology to be controlled?

The present era has seen an explosive growth in the capacity to gather, save, disseminate, and interpret information. In the age of information, privacy has become a public issue. While Canadians express concern about the issue of privacy, they are far from vigilant in ensuring its protection.

Social movements are conscious, collective, and organized attempts to bring about social change, to protect the status quo, or to restore society to a previous state. While discontent about some major aspect of society is a necessary condition for a social movement to emerge, to succeed it must be able to mobilize resources such as an ideology, effective leadership, connections to influential groups and individuals, funding, and networks of communication.

It is not uncommon for a social movement to be accompanied by a countermovement that is opposed to the position advocated by the social movement. A pattern of interdependence tends to emerge between the two movements, such that modifications may occur in both. We have examined the feminist movement and its anti-feminist counterpart in terms of this conceptual framework. Monolithic and pluralistic visions of family life provide the contested terrain on which these opposing movements meet.

ASSIGNMENTS

1. Do we have an obligation to consider the consequences that our behaviour may have on the welfare of future generations? Read *Thinking Intergenerationally* by Ron Hirshhorn (Working Paper No. 9, Economic Council of Canada, 1990). Is the concept of "intergenerational equity" reasonable? What are the liabilities he suggests we should be passing on? What do you think should be included in the concept of a "national heritage" to be held in trust for those who follow us?

2. Read two articles in one of the following books: (1) Liora Salter and David Wolfe, eds., *Managing Technology: Social Science Perspectives* (Toronto: Garamond, 1990); or (2) Henry Wiseman, Jokelee Vanderkop, and Jorge Nef, eds., *Critical Choices! Ethics, Science and Technology* (Toronto: Thompson Educational Publishing, 1991). What problems do the authors identify concerning the management of technological change? What strategies do they propose for addressing those problems?

3. Look up the editions of two newspapers that were issued on the day of your birth (or, if you were born on a Sunday, on the Monday edition). What things strike you as different than from what they are today? What seems not to have changed? Can any of the changes be attributed to the efforts of a social movement? What about technological innovation?

SUGGESTED READINGS

Nancy Adamson, Linda Briskin, and Margaret McPhail, *Feminist Organizing for Change: The Contemporary Women's Movement in Canada* (Toronto: Oxford University Press, 1988). The authors examine the ideology, practices, and strategies of one of the most influential social movements in this century and assess its successes and failures. While paying attention to the institutional aspects of the "second wave" of feminism, they also emphasize the grass-roots activities and ideology that gave impetus to, and continue to help shape, feminism's quest for a more equal society.

Gro Harlem Brundtland, *Our Common Future: Report of the World Commission on Environment and Development* (Oxford: Oxford University Press, 1987). Mandated in 1983 by the General Assembly of the United Nations to formulate "a global agenda for change," the Commission undertook a massive examination of the intricate relationships between the state of the environment and economic growth in the context of an increasingly international economy. The highly readable, and often shocking, report deals with such issues as population growth, food security, economic threats to ecological systems, urban concentration, Third World debt, and nuclear war. For a critique of the report that reproaches the Commission for assuming that economic growth is no longer possible or desirable, see Ted Trainer "A Rejection of the Brundtland Report," International Foundation for Development Alternatives, dossier 77 (May/June 1990), 72–84.

William Gibson, *Count Zero* (New York: Ace Books, 1986). Gibson is a prize-winning writer of cyberpunk, a subgenre of science fiction. *Count Zero* is the story of a small-time data thief, living in the twenty-first century, whose access to "cyberspace" is taken away because he has double-crossed his employers. In Gibson's works, electronic information technologies have created a global nervous system that is able to ignore traditional governmental institutions and regulations; the new "company man" is therefore devoid of national affiliations, and is legally bound to the company for life. Futurist Alvin Toffler has argued that the function of science fiction is to acclimatize us to the future, so that we will accept a world ruled by giant corporations. Gibson, on the contrary, seems to want to wake us up about what the future could hold, so that we will care enough not to let it happen.

Craig McKie and Keith Thompson, eds., *Canadian Social Trends, Vol. 2* (Toronto: Thompson Educational Publishing, Inc., 1994). The contributors to this valuable volume draw on a wealth of data about Canadians to analyze changes that have occurred in Canadian society. The picture they present is one of both stability and change.

Richard S. Rosenberg, *The Social Impact of Computers*, 2nd ed. (San Diego: Academic Press, Inc., 1992). This is a clear and interesting introduction to computer technology and its many applications. Rosenberg examines the hidden influences of computers, as microprocessors come to be embedded in more and more products. He assesses both the positive and negative impact that computers have on the nature of work and on personal freedom.

Eleanor Maticka-Tyndale, "Modification of Sexual Activities in the Era of AIDS: A Trend Analysis of Adolescent Sexual Activities," *Youth and Society*, 23:1, 31–49. The first Canadian case of Acquired Immune Deficiency Syndrome was reported in Montreal in 1981, and until the mid-eighties, the illness was portrayed as one pertaining only to male homosexuals. After 1985, when reports of heterosexual transmission of the HIV virus emerged, mass media and school campaigns to promote "safer sex" were launched. Maticka-Tyndale finds that there has been no marked shift among young adults to compliance with safer-sex guidelines, even though their knowledge about the disease has increased. See also the issue of *Current Sociology*, which is devoted to the subject of trends in the sociological study of AIDS; in particular Michael Pollack with Genevieve Poicheler and Janine Pierret; "AIDS: A Problem for Sociological Research," *Current Sociology* 40 (1992):3. With respect to AIDS and the workplace, see David Goss, Derek Adam-Smith, Gary Rees, and Adele Sinclair, "Organizational AIDS Policies as Data: Possibilities and Precautions," *Sociology*, 27:2, 299–305.

George Ritzer, *The McDonaldization of Society* (Newbury Park, Calif: Pine Forge Press, 1993). Using Weberian theory, Ritzer, who is a sociologist, examines McDonald's as the prime example of the process of rationalization that is changing the face of the social landscape. Video rentals, shopping malls, weight loss firms, universities, supermarkets, Disney World, medical clinics, churches, and suburban housing tracts are only a few of the items he tosses into his highly readable analysis. Some of the others may surprise you. In his final chapter, Ritzer makes some provocative suggestions as to how individuals can attempt to cope with, and resist, the ubiquitous process of McDonaldization.

NOTES

1. Nisbet illustrated the rather amusing side of this human tendency with a story:

   > During World War II in Britain ... time and motion studies were made of gun crews in the artillery ... In one such study of a gun crew numbering five men, two of the men simply stood at attention for three seconds, then resumed the work necessary to the next firing. This was puzzling. The men themselves could not explain it, it was a part of the technique they had learned in gunnery school. Neither the officers nor the instructors at gunnery school could explain it either. All any of them knew was that the three-second standing at attention was "a necessary" part of the process of firing the highly mechanized piece of artillery. One day, an old, long-retired artillery colonel was shown the time and motion pictures ... "Ah," he said when the performance was over "I have it. The two men are holding the horses." ... Not for close to half a century had horses drawn artillery, but they once had—holding the horses while the gun fired was necessary. The horses disappeared from the artillery, but the way of behaviour went on. We laugh, and say the story is one more illustration of military inertia ... But the history of the academic, legal, medical and engineering professions is not different, except in details. Nor is the rest of society different (1970, 316).

2. Privacy of information is only one of several types of privacy, but it is the one that concerns us here.

3. Notice that this legislation does not confront the issue of information abuse in the private sector. It concerns only the regulation of federal government data banks.

4. Exemptions are based on a number of considerations. For example, information is not released if it would harm the government's conduct of international affairs.

5. For a brief explanation of what this research entails, see Lewontin (1993).

6. Eugenics is an applied science that seeks to improve the human race's genetic heritage. The word also refers to a social movement that aims to popularize the principles and the practices of the science, and has come to be associated with racism. In the early part of the twentieth century, proponents of eugenics advocated sterilization as a means of reducing the costs to society of illness, moral depravation, and mental retardation. This practice was supported by state laws in the United States with respect to the mentally ill and the retarded. Eugenics fell into disrepute in the West when special eugenics health courts were established by the Nazis to deal with the "socially undesirable." The courts ordered the sterilization of over half a million individuals. In recent years, advances in genetics have revealed that certain diseases, such as diabetes and sickle cell anemia, are transmitted via the genes.

Couples who undergo genetic screening and are found to be at risk of passing on a hereditary illness may then decide not to have children. Eugenics has enthusiasts today, because of these scientific advances, but many people disapprove of any attempts to alter the human species' genetic heritage.

7. For a useful glossary of terms pertaining to these technologies, see McTeer (1993, 33–43). For an outline of their chronological development, see Corea (1988, 336–42).

8. The Ontario Law Reform Commission of 1985 recommended that artificial insemination and other technological "treatments" be confined to married women or to heterosexual women with partners (McDaniel, 1988a, 190).

9. Even as late as 1929, a decade after Canadian women had the vote in all jurisdictions except Quebec, women had to appeal to the British Privy Council for a ruling that they were persons and thus eligible to serve in the Senate.

10. For a description of the characteristics of pro-family adherents, see Erwin (1993).

Appendix

Writing to Learn: The Essay

Writing is a central skill in the acquisition of knowledge. Writing and learning are inextricably connected. That is, you learn to write *while* you are writing to learn. Often you don't know what you want to say until you have made a first attempt to write it down. As you write, you "discover" what you mean or want to say. Then, with the thoughts on the page, you can rethink what you have said before trying to express it in a revised form. (In fact, the word "revised" comes from the Latin for "see twice.") Writing, then, permits you to find meaning and to establish firmer ownership over your thoughts.

Thus, the ability to write is not acquired overnight, once and for all at a particular stage of your education. Rather, it is a skill to be developed, improved, and honed over a lifetime as you progress to more complex ways of thinking.

The academic essay is a particular form of writing, which begins with a problem or question that calls for resolution through research, study, and the presentation of evidence. It requires you to formulate a central idea (often referred to as a thesis) trying all the evidence together in response to the problem. The way the evidence is linked in support of the central idea is called the argument, an argument that you formulate in order to persuade a reader. As the writer of an essay, you are cast in the role of the courtroom lawyer arguing a case. The argument runs as a single thread throughout the essay, supporting, clarifying, or elaborating your central idea. The academic essay is, thus, a very disciplined form of thinking and writing.

GETTING STARTED

Faced with a task, most people worry about getting it done before actually buckling down to confront it. The longer you procrastinate, however, the larger the job looms. Something that is, in fact, quite manageable may grow into a major stumbling block. Students say that this is often true of writing essays. Focusing on a sequence of tasks, as described below, can help.

CHOOSING THE TOPIC

If you have been given a list of topics from which to choose, make that choice almost immediately. Once you've committed yourself, you have only one topic to worry about, instead of five or six.

An assignment that reads "Write a five-page essay on a subject of your choice" appears seductively simple but is one of the most difficult assignments of all because it leaves the field so open, obliging you to create a topic with appropriate limits.

Choosing your own topic does provide an opportunity to study something that interests you. However, it's wise to avoid a controversial issue about which you already hold strong opinions. You may fall into the trap of overstating your argument and presenting evidence in an excessively emotional way. Readers, like juries, are likely to dismiss this type of argument.

Limiting your topic is necessary, because you cannot write a short paper on a general subject such as "part-time work." *What* is it about part-time work that interests you? Perhaps you are curious about whether part-time workers are unionized. *Who* are the part-time workers that interest you most? Perhaps health-care workers. *Where?* In Canada? In a particular province? Perhaps you want to have a look at the situation in Saskatchewan. *When?* In the 1940s? In the last decade? Now your topic may look something like this: "The unionization of Saskatchewan part-time health-care workers in the 1980s." At this point, you are ready to turn your topic into a question that you can address in your essay, such as "What have been the obstacles to the unionization of these part-time health care workers?"

ANALYZING THE ASSIGNMENT

Your instructor may provide you with a topic rather than requiring you to create one. Before you rush off to read for an essay, it's important that you understand precisely what you are being asked to write about. Your first task, then, is to work carefully through the terms of the assignment. Make sure that you don't miss any dimension of the question. Use whatever method of analysis works best for you. For example, you can underline, circle, and define all of the key words. Or, if you have the kind of mind that tends to order things into a series of subtasks, reduce the assignment to a list of questions. Perhaps you like to map things out in a more visual way, playing with the relationships among the various parts of the question. You might come up with a rather messy-looking diagram that makes sense to *you*. Whatever your method, devoting some time to this phase of the project is a good investment.

WHAT ARE YOUR RESOURCES?

An essay assignment is not just an extra task designed to keep you busy. Rather, it's an opportunity for you to "try on for size" the material of the course. Place the question squarely in the context of the course, using as your primary resources the vocabulary, concepts, and theories that you have been acquiring along the way. Recall from Chapter 1 of this book the examination of different ways various disciplines, such as history, sociology, and economics, might approach the "simple" event of a birthday party. The questions posed by sociologists would not be the same as those posed by economists, even though both might be examining the same phenomenon. If your essay is for a sociology class, you need to respond to your assignment in sociological terms, asking sociological questions. Further, within a single discipline, such as sociology, there are different ways of defining a problem, depending on one's theoretical perspective. Be aware of these differences in considering your essay problem and in gathering the information for it.

After analyzing the assignment, you may think that the next step is to do research in the library, but you are not quite ready for that. First, ask yourself what you *already* know that will help you to undertake this essay. The contents of your lecture notes and course readings have provided you with basic analytical tools and perhaps some specific information. Other courses may also have given you useful data. This information will be easy to retrieve if you have taken a little time throughout each course to edit your lecture notes, culling out the basic concepts as you go along and making sure you have understood them. (Leaving a wide margin on each page of notes facilitates this process.) When you find, on going over your notes, that an idea or concept isn't clear in your mind, check with your instructor.

Our book can assist you in a number of ways, once you know what you are looking for. Think of key terms associated with your topic. Can you find any of them in the *Index*? If so, track them down in the text to see the context in which these terms are used. If they appear in several different chapters, you might pick up some hints about the sociological dimensions of your topic. Under what headings are these terms used? Are there any glossary terms in the passages under those headings? Check the *Glossary* for other terms that might also be useful. Are there any references to sociological studies in the passages you have located? Look them up in the list of *References* at the back of the book to see whether the book titles seem appropriate to your topic. Remember that there are *Suggested Readings* at the end of each chapter. One of them might be relevant to your question.

Review the major sociological perspectives introduced in Chapter 1. Which one might yield the most interesting approach to your topic? Remember that each perspective invites certain types of explanation and de-emphasizes others.

There is no "one best way" to go about this process of exploration. Just allow yourself the flexibility to search for clues by going back and forth between the chapters and the glossary, indexes, and list of references.

LIBRARY RESEARCH

The subject of the assignment now dictates what particular information you need to track down. Usually, you need to do some library research to gather information.

Become familiar with the library at your earliest opportunity, so it does not remain a forbidding mystery. Some libraries offer tours with explanations of how the catalogue system works, where the journals are located, and so on. Reference librarians are also there to assist you in locating appropriate material and to identify the general indexes and encyclopaedias that might be relevant (for example, *Social Sciences Index, Sociological Abstracts*, and *The Encyclopedia of the Social Sciences*).

SCANNING POTENTIAL MATERIAL

Once you have collected some books you think may be useful, there are a number of ways to determine whether they are actually relevant to your topic.

Scan the following:

- *The table of contents.* Does it show specific aspects of the general topic in which you are interested?
- *The index.* Is your topic mentioned here? Does the author make only passing reference to it, or is it dealt with extensively?
- *The introduction to the book.* Does the author indicate that he or she deals with the topic in a way that coincides with your interests? In a sociological work, watch for indications of the author's theoretical perspective.
- *The bibliography.* Does the author's research material seem to include the particular topic you are investigating? This bibliography may also lead you to other useful sources of information. Choose the most recent references first, and see what sources those have used.

Journal articles may begin with an abstract that states the essence of the author's argument. Otherwise, scan the introductory paragraphs and the conclusion to determine the article's usefulness.

NOTE-TAKING

When taking notes from books, journals, magazines, or newspapers, be sure to record the source of your material each time. This will save a great deal of backtracking later. Record the title, author, page number, place of publication, publisher, and date of publication. This information will go into your citations and bibliography, if you eventually use the material for your essay. Placing each note on a separate file card makes it easier to organize your bibliography later.

If you want to record the author's words, instead of just summing up (paraphrasing) the ideas, make sure that you copy the words exactly. Taking liberties with someone else's words is one of the deadly sins in the academic world.

Even when you are not actively working on your paper, the topic you are wrestling with will, no doubt, be simmering on a back burner of your mind. Thoughts about the topic may occur to you at the most unlikely times—on the bus, at the dinner table, or while reading for another course. It is useful to have a systematic way of capturing these ideas at the time that they occur to you. If you carry around a small notepad, you can jot down ideas in short form for future reference, since you cannot rely on their returning to you, like obedient children when summoned, at the time you sit down to write the essay. You may be surprised how quickly such ideas accumulate, and they will give you confidence when you are ready to begin writing.

WRITING THE ESSAY

As we have already noted, your assignment may have been given to you in the form of a general topic (such as "part-time work"). As we noted earlier, *within* this general topic, you must identify a problem that requires resolution, a question that calls out for an answer you are prepared to defend. Being driven by a "sense of problem" is somewhat like having a chicken bone stuck in your throat: something must be done about it!

The *thesis* of your essay is the answer to the question you have identified. It is the essence of your argument, a position for which you will present supporting (and possibly refuting) evidence throughout the essay.

Thus, when you have settled on an answer to the question your assignment raises, you can begin working on an outline of an argument that supports your answer (thesis). Unless your instructor requires a formal outline, you are not obliged to prepare one. However, it's wise to sketch out at least a skeleton of your argument—a plan for presenting your evidence—so that when you are writing, you don't lose sight of the essential points that will buttress your case. Writing and thinking almost never proceed in a simple linear fashion that is policed by an outline. You will find yourself moving back and forth between the thesis and ideas for the argument, modifying each as you go along. Linda Flower (1989) has aptly called writing a "mental three-ringed circus."

In organizing the essay, state your thesis or central idea and the essence of your argument in your introductory paragraph. An essay is not a whodunnit that entices the reader onwards with the promise of major revelations somewhere near the end. Just as you, when doing library research, want to know right from the beginning what a journal article is about, your reader, too, deserves to learn your point from a quick reading of your introduction. He or she will then be compelled to read on, not to learn *what* your central idea is, but why you believe it to be accurate.

The decision as to what evidence is important to advancing your case is determined by the question "What do my readers need to know in order to understand and accept my thesis?" Imagining that you have your readers by the hand and are leading them through the argument, step by step, is useful for ensuring that you are developing that argument in a clear, logical, and persuasive way. It will prevent you from darting about randomly in your notes for something to say next and will also facilitate clear transitions from paragraph to paragraph. If you include quotations, tables, or charts in your essay, integrate them into the text by explaining their significance for your thesis. No essay should contain "orphan information," unattached to the sentences that come before and after it.

You are the gatekeeper of your paper, the one who makes the decisions as to what should be allowed to stay and what should be excluded. With each piece of information you have gathered, ask yourself sceptically, "So what? Does it add anything to what I have already argued? Does it relate directly to my thesis? Have I already said this in another way?" It's always hard to discard data and ideas that you have painstakingly gathered but, inevitably, not everything you have read in preparation for the essay will be applicable when you write it. Deciding what to exclude is as important as deciding what to include.

A dictionary and a thesaurus are good to have on hand when you are writing. The latter provides synonyms for words, so that you can enlarge your vocabulary and avoid boring repetition.

Some campuses have writing labs or writing centres where students can seek assistance. Inquire whether your institution has one. Often, there is also special assistance for students for whom English is a second language.

ACKNOWLEDGING YOUR SOURCES

It is important to let your reader know where the material in your paper comes from. First, it is dishonest to represent someone else's words as your own, even if you have not used direct quotations from another author. To borrow someone else's ideas or information without acknowledgment is called *plagiarism*, and it is considered a serious offence.

If you quote someone else's words directly, cite the author and page number, or put the complete reference in a *endnote*.[1] If you paraphrase the author's words, do the same. Perhaps you are merely summing up the author's general argument in the book or article. In that case, you must still acknowledge your source in accordance with the method of referencing that you have chosen to adopt. Second, the interested reader may want to consult your sources, and you can make this possible.

If your instructor does not specify the form of acknowledging sources, consult a writing manual for optional forms of citation and for the bibliography that is presented at the end of the paper. A bibliography essentially provides your reader with a map of the territory that you have covered in writing the essay. Whatever form you choose, use it consistently.

In our book, we have chosen to use the referencing method used in many academic journals. Instead of using numbered footnotes, we insert the author's name, and date of publication, in the text itself. For example, in Chapter 9, "'The Family' and Families: A Heavy Freight," we say "Hochschild (1975) argues that 'emotion work' is the most invisible kind of domestic labour." In this example, since we are referring to her general argument rather than a specific passage, and are not using a direct quotation, we do not cite a page number. If you look for Hochschild in the alphabetical list of references at the back of our book, you will find the author's name, date of publication, title of book, place of publication, and the name of the publisher:

Hochschild, Arlie
1975 "The Sociology of Feeling and Emotion: Selected Possibilities." In M. Milkman and R. Kanter, eds., *Another Voice*. New York: Anchor Books.

Notice that some authors have multiple entries; these references are listed in chronological order, beginning with the earliest date of publication.

CHANGING YOUR MIND

The first completed version of an essay is called the first draft. Once you have written it, you can work on refining your argument and making it more coherent. You may even find that, in the course of writing the initial draft, you have actually changed your focus or the position you wish to take on the problem raised by the assignment. When you think about it, changing your mind means that you, as an individual and a thinker, have taken a significant step during the process of writing. This is what we mean when we say that you write to learn.

EDITING AND PROOFREADING

When you are satisfied that your second (or third or fourth!) draft is the version you want to submit, it is time for careful editing. Review the paper thoroughly to eliminate distractions for the reader: incorrect spelling; grammatical errors; awkward, convoluted, or incomplete sentences; words that are colloquial (those that come from casual speech), jargon, or words so heavy or pedantic that they intrude upon the page. Certainly, take the risk of trying out new words from time to time, but as a general rule, choose language that is simple and straightforward.

Even if someone else types your essay, you are responsible for the final product.

WHAT'S NEW?

You may well say, "But I'm just a student. My ideas all come from what I have read or from my professor. How can I possibly write something original at this stage? "

Yes, the theories and concepts that you employ do originate with other people, the "experts" of your discipline. Likewise, most of your information comes from other people's research. However, the way you bring these elements together in support of your argument is unique. The synthesis—the interplay of ideas and information—is yours and reflects your ability to assimilate information, think about it in theoretical terms, and advance a sound argument. As we said at the beginning, writing permits you to discover meaning and to establish firmer ownership over your thoughts. It can be an adventure.

SUGGESTED READINGS

Peter Elbow, *Writing Without Teachers* (London: Oxford, 1973). Elbow's purpose is to dispel people's worries about getting down to the business of writing. If you tend to get mired in the "getting started" stage, this short book may be helpful. Elbow suggests practical ways to generate pieces of text and then revise them.

Patricia Nelson Limerick, "Dancing With Professors: The Trouble With Academic Prose" (*The New York Times Book Review*, October 31, 1993), pp. 1, 23–24. When professors give students advice about writing clearly, it is sometimes a case of "do-as-I-say-and-not-as-I-do." Professor Limerick makes a plea for the detoxification of academic writing, and examines how the "cult of obscurity" is sustained by academic conventions. Is dreary, obscure, and polysyllabic prose really necessary? Limerick provides some wonderful examples, from the works of prominent professors, of sentences that beg to be put out of their misery. Only partly facetiously, she argues that professors tend to be the ones who were not asked to dance in high school. Therefore, they sat on the sidelines, thinking, "I am immersed in some very important thoughts, which unsophisticated people could not even begin to understand. Thus, I would not *want* to dance, even if one of you unsophisticated people were to ask me." When they become professors, she says, their writing tone continues to convey this message: "I would not *want* the attention of a wide-reading audience, even if a wide audience were to *ask* for me." This, she argues, is not only hard on students, it is also politically foolish at a time when the funding of educational institutions is coming under closer scrutiny by an unsympathetic public.

Jan Rehner, *Practical Strategies for Critical Thinking* (Boston: Houghton and Mifflin, 1994). Rehner, a Canadian professor, is a published poet and the author of several academic books. This book contains valuable advice for students concerning critical reading, thinking, and writing. See in particular the suggestions for generating a "context" for your assignment and applying it to your preparatory reading. Rehner gives good examples of how to do this with specific assignments and readings.

The Sociology Writing Group, *A Guide to Writing Sociology Papers*, 2nd ed. (New York: St. Martin's, 1991). The authors take you through all stages of the essay-writing process, and discuss ways of treating various kinds of sociological data. The examples provided are useful.

NOTES

1. We use our endnotes to expand or qualify ideas or information given in the text.

Glossary

Acculturation: The process by which groups or individuals who are in contact exchange cultural traits and acquire new ones.

Achieved status: A status attained through an individual's actions, for example, through education, occupation, and marriage.

Adult socialization: *See* Secondary socialization.

Affirmative action: A method used to facilitate employment equity; measures are taken to compensate a group for past discrimination. It may be a short-term measure to hire or promote members of one group at a faster rate than those in other groups so that their representation will more accurately reflect their numbers in the general population.

Agents of socialization: The people (for example, parents, siblings, teachers) with whom the individual interacts in the process of socialization.

Alienation: An individual's sense of powerlessness, meaninglessness, and isolation from other individuals and from society as a whole. For Marx, alienation on several levels is the inevitable, dehumanizing result of the fragmented work carried out by the mass of people under capitalism. *Cf.* Anomie.

Androcentrism: A view of the world from a (white) male perspective that assumes men's centrality in that world.

Anomia: A strain theory concept used by Robert Merton to refer to the state of "normlessness" that occurs when socially accepted goals are not matched by available institutionalized means for reaching them.

Anomie: A lack of clarity about established rules for conduct; normlessness. In Durkheim's analysis, this state arises when a person socialized to one set of values must live in a world in which they no longer apply. *Cf.* Alienation.

Anticipatory socialization: The process by which individuals prepare themselves for roles to which they aspire but that they do not yet occupy.

Ascribed status: A status assigned to individuals, usually at birth, based on the social categories to which they belong, for example, gender, race, and age.

Audience cult: The most diffuse and least organized kind of cult, requiring little commitment from members.

Authority: Power that has become legitimated and institutionalized in a society or other social group.

Basic socialization: The process, occurring in childhood, of the initial development of the self.

Behaviourism: The theory that human beings are almost infinitely plastic, within the bounds of basic biological needs, and are conditioned to behave in various ways; behaviour is a matter of stimulus and response.

Bilateral society: A society in which ancestry is traced through both the mother's and the father's line.

Biological determinism: The theory that each person is born with a certain temperament and abilities that can be only slightly modified.

Biotechnology: The technological applications of the biological sciences.

Bourgeoisie: In Marxian analysis of society, the class whose members own and control the means of production.

Bureaucracy: A hierarchical organization designed to accomplish stated goals. Each position carries with it specific authority, rights, and duties; is clearly related to other positions on an organizational chart; and is filled on the basis of achievement. Procedures are standardized and recorded in writing. For Weber, bureaucracy was the epitome of rationality and efficiency.

Capitalism: A system of production in which the principal means of production are privately owned by an elite class of people and in which the individual's labour power is also a commodity that is bought and sold. This is an approach that relies heavily on the Marxist model of capitalism.

Caste: An inherited social rank in a stratified society that determines its members' lives.

Census family: Defined by Statistics Canada as a now-married couple (with or without never-married sons or daughters of either or both spouses); a couple living common-law (with or without sons or daughters of either or both partners); or a lone parent of any marital status with at least one never-married son or daughter living in the same dwelling.

Charismatic leader: An individual whose claim to authority is based on personal qualities, rather than on her or his position in an organization.

Church: In the church/sect typology, a church generally supports the social status quo, has a bureaucratized structure, a hierarchy of authority, and a professional priesthood; worship is ritualized. *Cf.* Sect.

Class: The social position and life chances derived from an individual's or family's relation to the processes of production in the society.

Class consciousness: In Marxian social analysis, an individual's recognition that he or she is in a certain class position and has shared objectives with his or her own class members, and that these interests are in opposition to those of members of other classes.

Class society: A stratified society in which each stratum is made up of families and individuals who have similar socioeconomic status. Strict Marxists argue that economic criteria (relationship to the means of production) are the only determinants of social position in a class society; others add prestige, power, lifestyle, and attitudes.

Classical conditioning: Pavlov's discovery that when a stimulus is paired with another stimulus over time, the response engendered by the first stimulus will come to be associated with the paired stimulus; eventually the second stimulus alone will cause the same response.

Client cult: A cult in which the relationship between those who promote the cult and those who partake in it is similar to the relationship between therapist and patient, or consultant and client.

Cohabitation: An arrangement in which two people form a sexual union and live together without marrying.

Competitive race relations: A model of majority–minority relations in which members of the dominant group view their inferiors with hostility as potential competitors for societal rewards. Spatial segregation is common, reducing opportunities for informal mixing, but the rules for interaction may be fuzzy. *Cf.* Paternalistic race relations.

Conflict perspective: One of the major perspectives or orientations of sociology. It stresses the effect of power on relationships between competing status groups or between classes. Theorists using this perspective emphasize conflict rather than consensus, and constant societal change rather than stability.

Conservative bias: In studying families, the propensity to use analytic frameworks that either ignore or underestimate the significance of changes in patterns of family living.

Contest mobility: The allocation of social rewards in a stratified society on the basis of competition. *Cf.* Sponsorship mobility.

Counterculture: A subculture formed as a protest against mainstream values and norms.

Countermovement: A collective, organized attempt to resist or reverse social change in response to the changes pursued by another social movement.

Cult: A religious movement that expresses an unconventional, and often innovative, faith; a cult has a loosely defined membership, and is often headed by a charismatic leader.

Cult movement: The emergence of a cult into a fully fledged religious organization that attempts to satisfy all the religious needs of converts.

Cultural capital: The configuration of formal and informal knowledge and social skills that enables people to cope with their environment.

Cultural diffusion: The exchange of the material and symbolic elements of culture that occurs when two societies come in contact. Diffusion may be rapid or slow and may be more in one direction than in the other, but it always occurs.

Cultural relativism: The attempt to understand other people's behaviour from the viewpoint of their own culture or group.

Culture: A society's or group's shared way of life, including knowledge, beliefs, arts, morals, laws, customs, and symbols.

Culture lag: The delay between changes in material culture (technological change) and related adjustments in other aspects of social life.

Definition of situation: W.I. Thomas's theory that people respond to the meaning a situation has for them and not necessarily to the objective features of the situation.

Dependency theory: The theory that poor nations of the Third World and poor regions of developed capitalist economies are systematically exploited by capitalist centres of dominance, and become caught up in a downward spiral of dependence, further underdevelopment, and impoverishment.

Dependent variable: In a hypothesis, the variable assumed to be the effect.

Deviance: A special label put on behaviour or appearance that violates a society's salient norms. When a person is called deviant, a standard of judgment has been applied by observers who feel that the behaviour in question ought to be controlled.

Differential association: The central concept of a theory developed by Edwin Sutherland. It describes the balance of messages that support or contradict the violation of the law. The theory holds that when a person is associated mainly with messages that say law-breaking is a good thing, the person is more likely to become a criminal.

Discrimination: The maltreatment of minority group members.

Division of labour: The differentiation of tasks in the production of goods and services, and the bases on which these tasks are allocated to individuals and groups.

Domestic labour: Unpaid work, usually carried out by women, that includes looking after the daily needs of those family members who work for wages, bearing and raising children, performing household tasks, transforming wages brought into the household into goods and services for household consumption, and maintaining kin contact across households.

Drives: Internal feelings of dissatisfaction or tension that press for resolution, for example, hunger, thirst, and sex.

Education culture: A culture that places a high priority on formal education.

Ego: In Freud's theory of personality, the ego, one of the three major personality systems, functions to mediate, through intellectual and cognitive processes, between the individual's biological requirements and the conditions of the the social and physical environment. The ego develops at about the age of two. *Cf.* Id and Superego.

Elite: A set of persons who hold the top positions in any institutional hierarchy.

Endogamy: Rules (formal or informal) that prescribe marriage within one's own group, based on race, religion, ethnicity, or other social characteristics.

Environmental (social) determinism: The idea that individuals' behaviour is entirely learned within a particular environment. Behaviour is not affected by biological or genetic forces.

Estate societies: A stratified society in which each stratum is clearly separated from the others but comprises a variety of occupations and socioeconomic levels.

Ethnic group: Defined by Fleras and Elliott as "a social classification in which a particular group of people define themselves as a distinctive category on the basis of an identification that is felt with a particular set of customs, and language, religion, nationality, and homeland" (1992, 315).

Ethnocentrism: The belief that one's own culture or group is superior to others.

Exogamy: Rules that define as unacceptable marriage partners certain persons within one's own social group.

Expressive leader: The person who, through encouragement and nurturance, sees to it that tensions within a group are resolved.

Extended family: A family comprising people who are related to each other by blood or marriage; in addition to the father, mother, and unmarried children (the nuclear family), it includes other relatives, such as grandparents, siblings of the father or mother, or polygamous mates and their children. The family members usually live in one dwelling.

Family wage: An employment policy of paying a male worker sufficient money to support his wife and children.

Feminist movement: A social movement (also known as the "women's movement") aimed at promoting the interests of women and changing their subordinate status.

Feminist sociology: A general term for sociological perspectives that attempt to empower women by including women's concerns, viewpoints, and experiences.

Feudal system: An economic system in which a hereditary class of labourers (serfs) works the land for a hereditary class of landowners who belong to the nobility.

Folkways: Informal norms, usually not encoded in law, that change quite frequently. Violations of folkways may bring criticisms or reprimands, but are not as harshly sanctioned as violations of mores. *Cf.* Mores.

Functional illiteracy: An insufficiency of reading, writing, and numeracy skills to get by in daily life.

Functionalism: One of the major perspectives or orientations of sociology. It views society as a system, each of whose components contributes to supporting the others and maintaining the whole. Its proponents tend to explain behaviour and institutions in terms of their function within the social system and thus focus on the mechanisms by which society coheres.

Gemeinschaft: One of Tonnies's ideal types of society. It is a small, homogeneous, usually rural community with a high degree of self-sufficiency, simple division of labour, shared values, and personal relationships overlapping several spheres of life. Ascribed status is salient. *Cf. Gesellschaft.*

Gender: The social role assigned to each sex.

Gender socialization: Socialization that inculcates in children the values, attitudes, and patterns of behaviour deemed desirable for people in a society.

Generalized other: George Herbert Mead's term for the internal monitor of behaviour that consists of the internalized values and norms of the culture as transmitted by children's socializers. The generalized other is developed during the game stage of the development of the self.

Geographic mobility: Movement from one location to another. Often such movement is undertaken by those who want to move up or maintain their place in the socioeconomic hierarchy.

Gesellschaft: One of Tonnies's ideal types of society. It is large, heterogeneous, and urban, with a highly specialized division of labour, a diversity of world views, and segmented personal relationships. Achieved status is salient. *Cf. Gemeinschaft.*

Hidden curriculum: The educational practices, largely unintended and unrecognized, that transmit the values and attitudes necessary for people to adapt to the status quo.

Hierarchy of authority: A professional priesthood, formal rituals, and prescribed prayers addressed to a rather distant deity.

High culture: Fine arts, classical music, and drama patronized and financed by wealthy members of a society. *Cf.* Popular culture.

Hinterland: An underdeveloped area that provides developed centres (metropoles) with raw materials and cheap labour, and relies on developed centres for manufactured goods.

Homophobia: A fear and hatred of homosexuals.

Horizontal mobility: Movement among jobs at roughly the same socioeconomic level.

Human Genome Project: An administrative and financial organization created to facilitate cooperative research aimed at mapping out the genetic makeup of human beings.

Human Relations School: An approach to management based on the idea that developing better human relations in the workplace (by providing pleasant surroundings, involving workers in minor decisions, and so on) will reduce the discontent experienced by workers and thus make them more productive.

Hypothesis: A suggested explanation of the relationships among variables.

Id: In Freud's theory of personality, the id, one of the three major personality systems, consists of forces and drives (sex and aggression) that are inherited and present from birth. *Cf.* Ego and Superego.

Ideal types: A general model or prototype of a phenomenon that posits what it would be like if all the characteristics attributed to the phenomenon were present in pure form. An ideal is an abstract— an idea—and never exists in its pure form in reality. It is used as a measuring device.

Ideology: A system of values that justifies certain kinds of actions or ways of life, sometimes to the detriment of the interests of other people.

In vitro **fertilization:** A method of artificial insemination involving the uniting of the male sperm and the female ovum outside of a living body, and the implanting of the resulting embryo into a woman's uterus.

Independent variable: In a hypothesis, the variable assumed to be the cause.

Industrial Revolution: The period in eighteenth-century Europe when there was a shift from land as the primary means of production to factory production using machines.

Industrialization: The use of machine technology and fossil fuels for the production of goods, with a more complex division of labour and the fragmentation of tasks.

Instincts: Uncontrollable, universal, innate, complicated behaviour patterns in a species that emerge through maturation. Humans do not possess instincts.

Institution: A social arrangement that defines expected behaviour in important areas of social life.

Instrumental leader: The person who takes responsibility for ensuring that the tasks of a group are accomplished.

Intergenerational mobility: Vertical mobility between one generation and the next of a family.

Intragenerational mobility: (Also referred to as "career mobility.") Vertical (upward or downward) mobility within an individual's own work life, accomplished by change in occupation or by career movement.

Kinship: The patterns of relationships engaged in by a constellation of people related either by common ancestry, marriage, or adoption.

Law of Three Stages: A linear progression of society, described by Auguste Comte, in which society moves from the theological to the metaphysical to the "positive" or scientific stage.

Laws: Formally sanctioned norms enforced by public officials.

Liberation theology: An approach to religion that stresses the Christian obligation to pursue social justice.

Libido: The life energy, according to Freud, that includes sexuality.

Looking-glass self: In Cooley's theory of socialization, the basis of self-perception; it is determined by the ways the individual imagines he or she appears to others.

Macrolevel: The study of relationships among large groups of people.

Macrosociology: The study of relationships of large social groups.

Majority: The dominant group in society, holding disproportionate power and access to desired goods and services. According to the definition used in this book, a sociological majority may be a numerical minority in the society. *Cf.* Minority.

Male dominance: The situation in which men have highly preferential access, although not always exclusive rights, to those activities to which the society accords the greatest value, and the exercise of which permits a measure of control over others. *See* Patriarchy.

Margin of tolerance: The limits beyond which behaviour will be reacted to as bad or wrong. Some situations allow a wider range of behaviour (a wide margin of tolerance) than others.

Marriage: A socially legitimated union, intended to be enduring, of two people who assume certain rights and obligations toward each other.

Master status: A characteristic that is so important that it overrides other characteristics that might confer a status on the individual. For example, among soldiers, being a coward could be a master status, overriding other characteristics such as being a good shot, being good-looking, or being very intelligent.

Material rewards: Money or other tangible rewards, for example, board and lodging.

Materialist: In the Marxist sense, a person who believes that the economy forms the substructure that determines all other societal spheres.

Matrilineal society: A society in which ancestry is traced through the mother's line.

Matrilocal residence: The custom for a married couple to live with the wife's family.

Means of production: The natural resources, capital, and labour needed to produce the goods and services required by a society.

Mechanical solidarity: Emile Durkheim's term for the social bond created by the common experience of people living in small, homogeneous communities, engaged in similar work and hence in similar lifestyles, and thus coming to hold the same values and beliefs.

Meritocracy: A system in which social rewards are distributed unequally according to individual achievement rather than on the basis of ascribed characteristics. In functionalism, it is the notion that a system of unequal rewards is necessary to motivate the more competent individuals to fulfill society's difficult and important tasks.

Metropole: A dominant, developed centre that extracts resources from underdeveloped (hinterland) regions and sells finished goods to those regions.

Micro-chip: A miniature electronic circuit mounted on a tiny piece of material (often silicon). These circuits are the base of modern computer technology.

Microlevel: The study of relationships within and between small groups of people.

Microsociology: The study of relationships of small social groups.

Microstructural bias: In studying families, a bias that leads to a concentration on interpersonal relationships rather than on legal, economic, social, and cultural frameworks.

Minority: A group stigmatized and discriminated against by the dominant majority on the basis of presumed physical, cultural, and/or behavioural differences from the norm. According to the definition used in this book, a sociological minority may be a numerical majority (like women) in the society. *Cf.* Majority.

Modernization: The process of economic, social, and cultural change that traditional, undeveloped, societies are seen to undergo as they move toward becoming industrial.

Modernization theory: A theory that assumes that different societies develop from being traditional to being industrial in similar ways, but at different times.

Monogamy: The practice of being married to only one person at a time.

Monolithic bias: A bias that emphasizes uniformity and universality in studying the structure and functions of the family.

Mores: Norms considered so crucial to group maintenance that violation is severely sanctioned. Mores are often the basis of law. *Cf.* Folkways.

Neolocal residence: The custom for a married couple to establish its own household, separate from the parental household of either mate.

Norms: The formal and informal rules of behaviour in particular situations. The concrete ways in which the abstract conceptions of values are put into practice.

Nuclear family: A family comprised of a father, mother, and their unmarried children; they share a dwelling with each other but usually with no one else.

Oedipus Complex: Freud's theory that during the phallic state of psycho-sexual development the child wishes to possess the parent of the opposite sex and to remove the same-sex parent. The guilt and ambivalence that results is repressed in the unconscious and leads ultimately to the development of the superego and gender identity.

Operant conditioning: The process of learning behaviour via reward and punishment.

Organic solidarity: Emile Durkheim's term for the social bond created by the interdependence of people living in societies that have a highly specialized division of labour. Values and beliefs and, therefore, lifestyles may vary among groups, but each needs the others to survive.

Party: In Max Weber's analysis of social stratification, a group that participates in the political sphere.

Paternalistic race relations: (Also referred to as "paternalism.") A model of majority–minority relations in which members of the dominant group regard the inferiors as irresponsible, like children who need parental guidance; docility brings kindness and treats, but only menial tasks are allotted to the inferiors. The two groups live in close proximity but interaction is ritualized. *Cf.* Competitive race relations.

Patriarchy: A system of social stratification that ensures that biological sex differences, particularly childbearing, are socially constructed so that men have more power than women. *See* Male dominance.

Patrilineal society: A society in which ancestry is traced through the father's line.

Patrilocal residence: The custom for a married couple to live with the husband's family.

Pattern variables: A dichotomized set of typical choices that, according to Talcott Parsons, people confront in particular roles. The variables are ascription–achievement, affectivity–affective neutrality, diffuseness–specificity, particularism–universalism, and collectivity orientation–self-orientation. For each pair, the first listed is typical of primary groups and the *Gemeinschaft*, the second of secondary groups and the *Gesellschaft*.

Peer group: A group of individuals who occupy roughly similar statuses in a society and who tend to identify with each other.

Peripheral economy: Workers who have less job security, lower earnings, and fewer fringe benefits than employees of large firms.

Political economy perspective: A critical, interdisciplinary approach to understanding society in terms of the complex relationships between the economic and political orders.

Polyandry: The practice of one woman being married to two or more men at the same time.

Polygamy: The practice of being married to more than one person at the same time.

Polygyny: The practice of one man being married to two or more women simultaneously.

Popular culture: The culture of the masses, including television, movies, rock concerts, and rock videos. *Cf.* High culture.

Positive rituals: Referred to by Emile Durkheim as those rituals carried out when group members gather to reaffirm their commonality.

Post-industrial society: A concept to describe a society that produces primarily services rather than goods, and that relies heavily on the expertise of managers and "knowledge workers."

Power: The ability to impose one's will on others, to force groups or individuals to act in certain ways, even against their will. Power can come from physical strength, control of valued resources, or weapons.

Prejudice: Biased attitudes and negative or hostile evaluations of groups of people based on stereotypes.

Primary group: A group of people, usually few in number, who have face-to-face contact, know who the other members of the group are, engage in several kinds of joint activities, and hold common values and beliefs. Emotion, which may be positive or negative (love or hate), frequently plays a part in interaction. *Cf.* Secondary group.

Primary deviation: Any deviation that is not shaped by response to previous deviance. It may have any number of causes, such as anger or rule-testing, or may even occur by accident.

Profane: Referred to by Emile Durkheim as that sphere in which things are known empirically; worldly, ordinary.

Proletariat: In Marxian social analysis, the class whose members do not own or control the means of production and hence have nothing to sell but their labour.

Protestant ethic: A term used by Max Weber to describe the notion that hard work and frugality are spiritual obligations that can lead to worldly success as a sign of God's grace.

Qualitative methods: Research methods that yield nonnumerical data, for example, participant observation and in-depth interviewing.

Quantitative methods: Research methods used to obtain numerical data by way of enumeration or measurement, for example, census-taking and survey research.

Race: A group of people who share physical characteristics. Many scientists doubt that this is a useful concept for classifying people as there are no pure races. The significance of race is social.

Racism: Prejudice and discrimination on the basis of race.

Rape: Forced sexual intercourse.

Reconstituted families: Families in which one or both spouses has remarried and where one or both spouses may have biological children living in a different household.

Reference group: A group that provides a model of values, attitudes, and behaviour that an individual seeks to adopt or to emulate.

Reflex: Simple, uncontrollable, innate responses to stimuli, for example, babies' sucking and the "knee-jerk" reflex.

Refugee: (In this book, we are using part of The Geneva Convention definition.) Someone with a well-founded fear of persecution on the basis of race, religion, nationality, membership in a particular social group, or political opinion who takes asylum in another country.

Resocialization: Socialization aimed at stripping the individual of his or her identity and replacing it with a new one.

Role: The behaviour stemming from the occupancy of a certain status.

Role conflict: A clash between the obligations accruing from two or more roles.

Role models: Those who demonstrate the appropriate attitudes and actions of an occupant of the role.

Sacred: A term that refers to those things that are knowable only through extraordinary experience and that are given ritual significance in group worship.

Salient (or master) status: The status that is the source of an individual's social identity, overriding his or her other statuses.

Salient norms: The social rules that are actually in effect, as opposed to the rules or norms that are "on the books" or that are just "ideals."

Sample: The respondents or research subjects in a research study.

Sanctions: Rewards or punishments used to enforce norms.

Scientific management: (Sometimes referred to as "Taylorism," after its advocate, Frederick Taylor, who was an engineer.) An approach to organizing work that breaks jobs down into separate tasks requiring little skill in order to gain efficiency and that maximizes control over the workers by management.

Secondary group: A relatively impersonal group in which the focus is on some objective common to members, who may not meet or know each other. *Cf.* Primary group.

Secondary deviation: Deviation that occurs as a person develops a deviant role identity and conforms to it. It is created largely as a reaction to other people's responses to previous deviance. For example, the skid row alcoholic may drink partly because that way of life has become his or her social role in response to the reactions of others.

Secondary Socialization: The lifelong process of acquiring new roles and behaviours. Adult socialization is usually less potent than basic socialization, as individuals have more experience with which to evaluate what they are learning.

Sect: A religious body that lives in a high state of tension with society; is loosely organized and non-hierarchical; uses lay leadership; and encourages emotionalism and a "familiar" rather than formal relationship with the deity. *Cf.* Church.

Secularization: The process of moving from a predominantly sacred orientation to a worldly one. In a secular society, primary values are rational and utilitarian, change and innovation are a matter of routine, and major religious groups themselves become more worldly.

Self: A conception of who one is. According to Mead, the self is comprised of the impulsive "I" and the "me" that represents the aspects of culture absorbed during socialization.

Self-fulfilling prophecy: A false definition of situation that provokes behaviour that makes the initial false definition come true.

Serf: A labourer on a feudal estate who is "tied" to the land, that is, whose service is attached to the land.

Sexism: Prejudice and discrimination on the basis of sex.

Sexist bias: The failure to take into account that husbands and wives, and mothers and fathers, have different experiences of family life.

Significant others: The agents of socialization in Mead's I/me theory. Significant others are people important to the individual at various life stages who transmit the parts of the culture they deem relevant to successful functioning in society.

Social class: A large segment of a society made up of people who share a similar position on a hierarchy with respect to money, power, and prestige, as determined by level of education and occupation. Group members need not have an awareness of this commonality.

Social Gospel Movement: A movement that emerged in Canada in the 1890s to involve the church in social reform to ameliorate the excesses of the new industrial age; it stressed collective rather than individual responsibility.

Social inequality: The unequal distribution of opportunities and rewards in a society.

Social interaction: A fundamental process through which people exchange meanings and have a reciprocal effect on each other by communicating through language, symbols, and gestures.

Social mobility: Movement, whether vertically or horizontally, within a social stratification system. *Cf.* Vertical mobility, Intergenerational mobility, Intragenerational mobility, Horizontal mobility, Geographic mobility.

Social movement: A collective, organized attempt to bring about social change, protect the status quo, or return society to a former state.

Social organization: Social institutions make up the social organization of the society, the long-term, stable patterns of social relationships that give social interaction regularity and predictability.

Social stratification: The division of a society into strata or horizontal groups that arises from the unequal opportunity to control the acquisition and distribution of valued goods in that society.

Socialization: The process through which an individual develops by internalizing the ways of the culture. *Cf.* Basic socialization.

Society: A group of people living in the same geographical areas who have all the necessary institutions for meeting basic human needs.

Sociobiology: An approach to the study of social behaviour that stresses its biological bases.

Sociology: The scientific study of society and the relationships among and within social groups.

Sponsorship mobility: A mentoring system in a stratified society in which existing members of the elite choose and recruit newcomers to fill their ranks. *Cf.* Contest mobility.

Staples thesis: An approach to understanding society that stresses the importance of geography, natural resources, and technology in shaping the economy.

Status: 1. A culturally defined position in the social structure. Each individual occupies many statuses, which may be ascribed or achieved. 2. In Max Weber's analysis of social stratification, prestige or social honour.

Stereotypes: Overgeneralizations about groups of people based on the human tendency to simplify the world around them. These "mental cartoons" are formed by generalizing too much or exaggerating people's characteristics on the basis of too little information. Stereotypes are resilient as they are emotionally held and any evidence negating the stereotype is seen as the exception proving the rule.

Stigma: A social mark of unworthiness or discredit that affects a person's social identity.

Strain theories: Theories that argue that people deviate when they experience inconsistencies in the social structure, especially inconsistencies between cultural goals and the institutionalized means for achieving them.

Structural mobility: Socioeconomic (often occupational) mobility brought about by changes in the economy that facilitate or constrict opportunities for occupational advance.

Subculture: A group existing within mainstream society but differing from it in patterned ways, for example, ethnolinguistic groups in Canada.

Symbolic interactionism: One of the major perspectives or orientations of sociology. Focusing on the microlevel, it emphasizes individual actors' interpretations of situations. According to this perspective, interaction is both prompted and mediated via symbols.

Superego: In Freud's theory of personality, the superego, one of the three major personality systems, is often referred to as the conscience. It is the last system to develop at about five years of age. The superego represents the internalization of society's values. It is oriented to the ideal world rather than the actual environment, and pushes the individual to strive for perfection. *Cf.* Id and Ego.

Surplus value: Under capitalism, the difference between the wage paid to the worker and the profit that the owner earns in the market on what the worker has produced, after other costs (such as those for machinery) have been deducted.

Surrogate mother: A woman who is impregnated in order to have a child for somebody else.

Symbolic interactionism: A microsociological approach that focuses on how individuals interpret given situations. In other words, it is concerned with how individuals subjectively construct, and react to, social situations.

Symbolic rewards: Power, prestige, or other nonmaterial rewards.

Symbols: Signs that have shared meaning for members of a group.

Technological determinism: The idea that social change is a direct outcome of technological change.

Technology: Applied science; can be described as a system of artifacts, symbols, practices, organization, and mindset.

Totem: An ordinary object that serves as a sacred symbol for the collectivity.

Training culture: A culture that stresses the importance of providing people with job skills.

Urbanization: The shift of the population from the countryside to the cities.

Valued goods: Socially scarce goods that are shared within the public and not the private sphere of a society.

Values: Cultural themes that designate goals worth striving for and lay out standards for evaluating behaviour.

Variables: Concepts that change quantitatively or qualitatively.

Verstehen: (The German word for "understanding.") The social researcher's attempt to grasp the frame of mind of subjects, thus making it possible to give causal interpretations of behaviour.

Vertical mobility: Movement (or the ability to move) up and down a social hierarchy. The fact that a society permits vertical mobility does not mean that everyone actually moves.

Virtual reality: A "reality" created by electronic sensors and computer-generated images in which an individual has the sense of participating in fabricated events.

Women's movement: A collective, organized effort on the part of women to promote a particular interest that would benefit them. The term is sometimes used interchangeably with the term "feminist movement," but there had been women's movements long before the term "feminist" was adopted.

World-system theory: An approach to the world capitalist economy that views states in the core and the periphery as competing against each other for advantage, resulting in an increasing polarization among states.

Abbott, P., and C. Wallace
1993 *An Introduction to Sociology: Feminist Perspectives.*
New York: Routledge, 453.

Abelia, R.
1984 *Equality in Employment: A Royal Commission Report.* Ottawa: Ministry of Supply and Services.

Abella, I., and H. Troper
1983 *None is Too Many: Canada and the Jews of Europe, 1933–48.* Toronto: Lester & Orpen Dennys.

Acker, J.
1980 "Women and Stratification; A Review of Recent Literature." *Contemporary Sociology* 9.

1992 "Gendering Organizational Theory." In A.J. Mills and P. Tancred, eds., *Gendering Organizational Analysis.* London: Sage.

Acker, J. and D.R. Van Houten
1974 "Differential Recruitment and Control: The Sex Structuring of Organizations," *Administrative Science Quarterly,* 19:2, 152–63.

Adams, H.
1979 "Canada from the Native Point of View." In J.L. Leonard, ed., *Two Nations: Many Cultures.* Scarborough, Ont.: Prentice-Hall Canada.

Adamson, N., N. Briskin, and M. McPhail
1988 *Feminists Organizing for Change: The Contemporary Women's Movement in Canada.* Don Mills, Ont.: Oxford University Press.

Agnew, N.M., and S. Pyke
1987 *The Science Game,* 4th ed. Englewood Cliffs, N.J.: Prentice-Hall.

Agocs, C., and M. Boyd
1993 *The Canadian Ethnic Mosaic Recast for the 1990s.* In Curtis, J., E. Grabb, and N. Guppy, eds. *Social Inequality in Canada Patterns, Problems, Policies.*

Scarborough, Ont.: Prentice-Hall Canada, pp. 330–352.

Akyeampong, E.
1987 "Involuntary Part-Time Employment in Canada, 1975–1986." *Canadian Social Trends* (Autumn).

Alger, H., Jr.
1973 *Silas Snobden's Office Boy.* New York: Doubleday. First published in *Argosy,* 1889–1890.

Ambert, A.M.
1980 *Divorce in Canada.* Toronto: Academic Press.

1992 *The Effect of Children on Parents.* New York: Haworth Press.

Ames. H.B.
1972 *The City below the Hill.* Toronto: University of Toronto Press. First published in 1897.

Anderson, G.M.
1981 "Networks, Education, and Occupational Success." In K.L.P. Lundy, and B.D. Warme, eds., *Work in the Canadian Context.* Toronto: Butterworths.

Andrews, K.
1989 "We Are Family." *Healthsharing,* Fall, pp. 18–21.

Angelou, M.
1971 *I Know Why the Caged Bird Sings.* New York: Bantam.

Anisef, P.
1973 1974 *The Critical Juncture.* Toronto: Ontario Ministry of Colleges and Universities.

Anisef, P., T.D. Ashbury, and A.H. Turrittin
1992 "Differential Effects of University and Community College Education on Occupational Status Attainment in Ontario," *Canadian Journal of Sociology* 17:1, 69–84.

Anisef, P., J.G. Paasche, and A.H. Turrittin
1980 *Is the Die Cast?* Toronto: Ontario Ministry of Colleges and Universities.

Anthony, P.D.
1977 *The Ideology of Work.* London: Tavistock Publications.

Archibald, W.P.
1993 *Social Class and Social Interaction.* In J. Curtis, E. Grabb, and N. Guppy, eds., *Social Inequality in Canada Patterns, Problems, Policies.* Scarborough, Ont.: Prentice-Hall, Canada, pp. 539–554.

Arendt, H.
1964 *Eichmann in Jerusalem: A Report on the Banality of Evil.* New York: Viking.

Armstrong, P., and H. Armstrong
1983 *A Working Majority: What Women Must Do for Pay.* Ottawa: Canadian Advisory Council on the Status of Women.

1984 *The Double Ghetto.* Toronto: McClelland and Stewart.

1990 *Theorizing Women's Work.* Toronto: Garamond Press.

1993 *Women as Victims, Women as Actors.* In Curtis, J., E. Grabb, and N. Guppy, eds., *Social Inequality in Canada Patterns, Problems, Policies.* Scarborough, Ont.: Prentice-Hall Canada, pp. 299–310.

Arnold, G.F.
1915 "Ignorance of the Real Issues at Stake," *Women's Protest* 6 (April):14.

Aronowitz, S.
1976 "The Trap of Environmentalism." In R. Dale, G. Esland and M. MacDonald, *Schooling and Capitalism: A Sociological Reader.* London and Henley: Routledge & Kegan Paul in association with The Open University Press.

Ashton, D., and G. Lowe, eds.
1991 *Making Their Way: Education, Training, and the Labour Market in Canada and Great Britain.* Toronto: University of Toronto Press.

Assembly of First Nations
1988 *Tradition and Education: Vision of Our Future.*

Austen, J.
1962 *Pride and Prejudice.* New York: Airmont Books. First published in 1813.

Baar, E.
1983 "Patterns of Selective Accentuation Among Niagara Mennonites." *Canadian Ethnic Studies* 15 (2):77–91.

Babbie, E.
1986 *Observing Ourselves.* Belmont, Calif.: Wadsworth Publishing.

Backhouse, C., and D.H. Flaherty (eds.)
1992 *Challenging Times: The Women's Movement in Canada and the United States.* Montreal and Kingston: McGill-Queen's University Press.

Bacon, F.
1960 *The New Organon and Related Writings.* New York: Bobbs-Merrill. First published in 1620.

Badets, J.
1993 "Canada's Immigrants, Recent Trends," *Canadian Social Trends* (Summer). Ottawa: Ministry of Supply and Services, 8–10.

Badgley, R.F.
1984 *Sexual Offences Against Children*, Vol. 1. Ottawa: Ministry of Supply and Services Canada.

Bakan, D.
1971 *Slaughter of the Innocents: A Study of the Battered Child Phenomenon.* Toronto: CBC Learning Systems.

Baker, M., ed.
1984 The Family: Changing Trends in Canada. Toronto: McGraw-Hill Ryerson.

Baldwin, J.
1953 *Go Tell It on the Mountain.* New York: Knopf.

1964 *Blues for Mr. Charlie.* New York: Dial Press.

Ball, D.W.
1974 "The 'Family' as a Sociological Problem: Conceptualization of the Taken-for-Granted as a Prologue to Social Problems Analysis." In A. Skolnik and J.H. Skolnik, eds., *Intimacy, Family and Society.* Boston: Little, Brown, 25–40.

Ball-Rokeach, S.J. and M.G. Cantor, eds.
1986 *Media, Audience, and Social Structure.* Newbury Park, Calif.: Sage Publications.

Banting, K.G.
1987 "The Welfare State and Inequality in the
1980s," *Canadian Review of Sociology and Anthropology,*
24:3.

Bardach, A.L.
1993 "Tearing Off the Veil," *Vanity Fair.* (August).

Barnard, C.
1938 *The Functions of the Executive.* Cambridge, Mass.:
Harvard University Press.

Barrett, M., and M. McIntosh
1982 *The Anti-Social Family.* London: Verso.

Batcher, E.
1987 *Building the Barriers: Adolescent Girls Delimit the
Future.* In G. Nemiroff, ed., Women and Men.
Montreal: Fitzhenry & Whiteside, pp. 150–164.

Batten, J.
1984 *Lawyers.* Toronto: Gage.

Beattie, C.
1975 *Minority Men in a Majority Setting.* Toronto:
McClelland and Stewart.

Beaud, M.
1983 *A History of Capitalism 1500–1980.* New York:
Monthly Review.

Beccaria, C.
1819 *An Essay on Crimes and Punishments.*
Philadelphia: Nicklen.

Becker, H.S.
1952 "Social Class Variations in the Teacher–Pupil
Relationship," Journal of Educational Sociology
25:45–65.

1953 "The Teacher in the Authority Structure of the
School," *Journal of Educational Sociology* 27:128–41.

1963 *Outsiders: Studies in the Sociology of Deviance.* New
York: Free Press.

1964 *The Other Side: Perspectives on Deviance.* New
York: Free Press.

1967 *Social Problems.* New York: Wiley.

Becker, H., B. Geer, E.C. Hughes, and A.I. Straus
1961 *Boys in White: Student Culture in Medical School.*
Chicago: University of Chicago Press.

Belenky, M.F., B.M. Clinchy, N.R. Goldberger, and
J.M. Tarule
1986 *Women's Ways of Knowing.* New York: Basic
Books.

Bell, D.
1973 *The Coming of Post-Industrial Society.* New York:
Basic Books.

Bellah, R.
1970 *Beyond Belief: Essays on Religion in a Post-
Traditional World.* New York: Harper and Row.

Benedict, H.
1992 *Virgin or Vamp? How the Press Covers Sex Crimes.*
New York: Oxford University Press.

Benedict, R.
1934 *Patterns of Culture.* New York: Mentor.

Bennett, J.W.
1967 *Hutterian Brethren: The Agricultural, Economic and
Social Organization of a Communal People.* Palo Alto,
Calif.: Stanford University Press.

Bennett, R., and J. Cobb
1972 *The Hidden Injuries of Class.* New York: Random
House.

Benston, M.
1969 "The Political Economy of Women's
Liberation," cited in S. Hale, *Controversies in
Sociology.* Toronto: Copp Clark Pitman, 1990.

Berg, B.L.
1989 *Qualitative Research Methods.* Needham Heights,
Ma.: Allyn and Bacon.

Berger, B., ed.
1990 *Authors of Their Own Lives: Intellectual
Autobiographies by Twenty American Sociologists.*
Berkeley and Los Angeles: University of California
Press, The Regents of the University of California.

Berger, P.
1963 *Invitation to Sociology: A Humanistic Perspective.* New
York: Doubleday.

Berger, T.R.
1977 *Northern Frontier, Northern Homeland: The Report
of the Mackenzie Valley Pipeline Inquiry.* Ottawa, Supply
and Services Canada.

1981 *Fragile Freedoms: Human Rights and Dissent.* Toronto: Clarke, Irwin.

Berman, H.J.
1983 "The Origins of Western Legal Science." In J.C. Smith and D.V. Weisstub, eds., *The Western Idea of Law.* Toronto: Butterworths.

Bernard, J.
1981 *The Female World.* New York: Free Press.

Berry, J.W.
1991 *Sociopsychological Costs and Benefits of Multiculturalism.* Working Paper No. 24. Ottawa: Economic Council of Canada.

Bibby, R.W.
1987 *Fragmented Gods: The Poverty and Potential of Religion in Canada.* Toronto: Irwin.

1990 *Mosaic Madness: The Poverty and Potential of Life in Canada.* Toronto: Stoddart.

Bibby, R.W., and D.C. Posterski
1992 *Teen Trends: A Nation in Motion.* Toronto: Stoddart.

Billson, J.M.
1991 "Interlocking Identities: Gender, Ethnicity and Power in the Canadian Context," *International Journal of Canadian Studies* (Spring), 49–67.

Birnbaum, N.
1953 "Conflicting Interpretations of the Rise of Capitalism: Marx and Weber," *The British Journal of Sociology* 9:125–41.

Bissoondath, N.
1988 *A Casual Brutality.* Toronto: Macmillan of Canada.

Black, D.
1976 *The Behavior of Law.* New York: Academic Press.

1983 "Crime as Social Control," *American Sociological Review* 48 (February):34–45.

Blau, P.M. and O.D. Duncan
1967 *The American Occupational Structure.* New York: Wiley.

Blauner, R.
1964 *Alienation and Freedom: The Factory Worker and His Industry.* Chicago: University of Chicago Press.

Blishen, B.R., and H.A. McRoberts
1967 "A Revised Socio-Economic Index for Occupations in Canada," *Canadian Review of Sociology and Anthropology* 13:71–9.

Blishen, B.R., W.K. Carrol, and C. Moore
1987 "The 1981 Socioeconomic Index for Occupations in Canada," *The Canadian Review of Sociology and Anthropology* 24 (November 4):465–88.

Blishen, B.R., and H.A. McRoberts
1976 "A Revised Socioeconomic Index for Occupations in Canada," *Canadian Review of Sociology and Anthropology* 13:71–9.

Bliss, M.
1991 *Plague.* Toronto: HarperCollins.

Bloom, S.W.
1965 *The Doctor and His Patient.* New York: Free Press.

Blumer, H.
1987 *Symbolic Interactionism: Perspective and Method.* Berkeley: University of California Press.

Bly, R.
1990 *Iron John: A Book About Men.* Shaftesbury: Element Books.

Bogardus, E.S.
1993 "A Social Distance Scale," *Sociology and Social Research* 17 (January), 265–271.

Boston Women's Health Collective
1984 *The New Our Bodies, Ourselves.* New York: Anchor Books.

Bottomore, T.
1993 "Marxism." In W. Outhwaite and T. Bottomore, eds., *The Blackwell Dictionary of Twentieth-Century Social Thought.* Oxford: Blackwell Publishers.

Bottomore, T.B., and M. Rubel, eds.
1956 *Karl Marx: Selected Writings in Sociology and Social Philosophy.* London: Watts.

Boulding, K. E.
1969 "Technology and The Changing Social Order." In D. Popenoe, ed., *The Urban-Industrial Frontier.* New Brunswick, N.S.: Rutgers University Press.

Bourdieu, P.
1977 "Cultural Reproduction and Social

Reproduction." In J. Karabel and A.H. Halsey, eds., *Power and Ideology in Education*. New York: Oxford University Press, 487–511

Bowes, A.H.
1956 "The Ataractic Drugs: The Present Position of Chlorpromazine, Frenqual, Pacatal and Reserpine in the Psychiatric Hospital," *American Journal of Psychiatry* 1 (13):530–39.

Bowlby, J.
1951 *Maternal Care and Mortality*. World Health Organization (WHO) Monograph 2. Geneva: WHO.

1974 *Attachment*, Volume One of *Attachment and Loss*. London: The Hogarth Press and The Institute of Psycho-Analysis.

Bowles, S., and H. Gintis
1976 *Schooling in Capitalist America*. New York: Basic Books.

Bowra, C.M.
1985 *The Greek Experience*. Toronto: McClelland and Stewart.

Boyd, M.
1988 "Changing Canadian Family Forms: Issues for Women." In N. Mandell and A. Duffy, eds., *Restructuring the Canadian Family*. Toronto: Butterworths.

Boyd, M., and E.T. Pryor
1988 "The Cluttered Nest: The Living Arrangements of Young Canadian Adults." Paper presented at the annual meetings of the Canadian Population Society and the Canadian Sociological and Anthropological Association. Windsor, Ontario.

Boyd, N.
1988 *The Last Dance: Murder in Canada*. Scarborough, Ont.: Prentice-Hall Canada.

Boydell, C.L., C.F. Grindstaff, and P.C. Whitehead
1972 *Deviant Behaviour and Societal Reaction*. Toronto: Holt, Rinehart and Winston.

Brauner, R.
1964 *Alienation and Freedom: The Factory Worker and His Industry*. Chicago: University of Chicago Press.

Braverman, H.
1974 *Labour and Monopoly Capital: The Degradation of Work in the Twentieth Century*. New York: Monthly Review Press.

Brecht, B.
1981 *The Life of Galileo*. London: Eyre Methuen. First published in German, 1939.

Breton, R.
1964 "Institutional Completeness of Ethnic Communities and the Personal Relations of Immigrants," *American Journal of Sociology* 70:103–205.

1972 *Social and Academic Factors in the Career Decisions of Canadian Youth*. Ottawa: Information Canada.

Breton, R., and J. McDonald
1976 "Aspects of Parent–Adolescent Relationships: The Perceptions of Secondary School Students." In K. Ishwaren, ed., *The Canadian Family*, rev. ed. Toronto: Holt, Rinehart and Winston.

Breton, R., with J. McDonald and S. Richer
1972 *Special and Academic Factors in the Career Decisions of Canadian Youth*. Ottawa: Information Canada.

Breton, R., W. Isajiw, W. Kalbach, and J. Reitz
1990 *Ethnic Identity and Equality Varieties of Experience in a Canadian City*. Toronto: University of Toronto Press.

Brodribb, S.
1986 "Off the Pedestal and Onto the Block? Motherhood, Reproductive Technologies, and the Canadian State," *Canadian Journal of Women and the Law*, Vol. I, 407–25.

Bronfenbrenner, U.
1958 "Socialization and Social Class through Time and Class." In E.E. Maccoby, T.M. Newcomb, and E.L. Hartley, eds., *Readings in Social Psychology*, 3rd ed. New York: Holt, Rinehart and Winston.

Broverman, I.K., S.R. Vogel, D. Broverman, F. Clarkson, and P.S. Rosencrantz
1970 "Sex role stereotypes and clinical judgments of mental health." *Journal of Consulting and Clinical Psychology* 34:1–7.

Brown, M.
1974 *Seated Labour: A Study of Homework*. London: Low Pay Unit.

Brownmiller, S.
1975 *Against Our Will: Men, Women and Rape.* New York: Simon and Schuster.

Brundtland, G.H.
1987 *Our Common Future: Report of the World Commission on Environment and Development.* Oxford: Oxford University Press.

Bumpass, L., and J. Sweet
1988 "Preliminary Evidence on Cohabitation." University of Wisconsin, Center for Demographic Ecology, Working Paper #2.

Burch, T.
1985 *Family History Survey: Preliminary Findings.* Statistics Canada Catalogue 99-955, Ottawa: Minister of Supply and Services.

Burman, P.
1988 *Killing Time, Losing Ground: Experiences of Unemployment.* Toronto: Wall and Thompson.

Burnet, J., and H. Palmer, eds.
1988 *Generations: A History of Canada's People.* Toronto: McClelland and Stewart.

Burns, J.M.C.
1992 *Caught in the Riptide: Female Researcher in a Patricentric Setting.* In W.K. Carroll, L. Christiansen-Ruffman, R.F. Currie, and D. Harrison, eds., *Fragile Truths: Twenty-Five Years of Sociology and Anthropology in Canada.* Ottawa: Carleton University Press.

Burrell, G.
1992 "Sex and Organizational Analysis." In A.J. Mills and P. Tancred, eds., *Gendering Organizational Analysis.* London: Sage.

Calliste, A.
1989 *Canada's Immigration Policy and Domestics from the Caribbean: The Second Domestic Scheme.* In J. Vorst et al., eds., *Race, Class, Gender: Bonds and Barriers.* Winnipeg: Between the Lines in cooperation with the Society for Socialist Studies University of Manitoba.

Callwood, J.
1986 *Twelve Weeks in Spring.* Toronto: Lester & Orpen Dennys.

Cameron, B.J.
1990 "Fighting Infertility: Please Respect My Choice," *Globe and Mail* (November 5).

Campbell, R.M., and L.A. Powell
1989 *The Real Worlds of Canadian Politics: Cases in Process and Policy.* Peterborough: Broadview Press.

Canadian Social Trends
1990 Ottawa: Minister of Supply and Services Canada. No. 18 (Autumn).

1990 Ottawa: Minister of Supply and Services Canada. No. 19 (Winter).

1990 Ottawa: Minister of Supply and Services Canada No. 20 (Spring).

Canadian Woman Studies
1992 (Winter), Vol. 12, No. 2. Ottawa: Minister of Supply and Services Canada.

Caplan, P.
1985 *Class and Gender in India.* London and New York: Tavistock.

Carcopino, J.
1962 *Daily Life in Ancient Rome: The People and the City at the Height of the Empire.* Translated by E.O. Lorimer. London: Penguin.

Carey, A.
1967 "The Hawthorne Studies: A Radical Criticism," *American Sociological Review* 32:403–16.

Carlin, J.
1962 *Lawyers on Their Own.* New Brunswick, N.J.: Rutgers University Press.

Caron, R.
1978 *Go-Boy! The True Story of a Life Behind Bars.* Don Mills, Ont.: Nelson.

Carroll, W.K.
1986 *Corporate Power and Canadian Capitalism.* Vancouver: University of British Columbia Press.

1992 "The Political Economy of Canada." In J. Curtis and L. Tepperman, eds., *Understanding Canadian Society.* Toronto: McGraw-Hill Ryerson.

1993 "Introduction," Special Issue on New Directions in the Study of Social Movements, *Canadian Review of Sociology and Anthropology* 30:3, 309–311.

Carroll, W.K., L. Christiansen-Ruffman, R.F. Currie, and D. Harrison, eds.
1988 *Fragile Truths Twenty-Five Years of Sociology and*

Anthropology in Canada. Ottawa: Carleton University Press.

Carson, R.
1962 *The Silent Spring.* Greenwich, Conn.: Fawcett Publications.

Centre for Policy Studies in Education, University of British Columbia
1993 *The Changing Role of Vocational and Technical Education and Training, Canada.* Report prepared for the Council of Ministers of Education, Canada, the Department of Employment and Immigration Canada. Vancouver: Centre for Policy Studies in Education, University of British Columbia.

Chance, N.A.
1966 *The Eskimo of North Alaska.* New York: Holt, Rinehart and Winston.

Chatwin, B.
1987 *The Songlines.* Markham, Ont.: Penguin Books Canada.

Cheal, D.
1991 *Family and the State of Theory.* Toronto: University of Toronto Press.

Chodorow, N.
1978 *The Reproduction of Mothering.* Berkeley and Los Angeles: University of California Press, The Regents of the University of California.

Chodorow, N., and S. Contratto
1992 "The Fantasy of the Perfect Mother." In B. Thorne and M. Yalom, eds., *Rethinking the Family: Some Feminist Questions.* Boston: Northeastern University Press, 191–214.

Christopher, R.
1989 *Crashing the Gates: The De-Wasping of America's Power Elite.* New York: Simon and Schuster.

Cicourel, A.V.
1969 *The Organization of Juvenile Justice.* New York: John Wiley & Sons.

Clairmont, D.H., and D.W. Magill
1974 *Africville.* Toronto: McClelland and Stewart.

Clark, S.
1986 "Social Movements." In J.T. Teevan, ed.

Introduction to Sociology: A Canadian Focus. Scarborough, Ont.: Prentice-Hall Canada, 391–420.

Clark, S.D.
1948 *Church and Sect in Canada.* Toronto: University of Toronto Press.

1968 *The Developing Canadian Community,* 2nd ed. Toronto: University of Toronto Press.

Clarke, J.N.
1981 "The Clergy's Decline: A Historical Perspective on the Declining Power of Anglican and United Church Clergy." In K.L.P. Lundy and B.D. Warme, eds., *Work in the Canadian Context: Continuity Despite Change.* Toronto: Butterworths.

Clement, W.
1975 *The Canadian Corporate Elite An Analysis of Economic Power.* Toronto: McClelland and Stewart in association with the Institute of Canadian Studies, Carleton University.

1977 *Continental Corporate Power.* Toronto: McClelland and Stewart.

1981 *Hardrock Mining.* Toronto: McClelland and Stewart.

Clinard, M., and P. Yeager
1983 *Corporate Ethics and Crime: The Role of Middle Management.* London: Sage.

Cloward, R., and L. Ohlin
1960 *Delinquency and Opportunity: A Theory of Delinquent Gangs.* New York: Free Press.

Coates, M.L.
1988 "Part-Time Employment: Labour Market Flexibility and Equity Issues." In *Research and Current Issues Series No. 50.* Kingston: Industrial Relations Centre, Queen's University.

Coburn, J.
1987 "'I See and Am Silent': A Short History of Nursing in Ontario, 1850–1930." In D. Coburn et al., eds., *Health and Canadian Society,* 2nd ed. Toronto: Fitzhenry and Whiteside.

Cockburn, C.
1991 *In the Way of Women: Men's Resistance to Sex Equality in Organizations.* London: The Macmillan Press Ltd.

Code, L., S. Burt, and L. Dorney, eds.
1988 *Changing Patterns: Women in Canada.* Toronto: McClelland and Stewart.

Codere, H.
1961 "Kwakiutt." In E.H. Spicer, ed., *Perspectives on American Indian* Culture Change. Chicago: University of Chicago Press.

Cohen, A.K.
1963 *Delinquent Boys: The Culture of the Gang.* Glencoe, Ill.: Force Press.

1966 *Deviance and Control.* Englewood Cliffs, N.J.: Prentice-Hall.

Cohen, M.G.
1988 *Women's Work, Markets, and Economic Development in Nineteenth-Century Ontario.* Toronto: University of Toronto Press.

Cole, S.
1980 *The Sociological Method,* 3rd ed. Boston: Houghton Mifflin.

Coleman, J.R.
1971 *Blue Collar Journal: A College President's Sabbatical.* Philadelphia: J.B. Lippincott.

Coleman, J.S.
1963 *The Adolescent Society: The Social Life of The Teenager and Its Impact on Education.* New York: Free Press.

1968 "The Concept of Equality of Educational Opportunity," *Harvard Educational Review* 38:7–22.

Coleman, J., et al.
1966 *Equality of Educational Opportunity.* Washington: U.S. Department of Health, Education and Welfare, Office of Education.

Coles, R.
1964 *Children of Crisis.* Boston: Little, Brown.

Collins, P.H.
1992 "Black Women and Motherhood." In B. Thorne and M. Yalom, eds., *Rethinking the Family: Some Feminist Questions.* Boston: Northeastern University Press, 215–45.

Collins, R.
1979 *The Credential Society.* New York: Academic Press.

Collins, R., and M. Makowsky
1984 *The Discovery of Society,* 3rd ed. New York: Random House.

Comte, A.
1877 *System of Positive Polity.* London: Longmans, Green and Company.

1970 [1830–42] *Introduction to Positive Philosophy.* Indianapolis: Bobbs-Merrill.

Connell, R.W., et al.
1982 *Making the Difference: Schools, Families, and Social Division.* Sydney: Allen and Unwin.

Connelly, M.P., and L. Christiansen-Ruffman.
1977 "Women's Problems: Private Troubles or Public Issues?" *Canadian Journal of Sociology* 2(3):167–178.

Connelly, M.P., and M. MacDonald
1989 "Class and Gender in Fishing Communities in Nova Scotia," *Studies in Political Economy* 30 (Autumn):61–86.

Conniff, R.
1982 "21st Century Crime Stoppers," *Science Digest* 90 (August 8):60–5

Conrad, P., and R. Kern, eds.
1989 *The Sociology of Health and Illness: Critical Perspectives,* 3rd ed. New York: St. Martin's Press.

Cook, S.J.
1969 "Canadian Narcotics Legislation, 1908–1923: A Conflict Interpretation," *The Canadian Review of Sociology and Anthropology* 6 (1).

Cooke, K.
1986 *Report of the Task Force on Child Care.* Ottawa: Status of Women, Canada.

Cooley, C.H.
1902 *Human Nature and the Social Order.* New York: Scribners.

Corbett, G.A.
1981 *Bernardo Children in Canada.* Peterborough, Ont.: Woodland Publishing.

Corea, G.
1988 *The Mother Machine: Reproductive Technologies from Artificial Insemination to Artificial Wombs.* London: The Women's Press.

Coser, L.A.
1962 "Some Functions of Deviant Behavior and Normative Flexibility," *American Journal of Sociology* 68 (September):171–81.

Coward, R.
1985 *Female Desires: How They are Sought, Bought and Packaged.* New York: Grove Press.

Craven, M.
1973 *I Heard the Owl Call My Name.* New York: Dell Publishing.

Crawford, T., and T. Boyle
1993 "Embattled Trustees Defend their Role," *The Toronto Star* (June 3), A1, A14.

Croll, D.A.
1982 *Poverty Line Update.* Ottawa: Senate Report.

CRSA (The Canadian Review of Sociology and Anthropology)
1992 (May), vol. 29. Toronto: University of Toronto Press.

Crysdale, S.
1991 *Families Under Stress: Community, Work, and Economic Change.* Toronto: Thompson Educational Publishing, Inc.

Cuneo, C.
1990 *Pay Equity: The Labour-Feminist Challenge.* Toronto: Oxford University Press.

Currie, D.
1988 "Re-thinking What We Do and How We Do It: Study of Reproductive Decisions," *The Canadian Review of Sociology and Anthropology* 25 (2):231–53.

Curtis, J., E. Grabb, and N. Guppy, eds.
1993 *Social Inequality in Canada Patterns, Problems, Policies.* Scarborough: Prentice-Hall Canada.

Dahrendorf, R.
1959 *Class and Class Conflict in Industrial Society.* Palo Alto, Calif.: Stanford University Press.

1973 "Toward a Theory of Social Conflict." In A. Etzioni and E. Etzioni-Halevy, eds. *Social Change: Sources, Patterns, and Consequences.* New York: Basic Books.

Dalla Costa, M., and S. James
1972 *The Power of Women and the Subversion of the Community.* Bristol, England: Falling Wall Press.

Daly, M.
1978 Gyn\Ecology: *The Metaethics of Radical Feminism.* Boston: Beacon Press.

Daly, R.
1993 "More Parents Sending Children to Private Schools," *The Toronto Star,* (May 30), A1, A10.

Daniels, A.K.
1970 "Normal Mental Illness and Understandable Excuses: The Philosophy of Combat Psychiatry," *American Behavioral Scientist* 14:169–78; excerpts reprinted in E. Rubington and M.S. Weinberg, eds., *Deviance: The Interactionist Perspective,* 4th ed. New York: Macmillan, 1981.

Danylewycz, M.
1987 *Taking the Veil: An Alternative to Marriage, Motherhood and Spinsterhood in Quebec 1840–1920.* Toronto: McClelland and Stewart.

Darroch, G.A., and M. Ornstein
1984 "Family and Household in Nineteenth-Century Canada: Regional Patterns and Regional Economics," *Journal of Family History* (Summer).

Darwin, C.
[1859] 1959 *On the Origin of Species by Means of Natural Selection.* Philadelphia: University of Philadelphia Press.

Daudlin, R.
1984 Special Committee on Visible Minorities in Canadian Society, *Equality Now.* Ottawa: Queen's Printer.

Davies, B.
1989 *Frogs and Snails and Feminist Tales.* Sydney: Allen and Unwin.

Davies, S., C. Mosher, and B. O'Grady
1992 "Canadian Sociology and Anthropology Graduates in the 1980s Labour Market (Part II)," *Society Societe* (Newsletter of the Canadian Sociology and Anthropology Association), Vol. 16, No. 2 (May), Montreal: Concordia University.

Davis, K.
1948 *Human Society.* New York: Macmillan.

1961 "The Sociology of Prostitution." In R.K. Merton and R. Nisbet, eds., *Contemporary Social Problems.* New York: Harcourt Brace and World.

Davis, K., and W.E. Moore
1945 "Some Principles of Stratification," *American Sociological Review* 10:242–49.

Deal, T.E., and A.A. Kennedy
1982 *Corporate Cultures: The Rites and Rituals of Corporate Life.* Reading, Mass.: Addison Wesley.

Dean, J.
1976 *Blind Ambition.* New York: Simon & Schuster.

Deitz, M.L.
1983 *Killing for Profit: The Social Organization of Felony Homicide.* Chicago: Nelson-Hall.

DeKeseredy, W.S., and R. Hinch
1991 *Woman Abuse: Sociological Perspectives.* Toronto: Thomson Educational Publishing.

Demerath, N.J., and P.E. Hammond
1969 *Religion in Social Context.* New York: Random House.

Deming, R.
1970 *Man and Society.* New York: Dell Publishing.

DeMont, J.
1993 "New Activists: Angry Parents Press for Change," *Maclean's* (January 11), 40.

de Tocqueville, A.
1969 *Democracy in America.* New York: Anchor Books.

Devereaux, M.S., and C. Lindsay
1993 "Female Lone Parents in the Labour Market," *Perpectives on Labour and Income* 5:1. Statistics Canada Catalogue 75-001E.

Dickens, C.
1978 *Oliver Twist.* Oxford University Press. First published in 1837.

di Leonardo, M.
1992 "The Female World of Cards and Holidays." In B. Thorne and M. Yalom, eds., *Rethinking the Family: Some Feminist Questions.* Boston: Northeastern University Press, 246–61.

Dillard, A.
1987 *An American Childhood.* New York: Harper and Row.

Doctorow, E.L.
1989 *Billy Bathgate.* New York: Random House.

Dollard, J., N.E. Miller, L.W. Doob, O.H. Mower, and R.S. Sears
1939 *Frustration and Aggression.* New Haven, Conn.: Yale University Press.

Doyle, R., and L. Visano
1987 *A Time for Action.* Toronto: Social Planning Council of Metropolitan Toronto.

Drakich, J., and C. Guberman
1988 "Violence in the Family." In K.L. Anderson et al., eds. *Family Matters: Sociology and Contemporary Canadian Families.* Scarborough, Ont.: Nelson

Drummond, R.J.
1986 "Government and Employment in the Canadian Federal System." In K.L.P. Lundy and B.D. Warme, eds., *Work in the Canadian Context: Continuity Despite Change,* 2nd ed. Toronto: Butterworths.

Dubinsky, K.
1987 "REALly Dangerous: The Challenge of R.E.A.L. Women," *Canadian Dimension* 21:4–7.

Duffy, A.
1993 "Metro Schools Face Challenge of Teaching Immigrant Kids," *The Toronto Star.* (June 4), A1, A20.

Duffy, A., and R. Daly
1993 "Inquiry to Probe What Ails Ontario's Schools," *The Toronto Star* (June 7): A1, A6.

Duffy, A., N. Mandell, and N. Pupo
1989 *Few Choices: Women, Work and Family.* Toronto: Garamond Press.

Duffy, A., and N. Pupo
1992 *Part-Time Paradox: Connecting Gender, Work and Family.* Toronto: McClelland and Stewart.

Dulude, L.
1978 *Women and Aging: A Report on the Rest of Our Lives.* Ottawa: Canadian Advisory Council on the Status of Women.

Dumas, J., with Y. Lavoie
1992 *Report on the Demographic Situation in Canada 1992: Current Demographic Analysis.* Cat. 91-209E. Ottawa: Minister of Industry, Science and Technology.

Dumas, J., and Y. Péron
1992 *Marriage and Conjugal Life in Canada: Current Demographic Analysis.* Statistics Canada Cat. 91-534E. Ottawa: Minister of Industry, Service and Technology.

Duncombe, J., and D. Marsden
1993 "Love and Intimacy: The Gender Division of Emotion and 'Emotion Work,'" *Sociology* 27:2, 221–41.

Durkheim, E.
1947 *The Division of Labor in Society.* Trans. by G. Simpson. Glencoe, Ill.: Free Press. First published in 1893.

1950 *The Rules of Sociological Method.* Trans. by S.A. Soloway and J.H. Mueller; ed. by George E.G. Catlin. Glencoe, Ill.: Free Press. First published in 1895.

1952 *Suicide.* London: Routledge & Kegan Paul. First published in 1897.

1954 *The Elementary Forms of Religious Life.* New York: Free Press. First published in 1912.

1961 *Moral Education.* New York: Free Press. First published in 1925.

Durrenmatt, F.
1964 *The Physicists.* New York: Grove Press.

Dutton, D.G.
1988 *The Domestic Assault of Women.* Newton, Mass.: Allyn & Bacon.

Eaton, W.W.
1986 *The Sociology of Mental Disorders*, 2nd ed. New York: Praeger.

Economic Council of Canada
1990 *Good Jobs, Bad Jobs: Employment in the Service Economy.* Ottawa: Supply and Services Canada.

1991 *Employment in the Service Economy.* Ottawa: Canada Communication Group Publishing.

1992 *A Lot to Learn: Education and Training in Canada.* Ottawa: Minister of Supply and Services Canada.

Edwards, A.
1987 "Male Violence in Feminist Theory: An Analysis of the Changing Conceptions of Sex/Gender Violence and Male Dominance." In J. Hanmer, and M. Maynard, eds., *Women, Violence and Social Control.* Atlantic Highlands, N.J.: Humanities Press International, Inc.

Ehrenreich, B, and D. English
1989 "The Sexual Politics of Sickness." In P. Conrad and R. Kern, eds., *The Sociology of Health and Illness: Critical Perspectives*, 3rd ed. New York: St. Martin's Press.

Eichler, M.
1973 *Women as Personal Dependents.* In M. Stephenson, ed., *Women in Canada.* Toronto: New Press, 38–55.

1981 "Power Dependency, Love and the Sexual Division of Labour: A Critique of the Decision-Making Approach to Family Power and an Alternative Approach with an Appendix: On Washing My Dirty Linen in Public," *Women's Studies International Quarterly* 4:2, 151–175.

1985 "And the Work Never Ends: Feminist Contributions," *Canadian Review of Sociology and Anthropology* 22 (5):619–44.

1988 *Non-sexist Research Methods: A Practical Guide.* Winchester, Mass.: Unwin Hyman Inc.

Eichler, M., and J. Lapointe
1985 *On the Treatment of the Sexes in Research.* Ottawa: Social Sciences and Humanities Research Council of Canada.

1988 *Families in Canada Today: Recent Changes and Their Policy Consequences*, 2nd ed. Toronto: Gage Educational Publishing.

1992 "The Unfinished Transformation: Women and Feminist Approaches in Sociology and Anthropology." In W.K. Carroll, L. Christiansen-Ruffman, R.F. Currie, and D. Harrison, eds., *Fragile Truths: Twenty-Five Years of Sociology and Anthropology in Canada.* Ottawa: Carleton University Press.

Elbow, P.
1973 *Writing Without Teachers.* London: Oxford.Eliot, T.S.

1967 *Murder in the Cathedral.* London: Faber and Faber.

Ellis, V.
1988 *The Role of Trade Unions in the Promotion of Equal Opportunities.* London: Equal Opportunities Commission/Social Science Research Council.

Ember, C.R. and M. Ember
1993 *Cultural Anthropology.* Englewood Cliffs, N.J.: Prentice-Hall.

Engelhard, T.
1989 "To Boldly Go Where No Ad Has Gone Before," *In These Times* (May), 17–23.

Engels, F.
1986 *The Origin of the Family, Private Property and the State.* London: Penguin Books. First published in 1884.

Epstein, C.F.
1970 *Women's Place.* Berkeley, Calif.: University of California Press.

1990 "Personal Reflections with a Sociological Eye." In B.M. Berger, ed., *Authors of Their Own Lives: Intellectual Autobiographies by Twenty American Sociologists.* Berkeley: University of California Press, 349–62.

Ericson, R.V.
1981 *Making Crime: A Study of Detective Work.* Toronto: Butterworths.

Ericson, R.V., and P.M. Baranek
1982 *Ordering of Justice: A Study of Accused Persons as Defendants in the Criminal Process.* Toronto: University of Toronto Press.

Erikson, E.H.
1963 "The Eight Stages of Man," a chapter in *Childhood and Society,* 2nd ed. New York: Norton.

Ermann, M.D., and R.J. Lundman, eds.
1978 *Corporate and Government Deviance.* New York: Oxford University Press.

Erwin, L.
1993 "Neoconservatism and the Canadian Pro-Family Movement," *Canadian Review of Sociology and Anthropology,* 303: 401–20.

Etzioni, A.
1965 "Dual Leadership in Complex Organizations," *American Sociological Review* 30 (October 5).

1993 "Children of the Universe," *Utne Reader* (May/June).

Faludi, S.
1991 *Backlash: The Undeclared War Against American Women.* New York: Crown Publishers, Inc.

Fausto-Sterling, A.
1993 "Laboratory Languages," *The Women's Review of Books,* Vol. X, No. 8, 22–3.

Fennell, T.
1993 "Finding a New Life." *Maclean's* (May 10), 37.

Ferguson, J.
1993 "Lost Cities the Mayas Left Behind." *The Globe and Mail* (July 31), E5.

Finnie, R.
1993 "Women, Men, and the Economic Consequences of Divorce: Evidence from Canadian Longitudinal Data," *Canadian Review of Sociology and Anthropology* 30:2, 205–241.

Firestone, S.
1971 *The Dialectic of Sex.* New York: Morrow.

Fisher, M.
1989 "Two Cormie Firms Willfully Broke Law, U.S. Regulator Rules," *The Globe and Mail* (May 19).

Fitting, P.
1991 "The Lessons of Cyberpunk." In L. McCaffrey, ed., *Storming the Reality Studio: A Casebook of Cyberpunk and Postmodern Science Fiction.* Durham, N.C.: Duke University Press, 295–315.

Fleras, A.
1993 "From "Culture" to "Equality": Multiculturalism as Ideology and Policy." In J. Curtis, E. Grabb, and N. Guppy, eds., *Social Inequality in Canada Patterns, Problems, Policies.* Scarborough, Ont.: Prentice-Hall, 384–399.

Fleras, A., and J.L. Elliott
1992 *Multiculturalism in Canada.* Scarborough, Ont.: Nelson.

1992 *Unequal Relations: An Introduction to Race and Ethnic Dynamics in Canada.* Scarborough, Ont.: Prentice-Hall Canada.

Flower, L.
1989 *Problem-Solving Strategies for Writing,* 3rd ed. New York: Harcourt Brace Jovanovich.

Flynn, R.
1985 "Assessing the Effectiveness of Deinstitutionalization: Substantive and Methodological Conclusions from the Research Literature." In *Deinstitutionalization: Costs and Effects.* Ottawa: Canadian Council on Social Development.

Ford, R.C., B.R. Armandi, and C.P. Heaton
1988 *Organizational Theory: An Integrative Approach.* New York: Harper and Row.

Forman, F.J., and C. Sowton
1989 *Taking our Time: Feminist Perspectives on Temporality.* Oxford, U.K.: Pergamon Press.

Foucault, M.
1965 *Madness and Civilization.* New York: Random House.

1976 *Discipline and Punish.* London: Allan Lane.

Fowler, N.
1979 *After the Riots: The Police in Europe.* London: Davis Poynter.

Fox, B.J., and J. Fox
1987 "Occupational Gender Segregation in the Canadian Labour Force 1931–81," *The Canadian Review of Sociology and Anthropology* 24 (August 3).

Francis, D.
1988 *Contrepreneurs.* Toronto: Macmillan of Canada.

Frank, A.G.
1979 *Dependent Accumulation and Underdevelopment.* New York: Monthly Review Press.

Frankel-Howard, D.
1989 *Family Violence: A Review of Theoretical and Clinical Literature.* Ottawa: Minister of Supply and Services Canada.

Franklin, U.
1990 *The Real World of Technology.* Concord, Ont.: House of Anansi Press Limited.

Fraser, A.
1984 *The Weaker Vessel.* London: Weidenfeld and Nicholson.

Fraser, S.
1988 *My Father's House: A Memoir of Incest and Healing.* Don Mills, Ont.: Collins Paperbacks.

Freeman, D.
1972 *Creeps.* Toronto: University of Toronto Press.

Freidson, E.
1970 *Professional Dominance: The Social Structure of Medical Care.* New York: Aldine Publishing.

1990 *Professional Powers: A Study of the Institutionalization of Formal Knowledge.* Chicago: The University of Chicago Press.

Freire, P.
1972 *Pedagogy of the Oppressed.* Harmondsworth: Penguin.

Fretz, J.W.
1989 *The Waterloo Mennonites: A Community in Paradox.* Waterloo, Ont.: Wilfrid Laurier University Press and Conrad Grebel College.

Friedan, B.
1963 *The Feminine Mystique.* Harmondsworth: Penguin.

Friedl, E.
1975 *Women and Men: An Anthropologist's View.* New York: Holt, Rinehart and Winston.

Fry, A.
1970 *How a People Die: A Novel.* Toronto: Doubleday.

Gaines, E.
1983 *A Gathering of Old Men.* New York: Knopf.

Galbraith, J.K.
1973 *Economics and the Public Purpose.* Boston: Houghton Mifflin.

Gale, R.
1986 "Social Movements and the State: The Environmental Movement, Countermovements, and Government Agencies," *Sociological Perspectives* 29:202–40.

Gallese, L.R.
1985 *Women Like Us.* New York: Morrow.

Gambino, R.
1981 *Bread and Roses.* New York: Seaview Books.

Ganley, E.
1989 "Taxi 'hot seat' a crime stopper?" *The Globe and Mail,* (October 23).

Gannage, C.
1986 *Double Day, Double Bind: Women Garment Workers.* Toronto: Women's Press.

Garfinkel, H.
1967 *Studies in Ethnomethodology.* Englewood Cliffs, N.J.: Prentice-Hall.

Garrett, J.L., and E.G. Hinson
1983 *Are Southern Baptists "Evangelicals?"* Macon, Ga.: Mercer University Press.

Gaskell, J., and A.T. McLaren
1991 *Women and Education,* 2nd ed. Calgary: Detselig Enterprises Ltd.

Gavron, H.
1966 *The Captive Wife.* London: Routledge & Kegan Paul.

Gedge, P.
1977 *Child of the Morning.* Agincourt, Ont.: Gage.

Gerson, K.
1991 "Coping with Commitment: Dilemmas and Conflicts of Family Life." In A. Wolfe, ed., *America at Century's End.* Berkeley and Los Angeles: University of California Press.

Gerth, H.H., and C.W. Mills, eds.
1946 *From Max Weber: Essays in Sociology.* New York: Oxford University Press.

Gerver, I., and F.W. Howton, eds., *Mass Society in Crisis: Social Problems and Social Pathology.* New York: Macmillan.

Gibbs, N.R.
1993 "Bringing Up Father," *Time* (June 28), 30–36.

Giele, Janet Z.
1992 "Promise and Disappointment of the Modern Era." In H. Kahne and J.Z. Giele, eds., *Women's Work and Women's Lives: The Continuing Struggle Worldwide.* Boulder, Colo.: Westwood Press.

Gilbert, S., L. Barr, W. Clark, M. Blue, and D. Sunter
1991 *Leaving School: Results from a National Survey Comparing School Leavers and High School Graduates 18–20 Years of Age.* Cat. No. LM-294-07-93E. Ottawa: Human Resources and Labour Canada.

Gillespie, R.
1991 *Manufacturing Knowledge: A History of the Hawthorne Experiments.* New York: Cambridge University Press.

Gilligan, C.
1982 *In a Different Voice.* Cambridge, Ma.: Harvard University Press.

Gilligan, C., N.P. Lyons, and T.J. Hanmer
1990 *Making Connections.* Cambridge, Ma.: Harvard University Press.

Gintis, H.
1972 "Towards a Political Economy of Education: A Radical Critique of Ivan Illich's Deschooling Society," *Harvard Educational Review,* 42:1, 70–96.

Glenn, R.
1964 "Negro Religion and Negro Status in the United States." In L. Schneider, ed., *Religion, Culture and Society.* New York: Wiley.

Gluck, S.B.
1987 *Rosie the Riveter Revisited.* Boston: Twayne Publishers.

Glueck, S., and E. Glueck
1956 *Physique and Delinquency.* New York: Harper and Row.

Goethals, G.T.
1981 *The TV Ritual: Worship at the Video Altar.* Boston: Beacon Press.

Goffman, E.
1962 *Asylums.* Chicago: Aldine Publishing.

1963 *Stigma: Notes on the Management of a Spoiled Identity.* Englewood Cliffs, N.J.: Prentice-Hall.

1967 *Interaction Ritual: Essays on Face-to-Face Behavior.* New York: Doubleday.

1976 *Gender Advertisements.* New York: Harper Colophon Books.

Gold, R.I.
1964 "In the Basement—The Apartment Building Janitor." In. P.I. Berger, ed., *The Human Shape of Work.* New York: Macmillan.

Goldenberg, S.
1987 *Thinking Sociologically.* Belmont: Wadsworth.

Gonick, C.
1978 *Out of Work.* Toronto: James Lorimer and Company.

Goode, W.J.
1957 "Community within a Community: The Professions," *American Sociological Review* 22:194–200.

1970 *World Revolution and Family Patterns.* Glencoe, Ill.: Free Press.

1991 "Why Men Resist." In Barrie Thorne and Marilyn Yalom, eds., *Rethinking the Family: Some Feminist Questions.* Boston: Northeastern University Press, 287–310.

Gordon, L.
1992 "Family Violence, Feminism and Social Control." In B. Thorne and M. Yalom, eds., *Rethinking the Family: Some Feminist Questions,* 2nd ed. Boston: Northeastern University Press.

Goring, C.
1913 *The English Convict.* London: H.M. Stationery Office.

Gosse, E.
1979 *Father and Son.* Harmondsworth: Penguin. First published in 1907.

Gough, K.
1952 "Changing Kinship Usages in the Setting of Political and Economic Change Among the Nayars of Malabor," *Journal of the Royal Anthropological Institute of Great Britain and Ireland* 82:71–87.

Gould, S.J.
1981 *The Mismeasure of Man.* New York: W.W. Norton and Co.

Government of Canada
1991 *Learning Well … Living Well.* Ottawa: Minister of Supply and Services Canada.

Goyder, J.
1990 *Essentials of Canadian Society.* Toronto: McClelland and Stewart.

Grabb, E.G.
1984 *Social Inequality: Classical and Contemporary Theorists.* Toronto: Holt, Rinehart and Winston.

Grant, J., and P. Tancred
1992 "A Feminist Perspective on Bureaucracy." In A.J. Mills and P. Tancred, eds., *Gendering Organizational Analysis.* Newbury Park, Calif,: Sage Publications.

Grayson, J.P.
1986 *Plany Closures and De-Skilling: Three Case Studies.* Ottawa: Science Council of Canada.

Green, H.
1964 *I Never Promised You a Rose Garden.* New York: Holt, Rinehart and Winston.

Greenaway, W.K.
1980 "Crime and Class." In I. Harp and J.R. Hofley, eds., *Structured Inequality in Canada.* Toronto: Prentice-Hall Canada.

Greene, I.
1989 *The Charter of Rights.* Toronto: Lorimer.

Greenwood, E.
1957 "Attributes of a Profession," *Social Work* (July 2), 44–55.

Grescoe, P.
1987 "A Nation's Disgrace." In D. Coburn et al., eds., *Health and Canadian Society,* 2nd ed. Toronto: Fitzhenry and Whiteside, 127–140.

Griessman, B.E.
1975 *Minorities: A Text with Readings in Intergroup Relations.* Hinsdale, Ill.: Dryden Press.

Griswold, R.
1993 *Fatherhood in America: A History.* New York: Basic Books.

Guest, D.
1980 *The Emergence of Social Security in Canada.* Vancouver: University of British Columbia Press.

Guindon, H.
1978 "The Modernization of Quebec and the Legitimacy of the Canadian State," *Canadian Review of Sociology and Anthropology* 15:2, 227–45.

Guppy, N., and A.B. Arai
1993 "Who Benefits from Higher Education? Differences by Sex, Social Class, and Ethnic Background." In *Social Equality in Canada: Patterns, Problems, Policies,* 2nd ed. Scarborough, Ont.: Prentice-Hall Canada, 214–32.

Gusrield, J.R.
1963 *Symbolic Crusade: Status Politics and the American Temperance Movement.* Urbana, Ill.: University of Illinois Press.

Guteck, B.A.
1985 *Sex and the Workplace: The Impact of Sexual Behavior and Harrassment on Women, Men, and Organizations.* San Francisco: Jossey-Bass.

Hadden, J.K., and C.E. Swann
1981 *Prime Time Preachers: The Rising Power of Televangelism.* Reading, Mass.: Addison-Wesley.

Hagan, J., M. Huster, and P. Parker
1988 "Class Structure and Legal Practice: Inequality and Mobility among Toronto Lawyers," *Law and Society Review* 22 (1).

Hale, S.M.
1990 *Controversies in Sociology.* Mississauga, Ont.: Copp Clark Pitman.

Hall, E.T.
1959 *The Silent Language.* Garden City: Doubleday.

Hall, G.S., and G. Lindzey
1963 *Theories of Personality.* New York: Wiley.

Hall, O., and R. Carleton
1977 *Basic Skills at School and Work.* Toronto: Ontario Economic Council.

Hall, R.H.
1975 *Occupations and the Social Structure.* Englewood Cliffs, N.J.: Prentice-Hall.

1982 *Organizations: Structure and Process.* 3rd ed. Englewood Cliffs, N.J.: Prentice-Hall.

1987 *Organizations: Structures, Processes and Outcomes,* 4th ed. Englewood Cliffs, N.J.: Prentice-Hall.

Hall, R.M.
1982 *The Classroom Climate: A Chilly One for Women?* Washington: The Project on the Status and Education of Women, Association of American Colleges.

Hamilton, R.
1988 "Women, Wives and Mothers." In N. Mandell and A. Duffy, eds., *Reconstructing the Canadian Family: Feminist Perspectives.* Toronto: Butterworths.

1990 "A Politics of Intimate Life: A Funny Thing Happened on the Way Through the Eighties," *Atlantis* 15:2, 82–89.

Hammond, P.E., ed.
1964 *Sociologists at Work.* New York: Basic Books.

Hanmer, J., and M. Maynard, eds.
1987 *Women, Violence and Social Control.* Atlantic Highlands, N.J.: Humanities Press International.

Hannant, J.
1988 *The Rise of the New Right in Canada: Implications for the Women's Movement.* Ottawa: The National Action Committee on the Status of Women.

Hansen, D.A.
1976 *An Invitation to Critical Sociology.* New York: Free Press.

Harding, J.
1992 "The Ideological and Structural Roots of the Failure of Sociology as a Failure for English Canadian Social Policy." In W.K. Carroll, L. Christiansen-Ruffman, R.F. Currie, and D. Harrison, eds., *Fragile Truths: 25 Years of Sociology and Anthropology in Canada.* Ottawa: Carleton University Press.

Harding, Susan
1981 "Family Reform Movements: Recent Feminism and Its Opposition," *Feminist Studies* 7:1, 57–75.

Harding, Sandra
1987 *Feminism & Methodology.* Bloomington and Indianapolis: Indiana University Press.

Harkness, J.
1989 "The Economic Costs of AIDS in Canada," *Canadian Public Policy* 15 (December 4):405.

Harp, J., and J.R. Hofley, eds.
1971 *Poverty in Canada.* Scarborough, Ont.: Prentice-Hall Canada.

Harris, M.
1986 *Justice Denied.* Toronto: Macmillan of Canada.

Harrison, D., and L. Laliberté
1991 "Combat Idiology vs. Military Wives' Lived Reality." Paper presented at the Annual Meetings of the Canadian Sociological and Anthropological Association and the Society for Socialist Studies.

Hartley, R.E.
1958 "Sex-Role Pressure and the Socialization of the Male Child." In J. Fleck and J. Sawyer, eds., *Men and Masculinity.* Englewood Cliffs, N.J.: Prentice-Hall, 1974.

Harvey, D.
1989 *The Condition of Postmodernity.* Oxford: Basil Blackwell.

Harvey, E.B., and R. Kalwa
1983 "Occupational Status Attainments of University Graduates: Individual Attributes and Labour Market Effects Compared," *Canadian Review of Sociology and Anthropology* 20 (4):435–53.

Haviland, W.
1991 *Anthropology.* New York: Holt, Rinehart, Winston.

Hawkesworth, J.
1973 *Upstairs, Downstairs.* New York: Dell.

Heinz, J.P., and E.D. Laumann
1982 *Chicago Lawyers: The Social Structure of the Bar.* New York: Russell Sage Foundation and American Bar Foundation.

Hendricks, W.
1984 "The Theology of the Electronic Church," *Review and Exposition* 81:59–76.

Henry, F., and E. Ginzberg
1985 *Who Gets the Work? A Test of Racial Discrimination in Employment.* Toronto: The Urban Alliance on Race Relations and the Social Planning Council of Metropolitan Toronto.

1993 "Racial Discrimination in Employment." In J. Curtis, J.E. Grabb, and N. Guppy, eds., *Social Inequality in Canada Patterns, Problems, Policies.* Scarborough, Ont.: Prentice-Hall Canada, 353–360.

Herberg, E.N.
1989 *Ethnic Groups in Canada.* Scarborough, Ont.: Nelson Canada.

Herman, J.
1992 *Trauma and Recovery,* New York: Basic Books.

Heron, C.
1989 *The Canadian Labour Movement.* Toronto: Lorimer.

Herrnstein, R.
1971 "IQ," *Atlantic Monthly* (September), 228(3).

Hessing, M.
1993 "Mothers' Management of their Combined Workloads: Clerical Work and Household Needs." *Canadian Review of Sociology and Anthropology* 30:1.

Hewitt, W.E.
1991 "Roman Catholicism and Social Justice in Canada: A Comparative Case Study," *Canadian Review of Sociology and Anthropology* 28:3, 299–323.

Hewlett, S.
1986 *A Lesser Life.* New York: William Morrow and Company.

1991 *When the Bow Breaks: The Cost of Neglecting Our Children.* New York: Basic Books.

Himmelfarb, A., and C.J. Richardson
1979 *People Power and Process Sociology for Canadians.* Toronto: McGraw-Hill Ryerson.

1991 *Sociology for Canadians: Images of Canadian Society,* 2nd ed. Toronto: McGraw-Hill Ryerson.

Hinds, D.
1992 "Historic Debate that Creates a Broader Church," *The Independent* (November 12), 5.

Hirschi, T.
1969 *Causes of Delinquency.* Berkeley: University of California Press.

Hochschild, A.
1975 "The Sociology of Feeling and Emotion: Selected Possibilities." In M. Milkman and R. Kanter, eds., *Another Voice.* New York: Anchor.

Hochschild, A., and A. Machung
1989 *The Second Shift: Working Parents and the Revolution at Home.* New York: Viking Press.

Hoesteler, J.A., and G.E. Huntington
1967 *The Hutterites in North America.* New York: Holt, Rhinehart and Winston.

Holmes, H., and D. Taras, eds.
1992 *Seeing Ourselves: Media Power and Policy in Canada.* Toronto: Harcourt Brace Jovanovich.

Holmes, J., and E. Leslau Silverman
1992 *We're Here, Listen to Us! A Survey of Young Women in Canada.* Ottawa: Canadian Advisory Council on the Status of Women.

Holusha, J.
1993 "Carving Out Real-Life Uses for Virtual Reality," *The New York Times* (October 31), F11.

hooks, bell
1984 *From Margin to Center*. Boston: South End Press.

Hooton, E.A.
1939 "Crime and the Man." In B. Rosenberg, I. Gerver, and F.W. Howton, eds., *Mass Society in Crisis: Social Problems and Social Pathology*. New York: Macmillan.

Hospital, J.T.
1983 *The Tiger in the Tiger Pit*. Toronto: McClelland and Stewart.

Hotaling, G.T., and D.B. Sugarman
1986 "An Analysis of Risk Markers in Husband to Wife Violence: The Current State of Knowledge," *Violence and Victims* 1:2.

Houston, J.
1971 *The White Dawn*. New York: Harcourt Brace Jovanovich.

Howe, I.
1963 "Orwell's 1984." In I. Howe, ed., *The Fiction of Anti-Utopia*. New York: Harcourt Brace Jovanovich.

Howe, L.K.
1978 *Pink Collar Workers*. New York: Avon Books.

Huber, J.
1990 Presidential Address. American Sociological Association. *American Sociological Review* 55 (February):1–10.

Hughes, D.R., and E. Kallen
1982 *Ethnicity and Human Rights in Canada*. Toronto: Gage Educational Publishing Co.

Hughes, E.C.
1945 "Dilemmas and Contradictions of Status," *American Journal of Sociology* 50 (March):353–9.

1958 *Men and Their Work*. New York: Free Press.

Humphries, L.
1979 *Tearoom Trade*, 2nd ed. Chicago: Aldine.

Hundertmark, S.
1985 "Rural Feminism," *Healthsharing* (Winter), 14–17.

Hunter, A.A.
1981 *Class Tells*. Toronto: Butterworths.

Hunter, A.A., and J.M. Leiper
1993 "On Formal Education, Skills and Earnings: The Role of Educational Certificates in Earnings Determination," *Canadian Journal of Sociology* 18:1m, 21–42.

Huws, U.
1984 *The New Homeworkers*. London: Low Pay Unit.

Huxley, A.
1984 *Brave New World*. London: Penguin. First published in 1932.

Iacocca, L.
1984 *Iacocca*. Toronto: Bantam.

Ibn Khaldun
1967 [1377] *The Muquaddimah: An Introduction to History*. Princeton, N.J.: Princeton University Press.

Ignatieff, M.
1978 *A Just Measure of Pain: The Penitentiary in the Industrial Revolution, 1750–1850*. New York: Columbia University Press.

Illich, I.
1971 *Deschooling Society*. New York: Harper and Row.

Ingram, J.
1992 *Talk, Talk, Talk*. Toronto: Viking.

Inkeles, A., and D.H. Smith
1974 *Becoming Modern*. Cambridge, Mass.: Harvard University Press.

Innis, H.
1970 *The Fur Trade in Canada*, rev. ed. Toronto: University of Toronto Press. First published in 1930.

Ishwaren, K., ed.
1976 *The Canadian Family*, rev. ed. Toronto: Holt, Rinehart and Winston.

1980 *Canadian Families: Ethnic Variations*. Toronto: McGraw-Hill Ryerson.

Jackson, N.
1988 *Competence on Good Management Practice: A Study of Curriculum Reform in the Community College*. Unpublished Ph.D. dissertation, University of British Columbia.

1991 "Skill Training in Transition: Implications for Women." In Jane Gaskell and Arlene Tigar McLaren, *Women and Education*, 2nd ed. Calgary: Detselig Enterprises Ltd.

Jackson, P.
1967 *Life in Classrooms.* New York: Holt, Rinehart and Winston.

Jackson, S.
1993 "Even Sociologists Fall in Love: An Explanation in the Sociology of Emotions," *Sociology* 22:2, 201–220.

Jarvik, L., V. Klodin, and S.S. Matsuyama
1973 "Human Aggression and the Extra Y Chromosome," *American Psychologist* (August).

Jarvis, G.K.
1972 "Canadian Old People as Deviant." In C.L. Boydell, C.F. Grindstaff, and P.C. Whitehead, eds., *Deviant Behaviour and Societal Reaction.* Toronto: Holt, Rinehart and Winston.

Jencks, C., et al.
1972 *Inequality: A Reassessment of the Effect of Family and Schooling in America.* New York: Harper and Row.

1979 *Who Gets Ahead?* New York: Basic Books.

Jensen, A.R.
1969 "How Much Can We Boost IQ and Scholastic Achievement?," *Harvard Educational Review* 39 (Winter), 1–123.

Johnson, B.
1963 "On Church and Sect," *American Sociological Review* 28:539–549.

Johnson, L.C., and R.E. Johnson
1982 *The Seam Allowance: Industrial Home Sewing in Canada.* Toronto: Women's Press.

Jones, C., L. Marsden, and L. Tepperman
1990 *Lives of Their Own: The Individualization of Women's Lives.* Toronto: Oxford University Press.

Jones, S.R.G.
1990 "Worker Interdependence and Output: The Hawthorne Studies Reevaluated," *American Sociological Review* 55:176–90.

Kahne, H.
1985 *Re-Conceiving Part-Time Work: New Perspectives for Older Workers and Women.* Totowa, N.J.: Rowan and Allanheld.

1992 "Part-Time Work: A Hope and a Peril." In B.D. Lundy, K.L.P. Lundy and Larry A. Lundy, eds.,

Working Part-Time: Risks and Opportunities. New York: Praeger.

Kaihla, P., and R. Laver
1993 *Savage Messiah.* Toronto: Doubleday Canada.

Kallen, E.
1982 *Ethnicity and Human Rights in Canada.* Toronto: Gage.

1989 *Label Me Human: Minority Rights of Stigmatized Canadians.* Toronto: University of Toronto Press.

Kanter, R.M.
1977 *Men and Women of the Corporation.* New York: Basic Books.

1989 *Deceptive Distinctions.* New Haven: Yale University Press.

Kanter, R.M., and B. Stein
1979 *Life in Organizations: Workplaces as People Experience Them.* New York: Basic Books.

Karier, C.J.
1976 "Testing for Order and Control in the Corporate Liberal State," *Educational Theory* 22:2,154–70, 172–6, 178–80.

Kelner, M., 0. Hall, and I. Coulter
1980 *Chiropractors: Do They Help?* Toronto: Fitzhenry & Whiteside.

Kennedy, L.
1985 *The Airman and the Carpenter.* London: Collins.

Kessler, R.C., and J.A. McRea
1982 "The Effect of Wives' Employment on the Mental Health of Men and Women," *American Sociological Review* 47:216–27.

Kessler, S.J., and W. McKenna
1978 *Gender: An Ethnomethodological Approach.* Chicago: The University of Chicago Press.

Kett, J.F.
1981 "American and Canadian Medical Institutions 1800–1870." In S.E.D. Shortt, ed., *Medicine in Canadian Society.* Montreal: McGill-Queen's University Press.

Kevles, D.J., and L. Hood
1993 *The Code of Codes: Scientific and Social Issues in the Human Genome Project.* Cambridge, Mass.: Harvard University Press.

Kilduff, M., and R. Javers
1978 *The Suicide Cult.* New York: Bantam.

King, A.R.
1967 *The School at Mopass.* New York: Holt, Rinehart and Winston.

Kirby, S., and S. McKenna
1989 *Experience, Research and Social Change: Methods from the Margins.* Toronto: Garamond Press.

Kluckhohn, C., and A.L. Kroeber
1963 *Culture: A Critical Review of Concepts and Definitions.* New York: Vintage Books.

Knight, G.
1981 "Work Orientation and Mobility Ideology in the Working Class." In K.L.P. Lundy and B.D. Warme, eds., *Work in the Canadian Context: Continuity Despite Change.* Toronto: Butterworths.

Koestler, A.
1940 *Darkness at Noon.* Harmondsworth: Penguin.

Kogawa, J.
1981 *Obasan.* Toronto: Lester & Orpen Dennys.

Kohn, A.
1986 *False Profits: Fraud and Error in Silence and Medicine.* New York: Blackwell.

Kohn, M.L.
1963 "Social Class and Parent–Child Relationships," *American Journal of Sociology* 68:471-80.

Kolata, G.
1993 "Researcher Clones Embryos of Human in Fertility Effort," *The New York Times* (October 24), 1, 4.

Komarovsky, M.
1964 *Blue Collar Marriage.* New York: Random House.

Koss, M.P.
1992 "The Underdetection of Rape: Methodological Choices Influence Incidence Estimates." In *Journal of Social Issues,* 48:61–73.

Kostash, M.
1987 *No Kidding: Inside the World of Teenage Girls.* Toronto: McClelland and Stewart.

Kottak, C.P.
1991 *Anthropology: The Exploration of Human Diversity.* New York: McGraw-Hill.

Krahn, G.
1992 *Quality of Work in the Service Sector.* Ottawa: Statistics Canada, General Social Survey Analysis, Series 6 (Cat. No. 11–612E, No.6).

Krahn, H.J., and G.S. Lowe
1988 *Work, Industry and Canadian Society,* 2nd ed. Scarborough, Ont.: Nelson Canada.

Krahn, H.J., and G.S. Lowe
1993 *Work, Industry and Canadian Society,* 2nd ed. Scarborough, Ont.: Nelson Canada.

Krause, E.A.
1971 *The Sociology of Occupations.* Boston: Little, Brown.

Krauter, J.K., and M. Davis
1978 *Minority Canadians: Ethnic Groups.* Toronto: Nelson Canada.

Kreiner, P.
1987 *Contact Prints.* Toronto: Doubleday Canada.

Kroeber, T.
1962 *Ishi in Two Worlds.* Berkeley and Los Angeles: University of California Press.

Labour Canada
1986 *Women in the Labour Force, 1985–86 Edition.* Ottawa: Supply and Services Canada.

Lamy, P., and J. Levin
1986 "Punk and Middle-Class Values: A Content Analysis." In S.J. Ball-Rokeach, and M.G. Cantor, eds., *Media, Audience, and Social Structure.* Newbury Park, Calif.: Sage Publications, 338–48.

La Novara, P.
1993 "Changes in Family Living," *Canadian Social Trends* (Summer).

Lapidus, G.W.
1992 "The Interaction of Women's Work and Family Roles." In H. Kahn and J.Z. Giele, eds., *Women's Work and Women's Lives: The Continuing Struggle Worldwide.* Boulder, Colo.: Westwood Press.

Lasch, C.
1977 *Haven in a Heartless World.* New York: Basic Books.

Laurence, M.
1964 *The Stone Angel.* Toronto: McClelland and Stewart.

Law Reform Commission of Canada
1985 "Crimes Against the Environment," *Working Paper* 44.

Lawrence, P.R., and J.W. Lorseh
1968 *Organizations and Environment.* Cambridge: Harvard University Press.

Laxer, R., ed.
1973 *The Political Economy of Dependency.* Toronto: McClelland and Stewart.

Leach, B.
1993 "'Flexible' Work, Precarious Future: Some Lessons from the Canadian Clothing Industry," *Canadian Review of Sociology and Anthropology* 30:1, 64–82.

Lederer, W.J. and E. Burdick
1958 *The Ugly American.* New York: W.W. Norton.

Lee, H.
1960 *To Kill a Mockingbird.* Philadelphia: Lippincott.

Lemert, E.M.
1951 *Social Pathology.* New York: McGraw-Hill.

1967 *Human Deviance, Social Problems, and Social Control.* Englewood Cliffs, N.J.: Prentice-Hall.

Lenski, G.E.
1966 *Power and Privilege: A Theory of Social Stratification.* New York: McGraw-Hill.

Lenton, R. L.
1990 "Techniques of Child Discipline and Abuse by Parents," *Canadian Journal of Sociology and Anthropology* 27:2, 157–85.

Lessing, D.
1991 *Prisons We Choose to Live Inside.* Concord, Ont.: House of Anansi Press Limited.

Levin, J.S., and J.D. Dennison
1989 "Responsiveness and Renewal in Canada's Community Colleges: A Study of Organizations," *The Canadian Journal of Higher Education* XIX, 2, 41–57.

Levitt, K.
1970 *Silent Surrender: The Multinational Corporation in Canada.* Toronto: Macmillan.

Lewis, O.
1955 "Peasant Culture in India and Mexico." In McKim Marriott, ed., *Village India.* Chicago: University of Chicago Press.

1959 *Five Families.* New York: Basic Books.

Lewontin, R.C.
1991 *Biology as Ideology: The Doctrine of DNA.* Concord, Ont.: House of Anansi Press.

Lewontin, R.C., S. Rose, and L. Kamin
1984 *Not in Our Genes: Biology, Ideology, and Human Nature.* New York: Pantheon Books.

Li, P.S.
1988 *The Chinese in Canada.* Toronto: Oxford University Press.

Liebow, E.
1967 *Tally's Corner: A Study of Negro Streetcorner Men.* Boston: Little, Brown.

Lightfoot-Klein, H.
1989 *Prisoners of Ritual: An Odyssey into Female Genital Circumcision in Africa.* New York: Harrington Park Press.

Lindsay, C., and S. Donald
1988 "Income of Canada's Seniors," *Canadian Social Trends* (Autumn).

Linz, D., B.J. Wilson, and E. Donnerstein
1992 "Sexual Violence in the Mass Media: Legal Solution, Warnings and Mitigation Through Education," *Journal of Social Issues* 48:145–71.

Lippert, R.
1992 "The Construction of Satanism as a Social Problem in Canada," *Canadian Journal of Sociology* 15:4, 417–439.

1992 "Reply to Tucker," *Canadian Journal of Sociology* 17:2, 191–92.

Lips, H.N.
1991 *Women, Men, and Power.* Mountain View, Calif.: Mayfield Publishing Co.

Literacy in Canada: A Research Report Prepared for Southam News.
1987 Toronto: Creative Research Group.

Livingstone, D.W.
1993 "Lifelong Education and Chronic Underemployment: Exploring the Contradiction." In Paul Anisef and Paul Axelrod, eds., *Transitions: Schooling and Employment in Canada.* Toronto: Thompson Educational Publishing.

Lombroso, C.
1895 *The Female Offender.* London: Unwin.

1911 "Introduction" to G. Lombroso-Ferrero, *Criminal Man According to the Classification of Cesare Lombroso.* New York: Putnam.

1918 *Crime, Its Causes and Remedies.* Boston: Little, Brown. Originally published in French, 1899.

Lorimer, R., and J. McNulty
1991 *Mass Communication in Canada.* Toronto: McClelland and Stewart.

Lowe, G.S.
1981 "The Administrative Revolution in the Canadian Office." In K.L.P. Lundy and B.D. Warme, eds., *Work in the Canadian Context: Continuity Despite Change.* Toronto: Butterworths.

1987 "Jobs, Class and Gender in the Canadian Office," *Labour/Le Travail* 10 (Autumn).

Lowe, M.
1988 *Conspiracy of Brothers.* Toronto: McClelland-Bantam Seal Books.

Lower, A.R.M.
1977 *Colony to Nation: A History of Canada.* Toronto: McClelland and Stewart.

Lowrie, R.H.
1948 *Social Organization.* New York: Rinehart.

Lshwaran, K., ed.
1976 *The Canadian Family,* rev. ed. Toronto: Holt, Rinehart and Winston.

1980 *Canadian Families: Ethnic Variations.* Toronto: McGraw-Hill Ryerson.

Luker, K.
1984 *Abortion and the Politics of Motherhood.* Berkeley and Los Angeles: University of California Press.

Lundberg, F.
1969 *The Rich and the Super Rich: A Study of the Power of Money Today.* New York: Bantam.

Lundy, K.L.P.
1972 "The Toronto Chapter of the National Secretaries Association." Unpublished MA thesis, University of Toronto.

1977 "The Effect of Organizational Setting on Secretary-Executive Interaction." Ph.D. thesis, University of Toronto.

1982 "Who Sends Their Children to Private School and Why?" Unpublished paper. University of Toronto.

Lundy, K.L.P., and B.D. Warme
1986 *Work in the Canadian Context: Continuity Despite Change,.* 2nd ed. Toronto: Butterworths.

Lundy, L.A.
1969 "Learning the Ethical Norms of Practitioner-Client Relationships at a School of Social Work," D.W.S. thesis, University of Toronto.

Luxton, M.
1983 *More than a Labour of Love.* Toronto: Women's Educational Press.

1983 "Two Hands for the Clock: Changing Patterns in the Gendered Division of Labour in the Home," *Studies in Political Economy* 12 (Fall), 27–44.

1988 "Thinking about the Future." In K. Anderson et al., *Family Matters: Sociology and Contemporary Canadian Families.* Scarborough: Nelson Canada.

Luxton, M. and H. Rosenberg
1986 *Through the Kitchen Windows: The Politics of Home and Family.* Toronto: Garamond Press.

1993 "The Gendered Division of Labour in the Home." In J. Curtis, E. Grabb, and N. Guppy, eds., *Social Inequality in Canada Patterns, Problems, Policies.* Scarborough, Ont.: Prentice-Hall Canada, 285–98.

Lykken, D.
1982 "Fearlessness: Its Carefree Charm and Deadly Risks," *Psychology Today* (September), 20–7.

Maas, P.
1975 *King of the Gypsies.* New York: Viking.

1985 *Marie: A True Story.* New York: Praeger.

MacGill, E.G.
1955 *My Mother, the Judge: A Biography of Helen Gregory MacGill.* Toronto: The Ryerson Press.

MacKay, H., and H. Clifford
1982 "Choices for Day Care," *Policy Options* 3 (3).

Mackenzie, R.
1983 "Anguish of Being Homosexual Led Him to Shoplift: Charron," *Toronto Star* (May 30).

MacKinnon, M.H.
1981 "The Industrial Worker and the Job: Alienated or Instrumentalized?" In K.L.P. Lundy, and B.D. Warme, eds., *Work in the Canadian Context: Continuity Despite Change*, 2nd ed. Toronto: Butterworths.

MacLennan, H.
1945 *Two Solitudes*. Toronto: Macmillan of Canada.

Mahood, L.
1993 "Reconstructing Girlhood: Putting 'Clever' Girls in Science." *Canadian Woman Studies*, Vol. 13, No. 2.

Makin, K.
1993 "Memories of Abuse: Real or Imagined?," *The Globe and Mail*, (July 3), A1, A4.

Mandell, N., and A. Duffy, eds.
1988 *Reconstructing the Canadian Family: Feminist Perspectives*. Toronto: Butterworths.

Mann, W.E.
1967 *Society behind Bars: A Sociological Scrutiny of the Guelph Reformatory*. Toronto: Social Science Publishers.

Mann, W.E., and J.A. Lee
1979 *The RCMP vs. the People*. Don Mills, Ont.: General Publishing.

Manning, M.
1984 *The Hospice Alternative: Living with Dying*. London: Souvenir Press.

Mansbridge, J.
1986 *Why We Lost the E.R.A.* Chicago: University of Chicago Press.

Mantoux, P.
1961 *The Industrial Revolution in the Eighteenth Century*. London: Jonathan Cape.

Marchak, P.
1981 "Labour in a Staples Economy." In K.L.P. Lundy and B.D. Warme, eds., *Work in the Canadian Context: Continuity Despite Change*. Toronto: Butterworths.

Maroney, H.J.
1985 "Embracing Motherhood: New Feminist

Theory," *Canadian Journal of Political and Social Theory*, Vol. 9, 40–64.

Marriott, M.
1969 "Little Communities in an Indigenous Civilization." In McKim Marriott, ed., *Village India*. Chicago: University of Chicago Press.

Marshall, S.E.
1984 *Keep Us On the Pedestal: Women against Feminism in Twentieth-Century America*. In J. Freeman, ed., Women: A Feminist Perspective, 3rd ed. Palo Alto, Calif.: Mayfield, 568–81.

Marshall, V.H.
1987 *Aging in Canada: Social Perspectives*, 2nd ed. Toronto: Fitzhenry & Whiteside.

Mortell, G.
1989 "Labelling, Streaming, and Programming of Working Class Kids in School," *Our Schools/Ourselves: A Magazine for Canadian Education Activists* 1:8, 19–30.

Marten, G., ed.
1974 *The Politics of the Canadian Public School*. Toronto: Lorimer.

Martin, L.
1986 "Women Workers in a Masculine Domain: Jobs and Gender in a Yukon Mine." In K.L.P. Lundy and B.D. Warme, eds., *Work in the Canadian Context: Continuity Despite Change*, 3rd ed. Toronto: Butterworths.

Marx, G.T.
1981 "The Ironies of Social Control," *Social Problems* 28 (February).

Marx, K.
1932 *The Communist Manifesto*. New York: Modern Library. First published in 1848.

1971 *The Poverty of Philosophy*. New York: International Publishers.

1973 *Grundrisse*. Harmondsworth: Penguin. First published in 1857–58.

1976 *Capital*, Vol I. Harmondsworth: Penguin. First published in 1867.

Mason, B.A.
1988 *Spence and Lila*. New York: Harper and Row.

Matza, D.
1964 *Delinquency and Drift*. New York: John Wiley & Sons.

1969 *Becoming Deviant*. Englewood Cliffs, N.J.: Prentice-Hall.

Mauss, A.L., and D.W. Petersen
1973 "The Cross and the Commune: An Interpretation of the Jesus People." In R.R. Evans, ed., *Social Movements*. Chicago: Rand McNally.

Mayo, E.
1945 *The Social Problems of an Industrial Civilization*. Cambridge, Mass.: Harvard University Press.

McClintock, D.
1982 *Indecent Exposure: A True Story of Hollywood and Wall Street*. New York: Dell.

McDaniel, S.A.
1988a "Women's Roles, Reproduction, and the New Reproductive Technologies: A New Stork Rising." In N. Mandell and A. Duffy, eds., *Reconstructing the Canadian Family: Feminist Perspectives*. Toronto: Butterworths.

1988b "Women's Roles and Reproduction: The Changing Picture in Canada in the 1980's," *Atlantis*, 14:1, 1–12.

McHugh, F.P.
1993 "Liberation Theology." In W. Outhwaite and T. Bottomore, eds., *The Blackwell Dictionary of Twentieth-Century Social Thought*. Oxford: Blackwell Publishers.

McIntosh, M.
1971 "Changes in the Organization of Thieving." In S. Cohen, ed., *Image of Deviance*. Harmondsworth: Penguin.

McLaren A., and A.T. McLaren
1986 *The Bedroom and the State: The Changing Practices and Politics of Contraception and Abortion in Canada 1880–1980*. Toronto: McClelland and Stewart.

McLaren, P.
1980 *Cries from the Corridor*. Toronto: Methuen.

McLeod, L.
1982 *Wife Battering in Canada: The Vicious Circle*. Ottawa: Canadian Government Publishing Centre.

McNuity, F.
1981 *The Burning Bed*. New York: Bantam.

McRobbie, A., and T. McCabe, eds.
1981 *Feminism for Girls: An Adventure Story*. Boston: Routledge & Kegan Paul Ltd.

McRoberts, K.
1988 *Quebec: Social Change and Political Crisis*, 2nd ed. Toronto: McClelland and Stewart.

McRoberts, R., and D. Posgate
1980 *Quebec: Social Change and Political Crisis*, rev. ed. Toronto: McClelland and Stewart.

McTeer, M.
1992 *The Tangled Womb: The Politics of Human Reproduction*. Toronto: HarperCollins.

Mead, G.H.
1934 *Mind, Self and Society*. Chicago: University of Chicago Press.

Mednick, S.A., and J. Wolavka
1980 "Biology and Crime." In N. Morris and M. Tonry (eds.), *Crime and Justice*. Chicago: University of Chicago, 85–158.

Mehan, H.
1992 "Understanding Inequality in Schools: The Contribution of Interpretive Studies," *Sociology of Education* 65 (January), 1–20.Menzies, H.

1989 *Fast Forward and Out of Control*. Toronto: Macmillan Canada.

Merton, R.K.
1968 *Social Theory and Social Structure*. Glencoe, Ill.: Free Press.

Merton, R.K., G.K. Reader, and P.L. Kendall, eds.
1987 *The Student Physician*. Cambridge, Mass.: Harvard University Press.

Messing, K.
1987 *Guarantee Purity in the Search for Knowledge about the Nature of Women?* In G. Nemiroff, ed., Women and Men. Montreal: Fitzhenry & Whiteside.

Miedzian, M.
1991 *Boys will be Boys: Breaking the Link Between Masculinity and Violence*. New York: Anchor Books.

Milgram, S.
1974 *Obedience to Authority*. New York: Harper and Row.

1974 "The Frozen World of the Familiar Stranger," *Psychology Today* (June).

Miller, A.
1949 *Death of a Salesman.* New York: The Viking Press.

1977 *The Crucible.* Markham, Ont.: Penguin. First published in 1953.

Miller, D.C., and W.H. Form
1980 *Industrial Sociology: Work in Organizational Life,* 3rd ed. New York: Harper and Row.

Miller, G.
1978 *Odd Jobs: The World of Deviant Work.* Englewood Cliffs, N.J.: Prentice-Hall.

Miller, J.B.
1973 *Psychoanalysis and Women.* Baltimore: Penguin Books.

Miller, W.P.
1958 "Lower Class Culture as a Generating Milieu of Gang Delinquency," *Journal of Social Issues* 14 (Summer):5–19.

Millett, K.
1970 *Sexual Politics.* New York: Doubleday.

Mills, C.W.
1956 *White Collar.* New York: Oxford University Press.

1956 *The Power Elite.* New York: Oxford University Press.

1959 *The Sociological Imagination.* New York: Oxford University Press.

Mironowiez, M.
1985 "Faith, Hope and Charitable Donations," *The Globe and Mail* (April 18).

Mitchell, G.
1981 *Truth and Consequences: Seven Who Would Not Be Silenced.* New York: Dembner Books.

Mitchell, J.
1974 *Psychoanalysis and Feminism.* Toronto: Random House.

Molyneux, M.
1993 "Women's Movement." In W. Outhwaite and T. Bottomore, eds., *The Blackwell Dictionary of Twentieth-Century Social Thought.* Oxford: Blackwell Publishers.

Moore, W.E.
1974 *Social Change.* Englewood Cliffs, N.J.: Prentice-Hall.

Morgan, G.
1986 *Images of Organization.* Beverly Hills, Calif.: Sage.

Morris, J.
1974 *Conundrum.* New York: Harcourt Brace Jovanovich.

Morris, N., and G. Hawkins
1969 "The Overreach of the Criminal Law," *Midway* 9 (Winter).

1970 *The Honest Politician's Guide to Crime Control.* Chicago: University of Chicago Press.

Morrison, T.
1972 *The Bluest Eye.* New York: Pocket Books.

Morrissey, J.P., H.H. Goldman, and L.V. Klerman, eds.
1980 *The Enduring Asylum.* New York: Gruene and Stratton.

Mottl, T.L.
1980 "The Analysis of Countermovements," *Social Problems* 27:620–35.

Mukherjee, A.
1989 "Equity and Access: A Forum for Black, Asian and Native Women at York University." Unpublished paper.

Munan, H.
1988 *Culture Shock.* Singapore: Times Books International.

Munley, A.
1983 *The Hospice Alternative.* New York: Basic Books.

Murdock, G.
1949 *Social Structure.* New York: Macmillan.

Muszynski, A.
1989 What Is Patriarchy? In Jesse Vorst, et al., eds. *Race, Class, Gender: Bonds and Barriers.* Winnipeg: Between the Lines in cooperation with Society for Socialist Studies, University of Manitoba.

Myles, J.
1988 "The Expanding Middle: Some Canadian Evidence on the Deskilling Debate," *Canadian Review of Sociology and Anthropology,* 25:3, 335–364.

1993 "Post-Industrialism and the Service Economy." In H.J. Krahn and G.S. Lowe, eds. *Work in Canada: Readings in the Sociology of Work and Industry.* Scarborough, Ont.: Nelson, 124–34.

Myrdal, G.
1944 *An American Dilemma.* New York: Harper.

Naipaul, V.S.
1968 *An Area of Darkness.* Markham, Ont.: Penguin.

Nash, P., and C. Krzaniwski
1984 "Electronic Imprisonment," *Our Times* 3 (5):18–20.

National Anti-Poverty Organization
1992 *Literacy and Poverty: A View from the Inside.* Ottawa: National Anti-Poverty Association.

National Council of Welfare
1979 *Women and Poverty.* Ottawa: Minister of Supply and Services.

1988 *Poverty Profile.* Ottawa: Minister of Supply and Services

National Institute of Mental Health
1970 *Report on the XXY Chromosomal Abnormality.* (US) Public Health Service Publication 2103, Rockville, M.D.: NIMH.

Naylor, G.
1983 *The Women of Brewster Place.* London: Penguin.

Nef, J., J. Vanderkoop, and H. Wiseman, eds.
1989 *Ethics and Technology: Ethical Choices in the Age of Pervasive Technology.* Toronto: Thompson Educational Publishing.

1991 *Critical Choices! Ethics, Science and Technology.* Toronto: Thompson Educational Publishers.

Nemeth, M., with N. Underwood and J. Howse
1993 "God Is Alive: Special Report, Religion Poll," *Maclean's* (12 April 1993).

Nemiroff, G.H., ed.
1987 *Women and Men Interdisciplinary Reading on Gender.* Montreal: Fitzhenry & Whiteside.

Nett, E.
1981 "Canadian Families in Socio-Historical Perspective," *Canadian Journal of Sociology* 6 (3):239–60.

Nettler, G.
1982 *Criminal Careers,* 4 vols. Cincinnati, Oh.: Anderson Publishing.

Neuman, L.W.
1991 *Social Research Methods Qualitative and Quantitative Approaches.* Needham Heights. Ma.: Allyn and Bacon.

Newman, O.
1972 *Defensible Space: People and Design in the Violent City.* London: Architectural Press.

Newman, P.C.
1975 *The Canadian Establishment.* Toronto: McClelland and Stewart.

1978 *Bronfman Dynasty.* Toronto: McClelland and Stewart.

1981 *The Acquisitors.* Toronto: McClelland and Stewart.

Newson, J., and H. Buchbinder
1988 *The University Means Business.* Toronto: Garamond Press.

Ng, E.
1992 "Children and Elderly People: Sharing Public Income Resources," *Canadian Social Trends* 25 (Summer). Ottawa: Minister of Supply and Services Canada.

Ng, R.
1988 *The Politics of Community Services: Immigrant Women, Class and State.* Toronto: Garamond Press.

1989 "Sexism, Racism and Canadian Nationalism." In J. Vorst et al., eds. *Race, Class, Gender: Bonds and Barriers.* Winnipeg: Between the Lines in cooperation with Society for Socialist Studies, University of Manitoba.

1991 "Teaching Against the Grain: Contradictions for Minority Teachers," 99–115. In J. Gaskell and A.Tigar McLaren, eds., *Women in Education,* 2nd ed. Calgary: Detselig Enterprises Ltd.

Nicholson, N.
1973 *Portrait of a Marriage.* London: Weidenfeld and Nicholson.

Niebuhr, H.R.
1929 *The Social Sources of Denominationalism.* New York: Henry Holt.

Nielsen, J.McCarl, ed.
1990 *Feminist Research Methods: Exemplary Readings in the Social Sciences.* Boulder, Col.: Westview Press.

Nisbet, R.A.
1970 *The Social Bond.* New York: Albert A. Knopf.

Nock, D.A.
1987 "Cult, Sect and Church in Canada: A Re-Examination of Start and Bainbridge," *The Canadian Review of Sociology and Anthropology* 24(4):514–25.

Novak, M.
1971 *The Rise of the Unmeltable Ethnics: Politics and Culture in the Seventies.* New York: Macmillan.

O'Brien, M.
1981 *The Politics of Reproduction.* London: Routledge & Kegan Paul.

1987 "Loving Wisdom," *Resources for Feminist Research,* 16:3, 6–7.

O'Connor, J.S.
1989 "Welfare Expenditure and Policy Orientation in Canada in Comparative Perspective," *Canadian Review of Sociology and Anthropology,* 26:1, 127–50.

O'Malley, M.
1983 *Doctors.* Toronto: Macmillan of Canada.

1986 *Hospital.* Toronto: Macmillan of Canada.

Oakley, A.
1974 *The Sociology of Housework.* New York: Pantheon Books.

1986 "Feminism, Motherhood, and Medicine: WHO CARES?" In J. Mitchell and A. Oakley, eds., *What is Feminism?* Oxford: Basil Blackwell.

Oderkirk, J., and C. Lochhead
1992 "Lone Parenthood: Gender Differences," *Canadian Social Trends* (Winter): 16–19.

Ogburn, W.F.
1922 *Social Change.* New York: Viking Press.

Ogmundson, R. and J. McLaughlin,
1992 "Trends in the Ethnic Origins of Canadian Elites: the Decline of the BRITS?" *The Canadian Review of Sociology and Anthropology* 29 (2):227–42.

Okun, L.
1986 *Women Abuse: Facts Replacing Myths.* New York: State University of New York Press.

Olsen, M.E., and M.N. Marger, eds.
1993 *Power in Modern Societies.* Boulder: Westview Press.

Olson P., and G. Burns
1983 "Politics, Class and Happenstance: French Immersion in a Canadian Context," *Interchange* 14 (1).

Ontario Education Act
1985 Toronto: Queen's Printer.

Ontario Minister's Advisory Committee on the International Year of Shelter for the Homeless
1987 *More than Just a Roof: Action to End Homelessness in Ontario.* Toronto: Ministry of Housing.

Ontario Provincial Commission on Aims and Objectives of Education in the Schools of Ontario.
1968 *Living and Learning.* Toronto: Newton Publishing Co.

Ornstein, M.
1986 "The Political Ideology of the Canadian Capitalist Class," *Canadian Review of Sociology and Anthropology* 23:3, 182–209.

1989 *AIDS in Canada: Knowledge, Behaviour and Attitudes of Adults.* Toronto: Institute for Social Research, York University.

Ortner, S.
1974 "Is Female to Male as Nature is to Culture?" In M. Rosaldo and L. Lamphere, eds., *Woman Culture & Society.* Stanford Calif.: Stanford University Press, 67–87.

Orwell, G.
1949 *Nineteen Eighty-Four.* London: Secker and Warburg.

Orwen, P.
1991 "How Our Lives Are Changing." *The Toronto Star* (April 20) D1.

Osberg, L.
1981 *Economic Inequality in Canada.* Toronto: Butterworths.

Ostling, R.N.
1992 "The Second Reformation," *Time* (November 23).

Outhwaite, W., and T. Bottomore, eds.
1993 *The Blackwell Dictionary of Twentieth-Century Social Thought.* Oxford: Blackwell Publishers.

Palmer, B.D.
1986 *The Character of Class Struggle: Essays in Canadian Working Class History, 1850–1985.* Toronto: McClelland and Stewart.

Parker, G.
1983 *An Introduction to Criminal Law,* 2nd ed. Toronto: Nelson Canada.

Parrilo, V.N.
1980 *Strangers to These Shores.* Boston: Houghton Mifflin.

Parsons, T.
1937 *The Structure of Social Action.* New York: Free Press.

1951 *The Social System.* New York: Free Press.

1960 *Structure and Process in Modern Societies.* New York: Free Press.

1977 *The Evolution of Societies.* Englewood Cliffs, N.J.: Prentice-Hall.

Parsons, T., and R.F. Bales, eds.
1956 *Family, Socialization, and Interaction Practice.* London: Routledge & Kegan Paul.

Peck, M.S.
1983 *People of the Lie: The Hope for Healing Human Evil.* New York: Simon and Schuster.

Pelletier, W.
1971 *For Every North American Indian Who Begins to Disappear, I Also Begin to Disappear.* Toronto: The Neewin Publishing Co.

Peoples, J., and B. Bailey
1988 *Humanity: An Introduction to Cultural Anthropology.* West Publishing.

Perrow, C.
1986 *Complex Organizations: A Critical Essay.* New York: Random House.

Persell, C.H., S. Catsambis, and P.W. Cookson, Jr.
1992 "Differential Asset Conversion: Class and Gendered Pathways to Selective Colleges," *Sociology of Education* 65 (July):208–25.

Peters, T.J., and R.H. Waterman, Jr.
1984 *In Search of Excellence.* New York: Harper and Row.

Pettifer, S., and J. Torge
1987 *A Book About Sexual Assault.* Montreal: Montreal Health Press Inc.

Pfohl, S.
1985 *Images of Deviance and Control: A Sociological History.* New York: McGraw-Hill.

Phizachlea, A.
1990 *Unpacking the Fashion Industry: Gender, Racism and Class in Production.* London: Routledge.

Pike, R.M.
1988 "Education and the Schools." In J. Curtis and L. Tepperman, eds., *Understanding Canadian Society.* Toronto: McGraw-Hill Ryerson.

Pineos, P.C., and J. Porter
1967 "Occupational Prestige in Canada," *Canadian Review of Sociology and Anthropology* 4:24–40.

Pirie, M.
1988 "Women and the Illness Role: Re-thinking Feminist Theory," *Canadian Review of Sociology and Anthropology* 25 (4):628–48.

Platt, A.
1969 *The Child Savers.* Chicago: University of Chicago Press.

Pollack, O.
1950 *The Criminality of Women.* Philadelphia: University of Pennsylvania Press.

Polsky, N.
1969 *Hustlers, Beats and Others.* New York: Anchor Books.

Ponting, J.R.
1988 "Native-White Relations." In J. Curtis and L. Tepperman, eds., *Understanding Canadian Society.* Toronto: McGraw-Hill Ryerson, 619–44.

Pope, L.
1942 *Millhands and Preachers.* New Haven, CT: Yale University Press.

Porter, J.
1965 *The Vertical Mosaic: An Analysis of Social Class and Power in Canada.* Toronto: University of Toronto Press.

Porter, J., M.R. Porter, and B. Blishen
1973 *Does Money Matter? Prospects for Higher Education.* Toronto: Institute for Behavioural Research.

Porter, M.R., J. Porter, and B. Blishen
1982 *Stations and Callings: Making it Through the School System.* Toronto: Methuen.

Posner, J.
1980 "Old and Female: The Double Whammy." In V.H. Marshall, ed., *Aging in Canada: Social Perspectives.* Toronto: Fitzhenry & Whiteside.

Postman, N.
1985 *Amusing Ourselves to Death.* New York: Penguin.

1992 *Technopoly: The Surrender of Culture to Technology.* New York: Alfred A. Knopf.

Poulantzas, N.
1978 *Classes in Contemporary Capitalism.* London: Verso.

Poverty Profile, 1980–1990
1992 (Autumn) A Report by the National Council of Welfare. Ottawa: Minister of Supply and Services.

Poverty Profile Update for 1991
1993 (Winter) National Council of Welfare. Ottawa: Minster of Supply and Services.

Powell, B., and J. Martin
1980 "Economic Implications of Canada's Aging Society." In V.H. Marshall, ed., *Aging in Canada.* Toronto: Fitzhenry & Whiteside.

Prentice, A.
1977 *The School Promoters: Education and Social Class in Mid-Nineteenth Century Upper Canada.* Toronto: McClelland and Stewart.

Prentice, A., et al., eds.
1988 *Canadian Women: A History.* Toronto: Harcourt Brace Jovanovich.

Priest, L.
1989 *Conspiracy of Silence.* Toronto: McClelland and Stewart.

Privacy Commissioner
1993 *Annual Report 1992–1993.* Ottawa: Canadian Communication Group.

Quebedeauax, R.
1982 *By What Authority?* San Francisco: Harper and Row.

Radwanski, G.
1987 *Ontario Study of the Relevance of Education and the Issue of Dropouts.* Toronto: Ministry of Education.

Ram, M., and R. Holliday
1993 "Relative Merits: Family Culture and Kinship in Small Firms," *Sociology* 27:4, 629–48.

Rapp, R.
1992 "Family and Class in Contemporary America: Notes toward an Understanding of Ideology." In B. Thorne and M. Yalom, eds., *Rethinking the Family: Some Feminist Questions,* 2nd ed. Boston: Northeastern University Press.

Rayfield, J.R.
1970 *Maria in Markham Street: The Role of Italian Women in a Central City Neighbourhood.* Ethnic Studies Committee: Unpublished.

Redfield, R., et al.
1936 "Memorandum on the study of acculturation." Cited in Berry, J.W. *Sociopsychological Costs and Benefits of Multiculturalism.* Working Paper No. 24. Ottawa: Economic Council of Canada.

Sociopsychological Costs and Benefits of Multiculturalism. Working Paper No. 24. Ottawa: Economic Council of Canada.

Rehner, J.
1989 *Infertility: Old Myths, New Meanings.* Toronto: Second Story Press.

Reiter, E.
1991 *Making Fast Food: From the Frying Pan into the Fire.* Montreal and Kingston: McGill-Queen's University Press.

Reiter, R.R., ed.
1975 *Toward an Anthropology of Women.* New York: Monthly Review Press.

Reitz, J.S.
1980 *The Survival of Ethnic Groups.* Toronto: McGraw-Hill Ryerson.

Rendell, R.
1978 *A Judgement in Stone.* London: Avon Books.

Richardson, C.J.
1988 "Children of Divorce." In K. L. Anderson et al., eds., *Family Matters: Sociology and Contemporary Canadian Families.* Scarborough, Ont.: Nelson Canada, 163–200.

Richardson, L.
1988 *The Dynamics of Sex and Gender: A Sociological Perspective.* New York: Harper and Row.

Richardson, R.J.
1988 "'A Sacred Trust:' The Trust Industry and Canadian Economic Structure," *The Canadian Review of Sociology and Anthropology* 25 (February 1):1–22.

Richer, S.
1982 "Equality to Benefit from Schooling: The Issue of Educational Opportunity." In P. Forcese and S. Richer, eds., *Social Issues.* Scarborough, Ont.: Prentice-Hall Canada.

Richler, M.
1969 *The Apprenticeship of Duddy Kravitz.* Toronto: McClelland and Stewart.

Richmond, A.H., and W.E. Kalback
1980 *Factors in the Adjustment of Immigrants and Their Descendants.* Ottawa: Statistics Canada.

Ricks, C., and L. Michaels, eds.
1990 *The State of the Language,* 2nd ed. Berkeley: University of California Press.

Riley, M.W.
1988 *Sociological Lives.* Newbury Park: Sage Publications.

Rinehart, J.
1987 *The Tyranny of Work: Alienation and the Labour Process,* 2nd ed. Toronto: Harcourt Brace Jovanovich, Canada.

Ritzer, G.
1993 *The McDonaldization of Society: An Investigation into the Changing Character of Contemporary Social Life.* Newbury Park, Calif.: Pine Forge Press.

Robbins, T.
1988 "Cults, Converts and Charisma: The Sociology of New Religious Movements," *Current Sociology* 36:1 (Spring), Trend Report.

Roberts, O.
1974 *Twelve Greatest Miracles of My Ministry.* Tulsa, Okla: Pinoak Publications.

Robertson, J.R.
1992 "Sexual Orientation and Legal Rights," *Current Issue Review* 92-1E (October). Ottawa: Minister of Supplies and Services Canada.

Robinson, B.W., and E.D. Salamon eds.
1991 *Gender Roles: Doing What Comes Naturally.* Scarborough, Ont.: Nelson Canada.

Roche, P.
1984 "Bleak Dropout Picture Calls for Dramatic Change," *Globe and Mail* (November 10)

Roethlisberger F.J., and W.J. Dixon
1939 *Management and the Worker.* Cambridge, Mass.: Harvard University Press.

Rogers, R.G.
1990 *Reaching for Solutions: The Summary Report of the Special Advisor to the Minister of National Health and Welfare on Child Sexual Abuse in Canada.* Ottawa: National Clearinghouse on Family Violence, Health and Welfare Canada.

Rogoff, N.
1953 *Recent Trends in Occupational Mobility.* Glencoe, Ill.: Free Press.

Rosaldo, M. Zimbalist and L. Lamphere, eds.
1974 *Woman Culture & Society.* Stanford Calif.: Stanford University Press.

Rosen, G.
1963 "The Hospital: Historical Sociology of a Community Institution." In E. Freidson, ed., *The Hospital in Modern Society.* London: The Free Press.

Ross, D.P.
1980 *The Canadian Fact Book on Income Distribution.* Ottawa: The Canadian Council on Social Development.

1981 *The Working Poor.* Toronto: Lorimer.

Ross, E.A.
"Social Control," *American Journal of Sociology* 1:513–35.

Roszack, T.
1986 *The Cult of Information.* New York: Pantheon.

Rothman, R.
1987 *Working: Sociological Perspectives.* Englewood Cliffs, N.J.: Prentice-Hall.

Roy, G.
1947 *The Tin Flute.* Toronto: McClelland and Stewart.

1982 *The Fragile Lights of Earth.* Toronto: McClelland and Stewart.

Royal Commission on Bilingualism and Biculturalism
1969 *Report, Vol. 3, The Work World.* Ottawa: Queen's Printer.

Rubin, L.
1977 *Worlds of Pain: Life in the Working-Class Family.* New York: Basic Books.

1983 *Intimate Strangers: Men and Women Together.* New York: Harper and Row.

Ryan, T.J.
1972 *Poverty and the Child: A Canadian Study.* Toronto: McGraw-Hill Ryerson.

Sagan, C.
1977 *The Dragons of Eden.* New York: Random House.

Sagel, J.F.
1984 "Blowing the Whistle," *Ontario Lawyer's Weekly* (December 7).

1985 "Time for a Whistle-Blower Law," *The Globe and Mail* (January 14).

Salamon, E.D., and B.W. Robinson, eds.
1991 *Gender Roles: Doing What Comes Naturally.* Scarborough, Ont.: Nelson Canada.

Salter, L., and D. Wolfe, eds.
1990 *Managing Technology: Social Science Perspectives.* Toronto: Garamond Press.

Samenow, S.E.
1984 *Inside the Criminal Mind.* New York: Times Books.

Sampson, A.
1984 *The Seven Sisters: The Great Oil Companies and the World They Shaped.* Toronto: Bantam.

Sarsby, J.
1983 *Romantic Love and Society.* Harmondsworth: Penguin.

Sawyer, D.
1979 *Tomorrow Is School and I Am Sick to the Heart Thinking about it.* Vancouver: Douglas and McIntyre.

Schein, E.H.
1978 *Career Dynamics: Matching Individual and Organizational Needs.* Reading, Mass.: Addison-Wesley.

Scheleff, L.S.
1981 "The Relevance of Classical Criminology Today." In I. Barak-Glantz and C.R. Huff, eds., *The Mad, the Bad, and the Different.* Lexington, Mass.: Lexington Books/Heath.

Schlesinger, B.
1985 *The One Parent Family in the 1980's.* Toronto: University of Toronto Press.

Schnaiberg, A., and S. Goldenberg
1989 "From Empty Nest to Crowded Nest: The Dynamics of Incompletely-Launched Young Adults," *Social Problems* 36:3, 251–69.

Schur, E.M.
1965 *Crimes Without Victims.* Englewood Cliffs, N.J.: Prentice-Hall.

1979 *Interpreting Deviance.* New York: Harper and Row.

1980 *The Politics of Deviance: Stigma Contests and the Uses of Power.* Englewood Cliffs, N.J.; Prentice-Hall.

1984 *Labelling Women Deviant: Gender, Stigma and Social Control.* New York: Random House.

Schwartz, B.
1953 *The Supreme Court.* New York: Ronald Press.

Schwenger, C.W.
1974 "Keep the Old Folks at Home," *Canadian Journal of Public Health* 65.

Seaccombe, W.
1980 "Domestic Labour and the Working Class Household." Cited in S. Hale *Controversies in Sociology.* Toronto: Copp Clark Pitman, 1990.

Segal, E.
1989 *Doctors.* New York: Bantam.

Segal, L.
1990 *Slow Motion: Changing Masculinities, Changing Men.* London: Virago.

Selznick, P.
1957 *Leadership in Administration: A Sociological Interpretation.* New York: Harper and Row.

Sennett, R.
1970 "The Brutality of Modern Families," *Transaction* 7:4, 29–37.

Sennett, R., and J. Cobb
1973 *The Hidden Injuries of Class.* New York: Vintage Books.

Shapiro, B.J.
1985 *The Report of the Commission on Private Schools in Ontario.* Toronto.

Shapiro, M.
1978 *Getting Doctored: Critical Reflections on Becoming a Physician.* Kitchener, Ont.: Between the Lines.

Shaw, C.R.
1966 *The Jack Roller: A Delinquent Boy's Own Story.* Chicago: University of Chicago Press. First published in 1930.

Shaw, G.B.
1965 *Pygmalion: A Romance in Five Acts.* Harmondsworth: Penguin. First published in 1913.

Shea, C.
1990 "Changes in Women's Occupations." *Canadian Social Trends*, No. 18 (Autumn, 1990). Ottawa: Minister of Supply and Services.

Shearing, C.D., ed.
1981 *Organizational Police Deviance: Its Structure and Control.* Toronto: Butterworths.

Sheldon, W.H.
1948 *Varieties of Delinquent Youth: An Introduction to Constitutional Psychiatry.* New York: Harper and Row.

Shiva, V.
1988 *Staying Alive: Women, Ecology and Development.* Zed Books.

Shortall, S.
1993 "Canadian and Irish Farm Women: Some Similarities, Differences and Comments," *Canadian Review of Sociology and Anthropology*, 30:2, 172–189.

Shortt, S.E.D.
1986 *Victorian Lunacy.* Cambridge, U.K.: Cambridge University Press.

Shotland, R.L.
1992 "A Theory of the Causes of Courtship Rape: Part 2." In *Journal of Social Issues* 48 (1):127–143.

Shupe, A., and J.K. Hadden, eds.
1988 *The Politics of Religion and Social Change: Religion and the Political Order.* Toronto: McClelland and Stewart.

Sidel, R.
1990 *On Her Own: Growing Up in the Shadow of the American Dream.* New York: Viking.

Silberman, C.E.
1980 *Criminal Violence, Criminal Justice.* New York: Vintage Books.

Sills, D.L.
1980 *The Volunteers.* Salem, N.H.: Ayer Co. Publications. First published in 1957.

Silvester, N.
1991 "Can a Genital-Mutilation Fugitive Win Political Asylum?" In *Ms. Magazine* (September/October):16.

Silzer, K.
1985 "Deinstitutionalization of Psychiatrically Disabled Persons." In *Deinstitutionalization: Costs and Effects.* Ottawa: Canadian Council on Social Development.

Simmonds, C.
1981 "The Next Wave in Technology," *Policy Options* 2 (5).

Simmons, J.L.
1969 *Deviants.* California: Glendessary Press.

Singer, E., and P. Endreny
1986 "The Reporting of Social Science Research in the Mass Media." In Ball-Rokeach, J. Sandra, and M.G. Cantor, eds., *Media, Audience, and Social Structure.* Newbury Park, Calif.: Sage Publications, 293–312.

Skolnik, A.
1983 *The Intimate Environment: Exploring Marriage and the Family*, 3rd ed. Boston: Little, Brown.

Smigel, E.O
1964 *The Wall Street Lawyer.* Glencoe, Ill.: Free Press.

1969 "The Wall Street Lawyer Reconsidered," *New York* 36 (August 18).

Smith, B.
1943 *A Tree Grows in Brooklyn.* New York: Harper and Row.

Smith, D.E.
1977 "Women, the Family, and Corporate Capitalism." In M. Stephenson, ed., *Women in Canada.* Don Mills, Ont.: General Publishing, 17–48.

1983 "Women, Class and Family." In R. Miliband and J. Saville *The Socialist Register*. London: Merlin Press.

1987 *The Everyday World As Problematic: A Feminist Sociology*. Toronto: University of Toronto Press.

1992 "Whistling Women: Reflections on Rage and Rationality." In W.K. Carroll, L. Christiansen-Ruffman, R.F. Currie, and D. Harrison, eds. *Fragile Truths Twenty-Five Years of Sociology and Anthropology in Canada*. Ottawa: Carleton University Press.

1992 "Remaking a Life, Remaking Sociology: Reflections of a Feminist." In W.K. Carroll, L. Christiansen-Ruffman, R.F. Currie, and D. Harrison, eds., *Fragile Truths: Twenty-Five Years of Sociology and Anthropology in Canada*. Ottawa: Carleton University Press.

Snider, L.
1982 "The Criminal Justice System." In D. Forcese and S. Richer, eds., *Social Issues*. Scarborough, Ont.: Prentice-Hall Canada.

Sniderman, P.M., D.A. Northrup, J.F. Fletcher, P.H. Russell, and P.E. Tetlock
1993 "Psychological and Cultural Foundations of Prejudice: The Case of Anti-Semitism in Quebec." *The Canadian Review of Sociology and Anthropology* 30:2 (May): 242–270.

Sociology Writing Group (U.C.L.A.)
1986 *A Guide to Writing Sociology Papers*. Los Angeles: University of California Press.

Southam Literacy Report
1987 *Broken Words: Why Five Million Canadians are Illiterate*. Toronto: Southam Newspaper Group.

Speirs, R.
1983 "The Chip: Killing Jobs and Creating Peasants," *The Globe and Mail* (January 1).

Spergel, I.
1964 *Racketville, Slumtown and Haulberg: An Exploratory Study of Delinquent Subcultures*. Chicago: University of Chicago Press.

Spiro, M.E.
1958 *Children of the Kibbutz*. Cambridge: Harvard University Press.

1960 "Addendum, 1958." In N.W. Bell and E.F. Vogel, eds., *A Modern Introduction to the Family*. Glencoe, Ill.: Free Press.

Spradley, J.P. ,and B.J. Mann
1975 *The Cocktail Waitress*. New York: John Wiley.

Stacey, J.
1992 "Back Toward the Postmodern Family: Reflections on Gender, Kinship, and Class in the Silicon Valley." In B. Thorne and M. Yalom, eds., *Rethinking the Family: Some Feminist Questions*. Boston: Northeastern University Press.

Stack, C.B.
1974 *All Our Kin: Strategies for Survival in a Black Community*. New York: Harper and Row.

Stamp, R.
1984 "A History of Private Schools in Ontario." Appendix G in B.J. Shapiro, *The Report of the Commission on Private Schools in Ontario*. Toronto.

Stanton, A.H., and M.S. Schwartz
1954 *The Mental Hospital*. New York: Basic Books.

Stark, R., and W.S. Bainbridge
1983 "Concepts for a Theory of Religious Movements." In J.H. Fichter, ed., *Alternatives to Mainline Churches*. Barrytown, N.Y.: Unification Theological Seminary.

1985 *The Future of Religion*. Berkeley: University of California Press.

Statistics Canada
1984 *Universities: Enrolment and Degrees*. Cat. No. 81-20. Ottawa: Minister of Supply and Services Canada.

1992 *Age Structure in Transition: Two Centuries of Demographic Change*. Cat. 91-209E, Annual.

1993 *Earnings of Men and Women in 1991*. Cat. 13-217. Ottawa: Minister of Industry, Science, and Technology.

1993 *Occupation*. Cat. 93-327. Ottawa: Minister of Industry, Science, and Technology.

1993 *Religion in Canada*. Cat. 93-319. Ottawa: Minister of Industry, Science, and Technology.

Stebbins, R.
1987 *Canadian Football: The View from the Helmet*. London, Ont.: Centre for Social and Humanistic Studies.

1988 "Men, Husbands and Fathers: Beyond Patriarchal Relations." In N. Mandell and A. Duffy, eds., *Reconstructing the Canadian Family: Feminist Perspectives.* Toronto: Butterworths.

Steiner, G.
1974 *Nostalgia for the Absolute.* Toronto: CBC Publications.

Stern, P.C.
1979 *Evaluating Social Science Research.* New York: Oxford University Press.

Steur, E.B., J.M. Applerield, and R. Smith
1971 "Televised Aggression and Interpersonal Aggression of Preschool Children," *Journal Of Experimental Child Psychology* 11:442–7.

Steuter, E.
1992 "Women Against Feminism: An Examination of Feminist Social Movements and Anti-Feminist Countermovements," *Canadian Review of Sociology and Anthropology,* 29:3, 288–306.

Stewart, J.B.
1983 *The Partners: Inside America's Powerful Law Firms.* New York: Simon and Schuster.

Stone, S.D.
1993 "Getting the Message Out: Feminists, the Press and Violence against Women." *The Canadian Review of Sociology and Anthropology* 30:3 (August): 377–400.

Stouter, S.A.
1950 *The American Soldier.* Princeton, N.J.: Princeton University Press.

Strauss, S.
1984 "Human Ideas from Computer," *The Globe and Mail,* (January 19).

Struthers, J.
1983 *No Fault of Their Own: Unemployment and the Canadian State 1914–1941.* Toronto: University of Toronto Press.

Stuart, D.
1982 *Canadian Criminal Law: A Treatise.* Toronto: Carswell.

Stymeist, D.
1975 *Ethics and Indians.* Toronto: Peter Martin Associates.

Such, P.
1973 *Riverrun.* Toronto: Clarke Irwin.

Sudnow, D.
1965 "Normal Crimes: Sociological Features of the Penal Code in a Public Defender Office," *Social Problems* 12:255–76.

Sutherland, E.H.
1961 *White Collar Crime.* New York: Holt, Rinehart and Winston.

Suzuki, D.
1988 "Scientists Should Not Turn From Twisted Nazi Genetics," *The Globe and Mail* (January 9).

Suzuki, D., and P. Knudtson
1992 *Genetics: The Ethics of Engineering Life.* Cambridge, Mass.: Harvard University Press.

Swingewood, A.
1984 *A Short History of Sociological Thought.* London: Macmillan.

Sykes, G., and D. Matza
1957 "Techniques of Neutralization: A Theory of Delinquency," *American Sociological Review* 22 (December):664–70.

Symons, G.
1986 "Careers and Self-Concepts: Managerial Women in French and English Canada." In K.L.P. Lundy and B.D. Warme, eds., *Work in the Canadian Context: Continuity Despite Change,* 2nd ed. Toronto: Butterworths.

Talbott, J.E., ed.
1980 *State Mental Hospitals: Problems and Potentials.* New York: Human Sciences.

Tannen, D.
1991 *You Just Don't Understand: Men and Women in Conversation.* London: Virago.

Tannenbaum, F.
1938 *Crime and the Community.* New York: Columbia University Press.

Tanner, J.
1990 "Reluctant Rebels: A Case Study of Edmonton High School Drop-Outs," *Canadian Review of Sociology and Anthropology,* 271, 74–94.

Task Force on Human Relations
1977 *Now Is Not Too Late.* Toronto.

Taylor, F.W.
1919 *Shop Management.* New York: Harper and Row.

1947 *The Principles of Scientific Management.* New York: Harper and Row. First published in 1911.

Tepperman, L.
1975 *Social Mobility in Canada.* Toronto: McGraw-Hill Ryerson.

Terkel, S.
1972 *Working.* New York: Avon Books.

Terman, L.
1923 *Intelligence Tests and School Reorganization.* New York: World Book Co.

Theodorson, G.A., and A.A. Theodorson
1969 *A Modern Dictionary of Sociology.* New York: Crowell.

Thomas, A.M.
1993 "Transitions: From School to Work and Back—A New Paradigm." In P. Anisef and P. Axelrod, eds., *Transitions: Schooling and Employment in Canada.* Toronto: Thomson Educational Publishing.

Thorne, B.
1992 "Feminism and the Family: Two Decades of Thought." In B. Thorne and M. Yalom, eds., *Rethinking the Family: Some Feminist Questions.* Boston: Northeastern University Press, 3–30.

Tilly, C.
1990 *Short Hours, Short Shrift: Causes and Consequences of Growing Part-time Work.* Washington, D.C.: Employment Research Institute.

Tischler, H.L.
1993 *Introduction to Sociology,* 4th ed. New York: Harcourt Brace Jovanovich.

Toffler, A.
1980 *The Third Wave.* London: Collins.

Tomes, N.
1985 "Religion and the Earnings Function," *American Economic Review: Papers and Proceedings.*

Torrance, G.M.
1987 "Hospitals as Health Factories." In D. Coburn

et al., eds., *Health and Canadian Society,* 2nd ed. Toronto: Fitzhenry & Whiteside, 479–500.

Townsend, R.
1984 *Further Up The Organization: How To Stop Management From Stifling People and Strangling Productivity.* New York: Knopf.

Trainer, T.
1990 "A Rejection of the Brundtland Report," *International Foundation for Development Alternatives,* dossier 77 (May\June):72–84.

True, J.A.
1989 *Finding Out.* Belmont Calif.: Wadsworth.

Truzzi, M.
1971 "Lilliputians in Gulliver's Land: The Social Role of the Dwarf." In M. Truzzi, ed., *Sociology and Everyday Life.* Englewood Cliffs, N.J.: Prentice-Hall.

Tuchman, B.
1978 *A Distant Mirror.* New York: Alfred A. Knopf.

Tuchman, G.
1979 "Women's Depiction by the Mass Media," *Signs* 4 (3), (Spring):528–42.

Tucker, R.
1992 "Comment on Randy Lippert, 'The Construction of Satanism' as a Social Problem in Canada," *Canadian Journal of Sociology* 17(1992):2, 184–190.

Tumin, M.
1953 "Some Principles of Stratification: A Critical Analysis," *American Sociological Review* 18:387–93.

1967 *Social Stratification.* Englewood Cliffs, N.J.: Prentice-Hall.

Turner, R., and L. Killian
1972 *Collective Behavior.* Englewood Cliffs, N.J.: Prentice-Hall.

Turrittin, J.
1981 "Doing Domestic: Work Relationships in a Particularistic Setting." In K.L.P. Lundy and B.D. Warme, eds., *Work in the Canadian Context: Continuity Despite Change.* Toronto: Butterworths.

Tylor, E.B.
1970 *Primitive Culture,* 2nd ed. Gloucester: Smith.

Valaskakis, R., and P. Sendell
1980 *Industrial Strategy and the Information Economy: Towards a Game Plan for Canada.* Montreal: Gamma.

Van den Berghe, P.
1967 *Race and Racism.* New York: Wiley.

Vaz, E.W.
1976 *Aspects of Deviance.* Scarborough, Ont.: Prentice-Hall Canada.

Veevers, J.
1973 "The Child-Free Alternative: Rejection of the Motherhood Mystique." In Marylee Stephenson, ed., *Women in Canada.* Toronto: New Press, 183–99.

1980 *Childless by Choice.* Toronto: Butterworths.

Vickers, J.
1992 "The Intellectual Origins of the Women's Movements in Canada." In C. Backhouse and D.H. Flaherty, eds., *Challenging Times: The Women's Movement in Canada and the United States.* Kingston: McGill-Queen's University Press.

Vincent, C.L.
1979 *Policeman.* Toronto: Gage.

Visser, M.
1991 *The Rituals of Dinner: The Origins: Evolution, Eccentricities and Meaning of Table Manners.* Toronto: HarperCollins.

Vorst, J., ed.
1989 *Race, Class, Gender: Bonds and Barriers.* Winnipeg: Between the Lines in cooperation with Society for Socialist Studies, University of Manitoba.

Waddams, S.M.
1983 *Introduction to the Study of Law,* 2nd ed. Toronto: Carswell.

Walshok, M.L.
1981 *Blue-Collar Women.* Garden City, N.J.: Anchor Books.

Walby, S.
1988 *Gender Segregation at Work.* Milton Keynes: Open University Press.

Wallace, E., and E.A. Hochel
1952 *The Comanches: Lords of the South Plains.* Norman, Okla.: University of Oklahoma Press.

Wallace, J.
1983 *Part-time Work in Canada: Report of the Commission of Inquiry into Part-time Work.* Ottawa: Minister of Supply and Services.

Waller, W.
1932 *The Sociology of Teaching.* New York: John Wiley & Sons.

Wallerstein, I.
1974 *The Modern World-System Capitalist Agriculture and the Origins of European World-Economy in the Sixteenth Century.* New York: Academic Press.

Wallerstein, J., and S. Blakeslee
1989 *Second Chance: Men, Women and Children A Decade After Divorce.* New York: Ticknor and Fields.

Wallis, W.A., and M.V. Roberts
1962 *The Nature of Statistics.* New York: Free Press.

Waring, M.
1988 *If Women Counted.* New York: HarperCollins.

Warme, B.D.
1979 "Breaking the Cycle of Child Abuse," *Status of Women News* 5 (5).

Warme, B.D., and K.L.P. Lundy
1988 "Erosion of an Ideal: The 'Presence' of Part-Time Faculty," *Studies in Higher Education* 13 (2).

Warme, B.D., K.L.P. Lundy, and L.A. Lundy.
Working Part-time: Risks and Opportunities. New York: Praeger.

Warme, B.D., and S. Thomas
1978 "Wednesday's Parent and the Role of the Para-Professional." In M.A. Beyer-Gammon, ed., *Violence in Canada.* Toronto: Methuen, 112–27.

Warme, P.
1985 "Political Stability and Instability in Latin America." York University. Unpublished thesis.

Warner, W.L. Lloyd
1963 *Yankee City.* New Haven: Yale University Press. Abridged edition.

Weber, M.
1958 *The Protestant Ethic and the Spirit of Capitalism.* New York: Scribners Sons. First published in 1904–5.

1967 *Economy and Society: An Outline of Interpretive Sociology*, 3-vol. ed. New York: Bedminster Press. First published in 1921–2.

Wein, F.
1993 "Regional Inequality: Explanations and Policy Issues." In J. Curtis, E. Grabb, and N. Gluppy, eds., *Social Inequality in Canada Patterns, Problems, Policies*. Scarborough, Ont.: Prentice-Hall Canada, 449–68.

Weingarten, M.
1959 *Life in a Kibbutz*. Jerusalem: Jerusalem Post Press.

Weisser, M.
1982 *Crime and Punishment in Early Modern Europe 1350–1850*, 2nd ed. Sussex, U.K.: The Harvester Press.

Weitzman, L.J.
1985 *The Divorce Revolution: The Unexpected Social and Economic Consequences for Women and Children in America*. New York: Free Press.

Weldon, F.
1984 *Letters to Alice on First Reading Jane Austen*. Great Britain: Coronet Books Hoddard and Stoughton.

Welfare Council
1992 *Poverty Profile 1980–1990*. Ottawa: National Council of Welfare, Jeanne Mance Building.

Weston, K.
1992 "The Politics of Gay Families." In B. Thorne and M. Yalom, eds., *Rethinking the Family: Some Feminist Questions*. Boston: Northeastern University Press, 119–39.

Whitehead, B.D.
1993 "Dan Quayle Was Right." *The Atlantic Monthly* (April).

Whyte, W.F.
1943 *Street Corner Society: The Social Structure of an Italian Slum*. Chicago: University of Chicago Press.

Whyte, W.H., Jr.
1956 *The Organization Man*. New York: Simon and Schuster.

Williams, C.L.
1992 "The Glass Escalator: Hidden Advantages for Men in the 'Female' Professions," *Social Problems* 39:3, 253–267.

Williams, L.S.
1989 "Behind the Headlines: The Physical and Emotional Costs of In Vitro Fertilization," *Healthsharing* (Summer):20–25.

1990 "Motherhood, Ideology, and the Power of Technology: In Vitro Fertilization Use by Adoptive Mothers," *Women's Studies International Forum*, 13:6, 543–552.

Williams, T. MacBeth, ed.
1986 *The Impact of Television: A Natural Experiment in Three Communities*. Toronto: Academic Press, Inc.

Willis, P.
1978 *Learning to Labour: How Working-Class Kids Get Working-Class Jobs*. London: Saxon House.

Wilson, J.
1973 *Introduction to Social Movements*. New York: Basic Books.

1975 *Sociobiology: The New Synthesis*. Cambridge: Harvard University Press.

Winner, L.
1989 "Mythinformation in the High-Tech Era." In T. Forrester, ed., *Computers in the Human Context: Information Technology, Productivity and People*. Oxford: Blackwell.

Wolf, N.
1990 *The Beauty Myth*. Toronto: Random House.

Wolfe, Leslie R., ed.
1991 *Women, Work and School—Occupational Segregation and the Role of Education*. Boulder, Colo.: Westview Press.

Wolff, H.J.
1983 "Roman Law." In J.C. Smith and D.V. Weisstub, eds., *The Western Idea of Law*. Toronto: Butterworths.

Woliver, L.R.
1991 "The Influence of Technology on the Politics of Motherhood: An Overview of the United States," *Women's Studies International Forum* 14:5, 479–90.

Woodcock, G.
1988 *A Social History of Canada*. Toronto: Penguin.

Woodsworth, J.S.
1972 *Strangers Within Our Gates*. Toronto: University of Toronto Press. First published in 1909.

Woodward, J.
1965 *Industrial Organizations: Theory and Practice.*
London: Oxford University Press.

Wotherspoon, T.
1987 *The Political Economy of Canadian Schooling.*
Scarborough, Ont.: Nelson.

Wright, E.N.
1970 *Student's Background and Its Relationship to Class
and Programme in School.* Toronto: Toronto Board of
Education.

Wright, P.J.
1979 *On a Clear Day You Can See General Motors.*
Grosse Point: Wright Enterprises.

Wylie, P.
1942 *Generation of Vipers.* New York: Farrar, Rinehart.

Yinger, M.
1954 *The Scientific Study of Religion.* New York:
Macmillan.

1970 *The Scientific Study of Religion.* New York:
Macmillan.

1982 *Countercultures: The Promise and Peril of a World
Turned Upside Down.* New York: Free Press.

Yochelson, S., and S. Samenow
1976 *The Criminal Personality.* New York: Aronson.

Young, M.
1958 *The Rise of the Meritocracy.* Harmondsworth:
Penguin.

Yoxen, E.
1983 *The Gene Business: Who Should Control
Biotechnology?* Burgary Suffold: Richard Clay (The
Chaucer Press).

Zamyatin, E.I.
1975 *We.* Boston: Gregg Press.

Zeitlin, I.M.
1973 *Rethinking Sociology: A Critique of Contemporary
Theory.* Englewood Cliffs, N.J.: Prentice-Hall.

Zerker, S.F.
1982 *The Rise and Fall of the Toronto Typographical
Union 1832–1932: A Case Study of Foreign Domination.*
Toronto: University of Toronto Press.

Zuckerman, M., ed.
1983 *Biological Bases of Sensation-Seeking, Impulsivity
and Anxiety.* Hillsdale, N.J.: Lawrence Erlbaum
Associates.

To the owner of this book

We hope that you have enjoyed *Sociology: A Window on the World,* and we would like to know as much about your experiences with it as you would care to offer. Only through your comments and those of others can we learn how to make this a better text for future readers.

School _____ Your instructor's name _____

Course _____ Was the text required? _____ Recommended? _____

1. What did you like the most about *Sociology: A Window on the World*?

_____

_____

_____

2. How useful was this text for your course?

_____

_____

_____

3. Do you have any recommendations for ways to improve the next edition of this text?

_____

_____

_____

4. In the space below or in a separate letter, please write any other comments you have about the book. (For example, please feel free to comment on reading level, writing style, terminology, design features, and learning aids.)

_____

_____

_____

_____

Optional

Your name _____ Date _____

May Nelson Canada quote you, either in promotion for *Sociology: A Window on the World* or in future publishing ventures?

Yes _____ No _____

Thanks!

FOLD HERE

Nelson

TAPE SHUT

TAPE SHUT

MAIL ▶ POSTE

Canada Post Corporation / Société canadienne des postes

Postage paid
if mailed in Canada

Port payé
si posté au Canada

Business Reply

Réponse d'affaires

0107077099   01

0107077099-M1K5G4-BR01

Nelson Canada
College Editorial Department
1120 Birchmount Rd.
Scarborough, ON   M1K 9Z9

PLEASE TAPE SHUT. DO NOT STAPLE.